Essays

AN ANALYTIC READER

AN ANALYTIC READER

ESSAYS

RALPH W. RADER
SHELDON SACKS

University of California, Berkeley

BOSTON

TORONTO

Little, Brown and Company

ACKNOWLEDGMENTS

The authors are grateful to the following publishers, authors,
and agencies for permission to quote from the works listed:

GEORGE ALLEN & UNWIN LTD. for "Freedom and the Colleges," from *Why I Am Not a Christian,* by Bertrand Russell.

THE BEACON PRESS for "Afterthoughts on the Rosenbergs," from *An End to Innocence,* by Leslie Fiedler. Reprinted by permission of the author and the Beacon Press, copyright © 1954 Leslie Fiedler.

HAROLD J. BERMAN for "Constitutional Rights of Racial Minorities in the United States," by Arthur E. Sutherland, from *Talks on American Law,* ed. Harold J. Berman (Random House: 1961).

THE BOBBS-MERRILL COMPANY, INC. for "Individualism in America," from *Company Manners,* by Louis Kronenberger. Copyright 1951, 1953, 1954 by Louis Kronenberger, reprinted by permission of the publishers, The Bobbs-Merrill Company, Inc.

DOUGLAS BUSH for "The Humanities." Reprinted with the permission of the author and the editors of *The Key Reporter.*

CAMBRIDGE UNIVERSITY PRESS for "The Two Cultures," from *The Two Cultures and the Scientific Revolution,* by Sir Charles P. Snow, published by Cambridge University Press, 1959.

THE CARLETON COLLEGE BULLETIN for "The Idea of the Humanities," by R. S. Crane (*Carleton College Bulletin,* June, 1953). Reprinted by permission of the publisher and the author.

iv

CHATTO AND WINDUS LTD. for "The Arts of Selling," from *Brave New World Revisited*, by Aldous Huxley.

THE CLARENDON PRESS for "An Enquiry into the Origin of Moral Virtue," from *The Fable of the Bees*, by Bernard Mandeville (ed. F. B. Kaye) ; and for "History's Nature, Object, Method, and Value," from *The Idea of History* (Introduction, Section II), by R. G. Collingwood.

CONSTABLE & COMPANY LTD. for "Christmas Trees" and "The Man Who Knew Everybody," from *Small Talk*, by Sir Harold Nicolson.

R. S. CRANE for his article "The Idea of the Humanities" (from the *Carleton College Bulletin*, June, 1953). Reprinted by permission of the publisher and the author.

THE DIAL PRESS, INC. for "What it Means to be an American," from *Nobody Knows My Name*, by James Baldwin. © 1961, 1959 by James Baldwin and reprinted by permission of the publisher, the Dial Press Inc., New York, N.Y.

DOUBLEDAY & COMPANY, INC. for "R.M.S. Titanic," from *Sea Fights and Shipwrecks*, by Hanson Baldwin. Copyright © 1955, 1938 by Hanson W. Baldwin. Reprinted by permission of Doubleday & Company, Inc.

E. P. DUTTON & CO., INC. for "Something Defeasible," from the book *And Even Now*, by Max Beerbohm. Copyright 1921 by E. P. Dutton & Co., Inc. Renewal © 1949 by Max Beerbohm. Reprinted by permission of the publishers.

THE ESTATE OF ALBERT EINSTEIN for "Why Do They Hate the Jews?" and "The Laws of Science and the Laws of Ethics." Reprinted by permission of the Estate of Albert Einstein, the owner of the copyrights.

FARRAR, STRAUS & COMPANY, INC. for "Settling the Colonel's Hash," from *On the Contrary*, by Mary McCarthy. Copyright © 1961 by Mary McCarthy. Reprinted by permission of Farrar, Straus & Company, Inc.

INGE LEDERER GIBEL for her article "How *Not* to Integrate the Schools" (from *Harper's*, November, 1963).

HARCOURT, BRACE & WORLD, INC. for "Two Women," from *The Moment and Other Essays*, by Virginia Woolf, copyright 1948 by Harcourt, Brace & World, Inc.; for "Politics and the English Language" and "A Hanging," from *Shooting an Elephant and Other Essays*, by George Orwell, copyright 1945, 1946, 1950 by Sonia Brownell Orwell; for "The Invention of the Steamboat," from *Anthropology*, by A. L. Kroeber, copyright 1943, 1948 by Harcourt, Brace & World, Inc.; for "Christmas Trees" and "The Man Who Knew Everybody," from *Small Talk*, by Harold Nicolson, copyright 1937 by Harcourt, Brace & World, Inc.; for "Introductory: Language Defined," from *Language*, by Edward Sapir, copyright 1921 by Harcourt, Brace & World, Inc., renewed 1949 by Jean V. Sapir; and for "Captain Edward Gibbon," from *Abinger Harvest*, by E. M. Forster, copyright 1936 by E. M. Forster. All selections mentioned in this paragraph are reprinted by permission of the publisher, Harcourt, Brace & World, Inc.

HARPER & ROW, PUBLISHERS, INC. for "The Arts of Selling," from *Brave New World Revisited*, by Aldous Huxley, copyright © 1958 by Aldous Huxley; for "Crash!" from *Only Yesterday*, by Frederick Lewis Allen, copyright 1931 by Frederick Lewis Allen, renewed 1959 by Agnes Rogers Allen; for "Edmund G. Ross," from *Profiles in Courage*, by John F. Kennedy, copyright © 1955 by John F. Kennedy; and for "Calculating Machine," from *The Second Tree from the Corner*, by E. B. White, copyright 1951 by E. B. White. ("Calculating Machine," by E. B. White, originally appeared in *The New*

Yorker.) The selections mentioned in this paragraph are reprinted with the permission of Harper & Row, Publishers, Inc.

RUPERT HART-DAVIS LTD. for "Joe Louis" and "Roughing It," from *One Man's America,* by Alistair Cooke.

WILLIAM HEINEMANN LTD. for "Something Defeasible," from *And Even Now,* by Max Beerbohm.

HUMANITIES PRESS, INC. for "Motherhood and the Temptations of Incest," from *Sex and Repression in Savage Society,* by Bronislaw Malinowski.

THE KEY REPORTER, a publication of the United Chapters of Phi Beta Kappa, for "The Humanities" by Douglas Bush. The article appeared in *The Key Reporter,* Vol. XX, No. 2, February, 1955. (An earlier version of the article appeared in the January, 1955 issue of *The Educational Record,* and a portion of the article appeared in the Sunday Magazine of *The New York Times,* January 9, 1955.) Reprinted by permission of the editors of *The Key Reporter* and the author.

ALFRED A. KNOPF, INC. for "Joe Louis" and "Roughing It," copyright, 1952 by Alistair Cooke, reprinted from *One Man's America,* by Alistair Cooke; and for selections from *Democracy in America,* copyright, 1945 by Alfred A. Knopf, Inc., reprinted from *Democracy in America,* by Alexis de Tocqueville, translated by Phillips Bradley. The selections mentioned in this paragraph are reprinted by permission of Alfred A. Knopf, Inc.

McCLELLAN AND STEWART LTD. for "Dunkirk," from *Blood, Sweat and Tears,* by Sir Winston S. Churchill.

THE MACMILLAN COMPANY for "Progress," by Carl Becker, from *The Encyclopedia of the Social Sciences,* Vol. XII, by Seligman and Johnson. Copyright 1934, 1961 by The Macmillan Company.

THE NATION for "What Is a Good Review?" by Joseph Wood Krutch. Reprinted from *The Nation* by permission of the editors.

NATIONAL COUNCIL OF TEACHERS OF ENGLISH for "The Lexicographer's Uneasy Chair," by James Sledd (from *College English,* May, 1962). Reprinted with the permission of the National Council of Teachers of English and James Sledd.

THE NEW YORKER MAGAZINE, INC. for "The Case for the Daydreamer," by James Thurber, copyright © 1936 The New Yorker Magazine, Inc.; for "The String Untuned," by Dwight Macdonald, © 1962 The New Yorker Magazine, Inc.; "A Cloud of Smoke" by Thomas Whiteside, © 1963 The New Yorker Magazine, Inc. Reprinted by permission.

OXFORD UNIVERSITY PRESS, INC. for "The Gray Beginnings," from *The Sea Around Us,* by Rachel Carson, copyright © 1950, 1951, 1960 by Rachel L. Carson, reprinted by permission of Oxford University Press, Inc.; and for "The Implications for Us," from *The Uses of the Past,* by Herbert J. Muller, copyright © 1952 by Oxford University Press, Inc., and reprinted by permission.

G. P. PUTNAM'S SONS for "Dunkirk," from *Blood, Sweat and Tears,* by Winston S. Churchill. Copyright 1941 by Winston S. Churchill. Reprinted by permission of G. P. Putnam's Sons.

RANDOM HOUSE, INC. for "The First 'Fireside Chat'" from Volume II of *The Public Papers and Addresses of Franklin Delano Roosevelt,* copyright 1938 by Franklin Delano Roosevelt, reprinted by permission of Random House, Inc.

MARK SCHORER for "Two Houses, Two Ways: The Florentine Villas of Lewis and Lawrence, Respectively," by Mark Schorer (*New World Writing*, No. 4, 1953). Reprinted by permission of the author.

SCIENTIFIC AMERICAN for "The Army Ant," by T. C. Schneirla and Gerard Piel. Reprinted with permission. Copyright © 1948 by Scientific American, Inc. All rights reserved.

MARTIN SECKER & WARBURG LTD. for "A Hanging," from *Collected Essays*, by George Orwell; and for "Politics and the English Language," from *Shooting an Elephant and Other Essays*, by George Orwell.

SIMON AND SCHUSTER, INC. for "Freedom and the Colleges," from *Why I Am Not a Christian*, by Bertrand Russell, copyright © 1957 by George Allen and Unwin, Ltd.; and for "The Monster," from *Of Men and Music*, by Deems Taylor, copyright 1937 by Deems Taylor. Both selections reprinted by permission of Simon and Schuster, Inc.

THE VIKING PRESS, INC. for "The Kinsey Report," from *The Liberal Imagination*, by Lionel Trilling, copyright 1948 by Lionel Trilling; for "Benjamin Franklin," from *Studies in Classical American Literature*, by D. H. Lawrence, copyright 1923 by Thomas Seltzer, Inc., 1951 by Frieda Lawrence; and for "Suburbia, of Thee I Sing," from *A Short Walk from the Station*, by Phyllis McGinley, copyright 1949 by Phyllis McGinley. All selections mentioned in this paragraph are reprinted with the permission of the publishers, The Viking Press, Inc.

REBECCA WEST, D.B.E., for "The Meaning of Treason" (*Harper's*, October, 1947).

LEONARD WOOLF for "Two Women," from *The Moment and Other Essays*, by Virginia Woolf. Reprinted by permission of the publisher, Hogarth Press, and Leonard Woolf.

PREFACE

THIS BOOK OF ESSAYS is designed to give the student writer some knowledge of the principles upon which good compositions are constructed. With such knowledge, the editors believe, the student will not only be able to read essays more perceptively but he will also be able to solve more easily and intelligently the problems that arise as he constructs his own compositions. But between conscious knowledge of the principles upon which good compositions are built and the ability to write such compositions lies a gulf which, of course, is not at all easy to cross. The ability to write depends to a large extent upon the writer's native capacity as fostered by reading and by simple practice in composition. It depends, beyond that, on the writer's having something to say — some desire to express and shape his own thoughts and feelings in a way that will make them significant for other people. All of these things the student must have or get for himself. He cannot be given ability that he does not have, or a desire to express himself that he does not feel, but he can be taught principles that will enable him to make the most of the abilities he does have and to clarify the inchoate impulse to write that he does feel. The untalented student writer may not thereafter write good essays, but he will be able to write *formed* essays; the talented student may not write brilliant essays, but he will be able to discover the means available to him to perfect the imperfect essays he might otherwise have written.

We offer here what we believe to be a conceptually clear and pedagogically effective way of teaching the principles of good composition. Our assumption is that the form of any essay may be understood as resulting from the successful fusion of four component parts—*subject, purpose, disposition,* and *style.* Further, we assume that these component parts can be described in language with sufficient precision to enable a student to understand in concrete terms how they all function together to realize the form of the essay.

In the introduction to Part One we explain our approach and illustrate it through a description and revision of a short student theme. Our aim here is both to make the method clear and to indicate its practical relevance to the problems the student faces in his own compositions. For each of the professional essays grouped as "Guided Discussions" in Part One, we have provided an exploratory discussion followed by an analytic summary in which the four parts of the essay are specifically described and related to each other. This is followed, in turn, by a series of pointed questions, geared to the summary, and designed to help the student develop in full the conception of the form of the essay which has already been outlined. Following the questions are theme assignments intended to encourage the student to apply the formal insights he has gained by writing an essay parallel in form but different in subject.

The analyzed essays in Part One are arranged in groups to emphasize certain common and/or contrasting features of purpose and disposition. Each of these groups is followed by a group of unanalyzed essays similar in form to those that precede. Our intention here is to suggest, unobtrusively, the relevance to these fresh materials of the general analytic procedures previously developed.

In Part Two of the book the essays are grouped to emphasize connections in subject matter. This arrangement, we feel, will provide a basis for class discussion of substantial ideas which can lead to significant subjects for themes; on the other hand, it emphasizes, by the likeness in subject matter, the many contrasts of purpose, disposition, and style to be found among these essays. The selections both here and in Part One are nearly all distinguished pieces of writing, each of which is in itself stimulating to thought and interesting to read. Many have been reprinted before and were chosen partly because of that fact. Instructors are rarely happy to find an anthology in which all the faces are unfamiliar, and our feeling was that the virtues of our method, such as they are, would be all the more apparent if it were focused on some essays with which the instructor had already dealt. But there are also many new essays, fresh selections which the instructor should find pleasant and rewarding to teach.

The whole book, we venture to hope, is a useful tool for both teacher and student.

R. W. R.
S. S.

For

LOIS
ERIC
COLIN
MIKE
JAMES
NANCY
EMILY

TABLE OF CONTENTS

PART ONE: READING IN ORDER TO WRITE

The Four Components 1

Persuasion: Some Dispositions

Guided Discussions

JOHN STUART MILL, *Three Examples of Persecution for Belief* 13

LOUIS KRONENBERGER, *Individualism in America* 19

JAMES MADISON, *The Federalist, No. 10* 27

SAMUEL JOHNSON, *The Idler, No. 103* 36

For Further Analysis

PHYLLIS MC GINLEY, *Suburbia, of Thee I Sing* 40

BERTRAND RUSSELL, *Freedom and the Colleges* 48

HENRY DAVID THOREAU, *The War of the Ants* 57

ALEXIS DE TOCQUEVILLE, *Slavery in Ohio and Kentucky* 60

Persuasion for Particular Occasions

Guided Discussions

BENJAMIN FRANKLIN, *Speech in the Convention
on the Subject of Salaries* 65

WINSTON CHURCHILL, *Dunkirk* 71

For Further Analysis

FRANKLIN D. ROOSEVELT, *The First "Fireside Chat"* 84
JOHN F. KENNEDY, *The Soviet Threat to the Americas* .... 89 ·

Explanation: Coherence and Clarity

Guided Discussions

ALEXIS DE TOCQUEVILLE, *Why Democratic Nations Naturally
   Desire Peace, and Democratic Armies, War* 97
ALBERT EINSTEIN, *The Laws of Science and the Laws of Ethics* 106
R. G. COLLINGWOOD, *History's Nature, Object, Method, and Value* .. 110
A. L. KROEBER, *The Invention of the Steamboat* 115

For Further Analysis

DAVID HUME, *Of Tragedy* 123
T. C. SCHNEIRLA AND GERARD PIEL, *The Army Ant* 130
BRONISLAW MALINOWSKI, *Motherhood and the Temptations of Incest* 140
HENRI POINCARÉ, *Mathematical Creation* 146

Explanation with Emotive Force

Guided Discussions

THOMAS BABINGTON MACAULAY, *The Scottish Highlands
   in the Seventeenth Century* 159
RACHEL CARSON, *The Gray Beginnings* 169

For Further Analysis

HANSON BALDWIN, *R.M.S. Titanic* 181
FREDERICK LEWIS ALLEN, *Crash!* 193

Narrative and Character: Contrasting Purposes

Guided Discussions

GEORGE ORWELL, *A Hanging* 209
HAROLD NICOLSON, *The Man Who Knew Everybody* 216
JAMES BOSWELL, *The Wilkes Episode* 224

For Further Analysis

MAX BEERBOHM, *Something Defeasible* 236
SAMUEL CLEMENS, *The Boys' Ambition* 241
ALISTAIR COOKE, *Joe Louis* 245

PART TWO: ESSAYS FOR STUDY

Similar Subjects, Various Forms 251

Ideals and Action

Creeds in Crisis

LESLIE FIEDLER, *Afterthoughts on the Rosenbergs* 255
REBECCA WEST, *The Meaning of Treason* 273
JOHN F. KENNEDY, *Edmund G. Ross* 281
THOMAS PAINE, *The Crisis, No. 1* 298
EDMUND BURKE, from *Reflections on the Revolution in France* 306

Morals and Mores

BERNARD MANDEVILLE, *An Enquiry into the Origin of Moral Virtue* 325
JONATHAN SWIFT, *The Art of Political Lying* 334
ALDOUS HUXLEY, *The Arts of Selling* 338
THOMAS WHITESIDE, *A Cloud of Smoke* 346

JAMES THURBER, *The Case for the Daydreamer* 369

ALISTAIR COOKE, *Roughing It* 374

LIONEL TRILLING, *The Kinsey Report* 379

Freedom and Prejudice

ALBERT EINSTEIN, *Why Do They Hate the Jews?* 395

ARTHUR E. SUTHERLAND, *Constitutional Rights of Racial
   Minorities in the United States* 402

INGE LEDERER GIBEL, *How Not to Integrate the Schools* 410

HAROLD NICOLSON, *Christmas Trees* 421

VIRGINIA WOOLF, *Two Women* 425

JAMES BALDWIN, *The Discovery of What it Means to be an American* 431

Ideas and Men

Men and Letters

JOSEPH WOOD KRUTCH, *What Is a Good Review?* 439

THOMAS DE QUINCEY, *On the Knocking at the Gate in* Macbeth 442

DEEMS TAYLOR, *The Monster* 447

D. H. LAWRENCE, *Benjamin Franklin* 451

MARK SCHORER, *Two Houses, Two Ways: The Florentine Villas of
   Lewis and Lawrence, Respectively* 461

MARY MC CARTHY, *Settling the Colonel's Hash* 481

Men and Language

EDWARD SAPIR, *Language Defined* 494

GEORGE ORWELL, *Politics and the English Language* 509

E. B. WHITE, *Calculating Machine* 522

DWIGHT MACDONALD, *The String Untuned* 524

JAMES SLEDD, *The Lexicographer's Uneasy Chair* 547

Letters and Science

C. P. SNOW, *The Two Cultures* 557

DOUGLAS BUSH, *The Humanities* 569

R. S. CRANE, *The Idea of the Humanities* 577

THOMAS HENRY HUXLEY, *Science and Culture* 589

MATTHEW ARNOLD, *Literature and Science* 603

The Meaning of History

CARL BECKER, *Progress* 620

EDWARD GIBBON, *General Observations on the Fall of the
Roman Empire in the West* 629

E. M. FORSTER, *Captain Edward Gibbon* 637

HERBERT J. MULLER, *The Fall of Rome: Its Implications for Us* 643

Index of Authors and Titles 655

Reading

IN ORDER TO

Write

We have said in our preface that this book is designed to give the student some knowledge of the principles upon which good compositions are constructed, so that he will be able to solve more easily the problems which arise as he constructs his own compositions. But what are those principles, and how can they be applied to writing? Let us think, first of all, about the act of writing itself, about the writer as he sits down to write. He will have a subject to write about and will ordinarily know something about the subject. But though he may understand the subject in itself quite thoroughly and though he may have thought about his essay a great deal—planned it, outlined and even begun to draft it—he will not be able for that reason alone to complete his essay successfully. He will be able to complete it only when he has actively grasped his subject in relation to a specific purpose that will allow him to give it a form expressed in language appropriate to the realization of the purpose. Not until all of these come to be conceived as a functioning whole in his mind will he be able to write out, in a form which satisfies his inner sense of his task, the essay toward which he has been working.

THE FOUR COMPONENTS

What the writer grasps intuitively at the point where he is able to complete his essay is precisely the total form which makes an essay effective. This book is based upon the idea that, by learning to describe the forms of finished essays in terms analogous to the writer's original act of conception, the student can learn to understand abstractly what the principles of good compositions are. He will thus be able not only to appreciate fully just how a particular writer in a particular essay has met a particular problem, but he should also then be able to apply his knowledge to his own writing. He can use his insight to crystallize his own intuitive grasp of his compositions as he begins them, and at every stage along the way he can analyze the potential form of his essay and more surely guide, correct, and refine the product of his initial creative impulse.

The form of the whole composition which the successful writer intuits is, as we have already implied, made up of four components working together which the writer, consciously or unconsciously, brings into complete fusion. First of all, there is the *subject*—what is written about. Second, there is the *communicative purpose*—the end, in relation to a particular or generalized audience—to which the subject is shaped. The intent may be to present the subject so as to explain something about it to the reader, or to persuade him to feel a certain way about it, or to amuse or otherwise entertain him. Third, there is the *disposition*—the means employed to shape or develop the subject in such a way as to accomplish the communicative purpose. Such means would embrace various kinds and principles of development employed singly or in combination— examples, comparisons, narrative devices, etc. Finally, there is *style*—the selection of words, sentence structure, and other elements of language best suited for expressing the particular subject as shaped in the disposition to accomplish the particular communicative purpose of the essay. All these parts will be present in any complete and successful essay. No essay can be complete in which they are not present, and no essay successful in which they are not fused.

Let us emphasize again that the successful writer does not necessarily think of these as separate when he writes (though he may) but that he is more likely to fuse them, as we have said, intuitively. The point here is that if we wish to understand what goes on in a successful essay, above and beyond our own subjective feeling, we will do best to conceive it as a whole which works effectively precisely because these four components have been brought into concrete harmony.

The notion of these four interrelated components as the form of an essay is difficult to grasp, and you may not fully understand it until you have worked through a number of the essays below in terms of the discussions and questions given there. Before that, however, we will try to make the idea clearer by illustrating it through an analysis and progressive revision of the following short theme, written a few years back as a class exercise in one of the editors' composition classes.

PALOS VERDES

My home town, Palos Verdes, is a medium-sized community in Los Angeles county. Located on a peninsula extending into the ocean, it is sufficiently isolated for the purpose of industry as to encourage only residential housing, and indeed this has been the history of the town's development. Most of the residents live in the town and work elsewhere. A few stores provide local employment only for some of the older inhabitants. Palos Verdes has good schools and facilities for recreation in the town and in the nearby parks and beaches.

When our family first moved into Palos Verdes six years ago, I was struck by the beauty and quietness invoked by the large vistas of sea and mountains and by the isolation from the multitudes of "Angelenos." I thought then that this was the settled quiet kind of town that one could really call home.

But since then, first impressions have been changed or modified to the point where a totally new conception of Palos Verdes as a home town has emerged. Where once seclusion and permanence were felt to exist because of its location, continued living in the town showed a transience and unsettledness in the inhabitants. The rapid growth in population of Los Angeles county and the change of located people in the county from one place to another helped to make my town seem more and more like a way station—a stopover for catching one's breath and then moving on to somewhere else. Friends at school would often be gone the next day, and new faces would appear in their places.

I have nothing against change and growth as such, but I have a feeling that the essential ingredients of a home or home town are "roots" and permanence. If you are constantly on the move you feel like a nomad, but relativistically you still feel like a nomad when all around you is on the move.

Hills and trees, nice houses and big lawns—these things are important in making an area the kind of place that you want to make your home. But the most beautiful location is little more than a vacation land when there isn't the constant substructure of a permanent group of friends and acquaintances. My "home town" has exactly this feeling, and it is often that I feel like a visitor who will soon be moving on further, though rationally I realize that this will be my home for many years to come.

No doubt something wonderful is missed in not having the memories of a home town—a physical–spiritual base of operations somewhere back in one's history.

The first thing one notices about this composition, perhaps, is its general imprecision in statement and diction and its awkward syntax. Such shortcomings keep the language from being what we call "good writing," and we are likely to think that they are what keep the theme from success. Actually, however, the correction of these errors—which fall within our variable of style—will not make of this piece a good theme; for good writing, in the sense of clear, well-turned sentences, important as it is, does not by itself make a good composition. Just as fundamental are the other variables of subject, purpose, and disposition. Let us see what happens to the theme when we improve only the diction and syntax, leaving the subject, purpose, and disposition as they are.

PALOS VERDES

My home town, Palos Verdes, is a medium-sized community in Los Angeles county. Its isolated location on an ocean peninsula has precluded industrial development, and it remains, as it has always been, a residential community. Most of the residents live in the town and work elsewhere; only a few of the older inhabitants work in local stores. Palos Verdes has good schools and excellent recreational facilities both in the town and in the nearby parks and beaches.

When our family first moved to Palos Verdes six years ago, I was struck by the silent beauty of the wide vistas of sea and mountains and by the isolation from the multitudes of "Angelenos." I thought then that this was the quiet, settled kind of town that one could really call home.

But since then I have changed my mind about Palos Verdes as a home town. Where once I felt a seeming seclusion and permanence, I came after a time to sense a restlessness in the people and a transience in the life of the town. The rapid population growth of Los Angeles county brought a constant influx of new inhabitants, which together with the constant shifting of families out of the town, as they pursued the father's occupational transfers, made Palos Verdes seem more and more like a way station— a stopover where people merely caught their breath before moving on to someplace else. Friends at school would be there one day and gone the next, new faces appearing to take their places.

I have nothing against change and growth as such, but I feel that the essential ingredients of a home town are "roots" and permanence. In Palos Verdes I felt like a nomad, though it was not I but the people around me who moved.

Hills and trees, fine houses, and wide lawns—these things are important in making an area the kind of place that you want to make your home. But the most beautiful setting is little more than a vacation land when one cannot associate it with a permanent group of friends and acquaintances. In Palos Verdes I feel like a visitor who will soon be moving on, though rationally I know that it will be my home for many years to come.

No doubt one misses something very important and wonderful by not having the memory of a genuine home town—a physical and spiritual base of operations somewhere back in one's past.

We have now a reasonably sound theme. But it is sound not solely because the style has been improved but also because there was implicit in the original essay a working conception, not fully realized, of a true subject, a purpose, and an appropriate disposition. This fact makes it possible to work with this theme; it is, as many student papers are not, a potential whole. To make it fully coherent and effective, however, we will first have to understand what this potential wholeness is.

Let us ask, to begin with, what the subject of the piece is. We answer, Palos Verdes. But we immediately see that it is not just Palos Verdes. A large number of very different themes could be written about Palos Verdes, all very different in subject from this one. The true subject is *the writer's conception of a home town as it developed out of his experience of Palos Verdes*. What is his purpose? To make the reader share the writer's feeling that permanence is the crucial characteristic of a desirable home town. His subject and purpose together, therefore, might be stated as follows: to make the reader feel, through a presentation of the writer's experience of Palos Verdes, that permanence is the crucial characteristic of a desirable home town. A disposition appropriate to this subject–purpose, though

not fully worked out, is already present in the theme: the writer presents
first his early but erroneous impression of the town, causing the reader
imaginatively to share that impression, so that the shortcomings of the
town as a home, presented next, will strike him more forcibly and prepare
him to feel more strongly the truth of the concluding generalization. (Consider how unemphatic the reverse procedure would be.) This conception
of the disposition points to a simple, three-paragraph development, two
embodying the contrast, a third drawing out its implications.

What revisions does this analysis suggest? Looking back over the re-
written theme, we see first that a good bit of the material in the first paragraph is only potentially related to the true subject, whereas some of it
is not related at all. The last three sentences of the paragraph will need
to be altered so as to omit the details about the older inhabitants and industrial development and to make the other details appear not just as
neutral facts but as part of the writer's original feeling about Palos Verdes
as a home town. In order to make the first paragraph fully a part of the
subject the first sentence of the second paragraph will have to be introduced at the outset (after the first, stage-setting sentence, which could not,
without difficulty, be merged with it), so that we will have not Palos
Verdes but the writer's idea of it from the outset. More material will also
have to be added to the paragraph—description of the town's hills, trees,
etc. This will build up in the reader a sense of how these contribute to
the town's beauty, so that later, when their significance is re-evaluated, the
force of the contrast will be greater. As it is, the reference to the hills and
trees and fine houses comes in without effect because we hear of them
there for the first time, not, as should be the case, in a new and revealing
light which lets us see them not as sufficient constituents of a home town
but only as partial and incomplete ones.

Beyond this, we see that the middle part of the contrast as now revised serves its function reasonably well and can remain largely as it is.
We see, however, that after the writer begins to develop his concluding
generalization, he returns in two sentences (the last sentences, respectively,
of the fourth and fifth paragraphs) to reflections which are essentially con-
tinuations of the "true" perception of Palos Verdes as developed in the
second part of the contrast. These reflections will probably be more effectively disposed if they are placed at the end of the new second paragraph, so that they will give the generalization greater force and allow it,
when it comes, to develop more smoothly; as it is now, the force of the
generalization is dissipated. With all these changes the theme will be a

coherent whole, with subject, purpose, and disposition adjusted effectively to one another. We can add also a few further stylistic revisions to make the whole more fully effective—purposeful revisions now, since with our perception of the subject and purpose we can make stylistic choices not simply to make sentences clear and graceful but to make them effective expressions of the peculiar intent of the whole essay. These changes, however, will be of a very modest sort, since we wish mainly to illustrate what analysis of a form can do, not what greater inherent skill in writing can do. Here then is the final version.

PALOS VERDES

My home town, Palos Verdes, is a well-to-do suburban community located on an ocean peninsula in Los Angeles county. When our family first moved there six years ago, I was immediately struck by the silent beauty of the wide vistas of the surrounding sea and mountains and by the isolation from the multitudes of "Angelenos." Within the town itself the streets wound slowly through hills and trees, past substantial houses set on wide, well-kept lawns. There was no industry, no smoke— only a few stores and two very modern schools, together with a few pleasant playgrounds and parks. This, I remember thinking, was a town one could really call home.

But since then I have changed my mind about Palos Verdes as a home town. Where once I had felt a seeming seclusion and permanence, I came after a time to sense a restlessness in the people and a transience in the life of the town. The rapid population growth of Los Angeles county brought a constant influx of new inhabitants, which together with the equally constant shifting of families out of town, as they pursued the executive father's occupational transfers, made Palos Verdes seem more and more like a way station—a stopover where people merely caught their breath before moving on to someplace else. Friends at school would be there one day and gone the next, new faces appearing to take their places. I felt like a nomad, though it was not I but the people around me who moved. I knew rationally that Palos Verdes would continue to be my home, but I always felt, somehow, that I too would soon be moving on.

I have nothing against change and growth as such, but I do feel that the essential ingredients of a home town are "roots" and permanence, and that was what Palos Verdes lacked. The vistas, the hills, the trees, the wide lawns and fine homes are important in making an area the kind of place one wants for a home, but the most beautiful setting is little more than a vacation land when one cannot associate it with a permanent group of friends and acquaintances. A home town has to be more than a physically attractive place; it ought to be the secure center of one's life, a permanent base of spiritual operations.

We have tried here to perfect only the form which was implicit in the original essay. It is obvious that further thinking about the subject, deeper feeling, more specific memories, and greater skill in presentation could have made the essay much more impressive and praiseworthy than it is. But then it would have been a different essay from any which the writer could have envisaged when he turned in the draft with which we began. Our point, again, is to emphasize what conscious knowledge of the principles upon which good compositions are constructed can do to help a writer realize the potentialities of his work. Improvement on the basis of such knowledge is, as we see, quite possible, but the limits of the improvement will be set by the writer's native ability.

The essays in this section, together with the attached discussions, questions, and theme topics, are designed to further the student's understanding of the principles of analysis outlined above and to help him apply those principles in the writing of his own themes. The essays in the first group have in common the element of persuasive purpose. Though their specific purposes vary a good deal, what we wish to emphasize against the background of relatively homogeneous purpose is the variety of dispositions the selections illustrate and the contrast between the common purpose (persuasion) and the various principles or disposition employed. The following group of four speeches may be used to consolidate the knowledge gained through the study of the first group, since each speech is a notable example of forceful persuasion.

The third section, in contrast with the first two, is devoted to essays characterized by their explanatory purpose, whereas the essays in the fourth section illustrate the ways in which a simple explanatory purpose can be complicated by the addition of an element of emotive force. The final section is made up of essays similar in disposition (narration and characterization) and introduces a third general kind of purpose—entertainment.

Our over-all intention is not to set up any hard and fast categories either of purpose or disposition but rather to give the student some idea of the range of available purposes, dispositions, and styles. Categories are less important than precise description of the *particular* components of the individual essay.

To emphasize the importance of such description, we have provided, for each essay considered, an *analytic summary* specifically defining each of the four components and indicating their interrelationship.* The student may also wish to use these summaries as models for the description of his own essays. Such a description should be an aid to the student in writing an essay and to the instructor in criticizing it. Much more than an outline (which can be considered a chart of the disposition), such a description can reveal what is wrong—and right—with an essay. If the student is able to state for his essay a single subject in a clear nominal construction and a significant purpose in a clear verbal construction, and if he is able to construct an outline of a disposition which shapes precisely that subject to a meaningful realization of precisely that purpose, he will have gone a long way toward the construction of a successful essay. The statement might be drawn up, depending on the writer, either before or after a first draft has been written.

* *Style* is sometimes not specifically defined; where it is not, the student may assume that our implied description is "in language best suited to carry out this purpose in relation to this subject disposed in this fashion." Many of our questions will be designed to help the student to see how the authors make stylistic choices which effectively realize the other three variables.

PERSUASION: SOME DISPOSITIONS

Guided Discussions

JOHN STUART MILL, *Three Examples of Persecution for Belief*
LOUIS KRONENBERGER, *Individualism in America*
JAMES MADISON, *The Federalist, No. 10*
SAMUEL JOHNSON, *The Idler, No. 103*

For Further Analysis

PHYLLIS MC GINLEY, *Suburbia, of Thee I Sing*
BERTRAND RUSSELL, *Freedom and the Colleges*
HENRY DAVID THOREAU, *The War of the Ants*
ALEXIS DE TOCQUEVILLE, *Slavery in Ohio and Kentucky*

John Stuart Mill

THREE EXAMPLES
OF PERSECUTION FOR BELIEF

From *On Liberty*

*I*N ORDER more fully to illustrate the mischief of denying a hearing to opinions because we, in our own judgment, have condemned them, it will be desirable to fix down the discussion to a concrete case; and I choose, by preference, the cases which are least favorable to me—in which the argument against freedom of opinion, both on the score of truth and on that of utility, is considered the strongest. Let the opinions impugned be the belief in a God and in a future state, or any of the commonly received doctrines of morality. To fight the battle on such ground, gives a great advantage to an unfair antagonist; since he will be sure to say (and many who have no desire to be unfair will say it internally), Are these the doctrines which you do not deem sufficiently certain to be taken under the protection of law? Is the belief in a God one of the opinions, to feel sure of which, you hold to be assuming infallibility? But I must be permitted to observe, that it is not the feeling sure of a doctrine (be it what it may) which I call an assumption of infallibility. It is the undertaking to decide that question *for others,* without allowing them to hear what can be said on the contrary side. And I denounce and reprobate this pretension not the less, if put forth on the side of my most solemn convictions. However positive any one's persuasion may be, not only of the falsity but of the pernicious conse-quences—not only of the pernicious consequences, but (to adopt ex-pressions which I altogether condemn) the immorality and impiety of an opinion; yet if, in pursuance of that private judgment, though backed

13

by the public judgment of his country or his cotemporaries, he prevents
the opinion from being heard in its defence, he assumes infallibility.
And so far from the assumption being less objectionable or less dangerous
because the opinion is called immoral or impious, this is the case of
all others in which it is most fatal. These are exactly the occasions on
which the men of one generation commit those dreadful mistakes,
which excite the astonishment and horror of posterity. It is among such
that we find the instances memorable in history, when the arm of the
law has been employed to root out the best men and the noblest
doctrines; with deplorable success as to the men, though some of the
doctrines have survived to be (as if in mockery) invoked, in defence of
similar conduct towards those who dissent from *them,* or from their
received interpretation.

2   Mankind can hardly be too often reminded, that there was once a
man named Socrates, between whom and the legal authorities and
public opinion of his time, there took place a memorable collision.
Born in an age and country abounding in individual greatness, this
man has been handed down to us by those who best knew both him
and the age, as the most virtuous man in it; while *we* know him as
the head and prototype of all subsequent teachers of virtue, the source
equally of the lofty inspiration of Plato and the judicious utilitarianism
of Aristotle, *"i maëstri di color che sanno,"* the two headsprings of
ethical as of all other philosophy. This acknowledged master of all the
eminent thinkers who have since lived—whose fame, still growing after
more than two thousand years, all but outweighs the whole remainder of
the names which make his native city illustrious—was put to death
by his countrymen, after a judicial conviction, for impiety and immorality. Impiety, in denying the gods recognized by the State; indeed
his accuser asserted (see the "Apologia") that he believed in no gods
at all. Immorality, in being, by his doctrines and instructions, a "cor-
rupter of youth." Of these charges the tribunal, there is every ground
for believing, honestly found him guilty, and condemned the man
who probably of all then born had deserved best of mankind, to be
put to death as a criminal.

3   To pass from this to the only other instance of judicial iniquity, the
mention of which, after the condemnation of Socrates, would not be
an anti-climax: the event which took place on Calvary rather more than
eighteen hundred years ago. The man who left on the memory of those
who witnessed his life and conversation, such an impression of his moral
grandeur, that eighteen subsequent centuries have done homage to

him as the Almighty in person, was ignominiously put to death, as what? As a blasphemer. Men did not merely mistake their benefactor; they mistook him for the exact contrary of what he was, and treated him as that prodigy of impiety, which they themselves are now held to be, for their treatment of him. The feelings with which mankind now regard these lamentable transactions, especially the later of the two, render them extremely unjust in their judgment of the unhappy actors. These were, to all appearance, not bad men—not worse than men commonly are, but rather the contrary; men who possessed in a full, or somewhat more than a full measure, the religious, moral, and patriotic feelings of their time and people: the very kind of men who, in all times, our own included, have every chance of passing through life blameless and respected. The high-priest who rent his garments when the words were pronounced, which, according to all the ideas of his country, constituted the blackest guilt, was in all probability quite as sincere in his horror and indignation, as the generality of respectable and pious men now are in the religious and moral sentiments they profess; and most of those who now shudder at his conduct, if they had lived in his time, and been born Jews, would have acted precisely as he did. Orthodox Christians who are tempted to think that those who stoned to death the first martyrs must have been worse men than they themselves are, ought to remember that one of those persecutors was Saint Paul.

4   Let us add one more example, the most striking of all, if the impressiveness of an error is measured by the wisdom and virtue of him who falls into it. If ever any one, possessed of power, had grounds for thinking himself the best and most enlightened among his cotemporaries, it was the Emperor Marcus Aurelius. Absolute monarch of the whole civilized world, he preserved through life not only the most unblemished justice, but what was less to be expected from his Stoical breeding, the tenderest heart. The few failings which are attributed to him, were all on the side of indulgence: while his writings, the highest ethical product of the ancient mind, differ scarcely perceptibly, if they differ at all, from the most characteristic teachings of Christ. This man, a better Christian in all but the dogmatic sense of the word, than almost any of the ostensibly Christian sovereigns who have since reigned, persecuted Christianity. Placed at the summit of all the previous attainments of humanity, with an open, unfettered intellect, and a character which led him of himself to embody in his moral writings the Christian ideal, he yet failed to see that Christianity was to be a good and not an evil to the world, with his duties to which he was so

deeply penetrated. Existing society he knew to be in a deplorable state. But such as it was, he saw, or thought he saw, that it was held together, and prevented from being worse, by belief and reverence of the received divinities. As a ruler of mankind, he deemed it his duty not to suffer society to fall in pieces; and saw not how, if its existing ties were removed, any others could be formed which could again knit it together. The new religion openly aimed at dissolving these ties: unless, therefore, it was his duty to adopt that religion, it seemed to be his duty to put it down. Inasmuch then as the theology of Christianity did not appear to him true or of divine origin; inasmuch as this strange history of a crucified God was not credible to him, and a system which purported to rest entirely upon a foundation to him so wholly unbelievable, could not be foreseen by him to be that renovating agency which, after all abatements, it has in fact proved to be; the gentlest and most amiable of philosophers and rulers, under a solemn sense of duty, authorized the persecution of Christianity. To my mind this is one of the most tragical facts in all history. It is a bitter thought, how different a thing the Christianity of the world might have been, if the Christian faith had been adopted as the religion of the empire under the auspices of Marcus Aurelius instead of those of Constantine. But it would be equally unjust to him and false to truth, to deny, that no one plea which can be urged for punishing anti-Christian teaching, was wanting to Marcus Aurelius for punishing, as he did, the propagation of Christianity. No Christian more firmly believes that Atheism is false, and tends to the dissolution of society, than Marcus Aurelius believed the same things of Christianity; he who, of all men then living, might have been thought the most capable of appreciating it. Unless any one who approves of punishment for the promulgation of opinions, flatters himself that he is a wiser and better man than Marcus Aurelius—more deeply versed in the wisdom of his time, more elevated in his intellect above it—more earnest in his search for truth, or more single-minded in his devotion to it when found; let him abstain from that assumption of the joint infallibility of himself and the multitude, which the great Antoninus made with so unfortunate a result.

Discussion: This selection is an extract from Mill's famous work *On Liberty.* The chapter from which the extract is drawn has as its subject the problem of the limits that are to be set by society on the freedom of its individual members to think and to express their thoughts. Mill's purpose is to persuade the English public of his time—a public of firm religious beliefs and rather fixed prejudices but nevertheless of basic good will—that a society ought, for its own ultimate good, to give to all individuals the greatest possible freedom of expression. In the part of his work printed here Mill attempts to persuade his audience specifically that no one should ever feel justified in suppressing any opinion no matter how convinced he may personally be that it is false or dangerous. Mill develops this thesis, after his introduction of the specific subject, by means of three examples. In order to appreciate his accomplishment as a writer, we need to consider, among other things, the appropriateness to his thesis of the examples chosen and the appropriateness also of his ordering of the examples and his mode of developing each.

Analytic Summary: In this extract Mill treats the possible justifications for the suppression of opinion (subject) *by presenting and developing three examples in such a way* (disposition) *as to persuade a firmly religious audience of basic good will that it is never justifiable to suppress any opinion no matter how apparently false or dangerous it is* (purpose).

Questions

1. Why does Mill choose to focus his argument on beliefs proscribed for their impiety and immorality? Would he make the same choices today? Why?

2. State the general considerations which led Mill to choose these particular examples. Why, for instance, would he prefer any one of these to the example of Protestant martyrs in England, the stories of whom were quite familiar to his readers? State precisely the general historical truth which Mill wishes to drive home through these examples, as a means to enforcing his thesis.

3. Mill himself states his reason for treating Socrates before Christ. What is it?

4. Mill certainly wants us to feel that persecution for belief is heinous. Why then doesn't he dwell more than he does on the cruelty involved in putting Socrates and Christ to death?

5. Mill could assume that the stories of Socrates and Christ were both known to his readers. Given this fact and his purpose, account for the selection of facts that he recapitulates and the judgments that he makes in his opening reviews of their histories. Why does he refer to both their deaths, at the outset, only indirectly?

6. Why does Mill choose to mention the fact that Socrates was accused of believing in "no gods at all"? Would this have been a wise choice if the example were a man of less stature?

7. Why does Mill characterize in the way he does the men who put Christ to death? What possible reaction to this description does he forestall by his mention of St. Paul?

8. Mill apparently did not believe in the divinity of Christ. Analyze the way in which he manages not to conceal this fact and yet not to antagonize his audience.

9. The example of Marcus Aurelius is reserved for treatment after Christ. How does it differ in focus from the first two examples? How does this fact make it appropriate that it should be the last example? Comment specifically in this regard on the design and force of the last sentence.

10. Account specifically for the details Mill chooses in his discussion of the character and outlook of Marcus Aurelius. How does he keep the relevant traits of his character before us in the later discussion?

11. Why does Mill mention the fact that Marcus was a "better Christian" than most sovereigns who have reigned since? Is there more than one reason for the choice?

12. Why does Mill bring in the sentence about Constantine? Does it mend a possible weak point in his argument?

Theme Topics

1. Supporting a thesis through the presentation of a relevant example or examples is one of the basic ways of developing a composition either in whole or in part. Choose some thesis which you feel strongly is true but which is not generally accepted, and develop it, by example, in a paper designed to persuade those who do not share your opinion to change their views. Take care to choose and order your examples carefully and to select and emphasize relevant and telling details within the example.

2. Write a short essay in which you support Mill's thesis by using different examples or by using a different disposition entirely.

Louis Kronenberger

INDIVIDUALISM IN AMERICA

THE AMERICAN imagination has perhaps been stunted by a kind of paradox—by the fact that the whole basis of American living is a vivid dream. But it is a rigidly blueprinted dream, a series of set, established visions; and the average American has grown so accustomed to his own form of dreaming that he can comprehend no other. When one is pursuing an ideal at breakneck speed, how can one weigh the merits of other people's aspirations? In a sharply stratified society, those who acquiesce in their own way of life can thereafter turn their gaze outward, will have the time and the curiosity to grasp the nature of other ways of living, other beliefs and ideals. It is the realist, who studiously learns the strict value and use of things, that can in time assess the value and use of things not his own: the very ability to compare and distinguish fosters understanding. But the idealist, all of whose values are more or less theoretical, so many of whose acts are acts of faith, is nurtured by, is committed to, a dream. The materialistic idealism that governs American life, that on the one hand makes a chariot of every grocery wagon, and on the other a mere hitching post of every star, lets every man lead a very enticing double life, a life of strive and succeed alike, of go with the crowd and yet personally follow the gleam. What other road should he seek, what other will have a more exhilarating ascent, be more brightly lighted or prettily landscaped or widely traveled? Individuality in America is getting to be less and less sought after; hence it needn't even be proscribed. It is disappearing through lack of demand.

2   Here the fact that there is a whole network of conformities in America, rather than just a single pattern, strongly enters in. Americans

19

by no means all do things alike; they just don't do them differently
from everyone else. There are cliques as well as crowds, summer rules as
well as winter ones, group revolts no less than group conformities. Furthermore, the truly grown-up problem isn't how to be oneself *out* of
society, isn't Walden Pond as against Boston, but how to remain
oneself inside it. One of the saddest things about conformity is the
ghastly sort of non-conformity it breeds: the noisy protesting, the aggressive rebelliousness, the rigid counterfetishism. The village atheist
would have come to exist even with *God* for a next-door neighbor, for
he is an offshoot not of religion but of society; the avant-gardist, again,
is the last man to cultivate quietly his avant-garden. In terms of set
culture and community prejudices, Bohemia and Philistia are the same
things in reverse, like photograph and negative. In Greenwich Village
and Greenwich, Connecticut, there are probably an equal number of
things the inhabitants wouldn't be caught dead wearing, or furnishing
their houses with, or tolerating among their friends, or subscribing to as
beliefs; the two places are even necessary to each other—the one to
be shocked, the other to be shocking; the one to stare, the other to be
stared at—and each place will feel for the other an exactly equal
contempt. There are always places where a coat and trousers that match
are far worse form than where they don't.[1]

3   I suspect, too, that the American distaste for individualism is partly
due to our past forms of moral nonconformity, to our early crop of
militant puritans and cranks. In pioneer days it must have often seemed
as though cantankerousness were next to godliness. Our fetish of the
good guy may well owe something to our inherited fear of the Puritan;
the backslapper may well be a retort upon the bluenose; it has perhaps
required all of the American dream to blot out the Early American
nightmare. And once dissent has become associated with disapproval
of all normal pleasures, clearly the inducements of a conformist society
will prove very great; and the accompanying good-guy psychology will
in time prove quite decisive. Even now, to be sure, a sense of guilt
pervades the professional classes, the intellectual and quasi-intellectual
world, though this is a sense of guilt derived from Freud rather than
Jonathan Edwards. Something remains, of course, of the old New
England conscience—and with it, quite admirably, something of the old
New England character. But in general we are today a people who much
less fear God than hate themselves. Moreover, where our current guilts

1 I am speaking here of conformity as a thing in itself; in terms of basic tolerance
and essential *Gemütlichkeit,* Bohemia is enormously superior.

aren't Freudian, they seem rather Catholic than Protestant—rather the Catholic puritanism of Ireland than the Congregationalist puritanism of New England. What dominates, in any case, is much less guilt than self-righteousness, much less breast-beating than backslapping. Even the clergyman—whether priest, minister or rabbi—does well to prove a good mixer, the church or synagogue to stress its clubroom and recreation hall. America possesses a few, but only a few, truly august figures, whether real or symbolic; the others best flourish by blending authority with affability. In all of this there is a sound desire to avoid the pompous: nothing delights us more than to find that the President of our country, or of our college, or of our corporation, is really one of the boys. This seems to me a valuable trait, a real safeguard against Communist or Fascist blandishments; we want our leaders to display the human touch.

4   Our well-founded distaste for cranks has, however, rather blurred our ability to tell a crank from a mere eccentric, or even an eccentric from an individual. On a very rough-and-ready basis we might define an eccentric as a man who is a law unto himself, and a crank as one who, having determined what the law is, insists on laying it down to others. An eccentric[2] puts ice cream on steak simply because he likes it; should a crank do so, he would endow the act with moral grandeur and straightway denounce as sinners (or reactionaries) all who failed to follow suit. The crank, however, seldom deals in anything so agreeable as steak or ice cream; the crank prefers the glories of health bread or the splendors of soybeans. Cranks, at their most familiar, are a sort of peevish prophets, and it's not enough that they should be in the right; others must also be in the wrong. They are by definition obsessed, and, by connotation, obsessed with something odd. They mistake the part for the whole, the props for the play, the inconvenience for the efficacy; they are spoil-sport humanitarians, full of the sour milk of human kindness.[3]

5   The crank is for several reasons a fairly common figure in American

[2] Many "eccentrics" are, of course, mere poseurs and publicity seekers. But many are real, and I speak here only of such.

[3] They can be useful, at moments even invaluable, goads; but they fail of love no less than of humor, and seem most ready to plow the earth where they can spoil the lawn. John the Baptist *requires* the wilderness, and even a man of the critical excellence of Mr. F. R. Leavis evokes the workhouse. After all the gush of the Janeites, Mr. and Mrs. Leavis are well worth hearing on Jane Austen; but they, in the end, misrepresent her no less. They are the sort of people who, in assessing champagne, would give no consideration to the fizz.

life. To begin with, our reaction against cranks has helped breed more of them. A society that worships good-guyism brands the mere dissenter a misfit, and people who are shunned as square pegs will soon find something deeply immoral about round holes. A society, again, that runs to fads and crazes, that has a natural turn for the ingenious and inventive, will encourage some of its members to be cranks and will doom others. There must be, so to speak, lots of factory-damaged human products that, from being looked upon as rejects, come to crankhood rather than true creativity. Careerwise, there is frequently a missed-the-boat quality in cranks, a psychological origin for their moral obsessiveness; and their "flourishing" off failure is tied up with their having failed at the outset. The crank not only increasingly harangues his audience, but the audience increasingly yawns at, and even walks out on, the crank.[4]

6   Where a crank is either a moral crusader by nature or a man at war with his surroundings, an eccentric is neither given to crusading nor oppressed by the world. Perhaps a certain amount of enjoyment is essential to the eccentric—his life is satisfactory *because* it is pleasant— as a certain lack of enjoyment is essential to the crank. The great blessing of eccentricity is that, since it is a law unto itself, one isn't constantly torn between what is expedient on the one side and what is personally desirable on the other. Something of an anarchist (as your crank is something of a bigot), the eccentric will often display very unsound, or unsocial, habits and beliefs. But there is nothing self-righteous about his wrongheadedness; he doesn't drag God into keeping a pet leopard in his back yard, or Americanism into going in for rifle practice at 2:00 A.M.

7   True eccentrics, I would think, are fairly rare, for they must not only differ from other people but be quite indifferent to other peoples' ways: they must, in other words, be as well adjusted as they are odd. So soon as maladjustment enters in, they cease to be characters and turn into cases. On the other hand, many people who with a little encouragement might emerge as eccentrics are, from childhood on, judged—and hence turned into—misfits. Where their peculiarities are mocked, and

4 Just as many eccentrics are poseurs, so many cranks are charlatans. The charlatan shrewdly exploits human weakness where the true crank rails against it; the charlatan, preaching some form of nudism or trial marriage, some "holy" brand of licentiousness or God-sent type of laxative, may end up a millionaire. But the true crank has only a chip on his shoulder or bee in his bonnet, not a card up his sleeve.

certainly where they are penalized, the results can be very unhappy. In America, where even the slightest individualist must resist great pressure, the true eccentric is never free from it. In England there is a proud tradition of eccentricity: the English are far more given than we are to keeping strange pets, collecting strange objects, pursuing strange hobbies, adopting strange careers; even where they most conform, as in their club life, they will behave toward one another with what, to other races, seems a wild and splendid strangeness. This is so true that England's—and sometimes New England's—eccentrics have often a great air about them, possess style rather than mere singularity. Consider how Julia Margaret Cameron would walk the two miles from her house to the railway station stirring a cup of tea as she went. In England and New England on the one hand, and in most of America on the other, there may be a quite opposite basis for eccentricity: in the one case, the law unto oneself born of social privilege; in the other, the self-made world born of being left out of things. The English eccentric suggests a grande dame, the American a spinster.

8   The individualist is by no means an eccentric. He is for one thing aware of alternatives; he chooses—for the most part consciously—between the expedient and the self-satisfying; he refuses to play ball rather than doesn't know a game is in progress; and he will seldom seem freakish or even picturesque. Yet, more and more, the individualist is being looked on as an eccentric and perhaps even a crank: though this attitude is scarcely deliberate on the public's part, it yet subconsciously —or by force of repetition—constitutes a gimmick, a pressure to make people conform. The other method of diminishing individualism in America has been to foster and develop "personality." Though the difference between "personality" and individuality is vast, there exists a strong, however thoughtless, tendency to identify the one with the other. So greatly has conformity triumphed that, no matter how orthodox a man's opinions or conventional his behavior, if he happens to express or conduct himself with the slightest vividness or briskness, he is rated and touted a "person"—what might be supposed an individual! Actually, he may not even have an iota of real personality, may just possess a breezy, adaptable, quick-on-the-trigger manner that enables him to be the life of the party or the spark plug of the conference. In the same way, a woman with a gift for dinner-party chatter and a feminine, discreetly flirtatious air will be thought to have enormous personality.

9   And though such mere types must be written off, there yet *are* a
great many Americans with true personality—with an easy charm, a
distinctive way of doing and saying things, a regional tang, a surviving
girlishness or small-boy quality. They have the appeal, at the very
least, of not being like everyone else. But that, in the cliché sense, they
are "real persons" is to be doubted. One may go a year without hearing
them utter an original, not to say controversial, remark, or seeing them
perform a striking, not to say truly unorthodox, act. The centrifugal
and extrovert charm of personality is in many ways hostile to individualism, which more naturally manifests itself in withdrawal than in
contact, in quiet dissent than in eager acquiescence. Personality and
individuality are by no means mutually exclusive, nor is genuine personality necessarily engaging nor genuine individuality necessarily difficult. But the fact remains that we regard personality as a decided
blessing, as something a man can't have too much of, and individuality
as, oftener than not, a handicap. Individuality is almost by definition
antisocial; and the sound "social" maneuver—or it were perhaps better
called instinct—is to discredit individuality and eventually outlaw it
through enabling people to live *colorfully* alike. As for "personality,"
it has passed from having great social to acquiring great economic
importance: it is the prime mark, and prize asset, of the salesman. And
ours is the country where, in order to sell your product, you don't so
much point out its merits as you first work like hell to sell yourself.

Discussion: This lively piece of writing is interesting formally because it
helps us to be clear about a matter which is sometimes confused in textbooks
on writing. Kronenberger devotes a good deal of space to the definition of three
kinds of non-conformity, a fact which might lead us to call the piece a "definition" and to think of the definition as existing for its own sake as something
different, say, from an argument or persuasion. Actually, as we shall see, the
definitions are not at all ends in themselves but are clearly shaped by Kronenberger's persuasive purpose. Such distinctions seem elementary once they are
made, but purpose and disposition are often confused in this way. The result
may be to impose upon the student writer the task of defining or comparing
in a communicative vacuum, with no realization that his task will become
meaningful only when he has discovered for what *purpose* he is performing the
prescribed operation.

*Analytic Summary: In this selection Kronenberger endeavors,
through a consideration of American non-conformity* (subject),

to make his audience feel that the pervasive pressure of American society toward conformity stultifies the growth of genuine and harmonious individuality in its members (purpose). *He does this by characterizing several kinds of American non-conformity* (disposition). *His language suggests a man of quick intelligence, confident culture, and distinctive character, very much a part of the American milieu but nevertheless critical of and unhappy with it* (style).

Questions

1. A consistent feature of Kronenberger's style is his use of trite phrases as the basis for new and striking ones. Thus "hitch your wagon to a star" becomes "makes a chariot of every grocery wagon and a hitching post of every star"; "you can't fit round pegs into square holes" becomes "people who are shunned as square pegs will soon find something deeply immoral about round holes," etc. Can you find similar adaptations? Why, in view of Kronenberger's subject and purpose in the essay, is this particular stylistic device effective?

2. Why is Kronenberger's point about American bohemians an especially telling one for his purpose? Why are such pointed parallel phrasings as "Bohemia and Philistia" and "Greenwich Village and Greenwich, Connecticut" appropriate in this context? What aspect of his purpose leads Kronenberger to characterize the non-conformity of Bohemia as "ghastly," "noisy," and "rigid." Why do you think he adds the qualifying footnote about Bohemia?

3. In the third paragraph Kronenberger discusses for the moment not contemporary American society, with which he and the reader are familiar, but a somewhat uncertain hypothesis about the historical causes of the American attitude toward non-conformity. How does the uncertainty of the hypothesis influence Kronenberger's phrasing? Does the force of the paragraph depend entirely on the validity of the hypothesis?

4. Each of the definitions of the various kinds of non-conformists is shaped not by an intention to define for the sake of clear understanding but, as we have already said, as a means to the realization of Kronenberger's purpose. What attitude toward cranks does Kronenberger try to develop in the reader by the remarks in paragraph 4? What then is the force of showing in paragraph 5 that the crank is a "fairly common figure" in American society? Does the material in the paragraph (and in the one preceding) develop any general attitude toward social coercion in the reader that is relevant to the over-all purpose?

5. Why, in the same terms, are eccentrics characterized as they are and said to be "fairly rare"? What is the function of the contrast with the English situation?

6. Why is it to Kronenberger's purpose, in paragraph 8, to dwell only briefly on the characteristics of the individualist and then, in conclusion, to

develop at length his treatment of "personality" with subordinated comparisons to individuality?

7. We have already noticed Kronenberger's tendency toward euphonious, neatly balanced phrasing ("the backslapper may well be a retort on the blue-nose; it has perhaps required all of the American dream to blot out the Early American nightmare"). Such control of style is obviously an asset in writing, but is there any danger that it may turn into a liability? How might this be so? Does Kronenberger entirely avoid this danger?

Theme Topics

1. Write an essay with a persuasive purpose in which a central technique of the disposition is definition. You might, for example, try to persuade your audience of the correctness of a certain attitude toward college study by defining various types of students.

2. Define some abstract term—freedom, charity, peace, etc.—in such a way as to persuade your audience of the truth of a particular statement.

James Madison

THE FEDERALIST, No. 10

*A*MONG THE numerous advantages promised by a well-constructed Union, none deserves to be more accurately developed than its tendency to break and control the violence of faction. The friend of popular Governments never finds himself so much alarmed for their character and fate, as when he contemplates their propensity to this dangerous vice. He will not fail, therefore, to set a due value on any plan which, without violating the principles to which he is attached, provides a proper cure for it. The instability, injustice, and confusion introduced into the public councils, have, in truth, been the mortal diseases under which popular Governments have everywhere perished; as they continue to be the favorite and fruitful topics from which the adversaries to liberty derive their most specious declamations. The valuable improvements made by the American Constitutions on the popular models, both ancient and modern, cannot certainly be too much admired; but it would be an unwarrantable partiality, to contend that they have as effectually obviated the danger on this side, as was wished and expected. Complaints are everywhere heard from our most considerate and virtuous citizens, equally the friends of public and private faith, and of public and personal liberty, that our Governments are too unstable; that the public good is disregarded in the conflicts of rival parties; and that measures are too often decided, not according to the rules of justice, and the rights of the minor party, but by the superior force of an interested and overbearing majority. However anxiously we may wish that these complaints had no foundation, the evidence of known facts will not permit us to deny that they are in some degree true. It will be found, indeed, on a candid review of our situation, that some of the distresses under which we labor have been erroneously charged on the operation of our Governments; but it will be found, at the same time, that other causes will not alone account for many of our heaviest misfortunes; and, particularly, for that prevailing and increasing distrust of public engagements, and alarm for private rights, which are echoed from one end of the continent to the other. These must be chiefly, if not wholly, effects of the unsteadiness and injustice, with which a factious spirit has tainted our public administrations.

2   By a faction, I understand a number of citizens, whether amounting to a majority or minority of the whole, who are united and actuated by some common impulse of passion, or of interest, adverse to the rights of other citizens, or to the permanent and aggregate interests of the community.

3   There are two methods of curing the mischiefs of faction: the one, by removing its causes; the other, by controlling its effects.

4   There are again two methods of removing the causes of faction: the one, by destroying the liberty which is essential to its existence; the other, by giving to every citizen the same opinions, the same passions, and the same interests.

5   It could never be more truly said than of the first remedy, that it was worse than the disease. Liberty is to faction, what air is to fire, an aliment without which it instantly expires. But it could not be less folly to abolish liberty, which is essential to political life, because it nourishes faction, than it would be to wish the annihilation of air, which is essential to animal life, because it imparts to fire its destructive agency.

6   The second expedient is as impracticable, as the first would be unwise. As long as the reason of man continues fallible, and he is at liberty to exercise it, different opinions will be formed. As long as the connection subsists between his reason and his self-love, his opinions and his passions will have a reciprocal influence on each other; and the former will be objects to which the latter will attach themselves. The diversity in the faculties of men, from which the rights of property originate, is not less an insuperable obstacle to an uniformity of interests. The protection of these faculties is the first object of Government. From the protection of different and unequal faculties of acquiring property, the possession of different degrees and kinds of property immediately results; and from the influence of these on the sentiments and views of the respective proprietors, ensues a division of the society into different interests and parties.

⁷ The latent causes of faction, are thus sown in the nature of man; and we see them everywhere brought into different degrees of activity, according to the different circumstances of civil society. A zeal for different opinions concerning religion, concerning Government, and many other points, as well of speculation as of practice; an attachment to different leaders ambitiously contending for preëminence and power; or to persons of other descriptions whose fortunes have been interesting to the human passions, have, in turn, divided mankind into parties, inflamed them with mutual animosity, and rendered them much more disposed to vex and oppress each other, than to coöperate for their common good. So strong is this propensity of mankind to fall into mutual animosities, that where no substantial occasion presents itself, the most frivolous and fanciful distinctions have been sufficient to kindle their unfriendly passions, and excite their most violent conflicts. But the most common and durable source of factions has been the various and unequal distribution of property. Those who hold, and those who are without property, have ever formed distinct interests in society. Those who are creditors, and those who are debtors, fall under a like discrimination. A landed interest, a manufacturing interest, a mercantile interest, a moneyed interest, with many lesser interests, grow up of necessity in civilized nations, and divide them into different classes, actuated by different sentiments and views. The regulation of these various and interfering interests forms the principal task of modern Legislation, and involves the spirit of party and faction in the necessary and ordinary operations of the Government.

⁸ No man is allowed to be a judge in his own cause; because his interest would certainly bias his judgment, and, not improbably, corrupt his integrity. With equal, nay with greater reason, a body of men are unfit to be both judges and parties at the same time; yet what are many of the most important acts of legislation, but so many judicial determinations, not indeed concerning the rights of single persons, but concerning the rights of large bodies of citizens? and what are the different classes of Legislators, but advocates and parties to the causes which they determine? Is a law proposed concerning private debts? It is a question to which the creditors are parties on one side, and the debtors on the other. Justice ought to hold the balance between them. Yet the parties are, and must be, themselves the judges; and the most numerous party, or, in other words, the most powerful faction, must be expected to prevail. Shall domestic manufactures be encouraged, and in what degree, by restrictions on foreign manufactures? are questions which would be differently de-

cided by the landed and the manufacturing classes; and probably by neither, with a sole regard to justice and the public good. The apportionment of taxes on the various descriptions of property is an act which seems to require the most exact impartiality; yet there is, perhaps, no legislative act in which greater opportunity and temptation are given to a predominant party, to trample on the rules of justice. Every shilling, with which they overburden the inferior number, is a shilling saved to their own pockets.

9   It is in vain to say, that enlightened statesmen will be able to adjust these clashing interests, and render them all subservient to the public good. Enlightened statesmen will not always be at the helm: Nor, in many cases, can such an adjustment be made at all, without taking into view indirect and remote considerations, which will rarely prevail over the immediate interest which one party may find in disregarding the rights of another, or the good of the whole.

10   The inference to which we are brought is, that the *causes* of faction cannot be removed; and that relief is only to be sought in the means of controlling its *effects*.

11   If a faction consists of less than a majority, relief is supplied by the republican principle, which enables the majority to defeat its sinister views by regular vote. It may clog the administration, it may convulse the society; but it will be unable to execute and mask its violence under the forms of the Constitution. When a majority is included in a faction, the form of popular Government, on the other hand, enables it to sacrifice to its ruling passion or interest both the public good and the rights of other citizens. To secure the public good, and private rights, against the danger of such a faction, and at the same time to preserve the spirit and the form of popular Government, is then the great object to which our inquiries are directed: Let me add, that it is the great desideratum, by which alone this form of Government can be rescued from the opprobrium under which it has so long labored, and be recommended to the esteem and adoption of mankind.

12   By what means is this object attainable? Evidently by one of two only. Either the existence of the same passion or interest in a majority, at the same time, must be prevented; or the majority, having such co-existent passion or interest, must be rendered, by their number and local situation, unable to concert and carry into effect schemes of oppression. If the impulse and the opportunity be suffered to coincide, we well know that neither moral nor religious motives can be relied on as an adequate control. They are not found to be such on the injustice and violence

of individuals, and lose their efficacy in proportion to the number combined together; that is, in proportion as their efficacy becomes needful.
[13] From this view of the subject, it may be concluded, that a pure Democracy, by which I mean a Society consisting of a small number of citizens, who assemble and administer the Government in person, can admit of no cure for the mischiefs of faction. A common passion or interest will, in almost every case, be felt by a majority of the whole; a communication and concert results from the form of Government itself; and there is nothing to check the inducements to sacrifice the weaker party, or an obnoxious individual. Hence it is, that such Democracies have ever been spectacles of turbulence and contention; have ever been found incompatible with personal security, or the rights of property; and have in general been as short in their lives, as they have been violent in their deaths. Theoretic politicians, who have patronized this species of Government, have erroneously supposed, that by reducing mankind to a perfect equality in their political rights, they would, at the same time, be perfectly equalized and assimilated in their possessions, their opinions, and their passions.

[14] A Republic, by which I mean a Government in which the scheme of representation takes place, opens a different prospect, and promises the cure for which we are seeking. Let us examine the points in which it varies from pure Democracy, and we shall comprehend both the nature of the cure, and the efficacy which it must derive from the Union.

[15] The two great points of difference, between a Democracy and a Republic, are, first, the delegation of the Government, in the latter, to a small number of citizens elected by the rest: Secondly, the greater number of citizens, and greater sphere of country, over which the latter may be extended.

[16] The effect of the first difference is, on the one hand, to refine and enlarge the public views, by passing them through the medium of a chosen body of citizens, whose wisdom may best discern the true interest of their country, and whose patriotism and love of justice will be least likely to sacrifice it to temporary or partial considerations. Under such a regulation, it may well happen, that the public voice, pronounced by the representatives of the People, will be more consonant to the public good, than if pronounced by the People themselves, convened for the purpose. On the other hand, the effect may be inverted. Men of factious tempers, of local prejudices, or of sinister designs, may by intrigue, by corruption, or by other means, first obtain the suffrages, and then betray the interests of the people. The question resulting is, whether small or

extensive Republics are most favorable to the election of proper guardians of the public weal; and it is clearly decided in favor of the latter by two obvious considerations.

17   In the first place, it is to be remarked that however small the Republic may be, the Representatives must be raised to a certain number, in order to guard against the cabals of a few; and that however large it may be, they must be limited to a certain number, in order to guard against the confusion of a multitude. Hence, the number of Representatives in the two cases not being in proportion to that of the Constituents, and being proportionally greatest in the small Republic, it follows, that if the proportion of fit characters be not less in the large than in the small Republic, the former will present a greater option, and consequently a greater probability of a fit choice.

18   In the next place, as each Representative will be chosen by a greater number of citizens in the large than in the small Republic, it will be more difficult for unworthy candidates to practise with success the vicious arts, by which elections are too often carried; and the suffrages of the People, being more free, will be more likely to centre in men who possess the most attractive merit, and the most diffusive and established characters.

19   It must be confessed, that in this, as in most other cases, there is a mean, on both sides of which inconveniences will be found to lie. By enlarging too much the number of electors, you render the representative too little acquainted with all their local circumstances and lesser interests; as by reducing it too much, you render him unduly attached to these, and too little fit to comprehend and pursue great and National objects. The Federal Constitution forms a happy combination in this respect; the great and aggregate interests being referred to the National, the local and particular to the State Legislatures.

20   The other point of difference is, the greater number of citizens and extent of territory which may be brought within the compass of Republican, than of Democratic Government; and it is this circumstance principally which renders factious combinations less to be dreaded in the former, than in the latter. The smaller the society, the fewer probably will be the distinct parties and interests composing it; the fewer the distinct parties and interests, the more frequently will a majority be found of the same party; and the smaller the number of individuals composing a majority, and the smaller the compass within which they are placed, the more easily will they concert and execute their plans of oppression. Extend the sphere, and you take in a greater variety of parties and interests;

you make it less probable that a majority of the whole will have a common motive to invade the rights of other citizens; or if such a common motive exists, it will be more difficult for all who feel it to discover their own strength, and to act in unison with each other. Besides other impediments, it may be remarked, that where there is a consciousness of unjust or dishonorable purposes, communication is always checked by distrust, in proportion to the number whose concurrence is necessary.

21   Hence, it clearly appears, that the same advantage which a Republican has over a Democracy, in controlling the effects of faction, is enjoyed by a large over a small Republic,—is enjoyed by the Union over the States composing it. Does the advantage consist in the substitution of Representatives, whose enlightened views and virtuous sentiments render them superior to local prejudices, and to schemes of injustice? It will not be denied, that the Representation of the Union will be most likely to possess these requisite endowments. Does it consist in the greater security afforded by a greater variety of parties, against the event of any one party being able to outnumber and oppress the rest? In an equal degree does the increased variety of parties, comprised within the Union, increase this security. Does it, in fine, consist in the greater obstacles opposed to the concert and accomplishment of the secret wishes of an unjust and interested majority? Here, again, the extent of the Union gives it the most palpable advantage.

22   The influence of factious leaders may kindle a flame within their particular States, but will be unable to spread a general conflagration through the other States. A religious sect may degenerate into a political faction in a part of the Confederacy; but the variety of sects dispersed over the entire face of it, must secure the National Councils against any danger from that source; A rage for paper money, for an abolition of debts, for an equal division of property, or for any other improper or wicked project, will be less apt to pervade the whole body of the Union, than a particular member of it; in the same proportion as such a malady is more likely to taint a particular county or district, than an entire State.

23   In the extent and proper structure of the Union, therefore, we behold a Republican remedy for the diseases most incident to Republican Government. And according to the degree of pleasure and pride we feel in being Republicans, ought to be our zeal in cherishing the spirit, and supporting the character, of Federalists.

PUBLIUS

The New York Packet, Friday, November 23, 1787

Discussion: This piece of persuasion by Madison has a good many elements in common with the kind of essay called an explanation, of which the editors present examples later (see de Tocqueville's treatment of democratic armies, below). But though Madison's analysis of popular governments is intellectually completely honest and in itself a valuable contribution to political theory, still his purpose in the whole is to persuade his audience to adopt a particular belief and (implicitly) a course of action. It is therefore most useful, in analysis, to think of it as a persuasion, especially since, as will become obvious, the development and ordering of the parts is ultimately determined by persuasive and not explanatory needs.

Analytic Summary: In this essay Madison considers the possible remedies for the tendency toward faction inherent in popular government (subject) *in order to persuade a patriotic American audience, strongly in favor of individual liberty and suspicious of central government, that a large federal republic as envisaged in the proposed Constitution is the most satisfactory form for American government* (purpose). *He proceeds by considering in order, from least to most effective, various possible remedies for faction derived from an analysis of its causes and effects* (disposition).

Questions

1. If Madison had been writing merely an explanatory analysis of his subject, how much of the first paragraph would have been functional? What fact basic to his argument does Madison develop in the paragraph? What dangers, in regard to his audience, are involved in developing this fact? How does Madison make his point so as to avoid those dangers? How, particularly, is his choice of language affected?

2. Elimination of the causes of faction is not really, as Madison indicates, a very practicable remedy for the evils of faction. Why, then, after he has in effect dismissed (in paragraphs 5 and 6) the possibility of remedy through elimination of the causes, does he spend three paragraphs expanding on the causes? Could some of these points have been made, with specifically American examples, in the first paragraph? Why is it better to make them only as general points and at this point in the argument?

3. Notice that when Madison defines faction in the second paragraph he does not put particular emphasis on the danger of a majority as opposed to a minority faction, but that in paragraph 11 he gives it strong emphasis, saying that it is "the great object to which our inquiries are directed"? Why does he not initially stress this emphasis? How do the three paragraphs of expansion on the causes of faction referred to above (paragraphs 7, 8, and 9) help to prepare for this delayed emphasis?

4. The real alternatives which faced Madison and his audience were, of course, either the system of federal government offered by the Constitution or the looser, state-centered federation already in being. Why then does Madison deal with democracy (as he defines it) at all? In what ways does it help him establish his real point, that a large republic is to be preferred to a small one?

5. In what one sense does the possibility of a "small republic" exist in the actual situation confronting Madison? Where does he make this clear? Why is it to his purpose to admit that there are limits to the advantages of large over small republics?

6. What is the function, in relation to the whole, of the first two of the last three paragraphs? Of the last paragraph?

7. Although the principle of disposition in the *whole* of Madison's essay is that described in the analytic summary, some of the *parts* of the essay have different and distinctive principles of development. What principle is employed in paragraph 5? In paragraph 6? In paragraphs 14–16?

Theme Topics

1. Write an essay on a serious subject in which you endeavor to persuade a particular audience of a truth which would serve to justify a particular course of public action. Imitate, as much as your subject allows, Madison's sequential, cause-and-effect development. Appropriate subjects might be the possible solutions to the international nuclear arms race, or the relationship of capital punishment to the prevention of crime.

2. Write an essay on the relevance of Madison's analysis of popular government to some specific problem or problems of modern popular governments either at home or abroad. Remember, however, that the relation of Madison's essay to the modern problems is only the specific subject; you must shape it to a specific and significant purpose.

Samuel Johnson

THE IDLER, No. 103

Respicere ad longæ jussit spatia ultima vitæ.   Juv. [Sat. X. 275.]
"Bade him regard the last period of a long life."

*M*UCH OF the Pain and Pleasure of mankind arises from the conjectures which every one makes of the thoughts of others; we all enjoy praise which we do not hear, and resent contempt which we do not see. The *Idler* may therefore be forgiven, if he suffers his Imagination to represent to him what his readers will say or think when they are informed that they have now his last paper in their hands.

2   Value is more frequently raised by scarcity than by use. That which lay neglected when it was common, rises in estimation as its quantity becomes less. We seldom learn the true want of what we have till it is discovered that we can have no more.

3   This essay will, perhaps, be read with care even by those who have not yet attended to any other; and he that finds this late attention recompensed, will not forbear to wish that he had bestowed it sooner.

4   Though the *Idler* and his readers have contracted no close friendship, they are perhaps both unwilling to part. There are few things not purely evil, of which we can say, without some emotion of uneasiness, *this is the last.* Those who never could agree together, shed tears when mutual discontent has determined them to final separation; of a place which has been frequently visited, tho' without pleasure, the last look is taken with heaviness of heart; and the *Idler,* with all his chilness of tranquility, is not wholly unaffected by the thought that his last essay is now before him.

5   This secret horrour of the last is inseparable from a thinking being whose life is limited, and to whom death is dreadful. We always make a

secret comparison between a part and the whole; the termination of any period of life reminds us that life itself has likewise its termination; when we have done any thing for the last time, we involuntarily reflect that a part of the days allotted us is past, and that as more is past there is less remaining.

6   It is very happily and kindly provided, that in every life there are certain pauses and interruptions, which force consideration upon the careless, and seriousness upon the light; points of time where one course of action ends and another begins: and by vicissitude of fortune, or alteration of employment, by change of place, or loss of friendship, we are forced to say of something, *this is the last.*

7   An even and unvaried tenour of life always hides from our apprehension the approach of its end. Succession is not perceived but by variation; he that lives to-day as he lived yesterday, and expects that, as the present day is such will be the morrow, easily conceives time as running in a circle and returning to itself. The uncertainty of our duration is impressed commonly by dissimilitude of condition; it is only by finding life changeable that we are reminded of its shortness.

8   This conviction, however forcible at every new impression, is every moment fading from the mind; and partly by the inevitable incursion of new images, and partly by voluntary exclusion of unwelcome thoughts, we are again exposed to the universal fallacy; and we must do another thing for the last time, before we consider that the time is nigh when we shall do no more.

9   As the last *Idler* is published in that solemn week which the Christian world has always set apart for the examination of the conscience, the review of life, the extinction of earthly desires and the renovation of holy purposes, I hope that my readers are already disposed to view every incident with seriousness, and improve it by meditation; and that when they see this series of trifles brought to a conclusion, they will consider that by outliving the *Idler,* they have passed weeks, months, and years which are now no longer in their power; that an end must in time be put to every thing great as to every thing little; that to life must come its last hour, and to this system of being its last day, the hour at which probation ceases, and repentance will be vain; the day in which every work of the hand, and imagination of the heart shall be brought to judgment, and an everlasting futurity shall be determined by the past.

Saturday, April 5th, 1760

Discussion: This essay by a great eighteenth-century man of letters is, as he tells us, the last of a series which had appeared in a contemporary newspaper over a period of more than two years. Building upon this accidental fact, Johnson constructs a somber and moving essay of religious reflection. The essay shows how a specific and in itself limited occasional subject can be effectively turned to broader persuasive uses.

The essay also illustrates the importance of style in persuasive writing. It has been said that style is the man, and it is clear that in this essay Johnson, one of the great English stylists, gains his effect in large measure by revealing, through his style, as much of his own grand moral nature as was relevant to his subject and his purpose. One need only turn the piece into different language to see how much its force depends on the impression given by the language of the personality of the writer.

Analytic Summary: In this essay Johnson considers the last issue of The Idler *as an exemplification of all last things* (subject) *in order to persuade his reader that the brevity of life and the imminence of eternal judgment make self-examination and reformation urgent* (purpose). *He does this in three stages: (1) by attaching serious moral meaning to the appearance of the last* Idler *and developing out of this the idea that last things in general are reminders of death; (2) by then developing the connected idea that life in general is "happily" arranged so that "last" events continually remind us of the ultimate "last"; (3) by returning to the particular occasion of the last* Idler, *in the context now developed, as a basis for a final exhortation* (disposition). *The effect of the whole is greatly enhanced by choices of language which contribute to the revelation of the writer as a man who is given to serious moral reflection and who, without any sense of his own superiority, deeply feels his obligation to instruct others in a duty which he implicitly assumes that they recognize but, like himself, are too prone to forget* (style).

Questions

1. In the first three paragraphs Johnson uses a good many words to tell his readers two rather simple things: (1) that he wonders what they will think when they learn that this is the last *Idler;* and (2) that he believes they will read it with care. The accompanying generalizations do not seem immediately necessary. If we rewrite the paragraphs without them, however, we can see that they have a remarkably complex function. They serve to reveal Johnson's attitude toward himself, his audience, his work as an essayist, and toward human nature in a way directly relevant to the realization of his purpose. Specify as well as you can the content of these revelations and the effect that they have on the reader.

2. In the fourth paragraph Johnson (1) establishes his full subject and (2) does it in a way quite appropriate to his purpose. With respect to the first point, what is the function of the opening and closing references to the *Idler?* What is the function of the second sentence? What is the function of the first two clauses of the last sentence? With respect to the second point, what is the effect of the particular examples offered in the last sentence? (What truth about life, relevant to the purpose, do the phrases "mutual discontent" and "without pleasure" point to?) What is the effect of the revelation of the speaker's attitude in the last clause? Would the effect have been the same if the revelation had been made near the opening of the essay? Why?

3. What is the nature of the connection between paragraphs 5 and 4? What is the effect of the unqualified directness with which the assertions in paragraph 5 are made? What is the principle of the progression of the three clauses of the last sentence? Could the order have been reversed? Why not? What is the effect of the use of the words "secret" and "involuntarily"?

4. Considering the effect of paragraph 5, is it immediately obvious, in the paragraphs following, why the "last" things in life should be said to be very "happily and kindly provided"? What does the word "provided" imply? What does the fact that Johnson considers no further explanation of his meaning necessary reveal about his attitude toward life? Is the reader likely to feel a contrast between his own attitude and Johnson's? What will be the effect upon the reader?

5. What assumptions about human nature and human life, beyond the basic truth that Johnson is establishing, are implicit in paragraphs 6 through 8?

6. Notice that the last paragraph is one long sentence organized, after the initial introductory clause, as a series of telescoped *that* clauses. How does this patterning reinforce the effect of what Johnson is saying? How does Johnson arrange the elements within the last *that* clause so as to enhance still further the effect he seeks?

7. What is the effect of the adjective applied to *futurity* in relation to the subject of the essay and to the earlier references to "last hour" and "last day"?

Theme Topics

1. Write an essay focusing upon some specific event—some development in the news not notably significant in itself, or some happening in your own life— and expanding it into a more general but connected subject which is shaped to a clear purpose.

2. Write an essay on Johnson's subject (some last thing as an exemplification of all last things) but shape it to a different purpose. Such a purpose might be, for instance, to make the reader feel the hidden pathos of life.

Phyllis McGinley

SUBURBIA, OF THEE I SING

*T*WENTY miles east of New York City as the New Haven Railroad flies sits a village I shall call Spruce Manor. The Boston Post Road, there, for the length of two blocks, becomes Main Street, and on one side of that thundering thoroughfare are the grocery stores and the drug stores and the Village Spa where teen-agers gather of an afternoon to drink their cokes and speak their curious confidences. There one finds the shoe repairers and the dry cleaners and the second-hand stores which sell "antiques" and the stationery stores which dispense comic books to ten-year-olds and greeting cards and lending library masterpieces to their mothers. On the opposite side stand the bank, the fire house, the public library. The rest of this town of perhaps four or five thousand people lies to the south and is bounded largely by Long Island Sound, curving protectively on three borders. The movie theater (dedicated to the showing of second-run, single-feature pictures) and the grade schools lie north, beyond the Post Road, and that is a source of worry to Spruce Manorites. They are always a little uneasy about the children, crossing, perhaps, before the lights are safely green. However, two excellent policemen—Mr. Crowley and Mr. Lang—station themselves at the intersections four times a day, and so far there have been no accidents.

Spruce Manor in the spring and summer and fall is a pretty town, full of gardens and old elms. (There are few spruces, but the village Council is considering planting a few on the station plaza, out of sheer patriotism.) In the winter, the houses reveal themselves as comfortable, well-kept, architecturally insignificant. Then one can see the town for what it is and has been since it left off being farm and woodland some sixty years ago—the epitome of Suburbia, not the country and certainly not the city.

40

It is a commuter's town, the living center of a web which unrolls each morning as the men swing aboard the locals, and contracts again in the evening when they return. By day, with even the children pent in schools, it is a village of women. They trundle mobile baskets at the A & P, they sit under driers at the hairdressers, they sweep their porches and set out bulbs and stitch up slip covers. Only on weekends does it become hetero-geneous and lively, the parking places difficult to find.

Spruce Manor has no country club of its own, though devoted golfers have their choice of two or three not far away. It does have a small yacht club and a beach which can be used by anyone who rents or owns a house here. The village supports a little park with playground equipment and a counselor, where children, unattended by parents, can spend sum-mer days if they have no more pressing engagements.

It is a town not wholly without traditions. Residents will point out the two-hundred-year-old manor house, now a minor museum; and in the autumn they line the streets on a scheduled evening to watch the Volun-teer Firemen parade. That is a fine occasion, with so many heads of house-holds marching in their red blouses and white gloves, some with flaming helmets, some swinging lanterns, most of them genially out of step. There is a bigger parade on Memorial Day with more marchers than watchers and with the Catholic priest, the rabbi, and the Protestant ministers each delivering a short prayer when the paraders gather near the War Memorial. On the whole, however, outside of contributing generously to the Community Chest, Manorites are not addicted to municipal get-togethers.

No one is very poor here and not many families rich enough to be awesome. In fact, there is not much to distinguish Spruce Manor from any other of a thousand suburbs outside of New York City or San Francisco or Detroit or Chicago or even Stockholm, for that matter. Except for one thing. For some reason, Spruce Manor has become a sort of symbol to writers and reporters familiar only with its name or trivial aspects. It has become a symbol of all that is middle-class in the worst sense, of settled-downness or rootlessness, according to what the writer is trying to prove; of smug and prosperous mediocrity—or even, in more lurid novels, of lechery at the country club and Sunday morning hangovers.

To condemn Suburbia has long been a literary cliché, anyhow. I have yet to read a book in which the suburban life was pictured as the good life or the commuter as a sympathetic figure. He is nearly as much a stock character as the old stage Irishman: the man who "spends his life riding to and from his wife," the eternal Babbitt who knows all about Buicks and nothing about Picasso, whose sanctuary is the club locker room, whose ideas spring ready-made from the illiberal newspapers. His wife plays politics at the P.T.A. and keeps up with the Joneses. Or—if the scene is more gilded and less respectable—the commuter is the high-powered advertising executive with a station wagon and an eye for the ladies, his wife a restless baggage given to too many cocktails in the afternoon.

These clichés I challenge. I have lived in the country. I have lived in the city. I have lived in an average Middle Western small town. But for the best eleven years of my life I have lived in Suburbia and I like it.

"Compromise!" cried our friends when we came here from an expensive, inconvenient, moderately fashionable tenement in Manhattan. It was the period in our lives when everyone was moving somewhere. Farther uptown, farther downtown, across town to Sutton Place, to a half-dozen rural acres in Connecticut or New Jersey or even Vermont. But no one in our rather rarefied little group was thinking of moving to the suburbs except us. They were aghast that we could find anything appealing in the thought of a middle-class house on a middle-class street in a middle-class village full of middle-class people. That we were tired of town and hoped for children, that we couldn't afford both a city apartment and a farm, they put down as feeble excuses. To this day they cannot understand us. You see, they read the books. They even write them.

Compromise? Of course we compromise. But compromise, if not the spice of life, is its solidity. It is what makes nations great and marriages happy and Spruce Manor the pleasant place it is. As for its being middle-class, what is wrong with acknowledging one's roots? And how free we are! Free of the city's noise, of its ubiquitous doormen, of the soot on the windowsill and the radio in the next apartment. We have released ourselves from the seasonal hegira to the mountains or the seashore. We have only one address, one house to keep supplied with paring knives and blankets. We are free from the snows that block the countryman's roads in winter and its electricity which always goes off in a thunderstorm. I do not insist that we are typical. There is nothing really typical about any of our friends and neighbors here, and therein lies my point. The true suburbanite needs to conform less than anyone else; much less than the gentleman farmer with his remodeled salt-box or than the determined cliff dweller with his necessity for living at the right address. In Spruce Manor all addresses are right. And since we are fairly numerous here, we need not fall back on the people nearest us for total companionship. There is not here, as in a small city away from truly urban centers, some particular family whose codes must be ours. And we could not keep up with the Joneses even if we wanted to, for we know many Joneses and they are all quite different people leading the most various lives.

The Albert Joneses spend their weekends sailing, the Bertram Joneses cultivate their delphinium, the Clarence Joneses—Clarence being a handy man with a cello—are enthusiastic about amateur chamber music. The David Joneses dote on bridge, but neither of the Ernest Joneses understands it, and they prefer staying home of an evening so that Ernest Jones can carve his witty caricatures out of pieces of old fruit wood. We admire each other's gardens, applaud each other's sailing records; we are too busy to compete. So long as our clapboards are painted and our hedges decently trimmed, we have fulfilled our community obligations. We can live as anonymously as in a city or we can call half the village by their first names.

On our half-acre or three-quarters, we can raise enough tomatoes for our salads and assassinate enough beetles to satisfy the gardening urge. Or we can buy our vegetables at the store and put the whole place to lawn without feeling that we are neglecting our property. We can have privacy and shade and the changing of the seasons and also the Joneses next door from whom to borrow a cup of sugar or a stepladder. Despite the novelists, the shadow of the country club rests lightly on us. Half of us wouldn't be found dead with a golf stick in our hands, and loathe Saturday dances. Few of us expect to be deliriously wealthy or world-famous or divorced. What we do expect is to pay off the mortgage and send our healthy children to good colleges.

For when I refer to life here, I think, of course, of living with children. Spruce Manor without children would be a paradox. The summer waters are full of them, gamboling like dolphins. The lanes are alive with them, the yards overflow with them, they possess the tennis courts and the skating pond and the vacant lots. Their roller skates wear down the asphalt, and their bicycles make necessary the twenty-five mile speed limit. They converse interminably on the telephones and make rich the dentist and the pediatrician. Who claims that a child and a half is the American middle-class average? A nice medium Spruce Manor family runs to four or five, and we count proudly, but not with amazement, the many solid households running to six, seven, eight, nine even up to twelve. Our houses here are big and not new, most of them, and there is a temptation to fill them up, let the décor fall where it may.

Besides, Spruce Manor seems designed by providence and town planning for the happiness of children. Better designed than the city; better, I say defiantly, than the country. Country mothers must be constantly arranging and contriving for their children's leisure time. There is no neighbor child next door for playmate, no school within walking distance. The ponds are dangerous to young swimmers, the woods full of poison ivy, the romantic dirt roads unsuitable for bicycles. An extra acre or two gives a fine sense of possession to an adult; it does not compensate children for the give-and-take of our village, where there is always a contemporary to help swing the skipping rope or put on the catcher's mitt. Where in the country is the Friday evening dancing class or the Saturday morning movie (approved by the P.T.A.)? It is the greatest fallacy of all time that children love the country as a year-around plan. Children would take a dusty corner of Washington Square or a city sidewalk, even, in preference to the lonely sermons in stones and books in running brooks which their contemporaries cannot share.

As for the horrors of bringing up progeny in the city, for all its museums and other cultural advantages (so perfectly within reach of suburban families if they feel strongly about it), they were summed up for me one day last winter. The harried mother of one, speaking to me on the telephone just after Christmas, sighed and said, "It's been a really wonderful time for me, as vacations go. Barbara has had an engagement with a child in our apartment house every afternoon this week. I have had to take her almost nowhere." Barbara is eleven. For six of those eleven years, I realized, her mother must have dreaded Christmas vacation, not to mention spring, as a time when Barbara had to be entertained. I thought thankfully of my own daughters whom I had scarcely seen since school closed, out with their skis and their sleds and their friends, sliding down the roped-off hill half a block away, coming in hungrily for lunch and disappearing again, hearty, amused, and safe—at least as safe as any sled-borne child can be.

Spruce Manor is not Eden, of course. Our taxes are higher than we like, and there is always the eight-eleven in the morning to be caught, and we sometimes resent the necessity of rushing from a theater to a train on a weekday evening. But the taxes pay for our really excellent schools and for our garbage collections (so that the pails of orange peels need not stand in the halls overnight as ours did in the city) and for our water supply which does not give out every dry summer as it frequently does in the country. As for the theaters—they are twenty miles away and we don't get to them more than twice a month. But neither, I think, do many of our friends in town. The eight-eleven is rather a pleasant train, too, say the husbands; it gets them to work in thirty-four minutes and they read the papers restfully on the way.

"But the suburban mind!" cry our die-hard friends in Manhattan and Connecticut. "The suburban conversation! The monotony!" They imply that they and I must scintillate or we perish. Let me anatomize Spruce Manor, for them and for the others who envision Suburbia as a congregation of mindless housewives and amoral go-getters.

From my window, now, on a June morning, I have a view. It contains neither solitary hills nor dramatic skyscrapers. But I can see my roses in bloom, and my foxglove, and an arch of trees over the lane. I think comfortably of my friends whose houses line this and other streets rather like it. Not one of them is, so far as I know, doing any of the things that suburban ladies are popularly supposed to be doing. One of them, I happen to know, has gone bowling for her health and figure, but she has already tidied up her house and arranged to be home before the boys return from school. Some, undoubtedly, are ferociously busy in the garden. One lady is on her way to Ellis Island, bearing comfort and gifts to a Polish boy—a seventeen-year-old stowaway who did slave labor in Germany and was liberated by a cousin of hers during the war—who is being held for attempting to attain the land of which her cousin told him. The boy has been on the Island for three months. Twice a week she takes this tedious journey, meanwhile besieging courts and immigration authorities on his behalf. This lady has a large house, a part-time maid, and five children.

My friend around the corner is finishing her third novel. She writes daily from nine-thirty until two. After that her son comes back from school and she plunges into maternity; at six, she combs her pretty hair, refreshes her lipstick, and is charming to her doctor husband. The village dancing school is run by another neighbor, as it has been for twenty years. She has sent a number of ballerinas on to the theatrical world as well as having shepherded for many a successful season the white-gloved little boys and full-skirted little girls through their first social tasks.

Some of the ladies are no doubt painting their kitchens or a nursery; one of them is painting the portrait, on assignment, of a very distinguished personage. Some of them are nurses' aides and Red Cross workers and supporters of good causes. But all find time to be friends with their families and to meet the 5:32 five nights a week. They read something besides the newest historical novel, Braque is not unidentifiable to most of them, and their conversation is for the most part as agreeable as the tables they set. The tireless bridge players, the gossips, the women bored by their husbands live perhaps in our suburb, too. Let them. Our orbits need not cross.

And what of the husbands, industriously selling bonds or practicing law or editing magazines or looking through microscopes or managing offices in the city? Do they spend their evenings and their weekends in the gaudy bars of Fifty-second Street? Or are they the perennial householders, their lives a dreary round of taking down screens and mending drains? Well, screens they have always with them, and a man who is good around the house can spend happy hours with the plumbing even on a South Sea island. Some of them cut their own lawns and some of them try to break par and some of them sail their little boats all summer with their families for crew. Some of them are village trustees for nothing a year and some listen to symphonies and some think Milton Berle ought to be President. There is a scientist who plays wonderful bebop, and an insurance salesman who has bought a big old house nearby and with his own hands is gradually tearing it apart and reshaping it nearer to his heart's desire. Some of them are passionate hedge-clippers and some read Plutarch for fun. But I do not know many—though there may be such—who either kiss their neighbors' wives behind doors or whose idea of sprightly talk is to tell you the plot of an old movie.

It is June, now, as I have said. This afternoon my daughters will come home from school with a crowd of their peers at their heels. They will eat up the cookies and drink up the ginger ale and go down for a swim at the beach if the water is warm enough, that beach which is only three blocks away and open to all Spruce Manor. They will go unattended by me, since they have been swimming since they were four, and besides there are lifeguards and no big waves. (Even our piece of ocean is a compromise.) Presently it will be time for us to climb into our very old Studebaker—we are not car-proud in Spruce Manor —and meet the 5:32. That evening expedition is not vitally necessary, for a bus runs straight down our principal avenue from the station to the shore, and it meets all trains. But it is an event we enjoy. There is something delightfully ritualistic about the moment when the train pulls in and the men swing off, with the less sophisticated children running squealing to meet them. The women move over from the driver's seat, surrender the keys, and receive an absent-minded kiss. It is the sort of picture that wakes John Marquand screaming from his sleep. But, deluded people that we are, we do not realize how mediocre it all seems. We will eat our undistinguished meal, probably without even a cocktail to enliven it. We will drink our coffee at the table, not carry it into the living room; if a husband changes for dinner here it is into old and spotty trousers and more comfortable shoes. The children will then go through the regular childhood routine—complain about their homework, grumble about going to bed, and finally accomplish both ordeals. Perhaps later the Gerard Joneses will drop in. We will talk a great deal of unimportant chatter and compare notes on food prices; we will also discuss the headlines and disagree. (Some of us in the Manor are Republicans, some are Democrats, a few lean plainly leftward. There are probably anti-Semites and anti-Catholics and even anti-Americans. Most of us are merely anti-antis.) We will all have one highball, and the Joneses will leave early. Tomorrow and tomorrow and tomorrow the pattern will be repeated. This is Suburbia.

But I think that some day people will look back on our little interval here, on our Spruce Manor way of life, as we now look back on the Currier and Ives kind of living, with nostalgia and respect. In a world of terrible extremes, it will stand out as the safe, important medium.

Suburbia, of thee I sing!

Bertrand Russell

FREEDOM AND THE COLLEGES

I

BEFORE discussing the present status of academic freedom it may be as well to consider what we mean by the term. The essence of academic freedom is that teachers should be chosen for their expertness in the subject they are to teach and that the judges of this expertness should be other experts. Whether a man is a good mathematician, or physicist, or chemist, can only be judged by other mathematicians, or physicists, or chemists. By them, however, it can be judged with a fair degree of unanimity.

The opponents of academic freedom hold that other conditions besides a man's skill in his own department should be taken into consideration. He should, they think, have never expressed any opinion which controverts those of the holders of power. This is a sharp issue, and one on which the totalitarian states have taken a vigorous line. Russia never enjoyed academic freedom except during the brief reign of Kerenski, but I think there is even less of it now than there was under the Czars. Germany, before the War, while lacking many forms of liberty, recognized pretty fully the principle of freedom in university teaching. Now all this is changed, with the result that with few exceptions the ablest of the learned men of Germany are in exile. In Italy, though in a slightly milder form, there is a similar tyranny over universities. In Western democracies it is generally recognized that this state of affairs is deplorable. It cannot, however, be denied that there are tendencies which might lead to somewhat similar evils.

The danger is one which democracy by itself does not suffice to avert. A democracy in which the majority exercises its powers without restraint

48

may be almost as tyrannical as a dictatorship. Toleration of minorities is an essential part of wise democracy, but a part which is not always sufficiently remembered.

In relation to university teachers, these general considerations are reinforced by some that are especially applicable to their case. University teachers are supposed to be men with special knowledge and special training such as should fit them to approach controversial questions in a manner peculiarly likely to throw light upon them. To decree that they are to be silent upon controversial issues is to deprive the community of the benefit which it might derive from their training in impartiality. The Chinese empire, many centuries ago, recognized the need of licensed criticism and therefore established a Board of Censors, consisting of men with a reputation for learning and wisdom, and endowed with the right to find fault with the Emperor and his government. Unfortunately, like everything else in traditional China, this institution became conventionalized. There were certain things that the censors were allowed to censure, notably the excessive power of eunuchs, but if they wandered into unconventional fields of criticism the Emperor was apt to forget their immunity. Much the same thing is happening among us. Over a wide field criticism is permitted, but where it is felt to be really dangerous, some form of punishment is apt to befall its author.

Academic freedom in this country is threatened from two sources: the plutocracy and the churches, which endeavor between them to establish an economic and a theological censorship. The two are easily combined by the accusation of Communism, which is recklessly hurled against anyone whose opinions are disliked. For example, I have observed with interest that, although I have criticized the Soviet Government severely ever since 1920, and although in recent years I have emphatically expressed the opinion that it is at least as bad as the government of the Nazis, my critics ignore all this and quote triumphantly the one or two sentences in which, in moments of hope, I have suggested the possibility of good ultimately coming out of Russia.

The technique for dealing with men whose opinions are disliked by certain groups of powerful individuals has been well perfected and is a great danger to ordered progress. If the man concerned is still young and comparatively obscure, his official superiors may be induced to accuse him of professional incompetence, and he may be quietly dropped. With older men who are too well known for this method to be successful, public hostility is stirred up by means of misrepresentation. The majority of teachers naturally do not care to expose themselves to these risks and avoid giving public expression to their less orthodox opinions. This is a dangerous state of affairs, by which disinterested intelligence is partially muzzled, and the forces of conservatism and obscurantism persuade themselves that they can remain triumphant.

II

The principle of liberal democracy, which inspired the founders of the American Constitution, was that controversial questions should be decided by argument rather than by force. Liberals have always held that opinions should be formed by untrammeled debate, not by allowing only one side to be heard. Tyrannical governments, both ancient and modern, have taken the opposite view. For my part, I see no reason to abandon the liberal tradition in this matter. If I held power, I should not seek to prevent my opponents from being heard. I should seek to provide equal facilities for all opinions and leave the outcome to the consequences of discussion and debate. Among the academic victims of German persecution in Poland there are, to my knowledge, some eminent logicians who are completely orthodox Catholics. I should do everything in my power to obtain academic positions for these men, in spite of the fact that their coreligionists do not return the compliment.

The fundamental difference between the liberal and the illiberal outlook is that the former regards all questions as open to discussion and all opinions as open to a greater or less measure of doubt, while the latter holds in advance that certain opinions are absolutely unquestionable, and that no argument against them must be allowed to be heard. What is curious about this position is the belief that if impartial investigation were permitted it would lead men to the wrong conclusion, and that ignorance is, therefore, the only safeguard against error. This point of view is one which cannot be accepted by any man who wishes reason rather than prejudice to govern human action.

The liberal outlook is one which arose in England and Holland during the late seventeenth century, as a reaction against the wars of religion. These wars had raged with great fury for 130 years without producing the victory of either party. Each party felt an absolute certainty that it was in the right and that its victory was of the utmost importance to mankind. At the end, sensible men grew weary of the indecisive struggle and decided that both sides were mistaken in their dogmatic certainty. John Locke, who expressed the new point of view both in philosophy and in politics, wrote at the beginning of an era of growing toleration. He emphasized the fallibility of human judgments and ushered in an era of progress which lasted until 1914. It is owing to the influence of Locke and his school that Catholics enjoy toleration in Protestant countries, and Protestants in Catholic countries. Where the controversies of the seventeenth century are concerned, men have more or less learned the lesson of toleration, but in regard to the new controversies that have arisen since the end of the Great War the wise maxims of the philosophers of liberalism have been forgotten. We are no longer horrified by Quakers, as were the earnest Christians of Charles II's court, but we are horrified by the men who apply to present-day problems the same outlook and the same principles that seventeenth-century Quakers applied to the problems of their day. Opinions which we disagree with acquire a certain respectability by antiquity, but a new opinion which we do not share invariably strikes us as shocking.

There are two possible views as to the proper functioning of democracy. According to one view, the opinions of the majority should prevail absolutely in all fields. According to the other view, whenever a common decision is not necessary, different opinions should be represented, as nearly as possible, in proportion to their numerical frequency. The results of these two views in practice are very different. According to the former view, when the majority has decided in favor of some opinion, no other must be allowed to be expressed, or if expressed at all must be confined to obscure and uninfluential channels. According to the other view, minority opinions should be given the same opportunities for expression as are given to majority opinions, but only in a lesser degree.

This applies in particular to teaching. A man or woman who is to hold a teaching post under the state should not be required to express majority opinions, though naturally a majority of teachers will do so. Uniformity in the opinions expressed by teachers is not only not to be sought but is, if possible, to be avoided, since diversity of opinion among preceptors is essential to any sound education. No man can pass as educated who had heard only one side on questions as to which the public is divided. One of the most important things to teach in the educational establishments of a democracy is the power of weighing arguments, and the open mind which is prepared in advance to accept whichever side appears the more reasonable. As soon as a censorship is imposed upon the opinions which teachers may avow, education ceases to serve this purpose and tends to produce, instead of a nation of men, a herd of fanatical bigots. Since the end of the Great War, fanatical bigotry has revived until it has become over a great part of the world as virulent as during the wars of religion. All those who oppose free discussion and who seek to impose a censorship upon the opinions to which the young are to be exposed are doing their share in increasing this bigotry and in plunging the world further into the abyss of strife and intolerance from which Locke and his coadjutors gradually rescued it.

There are two questions which are not sufficiently distinguished: the one as to the best form of government; the other as to the functions of government. I have no doubt in my mind that democracy is the best *form* of government, but it may go as much astray as any other form in regard to the *functions* of government. There are certain matters on which common action is necessary; as to these, the common action should be decided by the majority. There are other matters on which a common decision is neither necessary nor desirable. These matters include the sphere of opinion. Since there is a natural tendency for those who have power to exercise it to the utmost, it is a necessary safeguard against tyranny that there should be institutions and organized bodies which possess, either in practice or in theory, a certain limited independence of the state. Such freedom as exists in the countries which derive their civilizations from Europe is traceable historically to the conflict between church and state in the Middle Ages. In the Byzantine Empire the church was subdued by the state, and to this fact we may trace the total absence of any tradition of freedom in Russia, which derived its civilization from Constantinople. In the West, first the Catholic Church and then the various Protestant sects gradually acquired certain liberties as against the state.

Academic freedom, in particular, was originally a part of the freedom of the church and accordingly suffered eclipse in England in the time of Henry VIII. In every state, I repeat, no matter what its form of government, the preservation of freedom demands the existence of bodies of men having a certain limited independence of the state, and among such bodies it is important that universities should be included. In America at the present day there is more academic freedom in private universities than in such as are nominally under a democratic authority, and this is due to a very widespread misconception as to the proper functions of government.

III

Taxpayers think that since they pay the salaries of university teachers they have a right to decide what these men shall teach. This principle, if logically carried out, would mean that all the advantages of superior education enjoyed by university professors are to be nullified, and that their teaching is to be the same as it would be if they had no special competence. "Folly, doctorlike, controlling skill" is one of the things that made Shakespeare cry for restful death. Yet democracy, as understood by many Americans, requires that such control should exist in all state universities. The exercise of power is agreeable, especially when it is an obscure individual who exercises power over a prominent one. The Roman soldier who killed Archimedes, if in his youth he had been compelled to study geometry, must have enjoyed a quite special thrill in ending the life of so eminent a malefactor. An ignorant American bigot can enjoy the same thrill in pitting his democratic power against men whose views are obnoxious to the uneducated.

There is perhaps a special danger in democratic abuses of power—namely, that being collective they are stimulated by mob hysteria. The man who has the art of arousing the witch-hunting instincts of the mob has a quite peculiar power for evil in a democracy where the habit of the exercise of power by the majority has produced that intoxication and impulse to tyranny which the exercise of authority almost invariably produces sooner or later. Against this danger the chief protection is a sound education designed to combat the tendency to irrational eruptions of collective hate. Such an education the bulk of university teachers desire to give, but their masters in the plutocracy and the hierarchy make it as difficult as possible for them to carry out this task effectively. For it is to the irrational passions of the mass that these men owe their power, and they know that they would fall if the power of rational thinking became common. Thus the interlocking power of stupidity below and love of power above paralyzes the efforts of rational men. Only through a greater measure of academic freedom than has yet been achieved in the public educational institutions of this country can this evil be averted.

The persecution of unpopular forms of intelligence is a very grave danger to any country and has not infrequently been the cause of national ruin. The stock example is Spain, where the expulsion of the Jews and Moors led to the decay of agriculture and the adoption of a completely mad finance. These two causes, though their effects were masked at first by the power of Charles V, were mainly responsible for the decline of Spain from its dominant position in Europe. It may safely be assumed that the same causes will produce the same effects in Germany, ultimately, if not in the near future. In Russia, where the same evils have been in operation for a longer time, the effects have become plainly visible, even in the incompetence of the military machine.

Russia is, for the moment, the most perfect example of a country where ignorant bigots have the degree of control that they are attempting to acquire in New York. Professor A. V. Hill quotes the following from the *Astronomical Journal of the Soviet Union* for December 1938:

> 1. Modern bourgeois cosmogony is in a state of deep ideological confusion resulting from its refusal to accept the only true dialectic-materialistic concept, namely, the infinity of the universe with respect to space as well as time.
>
> 2. The hostile work of the agents of Fascism, who at one time managed to penetrate to leading positions in certain astronomical and other institutions as well as in the press, has led to revolting propaganda of counterrevolutionary bourgeois ideology in the literature.
>
> 3. The few existing Soviet materialistic works on problems of cosmology have remained in isolation and have been suppressed by the enemies of the people, until recently.
>
> 4. Wide circles interested in science have been taught, at best, only in the spirit of indifference toward the ideological aspect of the current bourgeois cosmologic theories. . . .
>
> 5. The exposé of the enemies of the Soviet people makes necessary the development of a new Soviet materialistic cosmology. . . .
>
> 6. It is deemed necessary that Soviet science should enter the international scientific arena carrying concrete achievements in cosmologic theories on the basis of our philosophic methodology.

For "Soviet" substitute "American," for "Fascism" substitute "Communism," for "dialectic-materialism" substitute "Catholic truth," and you will obtain a document to which the enemies of academic freedom in this country might almost subscribe.

IV

There is one encouraging feature about the situation, which is that the tyranny of the majority in America, so far from being new, is probably less than it was a hundred years ago. Anybody may draw this conclusion from De Tocqueville's *Democracy in America*. Much of what he says is still applicable, but some of his observations are certainly no longer true. I can not agree, for example, "that in no country in the civilized world is less attention paid to philosophy than in the United States." But I think there is still some justice, though less than in De Tocqueville's day, in the following passage:

> In America the majority raises very formidable barriers to the liberty of opinion: within these barriers an author may write whatever he pleases, but he will repent it if he ever steps beyond them. Not

that he is exposed to the terrors of an auto-da-fé, but he is tormented by the slights and persecutions of daily obloquy. His political career is closed forever, since he has offended the only authority which is able to promote his success. Every sort of compensation, even that of celebrity, is refused to him. Before he published his opinions he imagined that he held them in common with many others; but no sooner has he declared them openly than he is loudly censured by his overbearing opponents, whilst those who think without having the courage to speak, like him, abandon him in silence. He yields at length, oppressed by the daily efforts he has been making, and he subsides into silence, as if he was tormented by remorse for having spoken the truth.

I think it must also be admitted that De Tocqueville is right in what he says about the power of society over the individual in a democracy:

> When the inhabitant of a democratic country compares himself individually with all those about him, he feels with pride that he is the equal of any one of them; but when he comes to survey the totality of his fellows, and to place himself in contrast to so huge a body, he is instantly overwhelmed by the sense of his own insignificance and weakness. The same quality which renders him independent of each of his fellow citizens, taken severally, exposes him alone and unprotected to the influence of the greater number. The public has therefore among a democratic people a singular power, of which aristocratic nations could never so much as conceive an idea; for it does not persuade to certain opinions, but it enforces them, and infuses them into the faculties by a sort of enormous pressure of the minds of all upon the reason of each.

The diminution in the stature of the individual through the hugeness of the Leviathan has, since De Tocqueville's day, taken enormous strides, not only, and not chiefly, in democratic countries. It is a most serious menace to the world of Western civilization and is likely, if unchecked, to bring intellectual progress to an end. For all serious intellectual progress depends upon a certain kind of independence of outside opinion, which cannot exist where the will of the majority is treated with that kind of religious respect which the orthodox give to the will of God. A respect for the will of the majority is more harmful than respect for the will of God, because the will of the majority can be ascertained. Some forty years ago, in the town of Durban, a member of the Flat Earth Society challenged the world to public debate. The challenge was taken up by a sea captain whose only argument in favor of the world's being round was that he had been round it. This argument, of course, was easily disposed of, and the Flat-Earth propagandist obtained a two thirds majority. The voice of the people having been thus declared, the true democrat must conclude that in Durban the earth is flat. I hope that from that time onward no one was allowed to teach in the public schools of Durban (there is, I believe, no university there) unless he subscribed to the declaration that the roundness of the earth is an infidel dogma designed to lead to Communism and the destruction of the family. As to this, however, my information is deficient.

Collective wisdom, alas, is no adequate substitute for the intelligence of individuals. Individuals who opposed received opinions have been the source of all progress, both moral and intellectual. They have been unpopular, as was natural. Socrates, Christ, and Galileo all equally incurred the censure of the orthodox. But in former times the machinery of suppression was far less adequate than it is in our day, and the heretic, even if executed, still obtained adequate publicity. The blood of the martyrs was the seed of the church, but this is no longer true in a country like modern Germany, where the martyrdom is secret and no means exists of spreading the martyr's doctrine.

The opponents of academic freedom, if they could have their way, would reduce this country to the level of Germany as regards the promulgation of doctrines of which they disapprove. They would substitute organized tyranny for individual thought; they would proscribe everything new; they would cause the community to ossify, and in the end they would produce a series of generations which would pass from birth to death without leaving any trace in the history of mankind. To some it may seem that what they are demanding at the moment is not a very grave matter. Of what importance, it may be said, is such a question as academic freedom in a world distracted by war, tormented by persecution, and abounding in concentration camps for those who will not be accomplices in iniquity? In comparison with such things, I admit, the issue of academic freedom is not in itself of the first magnitude. But it is part and parcel of the same battle. Let it be remembered that what is at stake, in the greatest issues as well as in those that seem smaller, is the freedom of the individual human spirit to express its beliefs and hopes for mankind, whether they be shared by many or by few or by none. New hopes, new beliefs, and new thoughts are at all times necessary to mankind, and it is not out of a dead uniformity that they can be expected to arise.

Henry David Thoreau

THE WAR OF THE ANTS

From *Walden*

ONE DAY when I went out to my wood-pile, or rather my pile of stumps, I observed two large ants, the one red, the other much larger, nearly half an inch long, and black, fiercely contending with one another. Having once got hold they never let go, but struggled and wrestled and rolled on the chips incessantly. Looking farther, I was surprised to find that the chips were covered with such combatants, that it was not a *duellum*, but a *bellum*, a war between two races of ants, the red always pitted against the black, and frequently two red ones to one black. The legions of these Myrmidons covered all the hills and vales in my wood-yard, and the ground was already strewn with the dead and dying, both red and black. It was the only battle which I have ever witnessed; the only battle-field I ever trod while the battle was raging; internecine war; the red republicans on the one hand, and the black imperialists on the other. On every side they were engaged in deadly combat, yet without any noise that I could hear, and human soldiers never fought so resolutely. I watched a couple that were fast locked in each other's embraces, in a little sunny valley amid the chips, now at noonday prepared to fight till the sun wet down, or life went out. The smaller red champion had fastened himself like a vice to his adversary's front, and through all the tumblings on that field never for an instant ceased to gnaw at one of his feelers near the root, having already caused the other to go by the board; while the stronger black one dashed him from side to side, and, as I saw on looking nearer, had already divested him of several of his members. They fought with more pertinacity than bulldogs. Neither manifested the least disposi-

57

tion to retreat. It was evident that their battlecry was "Conquer or die." In the meanwhile there came along a single red ant on the hillside of this valley, evidently full of excitement, who either had despatched his foe, or had not yet taken part in the battle; probably the latter, for he had lost none of his limbs; whose mother had charged him to return with his shield or upon it. Or perchance he was some Achilles, who had nourished his wrath apart, and had now come to avenge or rescue his Patroclus. He saw this unequal combat from afar,—for the blacks were nearly twice the size of the red,—he drew near with rapid pace till he stood on his guard within half an inch of the combatants; then, watching his opportunity, he sprang upon the black warrior, and commenced his operations near the root of his right fore leg, leaving the foe to select among his own members; and so there were three united for life, as if a new kind of attraction had been invented which put all other locks and cements to shame. I should not have wondered by this time to find that they had their respective musical bands stationed on some eminent chip, and playing their national airs the while, to excite the slow and cheer the dying combatants. I was myself excited somewhat even as if they had been men. The more you think of it, the less the difference. And certainly there is not the fight recorded in Concord history, at least, if in the history of America, that will bear a moment's comparison with this, whether for the numbers engaged in it, or for the patriotism and heroism displayed. For numbers and for carnage it was an Austerlitz or Dresden. Concord Fight! Two killed on the patriots' side, and Luther Blanchard wounded! Why here every ant was a Buttrick,—"Fire! for God's sake fire!" —and thousands shared the fate of Davis and Hosmer. There was not one hireling there. I have no doubt that it was a principle they fought for, as much as our ancestors, and not to avoid a three-penny tax on their tea; and the results of this battle will be as important and memorable to those whom it concerns as those of the battle of Bunker Hill, at least.

I took up the chip on which the three I have particularly described were struggling, carried into my house, and placed it under a tumbler on my window-sill, in order to see the issue. Holding a microscope to the first-mentioned red ant, I saw that, though he was assiduously gnawing at the near fore leg of his enemy, having severed his remaining feeler, his own breast was all torn away, exposing what vitals he had there to the jaws of the black warrior, whose breastplate was apparently too thick for him to pierce; and the dark carbuncles of the sufferer's eyes shone with ferocity such as war only could excite. They struggled half an hour longer under the tumbler, and when I looked again the black soldier had severed the heads of his foes from their bodies, and the still living heads were hanging on either side of him like ghastly trophies at his saddle-bow, still apparently as firmly fastened as ever, and he was endeavoring with feeble struggles, being without feelers and with only the remnant of a leg, and I know not how many other wounds, to divest himself of them; which at length, after half an hour more, he accomplished. I raised the glass, and he went off over the window-sill in that crippled state. Whether he finally survived that combat, and spent the remainder of his days in some Hôtel des Invalides, I do not know; but I thought that his industry would not be worth much thereafter. I never learned which party was victorious, nor the cause of the war; but I felt for the rest of that day as if I had had my feelings excited and narrowed by witnessing the struggle, the ferocity and carnage, of a human battle before my door.

Kirby and Spence tell us that the battles of ants have long been celebrated and the date of them recorded, though they say that Huber is the only modern author who appears to have witnessed them. "Æneas Sylvius," say they, "after giving a very circumstantial account of one contested with great obstinacy by a great and small species on the trunk of a pear tree," adds that " 'this action was fought in the pontificate of Eugenius the Fourth, in the presence of Nicholas Pistoriensis, an eminent lawyer, who related the whole history of the battle with the greatest fidelity.' A similar engagement between great and small ants is recorded by Olaus Magnus, in which the small ones, being victorious, are said to have buried the bodies of their own soldiers, but left those of their giant enemies a prey to the birds. This event happened previous to the expulsion of the tyrant Christiern the Second from Sweden." The battle which I witnessed took place in the Presidency of Polk, five years before the passage of Webster's Fugitive-Slave Bill.

Alexis de Tocqueville

SLAVERY IN OHIO AND KENTUCKY

From *Democracy in America*

HE STREAM that the Indians had distinguished by the name of Ohio, or the Beautiful River, waters one of the most magnificent valleys which have ever been made the abode of man. Undulating lands extend upon both shores of the Ohio, whose soil affords inexhaustible treasures to the laborer; on either bank the air is equally wholesome and the climate mild; and each of them forms the extreme frontier of a vast state: that which follows the numerous windings of the Ohio upon the left is called Kentucky; that upon the right bears the name of the river. These two states differ only in a single respect: Kentucky has admitted slavery, but the state of Ohio has prohibited the existence of slaves within its borders.[1] Thus the traveler who floats down the current of the Ohio to the spot where that river falls into the Mississippi may be said to sail between liberty and servitude; and a transient inspection of surrounding objects will convince him which of the two is more favorable to humanity.

Upon the left bank of the stream the population is sparse; from time to time one descries a troop of slaves loitering in the half-desert fields; the primeval forest reappears at every turn; society seems to be asleep, man to be idle, and nature alone offers a scene of activity and life.

From the right bank, on the contrary, a confused hum is heard, which proclaims afar the presence of industry; the fields are covered with abundant harvests; the elegance of the dwellings announces the taste and

[1] Not only is slavery prohibited in Ohio, but no free Negroes are allowed to enter the territory of that state or to hold property in it. See the statutes of Ohio.

activity of the laborers; and man appears to be in the enjoyment of that wealth and contentment which is the reward of labor.[2]

The state of Kentucky was founded in 1775, the state of Ohio only twelve years later; but twelve years are more in America than half a century in Europe; and at the present day the population of Ohio exceeds that of Kentucky by two hundred and fifty thousand souls.[3] These different effects of slavery and freedom may readily be understood; and they suffice to explain many of the differences which we notice between the civilization of antiquity and that of our own time.

Upon the left bank of the Ohio labor is confounded with the idea of slavery, while upon the right bank it is identified with that of prosperity and improvement; on the one side it is degraded, on the other it is honored. On the former territory no white laborers can be found, for they would be afraid of assimilating themselves to the Negroes; all the work is done by slaves; on the latter no one is idle, for the white population extend their activity and intelligence to every kind of employment. Thus the men whose task it is to cultivate the rich soil of Kentucky are ignorant and apathetic, while those who are active and enlightened either do nothing or pass over into Ohio, where they may work without shame.

It is true that in Kentucky the planters are not obliged to pay the slaves whom they employ, but they derive small profits from their labor, while the wages paid to free workmen would be returned with interest in the value of their services. The free workman is paid, but he does his work quicker than the slave; and rapidity of execution is one of the great elements of economy. The white sells his services, but they are purchased only when they may be useful; the black can claim no remuneration for his toil, but the expense of his maintenance is perpetual; he must be supported in his old age as well as in manhood, in his profitless infancy as well as in the productive years of youth, in sickness as well as in health. Payment must equally be made in order to obtain the services of either class of men: the free workman receives his wages in money; the slave in education, in food, in care, and in clothing. The money which a master spends in the maintenance of his slaves goes

[2] The activity of Ohio is not confined to individuals, but the undertakings of the state are surprisingly great: a canal has been established between Lake Erie and the Ohio, by means of which the valley of the Mississippi communicates with the river of the North, and the European commodities which arrive at New York may be forwarded by water to New Orleans across five hundred leagues of continent.

[3] The exact numbers given by the census of 1830 were: Kentucky, 688,844; Ohio, 937,679.

gradually and in detail, so that it is scarcely perceived; the salary of the
free workman is paid in a round sum and appears to enrich only him
who receives it; but in the end the slave has cost more than the free
servant, and his labor is less productive.[4]

The influence of slavery extends still further: it affects the character
of the master and imparts a peculiar tendency to his ideas and tastes.
Upon both banks of the Ohio the character of the inhabitants is enterprising and energetic, but this vigor is very differently exercised in the
two states. The white inhabitant of Ohio, obliged to subsist by his own
exertions, regards temporal prosperity as the chief aim of his existence;
and as the country which he occupies presents inexhaustible resources
to his industry, and ever varying lures to his activity, his acquisitive ardor
surpasses the ordinary limits of human cupidity: he is tormented by
the desire of wealth, and he boldly enters upon every path that fortune
opens to him; he becomes a sailor, a pioneer, an artisan, or a cultivator
with the same indifference, and supports with equal constancy the
fatigues and the dangers incidental to these various professions; the
resources of his intelligence are astonishing, and his avidity in the pursuit
of gain amounts to a species of heroism.

But the Kentuckian scorns not only labor but all the undertakings
that labor promotes; as he lives in an idle independence, his tastes are
those of an idle man; money has lost a portion of its value in his eyes;
he covets wealth much less than pleasure and excitement; and the energy
which his neighbor devotes to gain turns with him to a passionate love
of field sports and military exercises; he delights in violent bodily exertion, he is familiar with the use of arms, and is accustomed from a very
early age to expose his life in single combat. Thus slavery prevents the
whites not only from becoming opulent, but even from desiring to
become so.

4 Independently of these causes, which, wherever free workmen abound, render their
labor more productive and more economical than that of slaves, another cause may be
pointed out which is peculiar to the United States: sugar-cane has hitherto been
cultivated with success only upon the banks of the Mississippi, near the mouth of that
river in the Gulf of Mexico. In Louisiana the cultivation of sugar-cane is exceedingly
lucrative; nowhere does a laborer earn so much by his work; and as there is always a
certain relation between the cost of production and the value of the produce, the
price of slaves is very high in Louisiana. But Louisiana is one of the federal states, and
slaves may be carried thither from all parts of the Union; the price given for slaves
in New Orleans consequently raises the value of slaves in all the other markets. The
consequence of this is that in the regions where the land is less productive, the cost
of slave labor is still very considerable, which gives an additional advantage to the
competition of free labor.

PERSUASION FOR PARTICULAR OCCASIONS

Guided Discussions

BENJAMIN FRANKLIN, *Speech in the Convention
on the Subject of Salaries*
WINSTON CHURCHILL, *Dunkirk*

For Further Analysis

FRANKLIN D. ROOSEVELT, *The First "Fireside Chat"*
JOHN F. KENNEDY, *The Soviet Threat to the Americas*

Benjamin Franklin

SPEECH IN THE CONVENTION
ON THE SUBJECT OF SALARIES

S IR,
It is with reluctance that I rise to express a disapprobation of any one article of the plan, for which we are so much obliged to the honorable gentleman who laid it before us. From its first reading, I have borne a good will to it, and, in general, wished it success. In this particular of salaries to the executive branch, I happen to differ; and, as my opinion may appear new and chimerical, it is only from a persuasion that it is right, and from a sense of duty, that I hazard it. The committee will judge of my reasons when they have heard them, and their judgment may possibly change mine. I think I see inconveniences in the appointment of salaries; I see none in refusing them, but, on the contrary great advantages.

2 Sir, there are two passions which have a powerful influence in the affairs of men. These are *ambition* and *avarice;* the love of power and the love of money. Separately, each of these has great force in prompting men to action; but, when united in view of the same object, they have in many minds the most violent effects. Place before the eyes of such men a post of *honor,* that shall at the same time be a place of *profit,* and they will move heaven and earth to obtain it. The vast number of such places it is, that renders the British government so tempestuous. The struggles for them are the true source of all those factions which are perpetually dividing the nation, distracting its councils, hurrying it sometimes into fruitless and mischievous wars, and often compelling a submission to dishonorable terms of peace.

3   And of what kind are the men that will strive for this profitable preëminence, through all the bustle of cabal, the heat of contention, the infinite mutual abuse of parties, tearing to pieces the best of characters? It will not be the wise and moderate, the lovers of peace and good order, the men fittest for the trust. It will be the bold and the violent, the men of strong passions and indefatigable activity in their selfish pursuits. These will thrust themselves into your government, and be your rulers. And these, too, will be mistaken in the expected happiness of their situation; for their vanquished competitors, of the same spirit, and from the same motives, will perpetually be endeavouring to distress their administration, thwart their measures, and render them odious to the people.

4   Besides these evils, Sir, though we may set out in the beginning with moderate salaries, we shall find, that such will not be of long continuance. Reasons will never be wanting for proposed augmentations; and there will always be a party for giving more to the rulers, that the rulers may be able in return to give more to them. Hence, as all history informs us, there has been in every state and kingdom a constant kind of warfare between the governing and the governed; the one striving to obtain more for its support, and the other to pay less. And this has alone occasioned great convulsions, actual civil wars, ending either in dethroning of the princes or enslaving of the people. Generally, indeed, the ruling power carries its point, and we see the revenues of princes constantly increasing, and we see that they are never satisfied, but always in want of more. The more the people are discontented with the oppression of taxes, the greater need the prince has of money to distribute among his partisans, and pay the troops that are to suppress all resistance, and enable him to plunder at pleasure. There is scarce a king in a hundred, who would not, if he could, follow the example of Pharaoh,—get first all the people's money, then all their lands, and then make them and their children servants for ever. It will be said, that we do not propose to establish kings. I know it. But there is a natural inclination in mankind to kingly government. It sometimes relieves them from aristocratic domination. They had rather have one tyrant than five hundred. It gives more of the appearance of equality among citizens; and that they like. I am apprehensive, therefore,—perhaps too apprehensive,—that the government of these States may in future times end in a monarchy. But this catastrophe, I think, may be long delayed, if in our proposed system we do not sow the seeds of contention, faction, and tumult, by making our posts of honor places

of profit. If we do, I fear, that, though we employ at first a number and not a single person, the number will in time be set aside; it will only nourish the fœtus of a king (as the honorable gentleman from Virginia very aptly expressed it), and a king will the sooner be set over us.

5 It may be imagined by some, that this is an Uptopian idea, and that we can never find men to serve us in the executive department, without paying them well for their services. I conceive this to be a mistake. Some existing facts present themselves to me, which incline me to a contrary opinion. The high sheriff of a county in England is an honorable office, but it is not a profitable one. It is rather expensive, and therefore not sought for. But yet it is executed, and well executed, and usually by some of the principal gentlemen of the county. In France, the office of counsellor, or member of their judiciary parliaments, is more honorable. It is therefore purchased at a high price; there are indeed fees on the law proceedings, which are divided among them, but these fees do not amount to more than three per cent on the sum paid for the place. Therefore, as legal interest is there at five per cent, they in fact pay two per cent for being allowed to do the judiciary business of the nation, which is at the same time entirely exempt from the burthen of paying them any salaries for their services. I do not, however, mean to recommend this as an eligible mode for our judiciary department. I only bring the instance to show, that the pleasure of doing good and serving their country, and the respect such conduct entitles them to, are sufficient motives with some minds, to give up a great portion of their time to the public, without the mean inducement of pecuniary satisfaction.

6 Another instance is that of a respectable society, who have made the experiment, and practised it with success, now more than a hundred years. I mean the Quakers. It is an established rule with them that they are not to go to law, but in their controversies they must apply to their monthly, quarterly, and yearly meetings. Committees of these sit with patience to hear the parties, and spend much time in composing their differences. In doing this, they are supported by a sense of duty, and the respect paid to usefulness. It is honorable to be so employed, but it was never made profitable by salaries, fees, or perquisites. And indeed, in all cases of public service, the less the profit the greater the honor.

7 To bring the matter nearer home, have we not seen the greatest and most important of our offices, that of general of our armies, executed for eight years together, without the smallest salary, by a patriot whom

I will not now offend by any other praise; and this, through fatigues and distresses, in common with the other brave men, his military friends and companions, and the constant anxieties peculiar to his station? And shall we doubt finding three or four men in all the United States, with public spirit enough to bear sitting in peaceful council, for perhaps an equal term, merely to preside over our civil concerns, and see that our laws are duly executed? Sir, I have a better opinion of our country. I think we shall never be without a sufficient number of wise and good men to undertake, and execute well and faithfully, the office in question.

8   Sir, the saving of the salaries, that may at first be proposed, is not an object with me. The subsequent mischiefs of proposing them are what I apprehend. And therefore it is that I move the amendment. If it is not seconded or accepted, I must be contented with the satisfaction of having delivered my opinion frankly, and done my duty.

Discussion: Nothing more clearly illustrates the way in which the coherent development of a subject in appropriate language is controlled by a communicative purpose than a speech in which the writer attempts to shape a subject so that it will persuade a particular audience to a course of action.* An especially striking example of such a speech is Benjamin Franklin's attempt to discuss the effects of paying salaries to executive officers of government in order to persuade members of the Constitutional Convention to adopt an amendment precluding such salaries.

Franklin's task was not an easy one. As a careful reading of his speech will show, he was fully aware that he was espousing the unpopular side of the issue and was unlikely to convince the delegates to act as he wished them to. Since he believed firmly in the cause he espoused, it behooved him to write the most powerful appeal to the intellect, the passions, even the prejudices of the delegates. Only thus might he hope to move them to vote as he wished. On the other hand, the issue of executive salaries was relatively minor, and had Franklin, whose prestige was very great—second probably only to Washington's —put that prestige fully on the block, he would inevitably have sown dissension among the delegates. Increasing dissension in an atmosphere already tense with

* This text is, of course, a collection of essays—compositions fruitfully conceived as subjects shaped to a purpose in an appropriate medium. For obvious reasons it is useful to include a few works of rhetoric, but the editors are aware that even a work like Franklin's which is frequently advertised as "Speech in the Convention *on the Subject of Salaries*" may be considered as having no subject, but simply a variety of means, including topics, to persuade an audience to action. We have excluded from consideration all clear cases of persuasions without subject. We have, however, included a few peripheral cases where it seemed useful to consider the rhetorical work as a subject shaped for a communicative purpose.

major disagreements would have increased the danger of a number of delegates refusing to sign the Constitution of the United States. The adoption of the Constitution was a matter far more crucial to Franklin than the matter of salaries.

A more precise statement of the communicative purpose of his speech would in fact be "to persuade the delegates to the convention to adopt an amendment precluding salaries, but to argue in such a way that, whether the appeal failed or succeeded, the consequence would not be increased dissension." The fullest statement—one which would account for all details in the speech —would have to include also the conception of the audience the essay attempts to move: solid, highly patriotic citizens, with some fear of monarchy.

The ways in which Franklin fully shapes his subject to his purpose will become clearer as you answer the appended questions. As you answer each question refer back to the following summary.

Analytic Summary: In this speech Franklin treats the possible effects of paying salaries to high executive officers of government (subject). *He attempts to develop the subject so as to move the delegates (presumed to possess the qualities enumerated above) to vote for an amendment precluding executive salaries, but limits his appeals to those least likely to cause dissension whether the amendment passes or fails* (communicative purpose). *The means used to accomplish this end are three:* (1) *explicit revelation initially and finally of reluctance to differ with the initial proposal—reluctance overcome only by a sense of duty satisfied whether the proposal passes or is defeated;* (2) *a concatenation of proposed consequences to attaching power and wealth in a single office, which culminates in danger of monarchy;* (3) *a series of examples, each one progressively closer and dearer to the hearts of the delegates, to show that wise and good men are likely to undertake public office without remuneration* (disposition). *The choice of diction and, more especially, of sentence structure is frequently made to suggest the formal tone of a troubled man performing a responsible duty after mature deliberation, rather than one attempting to sway an audience through eloquence. At effective moments, though, the troubled man is permitted to emerge, and participial phrase is piled on participial phrase, or appositive is piled on appositive to achieve an effect of sudden intensity* (style).

Questions

1. A well-known historian has described the Constitutional Convention as "a body of men who were overwhelmingly conservative in their general philosophy of politics and overwhelmingly nationalistic in their views." In what ways

does Franklin show awareness of these traits? In what ways does he appeal to them? Does he make other presuppositions about the members of the convention? What are they?

2. How does Franklin characterize the men who will seek public office if salaries are paid? Why does he believe that paying salaries to executive officers in a republic will hasten the return of a monarchy? What effect is he trying to achieve by suggesting the reinstitution of monarchy as the final consequence of providing salaries?

3. In presenting examples of men who accept public office without financial reward, he begins with the High Sheriff of a county in England and ends with George Washington. What would be the effect of reversing the positions of the two examples? Why? Would the speech have been more or less effective if the position of the French Counsellor and the Quaker Committees were reversed?

4. Look carefully at the first sentence in paragraph 1 and the first sentence in paragraph 3. What would you infer about the state of mind of the man who wrote the former sentence? Why? What would you infer about the state of mind of the man who wrote the latter? What choices of style and diction might account for the differences in tone between the two sentences?

5. Does the last sentence seem somewhat anticlimactic? Why would the whole essay less effectively accomplish the communicative purpose if the last paragraph were omitted?

Theme Topics

1. Write an essay designed to persuade a particular audience to a course of action. Specify in a headnote both the specific audience and the action you wish them to perform.

2. Write an essay in which you consider to what extent Franklin's fears about the results of paying salaries to executive officers have been justified by American experience. Your purpose might be persuasive (salaries are injurious to good government) or explanatory (why Franklin was wrong).

Winston Churchill

DUNKIRK

*F*ROM THE moment that the French defenses at Sedan and on the Meuse were broken at the end of the second week of May, only a rapid retreat to Amiens and the south could have saved the British and French Armies who had entered Belgium at the appeal of the Belgian King; but this strategic fact was not immediately realized. The French High Command hoped they would be able to close the gap, and the Armies of the north were under their orders. Moreover, a retirement of this kind would have involved almost certainly the destruction of the fine Belgian Army of over 20 divisions and the abandonment of the whole of Belgium. Therefore, when the force and scope of the German penetration were realized and when a new French Generalissimo, General Weygand, assumed command in place of General Gamelin, an effort was made by the French and British Armies in Belgium to keep on holding the right hand of the Belgians and to give their own right hand to a newly created French Army which was to have advanced across the Somme in great strength to grasp it.

2   However, the German eruption swept like a sharp scythe around the right and rear of the Armies of the north. Eight or nine armored divisions, each of about four hundred armored vehicles of different kinds, but carefully assorted to be complementary and divisible into small self-contained units, cut off all communications between us and the main French Armies. It severed our own communications for food and ammunition, which ran first to Amiens and afterwards through Abbeville, and it shore its way up the coast to Boulogne and Calais, and almost to Dunkirk. Behind this armored and mechanized onslaught came a num-

71

ber of German divisions in lorries, and behind them again there plodded
comparatively slowly the dull brute mass of the ordinary German Army
and German people, always so ready to be led to the trampling down
in other lands of liberties and comforts which they have never known
in their own.

3   I have said this armored scythe-stroke almost reached Dunkirk—
almost but not quite. Boulogne and Calais were the scenes of desperate
fighting. The Guards defended Boulogne for a while and were then withdrawn by orders from this country. The Rifle Brigade, the 60th Rifles, and
the Queen Victoria's Rifles, with a battalion of British tanks and 1,000
Frenchmen, in all about four thousand strong, defended Calais to the
last. The British Brigadier was given an hour to surrender. He spurned
the offer, and four days of intense street fighting passed before silence
reigned over Calais, which marked the end of a memorable resistance.
Only 30 unwounded survivors were brought off by the Navy, and we do
not know the fate of their comrades. Their sacrifice, however, was not
in vain. At least two armored divisions, which otherwise would have
been turned against the British Expeditionary Force, had to be sent to
overcome them. They have added another page to the glories of the
light divisions, and the time gained enabled the Graveline water lines to
be flooded and to be held by the French troops.

4   Thus it was that the port of Dunkirk was kept open. When it was
found impossible for the Armies of the north to reopen their communications to Amiens with the main French Armies, only one choice remained.
It seemed, indeed, forlorn. The Belgian, British and French Armies were
almost surrounded. Their sole line of retreat was to a single port and
to its neighboring beaches. They were pressed on every side by heavy
attacks and far outnumbered in the air.

5   When, a week ago today, I asked the House to fix this afternoon as
the occasion for a statement, I feared it would be my hard lot to announce the greatest military disaster in our long history. I thought—and
some good judges agreed with me—that perhaps 20,000 or 30,000 men
might be re-embarked. But it certainly seemed that the whole of the
French First Army and the whole of the British Expeditionary Force
north of the Amiens-Abbeville gap would be broken up in the open field
or else would have to capitulate for lack of food and ammunition. These
were the hard and heavy tidings for which I called upon the House and
the nation to prepare themselves a week ago. The whole root and core
and brain of the British Army, on which and around which we were to

build, and are to build, the great British Armies in the later years of the war, seemed about to perish upon the field or to be led into an ignominious and starving captivity.

6   That was the prospect a week ago. But another blow which might well have proved final was yet to fall upon us. The King of the Belgians had called upon us to come to his aid. Had not this Ruler and his Government severed themselves from the Allies, who rescued their country from extinction in the late war, and had they not sought refuge in what has proved to be a fatal neutrality, the French and British Armies might well at the outset have saved not only Belgium but perhaps even Poland. Yet at the last moment, when Belgium was already invaded, King Leopold called upon us to come to his aid, and even at the last moment we came. He and his brave, efficient Army, nearly half a million strong, guarded our left flank and thus kept open our only line of retreat to the sea. Suddenly, without prior consultation, with the least possible notice, without the advice of his Ministers and upon his own personal act, he sent a plenipotentiary to the German Command, surrendered his Army, and exposed our whole flank and means of retreat.

7   I asked the House a week ago to suspend its judgment because the facts were not clear, but I do not feel that any reason now exists why we should not form our own opinions upon this pitiful episode. The surrender of the Belgian Army compelled the British at the shortest notice to cover a flank to the sea more than 30 miles in length. Otherwise all would have been cut off, and all would have shared the fate to which King Leopold had condemned the finest Army his country had ever formed. So in doing this and in exposing this flank, as anyone who followed the operations on the map will see, contact was lost between the British and two out of the three corps forming the First French Army, who were still farther from the coast than we were, and it seemed impossible that any large number of Allied troops could reach the coast.

8   The enemy attacked on all sides with great strength and fierceness, and their main power, the power of their far more numerous Air Force, was thrown into the battle or else concentrated upon Dunkirk and the beaches. Pressing in upon the narrow exit, both from the east and from the west, the enemy began to fire with cannon upon the beaches by which alone the shipping could approach or depart. They sowed magnetic mines in the channels and seas; they sent repeated waves of hostile aircraft, sometimes more than a hundred strong in one formation, to cast their bombs upon the single pier that remained, and upon the sand dunes upon

which the troops had their eyes for shelter. Their U-boats, one of which was sunk, and their motor launches took their toll of the vast traffic which now began. For four or five days an intense struggle reigned. All their armored divisions—or what was left of them—together with great masses of infantry and artillery, hurled themselves in vain upon the ever-narrowing, ever-contracting appendix within which the British and French Armies fought.

9   Meanwhile, the Royal Navy, with the willing help of countless merchant seamen, strained every nerve to embark the British and Allied troops; 220 light warships and 650 other vessels were engaged. They had to operate upon the difficult coast, often in adverse weather, under an almost ceaseless hail of bombs and an increasing concentration of artillery fire. Nor were the seas, as I have said, themselves free from mines and torpedoes. It was in conditions such as these that our men carried on, with little or no rest, for days and nights on end, making trip after trip across the dangerous waters, bringing with them always men whom they had rescued. The numbers they have brought back are the measure of their devotion and their courage. The hospital ships, which brought off many thousands of British and French wounded, being so plainly marked were a special target for Nazi bombs; but the men and women on board them never faltered in their duty.

10   Meanwhile, the Royal Air Force, which had already been intervening in the battle, so far as its range would allow, from home bases, now used part of its main metropolitan fighter strength, and struck at the German bombers and at the fighters which in large numbers protected them. This struggle was protracted and fierce. Suddenly the scene has cleared, the crash and thunder has for the moment—but only for the moment—died away. A miracle of deliverance, achieved by valor, by perseverance, by perfect discipline, by faultless service, by resource, by skill, by unconquerable fidelity, is manifest to us all. The enemy was hurled back by the retreating British and French troops. He was so roughly handled that he did not hurry their departure seriously. The Royal Air Force engaged the main strength of the German Air Force, and inflicted upon them losses of at least four to one; and the Navy, using nearly 1,000 ships of all kinds, carried over 335,000 men, French and British, out of the jaws of death and shame, to their native land and to the tasks which lie immediately ahead. We must be very careful not to assign to this deliverance the attributes of a victory. Wars are not won by evacuations. But there was a victory inside this deliverance, which should be noted.

It was gained by the Air Force. Many of our soldiers coming back have not seen the Air Force at work; they saw only the bombers which escaped its protective attack. They underrate its achievements. I have heard much talk of this; that is why I go out of my way to say this. I will tell you about it.

11   This was a great trial of strength between the British and German Air Forces. Can you conceive a greater objective for the Germans in the air than to make evacuation from these beaches impossible, and to sink all these ships which were displayed, almost to the extent of thousands? Could there have been an objective of greater military importance and significance for the whole purpose of the war than this? They tried hard, and they were beaten back; they were frustrated in their task. We got the Army away; and they have paid fourfold for any losses which they have inflicted. Very large formations of German aeroplanes—and we know that they are a very brave race—have turned on several occasions from the attack of one-quarter of their number of the Royal Air Force, and have dispersed in different directions. Twelve aeroplanes have been hunted by two. One aeroplane was driven into the water and cast away by the mere charge of a British aeroplane, which had no more ammunition. All of our types—the Hurricane, the Spitfire and the new Defiant— and all our pilots have been vindicated as superior to what they have at present to face.

12   When we consider how much greater would be our advantage in defending the air above this Island against an overseas attack, I must say that I find these facts a sure basis upon which practical and reassuring thoughts may rest. I will pay my tribute to these young airmen. The great French Army was very largely, for the time being, cast back and disturbed by the onrush of a few thousands of armored vehicles. May it not also be that the cause of civilization itself will be defended by the skill and devotion of a few thousand airmen? There never has been, I suppose, in all the world, in all the history of war, such an opportunity for youth. The Knights of the Round Table, the Crusaders, all fall back into the past—not only distant but prosaic; these young men, going forth every morn to guard their native land and all that we stand for, holding in their hands these instruments of colossal and shattering power, of whom it may be said that

> "Every morn brought forth a noble chance
> And every chance brought forth a noble knight,"

deserve our gratitude, as do all of the brave men who, in so many ways and on so many occasions, are ready, and continue ready, to give life and all for their native land.

13   I return to the Army. In the long series of very fierce battles, now on this front, now on that, fighting on three fronts at once, battles fought by two or three divisions against an equal or somewhat larger number of the enemy, and fought fiercely on some of the old grounds that so many of us knew so well—in these battles our losses in men have exceeded 30,000 killed, wounded and missing. I take occasion to express the sympathy of the House to all who have suffered bereavement or who are still anxious. The President of the Board of Trade is not here today. His son has been killed, and many in the house have felt the pangs of affliction in the sharpest form. But I will say this about the missing: We have had a large number of wounded come home safely to this country, but I would say about the missing that there may be very many reported missing who will come back home, some day, in one way or another. In the confusion of this fight it is inevitable that many have been left in positions where honor required no further resistance from them.

14   Against this loss of over 30,000 men, we can set a far heavier loss certainly inflicted upon the enemy. But our losses in material are enormous. We have perhaps lost one-third of the men we lost in the opening days of the battle of 21st March, 1918, but we have lost nearly as many guns— nearly one thousand—and all our transport, all the armored vehicles that were with the Army in the north. This loss will impose a further delay on the expansion of our military strength. That expansion had not been proceeding as fast as we had hoped. The best of all we had to give had gone to the British Expeditionary Force, and although they had not the numbers of tanks and some articles of equipment which were desirable, they were a very well and finely equipped Army. They had the first-fruits of all that our industry had to give, and that is gone. And now here is this further delay. How long it will be, how long it will last, depends upon the exertions which we make in this Island. An effort the like of which has never been seen in our records is now being made. Work is proceeding everywhere, night and day, Sundays and week days. Capital and Labor have cast aside their interests, rights, and customs and put them into the common stock. Already the flow of munitions has leaped forward. There is no reason why we should not in a few months overtake the sudden and serious loss that has come upon us, without retarding the development of our general program.

15 Nevertheless, our thankfulness at the escape of our Army and so many men, whose loved ones have passed through an agonizing week, must not blind us to the fact that what has happened in France and Belgium is a colossal military disaster. The French Army has been weakened, the Belgian Army has been lost, a large part of those fortified lines upon which so much faith had been reposed is gone, many valuable mining districts and factories have passed into the enemy's possession, the whole of the Channel ports are in his hands, with all the tragic consequences that follow from that, and we must expect another blow to be struck almost immediately at us or at France. We are told that Herr Hitler has a plan for invading the British Isles. This has often been thought of before. When Napoleon lay at Boulogne for a year with his flat-bottomed boats and his Grand Army, he was told by someone, "There are bitter weeds in England." There are certainly a great many more of them since the British Expeditionary Force returned.

16 The whole question of home defense against invasion is, of course, powerfully affected by the fact that we have for the time being in this Island incomparably more powerful military forces than we have ever had at any moment in this war or the last. But this will not continue. We shall not be content with a defensive war. We have our duty to our Ally. We have to reconstitute and build up the British Expeditionary Force once again, under its gallant Commander-in-Chief, Lord Gort. All this is in train; but in the interval we must put our defenses in this Island into such a high state of organization that the fewest possible numbers will be required to give effective security and that the largest possible potential of offensive effort may be realized. On this we are now engaged. It will be very convenient, if it be the desire of the House, to enter upon this subject in a secret Session. Not that the Government would necessarily be able to reveal in very great detail military secrets, but we like to have our discussions free, without the restraint imposed by the fact that they will be read the next day by the enemy; and the Government would benefit by views freely expressed in all parts of the House by Members with their knowledge of so many different parts of the country. I understand that some request is to be made upon this subject, which will be readily acceded to by His Majesty's Government.

17 We have found it necessary to take measures of increasing stringency, not only against enemy aliens and suspicious characters of other nationalities, but also against British subjects who may become a danger or a nuisance should the war be transported to the United Kingdom. I know

there are a great many people affected by the orders which we have made who are the passionate enemies of Nazi Germany. I am very sorry for them, but we cannot, at the present time and under the present stress, draw all the distinctions which we should like to do. If parachute landings were attempted and fierce fighting attendant upon them followed, these unfortunate people would be far better out of the way, for their own sakes as well as for ours. There is, however, another class, for which I feel not the slightest sympathy. Parliament has given us the powers to put down Fifth Column activities with a strong hand, and we shall use those powers, subject to the supervision and correction of the House, without the slightest hesitation until we are satisfied, and more than satisfied, that this malignancy in our midst has been effectively stamped out.

18   Turning once again, and this time more generally, to the question of invasion, I would observe that there has never been a period in all these long centuries of which we boast when an absolute guarantee against invasion, still less against serious raids, could have been given to our people. In the days of Napoleon the same wind which would have carried his transports across the Channel might have driven away the blockading fleet. There was always the chance, and it is that chance which has excited and befooled the imaginations of many Continental tyrants. Many are the tales that are told. We are assured that novel methods will be adopted, and when we see the originality of malice, the ingenuity of aggression, which our enemy displays, we may certainly prepare ourselves for every kind of novel stratagem and every kind of brutal and treacherous maneuver. I think that no idea is so outlandish that it should not be considered and viewed with a searching, but at the same time, I hope, with a steady eye. We must never forget the solid assurances of sea power and those which belong to air power if it can be locally exercised.

19   I have, myself, full confidence that if all do their duty, if nothing is neglected, and if the best arrangements are made, as they are being made, we shall prove ourselves once again able to defend our Island home, to ride out the storm of war, and to outlive the menace of tyranny, if necessary for years, if necessary alone. At any rate, that is what we are going to try to do. That is the resolve of His Majesty's Government—every man of them. That is the will of Parliament and the nation. The British Empire and the French Republic, linked together in their cause and in their need, will defend to the death their native soil, aiding each other like good

comrades to the utmost of their strength. Even though large tracts of Europe and many old and famous States have fallen or may fall into the grip of the Gestapo and all the odious apparatus of Nazi rule, we shall not flag or fail. We shall go on to the end, we shall fight in France, we shall fight on the seas and oceans, we shall fight with growing confidence and growing strength in the air, we shall defend our Island, whatever the cost may be, we shall fight on the beaches, we shall fight on the landing grounds, we shall fight in the fields and in the streets, we shall fight in the hills; we shall never surrender, and even if, which I do not for a moment believe, this Island or a large part of it were subjugated and starving, then our Empire beyond the seas, armed and guarded by the British Fleet, would carry on the struggle, until, in God's good time, the New World, with all its power and might, steps forth to the rescue and the liberation of the old.

Discussion: Rarely, indeed, does a course of events affecting all humanity depend in considerable measure on the skill and eloquence which a single man can bring to the prosaic task of shaping a subject to a communicative purpose in appropriate language. If any composition in recent history can lay claim to such a distinction, it is Winston Churchill's speech to Parliament on June 4, 1940, immediately following the successful evacuation of British troops from a nearly defeated France via the harbor of Dunkirk.

Churchill himself in *Their Finest Hour* has accurately described the complex communicative purpose of his speech "Parliament assembled on June 4, and it was my duty to lay the story [of Dunkirk] fully before them both in public and later in secret session . . . It was imperative to explain not only to our own people but to the world that our resolve to fight on was based on serious grounds, and was no mere despairing effort. It was also right to lay bare my own reasons for confidence."

The extent to which the whole speech is informed by the necessity to persuade the world and the British people that the "resolve to fight on was based on serious grounds, and was no mere despairing effort" can be seen quite clearly through even a cursory consideration of the relation between the final eloquent paragraph of Churchill's address and the relatively unemotive narration of events with which he begins it. For all its hortatory power the final paragraph, read in isolation, can easily be interpreted as a cry in the dark: a valiant attempt to inspire a doomed British people to an heroic last stand, coupled with a plea to the United States in particular to prevent the victory of Nazi barbarism. Such an interpretation would destroy, not accomplish, Churchill's purpose in delivering the speech. A cry in the dark, no matter how heroic, might elicit sympathy but not practical aid from a United States in which "liberalism" had been temporarily identified with pacifist sentiments, and "conservatism" temporarily identified with isolationist views. Such a cry would not help sustain a battered and now isolated France, nor would it cause the Germans many second thoughts about Great Britain's ability to defend her shores from air attack or from invasion itself.

It is necessary, in other words, that the early sections prepare the reader or listener to react to the last paragraph as a moving affirmation justified by a full knowledge of the practical consequences of the Dunkirk evacuation. Only when so justified will the eloquence of the final paragraph accomplish the communicative purpose of the whole address. A less astute statesman, a less gifted rhetorician might have attempted such justification by a narration of the events of Dunkirk in which the successful evacuation of British troops was interpreted as a victory, and in which the terribly serious consequences of the very real defeat were minimized. Churchill would not have had to lie if he had wished to tell the tale of Dunkirk in this manner, since the return to British shores of a large body of trained fighting men, as well as several other factors, had, in fact, made Churchill considerably more optimistic than parts of his speech suggest. But such an optimistic narrative of events would not have had the desired effect on the British public nor on "the world." Coddling the British people would not prepare them for the certainty of air attack nor steel them to the sacrifices they would have to make if the threat of invasion became reality. Denial of a real crisis would make even more difficult the necessary refusal to commit the R.A.F. wholly to the battle of France. Nor would it have been desirable completely to allay American fear of the consequences of a surrender of the British fleet to the Germans if American sympathies were to be converted into practical aid.

We can see that it would be far better, though far more difficult, to tell the story of Dunkirk, as Churchill did, in a manner that shows full awareness of the crisis consequent upon the defeat in France, but at the same time reveals more persuasively "serious grounds" for Britain's "resolve to fight on." Though the danger must never seem quite as convincing as the "serious grounds," the more forcefully Churchill conveys both the sense of crisis *and* the plausible reasons for continuing the war, the more fully will the communicative purpose of the essay be realized.

With this in mind, we should not find it difficult to comprehend the rationale behind the complex disposition of materials. The first major part, paragraphs 1 through 8, contains essentially a chronological narrative of the military events leading up to the Dunkirk evacuation. The narrative, though it gives full credit to German military might and though it fully emphasizes how desperate was the general military situation, constantly characterizes the victorious Germans as barbarous and evil. On the other hand, when the narrative touches upon a particular engagement between German and British troops, especially during the latter's attempt to keep the port open, it stresses the honor, heroism, and efficiency of the British forces. As a sub-part of the first section, paragraphs 5 through 8 describe the Belgian fiasco in terms which increase the sense of the possible disaster averted only by the evacuation, and which even further vindicate British honor. In other words, by the end of paragraph 8, the narrative, if effective, has made us feel that forces of evil had come perilously close to destroying heroic and blameless defenders of liberty.

The second section, consisting of paragraphs 9 through 13, deals with the deliverance, but not in a chronological narrative. Instead, Churchill presents a detailed and emotive account of the heroism and sacrifice with which each of the armed forces and the British public itself (note the effect of the mention of the absence of the President of the Board of Trade) contributed to the apparently impossible "deliverance."

It is only then, in paragraphs 15 through 18, that Churchill can meaningfully discuss the consequences of the defeat and the deliverance; if the first and second sections have adequately done their job, he can safely emphasize the danger to Britain, yet his assertion that within the defeat there was a very real victory will not ring hollow. And, indeed, each of the consequences he discusses suggests the drastic nature of the crisis, at the same time as it provides another "serious ground" for Britain's "resolve to fight on."

Finally, then, Churchill can plausibly assert his confidence in Britain's ability "to outlive the menace of tyranny" and in a passage which, through stylistic means, becomes almost an incantation, he can assert again and again Britain's resolve to fight on, no matter what the cost, in terms that do not suggest a cry in the night, but become, instead, an inspiration to free men everywhere.

Analytic Summary: In this address to Parliament Winston Churchill tells of the evacuation of Dunkirk (subject) *in such a way as to convince the British people and "the world that our resolve to fight on was based on serious grounds, and was no mere despairing effort"* (communicative purpose). *The speech contains four closely related sections: (1) an account of the military events which led to the necessity for the evacuation, presented in a chronological narrative which characterizes German might as evil and which stresses how close heroic British forces were to disaster; (2) a discussion of the evacuation by means of an emotive account of the noble contribution made of the "deliverance" by each of the armed forces and by the British public; (3) a discussion of the consequences of the evacuation so that each consequence emphasizes the drastic nature of the crisis at the same time as it provides us with a convincing, serious ground for Britain's resolve to fight on; (4) an inspiring affirmation of British resolve given a special power by a reiteration of that resolve in conjunction with a climactic enumeration of the most drastic imaginable consequences* (disposition). *The language varies from section to section, and even within sections. The relatively dispassionate, even impersonal sentences of the opening paragraphs give way to the rhetorical questions, the shifts from past to present tense, and the charged images of the middle paragraphs. The final section achieves a sense of inspired incantation, which is largely the result of a special use of reiterated parallel structure*

*in which Churchill exploits the fullest possible repetition of
parallel grammatical units, sometimes altering only one crucial
word in a series of otherwise identical clauses* (style).

Questions

1. Is there any indication at all, in the details or in the language of the first
paragraph, of Churchill's attitude toward the events he describes? What explanation can you offer for the disinterested tone of the opening?

2. What sentences or phrases are used to describe the German army in
paragraphs 2 through 6? How is its military efficiency described? How is it
characterized ethically?

3. Why is Churchill's description of the fighting in Calais so much more
detailed than his description of the struggle for Boulogne in paragraph 3? We
are told that the British Brigadier "spurned the offer" to surrender. Why is the
choice of "spurned" more effective than "rejected" or "refused" would have been
in this paragraph?

4. In paragraph 5 Churchill interrupts the narrative of events to summarize
what his fears were the previous week. Why? What is the difference between his
attitude toward the Belgian army and the Belgian king? Can you suggest a reason
for Churchill's stressing the difference in attitude at this point in the speech?
Considered only from the point of view of accomplishing the communicative
purpose of his address, was Churchill well-advised to give so much space and
prominence to King Leopold's actions and to their consequences?

5. Both paragraphs 9 and 10 begin with "meanwhile." Does this point to
some effect Churchill tried to achieve in the paragraphs? Why would Churchill
wish to achieve that effect at this point in the speech? How does he manipulate
grammatical tense in paragraph 10? What might he hope to achieve by such
manipulation?

6. Why, in paragraph 11, should Churchill go out of his way to emphasize
that the Germans are "a very brave race"?

7. List each fact or event revealed in the speech which might be construed
as a serious ground for Britain's continuing the war. What devices does Churchill
use to give each of these persuasive force?

8. In paragraph 15 Churchill insists that Dunkirk was "a colossal military
disaster." Would it have been better to have characterized the defeat in equally
honest but less forceful terms? How do you explain the fact that the anecdote
about Napoleon is included at the end of paragraph 15?

9. In the final paragraph Churchill begins with a statement of confidence,
but ends with a consideration of the subjugation of Great Britain; we would
normally expect the statement of confidence to be placed in the more emphatic
final position. What explanation can you offer for the reversal of expected procedure? How many times does Churchill use the phrase "we shall fight" in this
paragraph? The parallel series begins with the affirmation that "we shall fight
in France" and ends with "we shall fight in the hills"; what principle determines

the order in which the places where Britons will fight are listed? Churchill might more concisely have written, "We shall fight in France, on the seas and oceans, in the air, on the beaches and landing grounds, in the fields, the streets, the hills." Why doesn't he? Churchill partially breaks the parallel pattern at a number of points in the long sentence. How and why does he do this?

10. Briefly sum up the stylistic means employed in the last paragraph to emphasize the strength of Britain's resolve to fight on.

Theme Topics

1. Describe an event of national importance that has occurred in your lifetime in such a manner that an intelligent audience will be persuaded to share your attitude toward that event.

2. Write a letter in which you narrate a series of events which have led you into difficulties (losing a job, failing a course, etc.) in such a way as to elicit practical aid from your intended reader.

3. Included just below are John F. Kennedy's speech about Cuba and Franklin D. Roosevelt's speech about the closing of the banks in the United States. Like Churchill's, both these speeches were made by heads of government at moments of national crisis. In a coherent essay describe precisely how the subject, purpose, disposition, and style of one of those speeches differs from Churchill's. Organize your essay so that it will convince an intelligent reader that one of the speeches is superior to the other.

Franklin D. Roosevelt

THE FIRST "FIRESIDE CHAT"
An Intimate Talk with the People of the United States on Banking
March 12, 1933

I WANT TO talk for a few minutes with the people of the United States about banking—with the comparatively few who understand the mechanics of banking but more particularly with the overwhelming majority who use banks for the making of deposits and the drawing of checks. I want to tell you what has been done in the last few days, why it was done, and what the next steps are going to be. I recognize that the many proclamations from State capitols and from Washington, the legislation, the Treasury regulations, etc., couched for the most part in banking and legal terms, should be explained for the benefit of the average citizen. I owe this in particular because of the fortitude and good temper with which everybody has accepted the inconvenience and hardships of the banking holiday. I know that when you understand what we in Washington have been about I shall continue to have your cooperation as fully as I have had your sympathy and help during the past week.

First of all, let me state the simple fact that when you deposit money in a bank the bank does not put the money into a safe deposit vault. It invests your money in many different forms of credit—bonds, commercial paper, mortgages and many other kinds of loans. In other words, the bank puts your money to work to keep the wheels of industry and of agriculture turning around. A comparatively small part of the money you put into the bank is kept in currency—an amount which in

84

normal times is wholly sufficient to cover the cash needs of the average citizens. In other words, the total amount of all the currency in the country is only a small fraction of the total deposits in all of the banks.

What, then, happened during the last few days of February and the first few days of March? Because of undermined confidence on the part of the public, there was a general rush by a large portion of our population to turn bank deposits into currency or gold—a rush so great that the soundest banks could not get enough currency to meet the demand. The reason for this was that on the spur of the moment it was, of course, impossible to sell perfectly sound assets of a bank and convert them into cash except at panic prices far below their real value.

By the afternoon of March 3d scarcely a bank in the country was open to do business. Proclamations temporarily closing them in whole or in part had been issued by the Governors in almost all the States.

It was then that I issued the proclamation providing for the nationwide bank holiday, and this was the first step in the Government's reconstruction of our financial and economic fabric.

The second step was the legislation promptly and patriotically passed by the Congress confirming my proclamation and broadening my powers so that it became possible in view of the requirement of time to extend the holiday and lift the ban of that holiday gradually. This law also gave authority to develop a program of rehabilitation of our banking facilities. I want to tell our citizens in every part of the Nation that the national Congress—Republicans and Democrats alike—showed by this action a devotion to public welfare and a realization of the emergency and the necessity for speed that it is difficult to match in our history.

The third stage has been the series of regulations permitting the banks to continue their functions to take care of the distribution of food and household necessities and the payment of payrolls.

This bank holiday, while resulting in many cases in great inconvenience, is affording us the opportunity to supply the currency necessary to meet the situation. No sound bank is a dollar worse off than it was when it closed its doors last Monday. Neither is any bank which may turn out not to be in a position for immediate opening. The new law allows the twelve Federal Reserve Banks to issue additional currency on good assets and thus the banks which reopen will be able to meet every legitimate call. The new currency is being sent out by the

Bureau of Engraving and Printing in large volume to every part of the country. It is sound currency because it is backed by actual, good assets.

A question you will ask is this: why are all the banks not to be reopened at the same time? The answer is simple. Your Government does not intend that the history of the past few years shall be repeated. We do not want and will not have another epidemic of bank failures.

As a result, we start tomorrow, Monday, with the opening of banks in the twelve Federal Reserve Bank cities—those banks which on first examination by the Treasury have already been found to be all right. This will be followed on Tuesday by the resumption of all their functions by banks already found to be sound in cities where there are recognized clearing houses. That means about 250 cities of the United States.

On Wednesday and succeeding days banks in smaller places all through the country will resume business, subject, of course, to the Government's physical ability to complete its survey. It is necessary that the reopening of banks be extended over a period in order to permit the banks to make applications for necessary loans, to obtain currency needed to meet their requirements and to enable the Government to make common sense checkups.

Let me make it clear to you that if your bank does not open the first day you are by no means justified in believing that it will not open. A bank that opens on one of the subsequent days is in exactly the same status as the bank that opens tomorrow.

I know that many people are worrying about State banks not members of the Federal Reserve System. These banks can and will receive assistance from member banks and from the Reconstruction Finance Corporation. These State banks are following the same course as the National banks except that they get their licenses to resume business from the State authorities, and these authorities have been asked by the Secretary of the Treasury to permit their good banks to open up on the same schedule as the national banks. I am confident that the State Banking Departments will be as careful as the national Government in the policy relating to the opening of banks and will follow the same broad policy.

It is possible that when the banks resume a very few people who have not recovered from their fear may again begin withdrawals. Let me make it clear that the banks will take care of all needs—and it is my belief that hoarding during the past week has become an exceedingly unfashionable pastime. It needs no prophet to tell you that when the people find that they can get their money—that they can get it when they want it for all legitimate purposes—the phantom of fear will soon be laid. People will again be glad to have their money where it will be safely taken care of and where they can use it conveniently at any time. I can assure you that it is safer to keep your money in a reopened bank than under the mattress.

The success of our whole great national program depends, of course, upon the cooperation of the public—on its intelligent support and use of a reliable system.

Remember that the essential accomplishment of the new legislation is that it makes it possible for banks more readily to convert their assets into cash than was the case before. More liberal provision has been made for banks to borrow on these assets at the Reserve Banks and more liberal provision has also been made for issuing currency on the security of these goods assets. This currency is not fiat currency. It is issued only on adequate security, and every good bank has an abundance of such security.

One more point before I close. There will be, of course, some banks unable to reopen without being reorganized. The new law allows the Government to assist in making these reorganizations quickly and effectively and even allows the Government to subscribe to at least a part of new capital which may be required.

I hope you can see from this elemental recital of what your Government is doing that there is nothing complex, or radical, in the process.

We had a bad banking situation. Some of our bankers had shown themselves either incompetent or dishonest in their handling of the people's funds. They had used the money entrusted to them in speculations and unwise loans. This was, of course, not true in the vast majority of our banks, but it was true in enough of them to shock the people for a time into a sense of insecurity and to put them into a frame of mind where they did not differentiate, but seemed to assume that the acts of a comparative few had tainted them all. It was the Government's job to straighten out this situation and do it as quickly as possible. And the job is being performed.

I do not promise you that every bank will be reopened or that individual losses will not be suffered, but there will be no losses that possibly could be avoided; and there would have been more and greater losses had we continued to drift. I can even promise you salvation for some at least of the sorely pressed banks. We shall be engaged not merely in reopening sound banks but in the creation of sound banks through reorganization.

It has been wonderful to me to catch the note of confidence from all over the country. I can never be sufficiently grateful to the people for the loyal support they have given me in their acceptance of the judgment that has dictated our course, even though all our processes may not have seemed clear to them.

After all, there is an element in the readjustment of our financial system more important than currency, more important than gold, and that is the confidence of the people. Confidence and courage are the essentials of success in carrying out our plan. You people must have faith; you must not be stampeded by rumors or guesses. Let us unite in banishing fear. We have provided the machinery to restore our financial system; it is up to you to support and make it work.

It is your problem no less than it is mine. Together we cannot fail.

John F. Kennedy

THE SOVIET THREAT
TO THE AMERICAS

Good evening, my fellow citizens. This Government, as promised, has maintained the closest surveillance of the Soviet military buildup on the island of Cuba. Within the past week unmistakable evidence has established the fact that a series of offensive missile sites is now in preparation on that imprisoned island. The purpose of these bases can be none other than to provide a nuclear strike capability against the Western Hemisphere.

Upon receiving the first preliminary hard information of this nature last Tuesday morning [October 16] at 9:00 a.m., I directed that our surveillance be stepped up. And having now confirmed and completed our evaluation of the evidence and our decision on a course of action, this Government feels obliged to report this new crisis to you in fullest detail.

The characteristics of these new missile sites indicate two distinct types of installations. Several of them include medium-range ballistic missiles capable of carrying a nuclear warhead for a distance of more than 1,000 nautical miles. Each of these missiles, in short, is capable of striking Washington, D.C., the Panama Canal, Cape Canaveral, Mexico City, or any other city in the southeastern part of the United States, in Central America, or in the Caribbean area.

Additional sites not yet completed appear to be designed for intermediate-range ballistic missiles capable of traveling more than twice as far—and thus capable of striking most of the major cities in the Western Hemisphere, ranging as far north as Hudson Bay, Canada, and as far south as Lima, Peru. In addition, jet bombers, capable of carrying nuclear weapons, are now being uncrated and assembled in Cuba, while the necessary air bases are being prepared.

This urgent transformation of Cuba into an important strategic base—by the presence of these large, long-range, and clearly offensive weapons of sudden mass destruction—constitutes an explicit threat to the peace and security of all the Americas, in flagrant and deliberate defiance of the Rio Pact of 1947, the traditions of this nation and hemisphere, the Joint Resolution of the 87th Congress, the Charter of the United Nations, and my own public warnings to the Soviets on September 4 and 13.

This action also contradicts the repeated assurances of Soviet spokesmen, both publicly and privately delivered, that the arms buildup in Cuba would retain its original defensive character and that the Soviet Union had no need or desire to station strategic missiles on the territory of any other nation.

The size of this undertaking makes clear that it has been planned for some months. Yet only last month, after I had made clear the distinction between any introduction of ground-to-ground missiles and the existence of defensive antiaircraft missiles, the Soviet Government publicly stated on September 11 that, and I quote, "The armaments and military equipment sent to Cuba are designed exclusively for defensive purposes," and, and I quote the Soviet Government, "There is no need for the Soviet Government to shift its weapons for a retaliatory blow to any other country, for instance Cuba," and that, and I quote the Government, "The Soviet Union has so powerful rockets to carry these nuclear warheads that there is no need to search for sites for them beyond the boundaries of the Soviet Union." That statement was false.

Only last Thursday, as evidence of this rapid offensive buildup was already in my hand, Soviet Foreign Minister Gromyko told me in my office that he was instructed to make it clear once again, as he said his Government had already done, that Soviet assistance to Cuba, and I quote, "pursued solely the purpose of contributing to the defense capabilities of Cuba," that, and I quote him, "training by Soviet specialists of Cuban nationals in handling defensive armaments was by no means offensive," and that "if it were otherwise," Mr. Gromyko went on, "the Soviet Government would never become involved in rendering such assistance." That statement also was false.

Neither the United States of America nor the world community of nations can tolerate deliberate deception and offensive threats on the part of any nation, large or small. We no longer live in a world where only the actual firing of weapons represents a sufficient challenge to a nation's security to constitute maximum peril. Nuclear weapons are so destructive and ballistic missiles are so swift that any substantially increased possibility of their use or any sudden change in their deployment may well be regarded as a definite threat to peace.

For many years both the Soviet Union and the United States, recognizing this fact, have deployed strategic nuclear weapons with great care, never upsetting the precarious *status quo* which insured that these weapons would not be used in the absence of some vital challenge. Our own strategic missiles have never been transferred to the territory of any other nation under a cloak of secrecy and deception; and our history, unlike that of the Soviets since the end of World War II, demonstrates that we have no desire to dominate or conquer any other nation or impose our system upon its people. Nevertheless, American citizens have become adjusted to living daily on the bull's eye of Soviet missiles located inside the U.S.S.R. or in submarines.

In that sense missiles in Cuba add to an already clear and present danger—although it should be noted the nations of Latin America have never previously been subjected to a potential nuclear threat.

But this secret, swift, and extraordinary build-up of Communist missiles—in an area well known to have a special and historical relationship to the United States and the nations of the Western Hemisphere, in violation of Soviet assurances, and in defiance of American and hemispheric policy—this sudden, clandestine decision to station strategic weapons for the first time outside of Soviet soil—is a deliberately provocative and unjustified change in the *status quo* which cannot be accepted by this country if our courage and our commitments are ever to be trusted again by either friend or foe.

The 1930's taught us a clear lesson: Aggressive conduct, if allowed to grow unchecked and unchallenged, ultimately leads to war. This nation is opposed to war. We are also true to our word. Our unswerving objective, therefore, must be to prevent the use of these missiles against this or any other country and to secure their withdrawal or elimination from the Western Hemisphere.

Our policy has been one of patience and restraint, as befits a peaceful and powerful nation, which leads a worldwide alliance. We have been determined not to be diverted from our central concerns by mere irritants and fanatics. But now further action is required—and it is under way; and these actions may only be the beginning. We will not prematurely or unnecessarily risk the costs of worldwide nuclear war in which even the fruits of victory would be ashes in our mouth—but neither will we shrink from that risk at any time it must be faced.

Acting, therefore, in the defense of our own security and of the entire Western Hemisphere, and under the authority entrusted to me by the Constitution as endorsed by the resolution of the Congress, I have directed that the following *initial* steps be taken immediately:

First: To halt this offensive buildup, a strict quarantine on all offensive military equipment under shipment to Cuba is being initiated. All ships of any kind bound for Cuba from whatever nation or port will, if found to contain cargoes of offensive weapons, be turned back. This quarantine will be extended, if needed, to other types of cargo and carriers. We are not at this time, however, denying the necessities of life as the Soviets attempted to do in their Berlin blockade of 1948.

Second: I have directed the continued and increased close surveillance of Cuba and its military buildup. The Foreign Ministers of the OAS [Organization of American States] in their communique of October 3 rejected secrecy on such matters in this hemisphere. Should these offensive military preparations continue, thus increasing the threat to the hemisphere, further action will be justified. I have directed the Armed Forces to prepare for any eventualities; and I trust that, in the interest of both the Cuban people and the Soviet technicians at the sites, the hazards to all concerned of continuing this threat will be recognized.

Third: It shall be the policy of this nation to regard any nuclear missile launched from Cuba against any nation in the Western Hemisphere as an attack by the Soviet Union on the United States, requiring a full retaliatory response upon the Soviet Union.

Fourth: As a necessary military precaution I have reinforced our base at Guantanamo, evacuated today the dependents of our personnel there, and ordered additional military units to be on a standby alert basis.

Fifth: We are calling tonight for an immediate meeting of the Organ of Consultation, under the Organization of American States, to consider this threat to hemispheric security and to invoke articles 6 and 8 of the Rio Treaty in support of all necessary action. The United Nations Charter allows for regional security arrangements—and the nations of this hemisphere decided long ago against the military presence of outside powers. Our other allies around the world have also been alerted.

Sixth: Under the Charter of the United Nations, we are asking tonight that an emergency meeting of the Security Council be convoked without delay to take action against this latest Soviet threat to world peace. Our resolution will call for the prompt dismantling and withdrawal of all offensive weapons in Cuba, under the supervision of U.N. observers, before the quarantine can be lifted.

Seventh and finally: I call upon Chairman Khrushchev to halt and eliminate this clandestine, reckless, and provocative threat to world peace and to stable relations between our two nations. I call upon him further to abandon this course of world domination and to join in an historic effort to end the perilous arms race and transform the history of man. He has an opportunity now to move the world back from the abyss of destruction—by returning to his Government's own words that it had no need to station missiles outside its own territory, and withdrawing these weapons from Cuba—by refraining from any action which will widen or deepen the present crisis—and then by participating in a search for peaceful and permanent solutions.

This nation is prepared to present its case against the Soviet threat to peace, and our own proposals for a peaceful world, at any time and in any forum—in the OAS, in the United Nations, or in any other meeting that could be useful—without limiting our freedom of action.

We have in the past made strenuous efforts to limit the spread of nuclear weapons. We have proposed the elimination of all arms and military bases in a fair and effective disarmament treaty. We are prepared to discuss new proposals for the removal of tensions on both sides—including the possibilities of a genuinely independent Cuba, free to determine its own destiny. We have no wish to war with the Soviet Union, for we are a peaceful people who desire to live in peace with all other peoples.

But it is difficult to settle or even discuss these problems in an atmosphere of intimidation. That is why this latest Soviet threat—or any other threat which is made either independently or in response to our actions this week—must and will be met with determination. Any hostile move anywhere in the world against the safety and freedom of peoples to whom we are committed—including in particular the brave people of West Berlin—will be met by whatever action is needed.

Finally, I want to say a few words to the captive people of Cuba, to whom this speech is being directly carried by special radio facilities. I speak to you as a friend, as one who knows of your deep attachment to your fatherland, as one who shares your aspirations for liberty and justice for all. And I have watched and the American people have watched with deep sorrow how your nationalist revolution was betrayed and how your fatherland fell under foreign domination. Now your leaders are no longer Cuban leaders inspired by Cuban ideals. They are puppets and agents of an international conspiracy which has turned Cuba against your friends and neighbors in the Americas—and turned it into the first Latin American country to become a target for nuclear war, the first Latin American country to have these weapons on its soil.

These new weapons are not in your interest. They contribute nothing to your peace and well-being. They can only undermine it. But this country has no wish to cause you to suffer or to impose any system upon you. We know that your lives and land are being used as pawns by those who deny you freedom.

Many times in the past the Cuban people have risen to throw out tyrants who destroyed their liberty. And I have no doubt that most Cubans today look forward to the time when they will be truly free—free from foreign domination, free to choose their own leaders, free to select their own system, free to own their own land, free to speak and write and worship without fear or degradation. And then shall Cuba be welcomed back to the society of free nations and to the associations of this hemisphere.

My fellow citizens, let no one doubt that this is a difficult and dangerous effort on which we have set out. No one can foresee precisely what course it will take or what costs or casualties will be incurred. Many months of sacrifice and self-discipline lie ahead—months in which both our patience and our will will be tested, months in which many threats and denunciations will keep us aware of our dangers. But the greatest danger of all would be to do nothing.

The path we have chosen for the present is full of hazards, as all paths are; but it is the one most consistent with our character and courage as a nation and our commitments around the world. The cost of freedom is always high—but Americans have always paid it. And one path we shall never choose, and that is the path of surrender or submission.

Our goal is not the victory of might but the vindication of right—not peace at the expense of freedom, but both peace *and* freedom, here in this hemisphere and, we hope, around the world. God willing, that goal will be achieved.

EXPLANATION: COHERENCE AND CLARITY

Guided Discussions

ALEXIS DE TOCQUEVILLE, *Why Democratic Nations Naturally Desire Peace, and Democratic Armies, War*
ALBERT EINSTEIN, *The Laws of Science and the Laws of Ethics*
R. G. COLLINGWOOD, *History's Nature, Object, Method, and Value*
A. L. KROEBER, *The Invention of the Steamboat*

For Further Analysis

DAVID HUME, *Of Tragedy*
T. C. SCHNEIRLA *and* GERARD PIEL, *The Army Ant*
BRONISLAW MALINOWSKI, *Motherhood and the Temptations of Incest*
HENRI POINCARÉ, *Mathematical Creation*

Alexis de Tocqueville

WHY DEMOCRATIC NATIONS
NATURALLY DESIRE PEACE,
AND DEMOCRATIC ARMIES, WAR

From *Democracy in America*

THE SAME interests, the same fears, the same passions that deter democratic nations from revolutions deter them also from war; the spirit of military glory and the spirit of revolution are weakened at the same time and by the same causes. The ever increasing numbers of men of property who are lovers of peace, the growth of personal wealth which war so rapidly consumes, the mildness of manners, the gentleness of heart, those tendencies to pity which are produced by the equality of conditions, that coolness of understanding which renders men comparatively insensible to the violent and poetical excitement of arms, all these causes concur to quench the military spirit. I think it may be admitted as a general and constant rule that among civilized nations the warlike passions will become more rare and less intense in proportion as social conditions are more equal.

2 War is nevertheless an occurrence to which all nations are subject, democratic nations as well as others. Whatever taste they may have for peace, they must hold themselves in readiness to repel aggression, or, in other words, they must have an army. Fortune, which has conferred so many peculiar benefits upon the inhabitants of the United States, has placed them in the midst of a wilderness, where they have, so to speak, no neighbors; a few thousand soldiers are sufficient for their wants. But this is peculiar to America, not to democracy.

3 The equality of conditions and the manners as well as the institutions resulting from it do not exempt a democratic people from the neces-

97

sity of standing armies, and their armies always exercise a powerful influence over their fate. It is therefore of singular importance to inquire what are the natural propensities of the men of whom these armies are composed.

4   Among aristocratic nations, especially among those in which birth is the only source of rank, the same inequality exists in the army as in the nation; the officer is noble, the soldier is a serf; the one is naturally called upon to command, the other to obey. In aristocratic armies the private soldier's ambition is therefore circumscribed within very narrow limits. Nor has the ambition of the officer an unlimited range. An aristocratic body not only forms a part of the scale of ranks in the nation, but contains a scale of ranks within itself; the members of whom it is composed are placed one above another in a particular and unvarying manner. Thus one man is born to command of a regiment, another to that of a company. When once they have reached the utmost object of their hopes, they stop of their own accord and remain contented with their lot.

5   There is, besides, a strong cause that in aristocracies weakens the officer's desire of promotion. Among aristocratic nations an officer, independently of his rank in the army, also occupies an elevated rank in society; the former is almost always, in his eyes, only an appendage to the latter. A nobleman who embraces the profession of arms follows it less from motives of ambition than from a sense of the duties imposed on him by his birth. He enters the army in order to find an honorable employment for the idle years of his youth and to be able to bring back to his home and his peers some honorable recollections of military life; but his principal object is not to obtain by that profession either property, distinction, or power, for he possesses these advantages in his own right and enjoys them without leaving his home.

6   In democratic armies all the soldiers may become officers, which makes the desire of promotion general and immeasurably extends the bounds of military ambition. The officer, on his part, sees nothing that naturally and necessarily stops him at one grade more than at another; and each grade has immense importance in his eyes because his rank in society almost always depends on his rank in the army. Among democratic nations it often happens that an officer has no property but his pay and no distinction but that of military honors; consequently, as often as his duties change, his fortune changes and he becomes, as it were, a new man. What was only an appendage to his position in aristocratic armies has thus become the main point, the basis of his whole condition.

7   Under the old French monarchy officers were always called by their titles of nobility; they are now always called by the title of their military rank. This little change in the forms of language suffices to show that a great revolution has taken place in the constitution of society and in that of the army.

8   In democratic armies the desire of advancement is almost universal: it is ardent, tenacious, perpetual; it is strengthened by all other desires and extinguished only with life itself. But it is easy to see that, of all armies in the world, those in which advancement must be slowest in time of peace are the armies of democratic countries. As the number of commissions is naturally limited while the number of competitors is almost unlimited, and as the strict law of equality is over all alike, none can make rapid progress; many can make no progress at all. Thus the desire of advancement is greater and the opportunities of advancement fewer than elsewhere. All the ambitious spirits of a democratic army are consequently ardently desirous of war, because war makes vacancies and warrants the violation of that law of seniority which is the sole privilege natural to democracy.

9   We thus arrive at this singular consequence, that, of all armies, those most ardently desirous of war are democratic armies, and of all nations, those most fond of peace are democratic nations; and what makes these facts still more extraordinary is that these contrary effects are produced at the same time by the principle of equality.

10   All members of the community, being alike, constantly harbor the wish and discover the possibility of changing their condition and improving their welfare; this makes them fond of peace, which is favorable to industry and allows every man to pursue his own little undertakings to their completion. On the other hand, this same equality makes soldiers dream of fields of battle, by increasing the value of military honors in the eyes of those who follow the profession of arms and by rendering those honors accessible to all. In either case the restlessness of the heart is the same, the taste for enjoyment is insatiable, the ambition of success is great; the means of gratifying it alone are different.

11   These opposite tendencies of the nation and the army expose democratic communities to great dangers. When a military spirit forsakes a people, the profession of arms immediately ceases to be held in honor and military men fall to the lowest rank of the public servants; they are little esteemed and no longer understood. The reverse of what takes place in aristocratic ages then occurs; the men who enter the army are no longer

those of the highest, but of the lowest class. Military ambition is indulged only when no other is possible. Hence arises a circle of cause and consequence from which it is difficult to escape: the best part of the nation shuns the military profession because that profession is not honored, and the profession is not honored because the nation has ceased to follow it.

12   It is then no matter of surprise that democratic armies are often restless, ill-tempered, and dissatisfied with their lot, although their physical condition is commonly far better and their discipline less strict than in other countries. The soldier feels that he occupies an inferior position, and his wounded pride either stimulates his taste for hostilities that would render his services necessary or gives him a desire for revolution, during which he may hope to win by force of arms the political influence and personal importance now denied him.

13   The composition of democratic armies makes this last-mentioned danger much to be feared. In democratic communities almost every man has some property to preserve; but democratic armies are generally led by men without property, most of whom have little to lose in civil broils. The bulk of the nation is naturally much more afraid of revolutions than in the ages of aristocracy, but the leaders of the army much less so.

14   Moreover, as among democratic nations (to repeat what I have just remarked) the wealthiest, best-educated, and ablest men seldom adopt the military profession, the army, taken collectively, eventually forms a small nation by itself, where the mind is less enlarged and habits are more rude than in the nation at large. Now, this small uncivilized nation has arms in its possession and alone knows how to use them; for, indeed, the pacific temper of the community increases the danger to which a democratic people is exposed from the military and turbulent spirit of the army. Nothing is so dangerous as an army in the midst of an unwarlike nation; the excessive love of the whole community for quiet continually puts the constitution at the mercy of the soldiery.

15   It may therefore be asserted, generally speaking, that if democratic nations are naturally prone to peace from their interests and their propensities, they are constantly drawn to war and revolutions by their armies. Military revolutions, which are scarcely ever to be apprehended in aristocracies, are always to be dreaded among democratic nations. These perils must be reckoned among the most formidable that beset their future fate, and the attention of statesmen should be sedulously applied to find a remedy for the evil.

16   When a nation perceives that it is inwardly affected by the restless ambition of its army, the first thought which occurs is to give this in-

convenient ambition an object by going to war. I do not wish to speak ill of war: war almost always enlarges the mind of a people and raises their character. In some cases it is the only check to the excessive growth of certain propensities that naturally spring out of the equality of conditions, and it must be considered as a necessary corrective to certain inveterate diseases to which democratic communities are liable.

17 War has great advantages, but we must not flatter ourselves that it can diminish the danger I have just pointed out. That peril is only suspended by it, to return more fiercely when the war is over; for armies are much more impatient of peace after having tasted military exploits. War could be a remedy only for a people who were always athirst for military glory.

18 I foresee that all the military rulers who may rise up in great democratic nations will find it easier to conquer with their armies than to make their armies live at peace after conquest. There are two things that a democratic people will always find very difficult, to begin a war and to end it.

19 Again, if war has some peculiar advantages for democratic nations, on the other hand it exposes them to certain dangers which aristocracies have no cause to dread to an equal extent. I shall point out only two of these.

20 Although war gratifies the army, it embarrasses and often exasperates that countless multitude of men whose minor passions every day require peace in order to be satisfied. Thus there is some risk of its causing, under another form, the very disturbance it is intended to prevent.

21 No protracted war can fail to endanger the freedom of a democratic country. Not indeed that after every victory it is to be apprehended that the victorious generals will possess themselves by force of the supreme power, after the manner of Sulla and Cæsar; the danger is of another kind. War does not always give over democratic communities to military government, but it must invariably and immeasurably increase the powers of civil government; it must almost compulsorily concentrate the direction of all men and the management of all things in the hands of the administration. If it does not lead to despotism by sudden violence, it prepares men for it more gently by their habits. All those who seek to destroy the liberties of a democratic nation ought to know that war is the surest and the shortest means to accomplish it. This is the first axiom of the science.

22 One remedy, which appears to be obvious when the ambition of soldiers and officers becomes the subject of alarm, is to augment the num-

ber of commissions to be distributed by increasing the army. This affords temporary relief, but it plunges the country into deeper difficulties at some future period. To increase the army may produce a lasting effect in an aristocratic community, because military ambition is there confined to one class of men, and the ambition of each individual stops, as it were, at a certain limit, so that it may be possible to satisfy all who feel its influence. But nothing is gained by increasing the army among a democratic people, because the number of aspirants always rises in exactly the same ratio as the army itself. Those whose claims have been satisfied by the creation of new commissions are instantly succeeded by a fresh multitude beyond all power of satisfaction; and even those who were but now satisfied soon begin to crave more advancement, for the same excitement prevails in the ranks of the army as in the civil classes of democratic society, and what men want is, not to reach a certain grade, but to have constant promotion. Though these wants may not be very vast, they are perpetually recurring. Thus a democratic nation, by augmenting its army, allays only for a time the ambition of the military profession, which soon becomes even more formidable because the number of those who feel it is increased.

23   I am of the opinion that a restless and turbulent spirit is an evil inherent in the very constitution of democratic armies and beyond hope of cure. The legislators of democracies must not expect to devise any military organization capable by its influence of calming and restraining the military profession; their efforts would exhaust their powers before the object could be attained.

24   The remedy for the vices of the army is not to be found in the army itself, but in the country. Democratic nations are naturally afraid of disturbance and of despotism; the object is to turn these natural instincts into intelligent, deliberate, and lasting tastes. When men have at last learned to make a peaceful and profitable use of freedom and have felt its blessings, when they have conceived a manly love of order and have freely submitted themselves to discipline, these same men, if they follow the profession of arms, bring into it, unconsciously and almost against their will, these same habits and manners. The general spirit of the nation, being infused into the spirit peculiar to the army, tempers the opinions and desires engendered by military life, or represses them by the mighty force of public opinion. Teach the citizens to be educated, orderly, firm, and free and the soldiers will be disciplined and obedient.

25   Any law that, in repressing the turbulent spirit of the army, should tend to diminish the spirit of freedom in the nation and to overshadow

the notion of law and right would defeat its object; it would do much more to favor than to defeat the establishment of military tyranny.

26   After all, and in spite of all precautions, a large army in the midst of a democratic people will always be a source of great danger. The most effectual means of diminishing that danger would be to reduce the army, but this is a remedy that all nations are not able to apply.

Discussion: This chapter from de Tocqueville's great work on American democracy is different from the pieces we have so far considered in that it has a different kind of communicative purpose. It does not seek to persuade the reader—to shape a subject so as to make him feel the truth of a particular statement. Rather it seeks to explain the subject to him in a particular way— to make him understand it. The purpose of a persuasion is to produce a firm conviction; the reader's proper response is something like "I agree." The purpose of an explanation is to produce a clear conception; the proper response is "I understand." The success of an explanation will depend upon the interest and importance which the writer can give the subject and upon the cogency and adequacy of his analysis. The primary virtues requisite in an explanation are coherence and clarity.

Analytic Summary: In this essay de Tocqueville attempts to explain to intelligent and interested readers (purpose) *the problems posed for a democratic society by the special characteristics of democratic armies as a means to exploring possible solutions to those problems* (subject), *by establishing a series of related propositions each of which is dependent upon those which precede it* (disposition).

Questions

1. State succinctly the proposition which de Tocqueville tries to establish in the first paragraph. Do the same for the second paragraph. What is the relation of the first sentence of the third paragraph to the two opening paragraphs? What is the function of the first three paragraphs in relation to the rest of the essay?

2. Into what three parts does the rest of the essay fall? What is the subject of each? How is each part logically dependent upon what comes before?

3. For what purpose, in the first part, does de Tocqueville introduce the discussion of aristocratic armies? How does he mark the beginning and end of this discussion as more or less of a digression from the main line of his essay? What specifically would be lost if this discussion were omitted?

4. What is the function of the example from "the old French monarchy"? Why is it not introduced during the earlier discussion of aristocratic armies rather than here, after the introductory discussion of democratic armies?

5. What is the function of the first sentence of paragraph 8? What further, related proposition does the rest of the paragraph establish? What is the function of the next two paragraphs, in relation to what has gone before?

6. In what sentence is the transition between the first and second parts of the body of the essay effected? How does the form of the sentence reflect its function?

7. What proposition is established in paragraph 1 in the second part? How, specifically, does this proposition depend on what has gone before? What double proposition is established in the next paragraph? How is this dependent on the previous proposition? How is this last proposition further developed in paragraphs 13 and 14? Is this development solely an expansion of the implications of propositions already stated?

8. Describe the function of paragraph 15 as a summary of the argument to this point and as a transition to the third part.

9. How many possible remedies are proposed by de Tocqueville? Considering his subject and purpose, why, when he mentions the possible advantages of war as a remedy, does he not specify the "certain propensities" and "inveterate diseases" of democracy which war might eradicate?

10. The propositions advanced in paragraphs 17 and 18 are not fully related by de Tocqueville to what has gone before. Spell out the connections that he leaves implicit.

11. Where in the essay has de Tocqueville more fully established the specific fact about democratic societies upon which the proposition in paragraph 20 is built? Is it clear why aristocracies have "no cause to dread" the dangers discussed in paragraphs 20 and 21? Is the proposition developed in paragraph 21 dependent on what has gone before? Is it dependent in the same sense in which the previous propositions have been dependent?

12. On what earlier part of the essay is the analysis of the second remedy (paragraph 22) directly dependent? How is the third remedy different in kind from the other two? In relation to what general fact basic in the essay is it developed? The other two remedies are developed in relation to what other general fact? How much is this contrast indicated in the transition from the first two remedies to the third? Where is it directly stated? To what extent is the third remedy (paragraph 24) based upon facts already developed? On principles already developed? How is it thus the most effective remedy?

13. How does the point made in paragraph 24 help to make clear the inadequacy of the remedy discussed briefly in paragraph 25?

14. Suppose de Tocqueville had been writing a persuasion designed to convince his audience that because of the dangers inherent in democratic armies some particular course of preventive action ought to be followed. Would he have ended his essay with the material embodied in the last two paragraphs? Would he have treated the subject of war as he does? What other, more major changes might he have made?

Theme Topics

1. Write an essay designed to clarify a reasonably complex subject. Model your development upon de Tocqueville's progressive cause-and-effect procedure.

2. In a theme apply de Tocqueville's analysis to post-World War II America. As an initial step you will wish to recapitulate de Tocqueville's analysis clearly as it is relevant to the facts you wish to consider. Your piece might be either a persuasion or an explanation.

Albert Einstein

THE LAWS OF SCIENCE
AND THE LAWS OF ETHICS

*S*CIENCE searches for relations which are thought to exist independently of the searching individual. This includes the case where man himself is the subject. Or the subject of scientific statements may be concepts created by ourselves, as in mathematics. Such concepts are not necessarily supposed to correspond to any objects in the outside world. However, all scientific statements and laws have one characteristic in common: they are "true or false" (adequate or inadequate). Roughly speaking, our reaction to them is "yes" or "no."

2   The scientific way of thinking has a further characteristic. The concepts which it uses to build up its coherent systems are not expressing emotions. For the scientist, there is only "being," but no wishing, no valuing, no good, no evil; no goal. As long as we remain within the realm of science proper, we can never meet with a sentence of the type: "Thou shalt not lie." There is something like a Puritan's restraint in the scientist who seeks truth: he keeps away from everything voluntaristic or emotional. Incidentally, this trait is the result of a slow development, peculiar to modern Western thought.

3   From this it might seem as if logical thinking were irrelevant for ethics. Scientific statements of facts and relations, indeed, cannot produce ethical directives. However, ethical directives can be made rational and coherent by logical thinking and empirical knowledge. If we can agree on some fundamenal ethical propositions, then other ethical propositions can be derived from them, provided that the original premises are stated with sufficient precision. Such ethical premises play a similar role in ethics, to that played by axioms in mathematics.

106

4   This is why we do not feel at all that it is meaningless to ask such questions as: "Why should we not lie?" We feel that such questions are meaningful because in all discussions of this kind some ethical premises are tacitly taken for granted. We then feel satisfied when we succeed in tracing back the ethical directive in question to these basic premises. In the case of lying this might perhaps be done in some way such as this: Lying destroys confidence in the statements of other people. Without such confidence, social cooperation is made impossible or at least difficult. Such cooperation, however, is essential to make human life possible and tolerable. This means that the rule "Thou shalt not lie" has been traced back to the demands: "Human life shall be preserved" and "Pain and sorrow shall be lessened as much as possible."

5   But what is the origin of such ethical axioms? Are they arbitrary? Are they based on mere authority? Do they stem from experiences of men and are they conditioned indirectly by such experiences?

6   For pure logic all axioms are arbitrary, including the axioms of ethics. But they are by no means arbitrary from a psychological and genetic point of view. They are derived from our inborn tendencies to avoid pain and annihilation, and from the accumulated emotional reaction of individuals to the behavior of their neighbors.

7   It is the privilege of man's moral genius, impersonated by inspired individuals, to advance ethical axioms which are so comprehensive and so well founded that men will accept them as grounded in the vast mass of their individual emotional experiences. Ethical axioms are found and tested not very differently from the axioms of science. Truth is what stands the test of experience.

Discussion: The complexity of the ideas developed in this explanation may seem disproportionate to its brevity. Here economy of means is rigidly enforced—very few explanatory examples, a minimum of amplification of crucial propositions, act as signposts to make our path easier. No special knowledge—neither that of the scientist nor that of the philosopher—is required for us to comprehend what Einstein has written, but intelligence and an inquiring mind are indeed prerequisites. An essay such as this one results only when a serious inquirer makes a disinterested investigation of a subject presumed to have intrinsic importance for men. For the intelligent reader willing to make the initial effort, overcoming the difficulties of extreme concision will be rewarded by an impression of complete lucidity of explanation. We may disagree with Einstein, but, if we do, we will know precisely *what* we disagree with.

If one reads the first paragraphs rapidly, he may get the immediate impression that Einstein is primarily concerned with differentiating—with contrasting

—scientific and ethical statements: we can never, in science, form a sentence of the type, "Thou shalt not lie." The initial contrast, though, while it is never discarded, is considerably modified by the crucial observation that "ethical premises play a similar role in ethics, to that played by axioms in mathematics" —or, stated most generally—logical thought is not irrelevant for ethics. The final set of contrasts and comparisons enables us to see that, though "for pure logic all axioms are arbitrary," the discovery and testing of ethical precepts and logical axioms are not essentially different. The final statement in the essay, "Truth is what stands the test of experience," is seen to be applicable to scientific law and ethical statement alike.

> *Analytic Summary: In this essay Einstein treats the relation of sci-entific and ethical laws to truth (subject). He attempts to explain as clearly and concisely as possible to intelligent laymen how the similarities between scientific and ethical inquiries are more significant than the manifest differences between them (purpose). He shapes his subject to his purpose largely by exploiting a series of explicit or implied contrasts and comparisons (disposition).*

Questions

1. Throughout the first two paragraphs Einstein does not explicitly mention "ethics" or "the law of ethics." What sentences in these paragraphs make us aware that his explanation of the nature of scientific laws has been developed as an initial contrast to the nature of ethical statements?

2. Is there an explicit syntactical bridge from the second to the third paragraph? Does that bridge indicate that we are meant to think of the nature of scientific law as contrasting with the nature of ethical law? In the first sentence of paragraph 3, Einstein tells us that "it might seem as if logical thinking were irrelevant for ethics"; would the nature of the transition differ if "might seem" were altered to "seems"? How? State as precisely as possible why it is important for Einstein to prepare us at the beginning of paragraph 3 to expect a comparison rather than a further contrast between scientific and ethical laws.

3. In paragraph 3 are we allowed to lose sight of the fact that scientific law differs from ethical directive? What sentences, or phrases within sentences, in the paragraph remind us that premises do not play the *same* role in ethics as that played by axioms in mathematics? On the other hand, how does the order of presentation of elements in the paragraph help give greater force to the noted similarity than to the noted difference?

4. In paragraph 4, Einstein discusses the tacit ethical premises underlying the rule, "Thou shalt not lie," but makes no reference at all to the role played by axioms in mathematics. Why not? Is there a plausible relationship between the final assertion in paragraph 3 and the discussion in paragraph 4? Is that relationship stated explicitly anywhere in paragraph 4?

5. From the end of paragraph 4 to the end of the essay Einstein very briefly clarifies his contention that truth—whether that of science or that of ethics—"is what stands the test of experience"; nevertheless, he devotes one whole paragraph to posing a series of questions about the origin of ethical axioms. Does paragraph 5 make the essay more or less effective? Is each of the questions relevant to the final statement about the nature of truth? If the answers to questions 2 or 3 in paragraph 5 were affirmative, would Einstein's concluding arguments seem plausible?

6. In the last paragraph, what does the phrase "impersonated by" mean? If we omit the last sentence in the essay, to what extent could we regard the explanation as complete? Does the last sentence of the essay support, contradict, or qualify the first sentence of the essay?

Theme Topics

1. Explain the ways in which Einstein's views about science and ethics are similar to and the ways in which they are different from the views expressed by C. P. Snow in "The Two Cultures" (included below).

2. Consider any two fields which are ostensibly remote from each other, and explain clearly ways in which they might be related.

R. G. Collingwood

HISTORY'S NATURE, OBJECT, METHOD, AND VALUE

*W*HAT HISTORY is, what it is about, how it proceeds, and what it is for, are questions which to some extent different people would answer in different ways. But in spite of differences there is a large measure of agreement between the answers. And this agreement becomes closer if the answers are subjected to scrutiny with a view to discarding those which proceed from unqualified witnesses. History, like theology or natural science, is a special form of thought. If that is so, questions about the nature, object, method, and value of this form of thought must be answered by persons having two qualifications.

2   First, they must have experience of that form of thought. They must be historians. In a sense we are all historians nowadays. All educated persons have gone through a process of education which has included a certain amount of historical thinking. But this does not qualify them to give an opinion about the nature, object, method, and value of historical thinking. For in the first place, the experience of historical thinking which they have thus acquired is probably very superficial; and the opinions based on it are therefore no better grounded than a man's opinion of the French people based on a single week-end visit to Paris. In the second place, experience of anything whatever gained through the ordinary educational channels, as well as being superficial, is invariably out of date. Experience of historical thinking, so gained, is modelled on text-books, and text-books always describe not what is now being thought by real live historians, but what was thought by real live historians at some time in the past when the raw material was being created out of which the text-book has been put together. And it is not only the

110

results of historical thought which are out of date by the time they get into the text-book. It is also the principles of historical thought: that is, the ideas as to the nature, object, method, and value of historical thinking. In the third place, and connected with this, there is a peculiar illusion incidental to all knowledge acquired in the way of education: the illusion of finality. When a student is *in statu pupillari* with respect to any subject whatever, he has to believe that things are settled because the text-books and his teachers regard them as settled. When he emerges from that state and goes on studying the subject for himself he finds that nothing is settled. The dogmatism which is an invariable mark of immaturity drops away from him. He looks at so-called facts with a new eye. He says to himself: "My teacher and text-books told me that such and such was true; but is it true? What reasons had they for thinking it true, and were these reasons adequate?" On the other hand, if he emerges from the status of pupil without continuing to pursue the subject he never rids himself of this dogmatic attitude. And this makes him a person peculiarly unfitted to answer the questions I have mentioned. No one, for example, is likely to answer them worse than an Oxford philosopher who, having read Greats in his youth, was once a student of history and thinks that this youthful experience of historical thinking entitles him to say what history is, what it is about, how it proceeds, and what it is for.

3   The second qualification for answering these questions is that a man should not only have experience of historical thinking but should also have reflected upon that experience. He must be not only an historian but a philosopher; and in particular his philosophical thought must have included special attention to the problems of historical thought. Now it is possible to be a quite good historian (though not an historian of the highest order) without thus reflecting upon one's own historical thinking. It is even easier to be a quite good teacher of history (though not the very best kind of teacher) without such reflection. At the same time, it is important to remember that experience comes first, and reflection on that experience second. Even the least reflective historian has the first qualification. He possesses the experience on which to reflect; and when he is asked to reflect on it his reflections have a good chance of being to the point. An historian who has never worked much at philosophy will probably answer our four questions in a more intelligent and valuable way than a philosopher who has never worked much at history.

4   I shall therefore propound answers to my four questions such as I think any present-day historian would accept. Here they will be rough and ready answers, but they will serve for a provisional definition of our

subject-matter and they will be defended and elaborated as the argument proceeds.

5   (a) *The definition of history.* Every historian would agree, I think, that history is a kind of research or inquiry. What kind of inquiry it is I do not yet ask. The point is that generically it belongs to what we call the sciences: that is, the forms of thought whereby we ask questions and try to answer them. Science in general, it is important to realize, does not consist in collecting what we already know and arranging it in this or that kind of pattern. It consists in fastening upon something we do not know, and trying to discover it. Playing patience with things we already know may be a useful means towards this end, but it is not the end itself. It is at best only the means. It is scientifically valuable only in so far as the new arrangement gives us the answer to a question we have already decided to ask. That is why all science begins from the knowledge of our own ignorance: not our ignorance of everything, but our ignorance of some definite thing—the origin of parliament, the cause of cancer, the chemical composition of the sun, the way to make a pump work without muscular exertion on the part of a man or a horse or some other docile animal. Science is finding things out: and in that sense history is a science.

6   (b) *The object of history.* One science differs from another in that it finds out things of a different kind. What kind of things does history find out? I answer, *res gestae:* actions of human beings that have been done in the past. Although this answer raises all kinds of further questions many of which are controversial, still, however they may be answered, the answers do not discredit the proposition that history is the science of *res gestae,* the attempt to answer questions about human actions done in the past.

7   (c) *How does history proceed?* History proceeds by the interpretation of evidence: where evidence is a collective name for things which singly are called documents, and a document is a thing existing here and now, of such a kind that the historian, by thinking about it, can get answers to the questions he asks about past events. Here again there are plenty of difficult questions to ask as to what the characteristics of evidence are and how it is interpreted. But there is no need for us to raise them at this stage. However they are answered, historians will agree that historical procedure, or method, consists essentially of interpreting evidence.

8   (d) Lastly, *what is history for?* This is perhaps a harder question than the others; a man who answers it will have to reflect rather more widely than a man who answers the three we have answered already. He

must reflect not only on historical thinking but on other things as well, because to say that something is "for" something implies a distinction between A and B, where A is good for something and B is that for which something is good. But I will suggest an answer, and express the opinion that no historian would reject it, although the further questions to which it gives rise are numerous and difficult.

9   My answer is that history is "for" human self-knowledge. It is generally thought to be of importance to man that he should know himself: where knowing himself means knowing not his merely personal peculiarities, the things that distinguish him from other men, but his nature as man. Knowing yourself means knowing, first, what it is to be a man; secondly, knowing what it is to be the kind of man you are; and thirdly, knowing what it is to be the man *you* are and nobody else is. Knowing yourself means knowing what you can do; and since nobody knows what he can do until he tries, the only clue to what man can do is what man has done. The value of history, then, is that it teaches us what man has done and thus what man is.

Discussion: This is an excerpt from a work designed to present Collingwood's rather complicated conception of history and the nature of historical knowledge. In this section of his book Collingwood offers a provisional view of his subject, a starting point from which to build his later argument.

This selection is an excellent example of a composition governed by an explanatory purpose, which, specifically, is to answer the question posed in the first sentence. The piece is exceptionally well *composed*—that is, the form of the composition expresses the subject matter with nearly perfect clarity. The piece is so well ordered and so well marked that at no point is the reader in doubt about what is being explained or about how each stage is relevant to the whole.

Analytic Summary: *Collingwood here attempts to explain clearly* (purpose) *his conception of history's nature, object, method, and value* (subject) *by presenting a series of related conceptions each of which depends on one or more of those preceding it* (disposition).

Questions

1. What major part of his explanation might Collingwood have omitted and still remained with a coherent explanatory whole? Could the omission be made without changing any of the remaining sentences?

2. Can you account for the long elaboration of this apparently unnecessary part? Does it help to know that Collingwood is going to put a special emphasis

in his work on the idea that history is a "special form of thought"? (He is going to argue that historical knowledge is different in its very nature from the kind of knowledge offered by natural science and scientific philosophy and, further, that only those who have experienced this kind of knowledge can know what it is.) In view of the prestige of natural science, how does this account for his later appeal to the judgment of historians?

3. How does Collingwood mark the first and second parts of his digression? How, in turn, does he mark the three parts into which the first part is itself divided? Does this kind of marking add to the clarity of his explanation?

4. Trace out the means Collingwood uses to maintain sentence-to-sentence coherence within the digression. Does this also add to the clarity of the explanation?

5. How does Collingwood keep in our minds as he proceeds with his discussion the fact that he is offering only a provisional explanation of his conception of history?

6. Under point (a) Collingwood partially identifies history with science. Is there any indication that he is preparing for the later sharp distinction he is going to make in his work between the two forms of knowledge?

7. How is the explanation under (b) dependent on that in (a)? How is (c) dependent upon (b)? In what sentence does this appear?

8. In only one of his points does Collingwood fail to mention that historians generally will agree with what he is saying. Which part is this? Why doesn't he mention historians here?

9. At what point does the dependence of (d) on the earlier three points fully appear? Does this fact illustrate in any way the editors' statement about the perfect form of the composition?

Theme Topics

1. Write an essay in which you show how your having come to understand something about the past (your own past or the past in general) has enabled you to understand something about yourself. Take care to give your essay enough general significance to make it meaningful to your audience.

2. Show in an essay how some aspect of the American past illuminates in some significant way an aspect of the American present.

A. L. Kroeber

THE INVENTION
OF THE STEAMBOAT

$\mathcal{T}$HE STEAMBOAT belongs to a type of invention in which the elements
of fundamental insight and imagination are of fairly low order, and
the problems to be solved are overwhelmingly practical, industrial, or
economic. Once the steam engine was established, it required no great
originality to conceive of setting one up in a boat and having it turn
something like the familiar mill wheel or a pair of mill wheels, simply reversed from being a source of power to being an application of it. As a
matter of fact it was about eighty years from the original Newcomen
steam-and-atmospheric engine to the first steam-propelled boats, and just
over a hundred to the first commercially successful ones.[1] What follows is
essentially an account of the practical, not scientific, difficulties that had
to be overcome, and why and when they were overcome.

2   The first steamboats were French. In 1773 the Count d'Auxiron built
a steamboat on the Seine, which sank before it ever ran. In 1775 Périer
launched at Paris a one-horsepower boat, which is said to have moved,
but would not run against current, and was broken up. Next year the
Marquis Jouffroy designed and more or less ran a steamboat with a fold-
ing webfoot on the Doubs, an upper tributary of the Rhone, near Switzerland and Alsace, of all places. The webfoot failed to open as soon as the
boat gathered speed or was turned upstream. This was seven years after
the appearance of Watt's condensing engine; but when after another

[1] It was over forty years from Watt's first condensing steam engine to the operation of
the *Clermont* on the Hudson. In the Newcomen engine steam pushed one way; when it
was chilled back to water, atmospheric pressure pushed the piston back.

seven years, in 1783, Jouffroy put a 140-foot steamer on the Saône, it was
still with the old-fashioned Newcomen atmospheric engine, but with
paddle wheels this time. This vessel ran well against the current for a
quarter of an hour. Then the seams of both hull and boiler opened from
the pounding of the heavy engine, and the boat had to be beached.
Jouffroy did not get his expected monopoly rights and gave up. A long
lull followed. France was traversed by canals and towpaths and had then
the most and the best roads in the world, but its rivers were shallow and
crooked. Steamboats might run, but they could not compete with horse-
drawn transportation—not until they became a lot more efficient. In 1803,
Napoleon, on the advice of a committee of experts, turned down a boat of
Fulton's that developed three or four mph. Therewith, steamboating was
dead in France for another spell. Only in 1816, when there already were
steamboats in Russia and Java and 5000 tons of them on the Hudson
alone, did poor Jouffroy organize the first steam-vessel company in France,
forty years after he had sailed one on the Doubs—only to fail once more.
It was another decade before steam navigation began to prosper in
France: geography and competition were against it.

3   In Britain, canal and river conditions were similar to those of France,
and the first efforts were followed by a parallel period of complete cessa-
tion, during which the United States forged ahead. In 1788, Symington
ran a 25-foot steamboat on a Scotch lake, and next year a 60-foot, five-to-
seven mph one on a Scotch canal. During the 1790's there was a whole
series of vessels that actually ran in Scotch and English waters, designed
by Clarke, Lord Stanhope, Smith, Hunter, Dickinson, and the American
Rumsey, who used his favorite jet mechanism; but none of them paid,
and the inventors kept losing their financial backers.

4   In 1802 Symington found a new sponsor and perfected the *Charlotte
Dundas,* an efficient vessel, which however was soon barred from the
Forth-Clyde Canal because it was washing away the banks, or because
horse-towed competitors alleged that it might wash them away. For a
time British investors, like the contemporary French ones, became convinced that profitable operation was impossible, and laid off completely.
In 1812 there was a resumption by Bell, an innkeeper, who built the
Comet to carry excursionists on the Clyde to his hotel. The next year
saw improved vessels; and then came a rapid development and acceptance,
which was extended to the North and Irish seas by 1815 and 1818. In
the development, from then on, of the heavy-tonnage, sturdy, open-ocean
steamship, the British, with their world-wide commerce, took the lead.

5   In the United States, conditions were much more favorable for success of the weak craft of the early experimental period. There were good-sized rivers with prosperous towns on them, but not crowded with boats; there were no canals or towpaths, few and bad roads. It was on these waters—the Connecticut, Hudson, Delaware, Potomac, Savannah rivers, with Lake Champlain and the St. Lawrence—that the American steamer, a true river boat, worked its way to economic success in the very period of 1803–13 when navigation in Europe was in a lull of discouragement—in fact in suspension.

6   The first American efforts began soon after the Revolutionary War, a little after the earliest French experiments and a shade before Symington's in Scotland. Rumsey worked on the principle of steam-driven stern water jets. He is said to have tried such a boat on the Potomac in 1786 and 1787; it worked, but then failed. He was constructing a larger one on the Thames when he died in 1792. This boat later made four knots an hour, but was adjudicated not to have fulfilled its contract. Fitch, at Philadelphia, after a proving boat in 1786, built a paddle-wheel steamer that worked in 1787, and a better one in 1788. In 1790 he put a stern-wheeler of six to eight mph on a regular run on the Delaware from Philadelphia to Trenton. It traveled some two or three thousand miles during its life, and came near paying at least for its operation. This was seventeen years before Fulton; but the route was short, for once was paralleled by good roads, and Fitch was a difficult, restless person, who antagonized partners and sponsors. Stevens ran a high-pressure, steam-turbine, propeller-screw boat in New York Harbor in 1802; but American engines being still of bad workmanship, he reverted to low pressure and paddles, and built the famous *Phoenix* in 1808. This was probably as good a vessel as Fulton's *Clermont* of 1807, but Fulton had been given a monopoly of the Hudson River. So the *Phoenix* sailed, timorously and with stops and waits during thirteen days, the hundred and fifty miles from New York to the Delaware —the first steam voyage on the ocean—and ran the Philadelphia-Trenton route from 1809 to 1815.

7   Fulton came at the critical moment when, after thirty years of experiment, pioneering, and outlay, success was at last around the corner for someone operating in favorable American waters. Fulton had the advantage of knowing nearly all previous inventors, ships, or their plans. He had personality and charm, utilized these to form good connections, as with Livingston; and this connection not only financed him but secured the monopoly of New York State waters. This gave him the straight,

deep, well-populated Hudson River, its hundred and fifty miles flanked by hills instead of roads, as a proprietary right of way. His United States patent claims on his steamboats fell to pieces, as they deserved to, because as an inventor Fulton was belated and was more versatile than profound. The *Clermont's* Watt engine was imported bodily from England, and the main reason for her success was the engine. There was then no plant or shop in America that could produce a steamtight engine operating smoothly and reliably: that was Britain's contribution. Fulton had what was worth more to him than an invention—a virtual patent on a great river that nature had made as it were to order for steam transportation. So the *Clermont* finally made money, or convinced investors that steamboats would make money; and therewith the battle was definitely won for the now twenty-odd-year-old invention. By 1811 Fulton had a steamboat on the faraway Mississippi—while the whole of Europe was still in the phase of having given up the problem.

8   It is clear that in a case like this of the early steamboat, the term "invention," as generally used, includes a mass of factors—economic, geographic, and what not—that have nothing to do with science. Even on the wholly mechanical side, the real problem was the gradual overcoming of a long series of side-issue difficulties, such as perfection of an engine that would not rock or sink the boat, and would not give out. This overcoming of minor obstacles was the actual crux of the invention, and not the imaginatively obvious putting together of one and one to make two. That in fact had been done early in the 1700's, soon after the Newcomen and long before the Watt engine. English patents were granted to Allen in 1729 for a jet-propulsion steamboat and to Hulls in 1739 for a paddlewheel steamboat.

9   The question remains: Why the singling out of Fulton from among dozens of competitors as the outstanding hero of the occasion? Why is he the recipient, in American popular history, of from nine-tenths to ten-tenths of the glory, when his intrinsic earned credit, merely as inventor and engineer, could not have been over one-tenth? The basic reason is one we have already encountered: that naïve thinking refuses to deal with abstracted, generalizable factors, but demands a personalized, anthropomorphic story. It must be Caesar that wins the battle, not the myriad anonymous legionaries, still less their wholly impersonal armament or drill. So with inventions: an inventor must be found, or fabricated if necessary, on whom the dramatized tale can be hung.

10   That brings us to the specific question: Granted the emotional need for a hero, why was Fulton selected to be cast for the role? Here the an-

swer is that he was the first obvious success-boy in the story, in a way which a schoolchild, a shopkeeper, and a millionaire could all understand. He did make money, he did make headlines, he did get into the grammar-school histories and the Hudson-Fulton Centenary, and he was a fellow patriot American. So he must have been a great man—which he was; and therefore, folk reasoning runs, he must have been *the* great man, *the* inventor—which he was not.

11   Underneath this fairy tale, we can see the process of actual invention as something manifold and complicated, with no one individual really dominant, but with impersonal and economic factors like presence or absence of roads influential, reaching down even into geographical conditions, and determining within narrow limits both when and where the invention would become effective. Not that Fulton lacked ability: he had it; but without his predecessors, and Watt's engine, and his social connections, and the gift of the Hudson, most of us would never have heard of him, and the same success story, in only a slightly different version, would have been attached to some other name. Suppose Fulton had died in 1806. Even with nothing more to go on than the facts here skeletonized, we can scarcely doubt that someone else, perhaps Stevens, would in 1808 or 1809 or by 1810, in the United States and almost certainly in the vicinity of New York Harbor, have got far enough to be acclaimed as the finally successful inventor. Or, with some imaginary catastrophe blotting out America, it seems reasonably safe to believe that by say 1815 it would have been an Englishman.

12   It is in this sense that inventions can be said to come with inevitability. Not that their date and place and nationality are predetermined through all time, or are immanent in some great design of world pre-destination. What is meant by inevitability is that, given enough information on a certain status of a certain culture, it is possible to understand why particular inventions or innovations were made when, where, or how they were made, and not in other times, places, or contexts; and to understand this without denying personality but also without bringing into the argument any unique, God-given qualities of it. With sufficient knowledge, such explanations in social or cultural terms can be reasonably reliable in retrospect.

13   Predictions before the event would be less certain: first, because the facts of the whole story are not yet in; second, because there is bound to be less perspective and more emotional involvement while matters are still in the making.

Discussion: This selection is drawn from a well-known textbook on anthropology in which it is one of a series of discussions designed to illustrate the cultural conditions under which inventions emerge. The specific example of the steamboat is here used to validate the generalization about the dependence of invention upon cultural conditions which is made at the end of the essay. Kroeber's piece may fruitfully be compared with Collingwood's because, though both authors are in full intellectual control of their subject matter, Kroeber is much less successful than Collingwood in giving his explanation clear compositional form. Let us try to see why.

Kroeber says in the first paragraph that the essay is "an account of the practical, not scientific, difficulties that had to be overcome, and why and when they were overcome." It is that, but it is more. The statement implies that we are going to get a merely chronological account of the successive stages through which the steamboat passed on its way to functional perfection. Actually, as we see upon reading the piece, it is a more complex explanation of a more complex problem. In the first place it is not an account of the *invention* of the steamboat so much as it is an account of the emergence of the first commercially successful steamboat. (Kroeber intends this meaning, but he does not make it completely clear.) More specifically, the essay seeks to answer a question which might be phrased thus: why did the first commercially successful steamboat appear in America and not in Britain and France, and how does the answer to this question illustrate the fact that inventions are not the spontaneous products of individual geniuses but are conditioned by their cultural context? This question is clearly implicit in the essay and is answered by it. The trouble is that the question is not clear in the reader's mind from the outset, so that part of the force of the explanation is lost. The illustrative material itself, furthermore, is not arranged so as to make as clear as possible what its relation to the implicit question is. The answer to the question, it becomes clear, is this: the first successful steamboat appeared in the United States because there, for the first time, the several elements necessary for its success appeared together. What these elements were is fairly clear from the account of Fulton, but up to that point they have to be inferred piece-by-piece from the narrative. If the general problem had been stated clearly at the outset and the conditions had been set forth there also, the later exposition could have been very clearly and forcefully geared to it. The significance of the various conditions noted in France and Britain would have appeared more sharply, the reader would have been more aware of exactly what was lacking, and could then have been shown how all the conditions, lacking in the earlier examples in one degree or another, were now supplied. The relative chronology of the various projects in the three countries could also have been marked more clearly for the reader, so that he would have had a sharper grasp of the relative succession of events in all three countries. The account of the ultimately successful development of steamboats in France and Britain might also have been delayed for treatment after the account of Fulton.

Analytic Summary: In this essay Kroeber attempts to illustrate the cultural determination of inventions (purpose) *through an account of the emergence of the steamboat* (subject) *by tracing chronologically the successive stages of that emergence in three countries* (disposition).

Questions

1. What is the primary condition for the success of the steamboat in all countries? How clearly is this indicated in the first paragraph? How much of paragraph 2 is devoted to examples of the non-fulfillment of this condition in France? Are these examples referred to the general condition?

2. What two secondary general conditions for the success of the steamboat are introduced by example in paragraph 2? To what extent are the examples generalized so as to be relevant for later discussion?

3. What is the point of the sentence about Napoleon? Could this point have been made clearer by relating it to the previous sentence?

4. Does the discussion of British steamboating in paragraph 3 introduce any new conditions for the success of the steamboat? Does it develop further the interrelationship of the conditions? Is this given maximum clarity?

5. In paragraph 4 does the account of the ultimately successful British steamships without a chronological cross-reference to American developments make for any possible confusion? Actually, the chronological facts have already been stated. Where? Is this sufficient?

6. What is the relation of the "improved" British vessels to the secondary condition of commercial feasibility? Would the criterion of technical efficiency in Britain be different from that in the United States? The answer is implicit in the first sentence of the next paragraph, but is it sufficiently clear?

7. All the conditions so far developed are summed up in paragraph 5. Could the summing-up have been made more forceful by putting greater emphasis on the contrast with the European situation?

8. To what general condition do the American examples in paragraph 6 mostly refer? What two new, less significant conditions are introduced in this paragraph? If all the conditions had been stated at the outset, should these have been subordinated to those already developed?

9. Are all the conditions touched on in the discussion of Fulton's success? Could Kroeber, in listing them, have made useful contrasts with earlier examples? Would some general statement about the conditions also have made matters clearer?

10. Where does Kroeber begin to answer the second part of the implicit governing question?

11. What does the two-paragraph discussion of the Fulton legend contribute to the realization of Kroeber's full purpose? How is this contribution made clear in the next paragraph?

12. Does Kroeber's analysis of the development of the steamboat support his final generalization? What is the function of the very last paragraph?

Theme Topics

1. Write a short version of Kroeber's essay. Take into consideration all that you have learned through discussion and construct your explanation so that the problem will be clear at the outset and so that the relevance of all material to the problem will be manifest to the reader at each stage of the discussion.

2. Write an explanation of a particular fact, event, or process in such a way as to illustrate a larger truth.

David Hume

OF TRAGEDY

*I*T SEEMS an unaccountable pleasure, which the spectators of a well-written tragedy receive from sorrow, terror, anxiety, and other passions, that are in themselves disagreeable and uneasy. The more they are touched and affected, the more are they delighted with the spectacle; and as soon as the uneasy passions cease to operate, the piece is at an end. One scene of full joy and contentment and security is the utmost, that any composition of this kind can bear; and it is sure always to be the concluding one. If, in the texture of the piece, there be interwoven any scenes of satisfaction, they afford only faint gleams of pleasure, which are thrown in by way of variety, and in order to plunge the actors into deeper distress, by means of that contrast and disappointment. The whole heart of the poet is employed, in rouzing and supporting the compassion and indignation, the anxiety and resentment of his audience. They are pleased in proportion as they are afflicted, and never are so happy as when they employ tears, sobs, and cries to give vent to their sorrow, and relieve their heart, swoln with the tenderest sympathy and compassion.

The few critics who have had some tincture of philosophy, have remarked this singular phænomenon, and have endeavoured to account for it.

L'Abbé Dubos, in his reflections on poetry and painting, asserts, that nothing is in general so disagreeable to the mind as the languid, listless state of indolence, into which it falls upon the removal of all passion and occupation. To get rid of this painful situation, it seeks every amusement and pursuit; business, gaming, shews, executions; whatever will rouze the passions, and take its attention from itself. No matter what the passion is: Let it be disagreeable, afflicting, melancholy, disordered; it is still better than that insipid languor, which arises from perfect tranquility and repose.

It is impossible not to admit this account, as being, at least in part, satisfactory. You may observe, when there are several tables of gaming, that all the company run to those, where the deepest play is, even though they find not there the best players. The view, or, at least, imagination of high passions, arising from great loss or gain, affects the spectator by sympathy, gives him some touches of the same passions, and serves him for a momentary entertainment. It makes the time pass the easier with him, and is some relief to that oppression, under which men commonly labour, when left entirely to their own thoughts and meditations.

We find that common liars always magnify, in their narrations, all kinds of danger, pain, distress, sickness, deaths, murders, and cruelties; as well as joy, beauty, mirth, and magnificence. It is an absurd secret, which they have for pleasing their company, fixing their attention, and attaching them to such marvellous relations, by the passions and emotions, which they excite.

There is, however, a difficulty in applying to the present subject, in its full extent, this solution, however ingenious and satisfactory it may appear. It is certain, that the same object of distress, which pleases in a tragedy, were it really set before us, would give the most unfeigned uneasiness; though it be then the most effectual cure to languor and indolence. Monsieur Fontenelle seems to have been sensible of this difficulty; and accordingly attempts another solution of the phænomenon; at least makes some addition to the theory above mentioned.

'Pleasure and pain,' says he, 'which are two sentiments so different in themselves, differ not so much in their cause. From the instance of tickling, it appears, that the movement of pleasure, pushed a little too far, becomes pain; and that the movement of pain, a little moderated, becomes pleasure. Hence it proceeds, that there is such a thing as a sorrow, soft and agreeable: It is a pain weakened and diminished. The heart likes naturally to be moved and affected. Melancholy objects suit it, and even disastrous and sorrowful, provided they are softened by some circumstance. It is certain, that, on the theatre, the representation has almost the effect of reality; yet it has not altogether that effect. However we may be hurried away by the spectacle; whatever dominion the senses and imagination may usurp over the reason, there still lurks at the bottom a certain idea of falsehood in the whole of what we see. This idea, though weak and disguised, suffices to diminish the pain which we suffer from the misfortunes of those whom we love, and to reduce that affliction to such a pitch as converts it into a pleasure. We weep for the misfortune of a hero, to whom we are attached. In the same insant we comfort ourselves, by reflecting, that it is nothing but a fiction: And it is precisely that mixture of sentiments, which composes an agreeable sorrow, and tears that delight us. But as that affliction, which is caused by exterior and sensible objects, is stronger than the consolation which arises from an internal reflection, they are the effects and symptoms of sorrow, that ought to predominate in the composition.'

This solution seems just and convincing; but perhaps it wants still some new addition, in order to make it answer fully the phænomenon, which we here examine. All the passions, excited by eloquence, are agreeable in the highest degree, as well as those which are moved by painting and the theatre. The epilogues of Cicero are, on this account chiefly, the delight of every reader of taste; and it is difficult to read some of them without the deepest sympathy and sorrow. His merit as an orator, no doubt, depends much on his success in this particular. When he had raised tears in his judges and all his audience, they were then the most highly delighted, and expressed the greatest satisfaction with the pleader. The pathetic description of the butchery, made by Verres of the Sicilian captains, is a masterpiece of this kind: But I believe none will affirm, that the being present at a melancholy scene of that nature would afford any entertainment. Neither is the sorrow here softened by fiction: For the audience were convinced of the reality of every circumstance. What is it then, which in this case raises a pleasure from the bosom of uneasiness, so to speak; and a pleasure, which still retains all the features and outward symptoms of distress and sorrow?

I answer: This extraordinary effect proceeds from that very eloquence, with which the melancholy scene is represented. The genius required to paint objects in a lively manner, the art employed in collecting all the pathetic circumstances, the judgment displayed in disposing them: the exercise, I say, of these noble talents, together with the force of expression, and beauty of oratorial numbers, diffuse the highest satisfaction on the audience, and excite the most delightful movements. By this means, the uneasiness of the melancholy passions is not only overpowered and effaced by something stronger of an opposite kind; but the whole impulse of those passions is converted into pleasure, and swells the delight which the eloquence raises in us. The same force of oratory, employed on an uninteresting subject, would not please half so much, or rather would appear altogether ridiculous; and the mind, being left in absolute calmness and indifference, would relish none of those beauties of imagination or expression, which, if joined to passion, give it such exquisite entertainment. The impulse or vehemence, arising from sorrow, compassion, indignation, receives a new direction from the sentiments of beauty. The latter, being the predominant emotion, seize the whole mind, and convert the former into themselves, at least tincture them so strongly as totally to alter their nature. And the soul, being, at the same time, rouzed by passion, and charmed by eloquence, feels on the whole a strong movement, which is altogether delightful.

The same principle takes place in tragedy; with this addition, that tragedy is an imitation; and imitation is always of itself agreeable. This circumstance serves still farther to smooth the motions of passion, and convert the whole feeling into one uniform and strong enjoyment. Objects of the greatest terror and distress please in painting, and please more than the most beautiful objects, that appear calm and indifferent.[1] The affection, rouzing the mind, excites a large stock of spirit and vehemence; which is all transformed into pleasure by the force of the prevailing movement. It is thus the fiction of tragedy softens the passion, by an infusion of a new feeling, not merely by weakening or diminishing the sorrow. You may by degrees weaken a real sorrow, till it totally disappears; yet in none of its graduations will it ever give pleasure; except, perhaps, by accident, to a man sunk under lethargic indolence, whom it rouzes from that languid state.

To confirm this theory, it will be sufficient to produce other instances, where the subordinate movement is converted into the predominant, and gives force to it, though of a different, and even sometimes though of a contrary nature.

Novelty naturally rouses the mind, and attracts our attention; and the movements, which it causes, are always converted into any passion,

[1] Painters make no scruple of representing distress and sorrow as well as any other passion: But they seem not to dwell so much on these melancholy affections as the poets, who, tho' they copy every emotion of the human breast, yet pass very quickly over the agreeable sentiments. A painter represents only one instant; and if that be passionate enough, it is sure to affect and delight the spectator: But nothing can furnish to the poet a variety of scenes and incidents and sentiments, except distress, terror, or anxiety. Compleat joy and satisfaction is attended with security, and leaves no farther room for action.

belonging to the object, and join their force to it. Whether an event excite joy or sorrow, pride or shame, anger or good-will, it is sure to produce a stronger affection, when new or unusual. And though novelty of itself be agreeable, it fortifies the painful, as well as agreeable passions.

Had you any intention to move a person extremely by the narration of any event, the best method of encreasing its effect would be artfully to delay informing him of it, and first to excite his curiosity and impatience before you let him into the secret. This is the artifice practised by Iago in the famous scene of Shakespeare; and every spectator is sensible, that Othello's jealousy acquires additional force from his preceding impatience, and that the subordinate passion is here readily transformed into the predominant one.

Difficulties encrease passions of every kind; and by rouzing our attention, and exciting our active powers, they produce an emotion, which nourishes the prevailing affection.

Parents commonly love that child most, whose sickly infirm frame of body has occasioned them the greatest pains, trouble, and anxiety in rearing him. The agreeable sentiment of affection here acquires force from sentiments of uneasiness.

Nothing endears so much a friend as sorrow for his death. The pleasure of his company has not so powerful an influence.

Jealousy is a painful passion; yet without some share of it, the agreeable affection of love has difficulty to subsist in its full force and violence. Absence is also a great source of complaint among lovers, and gives them the greatest uneasiness: Yet nothing is more favourable to their mutual passion than short intervals of that kind. And if long intervals often prove fatal, it is only because, through time, men are accustomed to them, and they cease to give uneasiness. Jealousy and absence in love compose the *dolce peccante* of the Italians, which they suppose so essential to all pleasure.

There is a fine observation of the elder Pliny, which illustrates the principle here insisted on. *It is very remarkable,* says he, *that the last works of celebrated artists, which they left imperfect, are always the most prized, such as the* Iris *of Aristides, the* Tyndarides *of Nicomachus, the* Medea *of Timomachus, and the* Venus *of Appelles. These are valued even above their finished productions: The broken lineaments of the piece, and the half-formed idea of the painter are carefully studied; and our very grief for that curious hand, which had been stopped by death, is an additional encrease to our pleasure.*

These instances (and many more might be collected) are sufficient to afford us some insight into the analogy of nature, and to show us, that the pleasure, which poets, orators, and musicians give us, by exciting grief, sorrow, indignation, compassion, is not so extraordinary or paradoxical, as it may at first sight appear. The force of imagination, the energy of expression, the power of numbers, the charms of imitation; all these are naturally, of themselves, delightful to the mind: And when the object presented lays also hold of some affection, the pleasure still rises upon us, by the conversion of this subordinate movement into that which is predominant. The passion, though perhaps naturally, and when excited by the simple appearance of a real object, it may be painful; yet is so smoothed, and softened, and mollified, when raised by the finer arts, that it affords the highest entertainment.

To confirm this reasoning, we may observe, that if the movements of the imagination be not predominant above those of the passion, a contrary effect follows; and the former, being now subordinate, is converted into the latter, and still farther encreases the pain and affliction of the sufferer.

Who could ever think of it as a good expedient for comforting an afflicted parent, to exaggerate, with all the force of elocution, the irreparable loss, which he has met with by the death of a favourite child? The more power of imagination and expression you here employ, the more you encrease his despair and affliction.

The shame, confusion, and terror of Verres, no doubt, rose in proportion to the noble eloquence and vehemence of Cicero: So also did his pain and uneasiness. These former passions were too strong for the pleasure arising from the beauties of elocution; and operated, though from the same principle, yet in a contrary manner, to the sympathy, compassion, and indignation of the audience.

Lord Clarendon, when he approaches towards the catastrophe of the royal party, supposes, that his narration must then become infinitely disagreeable; and he hurries over the king's death, without giving us one circumstance of it. He considers it as too horrid a scene to be contemplated with any satisfaction, or even without the utmost pain and aversion. He himself, as well as the readers of that age, were too deeply concerned in the events, and felt a pain from subjects, which an historian and a reader of another age would regard as the most pathetic and most interesting, and, by consequence, the most agreeable.

An action, represented in tragedy, may be too bloody and atrocious. It may excite such movements of horror as will not soften into pleasure;

and the greatest energy of expression, bestowed on descriptions of that nature, serves only to augment our uneasiness. Such is that action represented in the *Ambitious Stepmother,* where a venerable old man, raised to the height of fury and despair, rushes against a pillar, and striking his head upon it, besmears it all over with mingled brains and gore. The English theatre abounds too much with such shocking images.

Even the common sentiments of compassion require to be softened by some agreeable affection, in order to give a thorough satisfaction to the audience. The mere suffering of plaintive virtue, under the triumphant tyranny and oppression of vice, forms a disagreeable spectacle, and is carefully avoided by all masters of the drama. In order to dismiss the audience with entire satisfaction and contentment, the virtue must either convert itself into a noble courageous despair, or the vice receive its proper punishment.

Most painters appear in this light to have been very unhappy in their subjects. As they wrought much for churches and convents, they have chiefly represented such horrible subjects as crucifixions and martyrdoms, where nothing appears but tortures, wounds, executions, and passive suffering, without any action or affection. When they turned their pencil from this ghastly mythology, they had commonly recourse to Ovid, whose fictions, though passionate and agreeable, are scarcely natural or probable enough for painting.

The same inversion of that principle, which is here insisted on, displays itself in common life, as in the effects of oratory and poetry. Raise so the subordinate passion that it becomes the predominant, it swallows up that affection which it before nourished and encreased. Too much jealousy extinguishes love: Too much difficulty renders us indifferent: Too much sickness and infirmity disgusts a selfish and unkind parent.

What so disagreeable as the dismal, gloomy, disastrous stories, with which melancholy people entertain their companions? The uneasy passion being there raised alone, unaccompanied with any spirit, genius, or eloquence, conveys a pure uneasiness, and is attended with nothing that can soften it into pleasure or satisfaction.

T. C. Schneirla and Gerard Piel

THE ARMY ANT

Wherever they pass, all the rest of the animal world is thrown into a state of alarm. They stream along the ground and climb to the summit of all the lower trees searching every leaf to its apex. Where booty is plentiful, they concentrate all their forces upon it, the dense phalanx of shining and quickly moving bodies, as it spreads over the surface, looking like a flood of dark-red liquid. All soft-bodied and inactive insects fall an easy prey to them, and they tear their victims in pieces for facility in carriage. Then, gathering together again in marching order, onward they move, the margins of the phalanx spread out at times like a cloud of skirmishers from the flanks of an army.

THAT IS how Henry Walter Bates, a Victorian naturalist, described the characteristic field maneuvers of a tribe of army ants. His language is charged with martial metaphor, but it presents with restraint a spectacle which other eyewitnesses have compared to the predatory expeditions of Genghis Khan and Attila the Hun.

Army ants abound in the tropical rain forests of Hispanic America, Africa and Asia. They are classified taxonomically into more than 200 species and distinguished as a group chiefly by their peculiar mode of operation. Organized in colonies 100,000 to 150,000 strong, they live off their environment by systematic plunder and pillage. They are true nomads, having no fixed abode. Their nest is a seething cylindrical cluster of themselves, ant hooked to ant, with queen and brood sequestered in a labyrinth of corridors and chambers within the ant mass. From these bivouacs they stream forth at dawn in tightly organized columns and swarms to raid the surrounding terrain. Their columns often advance as much as 35 meters an hour and may finally reach out 300 meters or more in an unbroken stream. For days at a time, they may keep their bivouacs fixed in a hollow tree or some other equally protected shelter. Then, for a restless period, they move on with every dusk. They swarm forth in a solemn, plodding procession, each ant holding to its place in line, its forward-directed antennae beating a hypnotic rhythm. At the rear come throngs of larvae-carriers and, at the very last, the big, wingless queen, buried under a melee of frenzied workers. Late at night they hang their new bivouac under a low branch or vine.

The army ant, observers are agreed, presents the most complex instance of organized mass behavior occurring regularly outside the home-site in any insect or, for that matter, in any subhuman animal. As such, it offers the student of animal psychology a subject rich in interest for itself. But it also provides an opportunity for original attack on some basic problems of psychology in general. The study here reported, covering the behavior of two of the Eciton species of army ants, was conducted by Schneirla over a 20-year period with extended field trips to the Biological Reservation on Barro Colorado Island in the Panama Canal Zone and to other ant haunts in Central America. In undertaking it, he had certain questions in mind. The central question, of course, was how such an essentially primitive creature as the ant manages such a highly organized and complex social existence. This bears on the more general consideration of organized group behavior as an adaptive device in natural selection. There was, finally, the neglected question of the nature of social organization. This is primarily a psychological problem because it concerns the contribution of individual behavior and relationships between individuals to the pattern of the group as a whole. It was expected that reliable data on these questions in the instance of the army ant might throw light on similar questions about human societies.

The ant commends itself to study by man. Measured by the dispassionate standard of survival, it stands as one of the most successful of nature's inventions. It is the most numerous of all land animals both in number of individuals and number of species (more than 3,500 at present count). It has occupied the whole surface of the globe between the margins of eternal frost.

The oldest of living families, the ant dates back more than 65 million years to the early Jurassic period. More significant, the societies of ants probably evolved to their present state of perfection no less than

50 million years ago. Man, by contrast, is a dubious experiment in evolution that has barely got under way.

Lord Avebury, a British myrmecologist, marveled at "the habits of ants, their large communities and elaborate habitations, their roadways, possession of domestic animals and, even, in some cases, of slaves!" He might have added that ants also cultivate agricultural crops and carry parasols. It is the social institutions of ants, however, that engender the greatest astonishment. The sight of an army ant bivouac put the British naturalist Thomas Belt in mind of Sir Thomas More's *Utopia*. The Swiss naturalist Auguste Forel urged the League of Nations to adopt the ant polity as the model for the world community.

The marvels of ant life have led some thinkers into giddy speculation on the nature of ant intelligence. Few have put themselves so quaintly on record as Lord Avebury, who declared: "The mental powers of ants differ from those of men not so much in kind as in degree." He ranked them ahead of the anthropoid apes. Maeterlinck was more cautious: "After all, we have not been present at the deliberations of the workers and we know hardly anything of what happens in the depths of the formicary." Others have categorically explained ant behavior as if the creatures could reason, exchange information, take purposeful action and feel tender emotion.

Obviously anthropomorphism can explain little about ants, and it has largely disappeared from the current serious literature about ant behavior. Its place has been taken, however, by errors of a more sophisticated sort. One such is the concept of the "superorganism." This derives from a notion entertained by Plato and Aquinas that a social organization exhibits the attributes of a superior type of individual. Extended by certain modern biologists, the concept assumes that the biological organism, a society of cells, is the model for social organizations, whether ant or human. Plausible analogies are drawn between organisms and societies: division of function, internal communication, rhythmic periodicity of life processes and the common cycle of birth, growth, senescence and death. Pursuit of these analogies, according to the protagonists of the superorganism, will disclose that the same forces of natural selection have shaped the evolution of both organism and superorganism, and that the same fundamental laws govern their present existence.

This is a thoroughly attractive idea, but it possesses a weakness common to all Platonistic thinking. It erects a vague concept, "organism" or "organization," as an ultimate reality which defies explanation. The danger inherent in this arbitrary procedure is the bias it encourages in the investigator's approach to his problem. The social scientist must impose on his work the same rules of repetition, systematic variation and control that prevail in the experimental sciences. Wherever possible he should subject his observations to experimental tests in the field and laboratory. In the area we are discussing this kind of work may at times seem more like a study of ants than an investigation of problems. But it yields dependable data.

The individual ant is not equipped for mammalian types of learning. By comparison with the sensitive perceptions of a human being, it is deaf and blind. Its hearing consists primarily in the perception of vibrations physically transmitted to it through the ground. In most species, its vision is limited to the discrimination of light and shadow. These deficiencies are partially compensated by the chemotactual perceptions of the ant, centered in its flitting antennae. Chiefly by means of its antennae, the army ant tells friend from foe, locates its booty, and, thanks to its habit of blazing its trail with organic products such as droplets from its anal gland, finds its way home to the nest. In any case, the ant has little need of learning when it crawls out of the cocoon. By far the greater part of its behavior pattern is already written in its genes.

How the essentially uncomplicated repertory of the individual ant contrives, when ants act in concert, to yield the exceedingly complex behavior of the tribe is one of the most intricate paradoxes in nature. This riddle has been fruitfully explored during the past generation under the guidance of the concept of "trophallaxis," originated by the late William Morton Wheeler of Harvard University, who ranks as the greatest of U. S. myrmecologists. Trophallaxis (from the Greek *trophe,* meaning food, and *allaxis,* exchange) is based upon the familiar observation that ants live in biological thrall to their nest-mates. Their powerful mutual attraction can be seen in the constant turning of one ant toward another, the endless antennal caresses, the licking and nuzzling. In these exchanges they can be seen trading intimate substances—regurgitated food and glandular secretions. Most ants are dependent for their lives upon this biosocial intercourse with their fellows. There is strong evidence that an interchange of co-enzymes among larvae, workers and queen is necessary to the survival of all three. Army ant queens unfailingly sicken and die after a few days of isolation.

The well-established concept of trophallaxis naturally suggests that clues to the complex behavior of the ant armies should be sought in the relationships among individuals within the tribe. Most investigators have looked elsewhere, with invariably mistaken results. In attempting to explain, for example, why an ant army alternates between periods of fixed bivouac and nomadic wandering, a half-dozen reputable scientists have jumped to the simplest and most disarmingly logical conclusion: food supply. The ants, they declared, stay in one place until they exhaust the local larder and then move on to new hunting grounds. Schneirla has shown, however, that the true explanation is quite different.

The migratory habits of the ant armies follow a rhythmically punctual cycle. The *Eciton hamatum* species, for example, wanders nomadically for a period of 17 days, then spends 19 or 20 days in fixed bivouac. This cycle coincides precisely with the reproductive cycle of the tribe. The army goes into bivouac when the larvae, hatched from the last clutch of eggs, spin their cocoons and, now quiescent, approach the pupal stage. At the end of the first week in permanent camp, the queen, whose abdomen has swollen to more than five times its normal volume, begins a stupendous five- to seven-day labor and delivers the 20,000 to 30,000 eggs of the next generation. The daily foraging raids, which meanwhile have dwindled to a minimum, pick up again as the eggs hatch into a great mass of larvae. Then, on about the 20th day, the cocoons yield a new complement of callow workers, and the army sets off once more on its evening marches. . . .

In determining this pattern of events Schneirla logged a dozen ant armies through one or more complete cycles, and upwards of 100 through partial cycles. Observations were set down in shorthand in the field. In the course of the last field trip, from February to July, 1953, broods of more than 80 colonies were sampled, most of them repeatedly at intervals of a few days.

A sentimentalist presented with this new picture of the army ant's domestic habits will perhaps decide that the ants stay in fixed bivouac to protect the queen and her helpless young through the time when they are most vulnerable. Doubtless this is the adaptive significance of the process. But the motivation which carries 100,000 to 150,000 individual ants through this precisely timed cycle of group behavior is not familial love and duty but the trophallactic relationship among the members of the tribe. A cocooned and slumberous pupa, for example, exerts a quieting influence upon the worker that clutches it in its mandible—somewhat as a thumb in the mouth pacifies an infant. But as it approaches maturity and quickens within its cocoon, the pupa produces precisely the reverse effect. Its stirring and twitching excite the workers to pick up the cocoon and snatch it from one another. As an incidental result, this manhandling effects the delivery of the cocoon's occupant.

The stimulus of the emerging brood is evident in a rising crescendo of excitement that seizes the whole community. Raiding operations increase in tempo as the hyperactive, newly delivered workers swarm out into the marching columns. After a day or two, the colony stages an exceptionally vigorous raid which ends in a night march. The bivouac site is left littered with empty cocoons. Later in the nomadic phase, as the stimulus of the callow workers wanes, the larvae of the next generation become the source of colony "drive." Fat and squirming, as big as an average worker, they establish an active trophallactic relationship with the rest of the tribe. Workers constantly stroke them with their antennae, lick them with their mouth parts and carry them bodily from place to place. Since the larvae at this stage are usually well distributed throughout the corridors and the chambers of the overnight bivouac, their stimulus reaches directly a large number of the workers. This is reflected in the sustained vigor of the daily raids, which continue until the larvae spin their cocoons.

These observations are supported by a variety of experimental findings in the field and laboratory. The role of the callow workers in initiating the movement to break bivouac was confirmed by depriving a number of colonies of their callow broods. Invariably, the raiding operations of the colony failed to recover from the lethargic state that is characteristic of the statary phases. Some tribes even extended their stay in fixed bivouac until the larvae grew large and active enough to excite the necessary pitch of activity. To test the role of the larval brood, captured tribes were divided into part-colonies of comparable size. The group with larvae showed much greater activity than those that had no larvae or that had cocoons in the early pupal state.

The interrelationships among members of the colony thus provide a complete explanation for the behavior cycle of the army ant. It should be observed, in conclusion, that the whole complex process is carried out by individuals which do not themselves originate the basic motivations of their behavior.

Long before the intricacies of its domestic existence were suspected, the army ant's reputation as a social animal was firmly established by its martial conduct in external affairs. It does not require an overactive imagination to perceive the classic doctrines of offensive warfare in the action of an ant army in the field. The swarm carries through the maneuvers of wheeling, flanking and envelopment with a ruthless precision. But to find its motivations and explain its mechanics, one must consult the ant, not von Clausewitz.

Army ant raids fall into one of two major patterns. They are organized either in dense swarms which form at the head of the column or in a delicate tracery of capillary columns branching out at the forward end of the main raiding column. Both types of raiding are found in subgenera of each of the common species of Central American army ant. Two species of Eciton (*Eciton*) were selected for this study because they lead their life almost altogether on or above the forest floor and are thus accessible to continuous observation. Whether the army ants raid in swarm or column, however, the essential mechanics of their behavior are substantially the same.

The bivouac awakes in the early dawn. The stir of activity begins when the light (as measured by photometer) reaches .05 foot candles, and it mounts steadily as the light increases. In strands and clusters, the workers tumble out of the bivouac into a churning throng on the ground. A crowding pressure builds up within this throng until, channeled by the path of least resistance, a raiding column suddenly bursts forth. The ants in the column are oriented rigidly along the line of travel blazed by the chemical trail of the leaders. The minims and medium-sized workers move in tight files in the center. The "workers major," displaced by the unstable footing afforded by the backs of their smaller fellows, travel along each side. This arrangement no doubt lends suggestive support to the major's legendary role of command. It has an adaptive significance in that it places the biggest and most formidable of the workers on the flanks. Unless disturbed, however, the majors hug the column as slavishly as the rest. The critical role of the tribal chemical in creating this drill sergeant's picture of order may be demonstrated by a simple field experiment. Removal of the chemically saturated litter from the trail brings the column to an abrupt halt. A traffic jam of ants piles up on the bivouac side of the break and is not relieved until enough ants have been pushed forward to re-establish the chemical trail.

Appearances are less ordered at the front of the column, where the "scouts" and "skirmishers" are most frequently observed. The timid individual behavior of the forward ants scarcely justifies such titles. The Eciton is a far from enterprising forager. It never ventures more than a few inches into the chemically-free area ahead. Even this modest pioneering is stimulated principally by physical impact from the rear. At the end of its brief sally, the Eciton rebounds quickly into the column. It is here that the critical difference between column and swarm raiding arises. The column-raiding ants are somewhat freer in their pioneering behavior and so open new pathways more readily. In the swarm raiders the comparatively reluctant progress of the forward elements creates a counterpressure against the progress of the column. This forces the head of the column into a broad elliptical swarm which arrays itself at right angles to the line of march. With ants pouring in from behind, the swarm grows steadily in size as it moves forward, often achieving a width of more than 15 meters.

The path of an ant army, whether in swarms or columns, shows no evidence of leadership. On the contrary, each individual makes substantially the same contribution to the group behavior pattern. The army's course is directed by such wholly chance factors as the stimulus of booty and the character of the terrain. On close inspection, therefore, it appears that the field operations of ant armies approximate the principles of hydraulics even more closely than those of military tactics. This impression is confirmed by analysis of the flanking maneuver as executed by the swarm raiders. A shimmering pattern of whirls, eddies and momentarily milling vortices of ants, the swarm advances with a peculiar rocking motion. First one and then the other end of the elliptical swarm surges forward. This action results in the outflanking of quarry, which is swiftly engulfed in the overriding horde of ants. It arises primarily, however, from an interplay of forces within the swarm. One of these forces is generated by the inrush of ants from the rear. Opposed by the hesitant progress of the swarm, the new arrivals are deflected laterally to the wing which offers least resistance. This wing moves forward in a wheeling motion until pressure from the slow advance of its frontal margins counterbalances the pressure from the rear. Pressure on the opposite wing has meanwhile been relieved by drainage of the ants into the flanking action. The cycle is therewith reversed, and a new flanking action gets under way from the other end. External factors, too, play a role in this cycle. The stimulus of booty will accelerate the advance of a flank. The capture of booty will halt it and bring ants stampeding in for a large-scale mopping-up party. But raiding activity as such is only incidental to the process. Its essential character is determined by the stereotyped behavior of the individual ant with its limited repertory of responses to external stimuli.

The profoundly simple nature of the beast is betrayed by an ironic catastrophe which occasionally overtakes a troop of army ants. It can happen only under certain very special conditions. But, when these are present, army ants are literally fated to organize themselves in a circular column and march themselves to death. Post-mortem evidence of this phenomenon has been found in nature; it may be arranged at will in the laboratory. Schneirla has had the good fortune to observe one such spectacle in nature almost from its inception to the bitter end.

The ants, numbering about 1,000, were discovered at 7:30 a.m. on a broad concrete sidewalk on the grounds of the Barrow Colorado laboratories. They had apparently been caught by a cloudburst which washed away all traces of their colony trail. When first observed, most of the ants were gathered in a central cluster, with only a company or two plodding, counterclockwise, in a circle around the periphery. By noon all of the ants had joined the mill, which had now attained the diameter of a phonograph record and was rotating somewhat eccentrically at fair speed. By 10:00 p.m. the mill had divided into two smaller counterclockwise spinning discs. At dawn the next day the scene of action was strewn with dead and dying Ecitons. A scant three dozen survivors were still trekking in a ragged circle. By 7:30, 24 hours after the mill was first observed, the various small myremicine and dolichoderine ants of the neighborhood were busy carting away the corpses.

This peculiarly Eciton calamity may be described as tragic in the classic meaning of the Greek drama. It arises, like Nemesis, out of the very aspects of the ant's nature which most plainly characterize its otherwise successful behavior. The general mechanics of the mill are fairly obvious. The circular track represents the vector of the individual ant's centrifugal impulse to resume the march and the centripetal force of trophallaxis which binds it to its group. Where no obstructions disturb the geometry of these forces, the organization of a suicide mill is almost inevitable. Fortunately for the army ant, the jungle terrain, with its random layout of roots and vines, leaves and stones, disarrays the symmetry of forces and liberates the ant from its propensity to destroy itself.

The army ant suicide mill provides an excellent occasion for considering the comparative nature of social behavior and organization at the various levels from ants to men. Other animals occasionally give themselves over to analogous types of mass action. Circular mills are common among schools of herring. Stampeding cattle, sheep jumping fences blindly in column and other instances of pell-mell surging by a horde of animals are familiar phenomena. Experience tells us that men, too, can act as a mob. These analogies are the stock-in-trade of the "herd instinct" schools of sociology and politics.

We are required, however, to look beyond the analogy and study the relationship of the pattern to other factors of individual and group behavior in the same species. In the case of the army ant, the circular column really typifies the animal. Among mammals, such simplified mass behavior occupies a clearly subordinate role. Their group activity patterns are chiefly characterized by great plasticity and capacity to adjust to new situations. This observation applies with special force to the social potentialities of man. When human societies begin to march in circular columns, the cause is to be found in the strait-jacket influence of the man-made social institutions which foster such behavior.

As for "specialization of functions," that is determined in insect societies by specialization in the biological make-up of individuals. Mankind, in contrast, is biologically uniform and homogeneous. Class and caste distinctions among men are drawn on a psychological basis. They break down constantly before the energies and talents of particular individuals.

Finally, the concept of "organization" itself, as it is used by the superorganism theorists, obscures a critical distinction between the societies of ants and men. The social organizations of insects are fixed and transmitted by heredity. But members of each generation of men may, by exercise of the cerebral cortex, increase, change and even displace given aspects of their social heritage. This is a distinction which has high ethical value for men when they are moved to examine the conditions of their existence.

Bronislaw Malinowski

MOTHERHOOD AND THE TEMPTATIONS OF INCEST

HE SUBJECT of the "origins" of incest prohibitions is one of the most discussed and vexed questions of anthropology. It is associated with the problem of exogamy or of primitive forms of marriage, with hypotheses of former promiscuity and so on. There is not the slightest doubt that exogamy is correlated with the prohibition of incest, that it is merely an extension of this taboo, exactly as the institution of the clan with its classificatory terms of relationship is simply an extension of the family and its mode of kinship nomenclature. We shall not enter into this problem, especially because in this we are in agreement with such anthropologists as Westermarck and Lowie.

To clear the ground it will be well to remember that biologists are in agreement on the point that there is no detrimental effect produced upon the species by incestuous unions. Whether incest in the state of nature might be detrimental if it occurred regularly is an academic question. In the state of nature the young animals leave the parental group at maturity and mate at random with any females encountered during rut. Incest at best can be but a sporadic occurrence. In animal incest, then, there is no biological harm nor obviously is there any moral harm. Moreover, there is no reason to suppose that in animals there is any special temptation.

While with the animal then there is neither biological danger nor temptation and in consequence no instinctive barriers against incest, with man, on the contrary, we find in all societies that the strongest barrier and the most fundamental prohibition are those against incest.

140

This we shall try to explain, not by any hypotheses about a primitive act of legislation nor by any assumptions of special aversion to sexual intercourse with inmates of the same household, but as the result of two phenomena which spring up under culture. In the first place, under the mechanisms which constitute the human family serious temptations to incest arise. In the second place, side by side with the sex temptations, specific perils come into being for the human family, due to the existence of the incestuous tendencies. On the first point, therefore, we have to agree with Freud and disagree with the well-known theory of Westermarck, who assumes innate disinclinaton to mate between members of the same household. In assuming, however, a temptation to incest under culture, we do not follow the psycho-analytic theory which regards the infantile attachment to the mother as essentially sexual.

This is perhaps the main thesis which Freud has attempted to establish in his three contributions to sexual theory. He tries to prove that the relations between a small child and its mother, above all in the act of suckling, are essentially sexual. From this it results that the first sexual attachment of a male towards the mother is, in other words, normally an incestuous attachment. "This fixation of libido," to use a psycho-analytic phrase, remains throughout life, and it is the source of the constant incestuous temptations which have to be repressed and as such form one of the two components of the Œdipus complex.

This theory it is impossible to adopt. The relation between an infant and its mother is essentially different from a sexual attitude. Instincts must be defined not simply by introspective methods, not merely by analysis of the feeling tones such as pain and pleasure, but above all by their function. An instinct is a more or less definite innate mechanism by which the individual responds to a specific situation by a definite form of behaviour in satisfaction of definite organic wants. The relation of the suckling to its mother is first of all induced by the desire for nutrition. The bodily clinging of a child to its mother again satisfies its bodily wants of warmth, protection and guidance. The child is not fit to cope with the environment by its own forces alone, and as the only medium through which it can act is the maternal organism it clings instinctively to the mother. In sexual relations the aim of bodily attraction and clinging is that union which leads to impregnation. Each of these two innate tendencies—the mother-to-child behaviour and the process of mating—cover a big range of preparatory and consummatory actions which present certain similarities. The line of division, however, is clear, because one set of acts, tendencies and feelings serves to complete the infant's unripe organism, to nourish, to protect and warm it; the other set of acts subserves the union of sexual organs and the production of a new individual.

We cannot therefore accept the simple solution that the temptation of incest is due to sexual relation between the infant and mother. The sensuous pleasure which is common to both relations is a component of every successful instinctive behaviour. The pleasure index cannot serve to differentiate instincts, since it is a general character of them all. But although we have to postulate different instincts for each emotional attitude yet there is one element common to them both. It is not merely that they are endowed with the general pleasure tone of all instincts, but there is also a sensuous pleasure derived from bodily contact. The active exercise of the drive which a child feels towards its mother's organism consists in the permanent clinging to the mother's body in the fullest possible epidermic contact, above all in the contact of the child's lips with the mother's nipple. The analogy between the preparatory actions of the sexual drive and the consummatory actions of the infantile impulse are remarkable. The two are to be distinguished mainly by their function and by the essential difference between the consummatory actions in each case.

What is the result of this partial similarity? We can borrow from psycho-analysis the principle which has now become generally accepted in psychology that there are no experiences in later life which would not stir up analogous memories from infancy. Again, from Shand's theory of sentiments we know that the sentimental attitudes in human life entail a gradual organization of emotions. To these we found it necessary to add that the continuity of emotional memories and the gradual building of one attitude on the pattern of another form the main principle of sociological bonds.

If we apply this to the formation of the sexual attitude between lovers we can see that the bodily contact in sexual relations must have a very disturbing retrospective effect upon the relation between mother and son. The caresses of lovers employ not only the same medium—epidermis; not only the same situation—embraces, cuddling, the maximum of personal approach; but they entail also the same type of sensuous feelings. When therefore this new type of drive enters it must invariably awaken the memories of earlier similar experiences. But these memories are associated with a definite object which remains in the foreground of an individual's emotional interests throughout life. This object is the person of the mother. With regard to this person the erotic life introduces disturbing memories which stand in direct contradiction to the attitude of reverence, submission and cultural dependence which in the growing boy has already completely repressed the early infantile sentimental attachment. The new type of erotic sensuality and the new sexual attitude blend disturbingly with the memories of early life and threaten to break up the organized system of emotions which has been built up around the mother. This attitude, for purposes of cultural education, has become less and less sensual, more and more coloured by mental and moral dependence, by interest in practical matters, by social sentiments associated with the mother as the centre of the household. . . . At this stage the relation between the boy and his mother is clouded over and . . . a reorganization of the sentiments has to take place. It is at this time that strong resistances arise in the individual's mind, that all sensuality felt towards the mother becomes repressed, and that the subconscious temptation of incest arises from the blending of early memories with new experiences.

The difference between this explanation and that of psycho-analysis consists in the fact that Freud assumes a continuous persistence from infancy of the same attitude towards the mother. In our argument we try to show that there is only a partial identity between the early and the later drives, that this identity is due essentially to the mechanism of sentiment formation; that this explains the non-existence of temptations among animals; and that the retrospective power of new sentiments in man is the cause of incestuous temptations.

We have now to ask why this temptation is really dangerous to man although it is innocuous to animals. We have seen that in man the development of emotions into organized sentiments is the very essence of social bonds and of cultural progress. As Mr. Shand has convincingly proved, such systems are subject to definite laws: they must be harmonious, i.e., emotions consistent with one another, and the sentiments so organized that they will allow of co-operation, continuity of blending. Now within the family the sentiment between mother and child begins with the early sensuous attachment which binds the two with a deep innate interest. Later on, however, this attitude has to change. The mother's function consists in educating, guiding and exercising cultural influence and domestic authority. As the son grows up he has to respond to this by the attitude of submission and reverence. During childhood, that is during this extremely long period in psychological reckoning which occurs after weaning and before maturity, emotions of reverence, dependence, respect, as well as strong attachment must give the leading tone to the boy's relation to his mother. At that time also a process of emancipation, of severing all bodily contacts must proceed and become completed. The family at this stage is essentially a cultural and not a biological workshop. The father and the mother are training the child into independence and into cultural maturity; their physiological rôle is already over.

Now into such a situation the inclination towards incest would enter as a destructive element. Any approach of the mother with sensual or erotic temptations would involve the disruption of the relationship so laboriously constructed. Mating with her would have to be, as all mating must be, preceded by courtship and a type of behavior completely incompatible with submission, independence and reverence. The mother, moreover, is not alone. She is married to another male. Any sensual temptation would not only upset completely the relation between son and mother but also, indirectly, that between son and father. Active hostile rivalry would replace the harmonious relationship which is the type of complete dependence and thorough submission to leadership. If, therefore, we agree with the psycho-analysts that incest must be a universal temptation, we see that its dangers are not merely psychological nor can they be explained by any such hypotheses as that of Freud's primeval crime. Incest must be forbidden because, if our analysis of the family and its rôle in the formation of culture be correct, incest is incompatible with the establishment of the first foundations of culture. In any type of civilization in which custom, morals, and law would allow incest, the family could not continue to exist. At maturity we would witness the breaking up of the family, hence complete social chaos and an impossibility of continuing cultural tradition. Incest would mean the upsetting of age distinctions, the mixing up of generations, the disorganization of sentiments and a violent exchange of rôles at a time when the family is the most important educational medium. No society could exist under such conditions. The alternative type of culture under which incest is excluded, is the only one consistent with the existence of social organization and culture.

Our type of explanation agrees essentially with the view of Atkinson and Lang, which makes the prohibition of incest the primal law, although our argument differs from their hypothesis. We differ also from Freud in that we cannot accept incest as due to the innate behaviour of the infant. From Westermarck we differ in so far as the aversion to incest does not appear to us as the natural impulse, a simple tendency not to cohabit with persons living in the same house from infancy, but rather as a complex scheme of cultural reactions. We have been able to deduce the necessity of the incest taboo from the change in instinctive endowment which must run parallel with social organization and culture. Incest, as a normal mode of behaviour, cannot exist in humanity, because it is incompatible with family life and would disorganize its very foundations. The fundamental pattern of all social bonds, the normal relation of the child to the mother and the father, would be destroyed. From the composition of each of these sentiments the instinct of sex must be eliminated. This instinct is the most difficult to control, the least compatible with others. The temptation to incest, therefore, has been introduced by culture, by the necessity of establishing permanent organized attitudes. It is therefore, in a sense, the original sin of man. This must be atoned for in all human societies by one of the most important and universal rules. Even then the taboo of incest haunts man throughout life, as psycho-analysis has revealed to us.

Henri Poincaré

MATHEMATICAL CREATION

$\mathcal{T}$HE GENESIS of mathematical creation is a problem which should intensely interest the psychologist. It is the activity in which the human mind seems to take least from the outside world, in which it acts or seems to act only of itself and on itself, so that in studying the procedure of geometric thought we may hope to reach what is most essential in man's mind.

This has long been appreciated, and some time back the journal called *L'Enseignement Mathématique*, edited by Laisant and Fehr, began an investigation of the mental habits and methods of work of different mathematicians. I had finished the main outlines of this article when the results of that inquiry were published, so I have hardly been able to utilize them and shall confine myself to saying that the majority of witnesses confirm my conclusions; I do not say all, for when the appeal is to universal suffrage unanimity is not to be hoped.

A first fact should surprise us, or rather would surprise us if we were not so used to it. How does it happen there are people who do not understand mathematics? If mathematics invokes only the rules of logic, such as are accepted by all normal minds; if its evidence is based on principles common to all men, and that none could deny without being mad, how does it come about that so many persons are here refractory?

That not every one can invent is nowise mysterious. That not every one can retain a demonstration once learned may also pass. But that not every one can understand mathematical reasoning when explained appears very surprising when we think of it. And yet those who can follow this reasoning only with difficulty are in the majority: that is undeniable, and will surely not be gainsaid by the experience of secondary-school teachers.

And further: how is error possible in mathematics? A sane mind should not be guilty of a logical fallacy, and yet there are very fine minds who do not trip in brief reasoning such as occurs in the ordinary doings of life, and who are incapable of following or repeating without error the mathematical demonstrations which are longer, but which after all are only an accumulation of brief reasonings wholly analogous to those they make so easily. Need we add that mathematicians themselves are not infallible?

The answer seems to me evident. Imagine a long series of syllogisms, and that the conclusions of the first serve as premises of the following: we shall be able to catch each of these syllogisms, and it is not in passing from premises to conclusion that we are in danger of deceiving ourselves. But between the moment in which we first meet a proposition as conclusion of one syllogism, and that in which we reencounter it as premise of another syllogism occasionally some time will elapse, several links of the chain will have unrolled; so it may happen that we have forgotten it, or worse, that we have forgotten its meaning. So it may happen that we replace it by a slightly different proposition, or that, while retaining the same enunciation, we attribute to it a slightly different meaning, and thus it is that we are exposed to error.

Often the mathematician uses a rule. Naturally he begins by demonstrating this rule; and at the time when this proof is fresh in his memory he understands perfectly its meaning and its bearing, and he is in no danger of changing it. But subsequently he trusts his memory and afterward only applies it in a mechanical way; and then if his memory fails him, he may apply it all wrong. Thus it is, to take a simple example, that we sometimes make slips in calculation because we have forgotten our multiplication table.

According to this, the special aptitude for mathematics would be due only to a very sure memory or to a prodigious force of attention. It would be a power like that of the whist-player who remembers the cards played; or, to go up a step, like that of the chess-player who can visualize a great number of combinations and hold them in his memory. Every good mathematician ought to be a good chess-player, and inversely; likewise he should be a good computer. Of course that sometimes happens; thus Gauss was at the same time a geometer of genius and a very precocious and accurate computer.

But there are exceptions; or rather I err; I can not call them exceptions without the exceptions being more than the rule. Gauss it is, on the contrary, who was an exception. As for myself, I must confess, I am absolutely incapable even of adding without mistakes. In the same way I should be but a poor chess-player; I would perceive that by a certain play I should expose myself to a certain danger; I would pass in review several other plays, rejecting them for other reasons, and then finally I should make the move first examined, having meantime forgotten the danger I had foreseen.

In a word, my memory is not bad, but it would be insufficient to make me a good chess-player. Why then does it not fail me in a difficult piece of mathematical reasoning where most chess-players would lose themselves? Evidently because it is guided by the general march of the reasoning. A mathematical demonstration is not a simple juxtaposition of syllogisms, it is syllogisms *placed in a certain order*, and the order in which these elements are placed is much more important than the elements themselves. If I have the feeling, the intuition, so to speak, of this order, so as to perceive at a glance the reasoning as a whole, I need no longer fear lest I forget one of the elements, for each of them will take its allotted place in the array, and that without any effort of memory on my part.

It seems to me then, in repeating a reasoning learned, that I could have invented it. This is often only an illusion; but even then, even if I am not so gifted as to create it by myself, I myself re-invent it in so far as I repeat it.

We know that this feeling, this intuition of mathematical order, that makes us divine hidden harmonies and relations, can not be possessed by every one. Some will not have either this delicate feeling so difficult to define, or a strength of memory and attention beyond the ordinary, and then they will be absolutely incapable of understanding higher mathematics. Such are the majority. Others will have this feeling only in a slight degree, but they will be gifted with an uncommon memory and a great power of attention. They will learn by heart the details one after another; they can understand mathematics and sometimes make applications, but they cannot create. Others, finally, will possess in a less or greater degree the special intuition referred to, and then not only can they understand mathematics even if their memory is nothing extraordinary, but they may become creators and try to invent with more or less success according as this intuition is more or less developed in them.

In fact, what is mathematical creation? It does not consist in making new combinations with mathematical entities already known. Any one could do that, but the combinations so made would be infinite in number and most of them absolutely without interest. To create consists precisely in not making useless combinations and in making those which are useful and which are only a small minority. Invention is discernment, choice.

How to make this choice I have before explained; the mathematical facts worthy of being studied are those which, by their analogy with other facts, are capable of leading us to the knowledge of a mathematical law just as experimental facts lead us to the knowledge of a physical law. They are those which reveal to us unsuspected kinship between other facts, long known, but wrongly believed to be strangers to one another.

Among chosen combinations the most fertile will often be those formed of elements drawn from domains which are far apart. Not that I mean as sufficing for invention the bringing together of objects as disparate as possible; most combinations so formed would be entirely sterile. But certain among them, very rare, are the most fruitful of all.

To invent, I have said, is to choose; but the word is perhaps not wholly exact. It makes one think of a purchaser before whom are displayed a large number of samples, and who examines them, one after the other, to make a choice. Here the samples would be so numerous that a whole lifetime would not suffice to examine them. This is not the actual state of things. The sterile combinations do not even present themselves to the mind of the inventor. Never in the field of his consciousness do combinations appear that are not really useful, except some that he rejects but which have to some extent the characteristics of useful combinations. All goes on as if the inventor were an examiner for the second degree who would only have to question the candidates who had passed a previous examination.

But what I have hitherto said is what may be observed or inferred in reading the writings of the geometers, reading reflectively.

It is time to penetrate deeper and to see what goes on in the very soul of the mathematician. For this, I believe, I can do best by recalling memories of my own. But I shall limit myself to telling how I wrote my first memoir on Fuchsian functions. I beg the reader's pardon; I am about to use some technical expressions, but they need not frighten him, for he is not obliged to understand them. I shall say, for example, that I have found the demonstration of such a theorem under such circumstances. This theorem will have a barbarous name, unfamiliar to many, but that is unimportant; what is of interest for the psychologist is not the theorem but the circumstances.

For fifteen days I strove to prove that there could not be any functions like those I have since called Fuchsian functions. I was then very ignorant; every day I seated myself at my work table, stayed an hour or two, tried a great number of combinations and reached no results. One evening, contrary to my custom, I drank black coffee and could not sleep. Ideas rose in crowds; I felt them collide until pairs interlocked, so to speak, making a stable combination. By the next morning I had established the existence of a class of Fuchsian functions, those which come from the hypergeometric series; I had only to write out the results, which took but a few hours.

Then I wanted to represent these functions by the quotient of two series; this idea was perfectly conscious and deliberate, the analogy with elliptic functions guided me. I asked myself what properties these series must have if they existed, and I succeeded without difficulty in forming the series I have called theta-Fuchsian.

Just at this time I left Caen, where I was then living, to go on a geologic excursion under the auspices of the school of mines. The changes of travel made me forget my mathematical work. Having reached Coutances, we entered an omnibus to go some place or other. At the moment when I put my foot on the step the idea came to me, without anything in my former thoughts seeming to have paved the way for it, that the transformations I had used to define the Fuchsian functions were identical with those of non-Euclidean geometry. I did not verify the idea; I should not have had time, as, upon taking my seat in the omnibus, I went on with a conversation already commenced, but I felt a perfect certainty. On my return to Caen, for conscience's sake I verified the result at my leisure.

Then I turned my attention to the study of some arithmetical questions apparently without much success and without a suspicion of any connection with my preceding researches. Disgusted with my failure, I went to spend a few days at the seaside, and thought of something else. One morning, walking on the bluff, the idea came to me, with just the same characteristics of brevity, suddenness and immediate certainty, that the arithmetic transformations of indeterminate ternary quadratic forms were identical with those of non-Euclidean geometry.

Returned to Caen, I meditated on this result and deduced the consequences. The example of quadratic forms showed me that there were

Fuchsian groups other than those corresponding to the hypergeometric series; I saw that I could apply to them the theory of theta-Fuchsian series and that consequently there existed Fuchsian functions other than those from the hypergeometric series, the ones I then knew. Naturally I set myself to form all these functions. I made a systematic attack upon them and carried all the outworks, one after another. There was one however that still held out, whose fall would involve that of the whole place. But all my efforts only served at first the better to show me the difficulty, which indeed was something. All this work was perfectly conscious.

Thereupon I left for Mont-Valérien, where I was to go through my military service; so I was very differently occupied. One day, going along the street, the solution of the difficulty which had stopped me suddenly appeared to me. I did not try to go deep into it immediately, and only after my service did I again take up the question. I had all the elements and had only to arrange them and put them together. So I wrote out my final memoir at a single stroke and without difficulty.

I shall limit myself to this single example; it is useless to multiply them. In regard to my other researches I would have to say analogous things, and the observations of other mathematicians given in *L'Enseignement Mathématique* would only confirm them.

Most striking at first is this appearance of sudden illumination, a manifest sign of long, unconscious prior work. The rôle of this unconscious work in mathematical invention appears to me incontestable, and traces of it would be found in other cases where it is less evident. Often when one works at a hard question, nothing good is accomplished at the first attack. Then one takes a rest, longer or shorter, and sits down anew to the work. During the first half-hour, as before, nothing is found, and then all of a sudden the decisive idea presents itself to the mind. It might be said that the conscious work has been more fruitful because it has been interrupted and the rest has given back to the mind its force and freshness. But it is more probable that this rest has been filled out with unconscious work and that the result of this work has afterward revealed itself to the geometer just as in the cases I have cited; only the revelation, instead of coming during a walk or a journey, has happened during a period of conscious work, but independently of this work which plays at most a rôle of excitant, as if it were the goad stimulating the results already reached during rest, but remaining unconscious, to assume the conscious form.

There is another remark to be made about the conditions of this unconscious work: it is possible, and of a certainty it is only fruitful, if it is on the one hand preceded and on the other hand followed by a period of conscious work. These sudden inspirations (and the examples already cited sufficiently prove this) never happen except after some days of voluntary effort which has appeared absolutely fruitless and whence nothing good seems to have come, where the way taken seems totally astray. These efforts then have not been as sterile as one thinks; they have set agoing the unconscious machine and without them it would not have moved and would have produced nothing.

The need for the second period of conscious work, after the inspiration, is still easier to understand. It is necessary to put in shape the results of this inspiration, to deduce from them the immediate consequences, to arrange them, to word the demonstrations, but above all is verification necessary. I have spoken of the feeling of absolute certitude accompanying the inspiration; in the cases cited this feeling was no deceiver, nor is it usually. But do not think this is a rule without exception; often this feeling deceives us without being any the less vivid, and we only find it out when we seek to put on foot the demonstration. I have especially noticed this fact in regard to ideas coming to me in the morning or evening in bed while in a semi-hypnagogic state.

Such are the realities; now for the thoughts they force upon us. The unconscious, or, as we say, the subliminal self plays an important rôle in mathematical creation; this follows from what we have said. But usually the subliminal self is considered as purely automatic. Now we have seen that mathematical work is not simply mechanical, that it could not be done by a machine, however perfect. It is not merely a question of applying rules, of making the most combinations possible according to certain fixed laws. The combinations so obtained would be exceedingly numerous, useless and cumbersome. The true work of the inventor consists in choosing among these combinations so as to eliminate the useless ones or rather to avoid the trouble of making them, and the rules which must guide this choice are extremely fine and delicate. It is almost impossible to state them precisely; they are felt rather than formulated. Under these conditions, how imagine a sieve capable of applying them mechanically?

A first hypothesis now presents itself: the subliminal self is in no way inferior to the conscious self; it is not purely automatic; it is capable of discernment; it has tact, delicacy; it knows how to choose, to divine.

What do I say? It knows better how to divine than the conscious self, since it succeeds where that has failed. In a word, is not the subliminal self superior to the conscious self? You recognize the full importance of this question. Boutroux in a recent lecture has shown how it came up on a very different occasion, and what consequences would follow an affirmative answer.

Is this affirmative answer forced upon us by the facts I have just given? I confess that, for my part, I should hate to accept it. Reëxamine the facts then and see if they are not compatible with another explanation.

It is certain that the combinations which present themselves to the mind in a sort of sudden illumination, after an unconscious working somewhat prolonged, are generally useful and fertile combinations, which seem the result of a first impression. Does it follow that the subliminal self, having divined by a delicate intuition that these combinations would be useful, has formed only these, or has it rather formed many others which were lacking in interest and have remained unconscious?

In this second way of looking at it, all the combinations would be formed in consequence of the automatism of the subliminal self, but only the interesting ones would break into the domain of consciousness. And this is still very mysterious. What is the cause that, among the thousand products of our unconscious activity, some are called to pass the threshold, while others remain below? Is it a simple chance which confers this privilege? Evidently not; among all the stimuli of our senses, for example, only the most intense fix our attention, unless it has been drawn to them by other causes. More generally the privileged unconscious phenomena, those susceptible of becoming conscious, are those which, directly or indirectly, affect most profoundly our emotional sensibility.

It may be surprising to see emotional sensibility invoked *à propos* of mathematical demonstrations which, it would seem, can interest only the intellect. This would be to forget the feeling of mathematical beauty, of the harmony of numbers and forms, of geometric elegance. This is a true esthetic feeling that all real mathematicians know, and surely it belongs to emotional sensibility.

Now, what are the mathematic entities to which we attribute this character of beauty and elegance, and which are capable of developing in us a sort of esthetic emotion? They are those whose elements are harmoniously disposed so that the mind without effort can embrace their totality while realizing the details. This harmony is at once a satisfaction of our esthetic needs and an aid to the mind, sustaining and guiding. And at the same time, in putting under our eyes a well-ordered whole, it makes us foresee a mathematical law. Now, as we have said above, the only mathematical facts worthy of fixing our attention and capable of being useful are those which can teach us a mathematical law. So that we reach the following conclusion: The useful combinations are precisely the most beautiful, I mean those best able to charm this special sensibility that all mathematicians know, but of which the profane are so ignorant as often to be tempted to smile at it.

What happens then? Among the great numbers of combinations blindly formed by the subliminal self, almost all are without interest and without utility; but just for that reason they are also without effect upon the esthetic sensibility. Consciousness will never know them; only certain ones are harmonious, and, consequently, at once useful and beautiful. They will be capable of touching this special sensibility of the geometer of which I have just spoken, and which, once aroused, will call our attention to them, and thus give them occasion to become conscious.

This is only a hypothesis, and yet here is an observation which may confirm it: when a sudden illumination seizes upon the mind of the mathematician, it usually happens that it does not deceive him, but it also sometimes happens, as I have said, that it does not stand the test of verification; well, we almost always notice that this false idea, had it been true, would have gratified our natural feeling for mathematical elegance.

Thus it is this special esthetic sensibility which plays the rôle of the delicate sieve of which I spoke, and that sufficiently explains why the one lacking it will never be a real creator.

Yet all the difficulties have not disappeared. The conscious self is narrowly limited, and as for the subliminal self we know not its limitations, and this is why we are not too reluctant in supposing that it has been able in a short time to make more different combinations than the whole life of a conscious being could encompass. Yet these limitations exist. Is it likely that it is able to form all the possible combinations, whose number would frighten the imagination? Nevertheless that would seem necessary, because if it produces only a small part of these combinations, and if it makes them at random, there would be small chance that the *good*, the one we should choose, would be found among them.

Perhaps we ought to seek the explanation in that preliminary period of conscious work which always precedes all fruitful unconscious labor. Permit me a rough comparison. Figure the future elements of our combinations as something like the hooked atoms of Epicurus. During the complete repose of the mind, these atoms are motionless, they are, so to speak, hooked to the wall; so this complete rest may be indefinitely prolonged without the atoms meeting, and consequently without any combination between them.

On the other hand, during a period of apparent rest and unconscious work, certain of them are detached from the wall and put in motion. They flash in every direction through the space (I was about to say the room) where they are enclosed, as would, for example, a swarm of gnats or, if you prefer a more learned comparison, like the molecules of gas in the kinematic theory of gases. Then their mutual impacts may produce new combinations.

What is the rôle of the preliminary conscious work? It is evidently to mobilize certain of these atoms, to unhook them from the wall and put them in swing. We think we have done no good, because we have moved these elements a thousand different ways in seeking to assemble them, and have found no satisfactory aggregate. But, after this shaking up imposed upon them by our will, these atoms do not return to their primitive rest. They freely continue their dance.

Now, our will did not choose them at random; it pursued a perfectly determined aim. The mobilized atoms are therefore not any atoms whatsoever; they are those from which we might reasonably expect the desired solution. Then the mobilized atoms undergo impacts which make them enter into combinations among themselves or with other atoms at rest which they struck against in their course. Again I beg pardon, my comparison is very rough, but I scarcely know how otherwise to make my thought understood.

However it may be, the only combinations that have a chance of forming are those where at least one of the elements is one of those atoms freely chosen by our will. Now, it is evidently among these that is found what I called the *good combination*. Perhaps this is a way of lessening the paradoxical in the original hypothesis.

Another observation. It never happens that the unconscious work gives us the result of a somewhat long calculation *all made*, where we have only to apply fixed rules. We might think the wholly automatic subliminal self particularly apt for this sort of work, which is in a way exclusively mechanical. It seems that thinking in the evening upon the factors of a multiplication we might hope to find the product ready made upon our awakening, or again that an algebraic calculation, for example a verification, would be made unconsciously. Nothing of the sort, as observation proves. All one may hope from these inspirations, fruits of unconscious work, is a point of departure for such calculations. As for the calculations themselves, they must be made in the second period of conscious work, that which follows the inspiration, that in which one verifies the results of this inspiration and deduces their consequences. The rules of these calculations are strict and complicated. They require discipline, attention, will, and therefore consciousness. In the subliminal self, on the contrary, reigns what I should call liberty, if we might give this name to the simple absence of discipline and to the disorder born of chance. Only, this disorder itself permits unexpected combinations.

I shall make a last remark: when above I made certain personal observations, I spoke of a night of excitement when I worked in spite of myself. Such cases are frequent, and it is not necessary that the abnormal cerebral activity be caused by a physical excitant as in that I mentioned. It seems, in such cases, that one is present at his own unconscious work, made partially perceptible to the over-excited consciousness, yet without having changed its nature. Then we vaguely comprehend what distinguishes the two mechanisms or, if you wish, the working methods of the two egos. And the psychologic observations I have been able thus to make seem to me to confirm in their general outlines the views I have given.

Surely they have need of it, for they are and remain in spite of all very hypothetical: the interest of the questions is so great that I do not repent of having submitted them to the reader.

Translated by George Bruce Halsted

EXPLANATION WITH EMOTIVE FORCE

Guided Discussions

THOMAS BABINGTON MACAULAY, *The Scottish Highlands
in the Seventeenth Century*
RACHEL CARSON, *The Gray Beginnings*

For Further Analysis

HANSON BALDWIN, *R.M.S. Titanic*
FREDERICK LEWIS ALLEN, *Crash!*

Thomas Babington Macaulay

THE SCOTTISH HIGHLANDS
IN THE SEVENTEENTH CENTURY

From *The History of England from the Accession of James II*

*I*T IS not easy for a modern Englishman, who can pass in a day from his club in St. James's Street to his shooting box among the Grampians, and who finds in his shooting box all the comforts and luxuries of his club, to believe that, in the time of his greatgrandfathers, St. James's Street had as little connection with the Grampians as with the Andes. Yet so it was. In the south of our island scarcely any thing was known about the Celtic part of Scotland; and what was known excited no feeling but contempt and loathing. The crags and the glens, the woods and the waters, were indeed the same that now swarm every autumn with admiring gazers and sketchers. The Trosachs wound as now between gigantic walls of rock tapestried with broom and wild roses: Foyers came headlong down through the birchwood with the same leap and the same roar with which he still rushes to Loch Ness; and, in defiance of the sun of June, the snowy scalp of Ben Cruachan rose, as it still rises, over the willowy islets of Loch Awe. Yet none of these sights had power, till a recent period, to attract a single poet or painter from more opulent and more tranquil regions. Indeed, law and police, trade and industry, have done far more than people of romantic dispositions will readily admit, to develop in our minds a sense of the wilder beauties of nature. A traveller must be freed from all apprehension of being murdered or starved before he can be charmed by the bold outlines and rich tints of the hills. He is not likely to be thrown into ecstasies by the abruptness of a precipice from which he is in imminent danger of falling two thousand feet perpen-

159

dicular; by the boiling waves of a torrent which suddenly whirls away his baggage and forces him to run for his life; by the gloomy grandeur of a pass where he finds a corpse which marauders have just stripped and mangled; or by the screams of those eagles whose next meal may probably be on his own eyes. About the year 1730, Captain Burt, one of the first Englishmen who caught a glimpse of the spots which now allure tourists from every part of the civilised world, wrote an account of his wanderings. He was evidently a man of a quick, an observant, and a cultivated mind, and would doubtless, had he lived in our age, have looked with mingled awe and delight on the mountains of Invernesshire. But, writing with the feeling which was universal in his own age, he pronounced those mountains monstrous excrescences. Their deformity, he said, was such that the most sterile plains seemed lovely by comparison. Fine weather, he complained, only made bad worse; for, the clearer the day, the more disagreeably did those misshapen masses of gloomy brown and dirty purple affect the eye. What a contrast, he exclaimed, between these horrible prospects and the beauties of Richmond Hill! Some persons may think that Burt was a man of vulgar and prosaical mind: but they will scarcely venture to pass a similar judgment on Oliver Goldsmith. Goldsmith was one of the very few Saxons who, more than a century ago, ventured to explore the Highlands. He was disgusted by the hideous wilderness, and declared that he greatly preferred the charming country round Leyden, the vast expanse of verdant meadow, and the villas with their statues and grottoes, trim flower beds, and rectilinear avenues. Yet it is difficult to believe that the author of the Traveller and of the Deserted Village was naturally inferior in taste and sensibility to the thousands of clerks and milliners who are now thrown into raptures by the sight of Loch Katrine and Loch Lomond. His feelings may easily be explained. It was not till roads had been cut out of the rocks, till bridges had been flung over the courses of the rivulets, till inns had succeeded to dens of robbers, till there was as little danger of being slain or plundered in the wildest defile of Badenoch or Lochaber as in Cornhill, that strangers could be enchanted by the blue dimples of the lakes and by the rainbows which overhung the waterfalls, and could derive a solemn pleasure even from the clouds and tempests which lowered on the mountain tops.

2   The change in the feeling with which the Lowlanders regarded the Highland scenery was closely connected with a change not less remarkable in the feeling with which they regarded the Highland race. It is not strange that the Wild Scotch, as they were sometimes called, should, in

the seventeenth century, have been considered by the Saxons as mere savages. But it is surely strange that, considered as savages, they should not have been objects of interest and curiosity. The English were then abundantly inquisitive about the manners of rude nations separated from our island by great continents and oceans. Numerous books were printed describing the laws, the superstitions, the cabins, the repasts, the dresses, the marriages, the funerals of Laplanders and Hottentots, Mohawks and Malays. The plays and poems of that age are full of allusions to the usages of the black men of Africa and of the red men of America. The only barbarian about whom there was no wish to have any information was the Highlander. Five or six years after the Revolution, an indefatigable angler published an account of Scotland. He boasted that, in the course of his rambles from lake to lake, and from brook to brook, he had left scarcely a nook of the kingdom unexplored. But, when we examine his narrative, we find that he had never ventured beyond the extreme skirts of the Celtic region. He tells us that even from the people who lived close to the passes he could learn little or nothing about the Gaelic population. Few Englishmen, he says, had ever seen Inverary. All beyond Inverary was chaos. In the reign of George the First, a work was published which professed to give a most exact account of Scotland; and in this work, consisting of more than three hundred pages, two contemptuous paragraphs were thought sufficient for the Highlands and the Highlanders. We may well doubt whether, in 1689, one in twenty of the well read gentlemen who assembled at Will's coffeehouse knew that, within the four seas, and at the distance of less than five hundred miles from London, were many miniature courts, in each of which a petty prince, attended by guards, by armour bearers, by musicians, by hereditary orator, by a hereditary poet laureate, kept a rude state, dispensed a rude justice, waged wars, and concluded treaties. While the old Gaelic institutions were in full vigour, no account of them was given by any observer, qualified to judge of them fairly. Had such an observer studied the character of the Highlanders, he would doubtless have found in it closely intermingled the good and the bad qualities of an uncivilised nation. He would have found that the people had no love for their country or for their king; that they had no attachment to any commonwealth larger than the clan, or to any magistrate superior to the chief. He would have found that life was governed by a code of morality and honour widely different from that which is established in peaceful and prosperous societies. He would have learned that a stab in the back, or a shot from behind a fragment of rock, were

approved modes of taking satisfaction for insults. He would have heard
men relate boastfully how they or their fathers had wreaked on hereditary
enemies in a neighbouring valley such vengeance as would have made
old soldiers of the Thirty Years' War shudder. He would have found that
robbery was held to be a calling, not merely innocent, but honourable. He
would have seen, wherever he turned, that dislike of steady industry, and
that disposition to throw on the weaker sex the heaviest part of manual
labour, which are characteristic of savages. He would have been struck
by the spectacle of athletic men basking in the sun, angling for salmon,
or taking aim at grouse, while their aged mothers, their pregnant wives,
their tender daughters, were reaping the scanty harvest of oats. Nor did
the women repine at their hard lot. In their view it was quite fit that
a man, especially if he assumed the aristocratic title of Duinhe Wassel
and adorned his bonnet with the eagle's feather, should take his ease,
except when he was fighting, hunting, or marauding. To mention
the name of such a man in connection with commerce or with any mechanical art was an insult. Agriculture was indeed less despised. Yet a
highborn warrior was much more becomingly employed in plundering
the land of others than in tilling his own. The religion of the greater
part of the Highlands was a rude mixture of Popery and Paganism. The
symbol of redemption was associated with heathen sacrifices and incanta-
tions. Baptized men poured libations of ale to one Dæmon, and set out
drink offerings of milk for another. Seers wrapped themselves up in bulls'
hides, and awaited, in that vesture, the inspiration which was to reveal
the future. Even among those minstrels and genealogists whose hereditary
vocation was to preserve the memory of past events, an enquirer would
have found very few who could read. In truth, he might easily have
journeyed from sea to sea without discovering a page of Gaelic printed
or written. The price which he would have had to pay for his knowledge
of the country would have been heavy. He would have had to endure
hardships as great as if he had sojourned among the Esquimaux or the
Samoyeds. Here and there, indeed, at the castle of some great lord who
had a seat in the Parliament and Privy Council, and who was accustomed
to pass a large part of his life in the cities of the South, might have been
found wigs and embroidered coats, plate and fine linen, lace and jewels,
French dishes and French wines. But, in general, the traveller would have
been forced to content himself with very different quarters. In many
dwellings the furniture, the food, the clothing, nay the very hair and skin
of his hosts, would have put his philosophy to the proof. His lodging
would sometimes have been in a hut of which every nook would have

swarmed with vermin. He would have inhaled an atmosphere thick with peat smoke, and foul with a hundred noisome exhalations. At supper grain fit only for horses would have been set before him, accompanied by a cake of blood drawn from living cows. Some of the company with which he would have feasted would have been covered with cutaneous eruptions, and others would have been smeared with tar like sheep. His couch would have been the bare earth, dry or wet as the weather might be; and from that couch he would have risen half poisoned with stench, half blind with the reek of turf, and half mad with the itch.

3   This is not an attractive picture. And yet an enlightened and dispassionate observer would have found in the character and manners of this rude people something which might well excite admiration and a good hope. Their courage was what great exploits achieved in all the four quarters of the globe have since proved it to be. Their intense attachment to their own tribe and to their own patriarch, though politically a great evil, partook of the nature of virtue. The sentiment was misdirected and ill regulated; but still it was heroic. These must be some elevation of soul in a man who loves the society of which he is a member and the leader whom he follows with a love stronger than the love of life. It was true that the Highlander had few scruples about shedding the blood of an enemy: but it was not less true that he had high notions of the duty of observing faith to allies and hospitality to guests. It was true that his predatory habits were most pernicious to the commonwealth. Yet those erred greatly who imagined that he bore any resemblance to villains who, in rich and well governed communities, live by stealing. When he drove before him the herds of Lowland farmers up the pass which led to his native glen, he no more considered himself as a thief than the Raleighs and Drakes considered themselves as thieves when they divided the cargoes of Spanish galleons. He was a warrior seizing lawful prize of war, of war never once intermitted during the thirty-five generations which had passed away since the Teutonic invaders had driven the children of the soil to the mountains. That, if he was caught robbing on such principles, he should, for the protection of peaceful industry, be punished with the utmost rigour of the law was perfectly just. But it was not just to class him morally with the pickpockets who infested Drury Lane Theatre, or the highwaymen who stopped coaches on Blackheath. His inordinate pride of birth and his contempt for labour and trade were indeed great weaknesses, and had done far more than the inclemency of the air and the sterility of the soil to keep his country poor and rude. Yet even here there was some compensation. It must in fairness be acknowledged that

the patrician virtues were not less widely diffused among the population of the Highlands than the patrician vices. As there was no other part of the island where men, sordidly clothed, lodged, and fed, indulged themselves to such a degree in the idle sauntering habits of an aristocracy, so there was no other part of the island where such men had in such a degree the better qualities of an aristocracy, grace and dignity of manner, self-respect, and that noble sensibility which makes dishonour more terrible than death. A gentleman of this sort, whose clothes were begrimed with the accumulated filth of years, and whose hovel smelt worse than an English hogstye, would often do the honours of that hovel with a lofty courtesy worthy of the splendid circle of Versailles. Though he had as little booklearning as the most stupid ploughboys of England, it would have been a great error to put him in the same intellectual rank with such ploughboys. It is indeed only by reading that men can become profoundly acquainted with any science. But the arts of poetry and rhetoric may be carried near to absolute perfection, and may exercise a mighty influence on the public mind, in an age in which books are wholly or almost wholly unknown. The first great painter of life and manners has described, with a vivacity which makes it impossible to doubt that he was copying from nature, the effect produced by eloquence and song on audiences ignorant of the alphabet. It is probable that, in the Highland councils, men who would not have been qualified for the duty of parish clerks sometimes argued questions of peace and war, of tribute and homage, with ability worthy of Halifax and Caermarthen, and that, at the Highland banquets, minstrels who did not know their letters sometimes poured forth rhapsodies in which a discerning critic might have found passages which would have reminded him of the tenderness of Otway or of the vigour of Dryden.

4   There was therefore even then evidence sufficient to justify the belief that no natural inferiority had kept the Celt far behind the Saxon. It might safely have been predicted that, if ever an efficient police should make it impossible for the Highlander to avenge his wrongs by violence and to supply his wants by rapine, if ever his faculities should be developed by the civilising influence of the Protestant religion and of the English language, if ever he should transfer to his country and to her lawful magistrates the affection and respect with which he had been taught to regard his own petty community and his own petty prince, the kingdom would obtain an immense accession of strength for all the purposes both of peace and of war.

5   Such would doubtless have been the decision of a well informed and impartial judge. But no such judge was then to be found. The Saxons who dwelt far from the Gaelic provinces could not be well informed. The Saxons who dwelt near those provinces could not be impartial. National enmities have always been fiercest among borderers; and the enmity between the Highland borderer and the Lowland borderer along the whole frontier was the growth of ages, and was kept fresh by constant injuries. One day many square miles of pasture land were swept bare by armed plunderers from the hills. Another day a score of plaids dangled in a row on the gallows of Crieff or Stirling. Fairs were indeed held on the debatable land for the necessary interchange of commodities. But to those fairs both parties came prepared for battle; and the day often ended in bloodshed. Thus the Highlander was an object of hatred to his Saxon neighbours; and from his Saxon neighbours those Saxons who dwelt far from him learned the very little that they cared to know about his habits. When the English condescended to think of him at all,—and it was seldom that they did so,—they considered him as a filthy abject savage, a slave, a Papist, a cutthroat, and a thief.

Discussion: A historian attempts to relate the events of the past in such a way as to explain their interconnection and give them meaning. His task in one sense is merely narrative and explanatory, and his work is rewarding to the reader for the understanding of the past that it brings. But the work of some historians seems to have a quality beyond this basic requirement which gives them a place not only in the annals of history but in those of literature as well. Such are Edward Gibbon, author of the *Decline and Fall of the Roman Empire,* and Thomas Macaulay, author of *The History of England.* The literary eminence which these historians have attained is often attributed to their narrative style, and it is true that the style of these authors is extremely finished and forceful. But the reader senses more than mere style as he reads. He feels that the whole history has been *shaped* in some definite way so as to give it a very specific power of arousing a particular pervasive emotional response to the historical materials—a response which leaves him stirred as if by a great drama or epic. One of the editors has tried to define the shaping power of Macaulay's *History* (which ends in 1702) by saying that Macaulay's purpose is to explain later events in English history by earlier events in such a way as to make the ordinary English reader of the nineteenth century take pride in the fact that the England of his own day is richer, more powerful, and more secure than seventeenth-century England; at the same time he wishes him to understand that nineteenth-century England is what it is only because of the particular course which the earlier events had taken, and that the contrast between the two periods does not detract from the inherent interest and proper dignity attaching to the earlier period. This statement was not drawn up with the section now before us in mind, and it will serve as some test of the description to see how far it can be applied to this one very short part of Macaulay's work. It will be necessary only to add, in our analytic summary, a statement of the particular subject of explanation at this point in the *History*. In order to understand the summary, you will need to know that at the time of which Macaulay writes England and Scotland were separate nations divided by many animosities and joined only by their allegiance to a common king; and that Scotland in turn was made up of what were also, in effect, two separate nations—the fierce Celtic inhabitants of the rugged Highlands, and the more civilized Saxon occupants of the Lowlands. After a period of instability and conflict, later English history was to produce a firm political union between England and Scotland and, still later, an assimilation of Highland life to Lowland life which were to make Scotland a strong, thriving nation and an important factor in the power and pre-eminence of nineteenth-century Britain.

Analytic Summary: In this essay Macaulay explains, in such a way as to evoke the general emotional response defined above (purpose), *the enmity and misunderstanding between Highlander on the one hand and Lowlander and Englishman on the other* (subject) *through the establishment of several general facts developed by contrast* (disposition), *in language of appropriate dignity and force* (style).

Questions

1. Where in the opening sentences does Macaulay state the immediate subject of his explanation? What general fact about the Highlands relevant to this subject does he develop in paragraph 1?

2. He chooses to develop this fact by contrasting the reactions to Highland scenery of the eighteenth- and nineteenth-century traveler. Can this choice be fully explained by the immediate explanatory purpose, or does the more general emotive purpose help us to explain it more fully? Does the general purpose allow us to understand better the reasons for the details presented in the first sentence?

3. Where is the specific proposition to be established in the opening paragraph first fully stated? Where is it next stated? What is the function of the first statement? Of the second?

4. Can the form in which the proposition is finally stated be explained by Macaulay's desire to relate it both to his immediate explanatory purpose *and* the more general purpose?

5. What is the function of the initial description of Highland scenery in relation to the first statement of the proposition? How are the sentences constructed so as to keep the reader constantly aware of the point that is to give

the proposition force? What, in itself, does the description contribute to the general purpose?

6. What is the relation of the first statement of the proposition to the series of sentences beginning "a traveller must be freed"? How are these sentences constructed so as to illustrate the proposition in terms of the contrast implicit in the previous description?

7. What specifically do the examples of Burt and Goldsmith contribute to the development of the proposition? Is the contrast with the present implicit in the initial description of the scenery maintained in these examples? How? Why does Macaulay feel that he should add the testimony of Goldsmith to that of Burt? Why then does he later refer to Goldsmith as the "author of the Deserted Village and the Traveller" instead of merely by his name? What is the point of mentioning, in both cases, the sort of scenery which Burt and Goldsmith did admire?

8. The second paragraph is really two paragraphs welded together by two transitional sentences. Where are these sentences? What ideational connection between the two parts provides the basis of the transition?

9. What is the subject of the first part of this paragraph? Of the second part? The first sentence of the second part states a proposition with two aspects, one of which is developed in the remainder of the paragraph, whereas the other is left for development in paragraph 3. Find the sentence and state its precise relationship to the subsequent material.

10. How, at the beginning of paragraph 3, does Macaulay remind the reader that he is picking up the second half of his earlier proposition? What is the relationship of the transitional device used to the device used between the two parts of paragraph 2?

11. How does paragraph 2 contribute to the furtherance of the immediate explanatory purpose? To which of the three aspects of the general purpose does the second part of paragraph 2 contribute? To which other aspect of the general purpose does paragraph 3 contribute?

12. How does paragraph 4 draw upon the specifics of paragraphs 2 and 3 to realize the remaining aspect of the general purpose? Look back particularly at the second half of paragraph 2 to see how the details there are calculated to perform not only their immediate function but also to prepare for this later paragraph.

13. How in the last paragraph does Macaulay move back from his general to his immediate purpose?

14. Look up the four men Macaulay mentions at the end of paragraph 3 to discover their relevance to the discussion. Does the way Macaulay brings in these names, and the name of Goldsmith above, contribute anything to the fulfillment of his general purpose?

Theme Topics

1. Narrate a true event or series of connected events in such a way as to tell the factual truth about it but at the same time to invest it with a particular kind

of emotional force for the reader. Some well-known episode in American history might be a proper subject.

2. Read the account of Highland life in G. M. Trevelyan's *England Under Queen Anne* and write an essay in which, by comparing Trevelyan's in some ways quite similar account to Macaulay's, you explain the marked difference in effect of the two treatments.

Rachel Carson

THE GRAY BEGINNINGS

And the earth was without form, and void;
and darkness was upon the face of the deep.   GENESIS

*B*EGINNINGS are apt to be shadowy, and so it is with the beginnings of that great mother of life, the sea. Many people have debated how and when the earth got its ocean, and it is not surprising that their explanations do not always agree. For the plain and inescapable truth is that no one was there to see, and in the absence of eyewitness accounts there is bound to be a certain amount of disagreement. So if I tell here the story of how the young planet Earth acquired an ocean, it must be a story pieced together from many sources and containing whole chapters the details of which we can only imagine. The story is founded on the testimony of the earth's most ancient rocks, which were young when the earth was young; on other evidence written on the face of the earth's satellite, the moon; and on hints contained in the history of the sun and the whole universe of star-filled space. For although no man was there to witness this cosmic birth, the stars and the moon and the rocks were there, and, indeed, had much to do with the fact that there is an ocean.

2   The events of which I write must have occurred somewhat more than 2 billion years ago. As nearly as science can tell that is the approximate age of the earth, and the ocean must be very nearly as old. It is possible now to discover the age of the rocks that compose the crust of the earth by measuring the rate of decay of the radioactive materials they contain. The oldest rocks found anywhere on earth—in Manitoba—are about 2.3 billion years old. Allowing 100 million years or so for the cool-

ing of the earth's materials to form a rocky crust, we arrive at the supposition that the tempestuous and violent events connected with our planet's birth occurred nearly 2½ billion years ago. But this is only a minimum estimate, for rocks indicating an even greater age may be found at any time.

3   The new earth, freshly torn from its parent sun, was a ball of whirling gases, intensely hot, rushing through the black spaces of the universe on a path and at a speed controlled by immense forces. Gradually the ball of flaming gases cooled. The gases began to liquefy, and Earth became a molten mass. The materials of this mass eventually became sorted out in a definite pattern: the heaviest in the center, the less heavy surrounding them, and the least heavy forming the outer rim. This is the pattern which persists today—a central sphere of molten iron, very nearly as hot as it was 2 billion years ago, an intermediate sphere of semiplastic basalt, and a hard outer shell, relatively quite thin and composed of solid basalt and granite.

4   The outer shell of the young earth must have been a good many millions of years changing from the liquid to the solid state, and it is believed that, before this change was completed, an event of the greatest importance took place—the formation of the moon. The next time you stand on a beach at night, watching the moon's bright path across the water, and conscious of the moon-drawn tides, remember that the moon itself may have been born of a great tidal wave of earthly substance, torn off into space. And remember that if the moon was formed in this fashion, the event may have had much to do with shaping the ocean basins and the continents as we know them.

5   There were tides in the new earth, long before there was an ocean. In response to the pull of the sun the molten liquids of the earth's whole surface rose in tides that rolled unhindered around the globe and only gradually slackened and diminished as the earthly shell cooled, congealed, and hardened. Those who believe that the moon is a child of earth say that during an early stage of the earth's development something happened that caused this rolling, viscid tide to gather speed and momentum and to rise to unimaginable heights. Apparently the force that created these greatest tides the earth has ever known was the force of resonance, for at this time the period of the solar tides had come to approach, then equal, the period of the free oscillation of the liquid earth. And so every sun tide was given increased momentum by the push of the earth's oscillation, and each of the twice-daily tides was larger than the one before it. Physi-

cists have calculated that, after 500 years of such monstrous, steadily increasing tides, those on the side toward the sun became too high for
stability, and a great wave was torn away and hurled into space. But
immediately, of course, the newly created satellite became subject to
physical laws that sent it spinning in an orbit of its own about the earth.
6   There are reasons for believing that this event took place after the
earth's crust had become slightly hardened, instead of during its partly
liquid state. There is to this day a great scar on the surface of the globe.
This scar or depression holds the Pacific Ocean. According to some
geophysicists, the floor of the Pacific is composed of basalt, the substance
of the earth's middle layer, while all other oceans are floored with a thin
layer of granite. We immediately wonder what became of the Pacific's
granite covering and the most convenient assumption is that it was torn
away when the moon was formed. There is supporting evidence. The
mean density of the moon is much less than that of the earth (3.3 compared with 5.5), suggesting that the moon took away none of the earth's
heavy iron core, but that it is composed only of the granite and some
of the basalt of the outer layers.
7   The birth of the moon probably helped shape other regions of the
world ocean besides the Pacific. When part of the crust was torn away,
strains must have been set up in the remaining granite envelope. Perhaps
the granite mass cracked open on the side opposite the moon scar. Perhaps, as the earth spun on its axis and rushed on its orbit through space,
the cracks widened and the masses of granite began to drift apart, moving
over a tarry, slowly hardening layer of basalt. Gradually the outer portions of the basalt layer became solid and the wandering continents
came to rest, frozen into place with oceans between them. In spite of
theories to the contrary, the weight of geologic evidence seems to be that
the locations of the major ocean basins and the major continental land
masses are today much the same as they have been since a very early
period of the earth's history.
8   But this is to anticipate the story, for when the moon was born
there was no ocean. The gradually cooling earth was enveloped in heavy
layers of cloud, which contained much of the water of the new planet.
For a long time its surface was so hot that no moisture could fall without
immediately being reconverted to steam. This dense, perpetually renewed
cloud covering must have been thick enough that no rays of sunlight
could penetrate it. And so the rough outlines of the continents and the
empty ocean basins were sculptured out of the surface of the earth in

darkness, in a Stygian world of heated rock and swirling clouds and gloom.

9   As soon as the earth's crust cooled enough, the rains began to fall. Never have there been such rains since that time. They fell continuously, day and night, days passing into months, into years, into centuries. They poured into the waiting ocean basins, or, falling upon the continental masses, drained away to become sea.

10   That primeval ocean, growing in bulk as the rains slowly filled its basins, must have been only faintly salt. But the falling rains were the symbol of the dissolution of the continents. From the moment the rains began to fall, the lands began to be worn away and carried to the sea. It is an endless, inexorable process that has never stopped—the dissolving of the rocks, the leaching out of their contained minerals, the carrying of the rock fragments and dissolved minerals to the ocean. And over the eons of time, the sea has grown ever more bitter with the salt of the continents.

11   In what manner the sea produced the mysterious and wonderful stuff called protoplasm we cannot say. In its warm, dimly lit waters the unknown conditions of temperature and pressure and saltiness must have been the critical ones for the creation of life from non-life. At any rate they produced the result that neither the alchemists with their crucibles nor modern scientists in their laboratories have been able to achieve.

12   Before the first living cell was created, there may have been many trials and failures. It seems probable that, within the warm saltiness of the primeval sea, certain organic substances were fashioned from carbon dioxide, sulphur, phosphorus, potassium, and calcium. Perhaps these were transition steps from which the complex molecules of protoplasm arose— molecules that somehow acquired the ability to reproduce themselves and begin the endless stream of life. But at present no one is wise enough to be sure.

13   Those first living things may have been simple microorganisms rather like some of the bacteria we know today—mysterious borderline forms that were not quite plants, not quite animals, barely over the intangible line that separates the non-living from the living. It is doubtful that this first life possessed the substance chlorophyll, with which plants in sunlight transform lifeless chemicals into the living stuff of their tissues. Little sunshine could enter their dim world, penetrating the cloud banks from which fell the endless rains. Probably the sea's first children lived on the organic substances then present in the ocean waters, or, like the

iron and sulphur bacteria that exist today, lived directly on inorganic food.

14 All the while the cloud cover was thinning, the darkness of the nights alternated with palely illumined days, and finally the sun for the first time shone through upon the sea. By this time some of the living things that floated in the sea must have developed the magic of chlorophyll. Now they were able to take the carbon dioxide of the air and the water of the sea and of these elements, in sunlight, build the organic substances they needed for life. So the first true plants came into being.

15 Another group of organisms, lacking the chlorophyll but needing organic food, found they could make a way of life for themselves by devouring the plants. So the first animals arose, and from that day to this, every animal in the world has followed the habit it learned in the ancient seas and depends, directly or through complex food chains, on the plants for food and life.

16 As the years passed, and the centuries, and the millions of years, the stream of life grew more and more complex. From simple, one-celled creatures, others that were aggregations of specialized cells arose, and then creatures with organs for feeding, digesting, breathing, reproducing. Sponges grew on the rocky bottom of the sea's edge and coral animals built their habitations in warm, clear waters. Jellyfish swam and drifted in the sea. Worms evolved, and starfish, and hard-shelled creatures with many-jointed legs. The plants, too, progressed, from the microscopic algae to branched and curiously fruiting seaweeds that swayed with the tides and were plucked from the coastal rocks by the surf and cast adrift.

17 During all this time the continents had no life. There was little to induce living things to come ashore, forsaking their all-providing, all-embracing mother sea. The lands must have been bleak and hostile beyond the power of words to describe. Imagine a whole continent of naked rock, across which no covering mantle of green had been drawn— a continent without soil, for there were no land plants to aid in its formation and bind it to the rocks with their roots. Imagine a land of stone, a silent land, except for the sound of the rains and winds that swept across it. For there was no living voice, and nothing moved over its surface except the shadows of the clouds.

18 Meanwhile, the gradual cooling of the planet, which had first given the earth its hard granite crust, was progressing into its deeper layers; and as the interior slowly cooled and contracted, it drew away from the

outer shell. This shell, accommodating itself to the shrinking sphere within it, fell into folds and wrinkles—the earth's first mountain ranges.
19   Geologists tell us that there must have been at least two periods of mountain building (often called "revolutions") in that dim period, so long ago that the rocks have no record of it, so long ago that the mountains themselves have long since been worn away. Then there came a third great period of upheaval and readjustment of the earth's crust, about a billion years ago, but of all its majestic mountains the only reminders today are the Laurentian hills of eastern Canada, and a great shield of granite over the flat country around Hudson Bay.
20   The epochs of mountain building only served to speed up the processes of erosion by which the continents were worn down and their crumbling rock and contained minerals returned to the sea. The uplifted masses of the mountains were prey to the bitter cold of the upper atmosphere and under the attacks of frost and snow and ice the rocks cracked and crumbled away. The rains beat with greater violence upon the slopes of the hills and carried away the substance of the mountains in torrential streams. There was still no plant covering to modify and resist the power of the rains.
21   And in the sea, life continued to evolve. The earliest forms have left no fossils by which we can identify them. Probably they were soft-bodied, with no hard parts that could be preserved. Then, too, the rock layers formed in those early days have since been so altered by enormous heat and pressure, under the foldings of the earth's crust, that any fossils they might have contained would have been destroyed.
22   For the past 500 million years, however, the rocks have preserved the fossil record. By the dawn of the Cambrian period, when the history of living things was first inscribed on rock pages, life in the sea had progressed so far that all the main groups of backboneless or invertebrate animals had been developed. But there were no animals with backbones, no insects or spiders, and still no plant or animal had been evolved that was capable of venturing onto the forbidding land. So for more than three-fourths of geologic time the continents were desolate and uninhabited, while the sea prepared the life that was later to invade them and make them habitable. Meanwhile, with violent tremblings of the earth and with the fire and smoke of roaring volcanoes, mountains rose and wore away, glaciers moved to and fro over the earth, and the sea crept over the continents and again receded.

23 It was not until Silurian time, some 350 million years ago, that the first pioneer of land life crept out on the shore. It was an arthropod, one of the great tribe that later produced crabs and lobsters and insects. It must have been something like a modern scorpion, but, unlike its descendants, it never wholly severed the ties that united it to the sea. It lived a strange life, half-terrestrial, half-aquatic, something like that of the ghost crabs that speed along the beaches today, now and then dashing into the surf to moisten their gills.

24 Fish, tapered of body and stream-molded by the press of running waters, were evolving in Silurian rivers. In times of drought, in the drying pools and lagoons, the shortage of oxygen forced them to develop swim bladders for the storage of air. One form developed an air-breathing lung and by its air could live buried in the mud for long periods.

25 It is very doubtful that the animals alone would have succeeded in colonizing the land, for only the plants had the power to bring about the first amelioration of its harsh conditions. They helped make soil of the crumbling rocks, they held back the soil from the rains that would have swept it away, and little by little they softened and subdued the bare rock, the lifeless desert. We know very little about the first land plants, but they must have been closely related to some of the larger seaweeds that had learned to live in the coastal shallows, developing strengthened stems and grasping, rootlike holdfasts to resist the drag and pull of the waves. Perhaps it was in some coastal lowlands, periodically drained and flooded, that some such plants found it possible to survive, though separated from the sea. This also seems to have taken place in the Silurian period.

26 The mountains that had been thrown up by the Laurentian revolution gradually wore away, and as the sediments were washed from their summits and deposited on the lowlands, great areas of the continents sank under the load. The seas crept out of their basins and spread over the lands. Life fared well and was exceedingly abundant in those shallow, sunlit seas. But with the later retreat of the ocean water into the deeper basins, many creatures must have been left stranded in shallow, land-locked bays. Some of these animals found means to survive on land. The lakes, the shores of the rivers, and the coastal swamps of those days were the testing grounds in which plants and animals either became adapted to the new conditions or perished.

27 As the lands rose and the seas receded, a strange fishlike creature emerged on the land, and over the thousands of years its fins became legs,

and instead of gills it developed lungs. In the Devonian sandstone this first amphibian left its footprint.

28   On land and sea the stream of life poured on. New forms evolved; some old ones declined and disappeared. On land the mosses and the ferns and the seed plants developed. The reptiles for a time dominated the earth, gigantic, grotesque, and terrifying. Birds learned to live and move in the ocean of air. The first small mammals lurked inconspicuously in hidden crannies of the earth as though in fear of the reptiles.

29   When they went ashore the animals that took up a land life carried with them a part of the sea in their bodies, a heritage which they passed on to their children and which even today links each land animal with its origin in the ancient sea. Fish, amphibian, and reptile, warm-blooded bird and mammal—each of us carries in our veins a salty stream in which the elements sodium, potassium, and calcium are combined in almost the same proportions as in sea water. This is our inheritance from the day untold millions of years ago, when a remote ancestor, having progressed from the one-celled to the many-celled stage, first developed a circulatory system in which the fluid was merely the water of the sea. In the same way, our lime-hardened skeletons are a heritage from the calcium-rich ocean of Cambrian time. Even the protoplasm that streams within each cell of our bodies has the chemical structure impressed upon all living matter when the first simple creatures were brought forth in the ancient sea. And as life itself began in the sea, so each of us begins his individual life in a miniature ocean within his mother's womb, and in the stages of his embryonic development repeats the steps by which his race evolved, from gill-breathing inhabitants of a water world to creatures able to live on land.

30   Some of the land animals later returned to the ocean. After perhaps 50 million years of land life, a number of reptiles entered the sea in Mesozoic time. They were huge and formidable creatures. Some had oarlike limbs by which they rowed through the water; some were web-footed, with long, serpentine necks. These grotesque monsters disappeared millions of years ago, but we remember them when we come upon a large sea turtle swimming many miles at sea, its barnacle-encrusted shell eloquent of its marine life. Much later, perhaps no more than 50 million years ago, some of the mammals, too, abandoned a land life for the ocean. Their descendants are the sea lions, seals, sea elephants, and whales of today.

31 Among the land mammals there was a race of creatures that took to an arboreal existence. Their hands underwent remarkable development, becoming skilled in manipulating and examining objects, and along with this skill came a superior brain power that compensated for what these comparatively small mammals lacked in strength. At last, perhaps somewhere in the vast interior of Asia, they descended from the trees and became again terrestrial. The past million years have seen their transformation into beings with the body and brain and the mystical spirit of man.

32 Eventually man, too, found his way back to the sea. Standing on its shores, he must have looked out upon it with wonder and curiosity, compounded with an unconscious recognition of his lineage. He could not physically re-enter the ocean as the seals and whales had done. But over the centuries, with all the skill and ingenuity and reasoning powers of his mind, he has sought to explore and investigate even its most remote parts, so that he might re-enter it mentally and imaginatively.

33 He fashioned boats to venture out on its surface. Later he found ways to descend to the shallow parts of its floor, carrying with him the air that, as a land mammal long unaccustomed to aquatic life, he needed to breathe. Moving in fascination over the deep sea he could not enter, he found ways to probe its depths, he let down nets to capture its life, he invented mechanical eyes and ears that could re-create for his senses a world long lost, but a world that, in the deepest part of his subconscious mind, he had never wholly forgotten.

34 And yet he has returned to his mother sea only on her own terms. He cannot control or change the ocean as, in his brief tenancy of earth, he has subdued and plundered the continents. In the artificial world of his cities and towns, he often forgets the true nature of his planet and the long vistas of its history, in which the existence of the race of men has occupied a mere moment of time. The sense of all these things comes to him most clearly in the course of a long ocean voyage, when he watches day after day the receding rim of the horizon, ridged and furrowed by waves; when at night he becomes aware of the earth's rotation as the stars pass overhead; or when, alone in this world of water and sky, he feels the loneliness of his earth in space. And then, as never on land, he knows the truth that his world is a water world, a planet dominated by its covering mantle of ocean, in which the continents are but transient intrusions of land above the surface of the all-encircling sea.

Discussion: This chapter from Miss Carson's *The Sea Around Us* has often been reprinted, a fact which tells us that it is an essay of more than usual interest. It is obviously an explanation, an account of a complex scientific subject designed for a lay audience. It is unlike most such explanations, however—and therefore remarkable—in that it seeks not merely to explain its subject but also to induce in the reader a particular emotional reaction to the subject. In this respect it is like the Macaulay selection printed above and unlike the Kroeber and de Tocqueville selections. It is the emotive element in their purposes, as realized in the disposition and style, which makes the Macaulay and Carson pieces seem more "literary" than the other explanations, even in comparison with an explanation like Collingwood's in which both disposition and style are fully controlled and finished.

Analytic Summary: In this essay Miss Carson deals with the evolutionary process which began with the creation of the sea and led to the emergence of man (subject). *Her attempt is to give a scientifically valid explanation of this process which will be understood by a lay reader but which will at the same time induce in him a sense of reverential awe at the magnitude and mystery of the process and an imaginative feeling of his own connection with it* (purpose). *She does this by tracing, largely in chronological order, the successive stages of the process, each of which is shown to be a condition of those which follow* (disposition). *The language is marked by choices of diction and syntax which emphasize the magnitude, power, and mystery of the events that make up the process and which facilitate the reader's imaginative empathy with it* (style).

Questions

1. The essay proper begins with paragraph 3, the first two paragraphs serving as prologue. How is the material in the introductory paragraphs dictated by the basic explanatory purpose, particularly by that aspect of it which requires the explanation to be "scientifically valid"? Why, in presenting the scientific basis for her account, does Miss Carson emphasize its uncertainty ("debated," "disagreement," "only imagine," "must have occurred," etc.)? How are the choices of diction and syntax in these paragraphs dictated by the emotive aspect of the purpose? (Consider, for example, the use of "evidence written on the face of the . . . moon" rather than "evidence derived from a study of the moon's surface"; or the expanded "the stars and the moon and the rocks" for "the stars, moon, and rocks.")

2. The third paragraph is required by the explanatory purpose because it defines the initial stage of the whole evolutionary process which conditions all

of the succeeding stages. Are the choices of language, however, wholly explainable in the same terms?

3. How much of the factual material in the paragraphs devoted to the moon (4–7) is made use of in the paragraphs which follow (8–9)? Could the relevant information have been stated more quickly? How do you account, then, for the expansion and emphasis given the material in paragraphs 4 through 7?

4. Trace out the connections of paragraphs 8–17 showing how each stage described is a condition of those which follow. At what point in the sequence is there a shift from what has to this point been the apparent subject? How is this shift (and the second shift at paragraph 29 below) accommodated in the description of subject in the analytic summary? Does Miss Carson emphasize or minimize these shifts? Why? (See also question 11).

5. Analyze paragraphs 11 and 12 in terms of the non-explanatory aspects of the purpose.

6. Paragraphs 17–20 are a digression from the main line of development. How does Miss Carson mark them as a digression at beginning and end? What do these paragraphs contribute to the explanation proper? How are they made to contribute to the emotive aspect of the purpose? (Consider paragraph 17 particularly in this regard. Is there a possible allusion in the last sentence? What is its function? Consider also, in this connection, the function of the epigraph of the whole essay.)

7. Although the evolutionary stage when life emerges from the sea is not arrived at till paragraph 23, there are a number of references, beginning with paragraph 17, to the fact that life has *not* emerged. Find these references. What is the effect of this series of anticipations?

8. Why, in both the explanatory and emotive aspects of the purpose, do the paragraphs treating the two semi-land creatures (23 and 24) precede rather than follow paragraphs 25–26?

9. Why is the long and complicated evolutionary development of land animals given such exceedingly short treatment in paragraph 28?

10. What creatures does the "us" of paragraph 29 seem to embrace? What is the effect of this usage? What is the function of the whole paragraph in relation to the purpose?

11. The subject of this essay, we have said in our summary, is the evolutionary process which began with the creation of the sea and led to the emergence of man. Notice, however, that in the first paragraph Miss Carson merely hints at the full subject and says directly only that she is going to tell "the story of how the young planet Earth acquired an ocean." It is this failure to make the true subject clear which results in the apparent shifts in subject referred to in question 4. Is this "failure" a shortcoming on Miss Carson's part or does it have a clear function in relation to the purpose? Consider also in this regard the way paragraph 31 is developed. Why is man not referred to directly as man until the very last word of the paragraph? What is the effect, when it comes, of

the reference? What view of man are we forced to take, and what is our emotional reaction?

12. Paragraph 30, though relevant to the subject, in a way seems somewhat on the fringes of it. What is the function of the paragraph generally in relation to the purpose and specifically in relation to paragraph 33?

13. Which aspects of the purpose are the last two paragraphs designed to complete? What is the effect of referring to man in these last paragraphs only in the third person? How is the description in paragraph 33 brought into harmony with earlier descriptions in the essay and thereby made effective to the purpose?

Theme Topics

1. Explain some natural process in a scientifically valid way but, as Miss Carson does, so as to invest it with a particular emotive force for the reader.

2. Rewrite the first 9 paragraphs of Miss Carson's essay in such a way as to realize only the explanatory aspect of her purpose. Paragraphs 4 through 7 can be greatly abridged.

Hanson Baldwin

R.M.S. TITANIC

The white star liner *Titanic,* largest ship the world had ever known, sailed from Southampton on her maiden voyage to New York on April 10, 1912. The paint on her strakes was fair and bright; she was fresh from Harland and Wolff's Belfast yards, strong in the strength of her forty-six thousand tons of steel, bent, hammered, shaped and riveted through the three years of her slow birth.

There was little fuss and fanfare at her sailing; her sister ship, the *Olympic*—slightly smaller than the *Titanic*—had been in service for some months and to her had gone the thunder of the cheers.

But the *Titanic* needed no whistling steamers or shouting crowds to call attention to her superlative qualities. Her bulk dwarfed the ships near her as longshoremen singled up her mooring lines and cast off the turns of heavy rope from the dock bollards. She was not only the largest ship afloat, but was believed to be the safest. Carlisle, her builder, had given her double bottoms and had divided her hull into sixteen watertight compartments, which made her, men thought, unsinkable. She had been built to be and had been described as a gigantic lifeboat. Her designers' dreams of a triple-screw giant, a luxurious, floating hotel, which could speed to New York at twenty-three knots, had been carefully translated from blue prints and mold-loft lines at the Belfast yards into a living reality.

The *Titanic's* sailing from Southampton, though quiet, was not wholly uneventful. As the liner moved slowly toward the end of her dock that April day, the surge of her passing sucked away from the quay the steamer *New York,* moored just to seaward of the *Titanic's* berth. There were sharp cracks as the manila mooring lines of the

181

New York parted under the strain. The frayed ropes writhed and whistled through the air and snapped down among the waving crowd on the pier; the *New York* swung toward the *Titanic's* bow, was checked and dragged back to the dock barely in time to avert a collision. Seamen muttered, thought it an ominous start.

Past Spithead and the Isle of Wight the *Titanic* steamed. She called at Cherbourg at dusk and then laid her course for Queenstown. At 1:30 P.M. on Thursday, April 11, she stood out of Queenstown harbor, screaming gulls soaring in her wake, with 2,201 persons—men, women, and children—aboard.

Occupying the Empire bedrooms and Georgian suites of the first-class accommodations were many well-known men and women—Colonel John Jacob Astor and his young bride; Major Archibald Butt, military aide to President Taft, and his friend, Frank D. Millet, the painter; John B. Thayer, vice-president of the Pennsylvania Railroad, and Charles M. Hays, president of the Grand Trunk Railway of Canada; W. T. Stead, the English journalist; Jacques Futrelle, French novelist; H. B. Harris, theatrical manager, and Mrs. Harris; Mr. and Mrs. Isidor Straus; and J. Bruce Ismay, chairman and managing director of the White Star line.

Down in the plain wooden cabins of the steerage class were 706 immigrants to the land of promise, and trimly stowed in the great holds was a cargo valued at $420,000: oak beams, sponges, wine, calabashes, and an odd miscellany of the common and the rare.

The *Titanic* took her departure on Fastnet Light and, heading into the night, laid her course for New York. She was due at Quarantine the following Wednesday morning.

Sunday dawned fair and clear. The *Titanic* steamed smoothly toward the west, faint streamers of brownish smoke trailing from the funnels. The purser held services in the saloon in the morning; on the steerage deck aft the immigrants were playing games and a Scotsman was puffing "The Campbells Are Coming" on his bagpipes in the midst of the uproar.

At 9 A.M. a message from the steamer *Caronia* sputtered into the wireless shack:

CAPTAIN, TITANIC—WESTBOUND STEAMERS REPORT BERGS GROWLERS AND FIELD ICE IN 42 DEGREES N. FROM 49 DEGREES TO 51 DEGREES W. 12TH APRIL.

COMPLIMENTS—

BARR.

It was cold in the afternoon; the sun was brilliant, but the *Titanic*, her screws turning over at 75 revolutions per minute, was approaching the Banks.

In the Marconi cabin Second Operator Harold Bride, earphones clamped on his head, was figuring accounts; he did not stop to answer when he heard MWL, Continental Morse for the nearby Leyland liner, *Californian*, calling the *Titanic*. The *Californian* had some message about three icebergs; he didn't bother then to take it down. About 1:42 P.M. the rasping spark of those days spoke again across the water. It was the *Baltic*, calling the *Titanic*, warning her of ice on the steamer track. Bride took the message down and sent it up to the bridge. The officer-of-the-deck glanced at it; sent it to the bearded master of the *Titanic*, Captain E. C. Smith, a veteran of the White Star service. It was lunch time then; the Captain, walking along the promenade deck, saw Mr. Ismay, stopped, and handed him the message without comment. Ismay read it, stuffed it in his pocket, told two ladies about the icebergs, and resumed his walk. Later, about 7:15 P.M., the Captain requested the return of the message in order to post it in the chart room for the information of officers.

Dinner that night in the Jacobean dining room was gay. It was bitter on deck, but the night was calm and fine; the sky was moonless but studded with stars twinkling coldly in the clear air.

After dinner some of the second-class passengers gathered in the saloon, where the Reverend Mr. Carter conducted a "hymn sing-song." It was almost ten o'clock and the stewards were waiting with biscuits and coffee as the group sang:

> O, hear us when we cry to Thee
> For those in peril on the sea.

On the bridge Second Officer Lightoller—short, stocky, efficient— was relieved at ten o'clock by First Officer Murdock. Lightoller had talked with other officers about the proximity of ice; at least five wireless ice warnings had reached the ship; lookouts had been cautioned to be alert; captains and officers expected to reach the field at any time after 9:30 P.M. At twenty-two knots its speed unslackened, the *Titanic* plowed on through the night.

Lightoller left the darkened bridge to his relief and turned in. Captain Smith went to his cabin. The steerage was long since quiet; in the first and second cabins lights were going out; voices were growing still, people were asleep. Murdock paced back and forth on the bridge, peering out over the dark water, glancing now and then at the compass in front of Quartermaster Hichens at the wheel.

In the crow's-nest, Lookout Frederick Fleet and his partner, Leigh, gazed down at the water, still and unruffled in the dim, starlit darkness. Behind and below them the ship, a white shadow with here and there a last winking light; ahead of them a dark and silent and cold ocean.

There was a sudden clang. "Dong dong. Dong-dong. Dong-dong. Dong!" The metal clapper of the great ship's bell struck out 11:30. Mindful of the warnings, Fleet strained his eyes, searching the darkness for the dreaded ice. But there were only the stars and the sea.

In the wireless room, where Phillips, first operator, had relieved Bride, the buzz of the *Californian's* set again crackled into the earphones:

Californian: "Say, old man, we are stuck here, surrounded by ice."
Titanic: "Shut up, shut up; keep out. I am talking to Cape Race; you are jamming my signals."

Then, a few minutes later—about 11:40 . . .

Out of the dark she came, a vast, dim, white, monstrous shape, directly in the *Titanic's* path. For a moment Fleet doubted his eyes. But she was a deadly reality, this ghastly *thing*. Frantically, Fleet struck three bells—*something dead ahead*. He snatched the telephone and called the bridge:

"Iceberg! Right ahead!"

The First Officer heard but did not stop to acknowledge the message.

"Hard astarboard!"

Hichens strained at the wheel; the bow swung slowly to port. The monster was almost upon them now.

Murdock leaped to the engine-room telegraph. Bells clanged. Far below in the engine room those bells struck the first warning. Danger! The indicators on the dial faces swung round to "Stop!" Then "Full speed astern!" Frantically the engineers turned great valve wheels; answered the bridge bells. . . .

There was a slight shock, a brief scraping, a small list to port. Shell ice—slabs and chunks of it—fell on the foredeck. Slowly the *Titanic* stopped.

Captain Smith hurried out of his cabin.

"What has the ship struck?"

Murdock answered, "An iceberg, sir. I hard-astarboarded and reversed the engines, and I was going to hard-aport around it, but she was too close. I could not do any more. I have closed the watertight doors."

Fourth Officer Boxhall, other officers, the carpenter, came to the bridge. The Captain sent Boxhall and the carpenter below to ascertain the damage.

A few lights switched on in the first and second cabins; sleepy passengers peered through porthole glass; some casually asked the stewards:

"Why have we stopped?"

"I don't know, sir, but I don't suppose it is anything much."

In the smoking room a quorum of gamblers and their prey were still sitting round a poker table; the usual crowd of kibitzers looked on. They had felt the slight jar of the collision and had seen an eighty-foot ice mountain glide by the smoking-room windows, but the night was calm and clear, the *Titanic* was "unsinkable"; they hadn't bothered to go on deck.

But far below, in the warren of passages on the starboard side forward, in the forward holds and boiler rooms, men could see that the *Titanic's* hurt was mortal. In No. 6 boiler room, where the red glow from the furnaces lighted up the naked, sweaty chests of coal-blackened firemen, water was pouring through a great gash about two feet above the floor plates. This was no slow leak; the ship was open to the sea; in ten minutes there were eight feet of water in No. 6. Long before then the stokers had raked the flaming fires out of the furnaces and had scrambled through the watertight doors into No. 5 or had climbed up the long steel ladders to safety. When Boxhall looked at the mail room in No. 3 hold, twenty-four feet above the keel, the mailbags were already floating about in the slushing water. In No. 5 boiler room a stream of water spurted into an empty bunker. All six compartments forward of No. 4 were open to the sea; in ten seconds the iceberg's jagged claw had ripped a three-hundred-foot slash in the bottom of the great *Titanic*.

Reports came to the bridge; Ismay in dressing gown ran out on deck in the cold, still, starlit night, climbed up the bridge ladder.

"What has happened?"

Captain Smith: "We have struck ice."

"Do you think she is seriously damaged?"

Captain: "I'm afraid she is."

Ismay went below and passed Chief Engineer William Bell fresh from an inspection of the damaged compartments. Bell corroborated the Captain's statement; hurried back down the glistening steel ladders to his duty. Man after man followed him—Thomas Andrews, one of the ship's designers, Archie Frost, the builder's chief engineer, and his twenty assistants—men who had no posts of duty in the engine room but whose traditions called them there.

On deck, in corridor and stateroom, life flowed again. Men, women, and children awoke and questioned; orders were given to uncover the lifeboats; water rose into the firemen's quarters; half-dressed stokers steamed up on deck. But the passengers—most of them—did not know that the *Titanic* was sinking. The shock of the collision had been so slight that some were not awakened by it; the *Titanic* was so huge that she must be unsinkable; the night was too calm, too beautiful, to think of death at sea.

Captain Smith ran to the door of the radio shack. Bride, partly dressed, eyes dulled with sleep, was standing behind Phillips, waiting.

"Send the call for assistance."

The blue spark danced: "CQD—CQD—CQD—CQ—"

Miles away Marconi men heard. Cape Race heard it, and the steamships *La Provence* and *Mt. Temple.*

The sea was surging into the *Titanic's* hold. At 12:20 the water burst into the seamen's quarters through a collapsed fore-and-aft wooden bulkhead. Pumps strained in the engine rooms—men and machinery making a futile fight against the sea. Steadily the water rose.

The boats were swung out—slowly; for the deckhands were late in reaching their stations, there had been no boat drill, and many of the crew did not know to what boats they were assigned. Orders were shouted; the safety valves had lifted, and steam was blowing off in a great rushing roar. In the chart house Fourth Officer Boxhall bent above a chart, working rapidly with pencil and dividers.

12:15 A.M.   Boxhall's position is sent out to a fleet of vessels: "Come at once; we have struck a berg."

To the Cunarder *Carpathia* (Arthur Henry Rostron, Master, New York to Liverpool, fifty-eight miles away): "It's a CQD, old man. Position 41–46 N.; 50–14 W."

The blue spark dancing: "Sinking; cannot hear for noise of steam."

12:30 A.M.   The word is passed: "Women and children in the boats." Stewards finish waking their passengers below; life preservers are tied on; some men smile at the precaution. "The *Titanic* is unsinkable." The *Mt. Temple* starts for the *Titanic;* the *Carpathia,* with a double watch in her stokeholds, radios, "Coming hard." The CQD changes the course of many ships—but not of one; the operator of the *Californian,* near by, has just put down his earphones and turned in.

The CQD flashes over land and sea from Cape Race to New York; newspaper city rooms leap to life and presses whir.

On the *Titanic,* water creeps over the bulkhead between Nos. 5 and 6 firerooms. She is going down by the head; the engineers—fighting a losing battle—are forced back foot by foot by the rising water. Down the promenade deck, Happy Jock Hume, the bandsman, runs with his instrument.

12:45 A.M. Murdock, in charge on the starboard side, eyes tragic, but calm and cool, orders boat No. 7 lowered. The women hang back; they want no boat ride on an ice-strewn sea; the *Titanic* is unsinkable. The men encourage them, explain that this is just a precautionary measure: "We'll see you again at breakfast." There is little confusion; passengers stream slowly to the boat deck. In the steerage the immigrants chatter excitedly.

A sudden sharp hiss—a streaked flare against the night; Boxhall sends a rocket toward the sky. It explodes, and a parachute of white stars lights up the icy sea. "God! Rockets!" The band plays ragtime.

No. 8 is lowered, and No. 5. Ismay, still in dressing gown, calls for women and children, handles lines, stumbles in the way of an officer, is told to "get the hell out of here." Third Officer Pitman takes charge of No. 5; as he swings into the boat Murdock grasps his hand. "Good-by and good luck, old man."

No. 6 goes over the side. There are only twenty-eight people in a lifeboat with a capacity of sixty-five.

A light stabs from the bridge; Boxhall is calling in Morse flashes, again and again, to a strange ship stopped in the ice jam five to ten miles away. Another rocket drops its shower of sparks above the ice-strewn sea and the dying ship.

1:00 A.M. Slowly the water creeps higher; the fore ports of the *Titanic* are dipping into the sea. Rope squeaks through blocks; lifeboats drop jerkily seaward. Through the shouting on the decks comes the sound of the band playing ragtime.

The "Millionaires' Special" leaves the ship—boat No. 1, with a capacity of forty people, carries only Sir Cosmo and Lady Duff Gordon and ten others. Aft, the frightened immigrants mill and jostle and rush for a boat. An officer's fist flies out; three shots are fired into the air, and the panic is quelled. . . . Four Chinese sneak unseen into a boat and hide in its bottom.

1:20 A.M. Water is coming into No. 4 boiler room. Stokers slice and shovel as water laps about their ankles—steam for the dynamos, steam for the dancing spark! As the water rises, great ash hoes rake the flaming coals from the furnaces. Safety valves pop; the stokers retreat aft, and the watertight doors clang shut behind them.

The rockets fling their splendor toward the stars. The boats are more heavily loaded now, for the passengers know the *Titanic* is sinking. Women cling and sob. The great screws aft are rising clear of the sea. Half-filled boats are ordered to come alongside the cargo ports and take on more passengers, but the ports are never opened—and the boats are never filled. Others pull for the steamer's light miles away but never reach it; the light disappears, the unknown ship steams off.

The water rises and the band plays ragtime.

1:30 A.M. Lightoller is getting the port boats off; Murdock the starboard. As one boat is lowered into the sea a boat officer fires his gun alongside the ship's side to stop a rush from the lower decks. A woman tries to take her Great Dane into a boat with her; she is refused and steps out of the boat to die with her dog. Millet's "little smile which played on his lips all through the voyage" plays no more; his lips are grim, but he waves good-by and brings wraps for the women.

Benjamin Guggenheim, in evening clothes, smiles and says, "We've dressed up in our best and are prepared to go down like gentlemen."

1:40 A.M. Boat 14 is clear, and then 13, 16, 15, and C. The lights still shine, but the *Baltic* hears the blue spark say, "Engine room getting flooded."

The *Olympic* signals, "Am lighting up all possible boilers as fast as can."

Major Butt helps women into the last boats and waves good-by to them. Mrs. Straus puts her foot on the gunwale of a lifeboat, then she draws back and goes to her husband: "We have been together many years; where you go I will go." Colonel John Jacob Astor puts his young wife in a lifeboat, steps back, taps cigarette on fingernail: "Good-by, dearie; I'll join you later."

1:45 A.M. The foredeck is under water, the fo'c'sle head almost awash; the great stern is lifted high toward the bright stars; and still the band plays. Mr. and Mrs. Harris approach a lifeboat arm in arm.

Officer: "Ladies first, please."

Harris bows, smiles, steps back: "Of course, certainly; ladies first."

Boxhall fires the last rocket, then leaves in charge of boat No. 2.

2:00 A.M.   She is dying now; her bow goes deeper, her stern higher. But there must be steam. Below in the stokeholds the sweaty firemen keep steam up for the flaring lights and the dancing spark. The glowing coals slide and tumble over the slanted grate bars; the sea pounds behind that yielding bulkhead. But the spark dances on.

The *Asian* hears Phillips try the new signal—SOS.

Boat No. 4 has left now; boat D leaves ten minutes later. Jacques Futrelle clasps his wife: "For God's sake, go! It's your last chance; go!" Madame Futrelle is half forced into the boat. It clears the side.

There are about 660 people in the boats, and 1,500 still on the sinking *Titanic*.

On top of the officers' quarters men work frantically to get the two collapsibles stowed there over the side. Water is over the forward part of A deck now; it surges up the companionways toward the boat deck. In the radio shack, Bride has slipped a coat and lifejacket about Phillips as the first operator sits hunched over his key, sending—still sending— "41–46N.; 50–14 W. CQD—CQD—SOS—SOS—"

The Captain's tired white face appears at the radio-room door: "Men, you have done your full duty. You can do no more. Now, it's every man for himself." The Captain disappears—back to his sinking bridge, where Painter, his personal steward, stands quietly waiting for orders. The spark dances on. Bride turns his back and goes into the inner cabin. As he does so, a stoker, grimed with coal, mad with fear, steals into the shack and reaches for the lifejacket on Phillips' back. Bride wheels about and brains him with a wrench.

2:10 A.M.   Below decks the steam is still holding, though the pressure is falling—rapidly. In the gymnasium on the boat deck the athletic instructor watches quietly as two gentlemen ride the bicycles and another swings casually at the punching bag. Mail clerks stagger up the boat-deck stairways, dragging soaked mail sacks. The spark still dances. The band still plays—but not ragtime:

> Nearer my God to Thee,
> Nearer to Thee . . .

A few men take up the refrain; others kneel on the slanting decks to pray. Many run and scramble aft, where hundreds are clinging above the silent screws on the great uptilted stern. The spark still dances and the lights still flare; the engineers are on the job. The hymn comes to its close. Bandmaster Hartley, Yorkshireman violinist, taps his bow against a bulkhead, calls for "Autumn" as the water curls about his feet, and the eight musicians brace themselves against the ship's slant. People are leaping from the decks into the nearby water—the icy water. A woman cries, "Oh save me, save me!" A man answers, "Good lady, save yourself. Only God can save you now." The band plays "Autumn":

> God of Mercy and Compassion!
> Look with pity on my pain . . .

The water creeps over the bridge where the *Titanic's* master stands; heavily he steps out to meet it.

2:17 A.M.   "CQ—" The *Virginian* hears a ragged, blurred CQ, then an abrupt stop. The blue spark dances no more. The lights flicker out; the engineers have lost their battle.

2:18 A.M.   Men run about blackened decks; leap into the night; are swept into the sea by the curling wave which licks up the *Titanic's* length. Lightoller does not leave the ship; the ship leaves him; there are hundreds like him, but only a few who live to tell of it. The funnels still swim above the water, but the ship is climbing to the perpendicular; the bridge is under and most of the foremast; the great stern rises like a squat leviathan. Men swim away from the sinking ship; others drop from the stern.

The band plays in the darkness, the water lapping upwards;

> Hold me up in mighty waters,
> Keep my eyes on things above,
> Righteousness, divine atonement,
> Peace and everlas . . .

The forward funnel snaps and crashes into the sea; its steel tons hammer out of existence swimmers struggling in the freezing water. Streams of sparks, of smoke and steam, burst from the after funnels. The ship upends to fifty—to sixty degrees.

Down in the black abyss of the stokeholds, of the engine rooms, where the dynamos have whirred at long last to a stop, the stokers and the engineers are reeling against hot metal, the rising water clutching at their knees. The boilers, the engine cylinders, rip from their bed plates; crash through bulkheads; rumble—steel against steel.

The *Titanic* stands on end, poised briefly for the plunge. Slowly she slides to her grave—slowly at first, and then more quickly—quickly—quickly.

2:20 A.M. The greatest ship in the world has sunk. From the calm, dark waters, where the floating lifeboats move, there goes up, in the white wake of her passing, "one long continuous moan."

The boats that the *Titanic* had launched pulled safely away from the slight suction of the sinking ship, pulled away from the screams that came from the lips of the freezing men and women in the water. The boats were poorly manned and badly equipped, and they had been unevenly loaded. Some carried so few seamen that women bent to the oars. Mrs. Astor tugged at an oar handle; the Countess of Rothes took a tiller. Shivering stokers in sweaty, coal-blackened singlets and light trousers steered in some boats; stewards in white coats rowed in others. Ismay was in the last boat that left the ship from the starboard side; with Mr. Carter of Philadelphia and two seamen he tugged at the oars. In one of the lifeboats an Italian with a broken wrist—disguised in a woman's shawl and hat—huddled on the floor boards, ashamed now that fear had left him. In another rode the only baggage saved from the *Titanic*—the carry-all of Samuel L. Goldenberg, one of the rescued passengers.

There were only a few boats that were heavily loaded; most of those that were half empty made but perfunctory efforts to pick up the moaning swimmers, their officers and crew fearing that they would endanger the living if they pulled back into the midst of the dying. Some boats beat off the freezing victims; fear-crazed men and women struck with oars at the heads of swimmers. One woman drove her fist into the face of a half-dead man as he tried feebly to climb over the gunwale. Two other women helped him in and stanched the flow of blood from the ring cuts on his face.

One of the collapsible boats, which had floated off the top of the officers' quarters when the *Titanic* sank, was an icy haven for thirty or forty men. The boat had capsized as the ship sank; men swam to it, clung to it, climbed upon its slippery bottom, stood knee-deep in water in the freezing air. Chunks of ice swirled about their legs; their soaked clothing clutched their bodies in icy folds. Colonel Archibald Gracie was cast up there, Gracie who had leaped from the stern as the *Titanic* sank; young Thayer who had seen his father die; Lightoller who had twice been sucked down with the ship and twice blown to the surface by a belch of air; Bride, the second operator, and Phillips, the first. There were many stokers, half-naked; it was a shivering company. They stood there in the icy sea, under the far stars, and sang and prayed—the Lord's Prayer. After a while a lifeboat came and picked them off, but Phillips was dead then or died soon afterward in the boat.

Only a few of the boats had lights; only one—No. 2—had a light that was of any use to the *Carpathia* twisting through the ice field to the rescue. Other ships were "coming hard" too; one, the *Californian*, was still dead to opportunity.

The blue sparks still danced, but not the *Titanic's*. *La Provence* to *Celtic*: "Nobody has heard the *Titanic* for about two hours."

It was 2:40 when the *Carpathia* first sighted the green light from No. 2 boat; it was 4:10 when she picked up the first boat and learned that the *Titanic* had foundered. The last of the moaning cries had just died away then.

Captain Rostron took the survivors aboard, boatload by boatload. He was ready for them, but only a small minority of them required much medical attention. Bride's feet were twisted and frozen; others were suffering from exposure; one died, and seven were dead when taken from the boats, and were buried at sea.

It was then that the fleet of racing ships learned they were too late; the *Parisian* heard the weak signals of MPA, the *Carpathia*, report the death of the *Titanic*. It was then—or soon afterward, when her radio operator put on his earphones—that the *Californian*, the ship that had been within sight as the *Titanic* was sinking, first learned of the disaster.

And it was then, in all its white-green majesty, that the *Titanic's* survivors saw the iceberg, tinted with the sunrise, floating idly, pack ice jammed about its base, other bergs heaving slowly near by on the blue breast of the sea.

Frederick Lewis Allen

CRASH!

I

*E*ARLY IN September the stock market broke. It quickly recovered, however; indeed, on September 19th the averages as compiled by the *New York Times* reached an even higher level than that of September 3rd. Once more it slipped, farther and faster, until by October 4th the prices of a good many stocks had coasted to what seemed first-class bargain levels. Steel, for example, after having touched 261¾ a few weeks earlier, had dropped as low as 204; American Can, at the closing on October 4th, was nearly twenty points below its high for the year; General Electric was over fifty points below its high; Radio had gone down from 114¾ to 82½.

A bad break, to be sure, but there had been other bad breaks, and the speculators who escaped unscathed proceeded to take advantage of the lesson they had learned in June and December of 1928 and March and May of 1929: when there was a break it was a good time to buy. In the face of all this tremendous liquidation, brokers' loans as compiled by the Federal Reserve Bank of New York mounted to a new high record on October 2nd, reaching $6,804,000,000—a sure sign that margin buyers were not deserting the market but coming into it in numbers at least undiminished. (Part of the increase in the loan figure was probably due to the piling up of unsold securities in dealers' hands, as the spawning of investment trusts and the issue of new common stock by every manner of business concern continued unabated.) History, it seemed, was about to repeat itself, and those who picked up Anaconda at 109¾ or American Telephone at 281 would count themselves wise investors. And sure enough, prices once more began to climb. They had already turned

193

upward before that Sunday in early October when Ramsay MacDonald sat on a log with Herbert Hoover at the Rapidan camp and talked over the prospects for naval limitation and peace.

Something was wrong, however. The decline began once more. The wiseacres of Wall Street, looking about for causes, fixed upon the collapse of the Hatry financial group in England (which had led to much forced selling among foreign investors and speculators), and upon the bold refusal of the Massachusetts Department of Public Utilities to allow the Edison Company of Boston to split up its stock. They pointed, too, to the fact that the steel industry was undoubtedly slipping, and to the accumulation of "undigested" securities. But there was little real alarm until the week of October 21st. The consensus of opinion, in the meantime, was merely that the equinoctial storm of September had not quite blown over. The market was readjusting itself into a "more secure technical position."

II

In view of what was about to happen, it is enlightening to recall how things looked at this juncture to the financial prophets, those gentlemen whose wizardly reputations were based upon their supposed ability to examine a set of graphs brought to them by a statistician and discover, from the relation of curve to curve and index to index, whether things were going to get better or worse. Their opinions differed, of course; there never has been a moment when the best financial opinion was unanimous. In examining these opinions, and the outgivings of eminent bankers, it must furthermore be acknowledged that a bullish statement cannot always be taken at its face value: few men like to assume the responsibility of spreading alarm by making dire predictions, nor is a banker with unsold securities on his hands likely to say anything which will make it more difficult to dispose of them, unquiet as his private mind may be. Finally, one must admit that prophecy is at best the most hazardous of occupations. Nevertheless, the general state of financial opinion in October, 1929, makes an instructive contrast with that in February and March, 1928, when, as we have seen, the skies had not appeared any too bright.

Some forecasters, to be sure, were so unconventional as to counsel caution. Roger W. Babson, an investment adviser who had not always been highly regarded in the inner circles of Wall Street, especially since he had for a long time been warning his clients of future trouble, predicted early in September a decline of sixty or eighty points in the averages. On October 7th the Standard Trade and Securities Service of the Standard Statistics Company advised its clients to pursue an "ultra-conservative policy," and ventured this prediction: "We remain of the opinion that, over the next few months, the trend of common-stock prices will be toward lower levels." Poor's *Weekly Business and Investment Letter* spoke its mind on the "great common-stock delusion" and predicted "further liquidation in stocks." Among the big bankers, Paul M. Warburg had shown months before this that he was alive to the dangers of the situation. These commentators—along with others such as the editor of the *Commercial and Financial Chronicle* and the financial editor of the *New York Times*—would appear to deserve the 1929 gold medal for foresight.

But if ever such medals were actually awarded, a goodly number of leather ones would have to be distributed at the same time. Not necessarily to the Harvard Economic Society, although on October 19th, after having explained that business was "facing another period of readjustment," it predicted that "if recession should threaten serious consequences for business (as is not indicated at present) there is little doubt that the Reserve System would take steps to ease the money market and so check the movement." The Harvard soothsayers proved themselves quite fallible: as late as October 26th, after the first wide-open crack in the stock market, they delivered the cheerful judgment that "despite its severity, we believe that the slump in stock prices will prove an intermediate movement and not the precursor of a business depression such as would entail prolonged further liquidation." This judgment turned out, of course, to be ludicrously wrong; but on the other hand the Harvard Economic Society was far from being really bullish. Nor would Colonel Leonard P. Ayres of the Cleveland Trust Company get one of the leather medals. He almost qualified when, on October 15th, he delivered himself of the judgment that "there does not seem to be as yet much real evidence that the decline in stock prices is likely to forecast a serious recession in general business. Despite the slowing down in iron and steel production, in automobile output, and in building, the conditions which result in serious business depressions are not present." But the skies, as Colonel Ayres saw them, were at least partly cloudy. "It seems probable," he said, "that stocks have been passing not so much from the strong to the weak as from the smart to the dumb."

Professor Irving Fisher, however, was more optimistic. In the newspapers of October 17th he was reported as telling the Purchasing Agents

Association that stock prices had reached "what looks like a permanent high plateau." He expected to see the stock market, within a few months, "a good deal higher than it is today." On the very eve of the panic of October 24th he was further quoted as expecting a recovery in prices. Only two days before the panic, the *Boston News Bureau* quoted R. W. McNeel, director of McNeel's Financial Service, as suspecting "that some pretty intelligent people are now buying stocks." "Unless we are to have a panic—which no one seriously believes—stocks have hit bottom," said Mr. McNeel. And as for Charles E. Mitchell, chairman of the great National City Bank of New York, he continuously and enthusiastically radiated sunshine. Early in October Mr. Mitchell was positive that, despite the stock-market break, "The industrial situation of the United States is absolutely sound and our credit situation is in no way critical. . . . The interest given by the public to brokers' loans is always exaggerated," he added. "Altogether too much attention is paid to it." A few days later Mr. Mitchell spoke again: "Although in some cases speculation has gone too far in the United States, the markets generally are now in a healthy condition. The last six weeks have done an immense amount of good by shaking down prices. . . . The market values have a sound basis in the general prosperity of our country." Finally, on October 22nd, two days before the panic, he arrived in the United States from a short trip to Europe with these reassuring words: "I know of nothing fundamentally wrong with the stock market or with the underlying business and credit structure. . . . The public is suffering from 'brokers' loanitis.' "

Nor was Mr. Mitchell by any means alone in his opinions. To tell the truth, the chief difference between him and the rest of the financial community was that he made more noise. One of the most distinguished bankers in the United States, in closing a deal in the early autumn of 1929, said privately that he saw not a cloud in the sky. Habitual bulls like Arthur Cutten were, of course, insisting that they were "still bullish." And the general run of traders presumbaly endorsed the view attributed to "one large house" in mid-October in the *Boston News Bureau's* "Broad Street Gossip," that "the recent break makes a firm foundation for a big bull market in the last quarter of the year." There is no doubt that a great many speculators who had looked upon the midsummer prices as too high were now deciding that deflation had been effected and were buying again. Presumably most financial opinion agreed also with the further statement which appeared in the "Broad Street Gossip" column on October 16th, that "business is now too big and diversified, and the country too rich, to be influenced by stock-market fluctuations"; and with the editorial opinion of the *News Bureau,* on October 19th, that "whatever recessions (in business) are noted, are those of the runner catching his breath. . . . The general condition is satisfactory and fundamentally sound."

The disaster which was impending was destined to be as bewildering and frightening to the rich and the powerful and the customarily sagacious as to the foolish and unwary holder of fifty shares of margin stock.

III

The expected recovery in the stock market did not come. It seemed to be beginning on Tuesday, October 22nd, but the gains made during the day were largely lost during the last hour. And on Wednesday, the 23rd, there was a perfect Niagara of liquidation. The volume of trading was over six million shares, the tape was 104 minutes late when the three-o'clock gong ended trading for the day, and the *New York Times* averages for fifty leading railroad and industrial stocks lost 18.24 points—a loss which made the most abrupt declines in previous breaks look small. Everybody realized that an unprecedented number of margin calls must be on their way to insecurely margined traders, and that the situation at last was getting serious. But perhaps the turn would come tomorrow. Already the break had carried prices down a good deal farther than the previous breaks of the past two years. Surely it could not go on much longer.

The next day was Thursday, October 24th.

On that momentous day stocks opened moderately steady in price, but in enormous volume. Kennecott appeared on the tape in a block of 20,000 shares. General Motors in another of the same amount. Almost at once the ticker tape began to lag behind the trading on the floor. The pressure of selling orders was disconcertingly heavy. Prices were going down. . . . Presently they were going down with some rapidity. . . . Before the first hour of trading was over, it was already apparent that they were going down with an altogether unprecedented and amazing violence. In brokers' offices all over the country, tape-watchers looked at one another in astonishment and perplexity. Where on earth was this torrent of selling orders coming from?

The exact answer to this question will probably never be known. But it seems probable that the principal cause of the break in prices during that first hour on October 24th was not fear. Nor was it short selling.

It was forced selling. It was the dumping on the market of hundreds of thousands of shares of stock held in the name of miserable traders whose margins were exhausted or about to be exhausted. The gigantic edifice of prices was honeycombed with speculative credit and was now breaking under its own weight.

Fear, however, did not long delay its coming. As the price structure crumbled there was a sudden stampede to get out from under. By eleven o'clock traders on the floor of the Stock Exchange were in a wild scramble to "sell at the market." Long before the lagging ticker could tell what was happening, word had gone out by telephone and telegraph that the bottom was dropping out of things, and the selling orders redoubled in volume. The leading stocks were going down two, three, and even five points between sales. Down, down, down. . . . Where were the bargain-hunters who were supposed to come to the rescue at times like this? Where were the investment trusts, which were expected to provide a cushion for the market by making new purchases at low prices? Where were the big operators who had declared that they were still bullish? Where were the powerful bankers who were supposed to be able at any moment to support prices? There seemed to be no support whatever. Down, down, down. The roar of voices which rose from the floor of the Exchange had become a roar of panic.

United States Steel had opened at 205½. It crashed through 200 and presently was at 193½. General Electric, which only a few weeks before had been selling above 400, had opened this morning at 315—now it had slid to 283. Things were even worse with Radio: opening at 68¾, it had gone dismally down through the sixties and the fifties and forties to the abysmal price of 44½. And as for Montgomery Ward, vehicle of the hopes of thousands who saw the chain store as the harbinger of the new economic era, it had dropped headlong from 83 to 50. In the space of two short hours, dozens of stocks lost ground which it had required many months of the bull market to gain.

Even this sudden decline in values might not have been utterly ter-rifying if people could have known precisely what was happening at any moment. It is the unknown which causes real panic.

Suppose a man walked into a broker's branch office between twelve and one o'clock on October 24th to see how things were faring. First he glanced at the big board, covering one wall of the room, on which the day's prices for the leading stocks were supposed to be recorded. The LOW and LAST figures written there took his breath away, but soon he was aware that they were unreliable: even with the wildest scrambling, the boys who slapped into place the cards which recorded the last prices shown on the ticker could not keep up with the changes: they were too numerous and abrupt. He turned to the shining screen across which ran an uninterrupted procession of figures from the ticker. Ordinarily the practiced tape-watcher could tell from a moment's glance at the screen how things were faring, even though the Exchange now omitted all but the final digit of each quotation. A glance at the Board, if not his own memory, supplied the missing digits. But today, when he saw a run of symbols and figures like

$$R \qquad\qquad WX$$
$$6.5\tfrac{1}{2}.5.4 \qquad\qquad 9.8\tfrac{7}{8}\tfrac{3}{4}\tfrac{1}{2}\tfrac{1}{4}.8.7\tfrac{1}{2}.7.$$

he could not be sure whether the price of "6" shown for Radio meant 66 or 56 or 46; whether Westinghouse was sliding from 189 to 187 or from 179 to 177. And presently he heard that the ticker was an hour and a half late; at one o'clock it was recording the prices of half-past eleven! All this that he saw was ancient history. What was happening on the floor now?

At ten-minute intervals the bond ticker over in the corner would hammer off a list of selected prices direct from the floor, and a brokers' clerk would grab the uncoiling sheet of paper and shear it off with a pair of scissors and read the figures aloud in a mumbling expressionless monotone to the white-faced men who occupied every seat on the floor and stood packed at the rear of the room. The prices which he read out were *ten or a dozen or more points below those recorded on the ticker.* What about the stocks not included in that select list? There was no way of finding out. The telephone lines were clogged as inquiries and orders from all over the country converged upon the Stock Exchange. Once in a while a voice would come barking out of the broker's rear office where a frantic clerk was struggling for a telephone connection: "Steel at ninety-six!" Small comfort, however, to know what Steel was doing; the men outside were desperately involved in many another stock than Steel; they were almost completely in the dark, and their imaginations had free play. If they put in an order to buy or to sell, it was impossible to find out what became of it. The Exchange's whole system for the recording of current prices and for communicating orders was hopelessly unable to cope with the emergency, and the sequel was an epidemic of fright.

In that broker's office, as in hundreds of other offices from one end of the land to the other, one saw men looking defeat in the face. One of them was slowly walking up and down, mechanically tearing a piece of paper into tiny and still tinier fragments. Another was grinning shame-facedly, as a small boy giggles at a funeral. Another was abjectly beseech-ing a clerk for the latest news of American & Foreign Power. And still another was sitting motionless, as if stunned, his eyes fixed blindly upon the moving figures on the screen, those innocent-looking figures that meant the smash-up of the hopes of years. . . .

GL.	AWW.	JMP.
8.7.5.2.1.90.89.7.6.	3.2½.2.	6.5.3.2½.

A few minutes after noon, some of the more alert members of a crowd which had collected on the street outside the Stock Exchange, expecting they knew not what, recognized Charles E. Mitchell, erstwhile defender of the bull market, slipping quietly into the offices of J. P. Morgan & Company on the opposite corner. It was scarcely more than nine years since the House of Morgan had been pitted with the shrapnel-fire of the Wall Street explosion; now its occupants faced a different sort of calamity equally near at hand. Mr. Mitchell was followed shortly by Albert H. Wiggin, head of the Chase National Bank; William Potter, head of the Guaranty Trust Company; and Seward Prosser, head of the Bankers Trust Company. They had come to confer with Thomas W. Lamont of the Morgan firm. In the space of a few minutes these five men, with George F. Baker, Jr., of the First National Bank, agreed in behalf of their respective institutions to put up forty millions apiece to shore up the stock market. The object of the two-hundred-and-forty-million-dollar pool thus formed, as explained subsequently by Mr. Lamont, was not to hold prices at any given level, but simply to make such purchases as were necessary to keep trading on an orderly basis. Their first action, they decided, would be to try to steady the prices for the leading securities which served as bellwethers for the list as a whole. It was a dangerous plan, for with hysteria spreading there was no telling what sort of *débâcle* might be impending. But this was no time for any action but the boldest.

The bankers separated. Mr. Lamont faced a gathering of reporters in the Morgan offices. His face was grave, but his words were soothing. His first sentence alone was one of the most remarkable understatements of all time. "There has been a little distress selling on the Stock Exchange," said he, "and we have held a meeting of the heads of several financial insti-tutions to discuss the situation. We have found that there are no houses in difficulty and reports from brokers indicate that margins are being maintained satisfactorily." He went on to explain that what had happened was due to a "technical condition of the market" rather than to any fundamental cause.

As the news that the bankers were meeting circulated on the floor of the Exchange, prices began to steady. Soon a brisk rally set in. Steel jumped back to the level at which it had opened that morning. But the bankers had more to offer the dying bull market than a Morgan partner's best bedside manner.

At about half-past one o'clock Richard Whitney, vice-president of the Exchange, who usually acted as floor broker for the Morgan interests, went into the "Steel crowd" and put in a bid of 205—the price of the last previous sale—for 10,000 shares of Steel. He bought only 200 shares and left the remainder of the order with the specialist. Mr. Whitney then went to various other points on the floor, and offered the price of the last previous sale for 10,000 shares of each of fifteen or twenty other stocks, reporting what was sold to him at that price and leaving the remainder of the order with the specialist. In short, within the space of a few minutes Mr. Whitney offered to purchase something in the neighborhood of twenty of thirty million dollars' worth of stock. Purchases of this magnitude are not undertaken by Tom, Dick, and Harry; it was clear that Mr. Whitney represented the bankers' pool.

The desperate remedy worked. The semblance of confidence returned. Prices held steady for a while; and though many of them slid off once more in the final hour, the net results for the day might well have been worse. Steel actually closed two points higher than on Wednesday, and the net losses of most of the other leading securities amounted to less than ten points apiece for the whole day's trading.

All the same, it had been a frightful day. At seven o'clock that night the tickers in a thousand brokers' offices were still chattering; not till after 7:08 did they finally record the last sale made on the floor at three o'clock. The volume of trading had set a new record—12,894,650 shares. ("The time may come when we shall see a five-million-share day," the wise men of the Street had been saying twenty months before!) Incredible rumors had spread wildly during the early afternoon—that eleven speculators had committed suicide, that the Buffalo and Chicago exchanges had been closed, that troops were guarding the New York Stock Exchange against an angry mob. The country had known the bitter taste of panic. And although the bankers' pool had prevented for the moment an utter collapse, there was no gainsaying the fact that the economic structure had cracked wide open.

IV

Things looked somewhat better on Friday and Saturday. Trading was still on an enormous scale, but prices for the most part held. At the very moment when the bankers' pool was cautiously disposing of as much as possible of the stock which it had accumulated on Thursday and was thus preparing for future emergencies, traders who had sold out higher up were coming back into the market again with new purchases, in the hope that the bottom had been reached. (Hadn't they often been told that "the time to buy is when things look blackest"?) The newspapers carried a very pretty series of reassuring statements from the occupants of the seats of the mighty; Herbert Hoover himself, in a White House statement, pointed out that "the fundamental business of the country, that is, production and distribution of commodities, is on a sound and prosperous basis." But toward the close of Saturday's session prices began to slip again. And on Monday the rout was under way once more.

The losses registered on Monday were terrific—17½ points for Steel, 47½ for General Electric, 36 for Allied Chemical, 34½ for Westinghouse, and so on down a long and dismal list. All Saturday afternoon and Saturday night and Sunday the brokers had been struggling to post their records and go over their customers' accounts and send out calls for further margin, and another avalanche of forced selling resulted. The prices at which Mr. Whitney's purchases had steadied the leading stocks on Thursday were so readily broken through that it was immediately clear that the bankers' pool had made a strategic retreat. As a matter of fact, the brokers who represented the pool were having their hands full plugging up the "air-holes" in the list—in other words, buying stocks which were offered for sale without any bids at all in sight. Nothing more than this could have been accomplished, even if it could have been wisely attempted. Even six great banks could hardly stem the flow of liquidation from the entire United States. They could only guide it a little, check it momentarily here and there.

Once more the ticker dropped ridiculously far behind, the lights in the brokers' offices and the banks burned till dawn, and the telegraph companies distributed thousands of margin calls and requests for more collateral to back up loans at the banks. Bankers, brokers, clerks, messengers were almost at the end of their strength; for days and nights they had been driving themselves to keep pace with the most terrific volume of business that had ever descended upon them. It did not seem as if they could stand it much longer. But the worst was still ahead. It came the next day, Tuesday, October 29th.

The big gong had hardly sounded in the great hall of the Exchange at ten o'clock Tuesday morning before the storm broke in full force. Huge blocks of stock were thrown upon the market for what they would bring. Five thousand shares, ten thousand shares appeared at a time on the laboring ticker at fearful recessions in price. Not only were innumerable small traders being sold out, but big ones, too, protagonists of the new economic era who a few weeks before had counted themselves millionaires. Again and again the specialist in a stock would find himself surrounded by brokers fighting to sell—and nobody at all even thinking of buying. To give one single example: during the bull market the common stock of the White Sewing Machine Company had gone as high as 48; on Monday, October 28th, it had closed at 11⅛. On that black Tuesday, somebody—a clever messenger boy for the Exchange, it was rumored —had the bright idea of putting in an order to buy at 1—and in the temporarily complete absence of other bids he actually got his stock for a dollar a share! The scene on the floor was chaotic. Despite the jamming of the communication system, orders to buy and sell—mostly to sell— came in faster than human beings could possibly handle them; it was on that day that an exhausted broker, at the close of the session, found a large waste-basket which he had stuffed with orders to be executed and had carefully set aside for safe-keeping—and then had completely forgotten. Within half an hour of the opening the volume of trading had passed three million shares, by twelve o'clock it had passed eight million, by half-past one it had passed twelve million, and when the closing gong brought the day's madness to an end the gigantic record of 16,410,030 shares had been set. Toward the close there was a rally, but by that time the average prices of fifty leading stocks, as compiled by the *New York Times,* had fallen nearly forty points. Meanwhile there was a near-panic in other markets—the foreign stock exchanges, the lesser American exchanges, the grain market.

So complete was the demoralization of the stock market and so exhausted were the brokers and their staffs and the Stock Exchange employees, that at noon that day, when the panic was at its worst, the Governing Committee met quietly to decide whether or not to close the Exchange. To quote from an address made some months later by Richard Whitney: "In order not to give occasion for alarming rumors, this meeting was not held in the Governing Committee Room, but in the office of the president of the Stock Clearing Corporation directly beneath the Stock Exchange floor. . . . The forty governors came to the meeting in groups of two and three as unobtrusively as possible. The office they met in was never designed for large meetings of this sort, with the result that most of the governors were compelled to stand, or to sit on tables. As the meeting progressed, panic was raging overhead on the floor. . . . The feeling of those present was revealed by their habit of continually lighting cigarettes, taking a puff or two, putting them out and lighting new ones— a practice which soon made the narrow room blue with smoke. . . ." Two of the Morgan partners were invited to the meeting and, attempting to slip into the building unnoticed so as not to start a new flock of rumors, were refused admittance by one of the guards and had to remain outside until rescued by a member of the Governing Committee. After some deliberation, the governors finally decided not to close the Exchange.

It was a critical day for the banks, that Tuesday the 29th. Many of the corporations which had so cheerfully loaned money to brokers through the banks in order to obtain interest at 8 or 9 per cent were now clamoring to have these loans called—and the banks were faced with a choice between taking over the loans themselves and running the risk of precipitating further ruin. It was no laughing matter to assume the responsibility of millions of dollars' worth of loans secured by collateral which by the end of the day might prove to have dropped to a fraction of its former value. That the call money rate never rose above 6 per cent that day, that a money panic was not added to the stock panic, and that several Wall Street institutions did not go down into immediate bankruptcy, was due largely to the nerve shown by a few bankers in stepping into the breach. The story is told of one banker who went grimly on authorizing the taking over of loan after loan until one of his subordinate officers came in with a white face and told him that the bank was insolvent. "I dare say," said the banker, and went ahead unmoved. He knew that if he did not, more than one concern would face insolvency.

The next day—Wednesday, October 30th—the outlook suddenly and providentially brightened. The directors of the Steel Corporation had declared an extra dividend; the directors of the American Can Company had not only declared an extra dividend, but had raised the regular dividend. There was another flood of reassuring statements—though by this time a cheerful statement from a financier fell upon somewhat skeptical ears. Julius Klein, Mr. Hoover's Assistant Secretary of Commerce, composed a rhapsody on continued prosperity. John J. Raskob declared that stocks were at bargain prices and that he and his friends were buying. John D. Rockefeller poured Standard Oil upon the waters: "Believing that fundamental conditions of the country are sound and that there is nothing in the business situation to warrant the destruction of values that has taken place on the exchanges during the past week, my son and I have for some days been purchasing sound common stocks." Better still, prices rose—steadily and buoyantly. Now at last the time had come when the strain on the Exchange could be relieved without causing undue alarm. At 1:40 o'clock Vice-President Whitney announced from the rostrum that the Exchange would not open until noon the following day and would remain closed all day Friday and Saturday—and to his immense relief the announcement was greeted, not with renewed panic, but with a cheer.

Throughout Thursday's short session the recovery continued. Prices gyrated wildly—for who could arrive at a reasonable idea of what a given stock was worth, now that all settled standards of value had been upset?—but the worst of the storm seemed to have blown over. The financial community breathed more easily; now they could have a chance to set their houses in order.

It was true that the worst of the panic was past. But not the worst prices. There was too much forced liquidation still to come as brokers' accounts were gradually straightened out, as banks called for more collateral, and terror was renewed. The next week, in a series of short sessions, the tide of prices receded once more—until at last on November 13th the bottom prices for the year 1929 were reached. Beside the figures hung up in the sunny days of September they made a tragic showing:

	High price Sept. 3, 1929	Low price Nov. 13, 1929
American Can	181⅞	86
American Telephone & Telegraph	304	197¼
Anaconda Copper	131½	70
General Electric	396¼	168⅛
General Motors	72¾	36
Montgomery Ward	137⅞	49¼
New York Central	256⅜	160
Radio	101	28
Union Carbide & Carbon	137⅞	59
United States Steel	261¾	150
Westinghouse E & M	289⅞	102⅝
Woolworth	100⅜	52¼
Electric Bond & Share	186¾	50¼

The *New York Times* averages for fifty leading stocks had been almost cut in half, falling from a high of 311.90 in September to a low of

164.43 on November 13th; and the *Times* averages for twenty-five leading industrials had fared still worse, diving from 469.49 to 220.95.

The Big Bull Market was dead. Billions of dollars' worth of profits—and paper profits—had disappeared. The grocer, the window-cleaner, and the seamstress had lost their capital. In every town there were families which had suddenly dropped from showy affluence into debt. Investors who had dreamed of retiring to live on their fortunes now found themselves back once more at the very beginning of the long road to riches. Day by day the newspapers printed the grim reports of suicides.

Coolidge-Hoover Prosperity was not yet dead, but it was dying. Under the impact of the shock of panic, a multitude of ills which hitherto had passed unnoticed or had been offset by stock-market optimism began to beset the body economic, as poisons seep through the human system when a vital organ has ceased to function normally. Although the liquidation of nearly three billion dollars of brokers' loans contracted credit, and the Reserve Banks lowered the rediscount rate, and the way in which the larger banks and corporations of the country had survived the emergency without a single failure of large proportions offered real encouragement, nevertheless the poisons were there: overproduction of capital; overambitious expansion of business concerns; overproduction of commodities under the stimulus of installment buying and buying with stock-market profits; the maintenance of an artificial price level for many commodities; the depressed condition of European trade. No matter how many soothsayers of high finance proclaimed that all was well, no matter how earnestly the President set to work to repair the damage with soft words and White House conferences, a major depression was inevitably under way.

Nor was that all. Prosperity is more than an economic condition; it is a state of mind. The Big Bull Market had been more than the climax of a business cycle; it had been the climax of a cycle in American mass thinking and mass emotion. There was hardly a man or woman in the country whose attitude toward life had not been affected by it in some degree and was not now affected by the sudden and brutal shattering of hope. With the Big Bull Market gone and prosperity going, Americans were soon to find themselves living in an altered world which called for new adjustments, new ideas, new habits of thought, and a new order of values. The psychological climate was changing; the ever-shifting currents of American life were turning into new channels.

The Post-war Decade had come to its close. An era had ended.

NARRATIVE AND CHARACTER: CONTRASTING PURPOSES

Guided Discussions

GEORGE ORWELL, *A Hanging*
HAROLD NICOLSON, *The Man Who Knew Everybody*
JAMES BOSWELL, *The Wilkes Episode*

For Further Analysis

MAX BEERBOHM, *Something Defeasible*
SAMUEL CLEMENS, *The Boys' Ambition*
ALISTAIR COOKE, *Joe Louis*

George Orwell

A HANGING

*I*T WAS in Burma, a sodden morning of the rains. A sickly light, like yellow tinfoil, was slanting over the high walls into the jail yard. We were waiting outside the condemned cells, a row of sheds fronted with double bars, like small animal cages. Each cell measured about ten feet by ten and was quite bare within except for a plank bed and a pot for drinking water. In some of them brown, silent men were squatting at the inner bars, with their blankets draped round them. These were the condemned men, due to be hanged within the next week or two.

2   One prisoner had been brought out of his cell. He was a Hindu, a puny wisp of a man, with a shaven head and vague liquid eyes. He had a thick, sprouting moustache, absurdly too big for his body, rather like the moustache of a comic man on the films. Six tall Indian warders were guarding him and getting him ready for the gallows. Two of them stood by with rifles and fixed bayonets, while the others handcuffed him, passed a chain through his handcuffs and fixed it to their belts, and lashed his arms tight to his sides. They crowded very close about him, with their hands always on him in a careful, caressing grip, as though all the while feeling him to make sure he was there. It was like men handling a fish which is still alive and may jump back into the water. But he stood quite unresisting, yielding his arms limply to the ropes, as though he hardly noticed what was happening.

3   Eight o'clock struck and a bugle call, desolately thin in the wet air, floated from the distant barracks. The superintendent of the jail, who was standing apart from the rest of us, moodily prodding the

gravel with his stick, raised his head at the sound. He was an army doctor, with grey toothbrush moustache and a gruff voice. "For God's sake hurry up, Francis," he said irritably. "The man ought to have been dead by this time. Aren't you ready yet?"

4   Francis, the head jailer, a fat Dravidian in a white drill suit and gold spectacles, waved his black hand. "Yes sir, yes sir," he bubbled. "All iss satisfactorily prepared. The hangman iss waiting. We shall proceed."

5   "Well, quick march, then. The prisoners can't get their breakfast till this job's over."

6   We set out for the gallows. Two warders marched on either side of the prisoner, with their rifles at the slope; two others marched close against him, gripping him by arm and shoulder, as though at once pushing and supporting him. The rest of us, magistrates and the like, followed behind. Suddenly, when we had gone ten yards, the procession stopped short without any order or warning. A dreadful thing had happened—a dog, come goodness knows whence, had appeared in the yard. It came bounding among us with a loud volley of barks and leapt round us wagging its whole body, wild with glee at finding so many human beings together. It was a large woolly dog, half Airedale, half pariah. For a moment it pranced round us, and then, before anyone could stop it, it had made a dash for the prisoner, jumping up tried to lick his face. Everybody stood aghast, too taken aback even to grab the dog.

7   "Who let that bloody brute in here?" said the superintendent angrily. "Catch it, someone!"

8   A warder detached from the escort, charged clumsily after the dog, but it danced and gambolled just out of his reach, taking everything as part of the game. A young Eurasian jailer picked up a handful of gravel and tried to stone the dog away, but it dodged the stones and came after us again. Its yaps echoed from the jail walls. The prisoner, in the grasp of the two warders, looked on incuriously, as though this was another formality of the hanging. It was several minutes before someone managed to catch the dog. Then we put my handkerchief through its collar and moved off once more, with the dog still straining and whimpering.

9   It was about forty yards to the gallows. I watched the bare brown back of the prisoner marching in front of me. He walked clumsily with his bound arms, but quite steadily, with that bobbing gait of the Indian who never straightens his knees. At each step his muscles slid neatly into

place, the lock of hair on his scalp danced up and down, his feet printed themselves on the wet gravel. And once, in spite of the men who gripped him by each shoulder, he stepped slightly aside to avoid a puddle on the path.

10   It is curious, but till that moment I had never realized what it means to destroy a healthy, conscious man. When I saw the prisoner step aside to avoid the puddle I saw the mystery, the unspeakable wrong-ness, of cutting a life short when it is in full tide. This man was not dying, he was alive just as we are alive. All the organs of his body were working—bowels digesting food, skin renewing itself, nails growing, tissues forming—all toiling away in solemn foolery. His nails would still be growing when he stood on the drop, when he was falling through the air with a tenth-of-a-second to live. His eyes saw the yellow gravel and the grey walls, and his brain still remembered, foresaw, reasoned—even about puddles. He and we were a party of men walking together, seeing, hearing, feeling, understanding the same world; and in two minutes, with a sudden snap, one of us would be gone—one mind less, one world less.

11   The gallows stood in a small yard, separate from the main grounds of the prison, and overgrown with tall prickly weeds. It was a brick erection like three sides of a shed, with planking on top, and above that two beams and a crossbar with the rope dangling. The hangman, a grey-haired convict in the white uniform of the prison, was waiting beside his machine. He greeted us with a servile crouch as we entered. At a word from Francis the two warders, gripping the prisoner more closely than ever, half led, half pushed him to the gallows and helped him clumsily up the ladder. Then the hangman climbed up and fixed the rope round the prisoner's neck.

12   We stood waiting, five yards away. The warders had formed in a rough circle round the gallows. And then, when the noose was fixed, the prisoner began crying out to his dog. It was a high reiterated cry of "Ram! Ram! Ram! Ram!" not urgent and fearful like a prayer or cry for help, but steady, rhythmical, almost like the tolling of a bell. The dog answered the sound with a whine. The hangman, still standing on the gallows, produced a small cotton bag like a flour bag and drew it down over the prisoner's face. But the sound, muffled by the cloth, still persisted, over and over again: "Ram! Ram! Ram! Ram! Ram!"

13   The hangman climbed down and stood ready, holding the lever. Minutes seemed to pass. The steady, muffled crying from the prisoner

went on and on, "Ram! Ram! Ram!" never faltering for an instant. The superintendent, his head on his chest, was slowly poking the ground with his stick; perhaps he was counting the cries, allowing the prisoner a fixed number—fifty, perhaps, or a hundred. Everyone had changed colour. The Indians had gone grey like bad coffee, and one or two of the bayonets were wavering. We looked at the lashed, hooded man on the drop, and listened to his cries—each cry another second of life; the same thought was in all our minds: oh, kill him quickly, get it over, stop that abominable noise!

14   Suddenly the superintendent made up his mind. Throwing up his head he made a swift motion with his stick. "Chalo!" he shouted almost fiercely.

15   There was a clanking noise, and then dead silence. The prisoner had vanished, and the rope was twisting on itself. I let go of the dog, and it galloped immediately to the back of the gallows; but when it got there it stopped short, barked, and then retreated into a corner of the yard, where it stood among the weeds, looking timorously out at us. We went round the gallows to inspect the prisoner's body. He was dangling with his toes pointed straight downwards, very slowly, as dead as a stone.

16   The superintendent reached out with his stick and poked the bare brown body; it oscillated slightly. *"He's* all right," said the superintendent. He backed out from under the gallows, and blew out a deep breath. The moody look had gone out of his face quite suddenly. He glanced at his wrist-watch. "Eight minutes past eight. Well, that's all for this morning, thank God."

17   The warders unfixed bayonets and marched away. The dog, sobered and conscious of having misbehaved itself, slipped after them. We walked out of the gallows yards, past the condemned cells with their waiting prisoners, into the big central yard of the prison. The convicts, under the command of warders armed with lathis, were already receiving their breakfast. They squatted in long rows, each man holding a tin pannikin, while two warders with buckets marched round ladling out rice; it seemed quite a homely, jolly scene, after the hanging. An enormous relief had come upon us now that the job was done. One felt an impulse to sing, to break into a run, to snigger. All at once everyone began chattering gaily.

18   The Eurasian boy walking beside me nodded towards the way we had come, with a knowing smile: "Do you know, sir, our friend (he

meant the dead man) when he heard his appeal had been dismissed, he pissed on the floor of his cell. From fright. Kindly take one of my cigarettes, sir. Do you not admire my new silver case, sir? From the boxwallah, two rupees eight annas. Classy European style."

19   Several people laughed—at what, nobody seemed certain.

20   Francis was walking by the superintendent, talking garrulously: "Well, sir, all hass passed off with the utmost satisfactoriness. It was all finished—flick! like that. It iss not always so—oah, no! I have known cases where the doctor wass obliged to go beneath the gallows and pull the prissoner's legs to ensure decease. Most disagreeable!"

21   "Wriggling about, eh? That's bad," said the superintendent.

22   "Ach, sir, it iss worse when they become refractory! One man, I recall, clung to the bars of hiss cage when we went to take him out. You will scarcely credit, sir, that it took six warders to dislodge him, three pulling at each leg. We reasoned with him. 'My dear fellow,' we said, 'think of all the pain and trouble you are causing to us!' But no, he would not listen! Ach, he wass very troublesome!"

23   I found that I was laughing quite loudly. Everyone was laughing. Even the superintendent grinned in a tolerant way. "You'd better all come out and have a drink," he said quite genially. "I've got a bottle of whisky in the car. We could do with it."

24   We went through the big double gates of the prison into the road. "Pulling at his legs!" exclaimed a Burmese magistrate suddenly, and burst into a loud chuckling. We all began laughing again. At that moment Francis' anecdote seemed extraordinarily funny. We all had a drink together, native and European alike, quite amicably. The dead man was a hundred yards away.

Discussion: In external form "A Hanging" is a personal narrative. A good many successful professional essays are organized as personal narratives, and, because such a form enables one to impart significance to his own experiences, it is frequently a favorite with student writers. Some teachers of writing, too, find it useful to assign such essays because they allow the student to make use of concrete details drawn from his experience and help him to avoid the concatenations of misty generalities which are the bane of freshman themes. On the other hand the student who, in writing such an essay, fails to recognize that a "narrative" is merely the external form, the "disposition," of an essay, is likely to select the details of his experience in a haphazard manner and he will succeed in imparting only a sense of the incoherent or trivial. Note, in contrast, how each detail that Orwell chooses to reveal to us about his *subject* is dictated by his *purpose* so that each detail in the narrative (disposition) contributes to it.

It is not until paragraph 10 that Orwell explicitly reveals his conviction that "cutting a life short when it is in full tide" is "unspeakable wrongness." But if he is to make us *share* this conviction, every detail in the first nine paragraphs must implicitly play its role in convincing us that the condemned man is a part of humanity and that the taking of his life is inhumane. You may see clearly how Orwell has attempted to accomplish this end if you will answer each of the appended questions carefully.

Analytic Summary: In "A Hanging" George Orwell reveals how his part in the execution of a prisoner in Burma convinced him that it is wrong to take a human life (subject). The choice of each detail included in his narrative (disposition) is designed to convince the reader that any execution is "unspeakable wrongness" (purpose). Wherever he has choice, he employs diction, sentence structure, and figurative comparisons (style) which most effectively accomplish his purpose.

Questions

1. Before his explicit statement in paragraph 10, Orwell describes in surprising detail "a dreadful thing" which had occurred. What was the "dreadful thing"? What was "dreadful" about it?

2. Orwell describes the dog as being "wild with glee at finding so many human beings together." Orwell could not actually have known the motivation for the dog's apparent joy; what effect does he achieve by ascribing the animal's high spirits to "finding so many human beings together"?

3. In describing the dog's arrival on the scene, Orwell writes, "It came bounding among us with a loud volley of barks and leapt round us wagging its whole body . . ." Would the incident more or less effectively accomplish Orwell's purpose if an editor altered the passage to read, "It ran among us barking and in high spirits . . ."? Why?

4. Why should the onlookers be described as standing "aghast" when the dog attempts to lick the condemned man's face?

5. Many an essayist describing the hanging Orwell saw might well omit the apparently trivial incident of the dog's appearance on the scene, or treat it cursorily. Is Orwell's essay made more or less effective by his detailed treatment of the incident? Why?

6. At various points throughout the essay, Orwell quotes some of the participants directly. Try to explain (a) what attitude or state of mind is revealed by the remarks of each of the following characters and (b) how these revelations help accomplish Orwell's purpose: (i) the superintendent, (ii) Francis, (iii) the Eurasian boy, (iv) the Burmese magistrate.

7. From the point, in paragraph 10, at which Orwell makes explicit his objection to "cutting a life short," he takes some pains to indicate that there are *general* implications to be drawn from the particular hanging he describes— *i.e.,* he tries subtly to convince us that it is not just *this* hanging that is wrong. Can you explain why he must accomplish this task if he is to fulfill his communicative purpose? Try to isolate and explain two techniques that Orwell employs to accomplish his task.

8. At a number of points in his essay, Orwell makes use of metaphor or simile. Describe as precisely as possible what each of the following figurative comparisons contributes to the effectiveness of the essay:

(a) "one mind less, one world less" (paragraph 10)

(b) a "cry . . . almost like the tolling of a bell" (paragraph 12)

(c) "Indians . . . gone gray like bad coffee" (paragraph 13)

(d) "as dead as a stone" (paragraph 15)

Theme Topics

1. Write an essay in which you attack or defend capital punishment, but do not employ a narrative disposition.

2. Write a narrative in which you attempt to convince an audience of the truth of some moral proposition you have come to believe.

Harold Nicolson

THE MAN WHO KNEW EVERYBODY

*M*R. BENINGSEN, as I now realize, spoke with an English accent. At the time (being ignorant of such matters) I imagined that his intonation was that of New England. Those elongated vowels, those stressed consonants, suggested to me Beacon Hill rather than Oxford; Rhode Island rather than Mayfair. "More unimaginable," he would say when speaking of Persepolis, "than can be conceived." The last syllable of "conceived" prolonged itself with the insistence of a factory siren, its final "d" cutting dentally across his ululation, producing a silence as abrupt as that which follows upon some distant hoot at night-time. I was much impressed by this New England accent on the part of Mr. Beningsen. And one afternoon, riding among the sand hills by Shimran, I confessed to the second secretary of the United States Legation how instructive, and withal traditional, I considered Mr. Beningsen's accent to be.

2 "New England?" he said. "What an idea! Why, he comes from Utah. He adopts an English accent because he thinks it tony."

3 "Thinks it what?" I asked him.

4 "Tony," he answered, leaving me still confused.

5 Mr. Beningsen was a man of wide acquaintanceship, precise culture, and the utmost gentility. The orbit—the almost cosmic orbit—of his personal relationships was conveyed to one by Mr. Beningsen with a mastery which to this day compels my admiration. Others might adopt the crude gambit of referring to the eminent of three continents by their actual or, in extreme cases, by their Christian names. Not so Julius Beningsen. He would not directly mention either Mr. Andrew Mellon, Lord Curzon, Mr. Ezra Pound, M. Salomon Reinach, Prince Bülow,

216

Marinetti, Tagore, Lyautey, or Nagaoka. The thick pile of addressed envelopes which would accumulate during the week in his neat Berber basket, in anticipation of Friday's outward mail, would be arranged in such a manner as to hide always behind his weekly letter to his sister at Pasadena. "Miss Amy Beningsen," one would read, "2110 Colorado Avenue, Pasadena, California, Etats Unis." Yet one was well aware that behind that domestic covering lurked envelopes addressed to Mussolini, Elsa Maxwell, Lord Willingdon, and Madame de Polignac.

6   Only on carefully selected occasions would Julius Beningsen lift for one second the discreet veil which separated his neat and modest foreground from the palatial brocades with which his background was so lavishly draped. "Yes," he would murmur, "I also saw that statement in the Reuter telegrams this morning. It may well be true. I had a cable yesterday from Mr. Morgan, asking me to join the yacht at Villefranche towards the end of next month. It is quite possible that he may be stopping off in London and Paris on the way. Yet I question whether he can have been charged with any semi-official mission on the part of the present administration. My more recent information from Washington points rather. . . ."

7   The attention of his auditors became fixed upon the unindicated summits of his Washington correspondence. "Yes," Mr. Beningsen would be saying a few minutes later, "middle Achaemenid, not in a very perfect state," indicating thereby the precision of his culture. "You will," he would add, "take a second cup of tea?" indicating thereby the extent of his gentility. Inevitably the conversation would drift towards Persepolis, from which encumbered parapet Mr. Beningsen had only recently returned. "More unimaginable," he would murmur, "than can well be conceived."

8   For Mr. Beningsen had been sent to Persia, was even then at Teheran, as a representative of the Metropolitan Museum. Invariably would he pronounce that word "museum" in the English way. He smoked Maryland cigarettes which he obtained from Paris; to his guests he would offer Balkan Sobranye direct from London. There would be scones for tea and little pots of Tiptree jam. The tea parties of Mr. Beningsen filled his compatriots at the American Legation with anger undisguised.

9   It took me some three months before I realized that behind the reticence, the disguises, of Julius Beningsen there was nothing at all. My interest in him was by no means diminished by this discovery. During

the period when I regarded Julius Beningsen as an authentic person I had
looked upon him with anxious awe. Once I had attained to a conviction
of his fraudulence I studied him with an entranced interest. On those
rare occasions when European travellers would come to Persia I made it
a point to invite Beningsen to meet them. With delight I would observe
the skill with which, always indirectly, he would indicate to them that
triumphant background. With cold delight would I observe the phases
through which they passed. Few were the intellectual interludes allowed
to one in Persia; my examination of Julius Beningsen became for me a
pastime of which I never tired.

10   After some eight months of unflagging experiment I came to the
conclusion that the two most exquisitely imaginative of all Julius
Beningsen's autobiographical disclosures were those which dealt respectively with André Gide and Oscar Wilde. It was easy enough to
evoke the Gide story, since one had only to mention Mauriac, and thereafter Proust for a bit, and thus by a natural transition one arrived at
l'Immoraliste.

11   "Yes," Beningsen would murmur, thrusting his arm to full length
and gazing intently at the Maryland held upwards between thumb and
forefinger, "yes—there is *l'Immoraliste* of course—and the *Porte Étroite*
—I admit them both—yet one has one's preferences—*Paludes*, for instance . . ." He would pause when he reached *Paludes*, hoping that one
would press him further.

12   "And the *Nourritures Terrestres?*" one would inquire nonchalantly.

13   It was at that moment that the most exquisite of all Beningsen's
hallucinations would descend upon him. He would admit a tiny little
laugh, dry and apologetic. "Well, perhaps," he would answer. "I can
scarcely be classed as an unbiased judge of *Les Nourritures.*" At which
he would repeat his little laugh, conveying with the subtlety of infinite
practice that the embarrassment from which it resulted was on your side
and not on his, that the indelicacy of the question was one which, in the
crude circumstances of your ignorance, he was prepared to forgive. A
pregnant pause would follow, which Beningsen would end abruptly by
flinging his cigarette towards the fireplace.

14   "It might interest you," he would say, "to see some Raghes fragments
which I have recently acquired." Yet the reproach which he had managed
to convey hung like the smoke of his extinguished Maryland upon the
air.

¹⁵ One was conscious that in asking Beningsen about the *Nourritures Terrestres* one had probed too deep into the arcana of his personal past, that in clumsy ignorance one had touched upon some still exposed nerve, upon a nerve sensitively yet gloriously exposed to immortality. Only a moron could fail to derive from this elaborately rehearsed ceremonial the impression that some twenty years ago Beningsen had inspired André Gide to write the *Nourritures*. One had before one an elderly archæologist of exquisite manners, against an immediate background of indifferent Turcoman embroideries and littered shards. Yet behind that background there had been the glint for a moment of a vital Parisian past. The effect upon the cultured newcomer of this half-disclosure was electric: I would lie back upon the divan hugging myself with pleasure at the sheer artistry of Beningsen's fraudulence.

¹⁶ The Oscar Wilde story, for its part, was less expressionist and more precise. It could be evoked by the direct method. The newcomer could be primed in advance to ask Beningsen whether, during his period at the South Kensington in the early 'nineties, he had been at all intimate with Oscar Wilde. "No," he would answer. "No—I never knew Wilde during those days. In fact I never saw him. Curiously enough, the only time that I saw him was some eight, or it may have been nine, years after his death." There would be a pause at this filled to the brim with implicit inquiry. Beningsen, who until then had been leaning back in a deck-chair, would gather his thin legs under him and crouch over his own joined knees, again holding his cigarette upwards between thumb and forefinger as if it were some medicinal herb. "Yes," he would continue, "it was extremely painful." During the pause that followed, he would gather himself up more tightly over his own crouch. And then, in accents of the utmost refinement, he would embark upon his story.

¹⁷ "Poor Wilde, as you may remember, died in circumstances of comparative poverty in the Hôtel d'Alsace. He was buried in a suburban cemetery in the *banlieu*. In 1908 a lady who much admired his work, and deeply regretted the dishonour which had been done to him, bequeathed a large sum of money whereby this dishonour might be posthumously repaired. This reparation, as you shall see, was vividly——" (and here Beningsen would pause for an exquisite moment, shaping his lips to give full length and emphasis to the ensuing word) "*posthumous*." At this stage he would be apt to fling himself back into his chair with a gesture of distaste. "No," he would protest, "I prefer to tell you some

other story. I have no liking myself for the macabre." His auditors would urge him to continue. Again he would assume that crouching position. "Well . . ." he would begin.

[18]   It was obvious that in spite of his repudiation of the macabre he enjoyed the story immensely. It seems that in order that the remains of Wilde might be removed from his suburban cemetery to the more enlightened splendours of Père Lachaise an exhumation order had been obtained. It seems that the transference of the coffin from one cemetery to the other had been regarded by the Ministry of Public Instruction as an occasion demanding discreet but laudable official notice. The gravediggers had been working over-night, they had removed the tombstone and dug down to the coffin, under which they had placed bands with the aid of which, at the fitting moment, the coffin might be raised to the upper air. A group of some twelve people had gathered that morning beside the open grave. "I have," said Beningsen, "a marked *Abneigung* from all such functions, yet I felt that I should be wounding people who were very dear to me were I to refuse to attend." He had thus been one of the twelve who gathered by the grave-side. There had been a few chosen words from an official of the Ministry. The little group pressed closer to the edge. The grave-diggers began to strain upon their bands. The coffin below them jerked slightly and then began to rise. And at that one of the tombstones which had been placed to the side of the grave was dislodged by the strain of the band which passed across its surface. It fell upon the coffin and split it open. It was in this manner that Beningsen had obtained a glimpse of Oscar Wilde. The rest of the story was too harrowing to be recorded. Beningsen's slim freckled fingers would clutch the air as he searched for the most telling epithets. He found them. It would be with a sense of magnificent horror that we bade him good night.

[19]   I remember particularly driving back one night under blue Persian stars with an intellectual of the Air Force who had come up from Baghdad. He had been much impressed, as I had hoped, by Beningsen's recitation. "Gosh," he exclaimed, "what an interesting man! What I mean is, he's seen such a lot, and yet he doesn't boast about it; one has to drag it all out . . ."

[20]   "Yes," I answered, "Beningsen's an artist in his way. An artist in fraudulence."

[21]   "You mean it wasn't true?"

22 "Of course it wasn't true—the whole thing is an elaborate and, I admit, convincing day-dream."

23 I was so convinced of Beningsen's fraudulence that it never occurred to me to verify even those of his reticences which it would have been easy for me to control. A few days before I left Teheran I rode round to his little house among the plane trees to bid him farewell. He was not in at the moment, and his servant asked me to wait. I strolled to the book-case and pulled out a copy of the *Nourritures Terrestres*. "*A* Julius Beningsen," I read, "*de la part de son ami André Gide.*" And underneath I read as follows in the same handwriting. "*Je sais maintenant qui était Nathanaël.*" When Beningsen entered, I gazed at him with a wild surmise.

Some months later I was dining at my club in London. They were talking of the early work of Epstein, and someone mentioned the Wilde memorial in Père Lachaise. An old gentleman who was present stated that he much admired that monument, but that it was associated in his mind with one of the most ghastly episodes in his experience.

"I was present," he added glumly, "at the exhumation. It was a most distressing affair."

It was then that I heard the same story again.

"Tell me," I said to him afterwards, "at that exhumation—was there a man there of the name of Beningsen?"

"You mean Julius Beningsen," he answered. "Yes, he was there. I wish now that I had not forced him to come. He hated it. Yet I felt somehow that an American of his standing—you see, Wilde would have been pleased. But I felt sorry for Beningsen. He minded more than the others."

Discussion: Like "A Hanging," "The Man Who Knew Everybody" has the external form of a personal narrative. Unlike Orwell, though, Nicolson does not select the details of his narrative for their ability to accomplish a rhetorical end, but, rather, for their ability to impart a special kind of delight to the reader. Although, like Orwell, he describes an event which leads to a discovery, he does so in such a way that we are not allowed to become concerned with some general moral principle, such as "do not judge too hastily," but react instead with pleasure to the surprise and mild consternation with which the narrator learns that the ostensible fraud, Beningsen, had indeed been truthful.

The "true" narrative, which is informed by an intention to entertain, is most difficult of all to write effectively. Truth is, surely, stranger than fiction precisely because most good writers of fiction sensibly eschew the remarkable coincidence, the odd—almost unbelievable—revelatory meeting that sometimes does occur in everyday life; it does the novelist or short-story writer little good to assure a reader who has lost faith in his fictional creations that such things really *do* occur in life, and any protestation that such and such an event actually occurred to *him* may be completely sincere but is also completely irrelevant. Nicolson once remarked that a story is nothing if it is not true—and this is certainly the case with "The Man Who Knew Everybody," which would be a very bad short story but which, if true, is a first-rate narration of a surprising discovery the writer made about an interesting character whom he actually knew. If we were to discover that, in fact, a Mr. Beningsen who knew Wilde, Gide, and others had existed only in Mr. Nicolson's mind, we should feel cheated indeed.

Yet even if Nicolson can convince us that the events he relates actually occurred, he has far to go to accomplish the communicative purpose of this essay. The pat reversal of his beliefs about Beningsen's honesty is likely to leave us still with a feeling of being cheated unless he has revealed the details of Beningsen's character and of his own attitude in such a manner that, though we can share his initial view of Beningsen's fraudulence, we can also feel, *when* we learn it, that the truth was there waiting to be discovered from the outset.

Analytic Summary: In "The Man Who Knew Everybody"
Harold Nicolson tells how he became convinced that Mr.
Beningsen's claim to friendship with celebrities was a pose, only
to discover that Beningsen was truthful (subject). *The choice of*
each detail in his narrative (disposition) *is designed to delight the*
reader by imparting to him a sense of complete surprise at,
without destroying the credibility of, the final discovery (purpose).

Questions

1. At the beginning of paragraph 9, Nicolson informs us that, "It took me some three months before I realized that behind the reticence, the disguises, of Julius Beningsen there was nothing at all." What traits of Nicolson and of Beningsen revealed in the first eight paragraphs make it plausible that the writer would have taken so long to recognize Beningsen's ostensible fraudulence? What is the nature of the evidence that initially convinces Nicolson of Beningsen's fraudulence? Is the evidence plausibly convincing in view of Nicolson's expressed attitude? Is the evidence convincing or ambiguous when considered by itself?

2. Once Nicolson is convinced that Beningsen is a fraud, his interest in his acquaintance continues, and he makes it a point to display Beningsen's ostensible fraudulence to European visitors to Persia. He tells us, "With delight I would observe the skill with which, always indirectly, he would indicate to them that triumphant background." Is Beningsen's "skill" susceptible of a different

interpretation at the end of the essay? What are some of the ways in which Beningsen's "skill" is convincingly illustrated? How does Nicolson's concentration on Beningsen's "skill" contribute to the realization of the communicative purpose described in the summary above?

3. In a brief paragraph, describe the techniques that Nicolson employs throughout the essay to increase the sense of surprise we are meant to feel when we discover the truth. In another paragraph, describe in detail how he has attempted to make the surprising discovery plausible.

4. It is unlikely that Nicolson would remember precisely actual remarks made in previous conversations. As Orwell did in "The Hanging," though, he includes direct quotations. He quotes Beningsen, for example, as saying, "It might interest you . . . to see some Raghes fragments which I have recently acquired." Suppose Nicolson had quoted Beningsen as saying instead, "You might like to see some Raghes fragments I just bought." How would our impression of Beningsen be altered in the latter version? Why is it important that our impression of Beningsen be that conveyed in Nicolson's sentence?

5. Find three other sentences in which Nicolson chooses sentence structure and diction in such a way as directly to contribute to his communicative purpose.

6. Describe as precisely as possible the changes Nicolson would have to make if he wished to use his experience with Beningsen to write another kind of essay in which he persuaded the reader that it was wrong to judge people too harshly.

Theme Topics

1. Using the experience described in Nicolson's essay, rewrite it so as to convince an audience that they should not judge too hastily.

2. Write an essay in which you tell about your relationship with an interesting character in such a manner that your reader will be entertained. Be sure that you yourself can describe the particular kind of pleasure you wish to evoke in the reader.

3. Do sufficient research in the library to discover whether or not Nicolson's tale is in fact true. Write an essay in which you either explain to an interested reader the conclusion to which the evidence leads, or use that evidence as material in an essay designed to persuade your reader that Nicolson was (or was not) justified in treating facts as he did.

James Boswell

THE WILKES EPISODE

From *The Life of Samuel Johnson, LL.D.*

I AM NOW to record a very curious incident in Dr. Johnson's life, which fell under my own observation; of which *pars magna fui,* and which I am persuaded will, with the liberal-minded, be much to his credit.

2   My desire of being acquainted with celebrated men of every description, had made me, much about the same time, obtain an introduction to Dr. Samuel Johnson and to John Wilkes, Esq. Two men more different could perhaps not be selected out of all mankind. They had even attacked one another with some asperity in their writings; yet I lived in habits of friendship with both. I could fully relish the excellence of each; for I have ever delighted in that intellectual chymistry, which can separate good qualities from evil in the same person.

3   Sir John Pringle, "mine own friend and my Father's friend," between whom and Dr. Johnson I in vain wished to establish an acquaintance, as I respected and lived in intimacy with both of them, observed to me once, very ingeniously, "It is not in friendship as in mathematicks, where two things, each equal to a third, are equal between themselves. You agree with Johnson as a middle quality, and you agree with me as a middle quality; but Johnson and I should not agree." Sir John was not sufficiently flexible; so I desisted; knowing, indeed, that the repulsion was equally strong on the part of Johnson; who, I know not from what cause, unless his being a Scotchman, had formed a very erroneous opinion of Sir John. But I conceived an irresistible wish, if possible, to bring Dr. Johnson and Mr. Wilkes together. How to manage it, was a nice and difficult matter.

224

4   My worthy booksellers and friends, Messieurs Dilly in the Poultry, at whose hospitable and well-covered table I have seen a greater number of literary men, than at any other, except that of Sir Joshua Reynolds, had invited me to meet Mr. Wilkes and some more gentlemen, on Wednesday, May 15. "Pray (said I,) let us have Dr. Johnson."—"What with Mr. Wilkes? not for the world, (said Mr. Edward Dilly;) Dr. Johnson would never forgive me."—"Come, (said I,) if you'll let me negotiate for you, I will be answerable that all shall go well." DILLY. "Nay, if you will take it upon you, I am sure I shall be very happy to see them both here."

5   Notwithstanding the high veneration which I entertained for Dr. Johnson, I was sensible that he was sometimes a little actuated by the spirit of contradiction, and by means of that I hoped I should gain my point. I was persuaded that if I had come upon him with a direct proposal, "Sir, will you dine in company with Jack Wilkes?" he would have flown into a passion, and would probably have answered, "Dine with Jack Wilkes, Sir! I'd as soon dine with Jack Ketch."[1] I therefore, while we were sitting quietly by ourselves at his house in an evening, took occasion to open my plan thus:—"Mr. Dilly, Sir, sends his respectful compliments to you, and would be happy if you would do him the honour to dine with him on Wednesday next along with me, as I must soon go to Scotland." JOHNSON. "Sir, I am obliged to Mr. Dilly. I will wait upon him—" BOSWELL. "Provided, Sir, I suppose, that the company which he is to have, is agreeable to you." JOHNSON. "What do you mean, Sir? What do you take me for? Do you think I am so ignorant of the world, as to imagine that I am to prescribe to a gentleman what company he is to have at his table?" BOSWELL. "I beg your pardon, Sir, for wishing to prevent you from meeting people whom you might not like. Perhaps he may have some of what he calls his patriotick friends with him." JOHNSON. "Well, Sir, and what then? What care *I* for his *patriotick friends?* Poh!" BOSWELL. "I should not be surprized to find Jack Wilkes there." JOHNSON. "And if Jack Wilkes *should* be there, what is that to *me,* Sir? My dear friend, let us have no more of this. I am sorry to be angry with you; but really it is treating me strangely to talk to me as if I could not meet any company whatever, occasionally." BOSWELL. "Pray, forgive me, Sir: I meant well. But you shall meet whoever comes, for me." Thus I secured him, and told Dilly that he would find him very well pleased to be one of his guests on the day appointed.

[1] This has been circulated as if actually said by Johnson; when the truth is, it was only *supposed* by me.

6   Upon the much expected Wednesday, I called on him about half an hour before dinner, as I often did when we were to dine out together, to see that he was ready in time, and to accompany him. I found him buffeting his books, as upon a former occasion, covered with dust, and making no preparation for going abroad. "How is this, Sir? (said I). Don't you recollect that you are to dine at Mr. Dilly's?" JOHNSON. "Sir, I did not think of going to Dilly's: it went out of my head. I have ordered dinner at home with Mrs. Williams." BOSWELL. "But, my dear Sir, you know you were engaged to Mr. Dilly, and I told him so. He will expect you, and will be much disappointed if you don't come." JOHNSON. "You must talk to Mrs. Williams about this."

7   Here was a sad dilemma. I feared that what I was so confident I had secured, would yet be frustrated. He had accustomed himself to shew Mrs. Williams such a degree of humane attention, as frequently imposed some restraint upon him; and I knew that if she should be obstinate, he would not stir. I hastened down stairs to the blind lady's room, and told her I was in great uneasiness, for Dr. Johnson had engaged to me to dine this day at Mr. Dilly's, but that he had told me he had forgotten his engagement, and had ordered dinner at home. "Yes, Sir, (said she, pretty peevishly,) Dr. Johnson is to dine at home."—"Madam, (said I,) his respect for you is such, that I know he will not leave you, unless you absolutely desire it. But as you have so much of his company, I hope you will be good enough to forego it for a day: as Mr. Dilly is a very worthy man, has frequently had agreeable parties at his house for Dr. Johnson, and will be vexed if the Doctor neglects him to-day. And then, Madam, be pleased to consider my situation; I carried the message, and I assured Mr. Dilly that Dr. Johnson was to come; and no doubt he has made a dinner, and invited a company, and boasted of the honour he expected to have. I shall be quite disgraced if the Doctor is not there." She gradually softened to my solicitations, which were certainly as earnest as most entreaties to ladies upon any occasion, and was graciously pleased to empower me to tell Dr. Johnson, "That all things considered, she thought he should certainly go." I flew back to him, still in dust, and careless of what should be the event, "indifferent in his choice to go or stay;" but as soon as I had announced to him Mrs. Williams's consent, he roared, "Frank, a clean shirt," and was very soon drest. When I had him fairly seated in a hackney-coach with me, I exulted as much as a fortune-hunter who has got an heiress into a post-chaise with him to set out for Gretna-Green.

8 When we entered Mr. Dilly's drawing-room, he found himself in the midst of a company he did not know. I kept myself snug and silent, watching how he would conduct himself. I observed him whispering to Mr. Dilly, "Who is that gentleman, Sir?"—"Mr. Arthur Lee."—JOHNSON. "Too, too, too," (under his breath,) which was one of his habitual mutterings. Mr. Arthur Lee could not but be very obnoxious to Johnson, for he was not only a *patriot,* but an *American.* He was afterwards minister from the United States at the court of Madrid. "And who is the gentleman in lace?"—"Mr. Wilkes, Sir." This information confounded him still more; he had some difficulty to restrain himself, and taking up a book, sat down upon a window-seat and read, or at least kept his eye upon it intently for some time, till he composed himself. His feelings, I dare say, were aukward enough. But he no doubt recollected his having rated me for supposing that he could be at all disconcerted by any company, and he, therefore, resolutely set himself to behave quite as an easy man of the world, who could adapt himself at once to the disposition and manners of those whom he might chance to meet.

9 The cheering sound of "Dinner is upon the table," dissolved his reverie, and we *all* sat down without any symptom of ill humour. There were present, beside Mr. Wilkes, and Mr. Arthur Lee, who was an old companion of mine when he studied physick at Edinburgh, Mr. (now Sir John) Miller, Dr. Lettsom, and Mr. Slater, the druggist. Mr. Wilkes placed himself next to Dr. Johnson, and behaved to him with so much attention and politeness, that he gained upon him insensibly. No man eat more heartily than Johnson, or loved better what was nice and delicate. Mr. Wilkes was very assiduous in helping him to some fine veal. "Pray give me leave, Sir;—It is better here—A little of the brown—Some fat, Sir—A little of the stuffing—Some gravy—Let me have the pleasure of giving you some butter—Allow me to recommend a squeeze of this orange;—or the lemon, perhaps, may have more zest."—"Sir, Sir, I am obliged to you, Sir," cried Johnson, bowing, and turning his head to him with a look for some time of "surly virtue,"[2] but, in a short while, of complacency.

10 Foote being mentioned, Johnson said, "He is not a good mimick." One of the company added, "A merry Andrew, a buffoon." JOHNSON. "But he has wit too, and is not deficient in ideas, or in fertility and variety of imagery, and not empty of reading; he has knowledge enough

2 Johnson's "London, a Poem," v. 145.

to fill up his part. One species of wit he has in an eminent degree, that of escape. You drive him into a corner with both hands; but he's gone, Sir, when you think you have got him—like an animal that jumps over your head. Then he has a great range for wit; he never let's truth stand between him and a jest, and he is sometimes mighty coarse. Garrick is under many restraints from which Foote is free." WILKES. "Garrick's wit is more like Lord Chesterfield's." JOHNSON. "The first time I was in company with Foote was at Fitzherbert's. Having no good opinion of the fellow, I was resolved not to be pleased; and it is very difficult to please a man against his will. I went on eating my dinner pretty sullenly, affecting not to mind him. But the dog was so very comical, that I was obliged to lay down my knife and fork, throw myself back upon my chair, and fairly laugh it out. No, Sir, he was irresistible.[3] He upon one occasion experienced, in an extraordinary degree, the efficacy of his powers of entertaining. Amongst the many and various modes which he tried of getting money, he became a partner with a small-beer brewer, and he was to have a share of the profits for procuring customers amongst his numerous acquaintance. Fitzherbert was one who took his small-beer; but it was so bad that the servants resolved not to drink it. They were at some loss how to notify their resolution, being afraid of offending their master, who they knew liked Foote much as a companion. At last they fixed upon a little black boy, who was rather a favourite, to be their deputy, and deliver their remonstrance; and having invested him with the whole authority of the kitchen, he was to inform Mr. Fitzherbert, in all their names, upon a certain day, that they would drink Foote's small-beer no longer. On that day Foote happened to dine at Fitzherbert's, and this boy served at table; he was so delighted with Foote's stories, and merriment, and grimace, that when he went down stairs, he told them, "This is the finest man I have ever seen. I will not deliver your message. I will drink his small-beer."

[11]   Somebody observed that Garrick could not have done this. WILKES. "Garrick would have made the small-beer still smaller. He is now leaving the stage; but he will play *Scrub* all his life." I knew that Johnson would let nobody attack Garrick but himself, as Garrick said to me, and I had heard him praise his liberality; so to bring out his commendation of his celebrated pupil, I said, loudly, "I have heard Garrick is liberal." JOHNSON. "Yes, Sir, I know that Garrick has given away more

[3] Foote told me, that Johnson said of him, "For loud obstreperous broad-faced mirth, I know not his equal."

money than any man in England that I am acquainted with, and that not from ostentatious views. Garrick was very poor when he began life; so when he came to have money, he probably was very unskilful in giving away, and saved when he should not. But Garrick began to be liberal as soon as he could; and I am of opinion, the reputation of avarice which he has had, has been very lucky for him, and prevented his having many enemies. You despise a man for avarice, but do not hate him. Garrick might have been much better attacked for living with more splendour than is suitable to a player: if they had had the wit to have assaulted him in that quarter, they might have galled him more. But they have kept clamouring about his avarice, which has rescued him from much obloquy and envy."

12   Talking of the great difficulty of obtaining authentick information for biography, Johnson told us, "When I was a young fellow I wanted to write the 'Life of Dryden,' and in order to get materials, I applied to the only two persons then alive who had seen him; these were old Swinney, and old Cibber. Swinney's information was no more than this, 'That at Will's coffee-house Dryden had a particular chair for himself, which was set by the fire in winter, and was then called his winter-chair; and that it was carried out for him to the balcony in summer, and was then called his summer-chair.' Cibber could tell no more but 'That he remembered him a decent old man, arbiter of critical disputes at Will's.' You are to consider that Cibber was then at a great distance from Dryden, had perhaps one leg only in the room, and durst not draw in the other." BOSWELL. "Yet Cibber was a man of observation?" JOHNSON. "I think not." BOSWELL. "You will allow his 'Apology' to be well done." JOHNSON. "Very well done, to be sure, Sir. That book is a striking proof of the justice of Pope's remark:

> " 'Each might his several province well command,
>   Would all but stoop to what they understand.' "

BOSWELL. "And his plays are good." JOHNSON. "Yes; but that was his trade; *l'esprit du corps;* he had been all his life among players and play-writers. I wondered that he had so little to say in conversation, for he had kept the best company, and learnt all that can be got by the ear. He abused Pindar to me, and then shewed me an ode of his own, with an absurd couplet, making a linnet soar on an eagle's wing. I told him that when the ancients made a simile, they always made it like something real."

[13]   Mr. Wilkes remarked, that "among all the bold flights of Shak-speare's imagination, the boldest was making Birnam-wood march to Dunsinane; creating a wood where there never was a shrub; a wood in Scotland! ha! ha! ha!" And he also observed, that "the clannish slavery of the Highlands of Scotland was the single exception to Milton's re-mark of 'The Mountain Nymph, sweet Liberty,' being worshipped in all hilly countries."—"When I was at Inverary (said he,) on a visit to my old friend Archibald, Duke of Argyle, his dependents congratulated me on being such a favourite of his Grace. I said, 'It is then, gentlemen, truly lucky for me; for if I had displeased the Duke, and he had wished it, there is not a Campbell among you but would have been ready to bring John Wilkes's head to him in a charger. It would have been only

'Off with his head! so much for *Aylesbury.*'

I was then member for Aylesbury."

[14]   Dr. Johnson and Mr. Wilkes talked of the contested passage in Horace's Art of Poetry, *"Difficile est proprie communia dicere."* Mr. Wilkes, according to my note, gave the interpretation thus: "It is difficult to speak with propriety of common things; as, if a poet had to speak of Queen Caroline drinking tea, he must endeavour to avoid the vulgarity of cups and saucers." But upon reading my note, he tells me that he meant to say, that "the word *communia,* being a Roman law-term, signi-fies here things *communis juris,* that is to say, what have never yet been treated by any body; and this appears clearly from what followed.

'————Tuque
Rectiùs Iliacum carmen deducis in actus
Quàm si proferres ignota indictaque primus.'

You will easier make a tragedy out of the Iliad than on any subject not handled before." JOHNSON. "He means that it is difficult to appropriate to particular persons qualities which are common to all mankind, as Homer has done."

[15]   WILKES. "We have no City-Poet now: that is an office which has gone into disuse. The last was Elkanah Settle. There is something in *names* which one cannot help feeling. Now *Elkanah Settle* sounds so *queer,* who can expect much from that name? We should have no hesita-tion to give it for John Dryden, in preference to Elkanah Settle, from the names only, without knowing their different merits." JOHNSON. "I suppose, Sir, Settle did as well for Aldermen in his time, as John Home could do now. Where did Beckford, and Trecothick learn English?"

16   Mr. Arthur Lee mentioned some Scotch who had taken possession of a barren part of America, and wondered why they should choose it. JOHNSON. "Why, Sir, all barrenness is comparative. The *Scotch* would not know it to be barren." BOSWELL. "Come, come, he is flattering the English. You have now been in Scotland, Sir, and say if you did not see meat and drink enough there." JOHNSON. "Why yes, Sir; meat and drink enough to give the inhabitants sufficient strength to run away from home." All these quick and lively sallies were said sportively, quite in jest, and with a smile, which showed that he meant only wit. Upon this topick he and Mr. Wilkes could perfectly assimilate; here was a bond of union between them, and I was conscious that as both of them had visited Caledonia, both were fully satisfied of the strange narrow ignorance of those who imagine that it is a land of famine. But they amused themselves with persevering in the old jokes. When I claimed a superiority for Scotland over England in one respect, that no man can be arrested there for a debt merely because another swears it against him; but there must first be the judgement of a court of law ascertaining its justice; and that a seizure of the person, before judgement is obtained, can take place only, if his creditor should swear that he is about to fly from the country, or, as it is technically expressed, is *in meditatione fugæ*: WILKES. "That, I should think, may be safely sworn of all the Scotch nation." JOHNSON. (To Mr. Wilkes) "You must know, Sir, I lately took my friend Boswell, and shewed him genuine civilized life in an English provincial town. I turned him loose at Lichfield, my native city, that he might see for once real civility: for you know he lives among savages in Scotland, and among rakes in London." WILKES. "Except when he is with grave, sober, decent people, like you and me." JOHNSON. (smiling) "And we ashamed of him."

17   They were quite frank and easy. Johnson told the story of his asking Mrs. Macaulay to allow her footman to sit down with them, to prove the ridiculousness of the arguments for the equality of mankind; and he said to me afterwards, with a nod of satisfaction, "You saw Mr. Wilkes acquiesced." Wilkes talked with all imaginable freedom of the ludicrous title given to the Attorney-General, *Diabolus Regis;* adding, "I have reason to know something about that officer; for I was prosecuted for a libel." Johnson, who many people would have supposed must have been furiously angry at hearing this talked of so lightly, said not a word. He was now, *indeed,* "a good-humoured fellow."

18   After dinner we had an accession of Mrs. Knowles, the Quaker lady, well known for her various talents, and of Mr. Alderman Lee. Amidst

some patriotick groans, somebody (I think the Alderman) said, "Poor old England is lost." JOHNSON. "Sir, it is not so much to be lamented that old England is lost, as that the Scotch have found it." WILKES. "Had Lord Blue governed Scotland only, I should not have taken the trouble to write his eulogy, and dedicate 'MORTIMER' to him."

[19]   Mr. Wilkes held a candle to shew a fine print of a beautiful female figure which hung in the room, and pointed out the elegant contour of the bosom with the finger of an arch connoisseur. He afterwards in a conversation with me waggishly insisted, that all the time Johnson shewed visible signs of a fervent admiration of the corresponding charms of the fair Quaker.

[20]   This record, though by no means so perfect as I could wish, will serve to give a notion of a very curious interview, which was not only pleasing at the time, but had the agreeable and benignant effect of reconciling any animosity, and sweetening any acidity, which, in the various bustle of political contest, had been produced in the minds of two men, who though widely different, had so many things in common—classical learning, modern literature, wit and humour, and ready repartee—that it would have been much to be regretted if they had been for ever at a distance from each other.

[21]   Mr. Burke gave me much credit for this successful *negotiation;* and pleasantly said, "that there was nothing equal to it in the whole history of the *Corps Diplomatique."*

[22]   I attended Dr. Johnson home, and had the satisfaction to hear him tell Mrs. Williams how much he had been pleased with Mr. Wilkes's company, and what an agreeable day he had passed.

Discussion: This selection is anthologized more frequently than any other from the *Life of Johnson,* perhaps because more than most parts of that work it is very nearly a complete compositional whole in itself. It is incomplete only in that Boswell assumes that the reader has the knowledge of Johnson's character already developed in the *Life* and that he knows something of Wilkes' character and Johnson's attitude toward him.

The episode is ordered primarily as an entertainment—that is, again, as a composition whose purpose is to shape its subject so as to produce in the reader a particular pleasure, in this case a comic pleasure. The pleasure results from the fact that the reader is induced to look forward to the projected meeting with mild apprehension because of Johnson's strong moral objections to Wilkes but is at the same time led to desire and indeed confidently to expect, in the context of civilized social intercourse set up by Boswell, that the meeting will not result in anything more painful than Johnson's being temporarily disconcerted. The result, when the potential conflict turns beautifully into sophisticated fellowship, is the pleasure of comic relief. In order to accomplish this end, Boswell had to control the reader's attitudes very carefully. He had to make him share the delight he felt in engineering the affair without making him feel that he was blamably manipulating Johnson; he had, on the other hand, to show Johnson as slightly but sympathetically ridiculous—enough so that the reader will enjoy the approaching threat to his self-possession, but not so much that he will lose any of his admiration for him and so fail to take pleasure in his final coming to terms with the challenge posed.

We have spoken of Boswell's composition almost as though it were a fiction which he was at liberty to shape as he would, but to write fiction, of course, was not his intention. He wanted, like all good biographers, to tell the truth. Now the shaping of a factual narrative so as to maximize its power as entertainment will ordinarily do some violence to its validity as fact, but Boswell was able to realize both ends—entertainment and truthfulness to fact—at once. The explanation for this is apparent in the narrative itself: Boswell had given the story form at the time it occurred, so that when he came to write it, he did not have to warp the facts to fit his purpose but had only to realize in words his own sense of what had actually happened. He was thus here, as so often in the *Life,* an artist twice over. This fact largely accounts for his pre-eminence as a biographer: he could maximize entertainment without evading, as do many biographers who set out to entertain, any of his obligation to the truth about his subject. Beyond this, since his primary endeavor, throughout his book, was to reveal fully to the reader the complex and fascinating character of Johnson, he could not have found a better means to this end than the vivid dramatic sketches which his own involvement in Johnson's life allowed him to present.

Analytic Summary: In "The Wilkes Episode," Boswell endeavors to give his reader comic pleasure (purpose) *by representing vividly the successive stages of his own involvement* (disposition) *in the potentially explosive but actually amicable meeting of Johnson and Wilkes.*

Questions

1. Considering the fact that this episode is intended to function as a whole in itself, what (in relation to the rest of Boswell's work) is the purpose of the first paragraph?

2. The second paragraph is designed of course simply to set up the basic situation of the later narrative. But how do Boswell's remarks about himself help to shape the reader's expectations toward what is to come so that it will be read with proper effect?

3. Boswell's conversation with Sir John Pringle about Johnson did not occur at this time. Why does Boswell bring it in here?

4. How do the last two sentences of paragraph 3 maintain and heighten in the reader the expectations set up in paragraph 2? How does the next paragraph develop them still further? Does the characterization of Dilly's table as "hospitable and well covered" etc. contribute anything necessary to shape our expectation? Does giving the conversation help, or would a summary by Boswell have been better?

5. The wonderful comic force of paragraph 5 strikes the reader immediately but is rather hard to analyze. Consider first what the effect would have been if the first two sentences had been omitted. What necessary awareness in the reader would have been lost? How much does the comedy of the rest of the paragraph depend on this awareness?

6. In paragraph 5, what attitudes do we develop toward Johnson and toward what Boswell is doing to him? How do Boswell's attitude and manner or procedure contribute to this? How does the fact that Johnson (after a fashion) agrees to meet Wilkes affect our feeling about what Boswell is doing and our sympathies for Johnson when he arrives at Dilly's? Is any direct use of this fact made later?

7. The problem of Mrs. Williams was of course something that came up by mere chance and is of no factual importance at all. How does Boswell use his account of the incident to further his purpose in the story? How does the role he plays here connect with the earlier part of the story and, through identification with him, shape the reader's attitude toward the story? How does the last sentence bring this attitude to climax? What is our feeling toward Johnson throughout the paragraph? How does Boswell's final description of Johnson contribute to this feeling?

8. Boswell characterizes his own attitude at the outset of the dinner party ("snug and silent") but then drops out of view. Why? What is the point, in shaping our attitude toward Johnson at this moment, of mentioning that Lee was later "minister from the United States to the court of Madrid"?

9. How does Wilkes' initial conduct maintain the particular expectations the reader has already formed? Where does Boswell remind us of Johnson's underlying attitude of censure toward Wilkes? Does Wilkes' conduct have anything in common with the view Boswell has taken and that we are to take toward the whole affair?

10. For some space the dinner conversation does not contribute directly to the force of the comedy. Boswell is recording talk that deserves in itself to be part of the Johnsonian record. But is it after all so irrelevant? Do Johnson's remarks on Foote make any contribution? To whom do Wilkes and Johnson seem to address themselves? Is this significant? How do the general subject and the spirit of conversation help to provide a basis for the final reconciliation?

11. The paragraph about Scotland brings the episode to its climax. Since the comedy has been built on our apprehension about a potential conflict between Johnson and Wilkes, that apprehension must be fully discharged if the piece is to have its full effect. What then is the function of the subject of Scotland? (Boswell tells us himself.)

12. The climactic exchange itself is worth close attention. In the first place, what does Johnson's turning to Wilkes with a (friendly) remark about Boswell imply? Is it significant that the remark is directed against Boswell? What does the reference to rakes bring out into the open that so far has been hidden? Why is it important that it be brought out in just the way that it is? What does Wilkes' answer imply? Johnson's final response then (consider the pronoun) has the effect of doing what? How does Boswell's following comment (paragraph 17) make this clear?

13. Is paragraph 18 necessary to the full comic effect? Why? Would the effect be diminished if paragraph 19 were left out?

14. How does Boswell's concluding comment (paragraph 20) serve almost as an analysis of his composition?

15. How does Boswell's remark bring to a close the view we have had of him throughout?

16. Why was it a good choice for Boswell to end the story with this mention of Mrs. Williams?

Theme Topics

1. Narrate some scene to which you were witness so as to maximize its effect as entertainment. Consider that you are not bound as much as Boswell was to tell the absolute truth since your subject probably will not in itself be factually important. You will probably have to develop the characters of the participants at greater length than Boswell, who could assume that his were to some extent known to the reader. Be sure to choose *all details* for their relevance to the over-all effect.

2. Write a narrative account of a series of events to which you were witness or of which you have, or can obtain, valid knowledge. Let the purpose of your account be to make clear some fact about the events which will be significant or interesting to your audience.

Max Beerbohm

SOMETHING DEFEASIBLE

$\mathcal{T}$HE COTTAGE had a good trim garden in front of it, and another behind it. I might not have noticed it at all but for them and their emerald greenness. Yet itself (I saw when I studied it) was worthy of them. Sussex is rich in fine Jacobean cottages; and their example, clearly, had not been lost on the builder of this one. Its proportions had a homely grandeur. It was long and wide and low. It was quite a yard long. It had three admirable gables. It had a substantial and shapely chimney-stack. I liked the look that it had of honest solidity all over, nothing anywhere scamped in the workmanship of it. It looked as though it had been built for all time. But this was not so. For it was built on sand, and of sand; and the tide was coming in.

Here and there in its vicinity stood other buildings. None of these possessed any points of interest. They were just old-fashioned "castles," of the bald and hasty kind which I myself used to make in childhood and could make even now—conic affairs, with or without untidily-dug moats, the nullities of convention and of unskilled labour. When I was a child the charm of a castle was not in the building of it, but in jumping over it when it was built. Nor was this an enduring charm. After a few jumps one abandoned one's castle and asked one's nurse for a bun, or picked a quarrel with some child even smaller than oneself, or went paddling. As it was, so it is. My survey of the sands this morning showed me that forty years had made no difference. Here was plenty of animation, plenty of scurrying and gambolling, of laughter and tears. But the actual spade-work was a mere empty form. For all but the builder of that cottage. For him, manifestly, a passion, a rite.

236

He stood, spade in hand, contemplating, from one angle and another, what he had done. He was perhaps nine years old; if so, small for his age. He had very thin legs in very short grey knickerbockers, a pale freckled face, and hair that matched the sand. He was not remarkable. But with a little good-will one can always find something impressive in anybody. When Mr. Mallaby-Deeley won a wide and very sudden fame in connexion with Covent Garden, an awe-stricken reporter wrote of him for *The Daily Mail*, "he has the eyes of a dreamer." I believe that Mr. Cecil Rhodes really had. So, it seemed to me, had this little boy. They were pale grey eyes, rather prominent, with an unwavering light in them. I guessed that they were regarding the cottage rather as what it should be than as what it had become. To me it appeared quite perfect. But I surmised that to him, artist that he was, it seemed a poor thing beside his first flushed conception.

He knelt down and, partly with the flat of his spade, partly with the palm of one hand, redressed some (to me obscure) fault in one of the gables. He rose, stood back, his eyes slowly endorsed the amendment. A few moments later, very suddenly, he scudded away to the adjacent breakwater and gave himself to the task of scraping off it some of the short green sea-weed wherewith he had made the cottage's two gardens so pleasantly realistic, oases so refreshing in the sandy desert. Were the lawns somehow imperfect? Anon, when he darted back, I saw what it was that his taste had required: lichen, moss, for the roof. Sundry morsels and patches of green he deftly disposed in the angles of roof and gables. His stock exhausted, off to the breakwater he darted, and back again, to and fro with the lightning directness of a hermit-bee making its nest of pollen. The low walls that enclosed the two gardens were in need of creepers. Little by little, this grace was added to them. I stood silently watching.

I kept silent for fear of discommoding him. All artists—by which I mean, of course all good artists—are shy. They are trustees of something not entrusted to us others; they bear fragile treasure, not safe in a jostling crowd; they must ever be wary. And especially shy are those artists whose work is apart from words. A man of letters can mitigate his embarrassment among us by a certain glibness. Not so can the man who works through the medium of visual form and colour. Not so, I was sure, could the young architect and landscape-gardener here creating. I would have moved away had I thought my mere presence was a bother to him; but I decided that it was not: being a grown-up person, I did not matter; he had no fear that I should offer violence to his work. It was his coevals that made him uneasy. Groups of these would pause in their wild career to stand over him and watch him in a fidgety manner that hinted mischief. Suppose one of them suddenly jumped—on to the cottage!

Fragile treasure, this, in a quite literal sense; and how awfully exposed! It was spared, however. There was even legible on the faces of the stolid little boys who viewed it a sort of reluctant approval. Some of the little girls seemed to be forming with their lips the word "pretty," but then they exchanged glances with one another, signifying "silly." No one of either sex uttered any word of praise. And so, because artists, be they never so agoraphobious, do want praise, I did at length break my silence to this one. "I think it splendid," I said to him.

He looked up at me, and down at the cottage. "Do you?" he asked, looking up again. I assured him that I did; and to test my opinion of him I asked whether he didn't think so too. He stood the test well. "I wanted it rather different," he answered.

"In what way different?"

He searched his vocabulary. "More comf'table," he found.

I knew now that he was not merely the architect and builder of the cottage, but also, by courtesy of imagination, its tenant; but I was tactful enough not to let him see that I had guessed this deep and delicate secret. I did but ask him, in a quite general way, how the cottage could be better. He said that it ought to have a porch—"but porches tumble in." He was too young an artist to accept quite meekly the limits imposed by his material. He pointed along the lower edge of the roof: "It ought to stick out," he said, meaning that it wanted eaves. I told him not to worry about that: it was the sand's fault, not his. "What really *is* a pity," I said, "is that your house can't last for ever." He was tracing now on the roof, with the edge of his spade, a criss-cross pattern, to represent tiles, and he seemed to have forgotten my presence and my kindness. "Aren't you sorry, I asked, raising my voice rather sharply, "that the sea is coming in?"

He glanced at the sea. "Yes." He said this with a lack of emphasis that seemed to me noble though insincere.

The strain of talking in words of not more than three syllables had begun to tell on me. I bade the artist good-bye, wandered away up the half-dozen steps to the Parade, sat down on a bench, and opened the morning paper that I had brought out unread. During the War one felt it a duty to know the worst before breakfast; now that the English polity is threatened merely from within, one is apt to dally. . . . Merely from within? Is that a right phrase when the nerves of unrestful Labour in any one land are interplicated with its nerves in any other, so vibrantly? News of the dismissal of an erring workman in Timbuctoo is enough nowadays to make us apprehensive of vast and dreadful effects on our own immediate future. How pleasant if we had lived our lives in the nineteenth century and no other, with the ground all firm under our feet! True, the people who flourished then had recurring alarms. But their alarms were quite needless; whereas ours—! Ours, as I glanced at this morning's news from Timbuctoo and elsewhere, seemed odiously needful. Withal, our Old Nobility in its pleasaunces was treading once more the old graceful measure which the War arrested; Bohemia had resumed its motley; even the middle class was capering, very noticeably. . . . To gad about smiling as though he were quite well, thank you, or to sit down, pull a long face, and make his soul,—which, I wondered, is the better procedure for a man knowing that very soon he will have to undergo a vital operation at the hands of a wholly unqualified surgeon who dislikes him personally? I inclined to think the gloomier way the less ghastly. But then, I asked myself, was my analogy a sound one? We are at the mercy of Labour, certainly; and Labour does not love us; and Labour is not deeply versed in statecraft. But would an unskilled surgeon, however ill-wishing, care to perform a drastic operation on a patient by whose death he himself would forthwith perish? Labour is wise enough—surely?—not to will us destruction. Russia has been an awful example. Surely! And yet, Labour does not seem to think the example so awful as I do. Queer, this; queer and disquieting. I rose from my bench, strolled to the railing, and gazed forth.

The unrestful, the well-organised and minatory sea had been advancing quickly. It was not very far now from the cottage. I thought of all the civilisations that had been, that were not, that were as though they had never been. Must it always be thus?—always the same old tale of growth and greatness and overthrow, nothingness? I gazed at the cottage, all so solid and seemly, so full of endearing character, so like to the "comf'table" polity of England as we have known it. I gazed away from it to a large-ish castle the sea was just reaching. A little, then quickly much, the waters swirled into the moat. Many children stood by, all a-dance with excitement. The castle was shedding its sides, lapsing, dwindling, landslipping—gone. O Nineveh! And now another—O Memphis? Rome?—yielded to the cataclysm. I listened to the jubilant screams of the children. What rapture, what wantoning! Motionless beside his work stood the builder of the cottage, gazing seaward, a pathetic little figure. I hoped the other children would have the decency not to exult over the unmaking of what he had made so well. This hope was not fulfilled. I had not supposed it would be. What did surprise me, when anon the sea rolled close up to the cottage, was the comportment of the young artist himself. His sobriety gave place to an intense animation. He leapt, he waved his spade, he invited the waves with wild gestures and gleeful cries. His face had flushed bright, and now, as the garden walls crumbled, and the paths and lawns were mingled by the waters' influence and confluence, and the walls of the cottage itself began to totter, and the gables sank, and all, all was swallowed, his leaps were so high in air that they recalled to my memory those of a strange religious sect which once visited London; and the glare of his eyes was less indicative of a dreamer than of a triumphant fiend.

I myself was conscious of a certain wild enthusiasm within me. But this was less surprising for that *I* had not built the cottage, and *my* fancy had not enabled me to dwell in it. It was the boy's own enthusiasm that made me feel, as never before, how deep-rooted in the human breast the love of destruction, of mere destruction, is. And I began to ask myself: "Even if England as we know it, the English polity of which that cottage was a symbol to me, were the work of (say) Mr. Robert Smillie's own unaided hands"—but I waived the question coming from that hypothesis, and other questions that would have followed; for I wished to be happy while I might.

July, 1919

Samuel Clemens

THE BOYS' AMBITION

*W*HEN I was a boy, there was but one permanent ambition among my comrades in our village on the west bank of the Mississippi River. That was, to be a steamboatman. We had transient ambitions of other sorts, but they were only transient. When a circus came and went, it left us all burning to become clowns; the first negro minstrel show that ever came to our section left us all suffering to try that kind of life; now and then we had a hope that, if we lived and were good, God would permit us to be pirates. These ambitions faded out, each in its turn; but the ambition to be a steamboatman always remained.

Once a day a cheap, gaudy packet arrived upward from St. Louis, and another downward from Keokuk. Before these events, the day was glorious with expectancy; after them, the day was a dead and empty thing. Not only the boys, but the whole village, felt this. After all these years I can picture that old time to myself now, just as it was then: the white town drowsing in the sunshine of a summer's morning; the streets empty, or pretty nearly so; one or two clerks sitting in front of the Water Street stores, with their splint-bottomed chairs tilted back against the walls, chins on breasts, hats slouched over their faces, asleep—with shingle-shavings enough around to show what broke them down; a sow and a litter of pigs loafing along the sidewalk, doing a good business in watermelon rinds and seeds; two or three lonely little freight piles scattered about the "levee"; a pile of "skids" on the slope of the stone-paved wharf, and the fragrant town drunkard asleep in the shadow of them; two or three wood flats at the head of the wharf, but nobody to listen to the peaceful lapping of the wavelets against them; the great Missis-

241

sippi, the majestic, the magnificent Mississippi, rolling its mile-wide tide along, shining in the sun; the dense forest away on the other side; the "point" above the town, and the "point" below, bounding the river-glimpse and turning it into a sort of sea, and withal a very still and brilliant and lonely one. Presently a film of dark smoke appears above one of those remote "points"; instantly a negro drayman, famous for his quick eye and prodigious voice, lifts up the cry, "S-t-e-a-m-boat a-comin'!" and the scene changes! The town drunkard stirs, the clerks wake up, a furious clatter of drays follows, every house and store pours out a human contribution, and all in a twinkling the dead town is alive and moving. Drays, carts, men, boys, all go hurrying from many quarters to a common center, the wharf. Assembled there, the people fasten their eyes upon the coming boat as upon a wonder they are seeing for the first time. And the boat *is* rather a handsome sight, too. She is long and sharp and trim and pretty; she has two tall, fancy-topped chimneys, with a gilded device of some kind swung between them; a fanciful pilot-house, all glass and "gingerbread," perched on top of the "texas" deck behind them; the paddle-boxes are gorgeous with a picture or with gilded rays above the boat's name; the boiler-deck, the hurricane-deck, and the texas deck are fenced and ornamented with clean white railings; there is a flag gallantly flying from the jack-staff; the furnace doors are open and the fires glaring bravely; the upper decks are black with passengers; the captain stands by the big bell, calm, imposing, the envy of all; great volumes of the blackest smoke are rolling and tumbling out of the chimneys—a husbanded grandeur created with a bit of pitch-pine just before arriving at a town; the crew are grouped on the forecastle; the broad stage is run far out over the port bow, and an envied deck-hand stands picturesquely on the end of it with a coil of rope in his hand; the pent steam is screaming through the gauge-cocks; the captain lifts his hand, a bell rings, the wheels stop; then they turn back, churning the water to foam, and the steamer is at rest. Then such a scramble as there is to get aboard, and to get ashore, and to take in freight and to discharge freight, all at one and the same time; and such a yelling and cursing as the mates facilitate it all with! Ten minutes later the steamer is under way again, with no flag on the jack-staff and no black smoke issuing from the chimneys. After ten more minutes the town is dead again, and the town drunkard asleep by the skids once more.

My father was a justice of the peace, and I supposed he possessed the power of life and death over all men, and could hang anybody that offended him. This was distinction enough for me as a general thing; but the desire to be a steamboatman kept intruding, nevertheless. I first wanted to be a cabin-boy, so that I could come out with a white apron on and shake a table-cloth over the side, where all my old comrades could see me; later I thought I would rather be the deck-hand who stood on the stage-plank with the coil of rope in his hand, because he was particularly conspicuous. But these were only day-dreams—they were too heavenly to be contemplated as real possibilities. By and by one of our boys went away. He was not heard of for a long time. At last he turned up as apprentice engineer or "striker" on a steamboat. This thing shook the bottom out of all my Sunday-school teachings. That boy had been notoriously worldly, and I just the reverse; yet he was exalted to this eminence, and I left in obscurity and misery. There was nothing generous about this fellow in his greatness. He would always manage to have a rusty bolt to scrub while his boat tarried at our town, and he would sit on the inside guard and scrub it, where we all could see him and envy him and loathe him. And whenever his boat was laid up he would come home and swell around the town in his blackest and greasiest clothes, so that nobody could help remembering that he was a steamboatman; and he used all sorts of steamboat technicalities in his talk, as if he were so used to them that he forgot common people could not understand them. He would speak of the "labboard" side of a horse in an easy, natural way that would make one wish he was dead. And he was always talking about "St. Looy" like an old citizen; he would refer casually to occasions when he was "coming down Fourth Street," or when he was "passing by the Planter's House," or when there was a fire and he took a turn on the brakes of "the old Big Missouri"; and then he would go on and lie about how many towns the size of ours were burned down there that day. Two or three of the boys had long been persons of consideration among us because they had been to St. Louis once and had a vague general knowledge of its wonders, but the day of their glory was over now. They lapsed into a humble silence, and learned to disappear when the ruthless "cub"-engineer approached. This fellow had money, too, and hair-oil. Also an ignorant silver watch and a showy brass watch-chain. He wore a leather belt and used no suspenders. If ever a youth was cordially admired and hated by his comrades, this one was. No girl could withstand his charms. He "cut out" every boy in the village. When his boat blew up at last, it diffused a tranquil contentment among us such as we had not known for months. But when he came home the next week, alive, renowned, and appeared in church all battered up and bandaged, a shining hero, stared at and wondered over by everybody, it seemed to us that the partiality of Providence for an undeserving reptile had reached a point where it was open to criticism.

This creature's career could produce but one result, and it speedily followed. Boy after boy managed to get on the river. The minister's son became an engineer. The doctor's and the postmaster's sons became "mud clerks"; the wholesale liquor dealer's son became a barkeeper on a boat; four sons of the chief merchant, and two sons of the county judge, became pilots. Pilot was the grandest position of all. The pilot, even in those days of trivial wages, had a princely salary—from a hundred and fifty to two hundred and fifty dollars a month, and no board to pay. Two months of his wages would pay a preacher's salary for a year. Now some of us were left disconsolate. We could not get on the river—at least our parents would not let us.

So, by and by, I ran away. I said I would never come home again till I was a pilot and could come in glory. But somehow I could not manage it. I went meekly aboard a few of the boats that lay packed together like sardines at the long St. Louis wharf, and humbly inquired for the pilots, but got only a cold shoulder and short words from mates and clerks. I had to make the best of this sort of treatment for the time being, but I had comforting day-dreams of a future when I should be a great and honored pilot, with plenty of money, and could kill some of these mates and clerks and pay for them.

Alistair Cooke

JOE LOUIS

THE DAY Joe Louis retired must have brought a moment's pause and a sigh from many people who don't care for sport, the sense of a promised date that would never be kept such as non-musical people felt when Caruso or Paderewski died. On the 1st of March 1949, it came home to some of us that we should very likely never again see him shuffle with great grace up to some wheezing hulk of a man, bait him with a long left before he brought up the shattering, awful thunderbolt of his right, and then toddle considerately away and wait for the referee to call the roll on yet another ruined reputation.

There are some idols you acquire too early, who later turn into walking parodies of themselves, like a favorite uncle who gets to be a vaudeville bore. There are others—the artists of popularity—who stay just far enough away from the hungry crowd and never glut the appetite they tease. Joe Louis was one of these. I doubt I should ever have seen him, or cared to, if he had not at one time connected with a private occasion. I went down to Baltimore the first day of summer in 1937 to stay with an old friend, a doctor at the Johns Hopkins Hospital, who promised himself next day an afternoon off from his messy labors with stomach-aches and corpses. We drove out into the blossoming Worthington and Green Spring valleys. The purple twilight fell. It had been a perfect day, of the kind that makes you grateful for your friendships and stirs the memory of how they first started. I had met this man years before on such an evening when he stopped by my room in college to admire a battered record I had carried across the Atlantic. It was Fats Waller singing the *Dallas Blues*. Driving back into Baltimore he remembered that

Fats was on tap in person just then. "How about," he said, "we go down to darktown and catch him?" There was a little vaudeville house deep in the colored section of town, and that's where we went. We packed ourselves in with several hundred Negroes too many. They clapped and stomped in time and sweated like the plebs at a Roman circus. It was possibly ninety-five degrees outdoors and a hundred and ten inside. Nobody seemed to care. In the middle of one number, though, something happened outside that rode above the rhythm of the band and the hallelujahs of the audience. Far off from somewhere came a high roar like a tidal wave. The band looked uneasy but played on. It came on nearer, a great sighing and cheering. Suddenly there was a noise of doors splintering and cops barking and women screaming and men going down grabbing their toes and snarling obscenities. The band stopped and the lights went up. The black faces all around us bobbed and flashed. Women threw their heads back and shrieked at the roof. Some people embraced each other and a little girl in pigtails cried. Other people cuffed and swung at each other. We managed to get out whole. Outside, in the villainously lit streets—they still have gaslight in darktown Baltimore—it was like Christmas Eve in darkest Africa. This, it turned out, was the night that Joe Louis won the heavyweight championship, and for one night, in all the lurid darktowns of America, the black man was king.

The memory of that night has terrified and exhilarated me ever since. The phrase, "Arise, you have nothing to lose but your chains," must have a terrible appeal to the Negro. Most Southerners know it, and it is why in some places they watch fearfully for every Negro flexing his muscles and wonder if he is somehow connected with the Communists. That immediate fear was not besetting America then as it is now. But the lesson was plain: one Negro had outboxed all the living contenders, no matter how white (and Braddock was whiter when he came out of the ring than when he went in), and he was a racial god.

It took several years, and a run of inevitable victories, and wide familiarity with Joe in the ring and on the newsreels, for Americans to learn a special respect for this quiet, beautiful, mannerly youth, who never thought of himself as anybody's god, who never played his color up or down, who never questioned a ruling, never flirted with the crowd, kept his mind on his work, stepped scrupulously aside when an opponent stumbled; and who, when it was all over, said such embarrassing things over the radio that they had to whisk the mike away from him to the loser, who would usually say the clichés that were expected of him. They pushed the microphone up to Joe in December 1947, when he had been fought into a dazed parody of his younger self by another old Joe— Jersey Joe Walcott. A sharp little announcer chattered, "Did he ever have you worried, Joe—at any time?" This is a question expecting the answer, "No, I felt fine all the time, never better," Joe said, "I was worried all the way through. Yes, sir, I ain't twenty-three any more."

I know it is hard, perhaps impossible, for any white man to appraise the character of any Negro. If you have lived all your life around Negroes, you inherit certain attitudes towards them. If you are a stranger to them, there is the danger of making them out to be quite the nicest people in America. In a way, nice Negroes have to be; for though Negroes are as good and as bad as anybody else, they have one thing in common: they have had, most of them, a worse deal than the white man. A variation of this condescension is to think so poorly of the Negro in general that when he does anything as well as a white man, you have to make him out to be unique. You hear a colored band and shout that nobody can play a trumpet like a black man (it depends, of course, which black man is being compared with which white). Then you run into Louis Armstrong, who tells you of the first time he heard a white boy—a very pasty-faced boy from Davenport, Iowa—play the cornet. And Armstrong broke into tears. "Man!" he said, "might as well lay you down and die, nigger."

When you come to look at the life and career of Joe Louis, there is the special dilemma that he is a black man, and that even when you have done your best to judge him as other men, there's no way of denying that if he is not the best boxer that ever lived, he is as near to it as we are ever likely to know. He was born in 1914 on a sharecropper's cotton patch in Alabama and was as country-poor as it is possible to be. In theory the farm was—it had been rented as—a cotton and vegetable farm. But the vegetables did not feed the family, not by the time Joe, the seventh child, came along. His father broke, as sharecroppers do, from the daily strain of not making enough in crops either to feed his children or to put shoes on them. They had no money to send him to a hospital. So he was carried off to a state institution where he died. A widower came to help out and soon married Joe's mother. And his five children moved in with the eight Louises. Joe got a little more food and went to a one-room school. Then the family moved to Detroit, where the stepfather worked in an automobile factory. Joe went on to trade-school and worked in the evenings doing the rounds with an ice-wagon. Then came the depression, and the family went on relief. This, said Joe, made his mother feel very bad. Years later Joe wrote out a careful check, for two hundred and sixty-nine dollars, which was the amount of the relief checks they had had from the Government. That, said Joe, made Mrs. Brooks, as she now was, feel better.

Whatever a big city means to the poor, Detroit meant to Joe. But it means something else to a hefty Negro lad short of cash. It means gymnasiums and the prospect of a quick take of two or three dollars in improvised fights. When Joe was eighteen he came home very late one night and found his stepfather blocking the door. "Where you been, Joe?" he asked.

"Over to the gym," said Joe, "working out."

"I thought so," said Mr. Brooks, and lectured him about the fate of no-goods getting punch-drunk in gymnasiums. "You go on foolin' around with boxing, you're never gonna to amount to nothin'."

He says this had him really worried. He asked his mother about it. She said it was all right to be a boxer if that's what you wanted to do most. And that was, in a way, the end of Joe's wayward life. The rest was practice, and workouts, and learning, learning, being knocked to pulp, and learning some more and coming again with a new trick or two.

There is a biography of Joe Louis, there may be several, that makes him talk the way sentimental writers always think simple men talk. It is a fairly nauseating work. But just before Joe retired, two first-rate newspapermen, Meyer Berger and Barney Negler, got hold of him for many long sessions and, presumably with one hand in their pockets, transcribed exactly how he talked and what he said, without paying any more attention than Joe Louis does to grammar, simplicity, or morals. From a few sentences of this report, I think you can get closer to the sort of man Louis is than from reams of official biographies. Take the bit about his being born with a catlike tread. "When I got up in fighting," he says, "newspaper writers put a lot of words in my mouth. They wrote I was born with movements like a panther, and how I was a born killer. I never said it was wrong before, but the real truth is I was born kind of clumsy-footed. My mother says I liked to stumble a lot when I was a baby. . . . That footwork the writers say was cat-sense was something Chappie Blackburn drilled into me. That was learned, it wasn't a born thing. He saw I couldn't follow my left hook with a right cross without gettin' my right foot off the floor. It takes a lot of learnin' before you can do it without thinking'." Or his explanation of why he never says much. "When I got to be champion, the writers made a lot of noise about how hard it was to get me to talk. My mother said I was no different when I was a kid. When I went to school the teacher made me say words over and over and by-and-by I got stubborn, I guess, and wouldn't say them at all."

After he lost a fight in early 1934, before his professional career was technically on the books, his manager told him to stop staying out late with the gang. "He treated me real good," says Joe. "I got to wear some of his clothes made over." The night he became champion, the night it seemed the whole population of darktown Baltimore poured into that vaudeville theater, Joe summed up his feelings in an immortal sentence or two:

"He fell in a face-down dive. That made me heavyweight champion. People figure that was my biggest thrill. But I don't remember no special feelin', I just felt good . . . maybe it was because I figured I wouldn't feel a real champ until I got that Schmeling. That's what I fixed on." (Schmeling it was who rang the only jarring note on Joe's professional record. At the end, it read—61 bouts, 51 knockouts, 9 decisions, knocked out once. That was in 1936. And exactly one year to the night after he became champion, Joe had his revenge. He did what he "fixed on.")

Maybe you will get from this the idea that Joe Louis is a simple soul with quiet manners, a good boy who never had a crafty thought. Of course, he doesn't talk about his respect for his opponents, or his decency and casualness with the crowd, because these are fundamental, the characteristics that a man hardly knows about, or, if he does, keeps quiet about. But there is one remark he makes about his pride in money that should round out the picture. "People ask me," he says, " 'Joe, what will you do when the big money from fightin' stops comin' in? Won't you have to cut down?' I tell 'em, I'm gonna live good, retired or not retired. I got investments and I got ideas. I'll keep on livin' good. It's them who lived off me who won't be livin' so good."

We ought to be able to stop there. And in a more artistic world, that is where Joe would have stopped too. But the Bureau of Internal Revenue is not noted for its artistic restraint or its sense of the dying close. Joe might announce his retirement, and the newspapers salute him with splendid tears. But there was a little matter of two hundred and twenty thousand unpaid dollars between Joe and the tax officials. He had "lived good" when the money was rolling in like a Kansas harvest. And, true, he had "got investments." But many of them were grubstakes handed out in the flush days to acquaintances more remarkable for their enthusiasm than their financial foresight or prospecting genius. Some of these investments could charitably be written off as bad debts, but not on the merciless forms of the income-tax boys. So Joe was thrown back on those "ideas" he had dared to boast about. In the end, there was only one idea that—in desperation and in decency—he could fall back on: it was the pitiful idea of going on fighting.

He won a fight and lost a fight, and then in the fall of 1950 he was battered like a sick old bull by a little dancing man called Ezzard Charles. With every beating, his price would go down. I suppose the Internal Revenue theory was that it was still Joe Louis fighting up there, with the terrible right hand that once earned about fifty thousand dollars per thrust. They allow working depreciation on a five-year-old car but not apparently on a worn-out thunderbolt. So the means to pay off the big debt grew limper every month.

There is no point in going on. Better far accept the word he gave in the spring of 1949, when he retired unbeaten in full view of a thousand fighters who dare not match him. Better recall only the memory of incredible speed, a slow shuffle, a solemn face, a gentleness, a shy acceptance of his greatness. All things considered—even the prospect of a fumbling end—a credit to his race; so long as you add Jimmy Cannon's good and necessary afterthought—the human race, that is.

Essays

FOR

Study

No essay has been included in this section because it fits neatly into one category or another. Each has been selected only if, in greater or lesser degree, it has entertained, informed, or moved the editors. We have, on the other hand, taken considerable pains to group the selections in ways we hope will prove interesting and useful to student writers—particularly those who have at least partially grasped the concept of coherence in essays advanced in the earlier parts of this book.

The headings, largely self-explanatory, define the thematic similarity among essays in any one section. Far from avoiding controversial subjects, we have included in "Ideals and Action" a substantial number of selections designed to challenge the student's beliefs and impel him to a defense of his own views. A desire to defend one's

SIMILAR SUBJECTS, VARIOUS FORMS

views frequently leads to the impulse to communicate them and, hopefully, to the recognition of a real need for their clarification. A student so moved is a student likely to have something that he wants to write *about*; without such a desire he will write, not essays, but fruitless exercises. If the essays concerning his own time and country move him to a desire for expression, perhaps those in the same section which deal with other times and nations will prompt him to reflection. It should prove provocative, after all, to discover that the American Leslie Fielder, troubled by the implications of an act of treason, has an eloquent counterpart in British writer Rebecca West, and that the concerns about a citizen's responsibilities to his country common to both these writers were shared by a great statesman some two centuries ago. And it is to encourage such reflection by suggesting, however cursorily, the scope of man's intellectual interests that we have organized the group of essays "Ideas and Men."

Finally, however, it must be remembered that the subject matter of this book is not men, nor politics, nor language itself; its focus is the principles upon which good compositions are constructed, and we hope that the thematic grouping, which facilitates the comparison of essays with similar subjects, will have as its final consequence a fuller awareness of how those subjects may be shaped to quite different ends, and a richer apprehension of how versatile and beautiful an instrument the English language may be in the hands of men who have mastered even part of its resources. Consideration of intellectually substantial essays should lead to fruitful discussion of significant ideas, but only when we understand how writers shape such thoughts to worthwhile ends in appropriate language can we begin to comprehend what enables some men to move the hearts of their fellows, or to convey to them those ideas which are mankind's heritage. We may even be able then to borrow a little of the masters' fire.

IDEALS AND ACTION

Creeds in Crisis

LESLIE FIEDLER, *Afterthoughts on the Rosenbergs*
REBECCA WEST, *The Meaning of Treason*
JOHN F. KENNEDY, *Edmund G. Ross*
THOMAS PAINE, *The Crisis, No. 1*
EDMUND BURKE, from *Reflections on the Revolution in France*

Morals and Mores

BERNARD MANDEVILLE, *An Enquiry into the Origin of Moral Virtue*
JONATHAN SWIFT, *The Art of Political Lying*
ALDOUS HUXLEY, *The Arts of Selling*
THOMAS WHITESIDE, *A Cloud of Smoke*
JAMES THURBER, *The Case for the Daydreamer*
ALISTAIR COOKE, *Roughing It*
LIONEL TRILLING, *The Kinsey Report*

Freedom and Prejudice

ALBERT EINSTEIN, *Why Do They Hate the Jews?*
ARTHUR E. SUTHERLAND, *Constitutional Rights of Racial Minorities in the United States*
INGE LEDERER GIBEL, *How Not to Integrate the Schools*
HAROLD NICOLSON, *Christmas Trees*
VIRGINIA WOOLF, *Two Women*
JAMES BALDWIN, *The Discovery of What it Means to be an American*

Leslie Fiedler

AFTERTHOUGHTS ON THE ROSENBERGS

Since the execution of the Rosenbergs, it has become possible to see clearly what was for a long time obscured: that there were *two* Rosenberg cases, quite distinct though referred to by a single name; and that this ambiguity made it difficult for the pro- and anti-Rosenberg forces ever to engage in a real dialogue. How often we were talking about quite different things under the same label!

The first Rosenberg case, which reached its climax with their trial in March 1951, involved certain questions of fact about the transmission of secrets to the Soviet Union, culminating in the handing over of sketches for the detonating device of the atom bomb. Implicated in this first case were: the brother of Ethel Rosenberg, David Greenglass, who made a full confession; Morton Sobell; Anatoli Yacovlev, the Russian vice-consul who had got safely out of the United States in December of 1946; and the notorious Communist "drop," Harry Gold. Through Gold, the Rosenberg case was linked with those of the confessed espionage agents, Klaus Fuchs and Allan Nunn May, woven inextricably into a context against which their guilt appeared clear beyond doubt. The denials of the Rosenbergs seemed merely the mendacious pleas of two people fighting for their lives in the face of overwhelming evidence.

In this initial open-and-shut case, scarcely anyone was very interested. In the United States, it did not stir up nearly as much discussion as the Hiss-Chambers affair, or even the trivial business of Judith Coplon. In Europe, it was ignored or meagerly reported, so that the European defenders of the Rosenbergs tended to be happily ignorant of the first or factual case in its real interconnections; and this ignorance in many cases

255

they fought desperately to preserve. The Communists themselves maintained a strange official silence about the Rosenbergs for more than a
year after their arraignment, wary, presumably, about identifying themselves with a pair at once so central to their whole espionage effort and
so flagrantly guilty; and baffled, no doubt, at how to defend two comrades
who had been underground for six years and who refused to admit their
party membership in court.

The second, or legendary, Rosenberg case was invented, along with
the Committee to Secure Justice in the Rosenberg Case, at the end of
October 1951 in Knickerbocker Village, a housing settlement in New
York City. The place of the double birth seems almost too apt; the
Rosenbergs themselves had once inhabited that melancholy block of
identical dwelling units that seem the visible manifestation of the Stalinized petty-bourgeois mind: rigid, conventional, hopelessly self-righteous—
the mind which dreamed the odd parody of the martyr which was the
role of the Rosenbergs in their second case.[1]

The Rosenbergs stood alone in the new version of their plight—
alone except for certain honorable ghosts. Gone were the real accomplices: Yacovlev and Sobell, Harry Gold, Klaus Fuchs and Allan Nunn
May, though "Davy" Greenglass, recruited to the Movement at the age of
twelve by his nineteen-year-old sister, remained to play the shadowy
villain—replaced by the evoked figures of Sacco and Vanzetti, Tom
Mooney, the Scottsboro Boys, and, especially, Dreyfus. The cue had been
given by the "progressive" National Guardian, which had opened the
defense campaign with a story headlined: "Is the Rosenberg Case the
Dreyfus Case of America's Cold War?" The revised Rosenbergs were no
longer spies, but "political prisoners" in the European sense, victims of
the class struggle and the Cold War, defenders of the peace, a persecuted
minority—these very people, it must be remembered, who would not
confess their political allegiance in court, and who for six years had been
under instructions not even to appear "progressive."

The long-drawn-out process of appeal in the American courts had
made it possible to set up the symbolic Rosenbergs in place of the real
ones; between the first exposure of two spies and the appeal of the

[1] The Rosenbergs of the second case possess a certain kind of immortality; that is, they
will continue to live in the official history and art of the Communist Movement, until,
for one reason or another, their particular segment of history is forgotten or refalsified.
But not yet! In 1954, the hit of the season on the Warsaw stage was a play called
Ethel and Julius.

"framed up victims before the bar of world opinion" came the year (soon two, and three) of separation and imprisonment and real suffering. The Communists banked on this stretch of time to screen their sleight-of-hand; and it worked. Even those who had followed the first trial carefully found it difficult to keep it in mind; and the maintenance of the anti-Rosenberg position soon fell largely into the hands of those who countered liberaloid sentimentality and rancor not with facts but with their own even more wretched "Down with the Communist Rats—God Bless America" sentimentality and rancor. The second, the legendary, Rosenberg case possessed the imagination of the world.

It is that second case which I wish to discuss. There is no point in rehearsing the first; as far as I am concerned, the legal guilt of the Rosenbergs was clearly established at their trial, and it is from an assumption of that guilt that I begin. What I want to examine (and this, after all, is the enduring point of the matter) is why the Rosenbergs, for all their palpable guilt, won their second case before the world; why there arose such a universal condemnation of their sentence; and why so many, in the teeth of the evidence, even believed in their innocence.

One can say in a general way that in the second case the Rosenbergs were not tried at all, but that by a bit of prestidigitation they, too, disappeared along with Gold, Yacovlev, and the rest; and that we were called upon to judge in their places Sacco and Vanzetti or Dreyfus. And how did they get in? Through the evocation of these almost traditional victims, a kind of moral blackmail was practiced on us; the flags of the gallant old causes were unfurled, and we were expected to respond by revivifying the battered belief that the political dissident (but in what sense is the present-day flag-waving Communist a dissident?), the proud rebel (but in what sense were the Rosenbergs, peering slyly out from behind the Fifth Amendment, rebellious or proud?), the Jew (but in what sense were the Rosenbergs Jews?) is always framed, that the guilt is always on the other side.

What a relief to be able to reassert that simple-minded article of faith after Fuchs and Nunn May and Hiss, and after the thousand betrayals of the Soviet Union. The fact that the Rosenbergs were remarkable chiefly for their difference from the older martyrs, that the whole point of their affair lay in that difference, was hardly remarked; scarcely anyone wanted to see them as they were, but merely to *use* them for self-exculpation—for joining together once more the ranks that had marched unbroken for Vanzetti, but had since fallen hopelessly apart.

And yet the question remains. Why this occasion rather than another; why this improbable pair; and why (outside of the United States itself) so nearly unanimous a response to their plight? To disentangle the motives that found a focus in the pro-Rosenberg movement is to write a thumbnail moral history of our time.

One must begin, I suppose, by separating out the absolute cynics, the Communist bureaucrats who used the case coldly when it was convenient to use it, as they had ignored it calmly when it was convenient to ignore it; and who knew that they could not lose in any event. For if the freeing of the Rosenbergs would have been for them a minor victory, their death was a major one in the struggle against the United States. After a certain point, the energies of such functionaries were patently directed at insuring that clemency would not be granted. I do not want to seem to make master-minds out of shabby Communist bureaucrats, but surely a certain elementary cunning rather than mere stupidity led them to do everything that would infuriate official American opinion, make any revision of the death sentence seem an admission of a judicial error.

It is no accident, I think, that the only plea which came near saving the Rosenbergs was prompted by an outsider who had been expelled from both the Communist party and the Communist-controlled defense committee. The suffering and death of the Rosenbergs were *willed* by the makers of Communist opinion and relished by them, as every new lynching in America, every bit of violence against the Jews, is willed and relished as further evidence that they are right! These are the professional accomplices of calamity; and if they cried "innocent," it was because they thought that the greatest possibility of disaster lay in such an assertion.

These conscious exploiters of the case were a tiny minority, yet one which had ready to hand a mass of naïve communicants already trained to believe, sincerely and even fervently, what that minority decided they should believe. In this sense, one can think of the bacterial-warfare campaign and the various "peace" petitions as preparations for the Rosenberg case, as the Rosenberg case in turn is no end in itself but a rehearsal for the next real or manufactured issue on the Communist agenda. This prefabricated public is made up not only of the naïver party members, activists to whom ideas are unknown and the mute attenders of meetings, but also of fellow-travelers and the "innocents" who read nothing but the Communist press, or even only the Communist posters (knowing, of course, that all other sources of information are "bought").

For such believers an event does not even *exist,* much less have a significance, until it is recognized by their journals; and so for them there had simply been *no* Rosenberg case until the party had given the go-ahead signal after months of discreet silence. For them, only the legendary case was real.

The Communists have long controlled in Europe large numbers of "advanced" workers, peasants, and petty bourgeois by manipulating a mythology inherited from a hundred years of political struggle: the belief that the state and its courts are always wrong; that the bourgeoisie is always wrong; and especially that the United States, the bastion of capitalism, is always wrong[2]—with the corollaries that no Negro, Jew, or "progressive" (i.e., Communist or sympathizer) can ever be anything but innocent. This group was joined by an even larger periphery, stalinized to the extent of not believing its own press and of accepting in critical instances the opinions screamed in the piazzas by those whom they consider more "devoted" and "unselfish" than themselves, because they are louder and more assured. Together these formed a sizable public which appears really to have believed that the Rosenbergs were innocent in the basic sense of the word, guiltless of the crime with which they were charged. This they knew, not from scrutinizing the record, but from consulting the opinions of those who had always defined for them the truth. They would have believed it quite as firmly if there had been no such people as the Rosenbergs—as, in a sense, there were not.

Such a rank and file, stalinized at second and third remove, did not exist in the United States, which possesses in their place a mass of people politically innocent and merely indifferent to such affairs in a way no European can understand. To this oppositely corresponding American group, the *second* Rosenberg case had no existence; so that between them and their European opposite numbers there was not even ground enough for real disagreement.

In both Europe and America, however, a substantial minority of intellectuals shared a third position which asserted the innocence of the Rosenbergs, or at least maintained the final irrelevance of their guilt. This position combined in varying proportions two complementary attitudes: the *wish* that the Rosenbergs might actually be innocent; and the conviction that they were *symbolically* guiltless whatever action they may have committed. The first feeling led to an incantatory declaration of the

[2] Only the notion that priests are always wrong could not be exploited in the Rosenberg case; otherwise it was a perfect ritual expression of the sub-Marxist catechism.

Rosenbergs' guiltlessness, based on the belief that what these intellectuals repeated with truly unselfish fervor could not help but prove true; and, in any event, the Rosenbergs *couldn't* have done it, couldn't have committed treason—or these intellectuals, too, might have been guilty of as sordid a crime when in their own heedless youth they also had been Communists or had at least defended in perfect self-righteousness their Communist friends against the "Red-baiters."

But, even if the Rosenbergs *had* performed the act, this line of argument continues, treason was not what they had meant; they had been acting for a better world, for all Humanity (i.e., for the Soviet Union, whose interests all the more enlightened had once known were identical with those of mankind); and, anyhow, Russia had been our ally when the Rosenbergs gave them a helping hand, standing with us side by side against the Nazis; and, after all, Russia had not yet used the Bomb, will never use it, never, never, *never* (to stop believing this would mean having to rethink their whole lives), so that sharing the atomic secret in this somewhat unorthodox fashion was really a blow for world peace: just look at the present *détente,* etc., etc. In light of all which, isn't it better simply to declare that the Rosenbergs are "innocent," as a kind of shorthand for an analysis too complicated to explain to the uninitiated without re-educating them completely.

How near the conscious surface such reasoning was carried on must have varied from case to case; but in almost every instance it led to the by-now-customary double bookkeeping of the Communists' friends, the exploitation of a vocabulary which makes it possible to say, at one and the same time, "They didn't do it at all; it's a frame-up!" and, "After all, they had a right; their hearts were pure!" This is a fantastic enough position in any event, but when held by the accused themselves (and it *was* held by the Rosenbergs, as I shall show), it becomes utterly fantastic, the obverse of those equally absurd "symbolic" declarations of guilt in the rigged Russian trials.

Finally,[3] one is left with those who cried only for mercy, for the conversion of the death sentence, "even if they were guilty as charged." It is difficult to disentangle the position itself from those who maintained it; to redeem it from the scandalous way it was used by the Communists,

---

[3] I am relegating to this footnote the "diplomatic" advocates of mercy—those who urged a revision of the sentence in order to "placate world opinion" or in order "not to give the Communists a martyr." This was not an important group, and the point of the whole case is precisely that the Rosenbergs were *incapable* of becoming martyrs.

who sought to confuse hopelessly the two kinds of protest, to make every cry for grace seem an assertion of innocence, and more: a condemnation of the United States, the Atlantic Pact, the European Army, and God knows what else. One is so appalled at the cynicism of many of the exploiters of "mercy," with their own record of political executions without appeal, without trials—and after the most ignominious of self-degradations—that he is tempted to discount the whole movement.

Even where the Communists played only a secondary role, there was evident in the shrillness of the cries of horror (rising from countries where only a little while before the lynching of political enemies was considered an act of virtue) a desire to celebrate the fall of America from innocence, to indulge in an orgy of self-righteousness at our expense. There is no political act (and the simplest cry for clemency was inevitably a political act) that is not marred these days by the obsessive envy and anguish of the Europeans in our regard. If the Europeans could only have believed as firmly as they pretended that we had utterly yielded to hysteria and persecution, the balance of guilt that tilts so annoyingly in their direction would have been righted; and they might have loved us more, not less. But they could only *want* to believe this, not really credit it—any more than they have been able to really accept the stories of germ warfare in Korea. In a Europe that tends to admire where it is horrified, and to be overwhelmed by the fascination of ruthlessness, even our approximate innocence, or the mere inefficiency at terror that is its equivalent, is a reproach.

Yet, allowing for all that was stage-managed or disingenuous in the pleas for clemency; discounting the rather professional nature of some of the ecclesiastical protests; allowing for the sob sisters who are ready to howl bitterly at the sentencing of the most sadistic wretch; setting aside the pleading based on a general condemnation of the death penalty, which does not bear precisely on this case; and discounting the almost mechanical reflex of those to whom since Hitler any threat to any Jew seems a recrudescence of the old horror, one comes to a residual protest that cannot be explained away, and in the face of which we must as Americans admit a real, a perhaps tragic, failure of the moral imagination.

The final protest that existed behind all the others based on stupidity or malice or official dogma was the humane one. Under their legendary role, there were, after all, *real* Rosenbergs, unattractive and vindictive but human; fond of each other and of their two children; concerned with operations for tonsillitis and family wrangles; isolated from each other during three years of not-quite-hope and deferred despair; at the end, prepared scientifically for the electrocution: Julius' mustache shaved off and the patch of hair from Ethel's dowdy head (and all this painfully documented by the morning papers in an America that can keep no secrets); finally capable of dying. This we had forgotten, thinking of the Rosenbergs as merely typical, seeing them in the context of a thousand other petty-bourgeois Stalinists we had known, each repeating the same shabby standard phrases. That they were individuals and would die they themselves had denied in every gesture—and we foolishly believed them. In the face of their own death, the Rosenbergs became, despite themselves and their official defenders, symbols of the conflict between the human and the political, the individual and the state, justice and mercy; and this symbolic conflict only those who knew they were guilty could fully appreciate.

It is, in the end, no mere matter of protesting an excessive sentence, but of realizing that they *count*, these people moved always like puppets from above, that they count as *human*, though they committed treason in disregard of all real human considerations in the name of an intolerably abstract "Humanity." It is wonderful in a way that two individuals did still count to so many people in a world as accustomed as ours to mass slaughter and injustice become mere routine.

There is no sense in becoming enraged at the fact that these two, our *only* two victims, should have stirred up the response that could not be brought to focus for the millions of victims of Soviet firing squads; that most of the world should have been crying out for the lives of two American spies, convicted by due process, at the very moment when Willy Goettling and a score of nameless others were being summarily shot in Soviet Berlin. We should rather be flattered that as a nation we continue to act on a plane where moral judgment is still possible; elsewhere assertions of human value seem merely pointless, and the only possible protest is silence, the resolve at least not to hail institutionalized murder as social justice.

Some Americans have, indeed, felt flattered at being among the last peoples to whom real protest is still conceivable, not merely permitted by law, but possible to the uncorrupted moral sense; and they have been willing to stop there, arguing that this very fact sanctions the execution of the Rosenbergs, by proving it the sort of exceptional act we can still morally afford when political considerations demand it. But the point is surely that clemency to the Rosenbergs was what we could *not* afford to deny. The world had turned to us (that part at least still not hopelessly stalinized) for a symbolic demonstration that somewhere a government existed willing to risk the loss of political face for the sake of establishing an unequivocal moral position. A minority at least understood that the Communists were doing everything in their power to make any concession on our part seem a cowardly retreat; but they hoped we would have the courage to seem in that sense cowardly. I cannot help feeling that even among the rank-and-file Stalinists there existed on some deeply buried level the shadowy desire for someone somewhere to assert that the political man was not all of man, that our humanity is neither fictional nor irrelevant.

This opportunity we let slip away from us, in part because of our political innocence, in part through a lack of moral imagination, but also through a certain incapacity to really believe in Communists as people. In the official declarations of Eisenhower, one senses behind the cold reasoning from cause to effect, and the shaky conclusion that the secrets transmitted by the Rosenbergs unleashed the Korean War, the failure of the military mind to see beyond a justice defined in codes. In the justifications of Judge Kaufman, on the other hand, one feels a personal hysteria—a fear of Communism magnified by the sense that in the United States, where so many Stalinists have been Jews, the acts of the Rosenbergs were an attainder of the whole Jewish population. But the Rosenbergs were not, after all, excessively punished merely because their fates happened to rest in the hands of a military man and a Jew, but because mass opinion in America, in so far as it took notice of them at all, *wanted* their deaths, as an example and token.

When counter-pickets to the Rosenberg defenders carried placards demanding "Death to the Communist Rats!" there was involved, beyond an old American metaphor for spies, a wish to believe that the enemy is subhuman, an animal to exterminate rather than a man to confront. Needless to say, the Communists themselves need no lessons in this sort of maneuver; we have only to remember the words of the Rosenbergs' lawyer before the White House on the eve of their death: "I don't know what animals I am dealing with, but I know that I am dealing with animals." Yet we have no right to let ourselves be provoked into answering the Communists with equivalent strategies; differently from them, we still have much to lose; and in trying to dehumanize our opponents we may end by dehumanizing ourselves.

When the news of the Rosenbergs' long-delayed execution was announced before the White House, the counter-pickets cheered. A critical episode in the moral and political coming of age of America had reached its climax; the hopes for a world of equity and peace that had moved the more sensitive and intelligent in the 1920's and 1930's, had been used as camouflage by a brutally imperialistic power and had ended by leading two undistinguished people into a trap of lies and espionage and death; and the counter-pickets *cheered!* One is tempted to echo the words of Irwin Edelman[4] just before he was chased out of Pershing Square by an irate crowd: "If you are happy about the execution of the Rosenbergs, you are rotten to the core!" But, if this reaction seems the final indignity, there is much worse to come.

Our failure placed in the hands of the Communists the advantage of being able to exploit the very human considerations that they were least capable of feeling. And there was an additional advantage in their cynicism itself, which left them able to *use* the Rosenberg children, the co-incidence of the electrocution date with the fourteenth wedding anniversary of Ethel and Julius, their frustrated love, and the shocking physical details of their death with a complete lack of squeamishness. On the hoardings of the whole world, the embraces of the Rosenbergs and their approach to the Chair were turned into clichés, occasions for public orgies of sentiment. The Judaism of the condemned pair was played on tearfully by the same activists who had screamed for the death of the Russian Jewish doctors until the line was changed; and the believers that religion is the opium of the people cried out against executing the Rosenbergs on the Sabbath.

But all this, it must never be forgot, was not until the leaders of the party had decided it was *safe* to be sorry—safe for the party, of course, and not for the Rosenbergs. The disregard of the Stalinists for the individuals whose causes they support, their willingness to compromise their very lives for the sake of making propitious propaganda, has been known to everyone since the days of the Scottsboro boys. But unlike those

---

[4] Edelman is one of the most extraordinary figures in the whole affair. Thrown out of the Communist party in Los Angeles in 1947 for advocating more inner party democracy, and expelled from the official Rosenberg defense committee as a heretic, he nonetheless provided the nearest thing to a legal out for the Rosenbergs. His pamphlet, *Freedom's Electrocution,* inspired two rather eccentric lawyers to make the plea which brought into special session the Supreme Court, which had recently reviewed a case against Edelman himself on a charge of vagrancy. He enters and exits from the affair in a style that provides a real contrast to the Rosenbergs' sly, maddeningly mendacious conduct. He seems a survival of the old-fashioned American radical, refreshingly honest beside the new "underground" models. One would bid those who think the Rosenbergs were killed for being radicals to notice that in a presumably hysterical America it was the real radical who was free to come to their aid.

boys, or Tom Mooney, or the other classic cases, the Rosenbergs were actual comrades. This did not mean, however, that there was any more real desire to save them; indeed, as enlightened and disciplined members they would be expected to approve the tactics that assured their deaths in order to blacken the United States in the eyes of the world. Their actual affiliation was, in fact, an embarrassment, something not to be played upon but concealed. The Manchester *Guardian* and other liberal journals might talk of "making martyrs for the Communists," but the Communists, victims of the frantic game of hide-and-seek they had been playing with themselves ever since the dawning of the Popular Front, expended a good deal of energy to hide the fact that these martyrs were "theirs."

"Death for the Rosenbergs Is a Victory for McCarthy!" the posters read, and who, in Europe, at least, remembered that McCarthy had never had anything to do with the affair? Surely the chief evil of McCarthyism consists in branding honest men as Communists out of malice and stupidity. But how does this concern calling a Communist a Communist, or with deciding by legal process that a spy is a spy? These creatures of Soviet foreign policy were labeled the defenders of all "freedom-loving peoples," sacrificed to nothing less than their love for "American Democracy."

There were no limits to the absurd masquerade. A hundred marching Communists in London put flowers at the foot of a statue of Franklin Roosevelt, with an attached card reading: "That Roosevelt's Ideas May Live the Rosenbergs Must Not Die!" Not Marx' or Lenin's ideas, please note, but Roosevelt's: It is all of a piece. Julius draped after his death not with a red flag but with the ritual prayer shawl of the Jews; not "The Internationale" sung but "Go Down, Moses" and the Psalms; the American flags still flying brazenly over the cortege and the rabbi to intone unbelieved-in prayers at the grave. But the hoax would not quite hold to the end, for the crowd at the funeral parlor booed when a rabbi invited for the sake of camouflage, reminded them that the Jewish religion teaches forgiveness of enemies. In an instant, the fake piety and humanity had disappeared from the carefully prepared faces, and those who had cried for mercy a little while before hooted down the mention of its name.

But there was worse yet. I was in Rome when the news of the Rosenbergs' death came through, and I can speak only of what I actually witnessed; but there, at least on the faces of the Communist crowds surging and screaming before the American Embassy, I saw evidence of

joy. They were glad, these young activists, that the Rosenbergs were
safely dead; for a little while they had been afraid that some last-minute
reprieve might cheat them out of their victory celebration, that they
would be unable to go through the streets in their Sunday best chalking
up "Death to the Killers of the Rosenbergs!" and to sit afterwards over
a bottle of wine content with a good day's work. But even this is not the
utterest obscenity.

That the American public should deny the humanity of their
enemies is terrible enough; that the Communists should deny the
humanity of their comrades much worse; but that two people should
deny their *own* humanity in the face of death is the ultimate horror, the
final revelation of a universal moral calamity. For even at the end the
Rosenbergs were not able to think of themselves as real people, only as
"cases," very like the others for which they had helped fight, Scottsboro
and Harry Bridges and the Trenton Ten, replaceable puppets in a manifestation that never ends. There is something touching in their own
accounts of reading each issue of the *National Guardian* (not the frank
Daily Worker, but the crypto-Communist sheet) to share in the ritualistic
exploitation of themselves. But even before the "progressive" journal
had begun to spread their story, they themselves had written to each other
the foreseeable platitudes of the propaganda on their behalf. From the
start, they had not been able to find any selves realer than those official
clichés. If there is a tragedy of the Rosenbergs, this is it.

The persistently evoked image of Sacco and Vanzetti had led many
to expect in the correspondence of the Rosenbergs some evidence of an
underlying honesty, some frank and simple declaration of faith; but they
could not hit upon any note that rang true. Reading the "death-house
letters" of the Rosenbergs, one has the sense that not only the Marxist
dream of social justice but the very possibilities of any heroism and
martyrdom are being blasphemed. It is a parody of martyrdom they give
us, too absurd to be truly tragic, too grim to be the joke it is always
threatening to become.

Ethel's last appeal to President Eisenhower was the first of their
letters I read; and it is surely among the most embarrassing, combining
with Ethel's customary attempts at a "literary" style, and the constitutional inability to be frank which she shared with her husband, a deliberate and transparent craftiness. She, who had already been writing
about Eisenhower in private as "our gnaedige Gauleiter," refers in a
painfully adulatory beginning to that embarrassment "which the ordinary

person feels in the presence of the great and famous" and which has kept her from writing to the President before. Only the example of Mrs. Oatis,[5] who "bared her heart to the head of a foreign state," has led Ethel, she explains, to look for "as much consideration from the head of her own." She has been unable to avoid the note of reproach in this comparison of mercy on either side of the Iron Curtain, but to take off the curse she hastens to protest her ignorance, in the typical gesture of the Communist who has felt obliged to praise, however mildly, something publicly identified with his real allegiance. "Of Czechoslovakia I know very little, of her President even less than that. . . ." This unconvincing avowal, however, does not satisfy even her, so she tries the alternative gambit of gratuitous flag-waving, announcing quite inconsequently that for America she "would be homesick anywhere in the world."

She then reminds Eisenhower that before he became President he was a "Liberator," but it is not really a congenial memory to her who has still ringing in her ear her own cry of "gauleiter" and the conventional Communist characterization of the American general staff as "heirs of the Nazis." The transition to this note is easy: her execution will be, she charges, "an act of vengeance," and not the first, she reminds Eisenhower, identifying herself and her husband with the 6,000,000 hounded Jews of Europe, and the President with the masters of Buchenwald—those "ghastly mass butchers, the obscene fascists," who are presently "graciously receiving the benefits of mercy," while "the great democratic United States is proposing the savage destruction of a small unoffending Jewish family. . . ."

At last she is at home. The hatred, the obvious irony, the ready-made epithets of the Communist press are released like a dog's saliva at the *ting* of a bell. How happily she forgets that she has been defending the concept of mercy, and using the word "democratic" of her own country without sarcasm. But "a small unoffending Jewish family"—it seems incredible that anyone could speak so about herself, her own children.

At last she is ready for the final series of elegantly unctuous appeals: in the name of "fealty to religious and democratic ideals," as "an offering

---

[5] The evocation of the Oatis case raises problems which demand another article: the prefabricated stalinoid public's celebration of Oatis' release as an unparalleled act of generosity; his own attitude toward himself and his sentence; etc. Here I would like to note merely how neatly this reference joins together two problems that are really one. Why do the guiltless confess on the other side of the Curtain, while the guilty protest their innocence here? In both cases, "symbolic" truth-telling, a shorthand for the uninitiate, is at stake.

to God," in the name of the President's wife who will "plead my cause
with grace and felicity," or of "the province of the affectionate grandfather, the sensitive artist, the devoutly religious man." And the rhetoric
reaches its high point with the reminder that "truly the stories of Christ,
Moses and Gandhi hold more sheer wonderment and spiritual treasure
than all the conquests of Napoleon." Against the shadow of these names
the alternating venom and flattery seem especially evident; and we are
left astonished at the self-righteousness that dared evoke them.

The letters which the Rosenbergs wrote to each other from their
cells in Sing Sing seem at first glance superior at least to this. Ethel, to
be sure, is still hopelessly the victim not only of her politics but of the
painfully pretentious style that is its literary equivalent; but Julius, more
the scientist in his view of himself, manages from time to time to seem
sincere and touching. One is moved by his feelings for his wife, which is
more than love—an almost frantic dependence and adulation; and by the
tears that stand in his eyes after the visits of his children. But even these
scenes, we remember, were, if not staged, at least edited for publication;
published in a context of the most banal thumbnail editorials ("I was
horrified to read . . . that our government is planning an accord with
Spain . . . to ally ourselves with the most reactionary, feudal, and Fascist
elements in order to defend democracy . . . something is very rotten in
Denmark . . .")[6] at the wish of the Rosenbergs themselves.

In part, their self-exposure was aimed, as they declared, at raising
money for their children; but, in part, it must have been intended to
make political capital out of their own misery and frustrated passion.
Finally, the letters are incomprehensible either as genuine expressions of
feeling or as partisan manifestoes, since they consist almost equally of
intimacies which should never have been published, and lay sermons
which should never have been written to each other by a husband and
wife confronting their deaths. The line between the person and the case,
between private and public, had been broken down for them long before
and could not be redrawn even in the extremest of situations. A single
logic connects the Communist hating on order the person he has never
seen; the activist ignoring on the street yesterday's best friend who has

6 The reader checking these quotations against the English text of the letters will
find certain discrepancies, for I am translating them back from the French text of
the *Figaro Littéraire,* the only one available to me. There is, however, a certain
justice in this procedure; for the documents of the legendary Rosenberg case were
intended primarily for Europe, and should be seen backward through Europe to be
truly appreciated.

become a deviationist; the wife leaving her husband the day after he is expelled from the party; the son informing on the father; the accused in Russia slavishly vilifying themselves in court—and the Rosenbergs exploiting their final intimacies to strike a blow in the Cold War.

It is in light of this failure to distinguish the person from the cause, the fact from its "dialectical" significance, that we must understand the lies (what are for us, at least, lies) of the letters. The most flagrant, of course, is the maintenance by the Rosenbergs of the pose of innocence to the very end and *to each other!* We have grown used to Communist spies lying in court with all the conviction and fervor of true victims; there was the recent example of Alger Hiss, to name only one; but we had always hoped that to their wives at least, in darkness and whispers, they spoke the truth. Yet the Rosenbergs played out their comedy to the end; and this we should have foreknown.

Some, I recall, advocated a conversion of their sentences on the tactical grounds that they might in the long run confess; and some have even been shaken by their consequent persistence in the cry, "We are innocent!" An occasional less-convinced Stalinist, bullied into complicity like David Greenglass, can be bullied out again into a frank admission; but the true believer believes above all in his own unimpeachable innocence. Precisely because the Rosenbergs could have committed espionage as they did, they could not ever confess it. A confession would, in a certain sense, have shed doubt on their complicity.

They were able to commit their kind of treason because they were incapable of telling treason from devotion, deceit from honesty. It was not even, though this would be easier to accept, that they chose deliberately between rival allegiances: the Soviet Union versus the United States. They did not know that such a choice existed; but believed in their own way what they continued to assert, that they had always loved and served "American Democracy." It is misleading to think of them as liars, though their relationship to everything, including themselves, was false. When Julius, who had stuck up in his cell a copy of the Declaration of Independence clipped out of the New York *Times,* refers to it as if in passing so that all the world will know he is really a misunderstood patriot, one is tempted to call him a poseur and a hypocrite; but he is something much more devious.

When he and his wife carefully observe the coming of each Jewish holiday and sentimentalize over their double heritage as Americans and Jews, they are not deliberately falsifying, though they neither know nor care what Judaism actually is about; they will use as much of it as they need, defining it as they go. "In two days," Julius writes, "it will be Passover, which recalls the search of our people for liberty. This cultural heritage has for us a special significance, because we are imprisoned . . . by the Pharaohs of today. . . ." And in another place he remarks that "the culture of my people, its fight to liberate itself from slavery in Egypt" is astonishingly like "the great traditions in the history of America"— and, one understands though it is left unsaid, like those of the Communist party.

Ethel, typically, insists on defining her enlightened position more clearly. Thrilled by the sound of the shofar, she thinks of the Jews everywhere hastening to the synagogues to pray for a Happy New Year, but hastens to remind them via her husband that "we must not use prayer to the Almighty as an excuse for avoiding our responsibilities to our neighbors . . . the daily struggle for social justice." And she concludes, astonishingly, with the appeal: "Jews and non-Jews, Black and White, we must all stand together, firm, solid, and strong." It is like the curtain line of an *agit-prop* choral production at the combined celebration of *Rosh Hashanah* and the anniversary of the Russian Revolution.

Judaism happens to lie closest to hand because of the accident of the Rosenbergs' birth, but any other tradition would have done as well—and does. Not only the Christ, Gandhi and Moses of Ethel's letter to the President, but Roosevelt and "Butch" LaGuardia in their letters to each other—the list might be extended indefinitely. For they have been told, and are prepared to believe a priori, that they are the heirs of all the ages: Lincoln, Washington, Jefferson, Isaiah, Confucius, Leonardo da Vinci, Ivan the Terrible, Charlie Chaplin, and Christopher Columbus have all contributed to their patrimony.

They even like to think of themselves as sharing in the peculiarly American mana of the Brooklyn Dodgers. "The victory of the Dodgers," Ethel writes, "over the Phillies quickly restored me to my customary good spirits," and one takes it for a relatively harmless example of the pursuit of the popular and folksy that led Ethel to sing folk songs in the death house. But she cannot leave it at that; the editorial follows the next day, between declarations of love: "It is the Dodgers' unconquerable spirit which makes people love them. But where they have especially covered themselves with glory is in making an important contribution to the rooting out of racial prejudice." We have moved from melodrama to comedy, but the point is always the same. What is involved is the system of moral double bookkeeping invented to fool the Examiners, but so successful that it has ended by bamboozling the bookkeeper himself.

Nothing is what it seems: the Communist parties advocate revolution, and they do not; the Communist International has been dissolved, but it exists; one commits crimes, but he is innocent. Anyone can call war peace, or lies the truth; but to believe such assertions so that one will face death for them requires a trained will and imagination. For such belief, the Rosenbergs had been in training ever since they had combined wooing with the study of Communist literature; and they had finally reached a degree of perfection which enabled them to attain the final stage of subterfuge, to go "underground."

To me, even more extraordinary (for it seems on the face of it *pointless*) than the assertion of their innocence is the Rosenbergs' stubborn silence about their political affiliations. In court, they had refused to speak on constitutional grounds; in their letters to each other, these "martyrs of the Communist cause" never mention the word "Communism," unless in quotation marks as an example of the slander of their enemies; while the name of the Soviet Union is, needless to say, avoided like a dirty word.

The expurgation goes sometimes to fantastic lengths, of which the most amusing example occurs in a letter of Ethel's written on June 21, 1951. "My beloved husband," she begins, "I feel so discouraged by this unjustifiable attack on a legally constituted American party! The specter of Fascism looms up, enormous and menacing . . ." But she does not identify the party beyond labeling it "American"; and the explanatory note attached by the defense committee in the published volume is equally coy. "Seventeen men and women had been arrested and convicted in New York under the recently passed Smith Act." If one already knows that those otherwise unqualified "men and women" were the leaders of the Communist party, all well and good. If not, it is apparently better to persist in one's ignorance.

The upshot of the whole business is that the Rosenbergs were quite incapable of saying in their last letters just what it was for which they thought they were dying. Not only had they excluded themselves from the traditional procedure of the old-style radical, who rises up in court to declare that he has acted in the teeth of accepted morality and law for the sake of certain higher principles; they could not even tell the world for what beliefs they were being framed. Beyond the cry of frame-up, they could only speak in hints and evasions; so that they finished by seeming martyrs only to their own double talk, to a handful of banalities: "democracy and human dignity," "liberty and peace," "the greatest good of our own children, our family, and all families," and finally "the interests of American Democracy, of justice and fraternity, of peace and bread and roses and the laughter of children."

To believe that two innocents had been falsely condemned for favoring "roses and the laughter of children," one would have to believe the judges and public officials of the United States to be not merely the Fascists the Rosenbergs called them, but monsters, insensate beasts; and perhaps this was partly their point. But one must look deeper, realize that a code is involved, a substitution of equivalents whose true meaning can be read off immediately by the insider. "Peace, democracy, and liberty," like "roses and the laughter of children," are only conventional ciphers for the barely whispered word "Communism," and Communism itself only a secondary encoding of the completely unmentioned "Defense of the Soviet Union." The Defense of the Soviet Union—here is the sole principle and criterion of all value—and to this principle the Rosenbergs felt that they had been true; in this sense, they genuinely believed themselves innocent, more innocent than if they had never committed espionage.

The final pity was that they could not say even so much aloud—except in certain symbolic outcries of frame-up and persecution, and only through the most palpable lies. It is for this reason that they failed in the end to become martyrs or heroes, or even men. What was there left to die?

Yet despite all this, *because* of it, we should have granted them grace. The betrayal of their essential humanity by their comrades and themselves left the burden of its defense with us. This obligation we failed, and our failure must be faced up to. Before the eyes of the world we lost an opportunity concretely to assert what all our abstract declarations can never prove: that for us at least the suffering person is realer than the political moment that produces him or the political philosophy for which he stands. Surely it is not even a paradox to assert that it is our special duty to treat as persons, as real human beings, those who most blasphemously deny their own humanity.

Rebecca West

THE MEANING OF TREASON

*F*ROM TIME to time during my career as a journalist I have reported notable law cases, and I know that it is not only morbidity which makes the public enjoy following the trial of a serious crime. It is very difficult for those who study life to find a story that comes to its end under their eyes. When we select an individual whose course we want to trace, it is as likely as not that he covers his tracks with secrecy, or moves to a field outside our view, or delays his end until we ourselves have ended. That is why classical history is a valuable study; we can see the whole story, the beginning, the middle, and the end of Greece and Rome, Egypt and Persia. That is why the lives of great men in the past teach us more than knowledge of great men in the present; we know their remoter consequences. The dock brings a like illumination.

Here an individual story comes to its end in a collision with the community. Every case has its unique intellectual and spiritual significance. The appearance of the accused person, the changes in his face and voice, his agreement with society as disclosed by the witnesses who approve of him, his conflict with society as disclosed by the witnesses who disapprove of him, his relation to the crime of which he is truly or falsely accused, always reveal a special case. But the crime which he committed, if he was justly accused, or the other crime which was committed by the representatives of society if he was falsely accused, has always the same cause: refusal to respect the individuality of another or others. A world in which each man respected the soul of all other men, no matter how little they seemed to merit respect, would be crimeless.

There is an obvious political implication to be drawn from this. The authoritarian state is *ipso facto* criminal. When I covered the trial

of William Joyce ("Lord Haw-Haw") for the *New Yorker* I saw a man
in the dock who was doubly criminal. He had committed crimes against
the law out of his desire to substitute a criminal state for a state which,
if not completely innocent, aimed at the innocence of freedom. It was
obviously doubtful if he would ever have been guilty of any offense
had he not been tainted by this political guilt. But when his actual
offense against the law was examined it was seen that he had acted in a
manner which had long been extolled by many who were in theory
pure of that guilt and firmly opposed to the authoritarian state.

Almost all contemporary left-wing writers of this generation and
the last attacked the idea of nationalism. It was true that many of these
attacks were made under the delusion that the words nationalism and
imperialism mean the same thing, whereas nationalism—which means
simply a special devotion of a people to its own material and spiritual
achievements—implies no desire for the annexation of other territories
and enslavement of other peoples. But a great many of these attacks were
made under no such apprehension. It was genuinely felt that it was pure
superstition which required a man to feel any warmer emotion about
his own land, race, and people than about any other. Why then should
any man feel a lump in his throat when he saw his flag or the statue at
the harbor gate of his native land, or feel that in a dispute between his
people and another he must obey the will of his kin and not aid their
enemy?

I watched the trial of William Joyce, and of all traitors who were
charged in courts which I could conveniently attend. They had all
cleared their throats of that lump, they had all made that transit of
frontiers recommended by the nationalists; and this had landed them
in the service of the persecutors of reason, the fanatical believers in
frontiers as the demarcation lines between the saved and the damned.
But as their lives were unfolded it appeared that none of them had
cast off their nationalist prejudice because of their strength, but had
been divested of it by maladjusted ambition, by madness, by cowardice,
by weakness. It seemed as if contemporary rationalists had been wrong,
and I remembered that the trouble about man is twofold. He cannot
learn truths which are too complicated; he forgets truths which are
too simple. After I had seen twenty traitors tried it seemed to me that
the reason why they were in the dock, why intellectuals preach against
nationalism, is that we have forgotten certain simple truths.

We have forgotten that we live outward from the center of a circle
and that what is nearest to the center is most real to us. If a man cut his

hand, it hurts him more than if he cuts some other man's hand; therefore he is more careful to guard his own. Even if he spend his whole life in teaching himself that we are all of one body, and that therefore his neighbor's pain is his also, he will still suffer more when his own hand is hurt, for the message then runs straight from his palm and fingers to his brain, traveling at a speed faster than light or sound, which bear the news of others' accidents. Throughout his life it remains true that what is nearest to his body is of greatest interest to his mind. When a baby is given food and held warmly by a certain woman, he grows up to feel a closer concern for her than for other women of her generation, and at her death will feel greatly disturbed. Should he be institution-bred and have no woman as his particular slave and tyrant, grievance will sour him till his last day.

If in his maturity he should live with a woman for any considerable period of time, he and she are apt, unless they are overtaken by certain obviously disagreeable circumstances, to behave as though there were a complete community of interest between them. There must have been some instinctive liking between them or they would never have been drawn together in the first place; they became involved in each other's prosperity; experience has taught each how the other will behave in most eventualities. Therefore they do better by one another than strangers would. Should he have children by this or any other woman, they will have great power over him, while other children will have little or none. He will know so much more about them. The veiled moment of their conception is his secret, and resemblances to him, to a familiar woman, or to his kin enable him to trace their inner lives, disguised though they be first by their inarticulateness and then by their articulateness. He can read them by the light of his own nature, and read his own nature by their light, and will have a sense of fusion between himself and those who are so inextricably tangled with that self.

If that man live in a house during the days of his childhood, he will know it better than any house he lives in later, though it shelter him forty years longer; and though the staircase wind as deviously as any in the world he will find his way down it in the darkness as surely as if it were straight. All his life long, when he hears talk of woods, he shall see beechwoods, if he come from a Buckinghamshire village, and a castle to him shall stand on Castle Rock, if Edinburgh was his home; and in the one case he shall know Southern English country folk, and in the other Lowland Scottish townsfolk, better than other Britons.

Born and bred in England, he will find it easier to understand the English than the rest of men, not for any mystical reason, but because their language is his, because he is fully acquainted with their customs, and because he is the product of their common history. So also each continent enjoys a vague unity of self-comprehension, and is divided from the others by a sharp disunity; and even those who profess the closest familiarity with the next world speak with more robust certainty of this world and seem not to want to leave it.

This is not to say that a man loves what is nearest to him. He may hate his parents, his wife, and his children. Millions have done so. On the tables of the Law it was written "Honor thy father and thy mother, as the Lord God hath commanded thee; that thy days may be prolonged, and that it may go well with thee in the land which the Lord thy God giveth thee," and it is advice of almost gross practicality aimed at preventing the faithful from abandoning themselves to their natural impulses and wasting all their force on family rows. St. Paul, that great artist who perpetually betrayed his art because he was also a great man of action, and constantly abandoned the search for truth to seek instead a myth to inspire vigorous action, tried to gild the bondage of man to the familiar. "So ought men to love their own wives as their own body," he says. "He that loveth his wife loveth himself. For no man ever yet hated his own flesh, but nourisheth it and cherisheth it, even as the Lord the Church." But countless men have hated their own flesh. Everywhere and at all times men have carried such hatred to the point of slaying it, and still more have persecuted it by abstinence and mortification and debauchery. It has a value to them far above their loathing or their liking. It is their own flesh and they can have no direct experience of any other. Not with all the gold in the world or by incessant prayer can we obtain another instrument-case, packed with these our only instruments, the five senses, by which alone we can irradiate the universe that is a black void around us, and build a small irradiated platform in that darkness. A wife is someone who has stood on that irradiated platform long enough to be fully examined and to add the testimony of her own senses as to the nature of that encircling mystery. She may be loved or hated, or loved and hated, and serve in that research.

A child knows that what is near is easier for him to handle than what is far. All men took it for granted till recent times, when it was challenged, together with some other traditional assumptions, not because they had proved unsound, but because a number of urbanized populations from which the intellectual classes were largely drawn had lost their sense of spiritual as well as material process. They had lost their sense of material process owing to the development of the machine; goods which had formerly been produced by simple and comprehensible processes, often carried on where they could be witnessed by the consumer, were now produced by elaborate processes, not to be grasped by people without mechanical training, and carried on in the privacy of the large factories.

The reason for their ignorance of spiritual process was the urban lack of the long memory and the omniscient gossip enjoyed by the village. The townsman is surrounded by people whose circumstances he does not know and whose heredities are the secrets of other districts; and he is apt to take their dissimulating faces and their clothed bodies as the sum of them. People began to think of each other in a new way; as simple with a simplicity in fact unknown in organic life. They ignored the metabolism of human nature, by which experiences are absorbed into the mind and magically converted into personality, which rejects much of the material life brings to it and handles the rest to serve the interests of love or hate, good or evil, life or death, according to an inhabiting daemon, whose reasons are never given. Man conceived himself as living reasonably under the instruction of the five senses, which tell him to seek pleasure and avoid pain.

The first effect of this rational conception of life was cheerful vulgarity; and there are worse things than that. Man might well have felt this view of his destiny as a relief after the Christian philosophy, which abased his origin to criminality, and started him so low only to elevate him to the height, most disagreeable to most people, of company with godhead, after dragging him through all sorts of unpalatable experiences, including participation in a violent and apparently unnecessary death. In so far as a man adopted the new and rationalist philosophy he could be compared to an actor who, after spending a lifetime playing Hamlet and Othello and King Lear, retires to keep a country pub. All was thenceforward to go at a peaceable jogtrot. Children were to grow up straight striplings of light, undeformed by repression, unscarred by conflicts, because their parents would hand them over in their earliest years to the care of pedagogic experts. Divorce was not to be reckoned as a disgrace nor as a tragedy nor even as a failure, but as a pleasurable extension of experience, like travel. Furthermore—and this was con-

sidered as the sanest adjustment of all—the ardors of patriotism were
to be abandoned, and replaced by a cool resolution to place one's country
on a level with all others in one's affections, and to hand it over without
concern to the dominion of any other power which could offer it greater
material benefits. It was not out of cynicism that the benefits demanded
were material: it was believed that the material automatically produced
the intellectual and the spiritual. These reasonable steps having been
taken, there was to follow harmony. The only peril was that it might
become too sweet.

But the five senses had evidently not been rightly understood. Such
children as were surrendered by their parents to expert treatment, complained against that surrender as if it had been any other kind of
abandonment. They quarreled with the pedagogues as much as they
would have quarreled with their parents; but, the bond of the flesh
being absent, there was something sapless in their quarrels, and there
was less energy engendered. Sexual life was not noticeably smoother than
it had been. The epic love of marriage and the lyric love-song of the
encounter both lost much by the pretense that they were the same. Nor,
as patriotism was discredited, did peace come nearer. Indeed, the certainty of war now arched over the earth like a second sky, inimical to the
first. If harmony had been our peril, we were preserved from it, both
within and without. For it was plain that, as Christian philosophy had
so harshly averred, the world was a stage on which an extraordinary
drama, not yet fully comprehended by the intellect, was being performed;
and its action was now an agony. But, owing to the adoption of the
rationalist philosophy, some of the actors filling the most important
parts were now incapable of speaking their lines. It appeared that
Hamlet and *Othello* and *King Lear* would be no longer cathartic tragedies but repellent and distressing farces if the leading characters had,
in the climactic scenes, been overtaken by the delusion that they had
retired and were keeping country pubs.

So the evil moment came and was clear: not surpassed in evil since
the days of the barbarian invasions. The devil of nationalism had been
driven out of man, but he had not become the headquarters of the dove.
Instead there had entered into him the seven devils of internationalism,
and he was torn by their frenzies. Then what is against all devils came
to his aid. The achievement (which, as yet, is unfinished, since peace
does not reign) was accomplished by a continuance of the drama in
spite of the difficulties created by the rationalist philosophy. Since the

actors cast to play the leading parts would not speak, the action was carried on by the peoples who used to walk to and fro at the back of the scene, softly laughing or softly weeping, or simply quietly being. Now these people streamed across the continents, inscribing their beliefs on the surface of the earth by the course of their flights, and on the sites of their martyrdoms. They defeated fascism by not being fascist. They showed the contrast between fascism and nonfascism so clearly that the world, wishing to live, defended their side because it could be seen that they were the representatives of life. As they exorcised the devils from the body of Europe they seemed to affirm certain values. It was perhaps true that the origin of man was in criminality, for once a community refused to make the effort of seeking the company of godhead it certainly became criminal. It was perhaps true that hedonism is an impotent gospel, for now it could be seen that pleasure means nothing to many men. As fast as those who ran to save their lives ran those who ran to slay them, even if their pursuit, pressed too hard, might change them into fugitives, whose own lives were in danger. Now the scorned bonds of the flesh asserted their validity. It was the final and unbearable misery of these flights that husbands were separated from their wives, and parents lost sight of their children. The men who performed the cruelest surgery on these families, who threw the husband and wife into the gas chamber while the children traveled by train to an unknown destination, had themselves been brought up to condemn their own ties of blood. The anguish of the divided was obviously holy. The contentment of those who felt no reluctance to divide was plainly damned.

In this day of exposition those who made the other sacrifice of the near for the far, and preferred other countries to their own, proved also to be unholy. The relationship between a man and a fatherland is always disturbed by conflict, if either man or fatherland is highly developed. A man's demands for liberty must at some point challenge the limitations the state imposes on the individual for the sake of the mass. If he is to carry on the national tradition he must wrestle with those who, speaking in its name, desire to crystallize it at the point reached by the previous generation. In any case national life itself must frequently exasperate him, because it is the medium in which he is expressing himself, and every craftsman or artist is repelled by the resistance of his medium to his will. All men should have a drop or two of treason in their veins, if the nations are not to go soft like so many sleepy pears.

Yet to be a traitor is most miserable. All the men I saw in the prisoner's dock were sad as they stood their trials, not only because they were going to be punished. They would have been sad even if they had never been brought to justice. They had forsaken the familiar medium; they had trusted themselves to the mercies of those who had no reason to care for them; knowing their custodians' indifference they had lived for long in fear; and they were aware that they had thrown away their claim on those who might naturally have felt affection for them. Strangers, as King Solomon put it, were filled with their wealth, and their labors were in the house of a stranger, and they mourned at the last when their flesh and body were consumed. As a divorce sharply recalls what a happy marriage should be, so the treachery of these men recalled what a nation should be; a shelter where all talents are generously recognized, all forgivable oddities forgiven, all viciousness quietly frustrated, and those who lack talent honored for equivalent contributions of graciousness. Each of these men was as dependent on the good opinion of others as one is oneself; they needed a nation which was also a hearth, and their capacity for suffering made it tragic that they had gone out from their own hearth to suffer among strangers, because the intellectual leaders of their time had professed a philosophy which was scarcely more than a lapse of memory, and had forgotten, that a hearth gives out warmth.

John F. Kennedy

EDMUND G. ROSS

*I*N A lonely grave, forgotten and unknown, lies "the man who saved a President," and who as a result may well have preserved for ourselves and posterity constitutional government in the United States—the man who performed in 1868 what one historian has called "the most heroic act in American history, incomparably more difficult than any deed of valor upon the field of battle"—a United States Senator whose name no one recalls: Edmund G. Ross of Kansas.

The impeachment of President Andrew Johnson, the event in which the obscure Ross was to play such a dramatic role, was the sensational climax to the bitter struggle between the President, determined to carry out Abraham Lincoln's policies of reconciliation with the defeated South, and the more radical Republican leaders in Congress, who sought to administer the downtrodden Southern states as conquered provinces which had forfeited their rights under the Constitution. It was, moreover, a struggle between Executive and Legislative authority. Andrew Johnson, the courageous if untactful Tennessean who had been the only Southern Member of Congress to refuse to secede with his state, had committed himself to the policies of the Great Emancipator to whose high station he had succeeded only by the course of an assassin's bullet. He knew that Lincoln prior to his death had already clashed with the extremists in Congress, who had opposed his approach to reconstruction in a constitutional and charitable manner and sought to make the Legislative Branch of the government supreme. And his own belligerent temperament soon destroyed any hope that Congress might now join hands in carrying out Lincoln's policies of permitting the

281

South to resume its place in the Union with as little delay and controversy as possible.

By 1866, when Edmund Ross first came to the Senate, the two
branches of the government were already at each other's throats, snarling
and bristling with anger. Bill after bill was vetoed by the President on
the grounds that they were unconstitutional, too harsh in their treatment
of the South, an unnecessary prolongation of military rule in peacetime
or undue interference with the authority of the Executive Branch. And
for the first time in our nation's history, important public measures
were passed over a President's veto and became law without his support.

But not all of Andrew Johnson's vetoes were overturned; and the
"Radical" Republicans of the Congress promptly realized that one final
step was necessary before they could crush their despised foe (and in
the heat of political battle their vengeance was turned upon their President far more than their former military enemies of the South). That
one remaining step was the assurance of a two-thirds majority in the
Senate—for under the Constitution, such a majority was necessary to
override a Presidential veto. And more important, such a majority was
constitutionally required to accomplish their major ambition, now an
ill-kept secret, conviction of the President under an impeachment and
his dismissal from office!

The temporary and unstable two-thirds majority which had enabled
the Senate Radical Republicans on several occasions to enact legislation
over the President's veto was, they knew, insufficiently reliable for an
impeachment conviction. To solidify this bloc became the paramount
goal of Congress, expressly or impliedly governing its decisions on other
issues—particularly the admission of new states, the re-admission of
Southern states and the determination of senatorial credentials. By
extremely dubious methods a pro-Johnson Senator was denied his seat.
Over the President's veto Nebraska was admitted to the Union, seating
two more anti-administration Senators. Although last minute maneuvers
failed to admit Colorado over the President's veto (sparsely populated
Colorado had rejected statehood in a referendum), an unexpected
tragedy brought false tears and fresh hopes for a new vote, in Kansas.

Senator Jim Lane of Kansas had been a "conservative" Republican
sympathetic to Johnson's plans to carry out Lincoln's reconstruction
policies. But his frontier state was one of the most "radical" in the Union.
When Lane voted to uphold Johnson's veto of the Civil Rights Bill of
1866 and introduced the administration's bill for recognition of the

new state government of Arkansas, Kansas had arisen in outraged heat. A mass meeting at Lawrence had vilified the Senator and speedily reported resolutions sharply condemning his position. Humiliated, mentally ailing, broken in health and laboring under charges of financial irregularities, Jim Lane took his own life on July 1, 1886.

With this thorn in their side removed, the Radical Republicans in Washington looked anxiously toward Kansas and the selection of Lane's successor. Their fondest hopes were realized, for the new Senator from Kansas turned out to be Edmund G. Ross, the very man who had introduced the resolutions attacking Lane at Lawrence.

There could be no doubt as to where Ross's sympathies lay, for his entire career was one of determined opposition to the slave states of the South, their practices and their friends. In 1854, when only twenty-eight, he had taken part in the mob rescue of a fugitive slave in Milwaukee. In 1856, he had joined that flood of antislavery immigrants to "bleeding" Kansas who intended to keep it a free territory. Disgusted with the Democratic party of his youth, he had left that party, and volunteered in the Kansas Free State Army to drive back a force of proslavery men invading the territory. In 1862, he had given up his newspaper work to enlist in the Union Army, from which he emerged a Major. His leading role in the condemnation of Lane at Lawrence convinced the Radical Republican leaders in Congress that in Edmund G. Ross they had a solid member of that vital two-thirds.

The stage was now set for the final scene—the removal of Johnson. Early in 1867, Congress enacted over the President's veto the Tenure-of-Office Bill which prevented the President from removing without the consent of the Senate all new officeholders whose appointment required confirmation by that body. At the time nothing more than the cry for more patronage was involved, Cabinet Members having originally been specifically exempt.

On August 5, 1867, President Johnson—convinced that the Secretary of War, whom he had inherited from Lincoln, Edward M. Stanton, was the surreptitious tool of the Radical Republicans and was seeking to become the almighty dictator of the conquered South—asked for his immediate resignation; and Stanton arrogantly fired back the reply that he declined to resign before the next meeting of Congress. Not one to cower before this kind of effrontery, the President one week later suspended Stanton, and appointed in his place the one man whom Stanton did not dare resist, General Grant. On January 13, 1868, an angry

Senate notified the President and Grant that it did not concur in the suspension of Stanton, and Grant vacated the office upon Stanton's return. But the situation was intolerable. The Secretary of War was unable to attend Cabinet meetings or associate with his colleagues in the administration; and on February 21, President Johnson, anxious to obtain a court test of the act he believed obviously unconstitutional, again notified Stanton that he had been summarily removed from the office of Secretary of War.

While Stanton, refusing to yield possession, barricaded himself in his office, public opinion in the nation ran heavily against the President. He had intentionally broken the law and dictatorially thwarted the will of Congress! Although previous resolutions of impeachment had been defeated in the House, both in committee and on the floor, a new resolution was swiftly reported and adopted on February 24 by a tremendous vote. Every single Republican voted in the affirmative, and Thaddeus Stevens of Pennsylvania—the crippled, fanatical personification of the extremes of the Radical Republican movement, master of the House of Representatives, with a mouth like the thin edge of an ax—warned both Houses of the Congress coldly: "Let me see the recreant who would vote to let such a criminal escape. Point me to one who will dare do it and I will show you one who will dare the infamy of posterity."

With the President impeached—in effect, indicted—by the House, the frenzied trial for his conviction or acquittal under the Articles of Impeachment began on March 5 in the Senate, presided over by the Chief Justice. It was a trial to rank with all the great trials in history— Charles I before the High Court of Justice, Louis XVI before the French Convention, and Warren Hastings before the House of Lords. Two great elements of drama were missing: the actual cause for which the President was being tried was not fundamental to the welfare of the nation; and the defendant himself was at all times absent.

But every other element of the highest courtroom drama was present. To each Senator the Chief Justice administered an oath "to do impartial justice" (including even the hot-headed Radical Senator from Ohio, Benjamin Wade, who as President Pro Tempore of the Senate was next in line for the Presidency). The chief prosecutor for the House was General Benjamin F. Butler, the "butcher of New Orleans," a talented but coarse and demagogic Congressman from Massachusetts. (When he lost his seat in 1874, he was so hated by his own party as well as his opponents that one Republican wired concerning the Democratic sweep,

"Butler defeated, everything else lost.") Some one thousand tickets were printed for admission to the Senate galleries during the trial, and every conceivable device was used to obtain one of the four tickets allotted each Senator.

From the fifth of March to the sixteenth of May, the drama continued. Of the eleven Articles of Impeachment adopted by the House, the first eight were based upon the removal of Stanton and the appointment of a new Secretary of War in violation of the Tenure-of-Office Act; the ninth related to Johnson's conversation with a general which was said to induce violations of the Army Appropriations Act; the tenth recited that Johnson had delivered "intemperate, inflammatory and scandalous harangues . . . as well against Congress as the laws of the United States"; and the eleventh was a deliberately obscure conglomeration of all the charges in the preceding articles, which had been designed by Thaddeus Stevens to furnish a common ground for those who favored conviction but were unwilling to identify themselves on basic issues. In opposition to Butler's inflammatory arguments in support of this hastily drawn indictment, Johnson's able and learned counsel replied with considerable effectiveness. They insisted that the Tenure-of-Office Act was null and void as a clear violation of the Constitution; that even if it were valid, it would not apply to Stanton, for the reasons previously mentioned; and that the only way that a judicial test of the law could be obtained was for Stanton to be dismissed and sue for his rights in the courts.

But as the trial progressed, it became increasingly apparent that the impatient Republicans did not intend to give the President a fair trial on the formal issues upon which the impeachment was drawn, but intended instead to depose him from the White House on any grounds, real or imagined, for refusing to accept their policies. Telling evidence in the President's favor was arbitrarily excluded. Prejudgment on the part of most Senators was brazenly announced. Attempted bribery and other forms of pressure were rampant. The chief interest was not in the trial or the evidence, but in the tallying of votes necessary for conviction.

Twenty-seven states (excluding the unrecognized Southern states) in the Union meant fifty-four members of the Senate, and thirty-six votes were required to constitute the two-thirds majority necessary for conviction. All twelve Democratic votes were obviously lost, and the forty-two Republicans knew that they could afford to lose only six of their own members if Johnson were to be ousted. To their dismay, at a preliminary Republican caucus, six courageous Republicans indicated that the evidence so far introduced was not in their opinion sufficient to convict Johnson under the Articles of Impeachment. "Infamy!" cried the Philadelphia *Press*. The Republic has "been betrayed in the house of its friends!"

But if the remaining thirty-six Republicans would hold, there would be no doubt as to the outcome. All must stand together! But one Republican Senator would not announce his verdict in the preliminary poll—Edmund G. Ross of Kansas. The Radicals were outraged that a Senator from such an anti-Johnson stronghold as Kansas could be doubtful. "It was a very clear case," Senator Sumner of Massachusetts fumed, "especially for a Kansas man. I did not think that a Kansas man could quibble against his country."

From the very time Ross had taken his seat, the Radical leaders had been confident of his vote. His entire background, as already indicated, was one of firm support of their cause. One of his first acts in the Senate had been to read a declaration of his adherence to Radical Republican policy, and he had silently voted for all of their measures. He had made it clear that he was not in sympathy with Andrew Johnson personally or politically; and after the removal of Stanton, he had voted with the majority in adopting a resolution declaring such removal unlawful. His colleague from Kansas, Senator Pomeroy, was one of the most radical leaders of the anti-Johnson group. The Republicans insisted that Ross's crucial vote was rightfully theirs, and they were determined to get it by whatever means available. As stated by De Witt in his memorable *Impeachment of Andrew Johnson,* "The full brunt of the struggle turned at last on the one remaining doubtful Senator, Edmund G. Ross."

When the impeachment resolution had passed the House, Senator Ross had casually remarked to Senator Sprague of Rhode Island, "Well, Sprague, the thing is here; and, so far as I am concerned, though a Republican and opposed to Mr. Johnson and his policy, he shall have as fair a trial as an accused man ever had on this earth." Immediately the word spread that "Ross was shaky." "From that hour," he later wrote, "not a day passed that did not bring me, by mail and telegraph and in personal intercourse, appeals to stand fast for impeachment, and not a few were the admonitions of condign visitations upon any indication even of lukewarmness."

Throughout the country, and in all walks of life, as indicated by the correspondence of Members of the Senate, the condition of the public mind was not unlike that preceding a great battle. The dominant party of the nation seemed to occupy the position of public prosecutor, and it was scarcely in the mood to brook delay for trial or to hear defense. Washington had become during the trial the central point of the politically dissatisfied and swarmed with representatives of every state of the Union, demanding in a practically united voice the deposition of the President. The footsteps of the anti-impeaching Republicans were dogged from the day's beginning to its end and far into the night, with entreaties, considerations, and threats. The newspapers came daily filled with not a few threats of violence upon their return to their constituents.

Ross and his fellow doubtful Republicans were daily pestered, spied upon and subjected to every form of pressure. Their residences were carefully watched, their social circles suspiciously scrutinized, and their every move and companions secretly marked in special notebooks. They were warned in the party press, harangued by their constituents, and sent dire warnings threatening political ostracism and even assassination. Stanton himself, from his barricaded headquarters in the War Department, worked day and night to bring to bear upon the doubtful Senators all the weight of his impressive military associations. The Philadelphia *Press* reported "a fearful avalanche of telegrams from every section of the country," a great surge of public opinion from the "common people" who had given their money and lives to the country and would not "willingly or unavenged see their great sacrifice made naught."

The New York *Tribune* reported that Edmund Ross in particular was "mercilessly dragged this way and that by both sides, hunted like a fox night and day and badgered by his own colleagues, like the bridge at Arcola now trod upon by one Army and now trampled by the other." His background and life were investigated from top to bottom, and his constituents and colleagues pursued him throughout Washington to gain some inkling of his opinion. He was the target of every eye, his name was on every mouth and his intentions were discussed in every newspaper. Although there is evidence that he gave some hint of agreement to each side, and each attempted to claim him publicly, he actually kept both sides in a state of complete suspense by his judicial silence.

But with no experience in political turmoil, no reputation in the Senate, no independent income and the most radical state in the Union to deal with, Ross was judged to be the most sensitive to criticism and the most certain to be swayed by expert tactics. A committee of Congress-

men and Senators sent to Kansas, and to the states of the other doubtful
Republicans, this telegram: "Great danger to the peace of the country
and the Republican cause if impeachment fails. Send to your Senators
public opinion by resolutions, letters, and delegations." A member of
the Kansas legislature called upon Ross at the Capitol. A general urged
on by Stanton remained at his lodge until four o'clock in the morning
determined to see him. His brother received a letter offering $20,000 for
revelation of the Senator's intentions. Gruff Ben Butler exclaimed of
Ross, "There is a bushel of money! How much does the damned
scoundrel want?" The night before the Senate was to take its first vote
for the conviction or acquittal of Johnson, Ross received this telegram
from home:

> Kansas has heard the evidence and demands the conviction of the
> President.
>   [signed] D. R. ANTHONY AND 1,000 OTHERS

And on that fateful morning of May 16 Ross replied:

> To D. R. Anthony and 1,000 Others: I do not recognize your right
> to demand that I vote either for or against conviction. I have taken an
> oath to do impartial justice according to the Constitution and laws,
> and trust that I shall have the courage to vote according to the dictates
> of my judgment and for the highest good of the country.
>   [signed]—E. G. Ross

That morning spies traced Ross to his breakfast; and ten minutes
before the vote was taken his Kansas colleague warned him in the
presence of Thaddeus Stevens that a vote for acquittal would mean
trumped up charges and his political death.

But now the fateful hour was at hand. Neither escape, delay nor
indecision was possible. As Ross himself later described it: "The galleries
were packed. Tickets of admission were at an enormous premium. The
House had adjourned and all of its members were in the Senate chamber.
Every chair on the Senate floor was filled with a Senator, a Cabinet
Officer, a member of the President's counsel or a member of the House."
Every Senator was in his seat, the desperately ill Grimes of Iowa being
literally carried in.

It had been decided to take the first vote under that broad Eleventh
Article of Impeachment, believed to command the widest support. As
the Chief Justice announced the voting would begin, he reminded "the
citizens and strangers in the galleries that absolute silence and perfect
order are required." But already a deathlike stillness enveloped the

Senate chamber. A Congressman later recalled that "Some of the members of the House near me grew pale and sick under the burden of suspense"; and Ross noted that there was even "a subsidence of the shuffling of feet, the rustling of silks, the fluttering of fans, and of conversation."

The voting tensely commenced. By the time the Chief Justice reached the name of Edmund Ross twenty-four "guilties" had been pronounced. Ten more were certain and one other practically certain. Only Ross's vote was needed to obtain the thirty-six votes necessary to convict the President. But not a single person in the room knew how this young Kansan would vote. Unable to conceal the suspense and emotion in his voice, the Chief Justice put the question to him: "Mr. Senator Ross, how say you? Is the respondent Andrew Johnson guilty or not guilty of a high misdemeanor as charged in this Article?" Every voice was still; every eye was upon the freshman Senator from Kansas. The hopes and fears, the hatred and bitterness of past decades were centered upon this one man.

As Ross himself later described it, his "powers of hearing and seeing seemed developed in an abnormal degree."

> Every individual in that great audience seemed distinctly visible, some with lips apart and bending forward in anxious expectancy, others with hand uplifted as if to ward off an apprehended blow . . . and each peering with an intensity that was almost tragic upon the face of him who was about to cast the fateful vote. . . . Every fan was folded, not a foot moved, not the rustle of a garment, not a whisper was heard. . . . Hope and fear seemed blended in every face, instantaneously alternating, some with revengeful hate . . . others lighted with hope. . . . The Senators in their seats leaned over their desks, many with hand to ear. . . . It was a tremendous responsibility, and it was not strange that he upon whom it had been imposed by a fateful combination of conditions should have sought to avoid it, to put it away from him as one shuns, or tries to fight off, a nightmare. . . . I almost literally looked down into my open grave. Friendships, position, fortune, everything that makes life desirable to an ambitious man were about to be swept away by the breath of my mouth, perhaps forever. It is not strange that my answer was carried waveringly over the air and failed to reach the limits of the audience, or that repetition was called for by distant Senators on the opposite side of the Chamber.

Then came the answer again in a voice that could not be misunderstood—full, final, definite, unhesitating and unmistakable: "Not guilty." The deed was done, the President saved; the trial as good as over and the conviction lost. The remainder of the roll call was unimportant,

conviction had failed by the margin of a single vote and a general rum-
bling filled the chamber until the Chief Justice proclaimed that "on
this Article thirty-five Senators having voted guilty and nineteen not
guilty, a two-thirds majority not having voted for conviction, the President is, therefore, acquitted under this Article."

A ten-day recess followed, ten turbulent days to change votes on
the remaining Articles. An attempt was made to rush through bills to
readmit six Southern states, whose twelve Senators were guaranteed to
vote for conviction. But this could not be accomplished in time. Again
Ross was the only one uncommitted on the other Articles, the only one
whose vote could not be predicted in advance. And again he was
subjected to terrible pressure. From "D. R. Anthony and Others," he
received a wire informing him that "Kansas repudiates you as she does
all perjurers and skunks." Every incident in his life was examined and
distorted. Professional witnesses were found by Senator Pomeroy to
testify before a special House committee that Ross had indicated a
willingness to change his vote for a consideration. (Unfortunately this
witness was so delighted in his exciting role that he also swore that
Senator Pomeroy had made an offer to produce three votes for acquittal
for $40,000.) When Ross, in his capacity as a Committee Chairman, took
several bills to the President, James G. Blaine remarked: "There goes
the rascal to get his pay." (Long afterward Blaine was to admit: "In
the exaggerated denunciation caused by the anger and chagrin of the
moment, great injustice was done to statesmen of spotless character.")

Again the wild rumors spread that Ross had been won over on the
remaining Articles of Impeachment. As the Senate reassembled, he was
the only one of the seven "renegade" Republicans to vote with the
majority on preliminary procedural matters. But when the second and
third Articles of Impeachment were read, the name of Ross was reached
again with the same intense suspense of eleven days earlier, again came
the calm answer "Not guilty."

Why did Ross, whose dislike for Johnson continued, vote "Not
guilty"? His motives appear clearly from his own writings on the
subject years later in articles contributed to *Scribner's* and *Forum*
magazines:

> In a large sense, the independence of the executive office as a
> coordinate branch of the government was on trial. . . . If . . . the
> President must step down . . . a disgraced man and a political outcast
> . . . upon insufficient proofs and from partisan considerations, the

office of President would be degraded, cease to be a coordinate branch of the government, and ever after subordinated to the legislative will. It would practically have revolutionized our splendid political fabric into a partisan Congressional autocracy. . . . This government had never faced so insidious a danger . . . control by the worst element of American politics. . . . If Andrew Johnson were acquitted by a non-partisan vote . . . America would pass the danger point of partisan rule and that intolerance which so often characterizes the sway of great majorities and makes them dangerous.

The "open grave" which Edmund Ross had foreseen was hardly an exaggeration. A Justice of the Kansas Supreme Court telegraphed him that "the rope with which Judas Iscariot hanged himself is lost, but Jim Lane's pistol is at your service." An editorial in a Kansas newspaper screamed:

> On Saturday last Edmund G. Ross, United States Senator from Kansas, sold himself, and betrayed his constituents; stultified his own record, basely lied to his friends, shamefully violated his solemn pledge . . . and to the utmost of his poor ability signed the death warrant of his country's liberty. This act was done deliberately, because the traitor, like Benedict Arnold, loved money better than he did principle, friends, honor and his country, all combined. Poor, pitiful, shriveled wretch, with a soul so small that a little pelf would outweigh all things else that dignify or ennoble manhood.

Ross's political career was ended. To the New York *Tribune,* he was nothing but "a miserable poltroon and traitor." The Philadelphia *Press* said that in Ross "littleness" had "simply borne its legitimate fruit," and that he and his fellow recalcitrant Republicans had "plunged from a precipice of fame into the groveling depths of infamy and death." The Philadelphia *Inquirer* said that "They had tried, convicted and sentenced themselves." For them there could be "no allowance, no clemency."

Comparative peace returned to Washington as Stanton relinquished his office and Johnson served out the rest of his term, later—unlike his Republican defenders—to return triumphantly to the Senate as Senator from Tennessee. But no one paid attention when Ross tried unsuccessfully to explain his vote, and denounced the falsehoods of Ben Butler's investigating committee, recalling that the General's "well known groveling instincts and proneness to slime and uncleanness" had led "the public to insult the brute creation by dubbing him 'the beast.' " He clung unhappily to his seat in the Senate until the expiration of his term, frequently referred to as "the traitor Ross," and complaining that his fellow Congressmen, as well as citizens on the street, considered association with him "disreputable and scandalous," and passed him by as if he were "a leper, with averted face and every indication of hatred and disgust."

Neither Ross nor any other Republican who had voted for the acquittal of Johnson was ever re-elected to the Senate, not a one of them retaining the support of their party's organization. When he returned to Kansas in 1871, he and his family suffered social ostracism, physical attack, and near poverty.

Who was Edmund G. Ross? Practically nobody. Not a single public law bears his name, not a single history book includes his picture, not a single list of Senate "greats" mentions his service. His one heroic deed has been all but forgotten. But who might Edmund G. Ross have been? That is the question—for Ross, a man with an excellent command of words, an excellent background for politics and an excellent future in the Senate might well have outstripped his colleagues in prestige and power throughout a long Senate career. Instead, he chose to throw all of this away for one act of conscience.

But the twisting course of human events eventually upheld the faith he expressed to his wife shortly after the trial: "Millions of men cursing me today will bless me tomorrow for having saved the country from the greatest peril through which it has ever passed, though none but God can ever know the struggle it has cost me." For twenty years later Congress repealed the Tenure-of-Office Act, to which every President after Johnson, regardless of party, had objected; and still later the Supreme Court, referring to "the extremes of that episode in our government," held it to be unconstitutional. Ross moved to New Mexico, where in his later years he was to be appointed Territorial Governor. Just prior to his death when he was awarded a special pension by Congress for his service in the Civil War, the press and the country took the opportunity to pay tribute to his fidelity to principle in a trying hour and his courage in saving his government from a devastating reign of terror. They now agreed with Ross's earlier judgment that his vote had "saved the country from . . . a strain that would have wrecked any other form of government." Those Kansas newspapers and political leaders who had bitterly denounced him in earlier years praised Ross for his stand against legislative mob rule: "By the firmness and courage of Senator Ross," it was said, "the country was saved from calamity greater than war, while it consigned him to a political martyrdom, the most cruel in our history. . . . Ross was the victim of a wild flame of intolerance which swept everything before it. He did his duty knowing that it meant his political death. . . . It was a brave thing for Ross to do, but Ross did it. He acted for his conscience and with a lofty patriotism, regardless of what he knew must be the ruinous consequences to himself. He acted right."

I could not close the story of Edmund Ross without some more adequate mention of those six courageous Republicans who stood with Ross and braved denunciation to acquit Andrew Johnson. Edmund Ross, more than any of those six colleagues, endured more before and after his vote, reached his conscientious decision with greater difficulty, and aroused the greatest interest and suspense prior to May 16 by his noncommittal silence. His story, like his vote, is the key to the impeachment tragedy. But all seven of the Republicans who voted against conviction should be remembered for their courage. Not a single one of them ever won re-election to the Senate. Not a single one of them escaped the unholy combination of threats, bribes and coercive tactics by which their fellow Republicans attempted to intimidate their votes; and not a single one of them escaped the terrible torture of vicious criticism engendered by the vote to acquit.

William Pitt Fessenden of Maine, one of the most eminent Senators, orators and lawyers of his day, and a prominent senior Republican leader, who admired Stanton and disliked Johnson, became convinced early in the game that "the whole thing is a mere madness."

> The country has so bad an opinion of the President, which he fully deserves, that it expects his condemnation. Whatever may be the consequences to myself personally, whatever I may think and feel as a politician, I will not decide the question against my own judgment. I would rather be confined to planting cabbages the remainder of my days. . . . Make up your mind, if need be, to hear me denounced a traitor and perhaps hanged in effigy. All imaginable abuse has been heaped upon me by the men and papers devoted to the impeachers. I have received several letters from friends warning me that my political grave is dug if I do not vote for conviction, and several threatening assassination. It is rather hard at my time of life, after a long career, to find myself the target of pointed arrows from those whom I have faithfully served. The public, when aroused and excited by passion and prejudice, is little better than a wild beast. I shall at all events retain my own self-respect and a clear conscience, and time will do justice to my motives at least.

The Radical Republicans were determined to win over the respected Fessenden, whose name would be the first question mark on the call of the roll, and his mail from Maine was abusive, threatening and pleading. Wendell Phillips scornfully told a hissing crowd that "it takes six months for a statesmanlike idea to find its way into Mr. Fessenden's head. I don't say he is lacking; he is only very slow."

Fessenden decided to shun all newspapers and screen his mail. But when one of his oldest political friends in Maine urged him to "hang Johnson up by the heels like a dead crow in a cornfield, to frighten all of his tribe," noting that he was "sure I express the unanimous feeling of every loyal heart and head in this state," Fessenden indignantly replied:

> I am acting as a judge . . . by what right can any man upon whom no responsibility rests, and who does not even hear the evidence, undertake to advise me as to what the judgment, and even the sentence, should be? I wish all my friends and constituents to understand that I, and not they, am sitting in judgment upon the President. I, not they, have sworn to do impartial justice. I, not they, am responsible to God and man for my action and its consequences.

On that tragic afternoon of May 16, as Ross described it, Senator Fessenden "was in his place, pale and haggard, yet ready for the political martyrdom which he was about to face, and which not long afterward drove him to his grave."

The first Republican Senator to ring out "not guilty"—and the first of the seven to go to his grave, hounded by the merciless abuse that had dimmed all hope for re-election—was William Pitt Fessenden of Maine.

John B. Henderson of Missouri, one of the Senate's youngest members, had previously demonstrated high courage by introducing the Thirteenth Amendment abolishing slavery, simply because he was convinced that it would pass only if sponsored by a slave-state Senator, whose political death would necessarily follow. But when the full delegation of Republican representatives from his state cornered him in his office to demand that he convict the hated Johnson, warning that Missouri Republicans could stomach no other course, Henderson's usual courage wavered. He meekly offered to wire his resignation to the Governor, enabling a new appointee to vote for conviction; and, when it was doubted whether a new Senator would be permitted to vote, he agreed to ascertain whether his own vote would be crucial.

But an insolent and threatening telegram from Missouri restored his sense of honor, and he swiftly wired his reply: "Say to my friends that I am sworn to do impartial justice according to law and conscience, and I will try to do it like an honest man."

John Henderson voted for acquittal, the last important act of his Senatorial career. Denounced, threatened and burned in effigy in Missouri, he did not even bother to seek re-election to the Senate. Years later his party would realize its debt to him, and return him to lesser offices, but for the Senate, whose integrity he had upheld, he was through.

Peter Van Winkle of West Virginia, the last doubtful Republican name to be called on May 16, was, like Ross, a "nobody"; but his firm "not guilty" extinguished the last faint glimmer of hope which Edmund Ross had already all but destroyed. The Republicans had counted on Van Winkle—West Virginia's first United States Senator, and a critic of Stanton's removal; and for his courage, he was labeled "West Virginia's betrayer" by the Wheeling *Intelligencer,* which declared to the world that there was not a loyal citizen in the state who had not been misrepresented by his vote. He, too, had insured his permanent withdrawal from politics as soon as his Senate term expired.

The veteran Lyman Trumbull of Illinois, who had defeated Abe Lincoln for the Senate, had drafted much of the major reconstruction legislation which Johnson vetoed, and had voted to censure Johnson upon Stanton's removal.

But, in the eyes of the Philadelphia *Press,* his "statesmanship drivelled into selfishness," for, resisting tremendous pressure, he voted against conviction. A Republican convention in Chicago had resolved "That any Senator elected by the votes of Union Republicans, who at this time blenches and betrays, is infamous and should be dishonored and execrated while this free government endures." And an Illinois Republican leader had warned the distinguished Trumbull "not to show himself on the streets in Chicago; for I fear that the representatives of an indignant people would hang him to the most convenient lamppost."

But Lyman Trumbull, ending a brilliant career of public service and devotion to the party which would renounce him, filed for the record these enduring words:

> The question to be decided is not whether Andrew Johnson is a proper person to fill the Presidential office, nor whether it is fit that he should remain in it. . . . Once set, the example of impeaching a President for what, when the excitement of the House shall have subsided, will be regarded as insufficient cause, no future President will be safe who happens to differ with a majority of the House and

two-thirds of the Senate on any measure deemed by them important.
. . . What then becomes of the checks and balances of the Constitution
so carefully devised and so vital to its perpetuity? They are all gone.
. . . I cannot be an instrument to produce such a result, and at the
hazard of the ties even of friendship and affection, till calmer times
shall do justice to my motives, no alternative is left me but the inflexible discharge of duty.

Joseph Smith Fowler of Tennessee, like Ross, Henderson, and Van
Winkle a freshman Senator, at first thought the President impeachable.
But the former Nashville professor was horrified by the mad passion of
the House in rushing through the impeachment resolution by evidence
against Johnson "based on falsehood," and by the "corrupt and dishonorable" Ben Butler, "a wicked man who seeks to convert the Senate of the
United States into a political guillotine." He refused to be led by the
nose by "politicians, thrown to the surface through the disjointed time
. . . keeping alive the embers of the departing revolution." Threatened,
investigated and defamed by his fellow Radical Republicans, the nervous
Fowler so faltered in his reply on May 16 that it was at first mistaken for
the word "guilty." A wave of triumph swept the Senate—Johnson was
convicted, Ross's vote was not needed! But then came the clear and distinct answer: "Not guilty."

His re-election impossible, Fowler quietly retired from the Senate at
the close of his term two years later, but not without a single statement in
defense of his vote: "I acted for my country and posterity in obedience to
the will of God."

James W. Grimes of Iowa, one of Johnson's bitter and influential
foes in the Senate, became convinced that the trial was intended only to
excite public passions through "lies sent from here by the most worthless
and irresponsible creatures on the face of the earth" (an indication, perhaps, of the improved quality of Washington correspondents in the last
eighty-seven years).

Unfortunately, the abuse and threats heaped upon him during the
trial brought on a stroke of paralysis only two days before the vote was
to be taken, and he was confined to his bed. The Radical Republicans,
refusing any postponement, were delightedly certain that Grimes would
either be too sick in fact to attend on May 16, or would plead that his
illness prevented him from attending to cast the vote that would end
his career. In the galleries, the crowd sang, "Old Grimes is dead, that
bad old man, we ne'er shall see him more." And in the New York

Tribune, Horace Greeley was writing: "It seems as if no generation could pass without giving us one man to live among the Warnings of history. We have had Benedict Arnold, Aaron Burr, Jefferson Davis, and now we have James W. Grimes."

But James W. Grimes was a man of great physical as well as moral courage, and just before the balloting was to begin on May 16, four men carried the pale and withered Senator from Iowa into his seat. He later wrote that Fessenden had grasped his hand and given him a "glorified smile. . . . I would not today exchange that recollection for the highest distinction of life." The Chief Justice suggested that it would be permissible for him to remain seated while voting—but with the assistance of his friends, Senator Grimes struggled to his feet and in a surprisingly firm voice called out "not guilty."

Burned in effigy, accused in the press of "idiocy and impotency," and repudiated by his state and friends, Grimes never recovered—but before he died he declared to a friend:

> I shall ever thank God that in that troubled hour of trial, when many privately confessed that they had sacrificed their judgment and their conscience at the behests of party newspapers and party hate, I had the courage to be true to my oath and my conscience. . . . Perhaps I did wrong not to commit perjury by order of a party; but I cannot see it that way. . . . I became a judge acting on my own responsibility and accountable only to my own conscience and my Maker; and no power could force me to decide on such a case contrary to my convictions, whether that party was composed of my friends or my enemies.

Thomas Paine

THE CRISIS, No. 1

*T*HESE ARE the times that try men's souls. The summer soldier and the sunshine patriot will, in this crisis, shrink from the service of his country; but he that stands it NOW, deserves the love and thanks of man and woman. Tyranny, like hell, is not easily conquered; yet we have this consolation with us, that the harder the conflict, the more glorious the triumph. What we obtain too cheap, we esteem too lightly: 'tis dearness only that gives every thing its value. Heaven knows how to put a proper price upon its goods; and it would be strange indeed, if so celestial an article as FREEDOM should not be highly rated. Britain, with an army to enforce her tyranny, has declared that she has a right (*not only to* TAX) but "to BIND *us in* ALL CASES WHATSOEVER," and if being *bound in that manner,* is not slavery, then is there not such a thing as slavery upon earth. Even the expression is impious, for so unlimited a power can belong only to God.

Whether the independence of the continent was declared too soon, or delayed too long, I will not now enter into as an argument; my own simple opinion is, that had it been eight months earlier, it would have been much better. We did not make a proper use of last winter, neither could we, while we were in a dependant state. However, the fault, if it were one, was all our own; we have none to blame but ourselves. But no great deal it lost yet; all that Howe has been doing for this month past, is rather a ravage than a conquest, which the spirit of the Jerseys a year ago would have quickly repulsed, and which time and a little resolution will soon recover.

I have as little superstition in me as any man living, but my secret opinion has ever been, and still is, that God Almighty will not give up a

298

people to military destruction, or leave them unsupportedly to perish, who have so earnestly and so repeatedly sought to avoid the calamities of war, by every decent method which wisdom could invent. Neither have I so much of the infidel in me, as to suppose that He has relinquished the government of the world, and given us up to the care of devils; and as I do not, I cannot see on what grounds the king of Britain can look up to heaven for help against us: a common murderer, a highwayman, or a house-breaker, has as good a pretence as he.

'Tis surprising to see how rapidly a panic will sometimes run through a country. All nations and ages have been subject to them: Britain has trembled like an ague at the report of a French fleet of flat bottomed boats; and in the fourteenth century the whole English army, after ravaging the kingdom of France, was driven back like men petrified with fear; and this brave exploit was performed by a few broken forces collected and headed by a woman, Joan of Arc. Would that heaven might inspire some Jersey maid to spirit up her countrymen, and save her fair fellow sufferers from ravage and ravishment! Yet panics, in some cases, have their uses; they produce as much good as hurt. Their duration is always short; the mind soon grows through them, and acquires a firmer habit than before. But their peculiar advantage is, that they are the touchstones of sincerity and hypocrisy, and bring things and men to light, which might otherwise have lain forever undiscovered. In fact, they have the same effect on secret traitors, which an imaginary apparition would have upon a private murderer. They sift out the hidden thoughts of man, and hold them up in public to the world. Many a disguised tory has lately shown his head, that shall penitentially solemnize with curses the day on which Howe arrived upon the Delaware.

As I was with the troops at fort Lee, and marched with them to the edge of Pennsylvania, I am well acquainted with many circumstances, which those who live at a distance, know but little or nothing of. Our situation there, was exceedingly cramped, the place being a narrow neck of land between the North River and the Hackensack. Our force was inconsiderable, being not one fourth so great as Howe could bring against us. We had no army at hand to have relieved the garrison, had we shut ourselves up and stood on our defence. Our ammunition, light artillery, and the best part of our stores, had been removed, on the apprehension that Howe would endeavor to penetrate the Jerseys, in which case fort Lee could be of no use to us; for it must occur to every thinking man, whether in the army or not, that these kind of field forts are only for temporary purposes, and last in use no longer than the enemy directs his force against the particular object, which such forts are raised to defend. Such was our situation and condition at fort Lee on the morning of the 20th of November, when an officer arrived with information that the enemy with 200 boats had landed about seven miles above: Major General Green, who commanded the garrison, immediately ordered them under arms, and sent express to General Washington at the town of Hackensack, distant by the way of the ferry, six miles. Our first object was to secure the bridge over the Hackensack, which laid up the river between the enemy and us, about six miles from us, and three from them. General Washington arrived in about three quarters of an hour, and marched at the head of the troops towards the bridge, which place I expected we should have a brush for; however, they did not choose to dispute it with us, and the greatest part of our troops went over the bridge, the rest over the ferry, except some which passed at a mill on a small creek, between the bridge and the ferry, and made their way through some marshy grounds up to the town of Hackensack, and there passed the river. We brought off as much baggage as the wagons could contain, the rest was lost. The simple object was to bring off the garrison, and march them on till they could be strengthened by the Jersey or Pennsylvania militia, so as to be enabled to make a stand. We staid four days at Newark, collected our out-posts with some of the Jersey militia, and marched out twice to meet the enemy, on being informed that they were advancing, though our numbers were greatly inferior to theirs. Howe, in my little opinion, committed a great error in generalship in not throwing a body of forces off from Staten Island through Amboy, by which means he might have seized all our stores at Brunswick, and intercepted our march into Pennsylvania: but if we believe the power of hell to be limited, we must likewise believe that their agents are under some providential control.

I shall not now attempt to give all the particulars of our retreat to the Delaware; suffice it for the present to say, that both officers and men, though greatly harrassed and fatigued, frequently without rest, covering, or provision, the inevitable consequences of a long retreat, bore it with a manly and martial spirit. All their wishes centered in one, which was, that the country would turn out and help them to drive the enemy back. Voltaire has remarked that king William never appeared to full advantage but in difficulties and in action; the same remark may be made on General Washington, for the character fits him. There is a natural firmness in some minds which cannot be unlocked by trifles, but which, when unlocked, discovers a cabinet of fortitude; and I reckon it among those kind of public blessings, which we do not immediately see, that God hath blest him with uninterrupted health, and given him a mind that can even flourish upon care.

I shall conclude this paper with some miscellaneous remarks on the state of our affairs; and shall begin with asking the following question, Why is it that the enemy have left the New-England provinces, and made these middle ones the seat of war? The answer is easy: New-England is not infested with tories, and we are. I have been tender in raising the cry against these men, and used numberless arguments to show them their danger, but it will not do to sacrifice a world either to their folly or their baseness. The period is now arrived, in which either they or we must change our sentiments, or one or both must fall. And what is a tory? Good God! what is he? I should not be afraid to go with a hundred whigs against a thousand tories, were they to attempt to get into arms. Every tory is a coward; for servile, slavish, self-interested fear is the foundation of toryism; and a man under such influence, though he may be cruel, never can be brave.

But, before the line of irrecoverable separation be drawn between us, let us reason the matter together: your conduct is an invitation to the enemy, yet not one in a thousand of you has heart enough to join him. Howe is as much deceived by you as the American cause is injured by you. He expects you will all take up arms, and flock to his standard, with muskets on your shoulders. Your opinions are of no use to him, unless you support him personally, for 'tis soldiers, and not tories, that he wants.

I once felt all that kind of anger, which a man ought to feel, against the mean principles that are held by the tories: a noted one, who kept a tavern at Amboy, was standing at his door, with as pretty a child in his hand, about eight or nine years old, as I ever saw, and after speaking his mind as freely as he thought was prudent, finished with this un-fatherly expression, *"Well! give me peace in my day."* Not a man lives on the continent but fully believes that a separation must some time or other finally take place, and a generous parent should have said, *"If there must be trouble, let it be in my day, that my child may have peace;"* and this single reflection, well applied, is sufficient to awaken every man to duty. Not a place upon earth might be so happy as America. Her situation is remote from all the wrangling world, and she has nothing to do but to trade with them. A man can distinguish in himself between temper and principle, and I am as confident, as I am that God governs the world, that America will never be happy till she gets clear of foreign dominion. Wars, without ceasing, will break out till that period arrives, and the continent must in the end be conqueror; for though the flame of liberty may sometimes cease to shine, the coal can never expire.

America did not, nor does not want force; but she wanted a proper application of that force. Wisdom is not the purchase of a day, and it is no wonder that we should err at the first setting off. From an excess of tenderness, we were unwilling to raise an army, and trusted our cause to the temporary defence of a well-meaning militia. A summer's experience has now taught us better; yet with those troops, while they were collected, we were able to set bounds to the progress of the enemy, and, thank God! they are again assembling. I always considered militia as the best troops in the world for a sudden exertion, but they will not do for a long campaign. Howe, it is probable, will make an attempt on this city; should he fail on this side the Delaware, he is ruined: if he succeeds, our cause is not ruined. He stakes all on his side against a part on ours; admitting he succeeds, the consequence will be, that armies from both ends of the continent will march to assist their suffering friends in the middle states; for he cannot go every where, it is impossible. I consider Howe as the greatest enemy the tories have; he is bringing a war into their country, which, had it not been for him and partly for themselves, they had been clear of. Should he now be expelled, I wish with all the devotion of a Christian, that the names of whig and tory may never more be mentioned; but should the tories give him encouragement to come, or assistance if he come, I as sincerely wish that our next year's arms may expel them from the continent, and the congress appropriate their possessions to the relief of those who have suffered in well-doing. A single successful battle next year will settle the whole. America could carry on a two years war by the confiscation of the property of disaffected persons, and be made happy by their expulsion. Say not that this is revenge, call it rather the soft resentment of a suffering people, who, having no object in view but the *good* of *all*, have staked their *own all* upon a seemingly doubtful event. Yet it is folly to argue against determined hardness; eloquence may strike the ear, and the language of sorrow draw forth the tear of compassion, but nothing can reach the heart that is steeled with prejudice.

Quitting this class of men, I turn with the warm ardor of a friend to those who have nobly stood, and are yet determined to stand the matter out: I call not upon a few, but upon all: not on *this* state or *that* state, but on *every* state; up and help us; lay your shoulders to the wheel; better have too much force than too little, when so great an object is at stake. Let it be told to the future world, that in the depth of winter, when nothing but hope and virtue could survive, that the city and the country, alarmed at one common danger, came forth to meet and to repulse it. Say not that thousands are gone, turn out your tens of thousands; throw not the burden of the day upon Providence, but *"show your faith by your works,"* that God may bless you. It matters not where you live, or what rank of life you hold, the evil or the blessing will reach you all. The far and the near, the home counties and the back, the rich and the poor, will suffer or rejoice alike. The heart that feels not now, is dead: the blood of his children will curse his cowardice, who shrinks back at a time when a little might have saved the whole, and made *them* happy. I love the man that can smile in trouble, that can gather strength from distress, and grow brave by reflection. 'Tis the business of little minds to shrink; but he whose heart is firm, and whose conscience approves his conduct, will pursue his principles unto death. My own line of reasoning is to myself as straight and clear as a ray of light. Not all the treasures of the world, so far as I believe, could have induced me to support an offensive war for I think it murder; but if a thief breaks into my house, burns and destroys my property, and kills or threatens to kill me, or those that are in it, and to *"bind me in all cases whatsoever,"* to his absolute will, am I to suffer it? What signifies it to me, whether he who does it is a king or a common man; my countryman or not my countryman; whether it be done by an individual villain, or an army of them? If we reason to the root of things we shall find no difference; neither can any just cause be assigned why we should punish in the one case and pardon in the other. Let them call me rebel, and welcome, I feel no concern from it; but I should suffer the misery of devils, were I to make a whore of my soul by swearing allegiance to one whose character is that of a sottish, stupid, stubborn, worthless, brutish man. I conceive likewise a horrid idea in receiving mercy from a being, who at the last day shall be shrieking to the rocks and mountains to cover him, and fleeing with terror from the orphan, the widow, and the slain of America.

There are cases which cannot be overdone by language, and this is one. There are persons too who see not the full extent of the evil which threatens them, they solace themselves with hopes that the enemy, if he succeed, will be merciful. It is the madness of folly, to expect mercy from those who have refused to do justice; and even mercy, where conquest is the object, is only a trick of war; the cunning of the fox is as murderous as the violence of the wolf; and we ought to guard equally against both. Howe's first object is partly by threats and partly by promises, to terrify or seduce the people to deliver up their arms and receive mercy. The ministry recommended the same plan to Gage, and this is what the tories call making their peace, "*a peace which passeth all understanding*" indeed! A peace which would be the immediate forerunner of a worse ruin than any we have yet thought of. Ye men of Pennsylvania, do reason upon these things! Were the back counties to give up their arms, they would fall an easy prey to the Indians; who are all armed: this perhaps is what some tories would not be sorry for. Were the home counties to deliver up their arms, they would be exposed to the resentment of the back counties, who would then have it in their power to chastise their defection at pleasure. And were any one state to give up its arms, *that* state must be garrisoned by all Howe's army of Britons and Hessians to preserve it from the anger of the rest. Mutual fear is the principal link in the chain of mutual love, and wo be to that state that breaks the compact. Howe is mercifully inviting you to barbarous destruction, and men must be either rogues or fools that will not see it. I dwell not upon the powers of imagination; I bring reason to your ears; and in language as plain as A, B, C, hold up truth to your eyes.

I thank God that I fear not. I see no real cause for fear. I know our situation well, and can see the way out of it. While our army was collected, Howe dared not risk a battle, and it is no credit to him that he decamped from the White Plains, and waited a mean opportunity to ravage the defenceless Jerseys; but it is great credit to us, that, with a handful of men, we sustained an orderly retreat for near an hundred miles, brought off our ammunition, all our field pieces, the greatest part of our stores, and had four rivers to pass. None can say that our retreat was precipitate, for we were near three weeks in performing it, that the country might have time to come in. Twice we marched back to meet the enemy, and remained out till dark. The sign of fear was not seen in our camp, and had not some of the cowardly and disaffected inhabitants spread false alarms through the country, the Jerseys had never been ravaged. Once more we are again collected and collecting, our new army at both ends of the continent is recruiting fast, and we shall be able to open the next campaign with sixty thousand men, well armed and clothed. This is our situation, and who will may know it. By perseverance and fortitude we have the prospect of a glorious issue; by cowardice and submission, the sad choice of a variety of evils—a ravaged country—a depopulated city—habitations without safety, and slavery without hope —our homes turned into barracks and bawdy-houses for Hessians, and a future race to provide for, whose fathers we shall doubt of. Look on this picture and weep over it! and if there yet remains one thoughtless wretch who believes it not, let him suffer it unlamented.

Common Sense, December 23, 1776

Edmund Burke

From REFLECTIONS ON
THE REVOLUTION IN FRANCE

GOVERNMENT is not made in virtue of natural rights, which may and do exist in total independence of it; and exist in much greater clearness, and in a much greater degree of abstract perfection: but their abstract perfection is their practical defect. By having a right to every thing they want every thing. Government is a contrivance of human wisdom to provide for human *wants*. Men have a right that these wants should be provided for by this wisdom. Among these wants is to be reckoned the want, out of civil society, of a sufficient restraint upon their passions. Society requires not only that the passions of individuals should be subjected, but that even in the mass and body as well as in the individuals, the inclinations of men should frequently be thwarted, their will controlled, and their passions brought into subjection. This can only be done *by a power out of themselves*; and not, in the exercise of its function, subject to that will and to those passions which it is its office to bridle and subdue. In this sense the restraints on men, as well as their liberties, are to be reckoned among their rights. But as the liberties and the restrictions vary with times and circumstances, and admit of infinite modifications, they cannot be settled upon any abstract rule; and nothing is so foolish as to discuss them upon that principle.

The moment you abate any thing from the full rights of men, each to govern himself, and suffer any artificial positive limitation upon those rights, from that moment the whole organization of government becomes a consideration of convenience. This it is which makes the constitution of a state, and the due distribution of its powers, a matter of the most

306

delicate and complicated skill. It requires a deep knowledge of human nature and human necessities, and of the things which facilitate or obstruct the various ends which are to be pursued by the mechanism of civil institutions. The state is to have recruits to its strength, and remedies to its distempers. What is the use of discussing a man's abstract right to food or to medicine? The question is upon the method of procuring and administering them. In that deliberation I shall always advise to call in the aid of the farmer and the physician, rather than the professor of metaphysics.

The science of constructing a commonwealth, or renovating it, or reforming it, is, like every other experimental science, not to be taught *à priori*. Nor is it a short experience that can instruct us in that practical science; because the real effects of moral causes are not always immediate; but that which in the first instance is prejudicial may be excellent in its remoter operation; and its excellence may arise even from the ill effects it produces in the beginning. The reverse also happens; and very plausible schemes, with very pleasing commencements, have often shameful and lamentable conclusions. In states there are often some obscure and almost latent causes, things which appear at first view of little moment, on which a very great part of its prosperity or adversity may most essentially depend. The science of government being therefore so practical in itself, and intended for such practical purposes, a matter which requires experience, and even more experience than any person can gain in his whole life, however sagacious and observing he may be, it is with infinite caution than any man ought to venture upon pulling down an edifice which has answered in any tolerable degree for ages the common purposes of society, or on building it up again, without having models and patterns of approved utility before his eyes.

These metaphysic rights entering into common life, like rays of light which pierce into a dense medium, are, by the laws of nature, refracted from their straight line. Indeed in the gross and complicated mass of human passions and concerns, the primitive rights of men undergo such a variety of refractions and reflections, that it becomes absurd to talk of them as if they continued in the simplicity of their original direction. The nature of man is intricate; the objects of society are of the greatest possible complexity; and therefore no simple disposition or direction of power can be suitable either to man's nature, or to the quality of his affairs. When I hear the simplicity of contrivance aimed at and boasted of in any new political constitutions, I am at no loss to decide that the artificers are grossly ignorant of their trade, or totally negligent of their duty. The simple governments are fundamentally defective, to say no worse of them. If you were to contemplate society in but one point of view, all these simple modes of polity are infinitely captivating. In effect each would answer its single end much more perfectly than the more complex is able to attain all its complex purposes. But it is better that the whole should be imperfectly and anomalously answered, than that, while some parts are provided for with great exactness, others might be totally neglected, or perhaps materially injured, by the over-care of a favourite member.

The pretended rights of these theorists are all extremes; and in proportion as they are metaphysically true, they are morally and politically false. The rights of men are in a sort of *middle,* incapable of definition, but not impossible to be discerned. The rights of men in governments are their advantages; and these are often in balances between differences of good; in compromise sometimes between good and evil, and sometimes, between evil and evil. Political reason is a computing principle; adding, subtracting, multiplying, and dividing, morally and not metaphysically or mathematically, true moral denominations.

By these theorists the right of the people is almost always sophistically confounded with their power. The body of the community, whenever it can come to act, can meet with no effectual resistance; but till power and right are the same, the whole body of them has no right inconsistent with virtue, and the first of all virtues, prudence. Men have no right to what is not reasonable, and to what is not for their benefit; for though a pleasant writer said, *Liceat perire poetis,*[1] when one of them, in cold blood, is said to have leaped into the flames of a volcanic revolution, *Ardentem frigidus Ætnam insiluit,*[2] I consider such a frolic rather as an unjustifiable poetic licence, than as one of the franchises of Parnassus; and whether he were poet or divine, or politician that chose to exercise this kind of right, I think that more wise, because more charitable thoughts would urge me rather to save the man, than to preserve his brazen slippers as the monuments of his folly.

The kind of anniversary sermons, to which a great part of what I write refers, if men are not shamed out of their present course, in commemorating the fact, will cheat many out of the principles, and deprive them of the benefits of the Revolution they commemorate. I confess to

[1] "Let poets have license to die as they please." [Editor]
[2] "Leaped in cold blood into burning Aetna." [Editor]

you, Sir, I never liked this continual talk of resistance and revolution, or the practice of making the extreme medicine of the constitution its daily bread. It renders the habit of society dangerously valetudinary: it is taking periodical doses of mercury sublimate, and swallowing down repeated provocatives of cantharides to our love of liberty.

This distemper of remedy, grown habitual, relaxes and wears out, by a vulgar and prostituted use, the spring of that spirit which is to be exerted on great occasions. It was in the most patient period of Roman servitude that themes of tyrannicide made the ordinary exercise of boys at school—*cum perimit sævos classis numerosa tyrannos*.[3] In the ordinary state of things, it produces in a country like ours the worst effects, even on the cause of that liberty which it abuses with the dissoluteness of an extravagant speculation. Almost all the high-bred republicans of my time have, after a short space, become the most decided, thorough-paced courtiers; they soon left the business of a tedious, moderate, but practical resistance to those of us whom, in the pride and intoxication of their theories, they have slighted, as not much better than tories. Hypocrisy, of course, delights in the most sublime speculations; for, never intending to go beyond speculation, it costs nothing to have it magnificent. But even in cases where rather levity than fraud was to be suspected in these ranting speculations, the issue has been much the same. These professors, finding their extreme principles not applicable to cases which call only for a qualified, or, as I may say, civil and legal resistance, in such cases employ no resistance at all. It is with them a war or a revolution, or it is nothing. Finding their schemes of politics not adapted to the state of the world in which they live, they often come to think lightly of all public principle; and are ready, on their part, to abandon for a very trivial interest what they find of very trivial value. Some indeed are of more steady and persevering natures; but these are eager politicians out of parliament, who have little to tempt them to abandon their favourite projects. They have some change in the church or state, or both, constantly in their view. When that is the case, they are always bad citizens, and perfectly unsure connexions. For, considering their speculative designs as of infinite value, and the actual arrangement of the state as of no estimation, they are at best indifferent about it. They see no merit in the good, and no fault in the vicious management of public affairs; they rather rejoice in the latter, as more propitious to revolution. They see

3 "When schoolboys [in their declamations] slay the cruel tyrants." [Editor]

no merit or demerit in any man, or any action, or any political principle, any further than as they may forward or retard their design of change: they therefore take up, one day, the most violent and stretched prerogative, and another time the wildest democratic ideas of freedom, and pass from the one to the other without any sort of regard to cause, to person, or to party.

In France you are now in the crisis of a revolution, and in the transit from one form of government to another—you cannot see that character of men exactly in the same situation in which we see it in this country. With us it is militant; with you it is triumphant; and you know how it can act when its power is commensurate to its will. I would not be supposed to confine those observations to any description of men, or to comprehend all men of any description within them—No! far from it. I am as incapable of that injustice, as I am of keeping terms with those who profess principles of extremes; and who under the name of religion teach little else than wild and dangerous politics. The worst of these politics of revolution is this; they temper and harden the breast, in order to prepare it for the desperate strokes which are sometimes used in extreme occasions. But as these occasions may never arrive, the mind receives a gratuitous taint; and the moral sentiments suffer not a little, when no political purpose is served by the depravation. This sort of people are so taken up with their theories about the rights of man, that they have totally forgot his nature. Without opening one new avenue to the understanding, they have succeeded in stopping up those that lead to the heart. They have perverted in themselves, and in those that attend to them, all the well-placed sympathies of the human breast.

This famous sermon of the Old Jewry breathes nothing but this spirit through all the political part. Plots, massacres, assassinations, seem to some people a trivial price for obtaining a revolution. A cheap, bloodless reformation, a guiltless liberty, appear flat and vapid to their taste. There must be a great change of scene; there must be a magnificent stage effect; there must be a grand spectacle to rouze the imagination, grown torpid with the lazy enjoyment of sixty years security, and the still unanimating repose of public prosperity. The Preacher found them all in the French revolution. This inspires a juvenile warmth through his whole frame. His enthusiasm kindles as he advances; and when he arrives at his peroration, it is in a full blaze. Then viewing, from the Pisgah of his pulpit, the free, moral, happy, flourishing, and glorious state of France, as in a bird-eye landscape of a promised land, he breaks out into the following rapture:

"What an eventful period is this! I am *thankful* that I have lived to it; I could almost say, *Lord, now lettest thou thy servant depart in peace, for mine eyes have seen thy salvation.*—I have lived to see a *diffusion* of knowledge, which has undermined superstition and error.—I have lived to see the *rights of men* better understood than ever; and nations panting for liberty which seemed to have lost the idea of it.—I have lived to see *Thirty Millions of People,* indignant and resolute, spurning at slavery, and demanding liberty with an irrestible voice. *Their King led in triumph, and an arbitrary monarch surrendering himself to his subjects.*"[4]

Before I proceed further, I have to remark, that Dr. Price seems rather to over-value the great acquisitions of light which he has obtained and diffused in this age. The last century appears to me to have been quite as much enlightened. It had, though in a different place, a triumph as memorable as that of Dr. Price; and some of the great preachers of that period partook of it as eagerly as he has done in the triumph of France. On the trial of the Rev. Hugh Peters for high treason, it was deposed, that when King Charles was brought to London for his trial, the Apostle of Liberty in that day conducted the *triumph.* "I saw," says the witness, "his majesty in the coach with six horses, and Peters riding before the king *triumphing.*" Dr. Price, when he talks as if he had made a discovery, only follows a precedent; for, after the commencement of the king's trial, this precursor, the same Dr. Peters, concluding a long prayer at the royal chapel at Whitehall, (he had very triumphantly chosen his place) said, "I have prayed and preached these twenty years; and now I may say with old Simeon, *Lord, now lettest thou thy servant depart in peace, for mine eyes have seen thy salvation.*"[5] Peters had not the fruits of his prayer; for he neither departed so soon as he wished, nor in peace. He became (what I heartily hope none of his followers may be in this country) himself a sacrifice to the triumph which he led as Pontiff. They dealt at the Restoration, perhaps, too hardly with this poor good man. But we owe it to his memory and his sufferings, that he had as much illumination, and as much zeal, and had as effectually undermined all *the superstition and error* which might impede the great business he was

---

[4] Another of these reverend gentlemen, who was witness to some of the spectacles which Paris has lately exhibited—expresses himself thus, *"A king dragged in submissive triumph by his conquering subjects* is one of those appearances of grandeur which seldom rise in the prospect of human affairs, and which, during the remainder of my life, I shall think of with wonder and gratification." These gentlemen agree marvellously in their feelings.

[5] State Trials, vol. ii. p. 360, p. 363.

engaged in, as any who follow and repeat after him, in this age, which would assume to itself an exclusive title to the knowledge of the rights of men, and all the glorious consequences of that knowledge.

After this sally of the preacher of the Old Jewry, which differs only in place and time, but agrees perfectly with the spirit and letter of the rapture of 1648, the Revolution Society, the fabricators of governments, the heroic band of *cashierers* of *monarchs,* electors of sovereigns, and leaders of kings in triumph, strutting with a proud consciousness of the diffusion of knowledge, of which every member had obtained so large a share in the donative, were in haste to make a generous diffusion of the knowledge they had thus gratuitously received. To make this bountiful communication, they adjourned from the church in the Old Jewry, to the London Tavern; where the same Dr. Price, in whom the fumes of his oracular tripod were not entirely evaporated, moved and carried the resolution, or address of congratulation, transmitted by Lord Stanhope to the National Assembly of France.

I find a preacher of the gospel prophaning the beautiful and prophetic ejaculation, commonly called *"nunc dimittis,"* made on the first presentation of our Saviour in the Temple, and applying it, with an inhuman and unnatural rapture, to the most horrid, atrocious, and afflicting spectacle, that perhaps ever was exhibited to the pity and indignation of mankind. This *"leading in triumph,"* a thing in its best form unmanly and irreligious, which fills our Creature with such unhallowed transports, must shock, I believe, the moral taste of every wellborn mind. Several English were the stupified and indignant spectators of that triumph. It was (unless we have been strangely deceived) a spectacle more resembling a procession of American savages, entering into Onondaga, after some of their murders called victories, and leading into hovels hung round with scalps, their captives, overpowered with the scoffs and buffets of women as ferocious as themselves, much more than it resembled the triumphal pomp of a civilized marital nation;—if a civilized nation, or any men who had a sense of generosity, were capable of a personal triumph over the fallen and afflicted.

This, my dear Sir, was not the triumph of France. I must believe that, as a nation, it overwhelmed you with shame and horror. I must believe that the National Assembly find themselves in a state of the greatest humiliation, in not being able to punish the authors of this triumph, or the actors in it; and that they are in a situation in which any enquiry they may make upon the subject, must be destitute even of the appearance of liberty or impartiality. The apology of that Assembly is found in their situation; but when we approve what they *must* bear, it is in us the degenerate choice of a vitiated mind.

With a compelled appearance of deliberation, they vote under the dominion of a stern necessity. They sit in the heart, as it were, of a foreign republic: they have their residence in a city whose constitution has emanated neither from the charter of their king, nor from their legislative power. There they are surrounded by an army not raised either by the authority of their crown, or by their command; and which, if they should order to dissolve itself, would instantly dissolve them. There they sit, after a gang of assassins had driven away some hundreds of the members; whilst those who held the same moderate principles, with more patience or better hope, continued every day exposed to outrageous insults and murderous threats. There a majority, sometimes real, sometimes pretended, captive itself, compels a captive king to issue as royal edicts, at third hand, the polluted nonsense of their most licentious and giddy coffeehouses. It is notorious, that all their measures are decided before they are debated. It is beyond doubt, that under the terror of the bayonet, and the lamp-post, and the torch to their houses, they are obliged to adopt all the crude and desperate measures suggested by clubs composed of a monstrous medley of all conditions, tongues, and nations. Among these are found persons, in comparison of whom Catiline would be thought scrupulous, and Cethegus a man of sobriety and moderation. Nor is it in these clubs alone that the publick measures are deformed into monsters. They undergo a previous distortion in academies, intended as so many seminaries for these clubs, which are set up in all the places of publick resort. In these meetings of all sorts, every counsel, in proportion as it is daring, and violent, and perfidious, is taken for the mark of superior genius. Humanity and compassion are ridiculed as the fruits of superstition and ignorance. Tenderness to individuals is considered as treason to the public. Liberty is always to be estimated perfect as property is rendered insecure. Amidst assassination, massacre, and confiscation, perpetrated or meditated, they are forming plans for the good order of future society. Embracing in their arms the carcases of base criminals, and promoting their relations on the title of their offences, they drive hundreds of virtuous persons to the same end, by forcing them to subsist by beggary or by crime.

The Assembly, their organ, acts before them the farce of deliberation with as little decency as liberty. They act like the comedians of a fair before a riotous audience; they act amidst the tumultuous cries of a mixed mob of ferocious men, and of women lost to shame, who, according to their insolent fancies, direct, control, applaud, explode them; and sometimes mix and take their seats amongst them; domineering over them with a strange mixture of servile petulance and proud presumptuous authority. As they have inverted order in all things, the gallery is in the place of the house. This Assembly, which overthrows kings and kingdoms, has not even the physiognomy and aspect of a grave legislative body— *nec color imperii, nec frons erat ulla senatus.* They have a power given to them, like that of the evil principle, to subvert and destroy; but none to construct, except such machines as may be fitted for further subversion and further destruction.

Who is it that admires, and from the heart is attached to national representative assemblies, but must turn with horror and disgust from such a profane burlesque, and abominable perversion of that sacred institute? Lovers of monarchy, lovers of republicks, must alike abhor it. The members of your Assembly must themselves groan under the tyranny of which they have all the shame, none of the direction, and little of the profit. I am sure many of the members who compose even the majority of that body, must feel as I do, notwithstanding the applauses of the Revolution Society.—Miserable king! miserable Assembly! How must that assembly be silently scandalized with those of their members, who could call a day which seemed to blot the sun out of Heaven, "un beau jour!"[6] How must they be inwardly indignant at hearing others, who thought fit to declare to them, "that the vessel of the state would fly forward in her course towards regeneration with more speed than ever," from the stiff gale of treason and murder, which preceded our Preacher's triumph! What must they have felt, whilst with outward patience and inward indignation they heard of the slaughter of innocent gentlemen in their houses, that "the blood spilled was not the most pure?" What must they have felt, when they were besieged by complaints of disorders which shook their country to its foundations, at being compelled coolly to tell the complainants, that they were under the protection of the law, and that they would address the king (the captive king) to cause the laws to be enforced for their protection; when the enslaved ministers of that captive king had formally notified to them, that there were neither law, nor authority, nor power left to protect? What must they have felt at being

[6] 6th of October, 1789.

obliged, as a felicitation on the present new year, to request their captive king to forget the stormy period of the last, on account of the great good which *he* was likely to produce to his people; to the complete attainment of which good they adjourned the practical demonstrations of their loyalty, assuring him of their obedience, when he should no longer possess any authority to command?

This address was made with much good-nature and affection, to be sure. But among the revolutions in France, must be reckoned a considerable revolution in their ideas of politeness. In England we are said to learn manners at secondhand from your side of the water, and that we dress our behaviour in the frippery of France. If so, we are still in the old cut; and have not so far conformed to the new Parisian mode of good-breeding, as to think it quite in the most refined strain of delicate compliment (whether in condolence or congratulation) to say, to the most humiliated creature that crawls upon the earth, that great public benefits are derived from the murder of his servants, the attempted assassination of himself and of his wife, and the mortification, disgrace, and degradation, that he has personally suffered. It is a topic of consolation which our ordinary of Newgate would be too humane to use to a criminal at the foot of the gallows. I should have thought that the hangman of Paris, now that he is liberalized by the vote of the National Assembly, and is allowed his rank and arms in the Herald's College of the rights of men, would be too generous, too gallant a man, too full of the sense of his new dignity, to employ that cutting consolation to any of the persons whom the *leze nation* might bring under the administration of his *executive powers*.

A man is fallen indeed, when he is thus flattered. The anodyne draught of oblivion, thus drugged, is well calculated to preserve a galling wakefulness, and to feed the living ulcer of a corroding memory. Thus to administer the opiate potion of amnesty, powdered with all the ingredients of scorn and contempt, is to hold to his lips, instead of "the balm of hurt minds," the cup of human misery full to the brim, and to force him to drink it to the dregs.

Yielding to reasons, at least as forcible as those which were so delicately urged in the compliment on the new year, the king of France will probably endeavour to forget these events, and that compliment. But history, who keeps a durable record of all our acts, and exercises her awful censure over the proceedings of all sorts of sovereigns, will not forget, either those events, or the aera of this liberal refinement in the

intercourse of mankind. History will record, that on the morning of the
6th of October 1789, the king and queen of France, after a day of confusion, alarm, dismay, and slaughter, lay down, under the pledged security of public faith, to indulge nature in a few hours of respite, and
troubled melancholy repose. From this sleep the queen was first startled
by the voice of the centinel at her door, who cried out to her, to save
herself by flight—that this was the last proof of fidelity he could give—
that they were upon him, and he was dead. Instantly he was cut down.
A band of cruel ruffians and assassins, reeking with his blood, rushed into
the chamber of the queen, and pierced with an hundred strokes of bayonets and poniards the bed, from whence this persecuted woman had but
just time to fly almost naked, and through ways unknown to the murderers had escaped to seek refuge at the feet of a king and husband, not
secure of his own life for a moment.

This king, to say no more of him, and this queen, and their infant
children (who once would have been the pride and hope of a great and
generous people) were then forced to abandon the sanctuary of the most
splendid palace in the world, which they left swimming in blood, polluted
by massacre, and strewed with scattered limbs and mutilated carcases.
Thence they were conducted into the capital of their kingdom. Two had
been selected from the unprovoked, unresisted, promiscuous slaughter,
which was made of the gentlemen of birth and family who composed the
king's body guard. These two gentlemen, with all the parade of an
execution of justice, were cruelly and publickly dragged to the block,
and beheaded in the great court of the palace. Their heads were stuck
upon spears, and led the procession; whilst the royal captives who followed in the train were slowly moved along, amidst the horrid yells, and
shrilling screams, and frantic dances, and infamous contumelies, and all
the unutterable abominations of the furies of hell, in the abused shape
of the vilest of women. After they had been made to taste, drop by drop,
more than the bitterness of death, in the slow torture of a journey of
twelve miles, protracted to six hours, they were, under a guard, composed
of those very soldiers who had thus conducted them through this famous
triumph, lodged in one of the old palaces of Paris, now converted into a
Bastille for kings.

Is this a triumph to be consecrated at alters? to be commemorated
with grateful thanksgiving? to be offered to the divine humanity with
fervent prayer and enthusiastick ejaculation?—These Theban and Thra-
cian Orgies, acted in France, and applauded only in the Old Jewry, I

assure you, kindle prophetic enthusiasm in the minds but of very few people in this kingdom; although a saint and apostle, who may have revelations of his own, and who has so completely vanquished all the mean superstitions of the heart, may incline to think it pious and decorous to compare it with the entrance into the world of the Prince of Peace, proclaimed in an holy temple by a venerable sage, and not long before not worse announced by the voice of angels to the quiet innocence of shepherds.

At first I was at a loss to account for this fit of unguarded transport. I knew, indeed, that the sufferings of monarchs make a delicious repast to some sort of palates. There were reflexions which might serve to keep this appetite within some bounds of temperance. But when I took one circumstance into my consideration, I was obliged to confess, that much allowance ought to be made for the Society, and that the temptation was too strong for common discretion; I mean, the circumstance of the Io Paean of the triumph, the animating cry which called "for *all* the BISHOPS to be hanged on the lamp-posts,"[7] might well have brought forth a burst of enthusiasm on the foreseen consequences of this happy day. I allow to so much enthusiasm some little deviation from prudence. I allow this prophet to break forth into hymns of joy and thanksgiving on an event which appears like the precursor of the Millenium, and the projected fifth monarchy, in the destruction of all church establishments. There was, however (as in all human affairs there is) in the midst of this joy something to exercise the patience of these worthy gentlemen, and to try the long-suffering of their faith. The actual murder of the king and queen, and their child, was wanting to the other auspicious circumstances of this *"beautiful day."* The actual murder of the bishops, though called for by so many holy ejaculations, was also wanting. A groupe of regicide and sacrilegious slaughter, was indeed boldly sketched, but it was only sketched. It unhappily was left unfinished, in this great history-piece of the massacre of innocents. What hardy pencil of a great master, from the school of the rights of men, will finish it, is to be seen hereafter. The age has not yet the compleat benefit of that diffusion of knowledge that has undermined superstition and error; and the king of France wants another object or two, to consign to oblivion, in consideration of all the good which is to arise from his own sufferings, and the patriotic crimes of an enlightened age.

7 *Tous les Eveques à la lanterne.*

Although this work of our new light and knowledge, did not go to the length, that in all probability it was intended it should be carried; yet I must think, that such treatment of any human creatures must be shocking to any but those who are made for accomplishing Revolutions. But I cannot stop here. Influenced by the inborn feelings of my nature, and not being illuminated by a single ray of this new-sprung modern light, I confess to you, Sir, that the exalted rank of the persons suffering, and particularly the sex, the beauty, and the amiable qualities of the descendant of so many kings and emperors, with the tender age of royal infants, insensible only through infancy and innocence of the cruel outrages to which their parents were exposed, instead of being a subject of exultation, adds not a little to my sensibility on that most melancholy occasion.

I hear that the august person, who was the principal object of our preacher's triumph, though he supported himself, felt much on that shameful occasion. As a man, it became him to feel for his wife and his children, and the faithful guards of his person, that were massacred in cold blood about him; as a prince, it became him to feel for the strange and frightful transformation of his civilized subjects, and to be more grieved for them, than solicitous for himself. It derogates little from his fortitude, while it adds infinitely to the honour of his humanity. I am very sorry to say it, very sorry indeed, that such personages are in a situation in which it is not unbecoming in us to praise the virtues of the great.

I hear, and I rejoice to hear, that the great lady, the other object of the triumph, has borne that day (one is interested that beings made for suffering should suffer well) and that she bears all the succeeding days, that she bears the imprisonment of her husband, and her own captivity, and the exile of her friends, and the insulting adulation of addresses, and the whole weight of her accumulated wrongs, with a serene patience, in a manner suited to her rank and race, and becoming the offspring of a sovereign distinguished for her piety and her courage; that like her she has lofty sentiments; that she feels with the dignity of a Roman matron; that in the last extremity she will save herself from the last disgrace, and that if she must fall, she will fall by no ignoble hand.

It is now sixteen or seventeen years since I saw the queen of France, then the dauphiness, at Versailles; and surely never lighted on this orb, which she hardly seemed to touch, a more delightful vision. I saw her just above the horizon, decorating and cheering the elevated sphere she just began to move in,—glittering like the morning-star, full of life, and splendor, and joy. Oh! what a revolution! and what an heart must I have, to contemplate without emotion that elevation and that fall! Little did I dream when she added titles of veneration to those of enthusiastic, distant, respectful love, that she should ever be obliged to carry the sharp antidote against disgrace concealed in that bosom; little did I dream that I should live to see such disasters fallen upon her in a nation of gallant men, in a nation of men of honour and of cavaliers. I thought ten thousand swords must have leaped from their scabbards to avenge even a look that threatened her with insult.—But the age of chivalry is gone.— That of sophisters, oeconomists, and calculators, has succeeded; and the glory of Europe is extinguished for ever. Never, never more, shall we behold that generous loyalty to rank and sex, that proud submission, that dignified obedience, that subordination of the heart, which kept alive, even in servitude itself, the spirit of an exalted freedom. The unbought grace of life, the cheap defence of nations, the nurse of manly sentiment and heroic enterprize is gone! It is gone, that sensibility of principle, that chastity of honour, which felt a stain like a wound, which inspired courage whilst it mitigated ferocity, which ennobled whatever it touched, and under which vice itself lost half its evil, by losing all its grossness.

This mixed system of opinion and sentiment had its origin in the antient chivalry; and the principle, though varied in its appearance by the varying state of human affairs, subsisted and influenced through a long succession of generations, even to the time we live in. If it should ever be totally extinguished, the loss I fear will be great. It is this which has given its character to modern Europe. It is this which has distinguished it under all its forms of government, and distinguished it to its advantage, from the states of Asia, and possibly from those states which flourished in the most brilliant periods of the antique world. It was this, which, without confounding ranks, had produced a noble equality, and handed it down through all the gradations of social life. It was this opinion which mitigated kings into companions, and raised private men to be fellows with kings. Without force, or opposition, it subdued the fierceness of pride and power; it obliged sovereigns to submit to the soft collar of social esteem, compelled stern authority to submit to elegance, and gave a domination vanquisher of laws, to be subdued by manners.

But now all is to be changed. All the pleasing illusions, which made power gentle, and obedience liberal, which harmonized the different shades of life, and which, by a bland assimilation, incorporated into politics the sentiments which beautify and soften private society, are to be dissolved by this new conquering empire of light and reason. All the decent drapery of life is to be rudely torn off. All the super-added ideas, furnished from the wardrobe of a moral imagination, which the heart owns, and the understanding ratifies, as necessary to cover the defects of our naked shivering nature, and to raise it to dignity in our own estimation, are to be exploded as a ridiculous, absurd, and antiquated fashion.

On this scheme of things, a king is but a man; a queen is but a woman; a woman is but an animal; and an animal not of the highest order. All homage paid to the sex in general as such, and without distinct views, is to be regarded as romance and folly. Regicide, and parricide, and sacrilege, are but fictions of superstition, corrupting jurisprudence by destroying its simplicity. The murder of a king, or a queen, or a bishop, or a father, are only common homicide; and if the people are by any chance, or in any way gainers by it, a sort of homicide much the most pardonable, and into which we ought not to make too severe a scrutiny.

On the scheme of this barbarous philosophy, which is the offspring of cold hearts and muddy understandings, and which is as void of solid wisdom, as it is destitute of all taste and elegance, laws are to be supported only by their own terrors, and by the concern, which each individual may find in them, from his own private speculations, or can spare to them from his own private interests. In the groves of *their* academy, at the end of every visto, you see nothing but the gallows. Nothing is left which engages the affections on the part of the commonwealth. On the principles of this mechanic philosophy, our institutions can never be embodied, if I may use the expression, in persons; so as to create in us love, veneration, admiration, or attachment. But that sort of reason which banishes the affections is incapable of filling their place. These public affections, combined with manners, are required sometimes as supplements, sometimes as correctives, always as aids to law. The precept given by a wise man, as well as a great critic, for the construction of poems, is equally true as to states. *Non satis est pulchra esse poemata, dulcia sunto.* There ought to be a system of manners in every nation which a well-formed mind would be disposed to relish. To make us love our country, our country ought to be lovely.

But power, of some kind or other, will survive the shock in which manners and opinions perish; and it will find other and worse means for its support. The usurpation which, in order to subvert antient institutions, has destroyed antient principles, will hold power by arts similar to those by which it has acquired it. When the old feudal and chivalrous spirit of *Fealty,* which, by freeing kings from fear, freed both kings and subjects from the precautions of tyranny, shall be extinct in the minds of men, plots and assassinations will be anticipated by preventive murder and preventive confiscation, and that long roll of grim and bloody maxims, which form the political code of all power, not standing on its own honour, and the honour of those who are to obey it. Kings will be tyrants from policy when subjects are rebels from principle.

When antient opinions and rules of life are taken away, the loss cannot possibly be estimated. From that moment we have no compass to govern us; nor can we know distinctly to what port we steer. Europe undoubtedly, taken in a mass, was in a flourishing condition the day on which your Revolution was compleated. How much of that prosperous state was owing to the spirit of our old manners and opinions is not easy to say; but as such causes cannot be indifferent in their operation, we must presume, that, on the whole, their operation was beneficial.

We are but too apt to consider things in the state in which we find them, without sufficiently adverting to the causes by which they have been produced, and possibly may be upheld. Nothing is more certain, than that our manners, our civilization, and all the good things which are connected with manners, and with civilization, have, in this European world of ours, depended for ages upon two principles; and were indeed the result of both combined; I mean the spirit of a gentleman, and the spirit of religion. The nobility and the clergy, the one by profession, the other by patronages, kept learning in existence, even in the midst of arms and confusions, and whilst governments were rather in their causes than formed. Learning paid back what it received to nobility and to priesthood; and paid it with usury, by enlarging their ideas, and by furnishing their minds. Happy if they had all continued to know their indissoluble union, and their proper place! Happy if learning, not debauched by ambition, had been satisfied to continue the instructor, and not aspired to be the master! Along with its natural protectors and guardians, learning will be cast into the mire, and trodden down under the hoofs of a swinish multitude.

If, as I suspect, modern letters owe more than they are always willing to own to antient manners, so do other interests which we value full as much as they are worth. Even commerce, and trade, and manufacture, the gods of our oeconomical politicians, are themselves perhaps but creatures; are themselves but effects, which, as first causes, we choose to worship. They certainly grew under the same shade in which learning flourished. They too may decay with their natural protecting principles. With you, for the present at least, they all threaten to disappear together. Where trade and manufactures are wanting to a people, and the spirit of nobility and religion remains, sentiment supplies, and not always ill supplies their place; but if commerce and the arts should be lost in an experiment to try how well a state may stand without these old fundamental principles, what sort of a thing must be a nation of gross, stupid, ferocious, and at the same time, poor and sordid barbarians, destitute of religion, honour, or manly pride, possessing nothing at present, and hoping for nothing hereafter?

I wish you may not be going fast, and by the shortest cut, to that horrible and disgustful situation. Already there appears a poverty of conception, a coarseness and vulgarity in all the proceedings of the assembly and of all their instructors. Their liberty is not liberal. Their science is presumptuous ignorance. Their humanity is savage and brutal.

It is not clear, whether in England we learned those grand and decorous principles, and manners, of which considerable traces yet remain, from you, or whether you took them from us. But to you, I think, we trace them best. You seem to me to be—*gentis incunabula nostræ.* France has always more or less influenced manners in England; and when your fountain is choaked up and polluted, the stream will not run long, or not run clear with us, or perhaps with any nation. This gives all Europe, in my opinion, but too close and connected a concern in what is done in France. Excuse me, therefore, if I have dwelt too long on the atrocious spectacle of the sixth of October 1789, or have given too much scope to the reflections which have arisen in my mind on occasion of the most important of all revolutions, which may be dated from that day, I mean a revolution in sentiments, manners, and moral opinions. As things now stand, with every thing respectable destroyed without us, and an attempt to destroy within us every principle of respect, one is almost forced to apologize for harbouring the common feelings of men.

Why do I feel so differently from the Reverend Dr. Price, and those of his lay flock, who will choose to adopt the sentiments of his discourse?—For this plain reason—because it is *natural* I should; because we are so made as to be affected at such spectacles with melancholy sentiments upon the unstable condition of mortal prosperity, and the tremendous uncertainty of human greatness; because in those natural feelings we learn great lessons; because in events like these our passions instruct our reason; because when kings are hurl'd from their thrones by the Supreme Director of this great drama, and become the objects of insult to the base, and of pity to the good, we behold such disasters in the moral, as we should behold a miracle in the physical order of things. We are alarmed into reflexion; our minds (as it has long since been observed) are purified by terror and pity; our weak unthinking pride is humbled, under the dispensations of a mysterious wisdom.—Some tears might be drawn from me, if such a spectacle were exhibited on the stage. I should be truly ashamed of finding in myself that superficial, theatric sense of painted distress, whilst I could exult over it in real life. With such a perverted mind, I could never venture to shew my face at a tragedy. People would think the tears that Garrick formerly, or that Siddons not long since, have extorted from me, were the tears of hypocrisy; I should know them to be the tears of folly.

Indeed the theatre is a better school of moral sentiments than churches, where the feelings of humanity are thus outraged. Poets, who have to deal with an audience not yet graduated in the school of the rights of men, and who must apply themselves to the moral constitution of the heart, would not dare to produce such a triumph as a matter of exultation. There, where men follow their natural impulses, they would not bear the odious maxims of a Machiavelian policy, whether applied to the attainment of monarchical or democratic tyranny. They would reject them on the modern, as they once did on the antient stage, where they could not bear even the hypothetical proposition of such wickedness in the mouth of a personated tyrant, though suitable to the character he sustained. No theatric audience in Athens would bear what has been borne, in the midst of the real tragedy of this triumphal day; a principal actor weighing, as it were in scales hung in a shop of horrors,—so much actual crime against so much contingent advantage,—and after putting in and out weights, declaring that the balance was on the side of the advantages. They would not bear to see the crimes of new democracy posted as in a ledger against the crimes of old despotism, and the book-keepers of politics finding democracy still in debt, but by no means unable or unwilling to pay the balance. In the theatre, the first intuitive glance, without any elaborate process of reasoning, would shew, that this method of political computation, would justify every extent of crime. They would see, that on these principles, even where the very worst acts were not perpetrated, it was owing rather to the fortune of the conspirators than to their parsimony in the expenditure of treachery and blood. They would see, that on these principles, even where the very worst acts were not perpetrated, it was owing rather to the fortune of the conspirators than to their parsimony in the expenditure of treachery and blood. They would soon see, that criminal means once tolerated are soon preferred. They present a shorter cut to the object than through the highway of the moral virtues. Justifying perfidy and murder for public benefit, public benefit would soon become the pretext, and perfidy and murder the end; until rapacity, malice, revenge, and fear more dreadful than revenge, could satiate their insatiable appetites. Such must be the consequences of losing in the splendour of these triumphs of the rights of men, all natural sense of wrong and right.

Bernard Mandeville

AN ENQUIRY INTO THE ORIGIN
OF MORAL VIRTUE

*A*LL UNTAUGHT Animals are only sollicitous of pleasing themselves, and naturally follow the bent of their own Inclinations, without considering the good or harm that from their being pleased will accrue to others. This is the Reason, that in the wild State of Nature those Creatures are fittest to live peaceably together in great Numbers, that discover the least of Understanding, and have the fewest Appetites to gratify; and consequently no Species of Animals is, without the Curb of Government, less capable of agreeing long together in Multitudes than that of Man; yet such are his Qualities, whether good or bad, I shall not determine, that no Creature besides himself can ever be made sociable: But being an extraordinary selfish and headstrong, as well as cunning Animal, however he may be subdued by superior Strength, it is impossible by Force alone to make him tractable, and receive the Improvements he is capable of.

The Chief Thing, therefore, which Lawgivers and other wise Men, that have laboured for the Establishment of Society, have endeavour'd, has been to make the People they were to govern, believe, that it was more beneficial for every Body to conquer than indulge his Appetites, and much better to mind the Publick than what seem'd his private Interest. As this has always been a very difficult Task, so no Wit or Eloquence has been left untried to compass it; and the Moralists and Philosophers of all Ages employed their utmost Skill to prove the Truth of so useful an Assertion. But whether Mankind would have ever believ'd it or not, it is not likely that any Body could have persuaded

325

them to disapprove of their natural Inclinations, or prefer the good of others to their own, if at the same time he had not shew'd them an Equivalent to be enjoy'd as a Reward for the Violence, which by so doing they of necessity must commit upon themselves. Those that have undertaken to civilize Mankind, were not ignorant of this; but being unable to give so many real Rewards as would satisfy all Persons for every individual Action, they were forc'd to contrive an imaginary one, that as a general Equivalent for the trouble of Self-denial should serve on all Occasions, and without costing any thing either to themselves or others, be yet a most acceptable Recompense to the Receivers.

They thoroughly examin'd all the Strength and Frailties of our Nature, and observing that none were either so savage as not to be charm'd with Praise, or so despicable as patiently to bear Contempt, justly concluded, that Flattery must be the most powerful Argument that could be used to Human Creatures. Making use of this bewitching Engine, they extoll'd the Excellency of our Nature above other Animals, and setting forth with unbounded Praises the Wonders of our Sagacity and Vastness of Understanding, bestow'd a thousand Encomiums on the Rationality of our Souls, by the Help of which we were capable of performing the most noble Atchievements. Having by this artful way of Flattery insinuated themselves into the Hearts of Men, they began to instruct them in the Notions of Honour and Shame; representing the one as the worst of all Evils, and the other as the highest Good to which Mortals could aspire: Which being done, they laid before them how becoming it was the Dignity of such sublime Creatures to be sollicitous about gratifying those Appetites, which they had in common with Brutes, and at the same time unmindful of those higher Qualities that gave them the preeminence over all visible Beings. They indeed confess'd, that those impulses of Nature were very pressing; that it was troublesome to resist, and very difficult wholly to subdue them. But this they only used as an Argument to demonstrate, how glorious the Conquest of them was on the one hand, and how scandalous on the other not to attempt it.

To introduce, moreover, an Emulation amongst Men, they divided the whole Species into two Classes, vastly differing from one another: The one consisted of abject, low-minded People, that always hunting after immediate Enjoyment, were wholly incapable of Self-denial, and without regard to the good of others, had no higher Aim than their private Advantage; such as being enslaved by Voluptuousness, yielded without Resistance to every gross desire, and made no use of their Rational Faculties but to heighten their Sensual Pleasure. These vile grov'ling Wretches, they said, were the Dross of their Kind, and having only the Shape of Men, differ'd from Brutes in nothing but their outward Figure. But the other Class was made up of lofty high-spirited Creatures, that free from sordid Selfishness, esteem'd the Improvements of the Mind to be their fairest Possessions; and setting a true value upon themselves, took no Delight but in embellishing that Part in which their Excellency consisted; such as despising whatever they had in common with irrational Creatures, opposed by the Help of Reason their most violent Inclinations; and making a continual War with themselves to promote the Peace of others, aim'd at no less than the Publick Welfare and the Conquest of their own Passion.

> *Fortior est qui se quàm qui fortissima Vincit*
> *Mœnia* ———— ———— ———— ————

These they call'd the true Representatives of their sublime Species, exceeding in worth the first Class by more degrees, than that it self was superior to the Beasts of the Field.

As in all Animals that are not too imperfect to discover Pride, we find, that the finest and such as are the most beautiful and valuable of their kind, have generally the greatest Share of it; so in Man, the most perfect of Animals, it is so inseparable from his very Essence (how cunningly soever some may learn to hide or disguise it) that without it the Compound he is made of would want one of the chiefest Ingredients: Which, if we consider, it is hardly to be doubted but Lessons and Remonstrances, so skilfully adapted to the good Opinion Man has of himself, as those I have mentioned, must, if scatter'd amongst a Multitude not only gain the assent of most of them, as to the Speculative part, but likewise induce several, especially the fiercest, most resolute, and best among them, to endure a thousand Inconveniences, and undergo as many Hardships, that they may have the pleasure of counting themselves Men of the second Class, and consequently appropriating to themselves all the Excellences they have heard of it.

From what has been said, we ought to expect in the first Place that the Heroes who took such extraordinary Pains to master some of their natural Appetites, and preferr'd the good of others to any visible Interest of their own, would not recede an Inch from the fine Notions they had receiv'd concerning the Dignity of Rational Creatures; and having ever

the Authority of the Government on their side, with all imaginable
Vigour assert the esteem that was due to those of the second Class, as
well as their Superiority over the rest of their kind. In the second, that
those who wanted a sufficient Stock of either Pride or Resolution to buoy
them up in mortifying of what was dearest to them, follow'd the sensual
dictates of Nature, would yet be asham'd of confessing themselves to be
despicable Wretches that belong'd to the inferior Class, and were generally reckon'd to be so little remov'd from Brutes; and that therefore in
their own Defence they would say, as others did, and hiding their own
Imperfections as well as they could, cry up Self-denial and Publick-
spiritedness as much as any: For it is highly probable, that some of
them, convinced by the real Proofs of Fortitude and Self Conquest they
had seen, would admire in others what they found wanting in themselves;
others be afraid of the Resolution and Prowess of those of the second
Class, and that all of them were kept in aw by the Power of their Rulers;
wherefore it is reasonable to think, that none of them (whatever they
thought in themselves) would dare openly contradict, what by every
body else was thought Criminal to doubt of.

This was (or at least might have been) the manner after which
Savage Man was broke; from whence it is evident, that the first Rudiments of Morality, broach'd by skilful Politicians, to render Men useful
to each other as well as tractable, were chiefly contrived that the Ambitious might reap the more Benefit from, and govern vast Numbers of
them with the greater Ease and Security. This Foundation of Politicks
being once laid, it is impossible that Man should long remain uncivilized:
For even those who only strove to gratify their Appetites, being continually cross'd by others of the same Stamp, could not but observe,
that whenever they check'd their Inclinations or but followed them with
more Circumspection, they avoided a world of Troubles, and often
escap'd many of the Calamities that generally attended the too eager
Pursuit after Pleasure.

First, they receiv'd, as well as others, the benefit of those Actions
that were done for the good of the whole Society, and consequently
could not forbear wishing well to those of the superior Class that perform'd them. Secondly, the more intent they were in seeking their own
Advantage, without Regard to others, the more they were hourly convinced, that none stood so much in their way as those that were most
like themselves.

It being the Interest then of the very worst of them, more than any,
to preach up Publick-spiritedness, that they might reap the Fruits of the

Labour and Self-denial of others, and at the same time indulge their own Appetites with less disturbance, they agreed with the rest, to call every thing, which, without Regard to the Publick, Man should commit to gratify any of his Appetites, VICE; if in that Action there cou'd be observed the least prospect, that it might either be injurious to any of the Society, or ever render himself less serviceable to others: And to give the Name of VIRTUE to every Performance, by which Man, contrary to the impulse of Nature, should endeavour the Benefit of others, or the Conquest of his own Passions out of a Rational Ambition of being good.

It shall be objected, that no Society was ever any ways civiliz'd before the major part had agreed upon some Worship or other of an over-ruling Power, and consequently that the Notions of Good and Evil, and the Distinction between *Virtue* and *Vice,* were never the Contrivance of Politicians, but the pure Effect of Religion. Before I answer this Objection, I must repeat what I have said already, that in this *Enquiry into the Origin of Moral Virtue,* I speak neither of *Jews* or *Christians,* but Man in his State of Nature and Ignorance of the true Deity; and then I affirm, that the Idolatrous Superstitions of all other Nations, and the pitiful Notions they had of the Supreme Being, were incapable of exciting Man to Virtue, and good for nothing but to aw and amuse a rude and unthinking Multitude. It is evident from History, that in all considerable Societies, how stupid or ridiculous soever People's received Notions have been, as to the Deities they worshipp'd, Human Nature has ever exerted it self in all its Branches, and that there is no earthly Wisdom or Moral Virtue, but at one time or other Men have excell'd in it in all Monarchies and Commonwealths, that for Riches and Power have been any ways remarkable.

The *Ægyptians,* not satisfy'd with having Deify'd all the ugly Monsters they could think on, were so silly as to adore the Onions of their own sowing; yet at the same time their Country was the most famous Nursery of Arts and Sciences in the World, and themselves more eminently skill'd in the deepest Mysteries of Nature than any Nation has been since.

No States or Kingdoms under Heaven have yielded more or greater Patterns in all sorts of Moral Virtues than the *Greek* and *Roman* Empires, more especially the latter; and yet how loose, absurd and ridiculous were their Sentiments as to Sacred Matters? For without reflecting on the extravagant Number of their Deities, if we only consider the infamous Stories they father'd upon them, it is not to be denied but that their Religion, far from teaching Men the Conquest of their Passions, and the Way to Virtue, seem'd rather contriv'd to justify their Appetites, and encourage their Vices. But if we would know what made 'em excel in Fortitude, Courage and Magnanimity, we must cast our Eyes on the Pomp of their Triumphs, the Magnificence of their Monuments and Arches; their Trophies, Statues, and Inscriptions; the variety of their Military Crowns, their Honours decreed to the Dead, Publick Encomiums on the Living, and other imaginary Rewards they bestow'd on Men of Merit; and we shall find, that what carried so many of them to the utmost Pitch of Self-denial, was nothing but their Policy in making use of the most effectual Means that human Pride could be flatter'd with.

It is visible then that it was not any Heathen Religion or other Idolatrous Superstition, that first put Man upon crossing his Appetites and subduing his dearest Inclinations, but the skilful Management of wary Politicians; and the nearer we search into human Nature, the more we shall be convinced, that the Moral Virtues are the Political Offspring which Flattery begot upon Pride.

There is no Man of what Capacity or Penetration soever, that is wholly Proof against the Witchcraft of Flattery, if artfully perform'd, and suited to his Abilities. Children and Fools will swallow Personal Praise, but those that are more cunning, must be manag'd with greater Circumspection; and the more general the Flattery is, the less it is suspected by those it is levell'd at. What you say in Commendation of a whole Town is receiv'd with Pleasure by all the Inhabitants: Speak in Commendation of Letters in general, and every Man of Learning will think himself in particular obliged to you. You may safely praise the Employment a Man is of, or the Country he was born in; because you give him an Opportunity of screening the Joy he feels upon his own account, under the Esteem which he pretends to have for others.

It is common among cunning Men, that understand the Power which Flattery has upon Pride, when they are afraid they shall be impos'd upon, to enlarge, tho' much against their Conscience, upon the Honour, fair Dealing and Integrity of the Family, Country, or sometimes the Profession of him they suspect; because they know that Men often will change their Resolution, and act against their Inclination, that they may have the Pleasure of continuing to appear in the Opinion of Some, what they are conscious not to be in reality. Thus Sagacious Moralists draw Men like Angels, in hopes that the Pride at least of Some will put 'em upon copying after the beautiful Originals which they are represented to be.

When the Incomparable Sir *Richard Steele,* in the usual Elegance of his easy Style, dwells on the Praises of his sublime Species, and with all the Embellishments of Rhetoric sets forth the Excellency of Human Nature, it is impossible not to be charm'd with his happy Turns of Thought, and the Politeness of his Expressions. But tho' I have been often moved by the Force of his Eloquence, and ready to swallow the ingenious Sophistry with Pleasure, yet I could never be so serious, but reflecting on his artful Encomiums I thought on the Tricks made use of by the Women that would teach Children to be mannerly. When an aukward Girl, before she can either Speak or Go, begins after many Intreaties to make the first rude Essays of Curt'sying, the Nurse falls in an ecstacy of Praise; *There's a delicate Curt'sy! O fine Miss! There's a pretty Lady! Mama! Miss can make a better Curt'sy than her Sister* Molly! The same is echo'd over by the Maids, whilst Mama almost hugs the Child to pieces; only Miss *Molly,* who being four Years older knows how to make a very handsome Curt'sy, wonders at the Perverseness of their Judgment, and swelling with Indignation, is ready to cry at the Injustice that is done her, till, being whisper'd in the Ear that it is only to please the Baby, and that she is a Woman, she grows proud at being let into the Secret, and rejoicing at the Superiority of her Understanding, repeats what has been said with large Additions, and insults over the Weakness of her Sister, whom all this while she fancies to be the only Bubble among them. These extravagant Praises would by any one, above the Capacity of an Infant, be call'd fulsome Flatteries, and, if you will, abominable Lies, yet Experience teaches us, that by the help of such gross Encomiums, young Misses will be brought to make pretty Curt'sies, and behave themselves womanly much sooner, and with less trouble, than they would without them. 'Tis the same with Boys, whom they'll strive to persuade, that all fine Gentlemen do as they are bid, and that none but Beggar Boys are rude, or dirty their Clothes; nay, as soon as the wild Brat with his untaught Fist begins to fumble for his Hat, the Mother, to make him pull it off, tells him before he is two Years old, that he is a Man; and if he repeats that Action when she desires him, he's presently a Captain, a Lord Mayor, a King, or something higher if she can think of it, till egg'd on by the force of Praise, the little Urchin endeavours to imitate Man as well as he can, and strains all his Faculties to appear what his shallow Noddle imagines he is believ'd to be.

The meanest Wretch puts an inestimable value upon himself, and the highest wish of the Ambitious Man is to have all the World, as to

that particular, of his Opinion: So that the most insatiable Thirst after
Fame that ever Heroe was inspired with, was never more than an un-
governable Greediness to engross the Esteem and Admiration of others in
future Ages as well as his own; and (what Mortification soever this Truth
might be to the second Thoughts of an *Alexander* or a *Cæsar*) the great
Recompence in view, for which the most exalted Minds have with so
much Alacrity sacrificed their Quiet, Health, sensual Pleasures, and
every Inch of themselves, has never been any thing else but the Breath
of Man, the Aerial Coin of Praise. Who can forbear laughing when he
thinks on all the great Men that have been so serious on the Subject of
that *Macedonian* Madman, his capacious Soul, that mighty Heart, in
one Corner of which, according to *Lorenzo Gratian,* the World was so
commodiously Lodged, that in the whole there was room for Six more?
Who can forbear Laughing, I say, when he compares the fine things that
have been said of *Alexander,* with the End he proposed to himself from
his vast Exploits, to be proved from his own Mouth; when the vast
Pains he took to pass the *Hydaspes* forced him to cry out? *Oh ye*
Athenians, *could you believe what Dangers I expose my self to, to be
praised by you!* To define then the Reward of Glory in the amplest
manner, the most that can be said of it, is, that it consists in a superlative
Felicity which a Man, who is conscious of having perform'd a noble
Action, enjoys in Self-love, whilst he is thinking on the Applause he
expects of others.

But here I shall be told, that besides the noisy Toils of War and
publick Bustle of the Ambitious, there are noble and generous Actions
that are perform'd in Silence; that Virtue being its own Reward, those
who are really Good have a Satisfaction in their Consciousness of being
so, which is all the Recompence they expect from the most worthy
Performances; that among the Heathens there have been Men, who,
when they did good to others, were so far from coveting Thanks and
Applause, that they took all imaginable Care to be for ever conceal'd
from those on whom they bestow'd their Benefits, and consequently that
Pride has no hand in spurring Man on to the highest pitch of Self-denial.

In answer to this I say, that it is impossible to judge of a Man's
Performance, unless we are throughly acquainted with the Principle and
Motive from which he acts. Pity, tho' it is the most gentle and the least
mischievous of all our Passions, is yet as much a Frailty of our Nature,
as Anger, Pride, or Fear. The weakest Minds have generally the greatest
Share of it, for which Reason none are more Compassionate than Women

and Children. It must be own'd, that of all our Weaknesses it is the most amiable, and bears the greatest Resemblance to Virtue; nay, without a considerable mixture of it the Society could hardly subsist: But as it is an Impulse of Nature, that consults neither the publick Interest nor our own Reason, it may produce Evil as well as Good. It has help'd to destroy the Honour of Virgins, and corrupted the Integrity of Judges; and whoever acts from it as a Principle, what good soever he may bring to the Society, has nothing to boast of but that he has indulged a Passion that has happened to be beneficial to the Publick. There is no Merit in saving an innocent Babe ready to drop into the Fire: The Action is neither good nor bad, and what Benefit soever the Infant received, we only obliged our selves; for to have seen it fall, and not strove to hinder it, would have caused a Pain, which Self-preservation compell'd us to prevent: Nor has a rich Prodigal, that happens to be of a commiserating Temper, and loves to gratify his Passions, greater Virtue to boast of when he relieves an Object of Compassion with what to himself is a Trifle.

But such Men, as without complying with any Weakness of their own, can part from what they value themselves, and, from no other Motive but their Love to Goodness, perform a worthy Action in Silence: Such Men, I confess, have acquir'd more refin'd Notions of Virtue than those I have hitherto spoke of; yet even in these (with which the World has yet never swarm'd) we may discover no small Symptoms of Pride, and the humblest Man alive must confess, that the Reward of a Virtuous Action, which is the Satisfaction that ensues upon it, consists in a certain Pleasure he procures to himself by Contemplating on his own Worth: Which Pleasure, together with the Occasion of it, are as certain Signs of Pride, as looking Pale and Trembling at any imminent Danger, are the Symptoms of Fear.

If the too scrupulous Reader should at first View condemn these Notions concerning the Origin of Moral Virtue, and think them perhaps offensive to Christianity, I hope he'll forbear his Censures, when he shall consider, that nothing can render the unsearchable depth of the Divine Wisdom more conspicuous, than that *Man,* whom Providence had designed for Society, should not only by his own Frailties and Imperfections be led into the Road to Temporal Happiness, but likewise receive, from a seeming Necessity of Natural Causes, a Tincture of that Knowledge, in which he was afterwards to be made perfect by the True Religion, to his Eternal Welfare.

Jonathan Swift

THE ART OF POLITICAL LYING

*W*E ARE told the devil is the father of lies, and was a liar from the beginning; so that, beyond contradiction, the invention is old; and, which is more, his first Essay of it was purely political, employed in undermining the authority of his prince, and seducing a third part of the subjects from their obedience: for which he was driven down from heaven, where (as Milton expresses it) he had been viceroy of a great western province; and forced to exercise his talent in inferior regions among other fallen spirits, poor or deluded men, whom he still daily tempts to his own sin, and will ever do so, till he be chained in the bottomless pit.

But although the devil be the father of lies, he seems, like other great inventors, to have lost much of his reputation by the continual improvements that have been made upon him.

Who first reduced lying into an art, and adapted it to politics, is not so clear from history, although I have made some diligent inquiries. I shall therefore consider it only according to the modern system, as it has been cultivated these twenty years past in the southern part of our own island.

The poets tell us that, after the giants were overthrown by the gods, the earth in revenge produced her last offspring, which was Fame. And the fable is thus interpreted: that when tumults and seditions are quieted, rumours and false reports are plentifully spread through a nation. So that, by this account, lying is the last relief of a routed, earth-born, rebellious party in a state. But here the moderns have made great additions, applying this art to the gaining of power and preserving it, as well as revenging themselves after they have lost it; as the same instruments are made use of by animals to feed themselves when they are hungry, and to bite those that tread upon them.

But the same genealogy cannot always be admitted for political lying; I shall therefore desire to refine upon it, by adding some circumstances of its birth and parents. A political lie is sometimes born out of a discarded statesman's head, and thence delivered to be nursed and dandled by the rabble. Sometimes it is produced a monster, and licked into shape: at other times it comes into the world completely formed, and is spoiled in the licking. It is often born an infant in the regular way, and requires time to mature it; and often it sees the light in its full growth, but dwindles away by degrees. Sometimes it is of noble birth, and sometimes the spawn of a stockjobber. Here it screams aloud at the opening of the womb, and there it is delivered with a whisper. I know a lie that now disturbs half the kingdom with its noise, [of] which, although too proud and great at present to own its parents, I can remember its whisperhood. To conclude the nativity of this monster; when it comes into the world without a sting it is still-born; and whenever it loses its sting it dies.

No wonder if an infant so miraculous in its birth should be destined for great adventures; and accordingly we see it has been the guardian spirit of a prevailing party for almost twenty years. It can conquer kingdoms without fighting, and sometimes with the loss of a battle. It gives and resumes employments; can sink a mountain to a mole-hill, and raise a mole-hill to a mountain; has presided for many years at committees of elections; can wash a blackmoor white; make a saint of an atheist, and a patriot of a profligate; can furnish foreign ministers with intelligence, and raise or let fall the credit of the nation. This goddess flies with a huge looking-glass in her hands, to dazzle the crowd, and make them see, according as she turns it, their ruin in their interest, and their interest in their ruin. In this glass you will behold your best friends, clad in coats powdered with *fleurs de lis* and triple crowns; their girdles hung round with chains, and beads, and wooden shoes; and your worst enemies adorned with the ensigns of liberty, property, indulgence, moderation, and a cornucopia in their hands. Her large wings, like those of a flying-fish, are of no use but while they are moist; she therefore dips them in mud, and, soaring aloft, scatters it in the eyes of the multitude, flying with great swiftness; but at every turn is forced to stoop in dirty ways for new supplies.

I have been sometimes thinking, if a man had the art of the second sight for seeing lies, as they have in Scotland for seeing spirits, how admirably he might entertain himself in this town, by observing the different shapes, sizes, and colours of those swarms of lies which buzz about the heads of some people, like flies about a horse's ears in summer; or those legions hovering every afternoon in Exchange-alley, enough to darken the air; or over a club of discontented grandees, and thence sent down in cargoes to be scattered at elections.

There is one essential point wherein a political liar differs from others of the faculty, that he ought to have but a short memory, which is necessary according to the various occasions he meets with every hour of differing from himself and swearing to both sides of a contradiction, as he finds the persons disposed with whom he has to deal. In describing the virtues and vices of mankind, it is convenient, upon every article, to have some eminent person in our eye, from whom we copy our description. I have strictly observed this rule, and my imagination this minute represents before me a certain great man famous for this talent, to the constant practice of which he owes his twenty years' reputation of the most skilful head in England for the management of nice affairs. The superiority of his genius consists in nothing else but an inexhaustible fund of political lies, which he plentifully distributes every minute he speaks, and by an unparalleled generosity forgets, and consequently contradicts, the next half-hour. He never yet considered whether any proposition were true or false, but whether it were convenient for the present minute or company to affirm or deny it; so that, if you think fit to refine upon him by interpreting everything he says, as we do dreams, by the contrary, you are still to seek, and will find yourself equally deceived whether you believe or not: the only remedy is to suppose that you have heard some inarticulate sounds, without any meaning at all; and besides, that will take off the horror you might be apt to conceive at the oaths wherewith he perpetually tags both ends of every proposition; although, at the same time, I think he cannot with any justice be taxed with perjury when he invokes God and Christ, because he has often fairly given public notice to the world that he believes in neither.

Some people may think that such an accomplishment as this can be of no great use to the owner, or his party, after it has been often practised and is become notorious; but they are widely mistaken. Few lies carry the inventor's mark, and the most prostitute enemy to truth may spread a thousand without being known for the author: besides, as the vilest writer has his readers, so the greatest liar has his believers; and it often happens that, if a lie be believed only for an hour, it has done its work, and there is no farther occasion for it. Falsehood flies, and truth comes limping after it, so that when men come to be undeceived it is too late; the jest is over, and the tale has had its effect: like a man who has thought of a good repartee when the discourse is changed or the company parted; or like a physician who has found out an infallible medicine after the patient is dead.

Considering that natural disposition in many men to lie, and in multitudes to believe, I have been perplexed what to do with that maxim so frequent in everybody's mouth, that truth will at last prevail. Here has this island of ours, for the greatest part of twenty years, lain under the influence of such counsels and persons, whose principle and interest it was to corrupt our manners, blind our understanding, drain our wealth, and in time destroy our constitution both in church and state, and we at last were brought to the very brink of ruin; yet, by the means of perpetual misrepresentations, have never been able to distinguish between our enemies and friends. We have seen a great part of the nation's money got into the hands of those who, by their birth, education, and merit, could pretend no higher than to wear our liveries; while others, who, by their credit, quality, and fortune, were only able to give reputation and success to the Revolution, were not only laid aside as dangerous and useless, but loaded with the scandal of Jacobites, men of arbitrary principles, and pensioners to France; while truth, who is said to lie in a well, seemed now to be buried there under a heap of stones. But I remember it was a usual complaint among the Whigs, that the bulk of the landed men was not in their interests, which some of the wisest looked on as an ill omen; and we saw it was with the utmost difficulty that they could reserve a majority, while the court and ministry were on their side, till they had learned those admirable expedients for deciding elections and influencing distant boroughs by powerful motives from the city. But all this was mere force and constraint, however upheld by most dexterous artifice and management, until the people began to apprehend their properties, their religion, and the monarchy itself in danger; when we saw them greedily laying hold on the first occasion to interpose. But of this mighty change in the dispositions of the people I shall discourse more at large in some following paper: wherein I shall endeavour to undeceive or discover those deluded or deluding persons who hope or pretend it is only a short madness in the vulgar, from which they may soon recover; whereas, I believe it will appear to be very different in its causes, its symptoms, and its consequences; and prove a great example to illustrate the maxim I lately mentioned, that truth (however sometimes late) will at last prevail.

The Examiner, No. 15, November 2–9, 1710

Aldous Huxley

THE ARTS OF SELLING

*T*HE SURVIVAL of democracy depends on the ability of large numbers of people to make realistic choices in the light of adequate information. A dictatorship, on the other hand, maintains itself by censoring or distorting the facts, and by appealing, not to reason, not to enlightened self-interest, but to passion and prejudice, to the powerful "hidden forces," as Hitler called them, present in the unconscious depths of every human mind.

In the West, democratic principles are proclaimed and many able and conscientious publicists do their best to supply electors with adequate information and to persuade them, by rational argument, to make realistic choices in the light of that information. All this is greatly to the good. But unfortunately propaganda in the Western democracies, above all in America, has two faces and a divided personality. In charge of the editorial department there is often a democratic Dr. Jekyll—a propagandist who would be very happy to prove that John Dewey had been right about the ability of human nature to respond to truth and reason. But this worthy man controls only a part of the machinery of mass communication. In charge of advertising we find an anti-democratic, because anti-rational, Mr. Hyde—or rather a Dr. Hyde, for Hyde is now a Ph.D in psychology and has a master's degree as well in the social sciences. This Dr. Hyde would be very unhappy indeed if everybody always lived up to John Dewey's faith in human nature. Truth and reason are Jekyll's affair, not his. Hyde is a motivation analyst, and his business is to study human weaknesses and failings, to investigate those unconscious desires and fears by which so much of men's conscious thinking and overt doing is deter-

mined. And he does this, not in the spirit of the moralist who would like
to make people better, or of the physician who would like to improve
their health, but simply in order to find out the best way to take advantage of their ignorance and to exploit their irrationality for the
pecuniary benefit of his employers. But after all, it may be argued,
"capitalism is dead, consumerism is king"—and consumerism requires the
services of expert salesmen versed in all the arts (including the more
insidious arts) of persuasion. Under a free enterprise system commercial
propaganda by any and every means is absolutely indispensable. But the
indispensable is not necessarily the desirable. What is demonstrably good
in the sphere of economics may be far from good for men and women as
voters or even as human beings. An earlier, more moralistic generation
would have been profoundly shocked by the bland cynicism of the
motivation analysts. Today we read a book like Mr. Vance Packard's
The Hidden Persuaders, and are more amused than horrified, more
resigned than indignant. Given Freud, given Behaviorism, given the
mass producer's chronically desperate need for mass consumption, this is
the sort of thing that is only to be expected. But what, we may ask, is
the sort of thing that is to be expected in the future? Are Hyde's activities
compatible in the long run with Jekyll's? Can a campaign in favor of
rationality be successful in the teeth of another and even more vigorous
campaign in favor of irrationality? These are questions which, for the
moment, I shall not attempt to answer, but shall leave hanging, so to
speak, as a backdrop to our discussion of the methods of mass persuasion
in a technologically advanced democratic society.

The task of the commercial propagandist in a democracy is in some
ways easier and in some ways more difficult than that of a political
propagandist employed by an established dictator or a dictator in the
making. It is easier inasmuch as almost everyone starts out with a prejudice in favor of beer, cigarettes and iceboxes, whereas almost nobody
starts out with a prejudice in favor of tyrants. It is more difficult inasmuch
as the commercial propagandist is not permitted, by the rules of his
particular game, to appeal to the more savage instincts of his public. The
advertiser of dairy products would dearly love to tell his readers and
listeners that all their troubles are caused by the machinations of a gang
of godless international margarine manufacturers, and that it is their
patriotic duty to march out and burn the oppressors' factories. This sort
of thing, however, is ruled out, and he must be content with a milder
approach. But the mild approach is less exciting than the approach

through verbal or physical violence. In the long run, anger and hatred are self-defeating emotions. But in the short run they pay high dividends in the form of psychological and even (since they release large quantities of adrenalin and noradrenalin) physiological satisfaction. People may start out with an initial prejudice against tyrants; but when tyrants or would-be tyrants treat them to adrenalin-releasing propaganda about the wickedness of their enemies—particularly of enemies weak enough to be persecuted—they are ready to follow him with enthusiasm. In his speeches Hitler kept repeating such words as "hatred," "force," "ruthless," "crush," "smash"; and he would accompany these violent words with even more violent gestures. He would yell, he would scream, his veins would swell, his face would turn purple. Strong emotion (as every actor and dramatist knows) is in the highest degree contagious. Infected by the malignant frenzy of the orator, the audience would groan and sob and scream in an orgy of uninhibited passion. And these orgies were so enjoyable that most of those who had experienced them eagerly came back for more. Almost all of us long for peace and freedom; but very few of us have much enthusiasm for the thoughts, feelings and actions that make for peace and freedom. Conversely almost nobody wants war or tyranny; but a great many people find an intense pleasure in the thoughts, feelings and actions that make for war and tyranny. These thoughts, feelings and actions are too dangerous to be exploited for commercial purposes. Accepting this handicap, the advertising man must do the best he can with the less intoxicating emotions, the quieter forms of irrationality.

Effective rational propaganda becomes possible only when there is a clear understanding, on the part of all concerned, of the nature of symbols and of their relations to the things and events symbolized. Irrational propaganda depends for its effectiveness on a general failure to understand the nature of symbols. Simple-minded people tend to equate the symbol with what it stands for, to attribute to things and events some of the qualities expressed by the words in terms of which the propagandist has chosen, for his own purposes, to talk about them. Consider a simple example. Most cosmetics are made of lanolin, which is a mixture of purified wool fat and water beaten up into an emulsion. This emulsion has many valuable properties: it penetrates the skin, it does not become rancid, it is mildly antiseptic and so forth. But the commercial propagandists do not speak about the genuine virtues of the emulsion. They give it some picturesquely voluptuous name, talk ecstatically and misleadingly about feminine beauty and show pictures of gorgeous blondes nourishing their tissues with skin food. "The cosmetic manufacturers," one of their number has written, "are not selling lanolin, they are selling hope." For this hope, this fraudulent implication of a promise that they will be transfigured, women will pay ten or twenty times the value of the emulsion which the propagandists have so skilfully related, by means of misleading symbols, to a deep-seated and almost universal feminine wish— the wish to be more attractive to members of the opposite sex. The principles underlying this kind of propaganda are extremely simple. Find some common desire, some widespread unconscious fear or anxiety; think out some way to relate this wish or fear to the product you have to sell; then build a bridge of verbal or pictorial symbols over which your customer can pass from fact to compensatory dream, and from the dream to the illusion that your product, when purchased, will make the dream come true. "We no longer buy oranges, we buy vitality. We do not buy just an auto, we buy prestige." And so with all the rest. In toothpaste, for example, we buy, not a mere cleanser and antiseptic, but release from the fear of being sexually repulsive. In vodka and whisky we are not buying a protoplasmic poison which, in small doses, may depress the nervous system in a psychologically valuable way; we are buying friendliness and good fellowship, the warmth of Dingley Dell and the brilliance of the Mermaid Tavern. With our laxatives we buy the health of a Greek god, the radiance of one of Diana's nymphs. With the monthly best seller we acquire culture, the envy of our less literate neighbors and the respect of the sophisticated. In every case the motivation analyst has found some deep-seated wish or fear, whose energy can be used to move the consumer to part with cash and so, indirectly, to turn the wheels of industry. Stored in the minds and bodies of countless individuals, this potential energy is released by, and transmitted along, a line of symbols carefully laid out so as to bypass rationality and obscure the real issue.

Sometimes the symbols take effect by being disproportionately impressive, haunting and fascinating in their own right. Of this kind are the rites and pomps of religion. These "beauties of holiness" strengthen faith where it already exists and, where there is no faith, contribute to conversion. Appealing, as they do, only to the aesthetic sense, they guarantee neither the truth nor the ethical value of the doctrines with which they have been, quite arbitrarily, associated. As a matter of plain historical fact, the beauties of holiness have often been matched and indeed surpassed by the beauties of unholiness. Under Hitler, for example, the yearly Nuremberg rallies were masterpieces of ritual and theatrical art.

"I had spent six years in St. Petersburg before the war in the best days of the old Russian ballet," writes Sir Nevile Henderson, the British ambassador to Hitler's Germany, "but for grandiose beauty I have never seen any ballet to compare with the Nuremberg rally." One thinks of Keats— "beauty is truth, truth beauty." Alas, the identity exists only on some ultimate, supramundane level. On the levels of politics and theology, beauty is perfectly compatible with nonsense and tyranny. Which is very fortunate; for if beauty were incompatible with nonsense and tyranny, there would be precious little art in the world. The masterpieces of painting, sculpture and architecture were produced as religious or political propaganda, for the greater glory of a god, a government or a priesthood. But most kings and priests have been despotic and all religions have been riddled with superstition. Genius has been the servant of tyranny and art has advertised the merits of the local cult. Time, as it passes, separates the good art from the bad metaphysics. Can we learn to make this separation, not after the event, but while it is actually taking place? That is the question.

In commercial propaganda the principle of the disproportionately fascinating symbol is clearly understood. Every propagandist has his Art Department, and attempts are constantly being made to beautify the billboards with striking posters, the advertising pages of magazines with lively drawings and photographs. There are no masterpieces; for masterpieces appeal only to a limited audience, and the commercial propagandist is out to captivate the majority. For him, the ideal is a moderate excellence. Those who like this not too good, but sufficiently striking, art may be expected to like the products with which it has been associated and for which it symbolically stands.

Another disproportionately fascinating symbol is the Singing Commercial. Singing Commercials are a recent invention; but the Singing Theological and the Singing Devotional—the hymn and the psalm—are as old as religion itself. Singing Militaries, or marching songs, are coeval with war, and Singing Patriotics, the precursors of our national anthems, were doubtless used to promote group solidarity, to emphasize the distinction between "us" and "them," by the wandering bands of paleolithic hunters and food gatherers. To most people music is intrinsically attractive. Moreover, melodies tend to ingrain themselves in the listener's mind. A tune will haunt the memory during the whole of a lifetime. Here, for example, is a quite uninteresting statement or value judgment. As it stands nobody will pay attention to it. But now set the words to a catchy and easily remembered tune. Immediately they become words of power. Moreover, the words will tend automatically to repeat themselves every time the melody is heard or spontaneously remembered. Orpheus has entered into an alliance with Pavlov—the power of sound with the conditioned reflex. For the commercial propagandist, as for his colleagues in the fields of politics and religion, music possesses yet another advantage. Nonsense which it would be shameful for a reasonable being to write, speak or hear spoken can be sung or listened to by that same rational being with pleasure and even with a kind of intellectual conviction. Can we learn to separate the pleasure of singing or of listening to song from the all too human tendency to believe in the propaganda which the song is putting over? That again is the question.

Thanks to compulsory education and the rotary press, the propagandist has been able, for many years past, to convey his messages to virtually every adult in every civilized country. Today, thanks to radio and television, he is in the happy position of being able to communicate even with unschooled adults and not yet literate children.

Children, as might be expected, are highly susceptible to propaganda. They are ignorant of the world and its ways, and therefore completely unsuspecting. Their critical faculties are undeveloped. The youngest of them have not yet reached the age of reason and the older ones lack the experience on which their new-found rationality can effectively work. In Europe, conscripts used to be playfully referred to as "cannon fodder." Their little brothers and sisters have now become radio fodder and television fodder. In my childhood we were taught to sing nursery rhymes and, in pious households, hymns. Today the little ones warble the Singing Commercials. Which is better—"Rheingold is my beer, the dry beer," or "Hey diddle-diddle, the cat and the fiddle"? "Abide with me" or "You'll wonder where the yellow went, when you brush your teeth with Pepsodent"? Who knows?

"I don't say that children should be forced to harass their parents into buying products they've seen advertised on television, but at the same time I cannot close my eyes to the fact that it's being done every day." So writes the star of one of the many programs beamed to a juvenile audience. "Children," he adds, "are living, talking records of what we tell them every day." And in due course these living, talking records of television commercials will grow up, earn money and buy the products of industry. "Think," writes Mr. Clyde Miller ecstatically, "think of what it can mean to your firm in profits if you can condition a million or ten million children, who will grow up into adults trained to buy your product, as soldiers are trained in advance when they hear the trigger words, Forward March!" Yes, just think of it! And at the same time remember that the dictators and the would-be dictators have been thinking about this sort of thing for years, and that millions, tens of millions, hundreds of millions of children are in process of growing up to buy the local despot's ideological product and, like well-trained soldiers, to respond with appropriate behavior to the trigger words implanted in those young minds by the despot's propagandists.

Self-government is in inverse ratio to numbers. The larger the constituency, the less the value of any particular vote. When he is merely one of millions, the individual elector feels himself to be impotent, a negligible quantity. The candidates he has voted into office are far away, at the top of the pyramid of power. Theoretically they are the servants of the people; but in fact it is the servants who give orders and the people, far off at the base of the great pyramid, who must obey. Increasing population and advancing technology have resulted in an increase in the number and complexity of organizations, an increase in the amount of power concentrated in the hands of officials and a corresponding decrease in the amount of control exercised by electors, coupled with a decrease in the public's regard for democratic procedures. Already weakened by the vast impersonal forces at work in the modern world, democratic institutions are now being undermined from within by the politicians and their propagandists.

Human beings act in a great variety of irrational ways, but all of them seem to be capable, if given a fair chance, of making a reasonable choice in the light of available evidence. Democratic institutions can be made to work only if all concerned do their best to impart knowledge and to encourage rationality. But today, in the world's most powerful democracy, the politicians and their propagandists prefer to make nonsense of democratic procedures by appealing almost exclusively to the ignorance and irrationality of the electors. "Both parties," we were told in 1956 by the editor of a leading business journal, "will merchandize their candidates and issues by the same methods that business has developed to sell goods. These include scientific selection of appeals and planned repetition. . . . Radio spot announcements and ads will repeat phrases with a planned intensity. Billboards will push slogans of proven power. . . . Candidates need, in addition to rich voices and good diction, to be able to look 'sincerely' at the TV camera."

The political merchandisers appeal only to the weakness of voters, never to their potential strength. They make no attempt to educate the masses into becoming fit for self-government; they are content merely to manipulate and exploit them. For this purpose all the resources of psychology and the social sciences are mobilized and set to work. Carefully selected samples of the electorate are given "interviews in depth." These interviews in depth reveal the unconscious fears and wishes most prevalent in a given society at the time of an election. Phrases and images aimed at allaying or, if necessary, enhancing these fears, at satisfying these wishes, at least symbolically, are then chosen by the experts, tried out on readers and audiences, changed or improved in the light of the information thus obtained. After which the political campaign is ready for the mass communicators. All that is now needed is money and a candidate who can be coached to look "sincere." Under the new dispensation, political principles and plans for specific action have come to lose most of their importance. The personality of the candidate and the way he is projected by the advertising experts are the things that really matter.

In one way or another, as vigorous he-man or kindly father, the candidate must be glamorous. He must also be an entertainer who never bores his audience. Inured to television and radio, that audience is accustomed to being distracted and does not like to be asked to concentrate or make a prolonged intellectual effort. All speeches by the entertainer-candidate must therefore be short and snappy. The great issues of the day must be dealt with in five minutes at the most—and preferably (since the audience will be eager to pass on to something a little livelier than inflation or the H-bomb) in sixty seconds flat. The nature of oratory is such that there has always been a tendency among politicians and clergymen to over-simplify complex issues. From a pulpit or a platform even the most conscientious of speakers finds it very difficult to tell the whole truth. The methods now being used to merchandise the political candidate as though he were a deodorant positively guarantee the electorate against ever hearing the truth about anything.

Thomas Whiteside

A CLOUD OF SMOKE

*W*HEN A manufactured product that most consumers accept as useful or pleasurable comes under strong suspicion of being harmful to certain users, a number of acute problems confront the manufacturer. To solve them, he can do one of several things. If he is quite satisfied that his product presents no risk, he can do his best to reassure the public—and, if the sale of his product is subject to official regulation, the government—of its harmlessness. If he recognizes that a risk exists for certain users, he can try to modify his product, in order to render it as harmless as he knows how, or he can warn buyers of the nature of the risk, or he can withdraw the product from the market until its safety is firmly established. Whichever course he follows, the nature of the difficulty before him is not only technical and economic but moral. Such moral dilemmas are recurrent in American industry. At present, one of the most serious of them involves the tobacco business—the oldest industry in the country. During the past decade and a half, a number of medical people have produced an increasing weight of evidence showing that an association exists between people's smoking habits and the incidence of various diseases, including coronary heart disease, chronic bronchitis, emphysema, and lung cancer.

Of all the associations alleged to exist between smoking and disease, none has received more public attention than that between smoking and lung cancer. During the last half century, the annual death rate from all causes in this country has declined, but the death rate from lung cancer, once looked upon as a rare disease, is known to have increased strikingly. Between 1935 and 1962, deaths from lung cancer in the United States

346

rose from four thousand to forty-one thousand, and while some of this increase is accounted for by population growth, the rate, standardized for age, is still about ten times what it was in the mid-thirties. Among men, who are seven times as likely to die of the disease as women, cancer of the lung has come to be the predominant form of fatal cancer in this country.

The extraordinary increase in the lung-cancer death rate first became the subject of intensive investigation among medical people in the late forties, and at that time (as subsequently) a number of possible causes were considered—among them the increase in various kinds of air pollution and the increase in the habit of cigarette smoking. The role of cigarette smoking attracted particular interest because of the rapid growth of the habit since the early part of the century, when most tobacco was smoked in pipes or chewed. Cigarettes became popular during the First World War, and between 1920 and 1948 the annual consumption of them rose from a rate of about seven hundred and fifty for each adult in the population to about twenty-four hundred. In 1949, Dr. E. Cuyler Hammond, reporting to the American Cancer Society on trends in cancer mortality, pointed to a strong statistical connection between heavy cigarette smoking and the incidence of lung cancer. Since then, scientific studies have been undertaken in various countries—the most elaborate of them in the United States being conducted by Dr. Hammond and Dr. Daniel Horn, and, in England, by Dr. W. R. Doll and Dr. A. B. Hill—and their principal result has been to implicate cigarette smoking as a factor intimately associated with lung cancer. In 1960, the Board of Directors of the American Cancer Society, having reviewed a number of these studies, gave as its judgment that "the clinical, epidemiological, experimental, chemical, and pathological evidence presented by the many studies reported in recent years indicates beyond reasonable doubt that cigarette smoking is the major cause of the unprecedented increase in lung cancer." In 1962, the Royal College of Physicians, in Britain, issued an extensive review of the subject. It concluded that "cigarette smoking is the most likely cause of the worldwide increase in deaths from lung cancer," and that the habit probably also contributed to the development of coronary heart disease, chronic bronchitis, and lesser diseases. Both societies have asserted that while lung cancer is rare among nonsmokers— and almost nonexistent among nonsmokers in rural areas—it is less rare among cigar and pipe smokers, and its incidence among cigarette smokers varies in direct ratio to the number of cigarettes smoked and the

amount of smoke inhaled. And both organizations have concluded that
ordinary urban air pollution seems to be a comparatively minor factor
in the incidence of lung cancer, although the disease can be induced by
prolonged exposure to certain industrial dusts and fumes. According to
a summary made by the American Cancer Society earlier this year, the
death rate from lung cancer—death certificates being taken at face value
—is seven times as great for people who smoke less than half a pack a
day as it is for nonsmokers, while for those who smoke two or more packs
a day, it is more than twenty times as great.

As a consequence of these and other assertions, which were accompanied by widespread publicity, the American tobacco industry has had
to cope with a lot of trouble. The trouble began to be very noticeable in
1953. In that year, the *Journal of the American Medical Association*
carried an article by Dr. Alton Ochsner—a physician who had been
warning his colleagues for at least seventeen years of a suspicious relationship between smoking and lung cancer—in which he flatly called smoking a principal cause of the disease. Also in that year, an article appeared
in *Cancer Research* reporting on the results of a study of the possible
carcinogenic effects of tobacco smoke by Dr. Ernest L. Wynder and Dr.
Evarts Graham, who concluded that cancer could be induced on the skin
of mice by tobacco-tar condensates, and yet another article, entitled
"Cancer by the Carton," appeared in *Reader's Digest*. Following this
publicity, cigarette sales declined for the first time in twenty-one years.
The situation was perturbing enough to induce the major tobacco manufacturing and handling companies to take full-page display ads in the
press at the beginning of 1954; these announced that the industry, while
it had full confidence that its products were not injurious to health, was
"pledging aid and assistance to the research effort into all phases of
tobacco use and health," and had set up a Tobacco Industry Research
Committee, to be directed by "a scientist of unimpeachable integrity and
national repute," which would have available the services of "an Advisory
Board of scientists disinterested in the cigarette industry." The scientific
director appointed was Dr. Clarence Cook Little, an eminent geneticist
and cancer specialist, who was then director of the Roscoe B. Jackson
Memorial Laboratory, at Bar Harbor, Maine, and who had formerly been
managing director of the American Society for Control of Cancer, the
predecessor of the American Cancer Society. Since its formation, the
Tobacco Industry Research Committee has spent over six million dollars,
contributed by tobacco manufacturers, for the support of research by

various medical groups into various aspects of smoking and cancer and other diseases. In the nearly ten years that the committee has been at work, Dr. Little has consistently maintained that the relationship between smoking and health has been insufficiently investigated and is too complex to warrant a conclusion that smoking is a cause of lung cancer or of other diseases; that it remains to be seen whether genetic, hormonal, emotional, or other differences between smokers and nonsmokers—as well as differences in their external environment—afford clues to their differing health risks; and that the cause of lung cancer, as of cancer in general, is still unknown.

Several eminent medical men agree with Dr. Little. However, various governments abroad have considered the weight of the evidence associating cigarette smoking with lung cancer so impressive that they have adopted a policy of discouraging cigarette smoking, especially among younger people. In Britain, where the lung-cancer death rate is even higher than in the United States, the Ministry of Health, acting on a recommendation of the Royal College of Physicians, has been engaging for the past year in an extensive publicity campaign to warn people that cigarette smoking is dangerous to health, and so far about a million posters—a typical one entitled "Before You Smoke, THINK: Cigarettes Cause Lung Cancer"—have been distributed to British schools, clinics, and post offices, and put up in various public places. As a result of the government's approach to the problem, the Independent Television Authority, the group that governs commercial television in Britain, has come to an agreement with British cigarette manufacturers to restrict the showing of cigarette commercials to the hours after 9 P.M., in order to minimize children's exposure to them. In Canada, too, after the Canadian Medical Association issued a report that characterized cigarette smoking as "a grave and extensive health problem," cigarette commercials have been voluntarily restricted to late-evening hours. Various restrictions on cigarette advertising have been put into effect by the governments of West Germany and Denmark, and even the Soviet Union has mounted a poster campaign asserting that smoking is an unhealthy habit. In the United States, the American Medical Association has not yet taken an official stand on the nature of the association between smoking and lung cancer. Nor has the United States government. But in October of last year, largely as a result of a letter sent to the President jointly by the American Cancer Society, the American Heart Association, the American Public Health Association, and the National Tuberculosis Associa-

tion asking that a committee be appointed to examine "the social responsibilities" of business and government in protecting the health of
the public, the Surgeon General of the United States Public Health
Service announced that he had appointed an Advisory Committee on
Smoking and Health to "make a comprehensive review of all available
data on smoking and other factors in the environment that may affect
health." This review, he said, would be followed by recommendations
for action, if necessary. The first phase of the study is now nearly completed, and it is expected to be finished and published before the end
of this year.

The American cigarette industry, while it has suffered some hard
blows, has by no means been laid low by them. If one were to match the
weight of all the unfavorable publicity about smoking against the weight
of cigarette advertising campaigns, advertising and smoking would unquestionably triumph. The initial drop in cigarette sales has long since
been recovered. Since 1953, the number of cigarettes smoked in this
country in a year has risen from three hundred and eighty-seven billion
to more than half a trillion. Only part of this increase can be accounted
for by the expansion of the population; on an adult per-capita basis, the
figures have risen from 3,559 cigarettes in 1953 to 4,005 this year. In
England, cigarette sales dipped about four per cent in the year following
the Royal College report on smoking, but the drop has since been recovered and the English tobacco manufacturers are now selling more
cigarettes than ever. As for the American cigarette industry, its prosperity,
whatever its difficulties, is greater than at any other period in its history.

In growing to its present state of affluence, the industry has under-
gone considerable changes in its patterns of cigarette merchandising over
the last few years. The most noticeable changes have been, of course, the
introduction of many new brand names and the rise in the popularity
of filter cigarettes. Twelve years ago, there were five big brands—Lucky
Strike, Camel, Chesterfield, Old Gold, and Philip Morris—which accounted for ninety-five per cent of all cigarette sales in the country. Now
fifteen brands account for roughly the same percentage. The large cigarette companies of that day and this—R. J. Reynolds, American Tobacco,
Liggett & Myers, Philip Morris, P. Lorillard, and Brown & Williamson—
are now manufacturing fifty-one different brands, in sixty-nine sizes and
packages. The familiarity of some brand names, like Philip Morris and
Old Gold, has faded in the public consciousness; now the big names include Kent, Winston, Marlboro, and L & M, and nobody can get through

an evening of television without encountering showers of commercials for such newer brands as Newport, Salem, Spring, Montclair, Belair, and Alpine. Among these newer brands, the majority are filter cigarettes of one length or another. The filter has perhaps been the principal merchandising device used by tobacco manufacturers in their attempt to reassure smokers about possible health hazards. In the early fifties, filter cigarettes constituted barely one per cent of all cigarettes sold; now they account for almost fifty-five per cent. Presumably, the function of a filter is to trap condensates—including nicotine and the so-called tars—from the smoke of a cigarette. The first filter cigarette to be promoted here in a big way was Kent, which was put on the market, at a premium price, by Lorillard, the makers of Old Gold, in 1952. At the time, the only other filter cigarettes were Brown & Williamson's Viceroy, which had a crêpe-paper filter, and Benson & Hedges' Parliament, which had a filter packed with a tuft of cotton. Lorillard, which had been failing with Old Gold and needed something new, introduced Kent with a great fanfare over its "exclusive Micronite filter," made of stuff that had been "developed by researchers in atomic-energy plants." In 1953, when the question of smoking and health had become a matter of general public discussion, the prospects for Kent, helped along by hygienic-sounding advertising about the material in the Micronite filter ("so safe, so pure, it's used to filter the air in leading hospitals"), looked promising to its makers. But Kent sales slumped not long thereafter, partly because many smokers found it so hard to draw smoke through the filter that they scarcely had the sensation of smoking at all. Nevertheless, Lorillard's competitors were all hard at work on filter cigarettes of their own. Brown & Williamson put new infusions of advertising money into promoting its Viceroy. Philip Morris not only bought out Benson & Hedges in order to get the cotton-filtered Parliament but proceeded to develop a filter cigarette of its own from one of its old properties, Marlboro. Reynolds, the makers of Camel, came along with Winston. American Tobacco, which already had the cork-tipped, king-size Herbert Tareyton, now dressed it up with a "new Selective Filter," featuring "an entirely new concept in cigarette filtration—a filter tip of purified cellulose, incorporating *Activated Charcoal,* a filtering substance world famous as a purifying agent." Liggett & Myers put out L & M, with a "Pure White Miracle Tip of Alpha-Cellulose" ("Just what the doctor ordered"). By 1955, the filter boom was on in earnest, with each tobacco company striving to outdo the others in claims for the efficiency of its particular filters. It was the beginning of an era known in the business as the Tar Derby. The boom was a great gift to the industry in that it counteracted many of the injurious effects that publicity about smoking and health had been having on sales. It was also a gift to the industry in that while most of the manufacturers charged premium prices for filter cigarettes, the filters actually cost less to produce than the tobacco they displaced. The filters used in some brands were capable of reducing, to some extent, the amount of tar and nicotine normally inhaled per cigarette, but the ones used in several other brands, in spite of their loudly proclaimed merits, weren't. According to Dr. Hammond, some of the filters actually strained out less tar and nicotine than the tobacco they displaced would have done. Furthermore, as time went on, most of the tobacco manufacturers compensated for the filter's reduction of flavor by packing their cigarettes with stronger-flavored grades of tobacco, some of which had a higher tar and nicotine content than before. Also, as time went on, they added, for reasons of economy, "reconstituted" or "homogenized" material, including tobacco remnants that in less efficient days would have been discarded. And, in order to let the customer know that he was indeed smoking a cigarette, several of the manufacturers began loosening up their filters. The net result of such changes was that smokers who switched from regular cigarettes to filters in the belief that they were reducing the risk to their health were sometimes exposing themselves to greater amounts of tar and nicotine than ever. (To take a couple of examples derived from a report published in 1958 by a congressional investigating committee and based on laboratory tests conducted by Consumers Union: A smoker of Lorillard's Old Gold who in 1953 switched to Lorillard's Kent in order to cut down on tar and nicotine would have accomplished his aim in that year, but by 1957, if he was still smoking Kent, he would have been inhaling, through the atomic-age Micronite filter, six per cent more tar and twenty-six per cent more nicotine per cigarette than he had inhaled when he smoked Old Gold in 1953; in the intervening years, Lorillard, to increase sales of Kent, had loosened the Micronite filter. Again, if a 1955 smoker of Reynolds' Camel switched to the same company's Winston, he would have found that in 1957 he was taking in sixteen per cent more nicotine and twenty-three per cent more tar than he had been with Camel. Of course, it might be argued that a Winston, being king-size and considerably longer than a Camel, would contain more tobacco, and hence more nicotine and tar, but in 1956 the president of Reynolds conceded to a Senate-House committee that a Winston actually contained eight per cent less tobacco than a Camel. In any case, it should be added that today the tar-and-nicotine content of all cigarettes—filtered and unfiltered—has been markedly lowered.)

The furious Tar Derby reached its climax in 1960, when the Federal Trade Commission, which hitherto had had little success in trying to get the tobacco manufacturers to moderate their claims for filter cigarettes, put its foot down and announced that no more tar-and-nicotine claims would be permitted in cigarette advertising, and that the tobacco companies had made a "voluntary" agreement to this effect. Since that time, cigarette advertising has carried on without making specific, as distinct from implied, claims about the effectiveness of filters. Nowadays, most of the overt claims made about the advantages of particular cigarettes revolve around considerations that are entirely subjective and beyond the reach of measure—considerations of "taste," "flavor," "mildness," and the like. Yet the issue of health seems to underlie cigarette advertising as strongly today as it ever did during the Tar Derby. In their glow of supreme physical well-being, the models in the cigarette ads—whether the man and the girl snuggling up to each other on the deck of a yacht and lighting up each other's Tareytons ("The Tareyton ring marks the real thing") or the champion water skier celebrating an exhibition of his skill by puffing away at a Camel ("Every inch a real smoke")—certainly seem to be living refutations of any theory that smoking might have something unhealthy about it. In the last few years, smoking—and romance between smoking couples—seems to have moved outdoors from more stuffy surroundings. This impression is reinforced by the ads for menthol-flavored cigarettes. Since 1957 or so, menthol cigarettes have become the fastest-growing segment of the business. They have been promoted for their "cool" or "fresh" taste, and the millions of smokers who have switched to them—partly, perhaps, in the understandable, if mistaken, belief that their smoke is somehow cleaner than that of other cigarettes—may have had this belief strengthened by gazing at some of the countless television commercials and four-color ads showing couples plunging in and out of the surf on Caribbean-looking shores ("Newport smokes fresher") or dallying by waterfalls or covered bridges surrounded by delicate greenery ("It's springtime every time you light up a Salem!"). And as the cigarette-ad models seem to have taken en masse to fresh air (in some commercials air itself seems to have become almost a commodity—as in Salem's claim that "Salem's high-porosity paper air-softens every puff"), so do they seem to have acquired the habit of inhaling.

Fifteen years ago, when network television was just getting started and visual cigarette advertising was pretty much confined to the printed media, tobacco ads did not even go as far as to show the models in the act of smoking, let alone inhaling; the cigarettes were merely held near the mouth. In the early television commercials, some of the girl models, while they were smokers, all right, didn't really inhale and weren't required to blow much smoke around. Now the tobacco companies require as a matter of course that models be able to inhale properly, and even the youngest-looking of the girls seem to be able to do so pretty deeply. (Dr. Hammond, in an article surveying a number of studies on smoking and health: "In relation to total death rates, the degree of inhalation is as important, perhaps more important, than the amount of smoking.") While specific claims about the value of filters in dissipating the effects of inhaling may be taboo, the filters themselves are very much in evidence in cigarette ads and commercials. Whatever uneasiness about his habit may lie in the mind of a smoker, he can always look to the ads for some kind of reassurance, and no doubt somewhere he can find it. A Parliament smoker, for example, might take comfort in hearing and seeing in commercial after commercial that "Parliament gives you Extra Margin." He can have little doubt that the Extra Margin is essentially one of safety, even though the word "safety" is never mentioned; Parliament commercials with the "Extra Margin" theme are keyed to activities that involve physical danger, such as speedboat racing, parachute jumping, bobsledding, and ice hockey, and the viewer is led to equate the cigarette with such safety devices as protective goggles, crash helmets, and life preservers. However, if Parliament with its recessed filter is indeed something like a life preserver, Parliament advertising is silent on the nature of any danger that the smoker is being preserved against. That issue is clouded in smoke, perhaps very like the smoke called for in a recent "story board," or illustrated script for a proposed Parliament commercial. A boy and a girl, looking happy and secure with the Extra Margins of seat belts and Parliaments, are jolting along in a jeep over sand dunes: "THEY LAUGH AS THEY SMOKE. CUT TO HER REACTING: LAUGHS AS SHE TAKES IN DEEP, DELICIOUS DRAG ON CIGARETTE. STAY ON HER AS SHE REMOVES CIG . . . LOOKS AT FILTER WITH QUIET APPROVAL. CUT TO HIM FAST. HE BLOWS OUT SMOKE SO YOU KNOW HE THINKS PARLIAMENTS ARE GREAT."

The scale on which cigarette advertising is conducted is enormous and is expanding steadily. During the last ten years, the tobacco companies have increased their annual expenditures on television commercials from forty million dollars in 1957 to about a hundred and fifteen million dollars last year, and as the number of brands on the market has increased, so has the competition between them—a struggle in which battalions of water skiers, airplane pilots, and speedboat racers are deployed to overwhelm the opposition and assure the fidelity of the public to a particular brand. A good deal of earnest conferring among the strategists of the tobacco wars involves considerations of "brand loyalty" and "brand image." The creation of a brand image involves the manufacture and assembly of prepackaged elements of a sort of daydream—a set of visual and aural associations that will be launched from Madison Avenue into the minds of scores of millions of actual and potential smokers, there to be kept orbiting incessantly around the periphery of consciousness. "Tremendous loyalties are built up for a product as personal as a cigarette," the vice-president of an advertising agency in charge of a big cigarette account says. "The food a man eats, the toothpaste he uses, the socks he wears are all pretty personal matters to him, but none of these things tend to be as personal to him as the cigarette he smokes. It attaches a tremendous personal significance. He has it on display all day long. He has it on his person. He has it in his mouth. He draws its smoke into his lungs. It is safe to say that many cigarettes have a satisfactory taste, but the principal thing is the personal identification with the brand."

A good example of the creation of a brand image occurred in the promotion of Philip Morris's Marlboro filter cigarette. It was introduced into the cigarette market on a national scale in 1955, when the filter boom was just getting under way. At that time, the use of filter cigarettes was still associated to a considerable extent with women. Furthermore, Marlboro itself, up to then, had been a woman's cigarette, available with either an ivory or a ruby tip, but no filter. When the Philip Morris people decided to go into the filter business, they picked the Marlboro name, with the help of market research, as a promising one, and then abandoned the old brand except for the name. In promoting the new filter Marlboro, they resolved to strike at the prevailing notion that "there was something sissy about smoking filter cigarettes," as a Philip Morris executive recently put it. "We decided to go in for male-oriented imagery," he said. The result was a barrage of Marlboro ads showing the filter brand being smoked by determined-looking males with tattoos on their arms. "The image of the Marlboro man that we projected was one of the successful, up-the-hard-way sort of guy, who got himself tattooed somewhere along the line," the same Philip Morris executive said. "Gray, mature, rugged—the wealthy-rancher type rather than the Arrow Collar type. The brand personality of Marlboro was altogether different from the personality of, say, our Parliament, which was a sort of friendly, gregarious spirit—a fella-and-girl kind of warmth. The Marlboro approach has been a kind of male, mood thing. Marlboro advertising uses women only secondarily. On TV, we do use Julie London—she sits and sings the Marlboro Song, 'You Get a Lot to Like with a Marlboro,' to a guy in a night club or in the back seat of a limousine—but, generally speaking, the Marlboro man is *alone*. He is reflective as he relaxes with the cigarette. There is masculinity, and I would even say moodiness, rather than just mood—although not fickle moodiness. This brand personality is very important to us. The consumer who lights up the product —we've conditioned him. We've told him what kind of product he's got." Within two or three years after its introduction, Marlboro, pushed by vigorous advertising campaigns, became one of the best-selling filter cigarettes on the market. And, thanks to a big chunk of the thirty million dollars that Philip Morris is estimated to spend annually on advertising, it still is. In an average week, perhaps ninety million people are exposed to Marlboro—or, in the language of Madison Avenue, "delivered" to the advertisers, at a certain cost per thousand viewers.

For all the manipulative air of such talk, it would be quite incorrect to assume that any given force of advertising automatically assures a given degree of success in persuading the public to buy a particular brand of cigarette. Of the fourteen new brands that the tobacco companies have introduced with extensive advertising and on a national scale in the last five years, very few have been taken up by the smoking public in a way that their manufacturers have considered satisfactory. The market place has been littered with what the merchandisers sadly refer to as "brand failures"—makes with names like Hit Parade, Brandon, Oasis, and Duke of Durham. "You never can count on what's going to happen when you introduce a brand, even with the best planning," a tobacco executive has said. "Let's say you see a niche in the market for a new product and you think you can put out something that will fill it. You go to your experts, who come up with acceptable combinations of tobacco blends and filters. You test these out on consumer panels, just as you do everything else—the color of the package, the design, the brand names you have in mind, and so on—and eventually you start manufacture and put the product on sale in a regional test market. You ask yourself questions: Is the media weight you're putting behind it sufficient? Is this an item acceptable to the retailers? Is it going to get repeats—you're getting the tryers, but are they coming back? Is the taste of the product more satisfying? You listen to consumer reaction—to the things they play back to you.

If you have a package innovation, is that playing back? How much do you need to remold your advertising to fit the things that play back? You need the answers to these and other questions before you make a commitment to go national. If you get a positive answer, you put it in the corporate mix and you're ready to go. Once you've committed yourself to going national, you've committed yourself to a multimillion-dollar decision.

The introduction of new and competing brands of cigarettes on a national scale resembles a game of chance in which the ante required for each player begins at something like eight million dollars and playing the game itself can be far more costly than that; the American Tobacco Company is estimated to have put between twenty and thirty million dollars into the promotion of its Hit Parade brand before it gave it up as a lost cause. However, the possible winnings are enough to insure no shortage of players, and hardly a season passes without the entry of some new brand from the test markets into the arena of full-scale national promotion. The competition being what it is, the contenders seldom pass up an opportunity to seize on a promotional point that they think may give them an edge, however slight, on their opponents—whether the edge is a newly coined word for a filter or a new and hygienic-looking set of surroundings for the television-commercial models to smoke in. Cigarette merchandisers are constantly concerned with "dimensions of difference" ("At that time, the brand's dimension of difference was provided by the flip-top box") and "product differences" ("Then Newport came along and added 'A Hint of Mint' and that was the product difference"). So far this year, no fewer than three new filter brands—Montclair, Paxton, and Lark—have been shot out of the corporate mix and into the national market, and their promoters have made the most of whatever differences exist between them. Montclair, with "a unique development in compound filters," is the only cigarette that "puts the menthol in the filter, where it cannot burn" and "makes the last puff taste as fresh as the first puff." Paxton, the "first menthol cigarette to meet the challenge of today's smoking needs," features a "new Humiflex pack" and a "new team of filters back to back," one of the filters being "fortified with Pecton." Lark features a "three-piece Keith filter" that contains "two modern outer filters plus an inner filter of charcoal granules—a basic material science uses to purify air."

What impurities, if any, these and other such portentously described filtering devices are actually supposed to filter out remains unexplained in the ads. In fact, it is difficult to find a tobacco manufacturer who will concede that cigarettes contain anything impure enough to require filtering out at all.

The fact that the tobacco industry never deals overtly in its advertising with the issue of smoking and health does not mean that it has no pronouncements to make on the subject. Most of its pronouncements are issued by the Tobacco Institute, Inc., a trade organization that was formed by the major tobacco manufacturers in 1958 to look after some of their common interests. (It is independent of Dr. Little's Tobacco Industry Research Committee.) The Tobacco Institute, which has its headquarters in Washington, is headed by George V. Allen, the former director of the United States Information Agency, and Mr. Allen, in speeches before various organizations, has set forth its position by saying that the answers to questions about smoking and health are unknown, that the whole subject remains a speculative one, and that while some statistical studies have pointed the way to further research, they have not provided answers to the original questions. "We are not on a crusade either for or against tobacco," Allen has been quoted as saying. "If we have a crusade, it is a crusade for research." During the pursuit of such research, he has called for a "respite from theories, resolutions, and emotional statements" about smoking and health. The Tobacco Institute, in fact, is quite vocal on the subject of research, and, with the help of Hill & Knowlton, a big public-relations outfit with headquarters in New York, it sends more than a hundred thousand physicians around the country a quarterly publication called *Tobacco and Health Research,* a summary and compendium of items having to do with research on these subjects. The items are presented under such headings as "Autopsy Study Fails to Support Smoking Tie to Vascular Ills," "Lung Cancer Deaths 20% Overstated," and "Experts Differ on Royal College Report."

Besides pointing out to doctors what it considers the statistical fallacies and misconceptions in the studies that have drawn a causal connection between smoking and certain diseases, the Institute has had to contend with public criticism not only of the industry's own use of statistics in the past ("More Doctors Smoke Camels Than Any Other Cigarette") but of the manner in which it has continued to promote its products, particularly among young people. In England, the advertising of cigarettes on commercial television—as here, the principal medium used—is governed by a quite elaborate set of "guidance notes," drawn up by the television companies and subscribed to by the tobacco manufacturers. They provide, among other things, that "advertisements should not encourage people, and young people in particular, to believe that they will have any advantage romantically, physically, socially, or in their jobs if they smoke." Among the specific appeals to be avoided are:

"Hero appeal" and the appeal to "manliness."

The appeal of social success, or the suggestion that smoking is part of the modern, smart, sophisticated, or fashionable way of life. . . .

The creation of a romantic atmosphere in which it is implied that cigarettes are an essential ingredient.

An impression of exaggerated satisfaction; e.g., deep inhaling or expressions of intense enjoyment associated with smoking.

The use in advertisements of young people *unmistakably* under the age of twenty-one.

The suggestion that cigarettes overcome "nerves" or strain, [or are] an aid to relaxation or concentration.

Nothing like this set of restraints exists in cigarette advertising on television here, of course, and nothing remotely as thoroughgoing seems to have been urged upon the American tobacco industry or the television broadcasters by their critics. However, last November, LeRoy Collins, the former Governor of Florida and the current president of the National Association of Broadcasters, who has the reputation of being a maverick in the broadcasting business, made a speech before a group of broadcasters in Portland, Oregon, in which he suggested that, because of what he called "mounting evidence that tobacco provides a serious hazard to health," broadcasters had a moral responsibility to consider taking "corrective action" against the televising of some types of cigarette commercials, notably those featuring well-known athletes and those expressly designed to influence young people. The reaction of the broadcasting industry to Collins' remarks was not at all favorable, and for a while there was talk that Collins would be asked to resign from his job. Nonetheless, his speech did have the effect of stirring up questions about the wisdom of aiming cigarette advertising at young people, and last June the Tobacco Institute, responding to this pressure, issued a statement declaring that the tobacco industry had always taken the position that "smoking is a custom for adults," and that, in conformity with this belief, a number of companies had decided to discontinue advertising in college publications and engaging in other campus promotional activities. For years, most of the tobacco companies had been conducting campaigns to persuade college students to smoke their particular brands, both through placing advertising in college publications (the cigarette industry became the biggest single source of revenue for many such publications) and through the promotional activities of paid "campus representatives" among the student body, to whom they gave quantities of sample packs for free distribution.

The Institute's declaration that smoking was "a custom for adults," and thus, presumably, not one for non-adults, did have one result that applied on a broader basis than merely the college-publication level. This fall, the American Tobacco Company began an extensive campaign for Lucky Strike cigarettes in which the advertising copy contained the statement that "smoking is a pleasure meant for adults." This sentiment appeared under a headline, spread over two pages, that asserted, "Lucky Strike Separates the Men from the Boys . . . But Not from the Girls." On the left-hand page, the first part of the headline was illustrated by a photograph of a helmeted, Lucky Strike-smoking racing-car driver who is smilingly flourishing a winner's cup as he receives the adulatory glances of youths pressing close behind him; on the right-hand page, the second part of the headline was illustrated by a shot of the same model—still equipped with his cigarette, smile, and cup but minus the young male fans—being hugged by a girl admirer. Unfortunately, the ad men, having presumably set out to illustrate the theme that cigarettes are not for boys, thus achieved just the opposite effect by making the smoking of Lucky Strike appear to be the act that turns a boy into a man. But such mistakes can happen in cigarette advertising. It is even possible that they will happen more frequently in the future. With the growth rate of the cigarette market slowing down and the competition between manufacturers becoming increasingly heavy, there is really only one way for the industry to maintain its rate of expansion, and that is by doing business with the great mass of young people who reach smoking age each year. This is a potential market that is literally getting bigger by the minute. Over the past decade, the number of people between eighteen and twenty-four in this country increased by only two per cent, owing to the low birth rate of the depression years, but over the next decade their number, owing to the high birth rate of the postwar boom period, will increase by fifty-two per cent. And in the young-adult population bulge ahead the eighteen-year-olds of 1966 are the fifteen-year-olds of 1963. As these fifteen-year-olds are maturing, so is the tobacco for them to smoke, as it lies waiting in millions of hogsheads in the curing warehouses of the tobacco manufacturers.

Because of my interest in the dilemma confronting the tobacco industry, and because it seemed to me too bad that, owing to the relative anonymity of so many of the responsible people in the industry, their personal views on the issue of smoking and health—as distinct from the formally phrased announcements issued on their collective behalf—should be so little known, I set out recently to interview several people who are concerned with the merchandising of cigarettes. While I cannot say that there was any great eagerness to see me and talk about this touchy subject, I must say that when I was received, it was always with great courtesy and attentiveness.

My first call was upon James C. Bowling, who is assistant to Joseph F. Cullman III, the president of Philip Morris, Inc., at the Philip Morris headquarters on Park Avenue—a very smart set of offices. Bowling is a well-dressed, round-faced man in his middle thirties who talks smoothly and equably in a Southern accent. He has spent all his working life with Philip Morris. Even when he was attending the University of Louisville, he worked for the company as a campus representative, and after his graduation he worked for it as a tobacco salesman and then as a supervisor of campus representatives, making his way up through the ranks to his present position. Bowling was smoking from a pack of his company's new Paxton cigarettes—the ones with the team of filters back to back—and, like every other executive I encountered, he seemed to smoke almost incessantly. I asked him for his views on the connection that has been said to exist between smoking and disease, and he told me that, like all his colleagues, he had given the matter a good deal of serious thought. "We believe that there is no connection, or we wouldn't be in the business," he said earnestly, and, in a phrase that was to become familiar to me, he went on to characterize the issue as "the health scare." "I remember a speaker last year at the three hundred and fiftieth anniversary celebration of America's first tobacco crop at Jamestown telling of the trials that the tobacco industry had at that time," he said. "They had a health scare at the inception of the industry in America. And the scare goes further back than that—King James issued his 'Counterblaste to Tobacco' in 1604. We've had these trials from time to time, and each time the industry has come through stronger, because people have demonstrated conclusively that they want to smoke. When the health scare hit in 1952 or '53, we were all staggered, though. The matter was put forward not as a thesis but as an absolute fact. Yet it was clear to us—and to a few eminent statisticians, like the late Sir Ronald Fisher—that the case was far from proved, and the industry did the correct thing by taking the attitude that nothing could or should be done until the facts were in.

The work of the Tobacco Industry Research Committee has been under way for ten years, and it has required a great deal of patience for the industry not to answer the attacks on tobacco during that time, while the research has been going on. It has required a great deal of restraint not to lash back at the anti-cigarette forces. The people on the T.I.R.C. are eminent people. We in the industry have no contact with them, but we read all we can about the research they're doing. Everybody in the industry has been forced to become an authority in his peer group on the subject. It's impossible for me, for example, to go somewhere without meeting someone who wants to talk about it. I wonder how many conversations about it take place without a full understanding of the facts. Gosh, we're awed at how a story can be told and retold by the anti-cigarette people, and how little attention is given in the press to claims *for* cigarettes. But I'm also impressed with the way many people are sifting the facts for themselves and coming up with the conclusion that the case against tobacco is not proved."

Bowling lit up another Paxton and went on, "It surprises people sometimes that we should take it so seriously. I don't know why we should take it lightly. I'm from Kentucky, and I know what tobacco has meant to that one state. Some people who attack the industry don't stop to think that we're *people*—and people with a social conscience. Just as I feel I'm personally committed in this business, so do other people. I don't know of one executive who has resigned as a result of the health scare. The purveyor of pleasure-feeling may have been put in some jeopardy by the attacks of the anti-cigarette people, and the attacks may have made us more than a trifle self-conscious, but we believe that we're right, and that history will show this to be so. Meanwhile, people are smoking and enjoying it. An eminent physician sat in the chair you're sitting in not so long ago, and he said that if people were to stop smoking, there had better be something pretty powerful to take its place or there would be more wife-beating and job dissatisfaction than people's natures could tolerate."

From Bowling's office I went on to see John T. Landry, a tall, clear-faced, curly-haired man who, at thirty-nine, is the company's director of brand management, which means that he is responsible for the advertising of all its brands. Landry came to Philip Morris in 1956; previously, he had been the advertising manager for the Blue Coal Corporation, in New York, and before that he was in the advertising-research department of *Newsweek*. He made it clear to me that he really enjoyed being in the tobacco business. "It's hectic, it's competitive, and there are a lot of easier ways to live, but it's a great business," he said. "It's a real big business, a very responsible and honest business." Although Landry had a pack of Paxtons on his desk, the cigarette he was smoking was a Marlboro. The executive in charge of the promotion of a particular brand of cigarette is expected to smoke that brand, but Landry, being in charge of all Philip Morris's brands, could smoke any of them with propriety, and he told me that his personal preference was for Marlboro. After some discussion of brand promotion, I brought the conversation around to the issue of smoking and health. "We all assume that, as Mr. Cullman, the president of our company, said at the last annual meeting, cigarettes will ultimately be exonerated," Landry told me with conviction. "We all feel that way or we wouldn't be selling them. We're parents, citizens, members of society, you know. This business has been a respectable business for hundreds of years. I frequently get asked by people I come across about my attitude toward cigarettes. I've seen our research facilities in Richmond, and I know that other companies have facilities just as big, and up to this point nobody has ever shown anything conclusive about cigarettes and health—lung cancer and all that. It just hasn't been proved. I think if it were proved I would give up smoking. I also think I'd get the heck out of the business. Not because the business would be hurt but because I would not like to sell a product that was harmful. Even now, I wouldn't try to convince anyone that cigarettes are physically good for him, but from an emotional point of view smoking eases tension, and if I didn't smoke I'd probably develop a tic or something. My wife smokes, I smoke, and we certainly don't have any fear of it. I don't think that cigarettes will ever be found to contain anything dangerous to health. The problem is being worked on, and in the meantime I am very happy in this business."

From the offices of Philip Morris I went to those of Benton & Bowles, the advertising agency that prepares the ads for about half of the company's products, where I had an appointment with Henry Pattison, the chairman of the agency's executive committee. Pattison, who has direct charge of the Philip Morris account, is a highly experienced advertising man, and has been with Benton & Bowles in an executive role for more than twenty years. He is a big man in his fifties, with a rather cherubic face and an affable manner, and he received me not from behind a desk but at a small, round table, topped with polished, tooled leather that was decorated with sample packages of Philip Morris products. He was smoking from a pack of Parliaments. After some talk about the merchandising of cigarettes, we got around to my main question. "I think that if it were ever conclusively shown that there was some connection between smoking and, say, lung cancer, most agencies would not be advertising cigarettes," he said. "But it's easy to get stampeded, and the tobacco industry is being very much maligned. Fifty years ago, when I was a boy, my grandfather was a druggist in Alexandria, and I remember how Coca-Cola was then under the worst attack you could conceive of. People used to spread the rumor that it was a dope—the most unbelievable stories, all completely without foundation. The same thing has happened to the tobacco industry, which has been under attack for a couple of hundred years. People have been *shot*. Now the industry has been presented as a bunch of ogres trying to corrupt American youth. The fact is that I have never met a finer group in my life than the people in the tobacco industry—I'll stack them up against *any* other group for morals, ethics, and beliefs. And tobacco has given pleasure to an awful lot of people. You should not act on hunches, suspicions, and stir-ups. This cancer business, now—nobody knows about it. I have to accept that there is some connection between smoking and health, but just what it is we don't know. You can concentrate on the negative side—build a negative case for cigarettes' being banned—and ignore the positive case. Some people may be immoderate users. But I don't think any industry should be persecuted for the immoderation of its users, provided the industry hasn't promoted immoderation—and certainly the tobacco industry hasn't. You won't find anybody in the cigarette business telling you to smoke two and a half packs a day. I was having lunch the other day with a doctor, and he said, '*There's* the biggest killer in the United States! What we're doing—eating!' This anti-cigarette campaign is not a haphazard thing; it's a well-conceived, well-directed campaign from some over-all headquarters—from the timing of releases to everything else. Some of what is being put out goes so far overboard that it makes me almost sure it isn't true. They say that sixteen thousand people died last year of lung cancer. The obvious conclusion is that they were victims of cigarettes. But nothing is said about how many would die of lung cancer if all cigarette smoking stopped. If *we* pulled that trick in the advertising business, we'd be put in jail."

I remarked that I had been wondering whether Parliament's claim about Extra Margin didn't presuppose, to some degree, an element of danger to smokers.

"I have a theory that everything around us has an element of danger," Pattison said. "Your swimming pool can kill you. Cars can kill you. Coffee can kill you. Justice Holmes said that security is not the logical end of man."

At the Ted Bates advertising agency, Howard Black is one of the executives in charge of the Brown & Williamson cigarette accounts—Kool, Viceroy, Life, and a couple of other brands. In discussing his attitude toward smoking and health, he said that the position of the tobacco manufacturers was analogous to that of an automobile manufacturer confronted by statistics about automobile accidents. "I don't think that the tobacco industry would think of disbanding because one per cent— or whatever the figure is—of heavy smokers died of lung cancer any more than the automobile manufacturers would think of going out of business because five hundred people get killed in auto accidents on the Fourth of July," he said. "The automobile industry is going to go on. So is the tobacco industry."

The president of Brown & Williamson is William S. Cutchins, a courteous, gray-haired Southerner, who took me to lunch at the Barclay Hotel and spoke to me of his philosophy. "I went into the tobacco industry years ago, because it was a perfectly honorable business, and I set out to reap the rewards of free enterprise," he said. "I'm doing what I'm doing today because of the rewards that the free-enterprise system has to offer." He went on to say that he was as anxious as anyone else to see a well-reasoned solution to the questions that had been raised in connection with smoking and health, adding that some of the attacks on the tobacco industry were entirely unjustified, and that while many of the scientists who held "anti-cigarette views" were absolutely sincere, he did not think that the case for cigarettes had been presented to the public as it deserved to be.

I asked Cutchins what he would do if he came to accept the position that there was a connection between smoking and certain diseases.

"The first thing I'd try to do would be to correct it," he said. "A fundamental of common decency as well as of enlightened self-interest." He advised me to read a red-covered booklet—a copy of which he had with him—called "Headline Hunting with Statistics," which was a reprint of a speech given before a group of security analysts by Robert K. Heimann, assistant to the president of the American Tobacco Company. Later, I did so. It was a full-scale attack on what the author called "the anti-cigarette crusade," and sharply questioned the statistical validity of various studies that have found a link between smoking and disease. One section of the speech wound up, "Not all of the questions are scientific ones. You might well ask whether the American Cancer Society would be spending so much time and money propagandizing anti-tobacco statistics if the millions of dollars they have solicited from the public for so many years had shed any light on the causes of cancer."

Some time later, I again encountered Heimann's name, in an article in the *Times* headlined "2 DOUBT SMOKING IS CANCER CAUSE." Here he was identified as "Dr. Robert K. Heimann, a sociologist and statistician" of the American Tobacco Company, but when I went to call on him, I saw him not in his capacity as a sociologist and statistician but in his capacity as assistant to the president of the American Tobacco Company in charge of public relations. He is a slightly built, rather poker-faced man, who was once the editor of *Forbes Magazine*. Among other things, he told me, with emphasis, that experiments using cigarette smoke had never induced lung cancer in an animal. (Dr. Hammond has said, with equal emphasis, that experimental animals have so little tolerance for cigarette smoke forced into their lungs that they do not live long enough for further investigation.)

A day or so later, Heimann arranged to have me meet his chief, Robert B. Walker, who in April of this year succeeded the late Paul Hahn as president of American Tobacco. In contrast to the New York headquarters of the other tobacco companies I visited—all of them very modern-looking, with lots of formica and blocks of colors—the offices of the American Tobacco Company have a certain grand, old-fashioned air, and the furniture there looks just as it must have looked in the days of the late George Washington Hill, the great tobacco-empire builder. The secretaries' filing cabinets, desks, and chairs are all made of solid oak, and on each desk is a small silver plate engraved with its occupant's name. Here and there are plaques bearing various office slogans devised by Hill, such as "Quality of Product Is Essential to Continuing Success" and "Get Your O.K. in Writing." The offices of nearly all the executives are equipped with solid-mahogany desks and chairs, and the office of the president is on an even more solid scale—a vast room, with panelled walls of bleached mahogany, chairs of mahogany and black leather, a couple of black leather sofas, and a huge desk of unbleached mahogany. When Heimann escorted me into this office, Walker, a masterful-looking, gray-haired man of fifty with a pink rose in his buttonhole, was sitting behind his great desk in what looked like a judge's chair. It was indeed a judge's chair, he told me when he got up to greet me; it had belonged to Judge Gary, the first chairman of the United States Steel Corporation.

Getting down to the purpose of my interview, Walker said, "We are facing some rough seas. But I am thoroughly convinced that the tobacco industry will survive and flourish. The people in this industry are loyal, dedicated people—people dedicated to the good of the country, people who have made a contribution to humanity. I don't want to paraphrase Winston Churchill, but I will. I don't think that any industry has given so much pleasure to so many people for so many centuries, and is so deserving of more consideration and fair play than it is now getting." Having said this, he looked across at Heimann, who was sitting on a sofa to one side of him, and remarked appraisingly, "That's pretty good. 'So much pleasure to so many people for so many centuries.' " He lit up a Lucky Strike and puffed at it with pleasure.

I said that some people felt there was a mounting weight of evidence implicating cigarettes as the source of some danger to health, and he replied, "There isn't a mounting weight of evidence. There's a mounting wave of propaganda. The hypothesis about smoking has not been proved. Now, under our American system everybody is innocent until proved guilty, and even then the verdict is subject to appeal and reappeal. This is not the case here. Many doctors subscribe to the cholesterol theory that we've all heard so much about. Cholesterol may be the killer of us all. But until it's proved, should the whole dairy industry be condemned? Should everybody give up ice cream even if it takes a few hours off your life? Some doctors say that we don't have the answers about cholesterol, and some say that we don't have the answers about tobacco. Is it fair to condemn the tobacco industry under the present circumstances? This is a seven-billion-dollar business, and the taxes on the tobacco industry last year could pay for the whole space program for a year."

Of all the tobacco-manufacturing people I talked to, Morgan J. Cramer, president of the P. Lorillard Company, which manufactures Kent and Newport cigarettes, was distinctive, for a couple of reasons. For one, he was the only executive who even mentioned (although he certainly did not elaborate on) an issue that I understood was troubling the tobacco industry—the pending lawsuits brought against individual tobacco companies by the heirs of victims of lung cancer. For another, he was the only man to concede that cigarettes might possibly contain substances worth filtering out. He didn't say that these substances were harmful, but he did say that "certain things in smoking that don't affect taste, enjoyment, or pleasure can be removed, and since there has been some question about them, they're better out than in." To that end, he said, his company had come up with a new filter that would remove phenol from the smoke. (In the available literature on smoking and health, it seems to be commonly recognized that phenol is one—but only one—of the many substances in tobacco smoke that are suspected of playing a carcinogenic role.) But beyond this I found no compromise. "I don't believe that cigarettes are causing all these diseases," he said. "Cigarette smoking has been in existence a long time, and we consider that we have a serious responsibility to the smoking public. If we were convinced that cigarettes were harmful, we wouldn't be in the cigarette business."

Did he think, I asked, that cigarette companies should inform the public—by labelling or by other means—of the statistical association that is supposed to exist between smoking and disease.

"The public has been informed," he replied. "The public knows all about it."

My final interview was with Adolph J. Toigo, the president of Lennen & Newell, the advertising agency that handles the ads and commercials for most of Lorillard's cigarette brands. Lennen & Newell annually handles about thirty million dollars' worth of Lorillard advertising. After the comparative frankness of Cramer on certain aspects of the issue of smoking and health, I hoped that Toigo might be equally informative. He is a short, gray-looking man, with graying hair, a gray mustache, and a rather pale face. He was wearing a gray suit. As we talked about the cigarette business in his big, panelled office, I found my hopes fading. "Kent has grown more than any other filter cigarette," he said. "We believe the right combination of filter and tobacco is responsible. That reflects our current campaign. Lorillard has spent a lot of money anticipating consumer requirements. There's a lot of idealism in the big corporations. I have quite an aversion to the opposite interpretation."

After a while, I asked him what he thought about the cigarette-health question.

"Well, I think it's a controversial subject on which there is no proof—no established proof—of cigarettes' being harmful," he said. "What's more, I think it's *beneficial* to smoke. Otherwise they wouldn't be doing it."

As I left Toigo's office—and the offices of Cramer, Bowling, Landry, Pattison, Black, Heimann, and Walker before him—I could have no doubt but that the lines had been drawn and the battle joined. And I could no more foresee an accommodation between the opposing forces than I could before I started.

The New Yorker, November 30, 1963

James Thurber

THE CASE FOR THE DAYDREAMER

ALL THE books in my extensive library on training the mind agree that realism, as against fantasy, reverie, daydreaming, and wool-gathering, is a highly important thing. "Be a realist," says Dr. James L. Mursell, whose "Streamline Your Mind" I have already discussed. "Take a definite step to turn a dream into a reality," says Mrs. Dorothea Brande, the "Wake-Up-and-Live!" woman. They allow you a certain amount of reverie and daydreaming (no woolgathering), but only when it is purposeful, only when it is going to lead to realistic action and concrete achievement. In this insistence on reality I do not see as much profit as these Shapers of Success do. I have had a great deal of satisfaction and benefit out of daydreaming which never got me anywhere in their definition of getting somewhere. I am reminded, as an example, of an incident which occurred this last summer.

I had been travelling about the country attending dog shows. I was writing a series of pieces on these shows. Not being in the habit of carrying press cards, letters of introduction, or even, in some cases, the key to my car or the tickets to a show which I am on my way to attend, I had nothing by which to identify myself. I simply paid my way in, but at a certain dog show I determined to see if the officials in charge would give me a pass. I approached a large, heavy-set man who looked somewhat like Victor McLaglen. His name was Bustard. Mr. Bustard. "You'll have to see Mr. Bustard," a ticket-taker had told me. This Mr. Bustard was apparently very busy trying to find bench space for old Miss Emily Van Winkle's Pomeranians, which she had entered at the last minute, and attending to a number of other matters. He glanced at me, saw that

369

he outweighed me some sixty pounds, and decided to make short shrift of whatever it was I wanted. I explained I was writing an article about the show and would like a pass to get in. "Why, that's impossible!" he cried. "That's ridiculous! If I gave you a pass, I'd have to give a pass to everyone who came up and asked me for a pass!" I was pretty much overwhelmed. I couldn't, as is usual in these cases, think of anything to say except "I see." Mr. Bustard delivered a brief, snarling lecture on the subject of people who expect to get into dog shows free, unless they are showing dogs, and ended with "Are you showing dogs?" I tried to think of something sharp and well-turned. "No, I'm not showing any dogs," I said, coldly. Mr. Bustard abruptly turned his back on me and walked away.

As soon as Mr. Bustard disappeared, I began to think of things I should have said. I thought of a couple of sharp cracks on his name, the least pointed of which was Buzzard. Finely edged comebacks leaped to mind. Instead of going into the dog show—or following Mr. Bustard—I wandered up and down the streets of the town, improving on my retorts. I fancied a much more successful encounter with Bustard. In this fancied encounter, I, in fact, enraged Mr. Bustard. He lunged at me, whereupon, side-stepping agilely, I led with my left and floored him with a beautiful right to the jaw. "Try that one!" I cried aloud. "Mercy!" murmured an old lady who was passing me at the moment. I began to walk more rapidly; my heart took a definite lift. Some people, in my dream, were bending over Bustard, who was out cold. "Better take him home and let the other bustards pick his bones," I said. When I got back to the dog show, I was in high fettle.

After several months I still feel, when I think of Mr. Bustard, that I got the better of him. In a triumphant daydream, it seems to me, there is felicity and not defeat. You can't just take a humiliation and dismiss it from your mind, for it will crop up in your dreams, but neither can you safely carry a dream into reality in the case of an insensitive man like Mr. Bustard who outweighs you by sixty pounds. The thing to do is to visualize a triumph over the humiliator so vividly and insistently that it becomes, in effect, an actuality. I went on with my daydreams about Mr. Bustard. All that day at the dog show I played tricks on him in my imagination, I outgeneralled him, I made him look silly, I had him on the run. I would imagine myself sitting in a living room. It was late at night. Outside it was raining heavily. The doorbell rang. I went to the door and opened it, and a man was standing there. "I wonder if you would let me use your phone?" he asked. "My car has broken down." It was, of all people, Mr. Bustard. You can imagine my jibes, my sarcasm, my repartee, my shutting the door in his face at the end. After a whole afternoon of this kind of thing, I saw Mr. Bustard on my way out of the show. I actually felt a little sorry about the tossing around I had given him. I gave him an enigmatic, triumphant smile which must have worried him a great deal. He must have wondered what I had been up to, what superior of his I had seen, what I had done to get back at him—who, after all, I was.

Now, let us figure Dr. Mursell in my place. Let us suppose that Dr. Mursell went up to Mr. Bustard and asked him for a pass to the dog show on the ground that he could streamline the dog's intuition. I fancy that Mr. Bustard also outweighs Dr. Mursell by sixty pounds and is in better fighting trim; we men who write treatises on the mind are not likely to be in as good shape as men who run dog shows. Dr. Mursell, then, is rebuffed, as I was. If he tries to get back at Mr. Bustard right there and then, he will find himself saying "I see" or "Well, I didn't know" or, at best, "I just asked you." Even the streamlined mind runs into this Blockage, as the psychologists call it. Dr. Mursell, like myself, will go away and think up better things to say, but, being a realist dedicated to carrying a dream into actuality, he will perforce have to come back and tackle Mr. Bustard again. If Mr. Bustard's patience gives out, or if he is truly stung by some crack of the Doctor's he is likely to begin shoving, or snap his fingers, or say "*'Raus!*," or even tweak the Doctor's nose. Dr. Mursell, in that case, would get into no end of trouble. Realists are always getting into trouble. They miss the sweet, easy victories of the daydreamer.

I do not pretend that the daydream cannot be carried too far. If at this late date, for instance, I should get myself up to look as much like Mr. Bustard as possible and then, gazing into the bathroom mirror, snarl "Bustard, you dog!," that would be carrying the daydream too far. One should never run the risk of identifying oneself with the object of one's scorn. I have no idea what complexes and neuroses might lie that way. The mental experts could tell you—or, if they couldn't, they would anyway.

Now let us turn briefly to the indomitable Mrs. Brande, eight of whose precious words of advice have, the ads for her book tell us, changed the lives of 860,000 people, or maybe it is 86,000,000—Simon & Schuster published her book. (These words are "act as if it were impossible to fail," in case your life hasn't been changed.) Discussing realistic action as against the daydream, she takes up the case of a person, any person, who dreams about going to Italy but is getting nowhere. The procedure she suggests for such a person is threefold: (1) read a current newspaper in Italian, buy some histories, phrase books, and a small grammar; (2) put aside a small coin each day; (3) do something in your spare time to make money—"if it is nothing more than to sit with children while their parents are at parties." (I have a quick picture of the parents reeling from party to party, but that is beside the point.)

I can see the newspaper and the books intensifying the dream, but I can't somehow see them getting anybody to Italy. As for putting a small coin aside each day, everybody who has tried it knows that it does not work out. At the end of three weeks you usually have $2.35 in the pig bank or the cooky jar, a dollar and a half of which you have to use for something besides Italy, such as a C.O.D. package. At that rate, all that you would have in the bank or the jar at the end of six years would be about $87.45. Within the next six years Italy will probably be at war, and even if you were well enough to travel after all that time, you couldn't get into the country. The disappointment of a dream nursed for six years, with a reality in view that did not eventuate, would be enough to embitter a person for life. As for this business of sitting with children while their parents are at parties, anybody who has done it knows that no trip to anywhere, even Utopia, would be worth it. Very few people can sit with children, especially children other than their own, more than an hour and a half without having their dispositions and even their characters badly mauled about. In fifteen minutes the average child whose parents are at a party can make enough flat statements of fact about one's personal appearance and ask enough pointed questions about one's private life to send one away feeling that there is little, if any, use in going on with anything at all, let alone a trip to Italy.

The long and hard mechanics of reality which these inspirationalists suggest are, it seems to me, far less satisfactory than the soft routine of a dream. The dreamer builds up for himself no such towering and uncertain structure of hope; he has no depleted cooky jar to shake his faith in himself. It is significant that the line "Oh, to be in England now that April's there," which is a definite dream line, is better known than any line the poet wrote about actually being in England. (I guess *that* will give the inspirationalists something to think about.) You can sit up with children if you want to, you can put a dime a day in an empty coffee tin, you can read the Fascist viewpoint in an Italian newspaper, but when it comes to a choice between the dream and the reality of present-day Italy, I personally shall sit in a corner by the fire and read "The Ring and the Book." And in the end it will probably be me who sends you a postcard from Italy, which you can put between the pages of the small grammar or the phrase book.

The New Yorker, December 19, 1936

Alistair Cooke

ROUGHING IT

A HUNDRED years ago the first ship sailed out of New York bound for San Francisco and the American River, where, according to the reports that had drifted East, you lowered a pan into a sluggish stream, shook it several times, and sifted out a fortune in gold. By ship round the Horn was only one way, the most tedious and the safest. You could go by way of Panama and Nicaragua and run the risk of malaria or yellow fever. You could sail down to Mexico and face a shorter journey across its width through almost trackless desert and the chance of epidemics and slaughter by bandits.

Most people in the East who for one reason or another felt the urge to Go West decided to go the overland way. Today it is impossible to experience the human ordeal of that great migration, one of the last epics of purely human function before the Industrial Revolution transformed our lives. These people, in New England, and New York and Maryland and Ohio, sat down and planned to walk nearly two thousand miles from St. Joseph, Missouri, or Independence, where the locomotive and the steamboat ended and the Middle Ages began. Independence was a more thriving place a century ago than it is today, because it was the outfitting center for the Forty-Niners. From there you were on your own. You went by mule and drove your wagons and cattle along with you for the remaining eighteen hundred miles. You used a route map drawn by somebody who had once made it and survived. You depended very much, too much, on the hearsay of these people to know where the water-holes were and where you could take a short cut through the mountains.

374

There was no archetype of the Forty-Niner. They were of every human kind. But early on they learned that they had better travel in packs, and most of them elected what they called a captain and two lieutenants. A quartermaster was chosen to look after the provisions. They may sound very martial in a noticeably non-military nation.[1] But they knew, the later companies at any rate, that there were certain unavoidable hazards: flash floods, the rotting of their food, Indians, disease, and the constant challenge to their discipline and courage of reducing the weight of their pack—their implements, even their food supply—when the route was too much for their animals, who set the pace. They figured correctly that no group of human beings, however individually noble, would be likely to stay noble in the desperation of thirst, or spontaneously organize themselves in the event of attack. By the time they started the long journey from Missouri, most of them had formed themselves into companies and agreed on written or unwritten laws. Many of them spent weeks in the East before they left, drawing up written constitutions. Some of these were abided by all the way to California. Others were torn up in anger, stuffed down the captain's throat, or buried with a dead cow.

Most of them through the late spring of '49 took far too many provisions. It was said that the summer companies had the routes laid out for them by trails of abandoned stoves, pillows, beds, pots and kettles, crowbars, drills, plows, harness, trunks, bellows, and dishpans. These, they found, were luxuries to a pioneer. And the word got across the continent that what you needed was one wagon to carry the supplies for every five persons, a mule apiece, rifles and shotguns, a rubber knapsack, an oil-cloth cap, two pairs of boots, eight shirts, an overcoat, one pair of drawers, three blankets, a hundred and fifty pounds of flour, twenty-five pounds of bacon, fifteen pounds of coffee, twenty-five of sugar, some baking powder, salt and pepper.

That's as far as I want to go in describing the famous journeys across the plains. But I suspect that any American who started out today, fitted out just this way, and got to California, even if he stuck to the countless cement highways that slam across hundreds of thousands of miles north and south and east and west—such a man would become some sort of national hero or crank. He would be paced by the newsreel

[1] As of 1776–1942.

boys, met at intervals by the advertising salesmen of whoever's flour and bacon he was carrying, he would be greeted by the Mayor of San Francisco, he would in the end be flown to Washington and shown in all the papers shaking the President's hand in the White House.

Nothing persists more in the fancy of Europeans, and in the superstitious pride of Americans themselves, than the conviction that Americans are tough and rough and ready, scornful of the European niceties and primmer ways of travel. The last thirty years have turned this belief into unmitigated legend.

One of the most precious books to American book collectors is a copy of Baedeker's *United States* for, I believe, 1906. In the conscientious Baedeker way, it warns the comparatively domesticated European of the coarse pleasures and inconveniences he will have to settle for if he decides to take a holiday in the United States. It is always Baedeker's consolation, however, to the intending tourist that no matter how constant the public spitting, how hard the beds, how ankle-deep the roads and primitive the hotels away from the big cities, the traveler who has any pioneering spirit in him will never regret his courageous visit to the United States because nowhere else will he see the singing color of the New England fall, the blossom of the South in the spring, the grandeur of the Yosemite, the Yellowstone, etc., etc. This guidebook is greatly sought after precisely because today it reads like such a gorgeous joke. If you changed the place-names and made them European, an American could read it with a straight face, since it would record most of his grouches about traveling in Europe today. The application of American technical genius to the mechanics of living has not merely turned the tables on Baedeker, it has turned the American, however reckless or self-reliant his individual character, into the world's most urbanized, most petted traveler.

Mr. Richard Neuberger, who lives in the Far West, in Portland, Oregon, has taken up this theme in a magazine piece. He was in Alaska during the war having, as he puts it, "the sort of experience we had read about eagerly as boys, in the tales of James Fenimore Cooper, Jack London, and Zane Grey." And, he adds, "we hated it . . . we talked nostalgically of percale sheets and fluffy towels, or breakfast in bed and tiled bathrooms." They complained—in Alaska, this is—about "drafty privies and the lack of dry-cleaning facilities." Mr. Neuberger concludes that "with a few bold exceptions, we Americans have come to regard the steam-heated hotel and the internal combustion engine as indispensable to any foray in the open." Nowadays, more millions than ever before (the latest annual count was 15,057,443) visit the American National Parks. But according to the Department of the Interior fewer and fewer people each year attempt the two-day hikes, or even drive up the highest peaks, or, having looked at the Grand Canyon, will undertake the day-long mule journey down to the overnight camp at the bottom. It is very hard to say how Americans would compare with other peoples in this new-found lassitude. Driving around most of the National Parks is pretty strenuous in itself. If you could put Yosemite and Yellowstone together, you would have something about the area of Wales, whose geography is a combination of Switzerland, Persia, and the Day of Judgment. But even so, these parks were lovingly created two generations ago by men who chopped through thousands of feet of lumber, who rode into them on a horse, who discovered the sublime with an ax, a botanist's kit, a piece of bacon, a tent and a stout heart. Now through all of them, even over the hair-raising pass into Tuolumne Meadows on top of the Yosemite, American engineers have built incomparable cement highways, blasted through prehistoric rock, encircling mountains where no other race would dream of cutting out a dirt road.

This suggests a cheerful contradiction. That even if the traveler *is* a sissy sitting over an internal combustion engine, the heroes who in his behalf comb cement to the smoothness of toothpaste under the desert sun, and build his highways through the Rockies and Sierras: they are Americans too. And this leads us into a famous cliché. I hope I can then lead us out of it. (I have nothing against clichés. Most of them are true, though you have to live through the denial of them to know it.) It is the assumption that the Americans have grown soft and unable to fend for themselves, that their enslaving gadgets, through which they flip their way so expertly, are crutches or props to living, essential to a people sinking contentedly into a decadence that out-Romans the Romans.

I'm sorry to report that the Americans' devotion to urban comfort, their ingenuity with gadgets, even their reliance on them, proves no such thing. In my own experience, the Americans who are most devoted to convertible automobiles and glass-enclosed showers made no complaint on this score when they ripped up Japanese jungles for airfields or waded ashore at Okinawa. The women I know who can whip up a delicious meal in ten minutes with the skilled aid of pressure cookers, bean slicers, electric beaters and deep-frozen vegetables are also the ones who can make the best meal the slow way with none of these things. And the most skillful fisherman I know is a man who can charm a trout with his fingernail, but prefers to have a compact tackle-box along, which contains exquisite scales the size of your thumb and a leader cutter which is a little circle of plastic molds that exudes fine wire and cuts it in one motion.

Most Americans, even rich ones, were brought up in a culture that never expected somebody else to do the rough work. Most boys in college who can afford good cars can also take them apart and put them together again. This may all be changing. Still, I doubt that a devotion to gadgets is a reflection in the American character of a terrified dependence on them. They are loved for themselves, for the humorous felicity with which they dispose of elementary labor. A Texan I know, whom I would never like to meet in anger whether the choice of weapons was a jet-propelled torpedo or the back of the raw hand, put it neatly once when he said to me, "I'll ride fifty miles on a horse for the fun of it, but out of necessity I drive." One of the irritating troubles about Americans, in violation of the best advice of the best English divines, is that they just don't believe that whatever is uncomfortable is good for the character.

Lionel Trilling

THE KINSEY REPORT

B Y VIRTUE of its intrinsic nature and also because of its dramatic reception, the Kinsey Report,[1] as it has come to be called, is an event of great importance in our culture. It is an event which is significant in two separate ways, as symptom and as therapy. The therapy lies in the large permissive effect the Report is likely to have, the long way it goes toward establishing the *community* of sexuality. The symptomatic significance lies in the fact that the Report was felt to be needed at all, that the community of sexuality requires now to be established in explicit quantitative terms. Nothing shows more clearly the extent to which modern society has atomized itself than the isolation in sexual ignorance which exists among us. We have censored the folk knowledge of the most primal things and have systematically dried up the social affections which might naturally seek to enlighten and release. Many cultures, the most primitive and the most complex, have entertained sexual fears of an irrational sort, but probably our culture is unique in strictly isolating the individual in the fears that society has devised. Now, having become somewhat aware of what we have perpetrated at great cost and with little gain, we must assure ourselves by statistical science that the solitude is imaginary. The Report will surprise one part of the population with some facts and another part with other facts, but really all that it says to society as a whole is that there is an almost universal involvement in the sexual life and therefore much variety of conduct. This was taken for granted in any comedy that Aristophanes put on the stage.

[1] *Sexual Behavior in the Human Male,* by Alfred C. Kinsey, Wardell B. Pomeroy, and Clyde E. Martin. Philadelphia: Saunders, 1948.

379

There is further diagnostic significance to be found in the fact that
our society makes this effort of self-enlightenment through the agency
of science. Sexual conduct is inextricably involved with morality, and
hitherto it has been dealt with by those representatives of our cultural
imagination which are, by their nature and tradition, committed to
morality—it has been dealt with by religion, social philosophy, and
literature. But now science seems to be the only one of our institutions
which has the authority to speak decisively on the matter. Nothing in
the Report is more suggestive in a large cultural way than the insistent
claims it makes for its strictly scientific nature, its pledge of indifference
to all questions of morality at the same time that it patently intends a
moral effect. Nor will any science do for the job—it must be a science as
simple and materialistic as the subject can possibly permit. It must be
a science of statistics and not of ideas. The way for the Report was prepared by Freud, but Freud, in all the years of his activity, never had the
currency or authority with the public that the Report has achieved in a
matter of weeks.

The scientific nature of the Report must be taken in conjunction
with the manner of its publication. The Report says of itself that it is
only a "preliminary survey," a work intended to be the first step in a
larger research; that it is nothing more than an "accumulation of scientific fact," a collection of "objective data," a "report on what people do,
which raises no question of what they should do," and it is fitted out with
a full complement of charts, tables, and discussions of scientific method.
A work conceived and executed in this way is usually presented only to
an audience of professional scientists; and the publishers of the Report,
a medical house, pay their ritual respects to the old tradition which
held that not all medical or quasi-medical knowledge was to be made
easily available to the general lay reader, or at least not until it had been
subjected to professional debate; they tell us in a foreword for what
limited professional audience the book was primarily intended—physicians, biologists, and social scientists and "teachers, social workers, personnel officers, law enforcement groups, and others concerned with the
direction of human behavior." And yet the book has been so successfully
publicized that for many weeks it was a national best seller.

This way of bringing out a technical book of science is a cultural
phenomenon that ought not to pass without some question. The public
which receives this technical report, this merely preliminary survey, this
accumulation of data, has never, even on its upper educational levels,

been properly instructed in the most elementary principles of scientific thought. With this public, science is authority. It has been trained to accept heedlessly "what science says," which it conceives to be a unitary utterance. To this public nothing is more valuable, more precisely "scientific," and more finally convincing than raw data without conclusions; no disclaimer of conclusiveness can mean anything to it—it has learned that the disclaimer is simply the hallmark of the scientific attitude, science's way of saying "thy unworthy servant."

So that if the Report were really, as it claims to be, only an accumulation of objective data, there would be some question of the cultural wisdom of dropping it in a lump on the general public. But in point of fact it is full of assumption and conclusion; it makes very positive statements on highly debatable matters and it editorializes very freely. This preliminary survey gives some very conclusive suggestions to a public that is quick to obey what science says, no matter how contradictory science may be, which is most contradictory indeed. This is the public that, on scientific advice, ate spinach in one generation and avoided it in the next, that in one decade trained its babies to rigid Watsonian schedules and believed that affection corrupted the infant character, only to learn in the next decade that rigid discipline was harmful and that cuddling was as scientific as induction.

Then there is the question of whether the Report does not do harm by encouraging people in their commitment to mechanical attitudes toward life. The tendency to divorce sex from the other manifestations of life is already a strong one. This truly absorbing study of sex in charts and tables, in data and quantities, may have the effect of strengthening the tendency still more with people who are by no means trained to invert the process of abstraction and to put the fact back into the general life from which it has been taken. And the likely mechanical implications of a statistical study are in this case supported by certain fully formulated attitudes which the authors strongly hold despite their protestations that they are scientific to the point of holding no attitudes whatever.

These, I believe, are valid objections to the book's indiscriminate circulation. And yet I also believe that there is something good about the manner of publication, something honest and right. Every complex society has its agencies which are "concerned with the direction of human behavior," but we today are developing a new element in that old activity, the element of scientific knowledge. Whatever the Report claims for itself, the social sciences in general no longer pretend that they can

merely describe what people do; they now have the clear consciousness
of their power to manipulate and adjust. First for industry and then for
government, sociology has shown its instrumental nature. A government
which makes use of social knowledge still suggests benignity; and in an
age that daily brings the proliferation of government by police methods
it may suggest the very spirit of rational liberalism. Yet at least one
sociologist has expressed the fear that sociology may become the instrument of a bland tyranny—it is the same fear that Dostoevski gave immortal expression to in "The Grand Inquisitor." And indeed there is
something repulsive in the idea of men being studied for their own
good. The paradigm of what repels us is to be found in the common
situation of the child who is *understood* by its parents, hemmed in, anticipated and lovingly circumscribed, thoroughly taped, finding it easier
and easier to conform internally and in the future to the parents' own
interpretation of the external acts of the past, and so, yielding to understanding as never to coercion, does not develop the mystery and wild-
ness of spirit which it is still our grace to believe is the mark of full
humanness. The act of understanding becomes an act of control.

If, then, we are to live under the aspect of sociology, let us at least
all be sociologists together—let us broadcast what every sociologist
knows, and let us all have a share in observing one another, including
the sociologists. The general indiscriminate publication of the Report
makes sociology a little less the study of many men by a few men and a
little more man's study of himself. There is something right in turning
loose the Report on the American public—it turns the American public
loose on the Report. It is right that the Report should be sold in stores
that never before sold books and bought by people who never before
bought books, and passed from hand to hand and talked about and
also snickered at and giggled over and generally submitted to humor:
American popular culture has surely been made the richer by the Report's
gift of a new folk hero—he already is clearly the hero of the Report—
the "scholarly and skilled lawyer" who for thirty years has had an
orgasmic frequency of thirty times a week.

As for the objection to the involvement of sex with science, it may
be said that if science, through the Report, serves in any way to free
the physical and even the "mechanical" aspects of sex, it may be that
much has acted to free the emotions it might seem to deny. And perhaps
only science could effectively undertake the task of freeing sexuality from
science itself. Nothing so much as science has reinforced the moralistic or

religious prohibitions in regard to sexuality. At some point in the history of Europe, some time in the Reformation, masturbation ceased to be thought of as merely a sexual sin which could be dealt with like any other sexual sin, and, perhaps by analogy with the venereal diseases with which the sexual mind of Europe was obsessed, came to be thought of as the specific cause of mental and physical disease, of madness and decay.[2] The prudery of Victorian England went forward with scientific hygiene; and both in Europe and in America the sexual mind was haunted by the idea of *degeneration,* apparently by analogy with the second law of thermodynamics—here is enlightened liberal opinion in 1896: "The effects of venereal disease have been treated at length, but the amount of vitality burned out through lust has never been and, perhaps, never can be adequately measured."[3] The very word *sex,* which we now utter so casually, came into use for scientific reasons, to replace *love,* which had once been indiscriminately used but was now to be saved for ideal purposes, and *lust,* which came to seem both too pejorative and too human: *sex* implied scientific neutrality, then vague devaluation, for the word which neutralizes the mind of the observer also neuterizes the men and women who are being observed. Perhaps the Report is the superfetation of neutrality and objectivity which, in the dialectic of culture, was needed before sex could be free of their cold dominion.

Certainly it is a great merit of the Report that it brings to mind the earliest and best commerce between sex and science—the best thing about the Report is the quality that makes us remember Lucretius. The dialectic of culture has its jokes, and *alma Venus* having once been called to preside protectively over science, the situation is now reversed. The Venus of the Report does not, like the Venus of *De Rerum Natura,* shine in the light of the heavenly signs, nor does the earth put forth flowers for her. She is rather fusty and hole-in-the-corner and no doubt it does not help her charm to speak of her in terms of mean frequencies of 3.2. No *putti* attend her: although Dr. Gregg in his Preface refers to sex as the reproductive instinct, there is scarcely any further indication in the book that sex has any connection with propagation. Yet clearly all things still follow where she leads, and somewhere in the authors' assumptions is buried the genial belief that still without her "nothing

[2] See Abram Kardiner, *The Psychological Frontiers of Society,* p. 32 and the footnote on p. 441.
[3] Article "Degeneration" in *The Encyclopedia of Social Reform.*

comes forth into the shining borders of light, nothing joyous and lovely is made." Her pandemic quality is still here—it is one of the great points of the Report how much of every kind of desire there is, how early it begins, how late it lasts. Her well-known jealousy is not abated, and prodigality is still her characteristic virtue: the Report assures us that those who respond to her earliest continue to do so longest. The Lucretian flocks and herds are here too. Professor Kinsey is a zoologist and he properly keeps us always in mind of our animal kinship, even though he draws some very illogical conclusions from it; and those who are honest will have to admit that their old repulsion by the idea of human-animal contacts is somewhat abated by the chapter on this subject, which is, oddly, the only chapter in the book which hints that sex may be touched with tenderness. This large, recognizing, Lucretian sweep of the Report is the best thing about it and it makes up for much that is deficient and confused in its ideas.

But the Report is something more than a public and symbolic act of cultural revision in which, while the Heavenly Twins brood benignly over the scene in the form of the National Research Council and the Rockefeller Foundation, Professor Kinsey and his coadjutors drag forth into the light all the hidden actualities of sex so that they may lose their dark power and become domesticated among us. It is also an early example of science undertaking to deal head-on with a uniquely difficult matter that has traditionally been involved in valuation and morality. We must ask the question very seriously: how does science conduct itself in such an enterprise?

Certainly it does not conduct itself the way it says it does. I have already suggested that the Report overrates its own objectivity. The authors, who are enthusiastically committed to their method and to their principles, make the mistake of believing that, being scientists, they do not deal in assumptions, preferences, and conclusions. Nothing comes more easily to their pens than the criticism of the subjectivity of earlier writers on sex, yet their own subjectivity is sometimes extreme. In the nature of the enterprise, a degree of subjectivity was inevitable. Intellectual safety would then seem to lie not only in increasing the number of mechanical checks or in more rigorously examining those assumptions which had been brought to conscious formulation, but also in straightforwardly admitting that subjectivity was bound to appear and inviting the reader to be on the watch for it. This would not have guaranteed an absolutely objectivity, but it would have made for a higher degree of relative objectivity. It would have done a thing even more important —it would have taught the readers of the Report something about the scientific processes to which they submit their thought.

The first failure of objectivity occurs in the title of the Report, *Sexual Behavior in the Human Male*. That the behavior which is studied is not that of the human male but only that of certain North American males has no doubt been generally observed and does not need further comment.[4] But the intention of the word *behavior* requires notice. By *behavior* the Report means behavioristic behavior, only that behavior which is physical. "To a large degree the present study has been confined to securing a record of the individual's overt sexual experiences." This limitation is perhaps forced on the authors by considerations of method, because it will yield simpler data and more manageable statistics, but it is also a limitation which suits their notion of human nature and its effect is to be seen throughout the book.

The Report, then, is a study of sexual behavior in so far as it can be quantitatively measured. This is certainly very useful. But, as we might fear, the sexuality that is measured is taken to be the definition of sexuality itself. The authors are certainly not without interest in what they call attitudes, but they believe that attitudes are best shown by "overt sexual experiences." We want to know, of course, what they mean by an experience and we want to know by what principles of evidence they draw their conclusions about attitudes.

We are led to see that their whole conception of a sexual experience is totally comprised by the physical act and that their principles of evidence are entirely quantitative and cannot carry them beyond the conclusion that the more the merrier. Quality is not integral to what they mean by experience. As I have suggested, the Report is partisan with sex, it wants people to have a good sexuality. But by good its means nothing else but frequent. "It seems safe to assume that daily orgasm would be within the capacity of the average male and that the more than daily rates which have been observed for some primate species could be matched by a large portion of the human population if sexual activity were unrestricted." The Report never suggests that a sexual experience is anything but the discharge of specifically sexual tension and therefore seems to conclude that frequency is always the sign of a robust sexuality.

[4] The statistical method of the report lies, necessarily, outside my purview. Nor am I able to assess with any confidence the validity of the interviewing methods that were employed.

Yet masturbation in children may be and often is the expression not
of sexuality only but of anxiety. In the same way, adult intercourse may
be the expression of anxiety; its frequency may not be so much robust
as compulsive.

The Report is by no means unaware of the psychic conditions of
sexuality, yet it uses the concept almost always under the influence of
its quantitative assumption. In a summary passage (p. 159) it describes
the different intensities of orgasm and the various degrees of satisfaction,
but disclaims any intention of taking these variations into account in its
record of behavior. The Report holds out the hope to respectable males
that they might be as frequent in performance as underworld characters
if they were as unrestrained as this group. But before the respectable
males aspire to this unwonted freedom they had better ascertain in how
far the underworld characters are ridden by anxiety and in how far their
sexuality is to be correlated with other ways of dealing with anxiety, such
as dope, and in how far it is actually enjoyable. The Report's own data
suggest that there may be no direct connection between on the one hand
lack of restraint and frequency and on the other hand psychic health;
they tell us of men in the lower social levels who in their sexual careers
have intercourse with many hundreds of girls but who despise their
sexual partners and cannot endure relations with the same girl more
than once.

But the Report, as we shall see, is most resistant to the possibility of
making any connection between the sexual life and the psychic structure.
This strongly formulated attitude of the Report is based on the assumption that the whole actuality of sex is anatomical and physiological;
the emotions are dealt with very much as if they were a "superstructure."
"The subject's awareness of the erotic situation is summed up by this
statement that he is 'emotionally' aroused; but the material sources of
the emotional disturbance are rarely recognized, either by laymen or
scientists, both of whom are inclined to think in terms of passion, or
natural drive, or a libido, which partakes of the mystic[5] more than it

5 We must observe how the scientific scorn of the "mystic" quite abates when the
"mystic" suits the scientist's purpose. The Report is explaining why the interviews were
not checked by means of narcosynthesis, lie-detectors, etc.: "In any such study which
needs to secure quantities of data from human subjects, there is no way except to win
their voluntary cooperation through the establishment of that intangible thing known
as rapport." This intangible thing is established by looking the respondent squarely
in the eye. It might be asked why a thing which is intangible but real enough to assure
scientific accuracy should not be real enough to be considered as having an effect in
sexual behavior.

does of solid anatomy and physiologic function." Now there is of course
a clear instrumental advantage in being able to talk about psychic or
emotional phenomena in terms of physiology, but to make a disjunction
between the two descriptions of the same event, to make the anatomical
and physiological description the "source" of the emotional and then to
consider it as the more real of the two, is simply to commit not only the
Reductive Fallacy but also what William James called the Psychologist's
Fallacy. It must bring under suspicion any subsequent generalization
which the Report makes about the nature of sexuality.[6]

The emphasis on the anatomical and physiological nature of sexuality is connected with the Report's strong reliance on animal behavior as
a norm. The italics in the following quotation are mine. *"For those who
like the term,* it is clear that there is a sexual drive which cannot be set
aside for any large portion of the population, by any sort of social convention. *For those who prefer to think in simpler terms of action and
reaction,* it is a picture of an animal who, however civilized or cultured,
continues to respond to the constantly present sexual stimuli, albeit with
some social and physical restraints." The Report obviously finds the
second formulation to be superior to the first, and implies with a touch
of irony that those who prefer it are on firmer ground.

Now there are several advantages in keeping in mind our own animal nature and our family connection with the other animals. The advantages are instrumental, moral, and poetic—I use the last word for
want of a better to suggest the mere pleasure in finding kinship with
some animals. But perhaps no idea is more difficult to use with precision
than this one. In the Report it is used to establish a dominating principle
of judgment, which is the Natural. As a concept of judgment this is
notoriously deceptive and has been belabored for generations, but the
Report knows nothing of its dangerous reputation and uses it with the
naïvest confidence. And although the Report directs the harshest language toward the idea of the Normal, saying that it has stood in the way

6 The implications of the Reductive Fallacy may be seen by paraphrasing the sentence
I have quoted in which Professor Kinsey commits it: "Professor Kinsey's awareness of
the intellectual situation is summed up by his statement that he 'has had an idea' or
'has come to a conclusion'; but the material sources of his intellectual disturbances are
rarely recognized, either by laymen or scientists, both of whom are inclined to think
in terms of 'thought' or 'intellection' or 'cognition,' which partakes of the mystic more
than it does of solid anatomy or physiologic function." The Psychologist's Fallacy is
what James calls "the confusion of his own standpoint with that of the mental fact
about which he is making a report." "Another variety of the psychologist's fallacy is
the assumption that the mental fact studied must be conscious of itself as the
psychologist is conscious of it." *Principles of Psychology,* vol. I, pp. 196–97.

of any true scientific knowledge of sex, it is itself by no means averse to letting the idea of the Natural develop quietly into the ideal of the Normal. The Report has in mind both a physical normality—as suggested by its belief that under optimal conditions men should be able to achieve the orgasmic frequency of the primates—and a moral normality, the acceptability, on the authority of animal behavior, or certain usually taboo practices.

It is inevitable that the concept of the Natural should haunt any discussion of sex. It is inevitable that it should make trouble, but most of all for a scientific discussion that bars judgments of value. Thus, in order to show that homosexuality is not a neurotic manifestation, as the Freudians say it is, the Report adduces the homosexual behavior of rats. But the argument *de animalibus* must surely stand by its ability to be inverted and extended. Thus, in having lost sexual periodicity, has the human animal lost its naturalness? Again, the female mink, as we learn from the Report itself, fiercely resists intercourse and must be actually coerced into submission. Is it she who is unnatural or is her defense of her chastity to be taken as a comment on the females, animal or human, who willingly submit or who merely play at escape? Professor Kinsey is like no one so much as Sir Percival in Malory, who, seeing a lion and a serpent in battle wtih each other, decided to help the lion, "for he was the more natural beast of the two."

This awkwardness in the handling of ideas is characteristic of the Report. It is ill at ease with any idea that is in the least complex and it often tries to get rid of such an idea in favor of another that has the appearance of not going beyond the statement of physical fact. We see this especially in the handling of certain Freudian ideas. The Report acknowledges its debt to Freud with the generosity of spirit that marks it in other connections and it often makes use of Freudian concepts in a very direct and sensible way. Yet nothing could be clumsier than its handling of Freud's idea of pregenital generalized infantile sexuality. Because the Report can show, what is interesting and significant, that infants are capable of actual orgasm, although without ejaculation, it concludes that infantile sexuality is not generalized but specifically genital. But actually it has long been known, though the fact of orgasm had not been established, that infants can respond erotically to direct genital stimulation, and this knowledge does not contradict the Freudian idea that there is a stage in infant development in which sexuality is generalized throughout the body rather than specifically centered in the genital area; the fact of infant orgasm must be interpreted in conjunction with other more complex manifestations of infant sexuality.[7]

The Report, we may say, has an extravagant fear of all ideas that do not seem to it to be, as it were, immediately dictated by simple physical fact. Another way of saying this is that the Report is resistant to any idea that seems to refer to a specifically human situation. An example is the position it takes on the matter of male potency. The folk feeling, where it is formulated on the question, and certainly where it is formulated by women, holds that male potency is not to be measured, as the Report measures it, merely by frequency, but by the ability to withhold orgasm long enough to bring the woman to climax. This is also the psychoanalytic view, which holds further that the inability to sustain intercourse is the result of unconscious fear or resentment. This view is very strongly resisted by the Report. The denial is based on mammalian behavior—"in many species" (but not in all?) ejaculation follows almost immediately upon intromission; in chimpanzees ejaculation occurs in ten to twenty seconds. The report therefore concludes that the human male who ejaculates immediately upon intromission "is quite normal [here the word becomes suddenly permissible] among mammals and usual among his own species." Indeed, the Report finds it odd that the term "impotent" should be applied to such rapid responses. "It would be difficult to find another situation in which an individual who was quick and intense in his responses was labeled anything but superior, and that in most instances is exactly what the rapidly ejaculating male probably is, however inconvenient and unfortunate his qualities may be from the standpoint of the wife in the relationship."

But by such reasoning the human male who is quick and intense in his leap to the lifeboat is natural and superior, however inconvenient and unfortunate his speed and intensity may be to the wife he leaves standing on the deck, as is also the man who makes a snap judgment, who bites his dentist's finger, who kicks the child who annoys him, who bolts his—or another's—food, who is incontinent of his feces. Surely the problem of the natural in the human was solved four centuries ago by Rabelais, and in the simplest naturalistic terms; and it is sad to have the issue all confused again by the naïveté of men of science. Rabelais'

---

[7] The Report also handles the idea of sublimation in a very clumsy way. It does not represent accurately what the Freudian theory of sublimation is. For this, however, there is some excuse in the change of emphasis and even in meaning in Freud's use of the word.

solution lay in the simple perception of the *natural* ability and tendency of man to grow in the direction of organization and control. The young Gargantua in his natural infancy had all the quick and intense responses just enumerated; had his teachers confused the traits of his natural infancy with those of his natural manhood, he would not have been the more natural but the less; he would have been a monster.

In considering the Report as a major cultural document, we must not underestimate the significance of its petulant protest against the inconvenience to the male of the unjust demand that is made upon him. This protest is tantamount to saying that sexuality is not to be involved in specifically human situations or to be connected with desirable aims that are conceived of in specifically human terms. We may leave out of account any ideal reasons which would lead a man to solve the human situation of the discrepancy—arising from conditions of biology or of culture or of both—between his own orgasmic speed and that of his mate, and we can consider only that it might be hedonistically desirable for him to do so, for advantages presumably accrue to him in the woman's accessibility and responsiveness. Advantages of this kind, however, are precisely the matters of quality in experience that the Report ignores.[8]

And its attitude on the question of male potency is but one example of the Report's insistence on drawing sexuality apart from the general human context. It is striking how small a role women play in *Sexual Behavior in the Human Male.* We learn nothing about the connection of sex and reproduction; the connection, from the sexual point of view, is certainly not constant yet it is of great interest. The pregnancy or possibility of pregnancy of his mate has a considerable effect, sometimes one way, sometimes the other, on the sexual behavior of the male; yet in the index under *Pregnancy* there is but a single entry—*"fear of."* Again, the contraceptive devices which *Pregnancy, fear of,* requires have a notable influence on male sexuality; but the index lists only *Contraception, techniques.* Or again, menstruation has an elaborate mythos which men take very seriously; but the two indexed passages which refer to menstruation give no information about its relation to sexual conduct.

Then too the Report explicitly and stubbornly resists the idea that sexual behavior is involved with the whole of the individual's character.

---

[8] It is hard not to make a connection between the Report's strong stand against any delay in the male orgasm and its equally strong insistence that there is no difference for the woman between a clitoral and vaginal orgasm, a view which surely needs more investigation before it is as flatly put as the Report puts it. The conjunction of the two ideas suggests the desirability of a sexuality which uses a minimum of sexual apparatus.

In this it is strangely inconsistent. In the conclusion of its chapter on masturbation, after saying that masturbation does no physical harm and, if there are no conflicts over it, no mental harm, it goes on to raise the question of the effect of adult masturbation on the ultimate personality of the individual. With a certain confusion of cause and effect which we need not dwell on, it says: "It is now clear that masturbation is relied upon by the upper [social] level primarily because it has insufficient outlet through heterosexual coitus. This is, to a degree, an escape from reality, and the effect upon the ultimate personality of the individual is something that needs consideration." The question is of course a real one, yet the Report strenuously refuses to extend the principle of it to any other sexual activity. It summarily rejects the conclusions of psychoanalysis which make the sexual conduct an important clue to, even the crux of, character. It finds the psychoanalytical view unacceptable for two reasons: (1) The psychiatric practitioner misconceives the relation between sexual aberrancy and psychic illness because only those sexually aberrant people who are ill seek out the practitioner, who therefore never learns about the large incidence of mental health among the sexually aberrant. (2) The emotional illness which sends the sexually aberrant person to find psychiatric help is the result of no flaw in the psyche itself that is connected with the aberrancy but is the result only of the fear of social disapproval of his sexual conduct. And the Report instances the many men who are well adjusted socially and who yet break, among them, all the sexual taboos.

The quality of the argument which the Report here advances is as significant as the wrong conclusions it reaches. "It is not possible," the Report says, "to insist that any departure from the sexual mores, or any participation in socially taboo activities, always, or even usually, involves a neurosis or psychosis, for the case histories abundantly demonstrate that most individuals who engage in taboo activities make satisfactory social adjustments." In this context either "neuroses and psychoses" are too loosely used to stand for all psychic maladjustment, or "social adjustment" is too loosely used to stand for emotional peace and psychic stability. When the Report goes on to cite the "socially and intellectually significant persons," the "successful scientists, educators, physicians," etc., who have among them "accepted the whole range of the so-called abnormalities," we must keep in mind that very intense emotional disturbance, known only to the sufferer, can go along with the efficient discharge of social duties, and that the psychoanalyst could counter with as long a list of distinguished and efficient people who do consult him.

Then, only an interest in attacking straw men could have led the Report to insist that psychoanalysis is wrong in saying that *any* departure from sexual mores, or *any* participation in sexually taboo activities, involves a neurosis or a psychosis, for psychoanalysis holds nothing like this view. It is just at this point that distinctions are needed of a sort which the Report seems not to want to make. For example: the Report comes out in a bold and simple way for the naturalness and normality and therefore for the desirability of mouth-genital contacts in heterosexual love-making. This is a form of sexual expression which is officially taboo enough, yet no psychoanalyst would say that its practice indicated a neurosis or psychosis. But a psychoanalyst would say that a person who disliked or was unable to practice any other form of sexual contact thereby gave evidence of a neurotic strain in his psychic constitution. His social adjustment, in the rather crude terms which the Report conceives of it, might not be impaired, but certainly the chances are that his psychic life would show signs of disturbance, not from the practice itself but from the psychic needs which made him insist on it. It is not the breaking of the taboo but the emotional circumstance of the breaking of the taboo that is significant.

The Report handles in the same oversimplified way and with the same confusing use of absolute concepts the sexual aberrancy which is, I suppose, the most complex and the most important in our cultural life, homosexuality. It rejects the view that homosexuality is innate and that "no modification of it may be expected." But then it goes on also to reject the view that homosexuality provides evidence of a "psychopathic personality." "Psychopathic personality" is a very strong term which perhaps few analysts would wish to use in this connection. Perhaps even the term "neurotic" would be extreme in a discussion which, in the manner of the Report, takes "social adjustment," as indicated by status, to be the limit of its analysis of character. But this does not leave the discussion where the Report seems to want to leave it—at the idea that homosexuality is to be accepted as a form of sexuality like another and that it is as "natural" as heterosexuality, a judgment to which the Report is led in part because of the surprisingly large incidence of homosexuality it finds in the population. Nor does the practice of "an increasing proportion of the most skilled psychiatrists who make no attempt to redirect behavior, but who devote their attention to helping an individual accept himself" imply what the Report seems to want it to, that these psychiatrists have thereby judged homosexuality to be an unexceptionable form of sexuality; it is rather that, in many cases, they are able to effect no change in the psychic disposition and therefore do the sensible and humane next best thing. Their opinion of the etiology of homosexuality as lying in some warp—as our culture judges it—of the psychic structure has not, I believe, changed. And I think that they would say that the condition that produced the homosexuality also produced other character traits on which judgment could be passed. This judgment need by no means be totally adverse; as passed upon individuals it need not be adverse at all; but there can be no doubt that a society in which homosexuality was dominant or even accepted would be different in nature and quality from one in which it was censured.

That the Report refuses to hold this view of homosexuality, or any other view of at least equivalent complexity, leads us to take into account the motives that animate the work, and when we do, we see how very characteristically *American* a document the Report is. In speaking of its motives, I have in mind chiefly its impulse toward acceptance and liberation, its broad and generous desire for others that they be not harshly judged. Much in the Report is to be understood as having been dictated by a recoil from the crude and often brutal rejection which society has made of the persons it calls sexually aberrant. The Report has the intention of habituating its readers to sexuality in all its manifestations; it wants to establish, as it were, a democratic pluralism of sexuality. And this good impulse toward acceptance and liberation is not unique with the Report but very often shows itself in those parts of our intellectual life which are more or less official and institutionalized. It is, for example, far more established in the universities than most of us with our habits of criticism of America, particularly of American universities, will easily admit; and it is to a considerable extent an established attitude with the foundations that support intellectual projects.

That this generosity of mind is much to be admired goes without saying. But when we have given it all the credit it deserves as a sign of something good and enlarging in American life, we cannot help observing that it is often associated with an almost intentional intellectual weakness. It goes with a nearly conscious aversion from making intellectual distinctions, almost as if out of the belief that an intellectual distinction must inevitably lead to a social discrimination or exclusion. We might say that those who most explicitly assert and wish to practice the democratic virtues have taken it as their assumption that all social facts—with the exception of exclusion and economic hardship—must be *accepted,* not merely in the scientific sense but also in the social sense, in the sense, that is, that no judgment must be passed on them, that any conclusion drawn from them which perceives values and consequences will turn out to be "undemocratic."

The Report has it in mind to raise questions about the official restrictive attitudes toward sexual behavior, including those attitudes that are formulated on the statute books of most states. To this end it accumulates facts with the intention of showing that standards of judgment of sexual conduct as they now exist do not have real reference to the actual sexual behavior of the population. So far, so good. But then it goes on to imply that there can be only one standard for the judgment of sexual behavior—that is, sexual behavior as it actually exists; which is to say that sexual behavior is not to be judged at all, except, presumably, in so far as it causes pain to others. (But from its attitude to the "inconvenience" of the "wife in the relationship," we must presume that not all pain is to be reckoned with.) Actually the Report does not stick to its own standard of judgment; it is, as I have shown, sometimes very willing to judge among behaviors. But the preponderant weight of its argument is that a fact is a physical fact, to be considered only in its physical aspect and apart from an idea or ideal that might make it a social fact, as having no ascertainable personal or cultural meaning and no possible consequences—as being, indeed, not available to social interpretation at all. In short, the Report by its primitive conception of the nature of fact quite negates the importance and even the existence of sexuality as a social fact. That is why, although it is possible to say of the Report that it brings light, it is necessary to say of it that it spreads confusion.

Albert Einstein

WHY DO THEY HATE THE JEWS?

J SHOULD like to begin by telling you an ancient fable, with a few minor changes—a fable that will serve to throw into bold relief the mainspring of political anti-Semitism:

The shepherd boy said to the horse: "You are the noblest beast that treads the earth. You deserve to live in untroubled bliss; and indeed your happiness would be complete were it not for the treacherous stag. But he practiced from youth to excel you in fleetness of foot. His faster pace allows him to reach the water holes before you do. He and his tribe drink up the water far and wide, while you and your foal are left to thirst. Stay with me! My wisdom and guidance shall deliver you and your kind from a dismal and ignominious state."

Blinded by envy and hatred of the stag, the horse agreed. He yielded to the shepherd lad's bridle. He lost his freedom and became the shepherd's slave.

The horse in this fable represents a people, and the shepherd lad a class or clique aspiring to absolute rule over the people; the stag, on the other hand, represents the Jews.

I can hear you say: "A most unlikely tale! No creature would be as foolish as the horse in your fable." But let us give it a little more thought. The horse had been suffering the pangs of thirst, and his vanity was often pricked when he saw the nimble stag outrunning him. You, who have known no such pain and vexation, may find it difficult to understand that hatred and blindness should have driven the horse to act with such ill-advised, gullible haste. The horse, however, fell an

395

easy victim to temptation because his earlier tribulations had prepared
him for such a blunder. For there is much truth in the saying that it
is easy to give just and wise counsel—to others!—but hard to act justly
and wisely for oneself. I say to you with full conviction: We all have
often played the tragic role of the horse and we are in constant danger
of yielding to temptation again.

The situation illustrated in this fable happens again and again in
the life of individuals and nations. In brief, we may call it the process
by which dislike and hatred of a given person or group are diverted to
another person or group incapable of effective defense. But why did the
role of the stag in the fable so often fall to the Jews? Why did the
Jews so often happen to draw the hatred of the masses? Primarily
because there are Jews among almost all nations and because they are
everywhere too thinly scattered to defend themselves against violent
attack.

A few examples from the recent past will prove the point: Toward
the end of the nineteenth century the Russian people were chafing
under the tyranny of their government. Stupid blunders in foreign
policy further strained their temper until it reached the breaking point.
In this extremity the rulers of Russia sought to divert unrest by inciting
the masses to hatred and violence toward the Jews. These tactics were
repeated after the Russian government had drowned the dangerous
revolution of 1905 in blood—and this maneuver may well have helped
to keep the hated regime in power until near the end of the World War.

When the Germans had lost the World War hatched by their
ruling class, immediate attempts were made to blame the Jews, first for
instigating the war and then for losing it. In the course of time, success
attended these efforts. The hatred engendered against the Jews not
only protected the privileged classes, but enabled a small, unscrupulous
and insolent group to place the German people in a state of complete
bondage.

The crimes with which the Jews have been charged in the course
of history—crimes which were to justify the atrocities perpetrated against
them—have changed in rapid succession. They were supposed to have
poisoned wells. They were said to have murdered children for ritual
purposes. They were falsely charged with a systematic attempt at the
economic domination and exploitation of all mankind. Pseudo-scientific
books were written to brand them an inferior, dangerous race. They

were reputed to foment wars and revolutions for their own selfish purposes. They were presented at once as dangerous innovators and as enemies of true progress. They were charged with falsifying the culture of nations by penetrating the national life under the guise of becoming assimilated. In the same breath they were accused of being so stubbornly inflexible that it was impossible for them to fit into any society.

Almost beyond imagination were the charges brought against them, charges known to their instigators to be untrue all the while, but which time and again influenced the masses. In times of unrest and turmoil the masses are inclined to hatred and cruelty, whereas in times of peace these traits of human nature emerge but stealthily.

Up to this point I have spoken only of violence and oppression against the Jews—not of anti-Semitism itself as a psychological and social phenomenon existing even in times and circumstances when no special action against the Jews is under way. In this sense, one may speak of latent anti-Semitism. What is its basis? I believe that in a certain sense one may actually regard it as a normal manifestation in the life of a people.

The members of any group existing in a nation are more closely bound to one another than they are to the remaining population. Hence a nation will never be free of friction while such groups continue to be distinguishable. In my belief, uniformity in a population would not be desirable, even if it were attainable. Common convictions and aims, similar interests, will in every society produce groups that, in a certain sense, act as units. There will always be friction between such groups— the same sort of aversion and rivalry that exists between individuals.

The need for such groupings is perhaps most easily seen in the field of politics, in the formation of political parties. Without parties the political interests of the citizens of any state are bound to languish. There would be no forum for the free exchange of opinions. The individual would be isolated and unable to assert his convictions. Political convictions, moreover, ripen and grow only through mutual stimulation and criticism offered by individuals of similar disposition and purpose; and politics is no different from any other field of our cultural existence. Thus it is recognized, for example, that in times of intense religious fervor different sects are likely to spring up whose rivalry stimulates religious life in general. It is well known, on the other hand, that centralization—that is, elimination of independent groups—leads to one-sidedness and barrenness in science and art because such centralization checks and even suppresses any rivalry of opinions and research trends.

JUST WHAT IS A JEW?

The formation of groups has an invigorating effect in all spheres of human striving, perhaps mostly due to the struggle between the convictions and aims represented by the different groups. The Jews too form such a group with a definite character of its own, and anti-Semitism is nothing but the antagonistic attitude produced in the non-Jews by the Jewish group. This is a normal social reaction. But for the political abuse resulting from it, it might never have been designated by a special name.

What are the characteristics of the Jewish group? What, in the first place, is a Jew? There are no quick answers to this question. The most obvious answer would be the following: A Jew is a person professing the Jewish faith. The superficial character of this answer is easily recognized by means of a simple parallel. Let us ask the question: What is a snail? An answer similar in kind to the one given above might be: A snail is an animal inhabiting a snail shell. This answer is not altogether incorrect; nor, to be sure, is it exhaustive; for the snail shell happens to be but one of the material products of the snail. Similarly, the Jewish faith is but one of the characteristic products of the Jewish community. It is, furthermore, known that a snail can shed its shell without thereby ceasing to be a snail. The Jew who abandons his faith (in the formal sense of the word) is in a similar position. He remains a Jew.

Difficulties of this kind appear whenever one seeks to explain the essential character of a group.

The bond that has united the Jews for thousands of years and that unites them today is, above all, the democratic ideal of social justice, coupled with the ideal of mutual aid and tolerance among all men. Even the most ancient religious scriptures of the Jews are steeped in these social ideals, which have powerfully affected Christianity and Mohammedanism and have had a benign influence upon the social structure of a great part of mankind. The introduction of a weekly day of rest should be remembered here—a profound blessing to all mankind. Personalities such as Moses, Spinoza and Karl Marx, dissimilar as they may be, all lived and sacrificed themselves for the ideal of social justice;

and it was the tradition of their forefathers that led them on this thorny path. The unique accomplishments of the Jews in the field of philanthropy spring from the same source.

The second characteristic trait of Jewish tradition is the high regard in which it holds every form of intellectual aspiration and spiritual effort. I am convinced that this great respect for intellectual striving is solely responsible for the contributions that the Jews have made toward the progress of knowledge, in the broadest sense of the term. In view of their relatively small number and the considerable external obstacles constantly placed in their way on all sides, the extent of those contributions deserves the admiration of all sincere men. I am convinced that this is not due to any special wealth of endowment, but to the fact that the esteem in which intellectual accomplishment is held among the Jews creates an atmosphere particularly favorable to the development of any talents that may exist. At the same time a strong critical spirit prevents blind obeisance to any mortal authority.

I have confined myself here to these two traditional traits, which seem to me the most basic. These standards and ideals find expression in small things as in large. They are transmitted from parents to children; they color conversation and judgment among friends; they fill the religious scriptures; and they give to the community life of the group its characteristic stamp. It is in these distinctive ideals that I see the essence of Jewish nature. That these ideals are but imperfectly realized in the group—in its actual everyday life—is only natural. However, if one seeks to give brief expression to the essential character of a group, the approach must always be by the way of the ideal.

WHERE OPPRESSION IS A STIMULUS

In the foregoing I have conceived of Judaism as a community of tradition. Both friend and foe, on the other hand, have often asserted that the Jews represent a race; that their characteristic behavior is the result of innate qualities transmitted by heredity from one generation to the next. This opinion gains weight from the fact that the Jews for thousands of years have predominantly married within their own group. Such a custom may indeed *preserve* a homogeneous race—if it existed originally; it cannot *produce* uniformity of the race—if there was originally a racial intermixture. The Jews, however, are beyond doubt a mixed race, just as are all other groups of our civilization. Sincere anthropologists are agreed on this point; assertions to the contrary all belong to the field of political propaganda and must be rated accordingly.

Perhaps even more than on its own tradition, the Jewish group has thrived on oppression and on the antagonism it has forever met in the world. Here undoubtedly lies one of the main reasons for its continued existence through so many thousands of years.

The Jewish group, which we have briefly characterized in the foregoing, embraces about sixteen million people—less than one per cent of mankind, or about half as many as the population of present-day Poland. Their significance as a political factor is negligible. They are scattered over almost the entire earth and are in no way organized as a whole—which means that they are incapable of concerted action of any kind.

Were anyone to form a picture of the Jews solely from the utterances of their enemies, he would have to reach the conclusion that they represent a world power. At first sight that seems downright absurd; and yet, in my view, there is a certain meaning behind it. The Jews as a group may be powerless, but the sum of the achievements of their individual members is everywhere considerable and telling, even though these achievements were made in the face of obstacles. The forces dormant in the individual are mobilized, and the individual himself is stimulated to self-sacrificing effort, by the spirit that is alive in the group.

Hence the hatred of the Jews by those who have reason to shun popular enlightenment. More than anything else in the world, they fear the influence of men of intellectual independence. I see in this the essential cause for the savage hatred of Jews raging in present-day Germany. To the Nazi group the Jews are not merely a means for turning the resentment of the people away from themselves, the oppressors; they see the Jews as a nonassimilable element that cannot be driven into uncritical acceptance of dogma, and that, therefore—as long as it exists at all—threatens their authority because of its insistence on popular enlightenment of the masses.

Proof that this conception goes to the heart of the matter is convincingly furnished by the solemn ceremony of the burning of the books staged by the Nazi regime shortly after its seizure of power. This act, senseless from a political point of view, can only be understood as a spontaneous emotional outburst. For that reason it seems to me more revealing than many acts of greater purpose and practical importance.

In the field of politics and social science there has grown up a justified distrust of generalizations pushed too far. When thought is too greatly dominated by such generalizations, misinterpretations of specific sequences of cause and effect readily occur, doing injustice to the actual multiplicity of events. Abandonment of generalization, on the other hand, means to relinquish understanding altogether. For that reason I believe one may and must risk generalization, as long as one remains aware of its uncertainty. It is in this spirit that I wish to present in all modesty my conception of anti-Semitism, considered from a general point of view.

In political life I see two opposed tendencies at work, locked in constant struggle with each other. The first, optimistic, trend proceeds from the belief that the free unfolding of the productive forces of individuals and groups essentially leads to a satisfactory state of society. It recognizes the need for a central power, placed above groups and individuals, but concedes to such power only organizational and regulatory functions. The second, pessimistic, trend assumes that free interplay of individuals and groups leads to the destruction of society; it thus seeks to base society exclusively upon authority, blind obedience and coercion. Actually this trend is pessimistic only to a limited extent: for it is optimistic in regard to those who are, and desire to be, the bearers of power and authority. The adherents of this second trend are the enemies of the free groups and of education for independent thought. They are, moreover, the carriers of political anti-Semitism.

Here in America all pay lip service to the first, optimistic, tendency. Nevertheless, the second group is strongly represented. It appears on the scene everywhere, though for the most part it hides its true nature. Its aim is political and spiritual dominion over the people by a minority, by the circuitous route of control over the means of production. Its proponents have already tried to utilize the weapon of anti-Semitism as well as of hostility to various other groups. They will repeat the attempt in times to come. So far all such tendencies have failed because of the people's sound political instinct.

And so it will remain in the future, if we cling to the rule: Beware of flatterers, especially when they come preaching hatred.

Arthur E. Sutherland

CONSTITUTIONAL RIGHTS OF RACIAL MINORITIES IN THE UNITED STATES

A Voice of America Broadcast

*L*INGERING consequences of human slavery—consequences not entirely eliminated even today, despite ninety-five years that have passed since our Constitution forbade all such servitude—have presented in our time to the United States its most troublesome racial problems. We have had other ethnic frictions, of course. Voluntary migration of over forty million people from every part of the globe to our country has made some such difficulties inevitable. But our main racial problem began in 1619 when a Dutch ship brought to our shores a cargo of Africans. The captives were sold as slaves at Jamestown, Virginia. This original wrong, and the succeeding wrongs which stemmed from the same human indignity, have brought trouble and sorrow throughout the following centuries for the people of the thirteen English colonies on the American seaboard, and for the United States into which these colonies organized themselves in 1776.

An appraisal of the present constitutional position of racial minorities in the United States must be made with some recollection of these three and a half centuries of history. Our constitutional ideals have not been stationary. They have, we hope, improved with the development of our moral concepts. But for some members of any society time works slowly. Some traces of old social attitudes still survive, some consequential residues of the beliefs of past centuries still remain among us, here and there, almost a century after a bitter war ended our human slavery. Our constitutionalism is partly a system of morals. And moral growth is a slow process.

Social and legal attitudes in the United States vary in space, as well as in time. A feature of our Constitution which must be remembered in appraising today's problems of racial minorities is the federal structure of our republic. Federalism is part of our deep commitment to a theory of limited government. Among us a cherished political doctrine insists that governmental power be restrained rather than absolute. And one means to this end is a measure of local autonomy, constitutionally guaranteed. Respecting some matters of government, our nation is divided in fifty separate polities, fifty states, each semi-independent as to those laws thought to govern matters essentially local rather than national. Schools, hotels, theaters have customarily been considered such local, state-controlled matters. Each state has its own elected governor, its own legislature and its own system of courts. In the same city often are found governmental officers of the central government and officers of the states, each performing his own separate duties in neighboring buildings. Of course, the Constitution of the United States and federal statutes passed under its authority are supreme. But in matters which the Constitution leaves to state control, state governments have the last word. This toleration of local autonomy, within reasonable limits, is one expression of our distrust of an all-powerful central rule.

Here then, I undertake a brief survey of these two great facts in our constitutional story: change for the better, during many generations, of our moral, and so of our legal, attitudes toward our fellow-men of different races; and the effect of this change on the peculiar, mosaic-like governmental structure of component states which makes up our federal union.

As the eighteenth century closed, people in many of the thirteen American states came to feel that the capture and sale of Africans, often by African tribesmen, and their importation for slavery was a great moral wrong. Our southern states, however, were largely dependent on slave labor for the conduct of their plantations. Deep sectional differences thus developed; resulting constitutional compromises are apparent in the now obsolete slavery provisions of the 1789 Constitution. One such clause permitted importation of slaves until 1808. But this provision did not prevent the Congress from enacting regulations governing the conduct of United States shipping. And so from 1794 on, the Congress imposed heavier and heavier penalties on any citizen engaging in the overseas slave trade. From January 1, 1808, the Congress prohibited all importation of slaves. In 1820 our Congress by statute treated overseas slave trading as piracy, punishable by death.

The legislatures of some of our states, too, began to pass antislave-trade laws. For example, the State of Maryland by a statute of 1796, provided that any Negro brought into that state for sale or residence should become free. State courts enforced such laws, and their judgments freeing slaves were affirmed by the Supreme Court of the United States.

Unfortunately, the law is a complicated business. In 1857 a man named Dred Scott, held as a slave, brought suit claiming that he had become a free man when his owner had removed him into the northerly frontier territory, once part of French Louisiana, in which, by an Act of the United States Congress, slavery had been forever prohibited. The Supreme Court of the United States, to which Dred Scott's case finally came, held that because of his slave ancestry, he was not a "citizen," and so was under certain procedural disabilities. It further held that the Act of Congress purporting to abolish slavery in the northerly territory was beyond the constitutional powers of the central government. The unfortunate Scott was thus neither a citizen nor a free human being.

Dred Scott's case, a symbol of the evils of slavery, became a rallying cry for antislavery sentiment in the northern part of the United States. Memory of Scott's case was one of the influences in the 1860 election of the antislavery President Abraham Lincoln. Civil war between the northern and southern states broke out early in 1861.

Four years of bitter conflict, costly in lives on both sides, ended with the defeat of the South; and three amendments to the federal Constitution soon wrote the result into our fundamental law. The Thirteenth Amendment of 1865 provided that slavery should not exist within the United States or in any place subject to its jurisdiction. The Fourteenth Amendment of 1868 provided that all persons born or naturalized in the United States should be citizens of the United States and of the state where they reside, and that no state should abridge the privileges or immunities of any citizen of the United States nor deprive any person of life, liberty, or property without due process of law, nor deny to any person equal protection of the laws. In 1870 the Fifteenth Amendment provided that rights of the citizens of the United States to vote should not be denied or abridged by any state or by the United States by reason of race, color, or previous condition of servitude.

The constitutional history of racial minorities since 1870 has been written in the judicial construction of these amendments. Within fifteen years after the end of the Civil War, Americans of African descent began to establish in the courts their right to equality in the administration of justice and equality in voting procedures. Our courts declared unconstitutional and invalid any state laws to the contrary. Most such cases, naturally, originated in states where slavery had prevailed and where the non-white population was substantial. In 1880, for example, the Supreme Court upheld a criminal charge against a Virginia state judge for failing to select Negroes as jurors. Administration of justice was to be color-blind.

The Fourteenth Amendment is subject to one important qualification. While that amendment forbids the states to discriminate unjustly against racial groups, its terms contain no prohibition against discrimination by private citizens. The federal Congress, under our theory of limited powers, can only legislate concerning those matters constitutionally entrusted to it, and the Fourteenth Amendment grants to Congress no authority to make laws against private racial discrimination; it forbids public, not private, injustice. An 1883 case, giving effect to this principle, was a disappointment for the former slaves and their children. The Supreme Court had before it an Act of Congress forbidding racial discrimination by hotels, theaters and passenger carriers, none of them operated by the public authorities. The Court held the Act of Congress invalid because it exceeded the federal powers; it attempted to regulate wrongs not perpetrated by a state.

In 1886 the Supreme Court, this time applying the "equal protection clause" of the Fourteenth Amendment in favor of some Chinese nationals, held that a California administrative official was constitutionally required to observe racial impartiality in granting or withholding licenses to conduct laundries. Chinese, alike with others, were entitled to earn a living.

In 1896 the Supreme Court faced a particularly difficult problem. A non-white railway passenger, traveling within Louisiana, challenged the constitutional validity of a statute of that state requiring railroads to provide "equal but separate" accommodations for the different races. The Supreme Court upheld the state law on the premise that separation of races was not inconsistent with their equal treatment.

That decision was not overruled until 1954; but during the interval the constitutional position of the minority races improved in other important respects. They made notable progress in political standing.

From 1885 on, the Court sturdily upheld the voting rights of non-whites. For example, in the United States, selection of candidates who stand for election to public office is ordinarily made in "primary elections," in which members of the political parties vote for those whom they wish as their party candidates in the final election. In some states, the predominant party undertook to limit party membership to white citizens, thus excluding non-whites from participation in primary elections, and effectively preventing them from influencing the final election. In a series of judgments during the thirty years following 1925 the Supreme Court struck down all such "white primary" devices.

In 1946 the Supreme Court found in the "commerce clause" of the Constitution a weapon to use against some "equal but separate" state laws. The Constitution entrusts to the central government control of commerce "among the several states." The Supreme Court held state "equal but separate" railway or omnibus laws invalid when applied to passengers on a journey in more than one state. Such a state travel-segregation law, if enforced at the state border, would oblige travelers to rearrange their seating and would thus interfere with interstate commerce, which is the peculiar concern of the federal government. So in 1946, on interstate journeys, "equal but separate" ceased to be the rule.

The Supreme Court made other great advances toward racial equality by a series of decisions holding unconstitutional any attempt by law to restrict non-whites to segregated residential areas. In 1917 that Court held invalid a city ordinance which, in effect, established by law some city blocks solely for the residence of whites, and others solely for non-whites. Some private persons, who were buying and selling houses, tried to avoid the effect of this judgment by writing in their deeds of conveyance a requirement that the premises never be occupied by any but white residents. In 1948 the Supreme Court frustrated this device; it held unconstitutional the judicial enforcement of any such private bargain. All branches of government, the judicial as well as the legislative and executive, are forbidden to have a hand in restricting the choice of residence of any of our people.

Meantime a series of courtroom contests went on over the provisions of law, in seventeen states and in the District of Columbia, permitting or requiring the maintenance of "equal but separate" facilities for public education. In a number of cases involving state universities the Supreme Court applied the requirement of equality with much strictness, directing that such public institutions, as a condition of racial separation, be in fact equal. The steady success of non-white citizens in so many different types of constitutional lawsuits began to suggest that before long the 1896 doctrine of "equal but separate" would itself be repudiated. The Supreme Court of the United States is not bound to follow its previous decisions when it becomes convinced that they were mistaken, and so there was a constitutional possibility of ending the legality of all "equal but separate" statutes.

Exactly this occurred on May 18, 1954, a notable date in our constitutional history. The Supreme Court on that day decided cases concerning "equal but separate" public schools in four states and in the federal District of Columbia. In all these cases that Court gave judgment in favor of school children who were protesting against compulsory attendance at segregated schools. It overruled its own 1896 precedent which had established the doctrine of "equal but separate." Shortly thereafter the Court rejected "equal but separate" laws governing local omnibuses and such places of public recreation as municipal golf courses and bathing beaches. The Supreme Court thus by 1956 established the constitutional invalidity of any law, state or national, requiring that non-white people keep to themselves.

The difficult constitutional progress of racial minorities in the United States since the historic decisions of 1954 can only be understood by keeping in mind the substantial degree of local governmental independence provided by our federal system. The ancient attitude toward non-whites still persists among many white citizens in some of the seventeen states where State law had long segregated the schools. In the State public educational systems schools are not maintained by federal, but by state officials. Such schools are regulated by laws passed by State Legislatures. State legislators are elected by constituents who, in a certain number of States, resent the Supreme Court's 1954 judgments, and are eager to find ways to avoid or delay compliance. Thus despite the Supreme Court's unequivocal declarations, practical problems of enforcement remain.

In justice to our people I should point out that a substantial degree of compliance with the desegregation decrees has in fact occurred. As soon as the Supreme Court ruled against segregated schools, the President of the United States directed that the District of Columbia desegregate at once. That area, of course, is entirely controlled by the national government; the District, containing the capital of the Union, falls within no state jurisdiction. In a majority of the seventeen segregated states, gradual desegregation began at once. In eight of the seventeen, there was delay. Three of these originally recalcitrant eight states, urged by subsequent Court decrees, have now begun the process of desegregation in part of their schools. In another of the eight—Louisiana—there is now substantial enrollment of non-whites in those state colleges formerly maintained for white students only. But in five of our fifty states the opportunities for delay, which are inherent in state autonomy, up to this time (1960) still obstruct implementation, in the lower schools, of the Supreme Court's 1954 opinion.

To those who are unfamiliar with the operation of our federal union, and with the theory of limited government under which we rule ourselves, it may seem inexplicable that our great and powerful nation, which has spoken through its Constitution and its Supreme Court against racial discrimination by any state, still delays forcible requirement of obedience by several of its states. But law in action differs from law in theory. A judicial decree, strictly speaking, operates only on the persons summoned to court. And thus far, comparatively few of the many thousands of state and local school officials in these areas where desegregation is unpopular have been summoned. Additional proceedings are continually being started, but all this takes much time. Practical human difficulties retard the transformation of custom among millions of people. The remarkable fact is that so many have complied, not that a comparatively small number still resist. Two years ago, when in Little Rock, Arkansas, the local and state authorities appeared to be using force to oppose the national will in desegregation, the President at once sent United States troops who promptly restored order without shooting. Little Rock was, fortunately, an isolated instance. Traditionally we proceed by persuasion, not by force.

The distant observer may ask why the federal Congress does not pass more laws to enforce the Constitution as construed by the Supreme Court. Such legislation has, indeed, been considered in the Congress during recent sessions. When such a statute is enacted, federal agents can be sent to the recalcitrant states to take appropriate measures. In 1957 the Congress passed just such a law to prevent local obstruction of voting. But as yet the national legislature has not provided federal enforcement of state school desegregation. Perhaps our Congress has waited in hope that the few resisting states will soon see the light.

This hope is not misplaced. The southern United States is changing rapidly. Its economy is turning from traditional concentration on agriculture to much manufacture and commerce. This change opens up new economic opportunities for technical employment of many non-white citizens who in the past have been field hands or unskilled laborers. Churches have used their influence for racial justice. Most important of all, political participation by non-whites is increasing. We move ahead.

In 1776, our Declaration of Independence expressed an ideal of human equality then unachieved. It recited:

> We hold these truths to be self-evident, that all men are created equal, that they are endowed by their Creator with certain unalienable Rights, that among these are Life, Liberty and the pursuit of Happiness. That to secure these rights, Governments are instituted among Men, deriving their just powers from the consent of the governed . . .

We only now seem to approach realization of that ideal among races. We can well hope that the next generation will find our whole nation believing, with that Declaration, as a truth ". . . self evident; that all men are created equal. . . ."

Inge Lederer Gibel

HOW *NOT* TO INTEGRATE
THE SCHOOLS

I AM ONE of those creatures equally repulsive to Governor Ross Barnett of Mississippi, the Black Muslims' Malcolm X, and to many other Americans—the white wife of a black man and the mother of two Negro children. Even worse, I am out of step with the civil-rights leaders at whose side I have fought for many years.

At a recent CORE workshop, held in Harlem's Hotel Theresa, I reached a disturbing conclusion that has been forced on me many times in the past months: something ugly is happening in the struggle to achieve full equality for all our citizens, something that can destroy the very goals we seek.

I had suggested that in the schools of New York, Chicago, and Detroit we are dealing with problems quite different from those of Birmingham and Biloxi, where segregation is based on the assumption that all Negro children are inferior to all white children. In our Northern cities, I pointed out, there is a large mass of Negro children whose cultural and economic background is so deprived, that merely placing them in "integrated" schools will accomplish nothing.

These are dirty words in civil-rights circles today. If you're white they brand you as a bigot; if you're black you're an Uncle Tom.

Nonetheless, I believe that, in the North at least, what we think of as the race struggle has become much more a problem of class and economics than of color. Unless we recognize this, the "Negro Revolution" will fizzle out into a mere statistical adjustment. At the top of our social and power structure, the black man will be represented in proportion to

410

his numbers; but the majority of black people—along with the ex-miners of West Virginia, the migrant workers, and the South's own "poor white trash"—will remain at the bottom.

If this should happen, the Negro people will be bereft even of the comforting belief espoused by their current leaders that *only* race prejudice is holding them back.

Like James Baldwin I sense the growing hatred stirring in the black community. I, who am black only by association, am choked by a murderous hatred when I confront an open bigot. And I think I feel what any mother of black children would feel when I am subtly patronized by white liberals. Sometimes I am simply shocked and repelled by the irrelevance of their ideas despite the nobility of their motives.

There was, for instance, the sweet-faced white matron who passionately urged New York's new Superintendent of Schools, Calvin Gross, at a meeting last summer, to integrate all the city's schools immediately. A hostile black audience gave her a standing ovation as she demanded that small white children be bussed to Harlem schools (and vice versa), no matter how their parents felt about it and without regard to their socio-economic and cultural levels. "The white families of New York have no right to save their children at the expense of the black children of our city," she wound up.

In a way, her words crystallized for me what has gone wrong in the civil-rights struggle in the North. Twenty-five years ago, when I was a refugee from Nazi Austria, I too saw the world in such simple terms: defend the underdog, fight for the oppressed, right old wrongs, and build a brave new world. This conviction, indeed, led me to spend most of my adult life working for civil-rights groups, in settlement houses, and in whatever causes seemed to further those ends.

I do not now repudiate my youthful "idealism." What I deplore is the fact that the very people who bewail conformity in our society are introducing a strict orthodoxy into the civil-rights movement. It is a crippling error, particularly when you are dealing with a problem as complex and vast as the schools of New York and other Northern cities.

Integration Northern Style

My eleven-year-old daughter Kathie attends an integrated public school. Out of a student body of approximately two thousand, 17 per cent are white and the rest are Negro and Puerto Rican, with a small sprinkling of Orientals. Public-school enrollment in Manhattan is around

76.5 per cent non-white. So this might be called a reasonable "racial balance." How does it work?

Our schools are run on a "track" system, which separates children, sometimes as early as kindergarten, into more or less intellectually homogeneous classes. In the process the concept of integration bogs down, for the middle-class white five-year-old and a child of the same age from a lower-class non-white home will seldom be assigned to the same group. The middle-class Negro or Puerto Rican child will fare better than the lower-class white child. But since most of the city's poor happen to be non-whites, the burden falls on their children, even though no race prejudice is involved. Kindergarten placement is determined by age *and* nursery-school experience. The many working mothers in our community cannot afford the tuition at our two best nursery schools (which care for the children only a few hours a day) plus the additional cost of a housekeeper. Yet it is the children from these two nursery schools who are usually put into the "best" kindergarten class.

The next step is to get into a "good" first grade. This requires, above all, "reading readiness." How can the child from a home where the main medium of communication is a television set running all day compete here with the one who has had books read to him since he was a toddler, who has already joined the library, who sees his parents immersed in a world of books and newspapers? By the time they reach third grade, the children have been exposed to very different types and levels of schooling. Now they are tested for the IGC classes (for the so-called Intellectually Gifted Children), which are scattered in schools throughout the city. My daughter has been in the IGC program since fourth grade, and—except for the fact that she changed schools at the beginning of her third year— she would still have the same classmates (with very few exceptions) as when she started school.

One day last year Kathie came to me rather disturbed. "Mommy," she said, "why do all the dumb classes have mostly Negro children and all the smart classes have most of the white children?"

Kathie has always been aware of differences, of course. A favorite family joke dates from the time she first learned colors in nursery school. At dinner that night she announced in three-year-old solemnity, "Mommy is vanilla pudding, and Daddy is chocolate pudding, and I'm butterscotch."

Kathie has accepted the differences, even been proud of herself and of us. She has learned the history of her people—the black and the

Hebrew—and is well up to date on the struggle against discrimination, North and South. What troubled her now was that the children seemed to *belong* in the classrooms where they were placed.

I told her that "smart" and "dumb" really didn't have much to do with it, that children whose mommies and daddies had to work long hours for low pay, and had many other troubles, did not have the same opportunities to enlarge their knowledge as children from a home like hers. When Kathie wanted to know what was being done about all this, I had no ready answer.

The racial breakdown in Kathie's class is around fifty-fifty, although the school has only a 20 per cent white enrollment. In other IGC classes in the same school there is a smaller proportion of whites. But throughout the city in our public elementary schools attended by *middle-class* white children and *lower-class* non-white children, the IGC classes and the "good" lower grades, have the most white children, the "slow" classes have the least.

One sad result is that you can actually see the children of first-generation liberals becoming second-generation snobs. This is their reaction to an environment which implies that the non-white children cannot compete with them intellectually or socially. In our own school and housing area, for example, there are many white parents who pride themselves on their progressive outlook, support all sorts of integration and freedom drives, and assiduously court Negro and Puerto Rican friends. But their children despise their Negro classmates and play only among themselves. Some of the Negro children retaliate, of course, by becoming withdrawn or aggressive.

What Negro Parents Want

I discussed this situation recently with a friend I will call Jean Brighton. She is the mother of three bright, charming children and lives on the edge of Harlem, in a large, low-income public housing project. Her husband is a fiercely ambitious father who works days in the post office and evenings as foreman of a maintenance crew. He is determined that his children shall have a better life than his. The Brightons are Negroes, just like over 90 per cent of their neighbors.

I asked Jean to conduct an informal survey for me in her building. Within a few days she reported her chief finding: What these parents want for their children is education, lots of it and the very best possible. The question of segregation is not uppermost in their thoughts. The parents she interviewed (in most cases it was the mother who spoke for the family) covered a wide income span. They ranged from a family with two children, whose father earns over a hundred dollars a week as a policeman, to the five children of a hospital orderly paid less than sixty dollars a week. With one exception, none of these people knows Jean well.

She began the interview by asking, "Have you heard about the school integration campaign? Do you know that they're thinking of bussing Negro children out of Harlem and bringing white children in so that all schools in New York will have white and colored kids together?" Most people had heard of this much-publicized plan. "What do you think if it?" she then asked.

Invariably, the answer, with slight variation, was, *"What, before they improve the schools?"*

When she said Yes, they were astonished. Jean explained that civil-rights organizations were putting complete school integration at the top of their list of demands, backed up by the threat of a boycott of the schools. Everyone she talked to was certain that such a boycott would not be supported by the mass of Harlem parents, even though they all believed in integration. But without hesitation they felt that forced integration of the kind proposed would only continue to drive middle-class white children out of the schools. What these Negro parents wanted from the schools—and what, unfortunately, they were not getting—was a longer day; more and better textbooks that would be more representative of the minority and urban groups in our culture; dedicated teachers (of any color); smaller classes; and special programs which really serve the low-income child and are not aimed just at the middle-class child the schools are trying desperately to retain. None of these parents, incidentally, consider themselves at the bottom of the heap. They all expressed worry about the "others" who lived next door. Their views, I believe, are representative of many Northern Negro parents'.

Ironically, in New York at least, many white middle-class "liberal" families agonize about whether to send their children to overcrowded, often understaffed schools with a high percentage of children from "deprived backgrounds," or to a nice, safe private school. Most middle-class Negro families, on the other hand, do not spend much time agonizing (except, like their white counterparts, over the tuition), but make the latter choice. An outstanding Negro civil-rights attorney whom I will call Mike Dawson is typical. I worked closely with him for several years when we were both volunteers with the New York Branch of the NAACP. In his courtroom presentations he often tried to prove that it is rank hypocrisy for the white community to use "cultural" reasons as an excuse for prolonging *de facto* segregation. (And sometimes he is absolutely right.) But Mike enrolled his own son in an exclusive, largely white private school.

The Dawsons live in central Harlem, in a middle-income segregated housing development. It was built by a leading insurance company which has recently decided to integrate a similar downtown development and future projects. Very likely, before long in New York, black lawyers, doctors, social workers, teachers, engineers, and their like will have a whole new world of about-to-be-integrated housing to choose from. Meanwhile very, very few of them send their children to the local public school. They do not feel they are being biased in this—how can they be, they ask, when they are black? They are merely protecting the interests of their own children. In other words, they too are worried about the cultural, social, and educational level of the mass of slum children. Some of them are very unhappy about it and some couldn't care less; they just don't want their own children dragged down. Mrs. Dawson, for one, did volunteer work in the nearby public school—while she sent her Jackie to private school. She taught art twice a week to some youngsters who had never owned a box of crayons. After she caught ringworm from one child, Mike made her quit because he didn't want her bringing slum diseases home to little Jackie.

Teacher's Double Standard

Of course the Dawsons know—as I know from firsthand experience—that there can be no equality of opportunity for children in any school so long as two built-in barriers remain. One is the track system which, in effect, creates its own ghettoes. I believe it can and should be abolished, although it will take some imaginative planning—including perhaps the use of team teaching—to see that the "best" and the "worst" students all progress at their maximum capacity.

A more formidable obstacle is the attitude of the teachers. I recall, for example, Miss Jeffers (that is not her real name). Her mouth dropped open when we met for the first time. Negroes too—I must confess—often react that way when they discover that pretty, brown little Kathie is the honest-to-goodness child of big pale me. Kathie liked Miss Jeffers. But then she started coming home with complaints. So did other Negro children. For instance, one day Johnny—offspring of white, middle-class professionals—got down on the floor of the classroom and attempted to peek up skirts. One of them was my daughter's. When she was upset, Miss Jeffers told her, "Don't worry about it, dear, he's just being nine years old." Miss Jeffers' relaxed attitude about the pranks of white children did not extend to the vagaries of her dark students.

A few days later, my doorbell rang. I opened the door and faced a tall, dark, and angry woman. I will call her Mrs. Drummond, mother of one of Kathie's Negro schoolmates. Yesterday her Tommy had quarreled with several girls, including Kathie. In the scuffle, according to Miss Jeffers, Tommy had tried to rip Kathie's dress. The teacher sent for Mrs. Drummond and told her Tommy would not be allowed back in the classroom until she took him to my house and apologized to me. Kathie was home with a cold. When I questioned her she said, yes, there had been an argument, and Tommy tried to hit her, but he didn't tear her dress. She wasn't in the least angry with him anymore. I tried to assure Mrs. Drummond that I did not feel this visit necessary, but her resentment and humiliation remained.

I asked Miss Jeffers why she had sent Mrs. Drummond to my home for almost nothing, when she had made light of Johnny's really questionable behavior. I accused her of setting different standards for the white and the Negro children in her class. Tearfully she admitted I might be right. Then she added a telling commentary on the track system. "I'm just so sick of some of these little geniuses that I don't know what I'm doing anymore," she said. "Their mothers breathe down my neck, threatening to send their children to private school if the curriculum doesn't prove advanced enough. . . . I just made up my mind to let their children do whatever they wanted. Next year I'm going to be teaching average children. No more IGC classes for me."

Mr. Burnstein (his name is invented too) had another bias. He preferred IGC classes and, I am certain, had no race prejudice. If a Negro professor, say, were refused an apartment in his building, I don't doubt he would join a picket line to protest. But Mr. Burnstein did not feel guilty about ignoring the needs of the dark-skinned majority of children in his class. He doted on the bright, verbal, alert children, the ones who went places and did things with intelligent parents. Most of these children just happened to be white. On the other hand, he was annoyed by the children who never went anywhere except to school and home again to their low-income housing development or tenement, where the parents were not well-read, aggressive college graduates. (In many home-assigned "projects," it is the parents who compete, and not the children.) Most of these children just happened to be colored.

Mr. Burnstein, it is true, liked "bright" Negro children better than "stupid" white children. But the former were too rare to make this nuance apparent to his students and their parents. They were convinced that Mr. Burnstein played favorites, and that they were usually white.

What Volunteers Could Do

If simply mixing Negro children from the slums with middle-class white children doesn't work in the schools of our Northern cities, what then do I believe—as the mother of Negro children, as an American and an integrationist—should be done to speed integration?

Some of my ideas are already being carried out in a few school systems. Some have been tried, on a very small scale, and abandoned as "too expensive." Some may be difficult to implement; and some, such as more teachers and smaller classes, have been repeated so often that I shall only mention them here in agreement.

The crucial factor, I think, is the teacher. Good salaries are important, of course, but salary and prestige can't buy dedication. A dedicated teacher can turn a rathole into a palace, she can turn slum children into empire builders.

I say this out of deep personal conviction. When I came to America in 1938, I was the sheltered, spoiled darling of an indulgent family, complete with governess. Overnight I became the non-English-speaking child of a harassed working mother. I went to four different schools between second grade and junior high school. In each I found warm, dedicated teachers (not all, of course, but enough) who really cared about me, despite my shabby clothes and poor English. They talked to me at lunchtime, during and after school. They helped me with the words to "America the Beautiful" before I really knew their meaning. And sometimes they even came on their summer vacation to take me, for a day, out of whatever steamy city block I was living in then. And they did this for many, many children.

There are still such teachers in some of our classrooms, and we must find ways to encourage them and add to their numbers. At the same time we must weed out the security seekers interested mainly in salary, vacations, free time, and pensions.

All our teachers—including the best—should be required to attend a seminar dealing with Negro and Puerto Rican history and culture, and to learn how to emphasize the positive elements in them to their students. The white and the Negro child must learn that Africa was not a place full of ignorant savages; that its people were not cattle who were saved from subhumanity only by exposure to white society; but that the slave system deliberately broke down family and group ties, language, and religion, so that the African would be easier to use as chattel. The middle-class Negro child can learn all this at home, but the child of the slum is usually doomed to remain ignorant of his own history.

I am not simply suggesting some more material for Brotherhood or Negro History Week. This knowledge should be used throughout the school year, in discussing literature, geography, and especially history.

Another aspect of the teacher's attitude which has stirred up a current tempest is the matter of so-called middle-class values. Obviously, an insecure middle-class teacher who resents her lower-class students will not teach them well. But what of those progressive-minded teachers who feel "we mustn't impose our values on these children"? The assumption is that all middle-class values are bad. But are they? What's wrong with being clean, honest, and hardworking? The average middle-class teacher is simply shocked when a slum child asks to go to the bathroom in a four-letter word. But the child is harmed just as much by the "enlightened" teacher who—in order not to make the child feel "inferior"—fails to teach him a more acceptable word. The child is not inferior, but his vocabulary is.

To extol slum culture is no service to our deprived Negro youth. Negro children have a glorious cultural heritage, but it does not lie in the winos, the dope addicts, the Cadillac-wealthy "numbers" overlords, bred by the crawling, stinking slums where these children must live.

A child who comes to school from an overcrowded home without a good night's rest or breakfast is in no state to receive an education. These children need an all-day neighborhood school which would open its doors around eight o'clock. A breakfast of, say, an orange, a bun, and hot cocoa (if schools can serve lunch, why not breakfast?) would be distributed by an early shift of volunteers. New York is brimming with good and dependable people who love the city and its children, and want to keep it from going any further downhill. Why not organize a local corps to use the talents and spare hours of thousands of potential volunteers—the society housewife, the local mother (even one on relief) who loves children. It should be simple to screen and train such people for emergency service, as has been done on a very small scale by existing school volunteer plans. It is too late for more pilot programs. We need an army of volunteers to take over the nonteaching jobs in our schools, leaving our teachers time to teach. And some of these same teachers and volunteers could carry on into the late afternoon (with extra pay for the teachers, naturally, and perhaps a small stipend for the volunteers), with remedial classes and ballet, art, cooking, sewing, and athletics.

The school would offer a late-afternoon snack of fruit, cookies, and milk for those who wished it, and a study hall for the children who want to read quietly, do their homework, or, indeed, just rest. In this way the innocent will be kept off the poisonous streets and working mothers will be freed of tormenting fear for their children's safety. With a start like this, many more children would go on to junior and senior high schools, which would no longer be battlegrounds where teachers are hostile and frightened guards and students are surly prisoners.

Such a plan would work only if we get rid of the most serious form of discrimination against the slum child. His schools today have a different, inferior curriculum compared to other schools in the city, poorer libraries, and fewer and older textbooks. The most glaring contrast is with New York's fabulous public elementary school, PS 6. It is located on the elegant upper East Side at 81st Street and Madison Avenue. Such schools should exist throughout the city.

Restitution or Rabble-rousing

There is an old Brazilian saying, "A rich Negro is a white man and a poor white man is a Negro." Our private schools have proved that there is no great trick to integrating middle-class Negro children into middle- and upper-class white classrooms. The problem is to integrate large numbers of lower-class Negro and Puerto Rican children into a shrinking white middle-class student body.

A step in the right direction would be to abolish the track system and to group the children in different ways throughout the day. The child who excels in math will very likely be poorest in art. Let every child have a chance to be at some time in the "best group" and in the "worst group," and it will still be possible to let each advance at his own pace. But children must learn that almost everyone excels at one thing and does poorly at something else. If we mix our student body racially, we must do the same with faculty and volunteers. And we must find something better than those awful textbooks (illustrated in the early grades) which show blue-eyed, blond Mary Beth and Dick going to the market with Mommy, while their dog, Buster, stays at home, guarding the little white-picket-fenced cottage to which Daddy will come home after a hard day at the office. Let's have texts with which our urban low-income non-white youngsters can identify.

It is obvious that new schools, wherever possible, should be built in fringe areas rather than in the heart of racial ghettoes. They should be located as near as possible to the more expensive districts to discourage wholesale emigration of middle-class white families from the schools.

And let us by all means intensify our attack on the housing barriers which create the Harlems of this nation and the slum schools in their midst. Bussing children around the city is no more than a feeble—and foredoomed—palliative for this underlying evil.

Meanwhile, what I am advocating is in effect a massive crash program for all schools in low-income areas. It will be expensive, but not nearly as expensive as the present costs of maintaining the much-studied "hard-core multi-problem family," of sending a boy through reform school and on to graduate study in the penitentiary, of more and more policemen, an ever-growing rate of illegitimate births and of addict-induced crime.

Continuation of the status quo is not the answer. Nor is the immediate, across-the-board integration that the civil-rights "leadership" is pushing for in such slum areas as Harlem in Manhattan and Bedford-Stuyvesant in Brooklyn.

White society deliberately raped the Negro of his culture, stripped him of his manhood, and weakened his family structure. Many Negroes have risen above these handicaps. But large numbers of poor urban Negroes (and many equally poor whites) cannot give their children either love or education. The society which robbed the parents must now restore to the children their lost birthright.

Harold Nicolson

CHRISTMAS TREES

THE MARK of Brandenburg, which encloses in its sandy wastes the populous city of Berlin, is thickly coated with conifers—little stubby green things lining the railway from Hanover with sad reiterance. My train stopped, the other day, for some unknown reason, in the middle of a solid wedge of these crowded but upright objects. The brakes hissed with steam; the radiators within my carriage radiated with re-doubled violence; the window became coated with mist. I rose and opened the window, pulling it down as far as it would go. The silence, the dank November silence, was broken only by the hiss of steam. I leant out to see what was happening. Nothing was happening. The fir trees opposite stood close up to the line. It was half-past four, and already it was getting dark and sad. I leant out farther and observed that some workmen on the line had lit a fire on the embankment, in the midst of which was balanced a little wobbly saucepan. A young man, coming up from the forest, carried some green fir-branches in his arms. He placed one of the branches upon the fire, laying the other two carefully beside the track. A puff of smoke drifted up from the fire and along the train. It reached my carriage. I became a child again, watching a pink candle smoulder among the fibres of a Christmas tree.

My eldest brother (we were in Constantinople at the time, and it was the winter of 1894), being already a militarist and reactionary, had conceived a marked dislike for Captain Dreyfus. This unfortunate officer had been arrested in October of that year for selling military secrets to the German Embassy. The incident had filled my brother, then aged seven, with passionate indignation. He determined to give me an example of what happened to people who sold secrets to the German Embassy. I had observed, and desired, when unpacking things for our Christmas tree, a little figure of a French soldier which jumped and dangled upon an elastic string. My brother told me that this entrancing and resilient figure was in reality Captain Alfred Dreyfus. He indicated that, for this officer, destiny had reserved a sentence of death by slow torture. He told me to wait till December 22, which was the date fixed for our party. *"You wait!"* he said, menacingly, observing doubtless that I showed signs of being a Dreyfusard. I asked my mother whether I might not be allowed to have the little French soldier as a special present, reserved for myself alone, detached from the Christmas tree. She said that I must not beg for things in advance, and that perhaps, *perhaps,* if I were very good she would see that this particular object was reserved for my portion. But I wanted it now. I wanted to hide Captain Dreyfus in my play-box before fate could overtake him. She merely smiled.

Four days later, after many sticky mouths had munched at an enormous tea, the sliding doors which led to the drawing-room were suddenly opened and there in front of us, glowing and crackling like the lights of Brighton from the sea, stood this pyramid of glistening pendant things starred with a thousand flickering candles. We said *"Oh!"*—knowing that it was expected of us. Our minds, however, were concentrated greedily upon what we could obtain. My brother reached the tree before me, and began to walk round it quickly, searching for Captain Dreyfus. This officer, for his part, had managed to hide himself away from the blaze of publicity in some shadowed recess of this sparkling conifer. I found him first. They had attached him to the branch, not by his own piece of elastic, which was frail enough, but by an additional hawser made of twisted golden string. I tugged silently at these moorings, my heart beating for fear lest my brother should emerge from behind the tree. I tugged and tugged. It was impossible to release Captain Dreyfus. I covered his little dangling body with my hand, praying that my mother would appear with the scissors. But it was my brother who appeared. He was two years older than I was, and he was allowed a knife. He detached Captain Dreyfus while I watched in agony. He was, as I still feel, really angry with the Captain for having sold those papers to the German Embassy, although even at the time the evidence of his guilt was questionable. I watched his indignant determination with increasing terror. He kept on saying "Traitor!" quite close to Captain Dreyfus's ear, and then he went and put that ear, in fact the whole face of the officer, in the flame of the nearest candle. Captain Dreyfus was made of papier-maché, and did not burn as briskly as other criminals. His face and figure were formed, indeed, by two profiles stuck together with glue; the glue melted in the heat of the flame, and the two profiles of Captain Dreyfus began at that to curl outwards and away from each other, smoking terribly. I let forth a howl of unutterable anguish, and dashed to the rescue. I showed great merit in seizing at the candle rather than at the figure itself, which was already held firmly in the stronger hands of my brother. I pulled the candle sideways, bending it down into the fibres of the Christmas tree. A sharp smell of burning pine-woods reached my nostrils. I howled again. It was then that I was rescued by my mother. Captain Dreyfus, as an organic substance, had by that time ceased to exist.

My people, I feel, displayed but little sympathy. They were more gratified by my brother's vicarious and (as was clearly shown by the Rennes courtmartial) mistaken patriotism, than by my own passionate defence of a man who was clearly being victimized by a rigid military system. Besides, I had looked forward to possessing Captain Dreyfus and allowing him to dance and dangle at the end of my bed. My father was amused by the incident and went and told the French Ambassador, who happened to be present at the party. He also was gratified. He came and tweaked my brother's ear, speaking words of commendation. This incident, I am convinced, had a profound influence on my later life. From that moment I became anti-militarist, pro-Jewish, and pacifist; from that moment the smell of a Christmas tree evoked associations, not of love, hope, charity, and material acquisition, but of hatred, torture, and injustice.

That my affection for Captain Dreyfus was no mere passing whim is brought home to me by the recollection of an incident which occurred five years later. It was in the autumn of 1899. I had been a year at my private school. The boys in the big schoolroom were allowed *The Daily Graphic,* and I had followed with feverish interest the progress of that famous trial by which Captain Dreyfus was vindicated. The paper would arrive about eight-thirty, at the very moment when we were released, after morning prayers, for a ten-minutes' run in the playground. I would linger behind, watching the little wooden rack near the green baize door of the headmaster's study. In a minute, I knew, the door would open, and the arm of the headmaster would appear round it stretching out to drop *The Daily Graphic* into the rack. On the day when the Rennes verdict was to be announced I watched that door with bated breath. I could hear the cries of the other boys from the playground. I was alone. I hid behind a desk so as not to be seen by the headmaster. The door opened, the arm appeared, *The Daily Graphic* dropped folded into its rack, the door closed again. I rushed for the paper. He had been acquitted; there was something about extenuating circumstances which I did not understand; but it was quite clear from *The Daily Graphic* that he had been acquitted. Wild with joy, I dashed into the playground, waving the paper above my head. "He's free! He's free!" I yelled. I was received somewhat coldly by my comrades. Such exhibitions of hysteria were not in the best traditions of the school. "He's free!" I shouted again, defiantly. But my voice was diminuendo. I retired to the racquet courts to enjoy my triumph, and my great happiness, alone.

Such were the memories which crowded into my mind the other day as I leant out, looking upon the darkening fir-trees on that stretch of railway between Stendhal and Berlin. Dreyfus? Christmas trees? That playground at my private school? The train hooted and began to move on slowly past the fire upon the embankment. I shut the window and returned to my book. I was reading Professor Fay's excellent work upon the origins of the European War.

Virginia Woolf

TWO WOMEN

*U*P TO the beginning of the nineteenth century the distinguished woman had almost invariably been an aristocrat. It was the great lady who ruled and wrote letters and influenced the course of politics. From the huge middle class few women rose to eminence, nor has the drabness of their lot received the attention which has been bestowed upon the splendours of the great and the miseries of the poor. There they remain, even in the early part of the nineteenth century, a vast body, living, marrying, bearing children in dull obscurity, until at last we begin to wonder whether there was something in their condition itself—in the age at which they married, the number of children they bore, the privacy they lacked, the incomes they had not, the conventions which stifled them, and the education they never received—which so affected them that, though the middle class is the great reservoir from which we draw our distinguished men, it has thrown up singularly few women to set beside them.

The profound interest of Lady Stephen's life of Miss Emily Davies[1] lies in the light it throws upon this dark and obscure chapter of human history. Miss Davies was born in the year 1830, of middle-class parents who could afford to educate their sons but not their daughters. Her education was, she supposed, much the same as that of other clergymen's daughters at that time. "Do they go to school? No. Do they have governesses at home? No. They have lessons and get on as they can." But if their positive education had stopped at a little Latin, a little history, a

---

[1] *Emily Davies and Girton College,* by Lady Stephen.

little housework, it would not so much have mattered. It was what may
be called the negative education, that which decrees not what you may
do but what you may not do, that cramped and stifled. "Probably only
women who have laboured under it can understand the weight of discouragement produced by being perpetually told that, as women, nothing
much is ever expected of them. . . . Women who have lived in the atmosphere produced by such teaching know how it stifles and chills; how
hard it is to work courageously through it." Preachers and rulers of both
sexes nevertheless formulated the creed and enforced it vigorously.
Charlotte Yonge wrote: "I have no hesitation in declaring my full belief
in the inferiority of woman, nor that she brought it upon herself." She
reminded her sex of a painful incident with a snake in a garden which
had settled their destiny, Miss Yonge said, for ever. The mention of
Women's Rights made Queen Victoria so furious that "she cannot contain herself." Mr. Greg, underlining his words, wrote that "the essentials
of a woman's being are *that they are supported by, and they minister to,
men.*" The only other occupation allowed them, indeed, was to become a
governess or a needlewoman, "and both these employments were naturally
overstocked." If women wanted to paint, there was, up to the year 1858,
only one life class in London where they could learn. If they were musical
there was the inevitable piano, but the chief aim was to produce a brilliant
mechanical execution, and Trollope's picture of four girls all in the same
room playing on four pianos, all of them out of tune, seems to have
been, as Trollope's pictures usually are, based on fact. Writing was the
most accessible of the arts, and write they did, but their books were
deeply influenced by the angle from which they were forced to observe
the world. Half occupied, always interrupted, with much leisure but little
time to themselves and no money of their own, these armies of listless
women were either driven to find solace and occupation in religion, or,
if that failed, they took, as Miss Nightingale said, "to that perpetual daydreaming which is so dangerous." Some, indeed, envied the working
classes, and Miss Martineau frankly hailed the ruin of her family with
delight. "I, who had been obliged to write before breakfast, or in some
private way, had henceforth liberty to do my own work in my own way,
for we had lost our gentility." But the time had come when there were
occasional exceptions, both among parents and among daughters. Mr.
Leigh Smith, for example, allowed his daughter Barbara the same income
that he gave his sons. She at once started a school of an advanced character. Miss Garrett became a doctor because her parents, though shocked

and anxious, would be reconciled if she were a success. Miss Davies had a brother who sympathised and helped her in her determination to reform the education of women. With such encouragement the three young women started in the middle of the nineteenth century to lead the army of the unemployed in search of work. But the war of one sex upon the rights and possessions of the other is by no means a straightforward affair of attack and victory or defeat. Neither the means nor the end itself is clear-cut and recognised. There is the very potent weapon, for example, of feminine charm—what use were they to make of that? Miss Garrett said she felt "so mean in trying to come over the doctors by all kinds of little feminine dodges." Mrs. Gurney admitted the difficulty, but pointed out that "Miss Marsh's success among the navvies" had been mainly won by these means, which, for good or bad, were certainly of immense weight. It was agreed therefore that charm was to be employed. Thus we have the curious spectacle, at once so diverting and so humiliating, of grave and busy women doing fancy work and playing croquet in order that the male eye might be gratified and deceived. "Three lovely girls" were placed conspicuously in the front row at a meeting, and Miss Garrett herself sat there looking "exactly like one of the girls whose instinct it is to do what you tell them." For the arguments that they had to meet by these devious means were in themselves extremely indefinite. There was a thing called "the tender home-bloom of maidenliness" which must not be touched. There was chastity, of course, and her handmaidens, innocence, sweetness, unselfishness, sympathy; all of which might suffer if women were allowed to learn Latin and Greek. The *Saturday Review* gave cogent expression to what men feared for women and needed of women in the year 1864. The idea of submitting young ladies to local university examinations "almost takes one's breath away," the writer said. If examined they must be, steps must be taken to see that "learned men advanced in years" were the examiners, and that the presumably aged wives of these aged gentlemen should occupy "a commanding position in the gallery." Even so it would be "next to impossible to persuade the world that a pretty first-class woman came by her honours fairly." For the truth was, the reviewer wrote, that "there is a strong and ineradicable male instinct that a learned or even an accomplished young woman is the most intolerable monster in creation." It was against instincts and prejudices such as these, tough as roots but intangible as sea mist, that Miss Davies had to fight. Her days passed in a round of the most diverse occupations. Besides the actual labour of raising money and fighting prejudice, she had to decide the most delicate moral questions which, directly victory was within sight, began to be posed by the students and their parents. A mother, for example, would only entrust her with her daughter's education on condition that she should come home "as if nothing had happened," and not "take to anything eccentric." The students, on the other hand, bored with watching the Edinburgh express slip a carriage at Hitchin or rolling the lawn with a heavy iron roller, took to playing football, and then invited their teachers to see them act scenes from Shakespeare and Swinburne dressed in men's clothes. This indeed was a very serious matter; the great George Eliot was consulted; Mr. Russell Gurney was consulted, and also Mr. Tomkinson. They decided that it was unwomanly; Hamlet must be played in a skirt.

Miss Davies herself was decidedly austere. When money for the college flowed in she refused to spend it on luxuries. She wanted rooms—always more and more rooms to house those unhappy girls dreaming their youth away in indolence or picking up a little knowledge in the family sitting-room. "Privacy was the one luxury Miss Davies desired for the student, and in her eyes it was not a luxury—she despised luxuries—but a necessity." But one room to themselves was enough. She did not believe that they needed armchairs to sit in or pictures to look at. She herself lived austerely in lodgings till she was seventy-two, combative, argumentative, frankly preferring a labour meeting at Venice to the pictures and the palaces, consumed with an abstract passion for justice to women which burnt up trivial personalities and made her a little intolerant of social frivolities. Was it worth while, she once asked, in her admirable, caustic manner, after meeting Lady Augusta Stanley, to go among the aristocracy? "I felt directly that if I went to Lady Stanley's again I must get a new bonnet. And is it well to spend one's money in bonnets and flys instead of on instructive books?" she wondered. For Miss Davies perhaps was a little deficient in feminine charm.

That was a charge that nobody could bring against Lady Augusta Stanley. No two women could on the surface have less in common. Lady Augusta, it is true, was no more highly educated in a bookish sense than the middle-class women whom Miss Davies championed. But she was the finest flower of the education which for some centuries the little class of aristocratic women had enjoyed. She had been trained in her mother's drawing-room in Paris. She had talked to all the distinguished men and women of her time—Lamartine, Merimée, Victor Hugo, the Duc de Broglie, Sainte-Beuve, Renan, Jenny Lind, Turgenev—everybody came to talk to old Lady Elgin and to be entertained by her daughters. There she developed that abounding sensibility, that unquenchable sympathy which were to be so lavishly drawn upon in after years. For she was very young when she entered the Duchess of Kent's household. For fifteen years of her youth she lived there. For fifteen years she was the life and soul of that "quiet affectionate dull household of old people at Frogmore and Clarence House." Nothing whatever happened. They drove out and she thought how charming the village children looked. They walked and the Duchess picked heather. They came home and the Duchess was tired. Yet not for a moment, pouring her heart out in profuse letters to her sisters, does she complain or wish for any other existence.

Seen through her peculiar magnifying-glass the slightest event in the life of the Royal Family was either harrowing in the extreme or beyond words delightful. Prince Arthur was more handsome than ever. The Princess Helena was so lovely. Princess Ada fell from her pony. Prince Leo was naughty. The Beloved Duchess wanted a green umbrella. The measles had come out, but, alas, they threatened to go in again. One might suppose, to listen to Lady Augusta exclaiming and protesting in alternate rapture and despair, that to read aloud to the old Duchess of Kent was the most exciting of occupations, and that the old lady's rheumatisms and headaches were catastrophes of the first order. For inevitably the power of sympathy, when so highly developed and discharged solely upon personal relations tends to produce a hothouse atmosphere in which domestic details assume prodigious proportions and the mind feeds upon every detail of death and disease with a gluttonous relish. The space devoted in this volume[2] to illness and marriage entirely outweighs any reference to art, literature, or politics. It is all personal, emotional, and detailed as one of the novels which were written so inevitably by women.

It was such a life as this, and such an atmosphere as this, that Mr. Greg and the *Saturday Review* and many men, who had themselves enjoyed the utmost rigours of education, wished to see preserved. And perhaps there was some excuse for them. It is difficult to be sure, after all, that a college don is the highest type of humanity known to us; and there is something in Lady Augusta's power to magnify the common and illumine the dull which seems to imply a very arduous education of some sort behind it. Nevertheless as one studies the lives of the two women side

[2] *Letters of Lady Augusta Stanley,* edited by the Dean of Windsor and Hector Bolitho.

by side one cannot doubt that Miss Davies got more interest, more
pleasure, and more use out of one month of her life than Lady Augusta
out of a whole year of hers. Some inkling of the facts seems to have
reached Lady Augusta even at Windsor Castle. Perhaps being a woman
of the old type is a little exhausting; perhaps it is not altogether satisfying. Lady Augusta at any rate seems to have got wind of other possibilities. She liked the society of literary people best, she said. "I had
always said that I had wished to be a fellow of a college," she added
surprisingly. At any rate she was one of the first to support Miss Davies
in her demand for a University education for women. Did Miss Davies
sacrifice her book and buy her bonnet? Did the two women, so different
in every other way, come together over this—the education of their sex?
It is tempting to think so, and to imagine sprung from that union of the
middle-class woman and the court lady some astonishing phoenix of
the future who shall combine the new efficiency with the old amenity,
the courage of the indomitable Miss Davies and Lady Augusta's charm.

James Baldwin

THE DISCOVERY OF WHAT
IT MEANS TO BE AN AMERICAN

*I*T IS a complex fate to be an American," Henry James observed, and the principal discovery an American writer makes in Europe is just how complex this fate is. America's history, her aspirations, her peculiar defeats, and her position in the world—yesterday and today—are all so profoundly and stubbornly unique that the very word "America" remains a new, almost completely undefined and extremely controversial proper noun. No one in the world seems to know exactly what it describes, not even we motley millions who call ourselves Americans.

I left America because I doubted my ability to survive the fury of the color problem here. (Sometimes I still do.) I wanted to prevent myself from becoming *merely* a Negro; or, even, merely a Negro writer. I wanted to find out in what way the *specialness* of my experience could be made to connect me with other people instead of dividing me from them. (I was as isolated from Negroes as I was from whites, which is what happens when a Negro begins, at bottom, to believe what white people say about him.)

In my necessity to find the terms on which my experience could be related to that of others, Negroes and whites, writers and non-writers, I proved, to my astonishment, to be as American as any Texas G.I. And I found my experience was shared by every American writer I knew in Paris. Like me, they had been divorced from their origins, and it turned out to make very little difference that the origins of white Americans were European and mine were African—they were no more at home in Europe than I was.

431

The fact that I was the son of a slave and they were the sons of free men meant less, by the time we confronted each other on European soil, than the fact that we were both searching for our separate identities. When we had found these, we seemed to be saying, why, then, we would no longer need to cling to the shame and bitterness which had divided us so long.

It became terribly clear in Europe, as it never had been here, that we knew more about each other than any European ever could. And it also became clear that, no matter where our fathers had been born, or what they had endured, the fact of Europe had formed us both was part of our identity and part of our inheritance.

I had been in Paris a couple of years before any of this became clear to me. When it did, I, like many a writer before me upon the discovery that his props have all been knocked out from under him, suffered a species of breakdown and was carried off to the mountains of Switzerland. There, in that absolutely alabaster landscape, armed with two Bessie Smith records and a typewriter, I began to try to re-create the life that I had first known as a child and from which I had spent so many years in flight.

It was Bessie Smith, through her tone and her cadence, who helped me to dig back to the way I myself must have spoken when I was a pickaninny, and to remember the things I had heard and seen and felt. I had buried them very deep. I had never listened to Bessie Smith in America (in the same way that, for years, I would not touch watermelon), but in Europe she helped to reconcile me to being a "nigger."

I do not think that I could have made this reconciliation here. Once I was able to accept my role—as distinguished, I must say, from my "place"—in the extraordinary drama which is America, I was released from the illusion that I hated America.

The story of what can happen to an American Negro writer in Europe simply illustrates, in some relief, what can happen to any American writer there. It is not meant, of course, to imply that it happens to them all, for Europe can be very crippling, too; and, anyway, a writer, when he has made his first breakthrough, has simply won a crucial skirmish in a dangerous, unending and unpredictable battle. Still, the breakthrough is important, and the point is that an American writer, in order to achieve it, very often has to leave this country.

The American writer, in Europe, is released, first of all, from the necessity of apologizing for himself. It is not until he *is* released from the habit of flexing his muscles and proving that he is just a "regular guy" that he realizes how crippling this habit has been. It is not necessary for him, there, to pretend to be something he is not, for the artist does not encounter in Europe the same suspicion he encounters here. Whatever the Europeans may actually think of artists, they have killed enough of them off by now to know that they are as real—and as persistent—as rain, snow, taxes or businessmen.

Of course, the reason for Europe's comparative clarity concerning the different functions of men in society is that European society has always been divided into classes in a way that American society never has been. A European writer considers himself to be part of an old and honorable tradition—of intellectual activity, of letters—and his choice of a vocation does not cause him any uneasy wonder as to whether or not it will cost him all his friends. But this tradition does not exist in America.

On the contrary, we have a very deep-seated distrust of real intellectual effort (probably because we suspect that it will destroy, as I hope it does, that myth of America to which we cling so desperately). An American writer fights his way to one of the lowest rungs on the American social ladder by means of pure bull-headedness and an indescribable series of odd jobs. He probably *has* been a "regular fellow" for much of his adult life, and it is not easy for him to step out of that lukewarm bath.

We must, however, consider a rather serious paradox: though American society is more mobile than Europe's, it is easier to cut across social and occupational lines there than it is here. This has something to do, I think, with the problem of status in American life. Where everyone has status, it is also perfectly possible, after all, that no one has. It seems inevitable, in any case, that a man may become uneasy as to just what his status is.

But Europeans have lived with the idea of status for a long time. A man can be as proud of being a good waiter as of being a good actor, and, in neither case, feel threatened. And this means that the actor and the waiter can have a freer and more genuinely friendly relationship in Europe than they are likely to have here. The waiter does not feel, with obscure resentment, that the actor has "made it," and the actor is not tormented by the fear that he may find himself, tomorrow, once again a waiter.

This lack of what may roughly be called social paranoia causes the American writer in Europe to feel—almost certainly for the first time in his life—that he can reach out to everyone, that he is accessible to everyone and open to everything. This is an extraordinary feeling. He feels, so to speak, his own weight, his own value.

It is as though he suddenly came out of a dark tunnel and found himself beneath the open sky. And, in fact, in Paris, I began to see the sky for what seemed to be the first time. It was borne in on me—and it did not make me feel melancholy—that this sky had been there before I was born and would be there when I was dead. And it was up to me, therefore, to make of my brief opportunity the most that could be made.

I was born in New York, but have lived only in pockets of it. In Paris, I lived in all parts of the city—on the Right Bank and the Left, among the bourgeoisie and among *les misérables,* and knew all kinds of people, from pimps and prostitutes in Pigalle to Egyptian bankers in Neuilly. This may sound extremely unprincipled or even obscurely immoral: I found it healthy. I love to talk to people, all kinds of people, and almost everyone, as I hope we still know, loves a man who loves to listen.

This perpetual dealing with people very different from myself caused a shattering in me of preconceptions I scarcely knew I held. The writer is meeting in Europe people who are not American, whose sense of reality is entirely different from his own. They may love or hate or admire or fear or envy this country—they see it, in any case, from another point of view, and this forces the writer to reconsider many things he had always taken for granted. This reassessment, which can be very painful, is also very valuable.

This freedom, like all freedom, has its dangers and its responsibilities. One day it begins to be borne in on the writer, and with great force, that he is living in Europe as an American. If he were living there as a European, he would be living on a different and far less attractive continent.

This crucial day may be the day on which an Algerian taxi-driver tells him how it feels to be an Algerian in Paris. It may be the day on which he passes a café terrace and catches a glimpse of the tense, intelligent and troubled face of Albert Camus. Or it may be the day on which someone asks him to explain Little Rock and he begins to feel that it would be simpler—and, corny as the words may sound, more honorable

—to *go* to Little Rock than sit in Europe, on an American passport, trying to explain it.

This is a personal day, a terrible day, the day to which his entire sojourn has been tending. It is the day he realizes that there are no untroubled countries in this fearfully troubled world; that if he has been preparing himself for anything in Europe, he has been preparing himself—for America. In short, the freedom that the American writer finds in Europe brings him, full circle, back to himself, with the responsibility for his development where it always was: in his own hands.

Even the most incorrigible maverick has to be born somewhere. He may leave the group that produced him—he may be forced to—but nothing will efface his origins, the marks of which he carries with him everywhere. I think it is important to know this and even find it a matter for rejoicing, as the strongest people do, regardless of their station. On this acceptance, literally, the life of a writer depends.

The charge has often been made against American writers that they do not describe society, and have no interest in it. They only describe individuals in opposition to it, or isolated from it. Of course, what the American writer is describing is his own situation. But what is *Anna Karenina* describing if not the tragic fate of the isolated individual, at odds with her time and place?

The real difference is that Tolstoy was describing an old and dense society in which everything seemed—to the people in it, though not to Tolstoy—to be fixed forever. And the book is a masterpiece because Tolstoy was able to fathom, and make us see, the hidden laws which really governed this society and made Anna's doom inevitable.

American writers do not have a fixed society to describe. The only society they know is one in which nothing is fixed and in which the individual must fight for his identity. This is a rich confusion, indeed, and it creates for the American writer unprecedented opportunities.

That the tensions of American life, as well as the possibilities, are tremendous is certainly not even a question. But these are dealt with in contemporary literature mainly compulsively; that is, the book is more likely to be a symptom of our tension than an examination of it. The time has come, God knows, for us to examine ourselves, but we can only do this if we are willing to free ourselves of the myth of America and try to find out what is really happening here.

Every society is really governed by hidden laws, by unspoken but profound assumptions on the part of the people, and ours is no exception. It is up to the American writer to find out what these laws and assumptions are. In a society much given to smashing taboos without thereby managing to be liberated from them, it will be no easy matter.

It is no wonder, in the meantime, that the American writer keeps running off to Europe. He needs sustenance for his journey and the best models he can find. Europe has what we do not have yet, a sense of the mysterious and inexorable limits of life, a sense, in a word, of tragedy. And we have what they sorely need: a new sense of life's possibilities.

In this endeavor to wed the vision of the Old World with that of the New, it is the writer, not the statesman, who is our strongest arm. Though we do not wholly believe it yet, the interior life is a real life, and the intangible dreams of people have a tangible effect on the world.

IDEAS AND MAN

Men and Letters

JOSEPH WOOD KRUTCH, *What is a Good Review?*
THOMAS DE QUINCEY, *On the Knocking at the Gate in* Macbeth
DEEMS TAYLOR, *The Monster*
D. H. LAWRENCE, *Benjamin Franklin*
MARK SCHORER, *Two Houses, Two Ways: The Florentine Villas of Lewis and Lawrence, Respectively*
MARY MCCARTHY, *Settling the Colonel's Hash*

Men and Language

EDWARD SAPIR, *Language Defined*
GEORGE ORWELL, *Politics and the English Language*
E. B. WHITE, *The Calculating Machine*
DWIGHT MACDONALD, *The String Untuned*
JAMES SLEDD, *The Lexicographer's Uneasy Chair*

Letters and Science

C. P. SNOW, *The Two Cultures*
DOUGLAS BUSH, *The Humanities*
R. S. CRANE, *The Idea of the Humanities*
THOMAS HENRY HUXLEY, *Science and Culture*
MATTHEW ARNOLD, *Literature and Science*

The Meaning of History

CARL BECKER, *Progress*

EDWARD GIBBON, *General Observations on the Fall of the Roman Empire in the West*

E. M. FORSTER, *Captain Edward Gibbon*

HERBERT J. MULLER, *The Fall of Rome: Its Implications for Us*

Joseph Wood Krutch

WHAT IS A GOOD REVIEW?

O F ALL literary forms the book review is the one most widely cultivated and least often esteemed. To many the very phrase "literary
form" may smack of pretense when applied to a kind of writing which
is usually so casual; and formlessness may, indeed, be the only form of
many commentaries on books. Book reviewing can, nevertheless, become
an art in itself and would be such more often if the ambitious reviewer
would only devote himself to the cultivation of its particular excellences
instead of attempting, as he so often does, to demonstrate his capacities
by producing something "more than a mere review." The best review is
not the one which is trying to be something else. It is not an independent
essay on the subject of the book in hand and not an aesthetic discourse
upon one of the literary genres. The best book review is the best review
of the book in question, and the better it is, the closer it sticks to its
ostensible subject.

To say this is not to say that a good review is easy to write; in certain
technical respects it is, indeed, the most difficult of all forms of literary
criticism for the simple reason that in no other is the writer called upon
to do so many things in so short a space. The critical essay, no matter how
extended it may be, is not compelled to aim at any particular degree of
completeness. It may—in fact it usually does—assume that the reader is
sufficiently familiar with the work under discussion to make description
unnecessary and it may also confine itself to whatever aspects of the subject the critic may choose.

But the book review as a literary form implies completeness; it has
not really performed its function unless, to begin with, it puts the reader

439

in possession of the facts upon which the criticism is based, and unless—no matter upon how small a scale—its consideration is complete. However penetrating a piece of writing may be, it is not a good review if it leaves the reader wondering what the book itself is like as a whole or if it is concerned with only some aspects of the book's quality.

I shall not pretend to say how large a proportion of the so-called reviews published in *The Nation* or anywhere else actually achieve the distinguishing characteristics of the book-review form, but a certain number of them do, and the sense of satisfactoriness which they give can always be traced to the fact that, whatever other qualities they may have, they accomplish the three minimum tasks of the book reviewer. They describe the book, they communicate something of its quality, and they pass a judgment upon it.

Each of these things is quite different from the others, but only the last is usually considered as carefully as it ought to be by either reader or writer. Adequate description implies a simple account of the scope and contents of the book; its presence guarantees that the reader will not be left wondering what, in the simplest terms, the book is about. "Communication of quality" implies, on the other hand, a miniature specimen of what is commonly called "impressionistic criticism"; it means that the reviewer must somehow manage to re-create in the mind of the reader some approximation of the reaction produced in his own mind by the book itself. And in however low esteem this form of criticism may be held as a be-all and end-all (Mr. Eliot calls it the result of a weak creative instinct rather than of a critical impulse), it is indispensable in a book review if that review is to perform the function it is supposed to perform, and if it is to become what it is supposed to be—namely, not merely an account of a book on the one hand or an independent piece of criticism on the other, but a brief critical essay which includes within itself all that is necessary to make the criticism comprehensible and significant.

Your "reviewer" often envies the more lofty "critic" because the critic is supposed to be read for his own sake while the reviewer must assume that the reader is attracted more by his interest in the book discussed than by the reviewer himself. For that very reason he is likely either to treat reviewing as a casual affair or to seek for an opportunity to write something else under the guise of a review. He might be happier himself and make his readers happier also if he would, instead, take the trouble to ask what a review ought to be and if he would examine his own work in the light of his conclusions. It is not easy to do within the space of a thousand words or less the three things enumerated. It is less easy still to combine the description, the impression, and the judgment into a whole which seems to be, not three things at least, but one.

How many reviewers of novels, for instance, seem to know how much of a particular story has to be told in order to provide a solid basis for the impression they intend to convey? And if it is decided that some part of the story must be told, how many know, as a story-teller must, whether the incidents are striking enough to come first or must be introduced with some comment which creates the interest? Yet a first-rate review, despite its miniature scale, raises precisely the same problems as long narratives or expositions raise, and each must be solved as artfully if the review is to have such beauty of form as it is capable of. Doubtless the finest reviewer can hardly hope to have his art fully appreciated by the public. But there is every reason why he should respect it himself.

Thomas De Quincey

ON THE KNOCKING AT THE GATE IN *MACBETH*

FROM MY boyish days I had always felt a great perplexity on one point in *Macbeth*. It was this:—the knocking at the gate which succeeds to the murder of Duncan produced to my feelings an effect for which I never could account. The effect was that it reflected back upon the murderer a peculiar awfulness and a depth of solemnity; yet, however obstinately I endeavored with my understanding to comprehend this, for many years I never could see *why* it should produce such an effect.

Here I pause for one moment to exhort the reader never to pay any attention to his understanding when it stands in opposition to any other faculty of his mind. The mere understanding, however useful and indispensable, is the meanest faculty in the human mind and the most to be distrusted; and yet the great majority of people trust to nothing else,—which may do for ordinary life, but not for philosophical purposes. Of this, out of ten thousand instances that I might produce, I will cite one. Ask of any person whatsoever who is not previously prepared for the demand by a knowledge of perspective, to draw in the rudest way the commonest appearance which depends upon the laws of that science—as, for instance, to represent the effect of two walls standing at right angles to each other, or the appearance of the houses on each side of a street, as seen by a person looking down the street from one extremity. Now, in all cases, unless the person has happened to observe in pictures how it is that artists produce these effects, he will be utterly unable to make the smallest approximation to it. Yet why? For he has actually seen the effect every day of his life. The reason is that he allows his understanding to overrule

442

his eyes. His understanding, which includes no intuitive knowledge of the laws of vision, can furnish him with no reason why a line which is known and can be proved to be a horizontal line should not *appear* a horizontal line; a line that made any angle with the perpendicular less than a right angle would seem to him to indicate that his houses were all tumbling down together. Accordingly he makes the line of his houses a horizontal line, and fails of course to produce the effect demanded. Here then is one instance out of many, in which not only the understanding is allowed to overrule the eyes, but where the understanding is positively allowed to obliterate the eyes, as it were; for not only does the man believe the evidence of his understanding in opposition to that of his eyes, but (what is monstrous) the idiot is not aware that his eyes ever gave such evidence. He does not know that he has seen (and therefore *quoad* his consciousness has *not* seen) that which he *has* seen every day of his life.

But to return from this digression. My understanding could furnish no reason why the knocking at the gate in *Macbeth* should produce any effect, direct or reflected. In fact, my understanding said positively that it could *not* produce any effect. But I knew better; I felt that it did; and I waited and clung to the problem until further knowledge should enable me to solve it. At length, in 1812, Mr. Williams made his *début* on the stage of Ratcliffe Highway, and executed those unparalleled murders which have procured for him such a brilliant and undying reputation. On which murders, by the way, I must observe, that in one respect they have had an ill effect, by making the connoisseur in murder very fastidious in his taste, and dissatisfied with anything that has been since done in that line. All other murders look pale by the deep crimson of his; and, as an amateur once said to me in a querulous tone, "There has been absolutely nothing *doing* since his time, or nothing that's worth speaking of." But this is wrong, for it is unreasonable to expect all men to be great artists, and born with the genius of Mr. Williams. Now it will be remembered that in the first of these murders (that of the Marrs) the same incident (of a knocking at the door soon after the work of extermination was complete) did actually occur which the genius of Shakespeare has invented; and all good judges, and the most eminent dilettanti, acknowledged the felicity of Shakespeare's suggestion as soon as it was actually realized. Here, then, was a fresh proof that I had the right in relying on my own feeling in opposition to my understanding; and again I set myself to study the problem. At length I solved it to my own satisfaction; and my solution is this:—Murder, in ordinary cases, where the sympathy is wholly directed to the case of the murdered person, is an incident of coarse and vulgar horror; and for this reason,—that it flings the interest exclusively upon the natural but ignoble instinct by which we cleave to life; an instinct which, as being indispensable to the primal law of self-preservation, is the same in kind (though different in degree) amongst all living creatures. This instinct, therefore, because it annihilates all distinctions, and degrades the greatest of men to the level of "the poor beetle that we tread on," exhibits human nature in its most abject and humiliating attitude. Such an attitude would little suit the purposes of the poet. What then must he do? He must throw the interest on the murderer. Our sympathy must be with *him* (of course I mean a sympathy of comprehension, a sympathy by which we enter into his feelings, and are made to understand them—not a sympathy of pity or approbation).[1] In the murdered person all strife of thought, all flux and reflux of passion and of purpose, are crushed by one overwhelming panic; the fear of instant death smites him "with its petrific mace." But in the murderer, such a murderer as a poet will condescend to, there must be raging some great storm of passion—jealousy, ambition, vengeance, hatred —which will create a hell within him; and into this hell we are to look.

In *Macbeth,* for the sake of gratifying his now enormous and teeming faculty of creation, Shakespeare has introduced two murderers; and, as usual in his hands, they are remarkably discriminated; but—though in Macbeth the strife of mind is greater than in his wife, the tiger spirit not so awake, and his feelings caught chiefly by contagion from her—yet, as both were finally involved in the guilt of murder, the murderous mind of necessity is finally to be presumed in both. This was to be expressed; and on its own account, as well as to make it a more proportionable antagonist to the unoffending nature of their victim, "the gracious Duncan," and adequately to expound "the deep damnation of his taking off," this was to be expressed with peculiar energy. We were to be made to feel that the human nature—i.e., the divine nature of love and mercy, spread through the hearts of all creatures, and seldom utterly withdrawn from man—was gone, vanished, extinct, and that the fiendish nature had taken

[1] It seems almost ludicrous to guard and explain my use of a word in a situation where it would naturally explain itself. But it has become necessary to do so, in consequence of the unscholarlike use of the word sympathy, at present so general, by which, instead of taking it in its proper sense, as the act of reproducing in our minds the feelings of another, whether for hatred, indignation, love, pity, or approbation, it is made a mere synonym of the word *pity;* and hence, instead of saying, "sympathy *with* another," many writers adopt the monstrous barbarism of "sympathy *for* another."

its place. And, as this effect is marvellously accomplished in the *dialogues* and *soliloquies* themselves, so it is finally consummated by the expedient under consideration; and it is to this that I now solicit the reader's attention. If the reader has ever witnessed a wife, daughter, or sister, in a fainting fit, he may chance to have observed that the most affecting moment in such a spectacle is that in which a sigh and a stirring announce the recommencement of suspended life. Or, if the reader has ever been present in a vast metropolis on the day when some great national idol was carried in funeral pomp to his grave, and, chancing to walk near the course through which it passed, has felt powerfully, in the silence and desertion of the streets and in the stagnation of ordinary business, the deep interest which at that moment was possessing the heart of man,— if all at once he should hear the death-like stillness broken up by the sound of wheels rattling away from the scene, and making known that the transitory vision was dissolved, he will be aware that at no moment was his sense of the complete suspension and pause in ordinary human concerns so full and affecting as at that moment when the suspension ceases, and the goings-on of human life are suddenly resumed. All action in any direction is best expounded, measured, and made apprehensible, by reaction. Now apply this to the case in *Macbeth*. Here, as I have said, the retiring of the human heart and the entrance of the fiendish heart was to be expressed and made sensible. Another world has stepped in; and the murderers are taken out of the region of human things, human purposes, human desires. They are transfigured: Lady Macbeth is "unsexed"; Macbeth has forgot that he was born of woman; both are conformed to the image of devils; and the world of devils is suddenly revealed. But how shall this be conveyed and made palpable? In order that a new world may step in, this world must for a time disappear. The murderers, and the murder, must be insulated—cut off by an immeasurable gulf from the ordinary tide and succession of human affairs—locked up and sequestered in some deep recess; we must be made sensible that the world of ordinary life is suddenly arrested—laid asleep—tranced— racked into a dread armistice; time must be annihilated, relation to things without abolished; and all must pass self-withdrawn into a deep syncope and suspension of earthly passion. Hence it is that, when the deed is done, when the work of darkness is perfect, then the world of darkness passes away like a pageantry in the clouds: the knocking at the gate is heard, and it makes known audibly that the reaction has commenced; the human has made its reflux upon the fiendish; the pulses of life are beginning to beat again; and the re-establishment of the goings-on of the world in which we live first makes us profoundly sensible of the awful parenthesis that had suspended them.

O mighty poet! Thy works are not as those of other men, simply and merely great works of art, but are also like the phenomena of nature, like the sun and the sea, the stars and the flowers, like frost and snow, rain and dew, hailstorm and thunder, which are to be studied with entire submission of our own faculties, and in the perfect faith that in them there can be no too much or too little, nothing useless or inert, but that, the farther we press in our discoveries, the more we shall see proofs of design and self-supporting arrangement where the careless eye had seen nothing but accident!

Deems Taylor

THE MONSTER

*H*E WAS an undersized little man, with a head too big for his body—a sickly little man. His nerves were bad. He had skin trouble. It was agony for him to wear anything next to his skin coarser than silk. And he had delusions of grandeur.

He was a monster of conceit. Never for one minute did he look at the world or at people, except in relation to himself. He was not only the most important person in the world, to himself; in his own eyes he was the only person who existed. He believed himself to be one of the greatest dramatists in the world, one of the greatest thinkers, and one of the greatest composers. To hear him talk, he was Shakespeare, and Beethoven, and Plato, rolled into one. And you would have had no difficulty in hearing him talk. He was one of the most exhausting conversationalists that ever lived. An evening with him was an evening spent in listening to a monologue. Sometimes he was brilliant; sometimes he was maddeningly tiresome. But whether he was being brilliant or dull, he had one sole topic of conversation: himself. What *he* thought and what *he* did.

He had a mania for being in the right. The slightest hint of disagreement, from anyone, on the most trivial point, was enough to set him off on a harangue that might last for hours, in which he proved himself right in so many ways, and with such exhausting volubility, that in the end his hearer, stunned and deafened, would agree with him, for the sake of peace.

It never occurred to him that he and his doing were not of the most intense and fascinating interest to anyone with whom he came

447

in contact. He had theories about almost any subject under the sun, including vegetarianism, the drama, politics, and music; and in support of these theories he wrote pamphlets, letters, books . . . thousands upon thousands of words, hundreds and hundreds of pages. He not only wrote these things, and published them—usually at somebody else's expense—but he would sit and read them aloud, for hours, to his friends and his family.

He wrote operas; and no sooner did he have the synopsis of a story, but he would invite—or rather summon—a crowd of his friends to his house and read it aloud to them. Not for criticism. For applause. When the complete poem was written, the friends had to come again, and hear *that* read aloud. Then he would publish the poem, sometimes years before the music that went with it was written. He played the piano like a composer, in the worst sense of what that implies, and he would sit down at the piano before parties that included some of the finest pianists of his time, and play for them, by the hour, his own music, needless to say. He had a composer's voice. And he would invite eminent vocalists to his house, and sing them his operas, taking all the parts.

He had the emotional stability of a six-year-old child. When he felt out of sorts, he would rave and stamp, or sink into suicidal gloom and talk darkly of going to the East to end his days as a Buddhist monk. Ten minutes later, when something pleased him, he would rush out of doors and run around the garden, or jump up and down on the sofa, or stand on his head. He could be grief-stricken over the death of a pet dog, and he could be callous and heartless to a degree that would have made a Roman emperor shudder.

He was almost innocent of any sense of responsibility. Not only did he seem incapable of supporting himself, but it never occurred to him that he was under any obligation to do so. He was convinced that the world owed him a living. In support of this belief, he borrowed money from everybody who was good for a loan—men, women, friends, or strangers. He wrote begging letters by the score, sometimes groveling without shame, at others loftily offering his intended benefactor the privilege of contributing to his support, and being mortally offended if the recipient declined the honor. I have found no record of his ever paying or repaying money to anyone who did not have a legal claim upon it.

What money he could lay his hands on he spent like an Indian rajah. The mere prospect of a performance of one of his operas was enough to set him to running up bills amounting to ten times the amount of his prospective royalties. On an income that would reduce a more scrupulous man to doing his own laundry, he would keep two servants. Without enough money in his pocket to pay his rent, he would have the walls and ceiling of his study lined with pink silk. No one will ever know—certainly he never knew—how much money he owed. We do know that his greatest benefactor gave him $6,000 to pay the most pressing of his debts in one city, and a year later had to give him $16,000 to enable him to live in another city without being thrown into jail for debt.

He was equally unscrupulous in other ways. An endless procession of women marched through his life. His first wife spent twenty years enduring and forgiving his infidelities. His second wife had been the wife of his most devoted friend and admirer, from whom he stole her. And even while he was trying to persuade her to leave her first husband he was writing to a friend to inquire whether he could suggest some wealthy woman—*any* wealthy woman—whom he could marry for her money.

He was completely selfish in his other personal relationships. His liking for his friends was measured solely by the completeness of their devotion to him, or by their usefulness to him, whether financial or artistic. The minute they failed him—even by so much as refusing a dinner invitation—or began to lessen in usefulness, he cast them off without a second thought. At the end of his life he had exactly one friend left whom he had known even in middle age.

He had a genius for making enemies. He would insult a man who disagreed with him about the weather. He would pull endless wires in order to meet some man who admired his work, and was able and anxious to be of use to him—and would proceed to make a mortal enemy of him with some idiotic and wholly uncalled-for exhibition of arrogance and bad manners. A character in one of his operas was a caricature of one of the most powerful music critics of his day. Not content with burlesquing him, he invited the critic to his house and read him the libretto aloud in front of his friends.

The name of this monster was Richard Wagner. Everything that I have said about him you can find on record—in newspapers, in police reports, in the testimony of people who knew him, in his own letters, between the lines of his autobiography. And the curious thing about this record is that it doesn't matter in the least.

Because this undersized, sickly, disagreeable, fascinating little man was right all the time. The joke was on us. He *was* one of the world's great dramatists; he *was* a great thinker; he *was* one of the most stupendous musical geniuses that, up to now, the world has ever seen. The world did owe him a living. People couldn't know those things at the time, I suppose; and yet to us, who know his music, it does seem as though they should have known. What if he did talk about himself all the time? If he had talked about himself for twenty-four hours every day for the span of his life he would not have uttered half the number of words that other men have spoken and written about him since his death.

When you consider what he wrote—thirteen operas and music dramas, eleven of them still holding the stage, eight of them unquestionably worth ranking among the world's great musico-dramatic masterpieces—when you listen to what he wrote, the debts and heartaches that people had to endure from him don't seem much of a price. Eduard Hanslick, the critic whom he caricatured in *Die Meistersinger* and who hated him ever after, now lives only because he was caricatured in *Die Meistersinger*. The women whose hearts he broke are long since dead; and the man who could never love anyone but himself has made them deathless atonement, I think, with *Tristan und Isolde*. Think of the luxury with which for a time, at least, fate rewarded Napoleon, the man who ruined France and looted Europe; and then perhaps you will agree that a few thousand dollars' worth of debts were not too heavy a price to pay for the *Ring* tetralogy.

What if he was faithless to his friends and to his wives? He had one mistress to whom he was faithful to the day of his death: Music. Not for a single moment did he ever compromise with what he believed, with what he dreamed. There is not a line of his music that could have been conceived by a little mind. Even when he is dull, or downright bad, he is dull in the grand manner. There is greatness about his worst mistakes. Listening to his music, one does not forgive him for what he may or may not have been. It is not a matter of forgiveness. It is a matter of being dumb with wonder that his poor brain and body didn't burst under the torment of the demon of creative energy that lived inside him, struggling, clawing, scratching to be released; tearing, shrieking at him to write the music that was in him. The miracle is that what he did in the little space of seventy years could have been done at all, even by a great genius. Is it any wonder that he had no time to be a man?

D. H. Lawrence

BENJAMIN FRANKLIN

THE PERFECTIBILITY of Man! Ah heaven, what a dreary theme! The perfectibility of the Ford car! the perfectibility of which man? I am many men. Which of them are you going to perfect? I am not a mechanical contrivance.

Education! Which of the various me's do you propose to educate, and which do you propose to suppress?

Anyhow I defy you. I defy you, oh society, to educate me or to suppress me, according to your dummy standards.

The ideal man! And which is he, if you please? Benjamin Franklin or Abraham Lincoln? The ideal man! Roosevelt or Porfirio Diaz?

There are other men in me, besides this patient ass who sits here in a tweed jacket. What am I doing, playing the patient ass in a tweed jacket? Who am I talking to? Who are you, at the other end of this patience?

Who are you? How many selves have you? And which of these selves do you want to be?

Is Yale College going to educate the self that is in the dark of you, or Harvard College?

The ideal self! Oh, but I have a strange and fugitive self shut out and howling like a wolf or a coyote under the ideal windows. See his red eyes in the dark? This is the self who is coming into his own.

The perfectibility of man, dear God! When every man as long as he remains alive is in himself a multitude of conflicting men. Which of these do you choose to perfect, at the expense of every other?

Old Daddy Franklin will tell you. He'll rig him up for you, the pattern American. Oh, Franklin was the first downright American. He knew

451

what he was about, the sharp little man. He set up the first dummy American.

At the beginning of his career this cunning little Benjamin drew up for himself a creed that should "satisfy the professors of every religion, but shock none."

Now wasn't that a real American thing to do?

"That there is One God, who made all things."

(But Benjamin made Him.)

"That He governs the world by His Providence."

(Benjamin knowing all about Providence.)

"That He ought to be worshipped with adoration, prayer, and thanksgiving."

(Which cost nothing.)

"But—" But me no buts, Benjamin, saith the Lord.

"But that the most acceptable service of God is doing good to men."

(God having no choice in the matter.)

"That the soul is immortal."

(You'll see why, in the next clause.)

"And that God will certainly reward virtue and punish vice, either here or hereafter."

Now if Mr. Andrew Carnegie, or any other millionaire, had wished to invent a God to suit his ends, he could not have done better. Benjamin did it for him in the eighteenth century. God is the supreme servant of men who want to get on, to produce. Providence. The provider. The heavenly store-keeper. The everlasting Wanamaker.

And this is all the God the grandsons of the Pilgrim Fathers had left. Aloft on a pillar of dollars.

"That the soul is immortal."

The trite way Benjamin says it!

But man has a soul, though you can't locate it either in his purse or his pocket-book or his heart or his stomach or his head. The *wholeness* of a man is his soul. Not merely that nice little comfortable bit which Benjamin marks out.

It's a queer thing, is a man's soul. It is the whole of him. Which means it is the unknown him, as well as the known. It seems to me just funny, professors and Benjamins fixing the functions of the soul. Why the soul of man is a vast forest, and all Benjamin intended was a neat back garden. And we've all got to fit in to his kitchen garden scheme of things. Hail Columbia!

The soul of man is a dark forest. The Hercynian Wood that scared the Romans so, and out of which came the white-skinned hordes of the next civilization.

Who knows what will come out of the soul of man? The soul of man is a dark vast forest, with wild life in it. Think of Benjamin fencing it off!

Oh, but Benjamin fenced a little tract that he called the soul of man, and proceeded to get it into cultivation. Providence, forsooth! And they think that bit of barbed wire is going to keep us in pound forever? More fools them.

This is Benjamin's barbed wire fence. He made himself a list of virtues, which he trotted inside like a grey nag in paddock.

1 TEMPERANCE Eat not to fulness; drink not to elevation.

2 SILENCE Speak not but what may benefit others or yourself; avoid trifling conversation.

3 ORDER Let all your things have their places; let each part of your business have its time.

4 RESOLUTION Resolve to perform what you ought; perform without fail what you resolve.

5 FRUGALITY Make no expense but to do good to others or yourself—i.e., waste nothing.

6 INDUSTRY Lose no time, be always employed in something useful; cut off all unnecessary action.

7 SINCERITY Use no hurtful deceit; think innocently and justly, and, if you speak, speak accordingly.

8 JUSTICE Wrong none by doing injuries, or omitting the benefits that are your duty.

9 MODERATION Avoid extremes, forbear resenting injuries as much as you think they deserve.

10 CLEANLINESS Tolerate no uncleanliness in body, clothes, or habitation.

11 TRANQUILLITY Be not disturbed at trifles, or at accidents common or unavoidable.

12 CHASTITY Rarely use venery but for health and offspring, never to dulness, weakness, or the injury of your own or another's peace or reputation.

13 HUMILITY Imitate Jesus and Socrates.

A Quaker friend told Franklin that he, Benjamin, was generally considered proud, so Benjamin put in the Humility touch as an after-thought. The amusing part is the sort of humility it displays. "Imitate Jesus and Socrates," and mind you don't outshine either of these two. One can just imagine Socrates and Alcibiades roaring in their cups over Philadelphian Benjamin, and Jesus looking at him a little puzzled, and murmuring: "Aren't you wise in your own conceit, Ben?"

"Henceforth be masterless," retorts Ben. "Be ye each one his own master unto himself, and don't let even the Lord put his spoke in." "Each man his own master" is but a puffing up of masterlessness.

Well, the first of Americans practised this enticing list with assiduity, setting a national example. He had the virtues in columns, and gave himself good and bad marks according as he thought his behaviour deserved. Pity these conduct charts are lost to us. He only remarks that Order was his stumbling block. He could not learn to be neat and tidy.

Isn't it nice to have nothing worse to confess?

He was a little model, was Benjamin. Doctor Franklin. Snuff-coloured little man! Immortal soul and all!

The immortal soul part was a sort of cheap insurance policy.

Benjamin had no concern, really, with the immortal soul. He was too busy with social man.

1. He swept and lighted the streets of young Philadelphia.
2. He invented electrical appliances.
3. He was the centre of a moralizing club in Philadelphia, and he wrote the moral humorisms of Poor Richard.
4. He was a member of all the important councils of Philadelphia, and then of the American colonies.
5. He won the cause of American Independence at the French Court, and was the economic father of the United States.

Now what more can you want of a man? And yet he is *infra dig*, even in Philadelphia.

I admire him. I admire his sturdy courage first of all, then his sagacity, then his glimpsing into the thunders of electricity, then his common-sense humour. All the qualities of a great man, and never more than a great citizen. Middle-sized, sturdy, snuff-coloured Doctor Franklin, one of the soundest citizens that ever trod or "used venery."

I do not like him.

And, by the way, I always thought books of Venery were about hunting deer.

There is a certain earnest naïveté about him. Like a child. And like a little old man. He has again become as a little child, always as wise as his grandfather, or wiser.

Perhaps, as I say, the most complete citizen that ever "used venery."

Printer, philosopher, scientist, author and patriot, impeccable husband and citizen, why isn't he an archetype?

Pioneer, Oh Pioneers! Benjamin was one of the greatest pioneers of the United States. Yet we just can't do with him.

What's wrong with him then? Or what's wrong with us?

I can remember, when I was a little boy, my father used to buy a scrubby yearly almanack with the sun and moon and stars on the cover. And it used to prophesy bloodshed and famine. But also crammed in corners it had little anecdotes and humorisms, with a moral tag. And I used to have my little priggish laugh at the woman who counted her chickens before they were hatched, and so forth, and I was convinced that honesty was the best policy, also a little priggishly. The author of these bits was Poor Richard, and Poor Richard was Benjamin Franklin, writing in Philadelphia well over a hundred years before.

And probably I haven't got over those Poor Richard tags yet. I rankle still with them. They are thorns in young flesh.

Because although I still believe that honesty is the best policy, I dislike policy altogether; though it is just as well not to count your chickens before they are hatched, it's still more hateful to count them with gloating when they *are* hatched. It has taken me many years and countless smarts to get out of that barbed wire moral enclosure that Poor Richard rigged up. Here am I now in tatters and scratched to ribbons, sitting in the middle of Benjamin's America looking at the barbed wire, and the fat sheep crawling under the fence to get fat outside and the watchdogs yelling at the gate lest by chance anyone should get out by the proper exit. Oh America! Oh Benjamin! And I just utter a long loud curse against Benjamin and the American corral.

Moral America! Most moral Benjamin. Sound, satisfied Ben!

He had to go to the frontiers of his State to settle some disturbance among the Indians. On this occasion he writes:

> "We found that they had made a great bonfire in the middle of the square; they were all drunk, men and women quarrelling and fighting. Their dark-coloured bodies, half naked, seen only by the gloomy light of the bonfire, running after and beating one another with fire-brands,

accompanied by their horrid yellings, formed a scene the most resembling our ideas of hell that could well be imagined. There was no
appeasing the tumult, and we retired to our lodging. At midnight a
number of them came thundering at our door, demanding more rum,
of which we took no notice.

"The next day, sensible they had misbehaved in giving us that
disturbance, they sent three of their counsellors to make their apology.
The orator acknowledged the fault, but laid it upon the rum, and then
endeavoured to excuse the rum by saying: 'The Great Spirit, who made
all things, made everything for some use; and whatever he designed
anything for, that use it should always be put to. Now, when he had
made rum, he said: "Let this be for the Indians to get drunk with."
And it must be so.'

"And, indeed, if it be the design of Providence to extirpate these
savages in order to make room for the cultivators of the earth, it
seems not improbable that rum may be the appointed means. It has
already annihilated all the tribes who formerly inhabited all the sea-
coast . . ."

This, from the good doctor, with such suave complacency is a little
disenchanting. Almost too good to be true.

But there you are! The barbed wire fence. "Extirpate these savages
in order to make room for the cultivators of the earth." Oh, Benjamin
Franklin! He even "used venery" as a cultivator of seed.

Cultivate the earth, ye gods! The Indians did that, as much as they
needed. And they left off there. Who built Chicago? Who cultivated the
earth until it spawned Pittsburgh, Pa.?

The moral issue! Just look at it! Cultivation included. If it's a mere
choice of Kultur or cultivation, I give it up.

Which brings us right back to our question, what's wrong with
Benjamin, that we can't stand him? Or else, what's wrong with us, that we
find fault with such a paragon?

Man is a moral animal. All right. I am a moral animal. And I'm
going to remain such. I'm not going to be turned into a virtuous little
automaton as Benjamin would have me. "This is good, that is bad. Turn
the little handle and let the good tap flow," saith Benjamin and all
America with him. "But first of all extirpate those savages who are always
turning on the bad tap."

I am a moral animal. But I am not a moral machine. I don't work
with a little set of handles or levers. The Temperance-silence-order-
resolution-frugality-industry-sincerity-justice-moderation-cleanliness-tran-
quillity-chastity-humility keyboard is not going to get me going. I'm really

not just an automatic piano with a moral Benjamin getting tunes out of me.

Here's my creed, against Benjamin's. This is what I believe:

"That I am I."

"That my soul is a dark forest."

"That my known self will never be more than a little clearing in the forest."

"That gods, strange gods, come forth from the forest into the clearing of my known self, and then go back."

"That I must have the courage to let them come and go."

"That I will never let mankind put anything over me, but that I will try always to recognize and submit to the gods in me and the gods in other men and women."

There is my creed. He who runs may read. He who prefers to crawl, or to go by gasoline, can call it rot.

Then for a "list." It is rather fun to play at Benjamin.

1   TEMPERANCE   Eat and carouse with Bacchus, or munch dry bread with Jesus, but don't sit down without one of the gods.

2   SILENCE   Be still when you have nothing to say; when genuine passion moves you, say what you've got to say, and say it hot.

3   ORDER   Know that you are responsible to the gods inside you and to the men in whom the gods are manifest. Recognize your superiors and your inferiors, according to the gods. This is the root of all order.

4   RESOLUTION   Resolve to abide by your own deepest promptings, and to sacrifice the smaller thing to the greater. Kill when you must, and be killed the same: the *must* coming from the gods inside you, or from the men in whom you recognize the Holy Ghost.

5   FRUGALITY   Demand nothing; accept what you see fit. Don't waste your pride or squander your emotion.

6   INDUSTRY   Lose no time with ideals; serve the Holy Ghost; never serve mankind.

7   SINCERITY   To be sincere is to remember that I am I, and that the other man is not me.

8   JUSTICE   The only justice is to follow the sincere intuition of the soul, angry or gentle. Anger is just, and pity is just, but judgment is never just.

9   MODERATION   Beware of absolutes. There are many gods.

10 CLEANLINESS   Don't be too clean. It impoverishes the blood.

11 TRANQUILLITY   The soul has many motions, many gods come and go. Try and find your deepest issue, in every confusion, and abide by that. Obey the man in whom you recognize the Holy Ghost; command when your honour comes to command.

12 CHASTITY   Never "use" venery at all. Follow your passional impulse, if it be answered in the other being; but never have any motive in mind, neither off-spring nor health nor even pleasure, nor even service. Only know that "venery" is of the great gods. An offering-up of yourself to the very great gods, the dark ones, and nothing else.

13 HUMILITY   See all men and women according to the Holy Ghost that is within them. Never yield before the barren.

There's my list. I have been trying dimly to realize it for a long time, and only America and old Benjamin have at last goaded me into trying to formulate it.

And now I, at least, know why I can't stand Benjamin. He tries to take away my wholeness and my dark forest, my freedom. For how can any man be free, without an illimitable background? And Benjamin tries to shove me into a barbed-wire paddock and make me grow potatoes or Chicagoes.

And how can I be free, without gods that come and go? But Benjamin won't let anything exist except my useful fellow-men, and I'm sick of them; as for his Godhead, his Providence, He is Head of nothing except a vast heavenly store that keeps every imaginable line of goods, from victrolas to cat-o-nine tails.

And how can any man be free without a soul of his own, that he believes in and won't sell at any price? But Benjamin doesn't let me have a soul of my own. He says I am nothing but a servant of mankind—galley-slave I call it—and if I don't get my wages here below—that is, if Mr. Pierpont Morgan or Mr. Nosey Hebrew or the grand United States Government, the great US, US or SOMEOFUS, manages to scoop in my bit along with their lump—why, never mind, I shall get my wages HEREAFTER.

Oh Benjamin! Oh Binjum! You do NOT suck me in any longer.

And why oh why should the snuff-coloured little trap have wanted to take us all in? Why did he do it?

Out of sheer human cussedness, in the first place. We do all like to get things inside a barbed-wire corral. Especially our fellow-men. We love to round them up inside the barbed-wire enclosure of FREEDOM, and make 'em work. *"Work, you free jewel,* WORK!" shouts the liberator, cracking his whip. Benjamin, I will not work. I do not choose to be a free democrat. I am absolutely a servant of my own Holy Ghost.

Sheer cussedness! But there was as well the salt of a subtler purpose. Benjamin was just in his eyeholes—to use an English vulgarism meaning he was just delighted—when he was at Paris judiciously milking money out of the French monarchy for the overthrow of all monarchy. If you want to ride your horse to somewhere you must put a bit in his mouth. And Benjamin wanted to ride his horse so that it would upset the whole apple-cart of the old masters. He wanted the whole European apple-cart upset. So he had to put a strong bit in the mouth of his ass.

"Henceforth be masterless."

That is, he had to break-in the human ass completely, so that much more might be broken, in the long run. For the moment it was the British Government that had to have a hole knocked in it. The first real hole it ever had: the breach of the American rebellion.

Benjamin, in his sagacity, knew that the breaking of the old world was a long process. In the depths of his own under-consciousness he hated England, he hated Europe, he hated the whole corpus of the European being. He wanted to be American. But you can't change your nature and mode of consciousness like changing your shoes. It is a gradual shedding. Years must go by, and centuries must elapse before you have finished. Like a son escaping from the domination of his parents. The escape is not just one rupture. It is a long and half-secret process.

So with the American. He was a European when he first went over the Atlantic. He is in the main a recreant European still. From Benjamin Franklin to Woodrow Wilson may be a long stride, but it is a stride along the same road. There is no new road. The same old road, become dreary and futile. Theoretic and materialistic.

Why then did Benjamin set up this dummy of a perfect citizen as a pattern to America? Of course he did it in perfect good faith, as far as he knew. He thought it simply was the true ideal. But what we *think* we do is not very important. We never really know what we are doing. Either we are materialistic instruments, like Benjamin, or we move in the gesture of creation, from our deepest self, usually unconscious. We are only the actors, we are never wholly the authors of our own deeds or works. IT is the author, the unknown inside us or outside us. The best we can do is to try to hold ourselves in unison with the deeps which are inside us.

And the worst we can do is to try to have things our own way, when we run counter to IT, and in the long run get our knuckles rapped for our presumption.

So Benjamin contriving money out of the Court of France. He was contriving the first steps of the overthrow of all Europe, France included. You can never have a new thing without breaking an old. Europe happens to be the old thing. America, unless the people in America assert themselves too much in opposition to the inner gods, should be the new thing. The new thing is the death of the old. But you can't cut the throat of an epoch. You've got to steal the life from it through several centuries.

And Benjamin worked for this both directly and indirectly. Directly, at the Court of France, making a small but very dangerous hole in the side of England, through which hole Europe has by now almost bled to death. And indirectly in Philadelphia, setting up this unlovely, snuff-coloured little ideal, or automaton, of a pattern American. The pattern American, this dry, moral, utilitarian little democrat, has done more to ruin the old Europe than any Russian nihilist. He has done it by slow attrition, like a son who has stayed at home and obeyed his parents, all the while silently hating their authority, and silently, in his soul, destroying not only their authority but their whole existence. For the American spiritually stayed at home in Europe. The spiritual home of America was and still is Europe. This is the galling bondage, in spite of several billions of heaped-up gold. Your heaps of gold are only so many muck-heaps, America, and will remain so till you become a reality to yourselves.

All this Americanizing and mechanizing has been for the purpose of overthrowing the past. And now look at America, tangled in her own barbed wire, and mastered by her own machines. Absolutely got down by her own barbed wire of shalt-nots, and shut up fast in her own "productive" machines like millions of squirrels running in millions of cages. It is just a farce.

Now is your chance, Europe. Now let Hell loose and get your own back, and paddle your own canoe on a new sea, while clever America lies on her muck-heaps of gold, strangled in her own barbed-wire of shalt-not ideals and shalt-not moralisms. While she goes out to work like millions of squirrels in millions of cages. Production!

Let Hell loose, and get your own back, Europe!

Mark Schorer

TWO HOUSES, TWO WAYS: THE FLORENTINE VILLAS OF LEWIS AND LAWRENCE, RESPECTIVELY

*T*wo NOVELISTS both chose more or less to close their worldly accounts near Florence; not in Florence, but in houses just outside it, looking down upon it from different hilltops—Sinclair Lewis' to the south, D. H. Lawrence's to the southwest. The pursuit of these two men, and of what remains of them in the memory of people still in Florence who knew them, leads in fascinatingly divergent directions, but perhaps nothing about them, not even their writing, is so diverse as the houses they lived in. These were, in reality, their last houses although neither died here; at the end each staggered away from Florence in the weary daze of his ultimate illness, Lewis for only a few months to the lakes and then to Rome, Lawrence, for less than two years, to wander uneasily and then to perch at Bandol and at last to die at Vence one day after he had been removed from a sanatorium called "Ad Astra."

Lewis' house was Villa La Costa. Having the American ear, attuned perhaps first of all to that question, *"Quanto costa?"* you are challenged even before you have seen the house by the unhappy accident of its name to consider its price, and relevant as this sullen intuition proves to be, the name is in fact as ordinary as "Elmwood" or "Lakeview," meaning only the house on the hillside. To reach it most directly, you leave Florence by the Porta Romana and the Viale del Poggio Imperiale, already ascending, and after a sharp, short jog to the left you are on the street you want, the Via del Pian dei Guillari. This is a narrow

461

road that winds up between high, gray stone walls that shut from sight the estates behind them, and all that one sees are occasional heavy, closed gates, olive branches reaching out over the walls, their pale green leaves shimmering in the sunlight, and now and then the top of a towering grove of cypresses, blackly green against the brilliantly clear blue of the Italian sky in spring. Abruptly this road opens into a little country square, the Plain of the Jesters. Here, in the Renaissance and before, troops of traveling buffoons camped at night, for the ground levels out and the square lies at the center of a group of great, ancient houses where employment was certain. And very near here our latter-day jester lived out his jittery life in a very different kind of house.

You continue on out through the square by the same road, again between walls, and presently, after only a few meters, you are outside the walls of Number 124, Villa La Costa. There is the usual bell pull; the gates clang open; and you are confronted by two *carabinieri* in their dark blue uniform with the broad, brilliantly red stripes down each leg, and by a young American air policeman in his lighter blue who emerges from a sentry box just inside the gate. Villa La Costa is now occupied by the commanding officer of the Southern European arm of the Allied Air Forces, Lieutenant-General D. M. Schlatter, and his family. Mrs. Schlatter is a gracious southerner who made this inspection easy.

The house presents not so much a formidable as a blank front, a glare of yellow plaster in the sunlight, with eight or ten windows that seem rather small in such a long expanse, and an enormous, arched, oak door that, like a number of other doors in the house, you later learn, was appropriated by the owner from the storerooms of that great national monument in the city, the Palazzo Strozzi. Inside, such a rude assault is made upon the senses by the accumulated glitter of marble, gilt, dead white paint, glass, and crystal, that it is impossible, at once, to separate this general splendor into its parts. You are, you see, in a foyer as large as a moderately sized living room, your feet upon dark brown letters of marble laid in the beige marble of the floor, the letters forming the words PAX ET BONUM, and at the opposite end of the foyer, similar letters spell out that greeting you may already have observed over the northern gate of Siena, COR TIBI PANDIT. On both sides are expanses of glass, double sets of French doors set in heavy granite arches lined with oak arches. These doors, like all the windows in the house, consist of small leaded panes tinted in light pastel shades—blue, orchid, pink, yellow—and in the arch over each appears a crest of no significance in the history of Florence. PAX ET BONUM. This house was built in 1939, on the foundations of a modest but ancient villa, by a small official then in the Italian consulate at Madrid, and in its showy, shell-like opulence (the walls, under the burden of gilt, are very thin, so that the house rattles with human sounds) it shares with many another Italian monument of those years the atmosphere of minor and ephemeral officialdom on the loose, a truly horrendous taste. The Lewis rent in 1949–1950, when rents in Florence were still quite low, was $150 a month. Now, Villa La Costa is for sale: it can be had for fifty million lire, or about eighty thousand dollars.

The doors to the right open into a drawing room that, while it contains an elegant Strozzi mantelpiece, is nevertheless dominated by a flat and perfectly enormous modern portrait, perhaps five by six feet, of a lady associated with the owner's family, in ballroom dress. Here the relentlessness of marble under the feet is alleviated by rugs, and here stands an elderly servant who was attached to the house when Lewis had it. On the subject with which the world, alas, is most familiar, his drinking, she shows an engaging reticence, offering a few gently sad reflections that do not at all share the brutal tone of the obituary notices which the Florentine newspapers published with such energetic conviction. (*"Quando Arrivò a Firenze,"* reads the headline in *La Nazione,* a highly respectable journal, *"Era Già un Uomo Finito,"* and then quotes with relish in its opening paragraph an anonymous friend who purportedly announced eighteen months before his death that *"Lewis è già morto"*—Lewis is already dead. The obituary itself is not so much the recognition of the passing of a distinguished man as it is a diatribe on the evils of drink—*"il vizio di bere"*—which, we are assured, broke up each of Lewis' three marriages, one more than in fact he had.) The old servant prefers another tone, and repeats over and over again that he was *gentilissimo, gentilissimo,* and ill, ill, ill. At La Costa, she says, he saw very few people, but every day he worked for long hours, on the terrace, in the tower, and he lived, she thought, in some great fear. In the management of the household he had small interest; she took her orders from the secretary. Knowing of Lewis' detailed interest in the management of some earlier houses—at Williamstown, where in his meticulous handwriting he had himself labelled the whole array of keys; at Duluth, where an itemized examination of various materials led to a smashing quarrel

with his decorator—you begin to sense the lonely pathos and perhaps the
terror of his butt-end days. This sense of pathos is not diminished if one
considers another impression, from one of Lewis' new American acquaintances in Florence at that time, that he was enormously proud of La Costa
and all its tinsel. Buried in his Baedeker, determined to master all the
facts of art and architecture, history and hagiography in this city, he, who
always had the sharpest eye for the human phony, yet felt—it is said—
that in La Costa he had found the real thing, the truly elegant Italian
establishment.

Beyond the drawing room is a commodious library that contains
few books. At one end is an enormous fireplace so badly designed that
a fire on the hearth merely pours smoke into the room; to use it at all, a
small firebox on metal legs four or five feet high has been placed inside
the great opening, to bring the fire near the draft. In the drawing room
again, over excellent martinis, one can contemplate the kind of genius
Lewis had for choosing to live in houses that were quite beyond the possibility of being shaken down into homes (the Williamstown house has
been purchased by the Carmelite Order as a monastery), houses that, for
all their richness, are somehow characterized by a gaunt impersonality;
and the kind of genius he had, further, for losing friends, so that in the
end he was surrounded by strangers (his last secretary was an employee
of Cook's whom he had picked up as he contemplated the Giottos at
Assisi), and badly painted portraits of ladies he did not know at all who
were ready for a hypothetical dance with someone else.

Driven all his life, all over the world, from house to house, by his
unmanageable restlessness, he was, perhaps, never at home, only always
wishing to be. His first like his last novel is concerned with a hero who
desires "the land of elsewhere," and then cannot abide it. The last hero
goes to the American Church in Florence and longs for Colorado. "He
knew then that he was unalterably an American; he knew what a special
and mystical experience it is, for the American never really emigrates
but only travels; perhaps travels for two or three generations but at the
end is still marked with the gaunt image of Tecumseh." And how many
Americans there are, how many American writers especially, who are as
little at home out of the United States as they are in them! Certainly this
gaudy villa, so near the Pian dei Guillari, was only another camp for a
dark night.

On our way to the luncheon table, we cross the foyer into a sitting
room about the size of the drawing room, with more white enameled

walls and ornamental gilt embossments, a crystal chandelier large enough
for a theater lobby, a white enameled grand piano that requires a ten-
piece orchestra in white tuxedos and a singer like Ella Fitzgerald, another
even larger portrait of a lady in yards and yards of extravagant chiffon
gown, and, at one end of the room, most remarkable, a stairway that
winds up to the higher floors. Its balustrade is made of Venetian spun
glass in blue and milky white, and the stairs themselves are of that same
slippery beige marble of which the floors are made. Small wonder that
Lewis, with his famously ill-coördinated body, once came plummeting
headlong down these stairs and that thereafter the owner boxed the
balustrade in wood, and that at the bottom, Lewis' servants spread out
all available rugs in the event of another fall! In this hard glitter, what
heart had opened to him?

Beyond the blinding salon is a soberer, shadowed writing room, and
then the pleasantly spacious dining room that opens out onto a capacious
loggia overlooking the terraced, somber garden. We lunch beautifully on
pheasant shot by the General in Germany, and the easy, amiable conversation permits us to reflect on those more melancholy meals that were
served to Lewis at this table. A distinguished British woman of title
whom Lewis met at a cocktail party just before he took La Costa had
told me that, on this occasion, he devoted himself entirely to her and
that, as soon as he had moved into the house, called to say that he wanted
her to be his first dinner guest. She was a new acquaintance whom he
tried to treat as though she were his oldest, dearest friend; and out of
her great respect and great pity, she played his make-believe. (Perry
Miller, in his brilliantly sympathetic *Atlantic* piece, "The Incorruptible
Sinclair Lewis," has made the same point: "We perfected a little fiction
between us that my wife and I, his newest friends, were his oldest and
only friends.") With this British lady he took many drives into the country in his black Studebaker (this was his favorite relaxation—to drive out
to some isolated country *trattoria* and, to understate, sample the wines),
and with her he planned innumerable fascinating journeys abroad, with
detailed itineraries, to be pursued as soon as he had recovered his health.
Beginning in a kind of feverish exaltation, assisted by that nearly inexhaustible gift of verbal improvisation that never left him, he would build
what she calls "fantastic paper castles." They would go here, there, and
then on to that place; always different places, but always planned for
with the same mounting excitement. They would have the most marvel-
ous time! But he believed none of it, and at the pitch of his excitement,

the paper castle suddenly fell apart in the air before him, and then he
fell in upon himself, the long meager body collapsing in a hump on the
table as he groaned, "Oh God, no man has ever been so miserable!" This
misery, recollected in that brash, expensive house, is piercing, for it is the
bright, cold house itself that makes one feel that he might well have been
stating a quite simple truth.

Then there is Father Fosco Martinelli whose church, Santa Mar-
gherita a Montici, is just a few steps up beyond Villa La Costa. It is one
of the oldest churches in the environs of the city and stands at the highest
point of the hills that fall down to the valley of the Arno on one side,
the valley of the Ema on the other. On the Arno side the slopes are covered with guide-book gardens cut out sharply by walls and hedges from
scraggly olive groves; on the Ema side, the small, highly cultivated fields
step down to the river and then rise up from it again, precisely, thriftily,
as carefully tended as flowerbeds, and as different as it is agriculturally
possible to be from the wanton spread of "wheat, a golden sea for miles
about," of which Lewis liked to sing. Father Martinelli is a gravely handsome young man whose study is a rude, plastered cell. Behind the work
table hangs a *certificato al patriota,* signed by Marshal Montgomery, that
attests to his partisan activities, and recently he has published a small
novel for youngsters about boys in the partisan movement—*I Romani
Siamo Noi.* Propped up on top of a wardrobe is an unframed expressionist
painting in oil that had been given to Lewis and that Lewis gave to him
on the occasion when Father Martinelli was invited to dine at La Costa.
It was one of those frequent, half-hearted gestures Lewis made in an
attempt to come to know Italians, and like most, a failure. There was a
little preliminary conversation in which Lewis ambiguously said that to
be an artist, one really needed to learn to think in Italian. At the table,
they talked of his work habits and of Italian writers, but Lewis was
remote from the conversation, abstracted in gloom. After dinner he gave
the priest the picture—Christ before the Sanhedrin—"as a remembrance
of this evening," and sank into a chair. When Father Martinelli left,
Lewis said, "Friend, friend, we will see each other often." They never
saw each other again. Was he not interested in the Father's political
views? "That evening he was interested in nothing. An inspiration was
upon him."

One would have to search for a better example of the cultural barrier, for of inspiration there was unhappily very little at La Costa, but
of drudgery, much. The gap that acquaintances could not fill, work

might. We rise from the table and walk out in that loggia where, on fine days, Lewis did much of the writing on *World So Wide* and on those poems that he took to after this last novel. This is the north side of the house and lies entirely in deep shadow. We walk in the garden, contemplating the struggling box hedges, counting cypresses: there are seven. A gardener is raking over hard lumps of clay-ey earth. He says this is where Lewis always walked, alone, in the shadows, back and forth, never on the sunny side of the house. And we are reminded of a prophetic passage in *Our Mr. Wrenn*, his first novel, published in 1915: ". . . his loneliness shadowed him. Of that loneliness one could make many books; how it sat down with him; how he crouched in his chair, bespelled by it, till he violently rose and fled, with loneliness for companion in his flight. He was lonely. He sighed that he was 'lonely as fits.' Lonely—the word obsessed him. Doubtless he was a bit mad, as are all the isolated men who sit in distant lands longing for the voice of friendship."

But mainly he fled into work. According to the recently published collection, *The Man From Main Street,* Lewis finished *Main Street* on a certain day in 1920 "only by working eight hours a day, seven days in most weeks . . . I never worked so hard, and never shall work so hard again." But thirty years later, when he was about to die, he did. His secretary has written that he worked from nine to ten hours every day, and he told Father Martinelli that he got up at five and worked until seven, then had breakfast; at eight he was back at his desk and worked until eleven; at four in the afternoon he returned to it and worked until eight; and then, during the night he would wake up and write some more. It was a kind of fury. In 1941, when Lewis was directing Jack Levin's play, *Good Neighbor,* he described "a working day which, extending from 6 A.M. to midnight, has kept me out of the more vigorous forms of dissipation." But it would seem that, at the end, work itself, more than drink or any other *vizio,* had become the most vigorous of all forms of dissipation, if by dissipation one happens to mean any drugging activity that helps us to forget the intolerable.

But there we are, on the terrace, remembering that (according to the secretary) Lewis had only three demands of a house: a place to work, decent servants' quarters, and the view. We study the view that lies beyond the falling hill: it is of the new, industrialized area of Florence, with none of the monuments that a Florentine would expect in a "view" except, at the extreme left, a section of the cupola of the Duomo; and yet, hideous as it is when you are near it, the new Florence is adequately

far from Villa La Costa to look quite pretty, with its white and yellow
planes in the sunlight. But the best thing in the view is quite near by,
that Torre del Gallo on the site of which John Milton placed Galileo
(". . . the sad Tuscan, who with Optic glass, Exalted, saw the Constella-
tions pass . . ."), and where Lewis in that last novel he was writing located
the villa of Sam Dodsworth, as if to have an old friend near him while he
suffered in the higher splendor of La Costa. Father Martinelli says of
their moment in the loggia, "To the left appeared the city lights; above,
the stars." The observation seems important.

On bad days, Lewis worked in the tower. We mount those giddy
stairs and pause for a moment on the second floor, where, in the large
open hallway, a huge mirror in a floreated gilt frame doubles the vengeance on the eyes of white and gold and crystal-dripping chandelier, and
then, as the stairs continue, we continue up into the square tower that
juts up from the middle of the roof. It is a room about fifteen by fifteen
feet, containing only a large work table and a few straight chairs, and
entirely enclosed in long casement windows made up of hundreds of those
tinted, leaded panes. Here, in full visual command of all his ancient surroundings, he finished his novel about Americans from a town called
Newlife, uneasily attempting to make something of the old.

He could look, if he wished, straight north to Settignano, and on
clear days, with ordinary field glasses, would probably have been able to
pick out the clock tower among the cypresses of I Tatti, the house of his
old friend, Bernard Berenson. Why, in his last year, after the warmest
association beginning on that first day when, a dear friend of a dear
friend, Edith Wharton, he was brought to Berenson—why he let the
friendship lapse, too, is not yet clear, not even to Mr. Berenson. Nor is
the situation made clearer when we observe that in *World So Wide* Lewis
attributes to one of his shabbiest characters, an old fake of a connoisseur,
a remark that, according to the secretary, caused Lewis to lose his temper
at dinner one night at I Tatti; the remark was that civilization ended
with the fall of the Bastille. All that one can be sure of is that if Berenson
made this remark, he made it out of his uncanny instinct for the remark
that will command a rise, which he got—twice. The juggling of values
in this story—Lewis' remembering it at all, then attributing it to a mean
character, then omitting entirely his own response—all this suggests the
self-reproach from which he was suffering. It is shown more simply in
another anecdote. A brilliant Florentine man of letters whose first name
is Arturo has told me with a kind of humorous horror, that after their

first meeting, Lewis called him Art—most insignificant, unless you can hear a distinguished Florentine named Arturo and armed in all the chilly pride of these people speak that nickname, "Art." But then how pathetic it is to find, again in *World So Wide,* the shabbiest American of all saying, "This is . . . Mrs. Baccio . . . married to a fine young Italian businessman, friend of mine, Art Baccio." And, in fact, as one tries to see clearly through all that faintly tinted glass, one's emotion there in Lewis' tower, his last writing place, is almost entirely the emotion of pathos; for it is impossible not to juxtapose the sentimental coziness of entirely fabricated feeling that characterizes the end of his last novel with the desperation of the end of his life there in La Costa: the loneliness, the self-reproach, the shadowed isolation amidst the garish splendor, the desperate shame that kept him from people, especially his true friends, and then always the destructive forgetting. His Florentine doctor warned him: "You will die in the worst way; you will just go down a hole."

We think of this admonition as we go down to look at his bedroom, pausing to peer into two most un-Italian bathrooms, one apple green, one orchid, the two separated by a wall most of which consists of an aquarium where big goldfish sluggishly flaunt themselves. The room is large, but, with all its new green and gold furniture in heavy imitation of the Renaissance style it seems crowded. There is no rest from the gilt: on the doors, on the ceiling, on the fireplace, on the wide headboard of the bed. This is the bed on which Lewis' Florentine doctor first saw him. The occasion was a black, stormy night when he had suffered his initial heart attack, and the decanter on the bedside table contained not water but straight whisky. The doctor is the most fashionable in Florence, a cultivated man who buys pictures and reads widely, and who was more than merely respectfully aware of the great reputation of this new patient. He made it his personal rather than professional business to rehabilitate Sinclair Lewis, but it was a losing struggle. "Only gods and geniuses are as lonely as that man," he says, but then adds that this was a genius with a special problem. As is well known, Lewis suffered for most of his life from a violent form of acne that disfigured his face, and in his last years this ailment had become more acute causing in Lewis a gnawing self-consciousness and shame that impelled him, at last, to cut himself off from the sight of others, especially others who knew him well. Two things spared him: drink, and the dizzying kind of dramatic improvisation into which he loved to throw himself. His gifts of mimicry were great, and his mind, like his memory, like his blue eyes, remained brilliant to the

end (so say all his acquaintances), and with a kind of compulsive exaltation he spun out his verbal fantasies, his imitations, his imaginary travels,
giving his listeners the sometimes uncomfortable feeling that he could
not stop, until the effort reached its peak and suddenly collapsed completely. Then a deeper mood controlled him and sent him to his other
solace, a mood that arose from what his doctor calls the "interior tragedy,
a deep will to death, a real *cupio dissolvi*." We study the bed, and remind
ourselves that he was a novelist who never wrote of death at all. Then
outside a small white cloud moves, and the sunlight suddenly strikes into
the room and dances with a frenzy on the glitter.

In April or May of 1926, D. H. Lawrence, who was careless about
dating his letters, wrote to Dorothy Brett from a Lungarno *pensione* that
"Perhaps now we shall take a little flat in the country here—outside
Florence—for a couple of months, and I wander about to my Etruscans."[1]
How he found Villa Mirenda, isolated in the country beyond that ugly
little town of Scandicci and the mere crossroads of Vingone, I have been
unable to discover, but to find it today is easy enough, since we have only
to follow Lawrence's own directions. "When is your sister Margaret coming out? [This to Rolf Gardiner.] Here we are—if nothing drives us away
—so tell her to come and see us when she will. If she will walk out, then
tram *No.* 16 from the Duomo to *Vingone* to the very terminus and dead
end (½ hour). Then there's another 25 minutes' walk—straight ahead
uphill from Vingone till you come to two cypresses, just beyond the house
marked *Podere Nuovo.* Turn to the left there, and dip into the little
valley. Our house is the square big box on top of the *poggio,* near the
little church of San Paolo."

How the Lawrences found Villa Mirenda remains a mystery, but
why they did is clear enough. Lawrence was suffering with the tubercular
infection that killed him, and from that point of view, he should have
been back on his ranch in Taos, but he could not bring himself to go
back; England was out of the question, he found it so intolerable ("a
kingdom, a tight and unsatisfactory one in which I should die outright
if pinned to it"); he was not at work on a major effort, but he had interested himself in doing a series of essays on Etruscan art and life, and the
monuments of that civilization were scattered all over to the south and
west of Florence; he wanted a particular kind of isolation, separation,

[1] This and other quotations in this article are from *Letters of D. H. Lawrence,* edited
by Aldous Huxley, Viking Press.

loneliness; finally, they needed a *pied à terre,* and they needed it cheaply: they rented Villa Mirenda (or their top half of it) for three thousand lire, which was then twenty-five pounds, or about one hundred and twenty dollars a year. They kept it for two years.

We do not take tram No. 16, but drive out through the Porta San Frediano, and then follow directions and the trolley tracks. Through the long narrow Via Scandicci, with its scaling walls off which posters peel almost as soon as they are pasted up, but on which they are nevertheless pasted in great number—out through this hazardous street we circumspectly ease the second-hand Austin. It is a poor district, and the hazards are not provided by other cars, because there are few, but by the multitude of mule-drawn carts, bicycles, Vespas and Lambrettas, and, since it is a Sunday afternoon, half the Vespas are charging out into the country carrying hunters, their thick thighs splayed widely on the broad seats, their guns strapped to their backs, off to the tidy woods and fields to shoot the small birds, the larks and nightingales, for the markets and their own tables. Twenty-five years ago, when there must have been more birds in Italy than there are now, the hunters bothered Lawrence, who wrote to Aldous Huxley from Villa Mirenda, "Under cover of the mist, the Cacciatori are banging away—it's a wonder they don't blow one another to bits—but I suppose sparrow-shot is small dust. And it's Sunday, *sacra festa.*"

Driving slowly, we peer into the dark one-room dwellings that open immediately upon the street and each of which houses at least one large family, many of them more than one. Here there are no great houses nor a long history to invite our speculation, but only, for block after block, the terrible evidence of the life of the European poor. Then at last the houses thin out, the solid walls of low buildings break up, we pass more rapidly through Vingone, and presently we see a square house painted orange, and under the paint we can still read the words *Podere Nuovo.* We decide to walk, park the car beyond the two cypresses, and proceed uphill. Now we are in open country, and the landscape is soft and still curiously precise, as only Tuscany can be, but the road is narrow, rutted, and covered with loose gravel, and, as bumblingly we climb, we wonder not only whether Sister Margaret ever made it, but, aware of our own clumsy progress, remember also Lawrence's lines about inveterate motorists: ". . . the vibration of the motor-car has bruised their insensitive bottoms into rubber-like deadness." The Lawrences never had a car; they always walked, and not only on this rough road, but on every kind of road all over Europe.

The house is a great square block of whitish-gray stone that stands, like the typical farm villa of Tuscany, alone on its hill, its fields and vineyards falling away from it in all directions, and the matchstick dwellings of the *contadini* scattered here and there among the fields. Our gravel road climbs up toward it, then drops down again, then up once more, and at last we leave the road and climb up to the house by its own circuitous dirt path that brings us to a long, low, peasant house and an iron gate. A woman is spreading bits of laundry on stones in the sun, and we ask if this is Villa Mirenda. It is. Is there a dog? None but this, she tells us, and indicates a sleeping creature near her that has hardly lifted its ears at our approach. So we push open the gate and proceed. Near the great central door of the house, standing open, is a well—again, the characteristically Tuscan well, charming in its symmetry, a round gray stone cylinder perhaps six feet across and ten feet high, simply domed, with a small lion's head looking out in each of the four directions from the base of the dome. At the well is a young girl who is staring curiously at us as we approach. Is the owner at home? She turns her head and calls sharply to the open door, *"Zia! Zia!"* and in a moment her aunt, who is Signora Mirenda, appears, wiping her hands on her white apron. Then the explanations: who we are, why we are there, what we would like. *"Il gran scrittore inglese, Signor Lawrence . . . molto tempo fa, venticinque anni fa . . . abitò a qui?"* we stumble half convinced by her stern, questioning regard that we have surely come to the wrong place in spite of those detailed instructions. But the name of Lawrence brings recognition and a smile; suddenly she understands us and bursts into a string of *si, si, si*'s, and calls her husband with a shout flung over her shoulder. In a moment he appears in the doorway behind her, and now she explains to him, and we are welcomed.

Signor Mirenda appears to be a moderately successful farmer. He is wearing breeches and polished black boots to his knees, a rough jacket, and a curiously high corduroy cap. The boots are new and creak at every step, and the cap remains on his head, inside the house and out, through the entire time of our visit. He explains that the Lawrences used a different entrance, and leads us around the house so that we may enter as they did. How old is the house? *"Quattrocento,"* he replies, but that you do not take seriously, since it is the answer that nearly every Italian gives when you ask about the age of any structure, and you conclude that it is more probably eighteenth or early nineteenth century. At the front of the house are a wide green lawn and pleasant trees and, in line with the door, a straight avenue of cypresses that leads for perhaps a quarter of a mile downhill to the house of the peasants who helped the Lawrences. The double door, a handsome, arched affair painted dark green and standing at the head of five or six wide, stone steps, opens from the inside, and Signora Mirenda appears again.

We enter a large, cool, rather dark room, entirely devoid of furniture, and are startled by the walls, which are decorated with evenly spaced, quite large and very badly painted murals of allegorical subjects, and for a moment we wonder whether it is possible that Lawrence, who first took seriously to painting in this house, could have exercised his talent in these dubious studies of nymphs and clouds and winged heroes. But no; they were painted, Signor Mirenda says, by someone's mother— we cannot be sure whose. They were here in the time of Lawrence? Ah, yes. We do not ask what he thought of them, but go silently up a flight of rather narrow wooden stairs to the second floor.

Now huge keys are produced. The flat is used by Signor Mirenda's brother, but only in the summers, and it is differently furnished, but the rooms are of course the same. The narrow hall in which we are standing divides the apartment in two. Signor Mirenda unlocks one door and shows us into a living room. The floors are of dull red brick. There is a plain tile stove. The thick walls are plastered and scarcely finished off with whitewash. The deep windows are barred with iron grilles. (I have not inquired, but these grilles, which appear so frequently in old Tuscan houses even on high windows, must have been a mode of protection against the more ingenious of those bandits who thrived in such lively numbers in this part of Italy in past centuries.) The furniture is moderately comfortable and scanty. Beyond this room are two ample bedrooms, each containing a large dark bed, a chest, a chair, little else. We remember how Lawrence described the apartment in his *Letters:* "The rooms inside are big and rather bare . . . spacious, rather nice, and very still. Life doesn't cost much here. . . . I told you we'd fix up the *salotto* nice and warm, with matting and stove going and Vallombrosa chairs." The description suits, except that the stove is cold and those particular chairs do not seem to be here.

On the other side of the hall we see three more rooms. First, the kitchen, with an enormous open fireplace that still serves for cooking, the hearth raised about a foot from the floor, a black kettle hanging from a hook over a neat pile of dead ashes. Beyond the kitchen is a room for dining and intimate sitting, and beyond that, another bedroom, smaller.

And that is all. Very simple, very plain, and although the rooms carry
now the musty air of shut-up places, we are vividly reminded of
Lawrence's preferences, of the things he loved and the things he despised,
and particularly of one of these as set down in a poem written late in
his life, perhaps here:

> Some women live for the idiotic furniture of their houses,
> some men live for the conceited furniture of their minds,
> some only live for their emotional furnishing—
>
> and it all amounts to the same thing, furniture,
> usually in "suites."

The house speaks of him, and bears, in fact, an uncanny resemblance to
another house of his that we had previously seen and where he also
lived for exactly two years—at the edge of Taormina, where a vegetable
garden grows just outside the kitchen door and barnyard fowl ener-
getically peck away on the terraces.

Where did Lawrence work? In bad weather, in the *salotto,* but in all
good weather, either in the tower or in the woods. From the narrow hall,
we ascend by tight stairs to the tower. It is not much more than six feet
square, with two deep romanesque arches open to all weather. The sun
streams in, and we look out through one arch to the valley of the Arno
and the whole miniature spectacle of Florence, every dome and tower
as clearly limned as in an old engraving, and to the mountains beyond
it, and immediately below to the vineyards and the olive groves and
the small fields of grain that belong to the Mirendas, and we watch two
white bullocks slowly moving up a field, and near a road, a flock of long-
legged, gray and black sheep munching grass under the supervision of a
placid dog and a girl asleep in a ditch. From the other arch, we look out
at other villas on other hills, at clumps of cypresses like omnipresent senti-
nels, and at the spread of the *pinéta,* the pine woods, where Lawrence
took his daily walks and worked when he could. It is spring, and everything is green and stands out with gemlike clarity, but we remember
Lawrence's reference in a letter written in mistier autumn, to the yellow
leaves dropping from the vines against the barbarous red of sumac.

I begin to take some notes, and when the others thread down the
narrow stairs, I stay behind, for it is possible here, high up and looking

out and down, to feel a number of things that Lawrence felt, chiefly his desire to be out of the social world, to make something positive of his loneliness. In one quarrel after another, he, too, had lost many friends, but he had retained those he wanted ("*Tu stai con me, lo so*," he wrote to one of them from Villa Mirenda). Now, however, he did not want to see even them, and in this outlandish place he was quite safe. Few visitors came. An English couple living in a nearby villa came occasionally—the Wilkinsons, "sort of village arty people who went round with a puppet show, quite nice, and not at all intrusive." The Huxleys, who lived in nearby Forte dei Marmi, the Lawrences saw in this period, but not at Villa Mirenda. A daughter of Frieda Lawrence came once for a short stay. An occasional British friend trekked out from Florence now and then, and the Lawrences went into Florence once or twice a week. But chiefly they had the peasants and themselves. One reason that they took the place was because it was "a region of *no* foreigners." Lawrence knew quite well what he was facing ("Have you built your ship of death, oh, have you?") and he was trying to face it. ". . . people don't mean much to me, especially casuals: them I'd rather be without," he wrote; and, "the Florence society is no menace." He did not want what he could have, and he could not have what he felt he needed. "I suffer badly from being so cut off. But what is one to do? One can't link up with the social unconscious. [This is a letter of August 1927 to Dr. Trigant Burrow.] At times, one is *forced* to be essentially a hermit. I don't want to be. But anything else is either a personal tussle, or a money tussle: sickening: except, of course, just for ordinary acquaintance, which remains acquaintance. One has no real human relations—that is so devastating." Better to have no social relations at all than to have them and pretend that they are real! So he wrote disgustedly to Huxley of Beethoven, "always in love with somebody when he wasn't really, and wanting contacts when he didn't really—part of the crucifixion into isolated individuality—*poveri noi*." Every future holds but one final fact, and what Lawrence loved about Villa Mirenda was that it served to school him in that ultimate isolation.

I never know what people mean when they complain of loneliness.
To be alone is one of life's greatest delights, thinking one's own thoughts,
doing one's own little jobs, seeing the world beyond

and feeling oneself uninterrupted in the rooted connection
with the centre of all things.

In these bare quiet rooms, in this quiet country landscape, the rooted
connection might be found.

> There is nothing to save, now all is lost,
> but a tiny core of stillness in the heart
> like the eye of a violet.

Most of those many poems that Lawrence scribbled in his note-books
toward the end of his life have no interest as poems, but, as I flatten my
palms on the crusty gray walls of his tower and look out toward his pine
woods where just now the violets are blooming, I feel their charge as
facts.

He was ill much of the time, of course—with an illness that could
only be alleviated, not cured, and, in spite of his somewhat fantastic
notions about sickness and health, about the relation of physiology to
temperament, he knew this fact, and knew what he must expect. "My
bronchials," is a kind of refrain in the letters of these years. "I am itchy."
But it was worse than that: "I've been in bed the last eight days with
bronchial haemorrhage—and Dr. Giglioli!" It was this illness quite as
much as his native restlessness, his spirit of *andiamo,* as he called it, that
took the Lawrences away from Villa Mirenda and the Florentine climate
so frequently. Five or six times in two years they left it for a month or
two at a time—for Switzerland, for Germany, for Austria, for Ravello,
even briefly for England—but always to return; and even when they left
it for good, it was the Mirenda that they hoped to find in duplicate
somewhere else. Yet their two years in Villa Mirenda were punctuated
with outbursts of dislike for Italy. "I've had a spell of loathing the Italian
countryside altogether," Lawrence wrote to Earl Brewster, "and feeling
that Italy is no place for a *man* to live in. I nearly decided to go off to
Bavaria. But it all costs so much—and I think the discontent is inside
me, and I'd better abide and wait a bit. But O miserere!—I've taken the
house at least for six months more." In this mood, he could build up his
own "paper castles," and with his own excitement. "I *am* somehow bored
by Italy, and when a place goes against my grain I'm never well in it.
I do really think one is heaps better off in New Mexico—sometimes I

pine for it. Let's go in spring—and you help me chop down trees and irrigate pasture on the ranch. I'm sure you'd be happier—if we were all there. After all one *moves*—and this deadening kind of hopeless-helplessness one has in Europe passes off. Let's all go in March, let's go. I'm sick of Here. . . . And let's make an exhibition of pictures in New York. What fun! For Easter, an exhibition of pictures in New York, then go west. We might afterwards sail to China and India from San Francisco—there's always that door out. Let's do it! Anything, anything to shake off this stupor and have a bit of fun in life, I'd even go to Hell, en route."

If illness and the image of a black ship lay under this restlessness, they also affected in a curious way Lawrence's attitude toward his work. A lethargic indifference, a weary kind of rest after all the high-strung battles, came over him: "In the real summer," he wrote his British publisher, "I always lose interest in literature and publications. The *cicadas* rattle away all day in the trees, the girls sing, cutting the corn with the sickles, the sheaves of wheat lie all the afternoon like people dead asleep in the heat. *E più non si frega.* I don't work, except at an occasional scrap of an article. I don't feel much like doing a book, of any sort. Why do any more books? There are so many, and such a small demand for what there are. So why add to the burden, and waste one's vitality over it. Because it costs one a lot of blood. Here we can live very modestly, and husband our resources. It is as good as earning money, to have very small expenses. *Dunque*—" And to his agent: "I think perhaps it's a waste to write any more novels. I could probably live by little things. I mean in magazines." And yet, he did work, and under circumstances that few except Lawrence among modern writers could have found advantageous: "We have come to the lying in the garden stage, and I go off into the woods to work, where the nightingales have a very gay time singing to me. They are very inquisitive and come nearer to watch me turn a page. They seem to love to see the pages turned." The result of this kind of work was not only the articles that finally made up *Etruscan Places* (which called for a tour of cemeteries to the south and west in March and April of 1927, the essays themselves written rapidly in June when he was back at the Mirenda) but also the revision of all his poetry for the collected edition, that remarkable fable called *The Man Who Died,* a good deal of short work, and the three quite different versions of *Lady Chatterley's Lover,* all written here between February of 1927 and January of 1928. After that, Lawrence waited until June, when his queer friend Orioli, the Florentine bookseller and publisher, produced the private first edition, and then he left.

Downstairs, the others are standing in the doorway to a room off the big, shadowy hall. They are studying two plain chairs and a table, and Signora Mirenda explains that these belonged to the Lawrences, who gave them to the Mirendas when they left Scandicci. The Vallombrosa chairs! They are upright, walnut chairs with slim arms and straw seats, and this one, the signora continues, was his, and that, somewhat less comfortable with its single crosspiece in the center of the back, was hers. The room seems to be used for storage; on the floor, spread out on a large cane mat, are many lemons, and their fragrance fills the room.

The Mirendas invite us into their apartment, and we walk through rooms identical with those upstairs, through the kitchen with the same vast fireplace, and sit around the dining table with them. Signora Mirenda produces a decanter of white Chianti. Theirs? *Si, si.* ("They finished bringing in the grapes on Wednesday, so the whole place smells sourish, from the enormous vats of grapes downstairs, waiting to get a bit squashy, for the men to tread them out.") Now Signor Mirenda produces a photograph album and shows us a dim snapshot of the villa taken by Lawrence for them. Did the Lawrences have servants, we ask. They had the help of the *contadini*, but Lawrence liked to do the marketing himself, walking to and back from Scandicci, and he liked much to work around his house. He cooked, the signora says with a chuckle, and he washed the floors, he washed the clothes. He was very handy with the needle, and he turned his own shirt collars. He was *molto simpatico, molto, molto.* Was Signora Lawrence happy here? They do not know, but she cried much of the time. Did they quarrel? Was he cruel to her? Again, *"Non lo so,"* and the discreet Italian shrug. But he was very kind to the poor.

"The poor" must mean the peasants, of which there were twenty-seven on the place in the Lawrences' time. Lawrence has written in his letters how on each of their two Christmases at Villa Mirenda, they gave a party for all the *contadini*, with a tree brought in from the *pinéta*, presents for all the women and children, cigars for the men. Once, when they returned from Switzerland, all the peasants were "out to meet us, with primroses and violets and scarlet and purple anemones," and the peasants, say the Mirendas, enjoyed Lawrence's pictures and liked to watch him paint them. Lawrence pointed out that in this taste, they were rather different from the British magistrates who ordered the raid on the London gallery where they were shown.

Somewhere in another room a radio begins to sputter over an Italian version of *I Want To Be Happy,* perhaps to the young girl we saw by the well, and it jars the easy flow of reminiscence to a stop. We ask whether we can walk to the wood, and the Mirendas take us on a sunny terrace on the south side of the house and point out the way. From a wicker rack on the wall of the house, Signora Mirenda takes a handful of figs ("great big figs that they call *fiori*") and offers them to us. We thank her and thank her husband, and they come to the door with us and wave as we go.

We take the path through the vineyard that stretches out beyond the well. A turkey puffs and swells at us, and spreads his feathers protectively between us and his unconcerned hens. Eating the figs, we pass the stream where, in warm weather, the Lawrences picnicked ("I can go about in shirt and trousers and sandals, and it's hot, and all relaxed"), and then walk over the fields for about a half mile and presently we are in the woods. They are deep and cool, the umbrella pines old and tall, with straight, thick trunks, and high above, their curious spread of branches. Nearer the ground grow bushier trees with very small dark leaves that one Italian has told me are "elms" (when you solicit this kind of information, most Italians would rather misinform you than tell you nothing at all), and under them and all over the ground is that whole array of spring flowers which Lawrence so liked to catalogue and describe: crocuses and grape hyacinth, primroses and violets, enormous purple anemones, and some heavy-petaled chartreuse lilies that are strange to us. Here Lawrence once found a white orchid, but we find none; and here, in this most Italian wood, he imagined his English forest on the estate of Clifford Chatterley.

Lady Chatterley's Lover, like almost everything that Lawrence wrote, is a protest against the mechanization of human nature. At one point his heroine reflects that "civilized society is insane," and the novel opens with the assertion that "Ours is essentially a tragic age, so we refuse to take it tragically." This is a strange old wood to which Lawrence came every day: he had backed almost entirely out of society in order to give us this measure of it.

Then they moved again. ". . . at a certain point the business of the thistle is to roll and roll on the wind," he wrote about three months before they gave away their chairs and left for good. "We've given up the

Villa Mirenda, and are once more wanderers in the wide, wide world."
Much of what Lawrence wrote at Villa Mirenda was bitter, but the place
seems to have preserved him from his final savagery of feeling. When,
in his tower and in these woods, he worked over his many poems for
the collected edition, he felt, he said, "like an autumn morning, a perfect
maze of gossamer of rhythms and rhymes and loose lines floating in the
air." It was only after he left that he was impelled to write the inscription
for a hypothetical tombstone in Gsteig churchyard: "Departed this life,
etc. etc.—*He was fed up!*"

Here in his woods the nightingales are singing like mad.

By the most direct route, Villa Mirenda is twenty kilometers or about
twelve miles from Villa La Costa; in another measurement they are
light years apart. Yet they are perhaps not so far from each other as one is
from the coal mines of Nottinghamshire, the other from the wheat fields
around Sauk Center, Minnesota. They were different men, Sinclair Lewis
and D. H. Lawrence, very different writers, and they went by different
routes to very different kinds of houses. And they were both a long way
from home.

Mary McCarthy

SETTLING THE COLONEL'S HASH

SEVEN YEARS ago, when I taught in a progressive college, I had a pretty girl student in one of my classes who wanted to be a short-story writer. She was not studying writing with me, but she knew that I sometimes wrote short stories, and one day, breathless and glowing, she came up to me in the hall, to tell me that she had just written a story that her writing teacher, a Mr. Converse, was terribly excited about.

"He thinks it's wonderful," she said, "and he's going to help me fix it up for publication."

I asked what the story was about; the girl was a rather simple being who loved clothes and dates. Her answer had a deprecating tone. It was just about a girl (herself) and some sailors she had met on the train. But then her face, which had looked perturbed for a moment, gladdened.

"Mr. Converse is going over it with me and we're going to put in the symbols."

Another girl in the same college, when asked by us in her sophomore orals why she read novels (one of the pseudo-profound questions that ought never to be put) answered in a defensive flurry: "Well, *of course,* I don't read them to find out what happens to the hero."

At the time, I thought these notions were peculiar to progressive education: it was old-fashioned or regressive to read a novel to find out what happens to the hero or to have a mere experience empty of symbolic pointers. But I now discover that this attitude is quite general, and that readers and students all over the country are in a state of apprehension, lest they read a book or story literally and miss the presence of a symbol. And like everything in America, this search for meanings has

481

become a socially competitive enterprise; the best reader is the one who detects the most symbols in a given stretch of prose. And the benighted reader who fails to find any symbols humbly assents when they are pointed out to him; he accepts his mortification.

I had no idea how far this process had gone until last spring, when I began to get responses to a story I had published in *Harper's*. I say "story" because that was what it was called by *Harper's*. I myself would not know quite what to call it; it was a fragment of autobiography—an account of my meeting with an anti-Semitic army Colonel. It began in the club car of a train going to St. Louis; I was wearing an apple-green shirtwaist and a dark-green skirt and pink earrings; we got into an argument about the Jews. The Colonel was a rather dapper, flashy kind of Irish-American with a worldly blue eye; he took me, he said, for a sculptress, which made me feel, to my horror, that I looked Bohemian and therefore rather suspect. He was full of the usual profound clichés that anti-Semites air, like original epigrams, about the Jews: that he could tell a Jew, that they were different from other people, that you couldn't trust them in business, that some of his best friends were Jews, that he distinguished between a Jew and a kike, and finally that, of course, he didn't agree with Hitler: Hitler went too far: the Jews were human beings.

All the time we talked, and I defended the Jews, he was trying to get my angle, as he called it; he thought it was abnormal for anybody who wasn't Jewish not to feel as he did. As a matter of fact, I have a Jewish grandmother, but I decided to keep this news to myself: I did not want the Colonel to think that I had any interested reason for speaking on behalf of the Jews, that is, that I was prejudiced. In the end, though, I got my come-uppance. Just as we were parting, the Colonel asked me my married name, which is Broadwater, and the whole mystery was cleared up for him, instantly: he supposed I was married to a Jew and that the name was spelled B-r-o-dwater. I did not try to enlighten him; I let him think what he wanted; in a certain sense, he was right; he had unearthed my Jewish grandmother or her equivalent. There were a few details that I must mention to make the next part clear: in my car, there were two nuns, whom I talked to as a distraction from the Colonel and the moral problems he raised. He and I finally had lunch together in the St. Louis railroad station, where we continued the discussion. It was a very hot day. I had a sandwich; he had roast-beef hash. We both had an old-fashioned.

Where Are the Symbols?

The whole point of this "story" was that it really happened; it is written in the first person; I speak of myself in my own name, McCarthy: at the end, I mention my husband's name, Broadwater. When I was thinking about writing the story, I decided not to treat it fictionally; the chief interest, I felt, lay in the fact that it happened, in real life, last summer, to the writer herself, who was a good deal at fault in the incident. I wanted to embarrass myself and, if possible, the reader too.

Yet, strangely enough, many of my readers preferred to think of this account as fiction. I still meet people who ask me, confidentially, "That story of yours about the colonel—was it really true?" It seemed to them perfectly natural that I would write a fabrication, in which I figured under my own name, and sign it, though in my eyes this would be like perjuring yourself in court or forging checks. Shortly after the story was published, I got a kindly letter from a man in Mexico, in which he criticized the menu from an artistic point of view: he thought salads would be better for hot weather and it would be more in character for the narrator-heroine to have a martini. I did not answer the letter, though I was moved to, because I had the sense that he would not understand the distinction between what *ought* to have happened and what *did* happen.

Then in April I got another letter, from an English teacher in a small college in the Middle West, that reduced me to despair. I am going to cite it at length. "My students in freshman English chose to analyze your story, 'Artists in Uniform,' from the March issue of *Harper's*. For a week I heard oral discussions on it and then the students wrote critical analyses. In so far as it is possible, I stayed out of their discussions, encouraging them to read the story closely with your intentions as a guide to their understanding. Although some of them insisted that the story has no other level than the realistic one, most of them decided it has symbolic overtones.

"The question is: how closely do you want the symbols labeled? They wrestled with the nuns, the author's two shades of green with pink accents, with the 'materialistic godlessness' of the Colonel. . . . A surprising number wanted exact symbols; for example, they searched for the significance of the Colonel's eating hash and the author eating a sandwich. . . . From my standpoint, the story was an entirely satisfactory springboard

for understanding the various shades of prejudice, for seeing how much
of the artist goes into his painting. If it is any satisfaction to you, our
campus was alive with discussion about 'Artists in Uniform.' We liked
the story and we thought it amazing that an author could succeed in
making readers dislike the author—for a purpose, of course!"

I probably should have answered this letter, but I did not. The gulf
seemed to me too wide. I could not applaud the backward students who
insisted that the story has no other level than the realistic one without
giving offense to their teacher, who was evidently a well-meaning person.
But I shall try now to address a reply, not to this teacher and her unfortunate class, but to a whole school of misunderstanding. There were no
symbols in this story; there was no deeper level. The nuns were in the
story because they were on the train; the contrasting greens were the
dress I happened to be wearing; the Colonel had hash because he had
hash; materialistic godlessness meant just what it means when a priest
thunders it from the pulpit—the phrase, for the first time, had meaning
for me as I watched and listened to the Colonel.

But to clarify the misunderstanding, one must go a little further and
try to see what a literary symbol is. Now in one sense, the Colonel's hash
and my sandwich can be regarded as symbols; that is, they typify the
Colonel's food tastes and mine. (The man in Mexico had different food
tastes which he wished to interpose into our reality.) The hash and the
sandwich might even be said to show something very obvious about our
characters and bringing-up, or about our sexes; I was a woman, he was a
man. And though on another day I might have ordered hash myself, that
day I did not, because the Colonel and I, in our disagreement, were
polarizing each other.

The hash and the sandwich, then, could be regarded as symbols of
our disagreement, almost conscious symbols. And underneath our discussion of the Jews, there was a thin sexual current running, as there
always is in such random encounters or pickups (for they have a strong
suggestion of the illicit). The fact that I ordered something conventionally feminine and he ordered something conventionally masculine represented, no doubt, our awareness of a sexual possibility; even though I
was not attracted to the Colonel, nor he to me, the circumstances of our
meeting made us define ourselves as a woman and a man.

The sandwich and the hash were our provisional, *ad hoc* symbols
of ourselves. But in this sense all human actions are symbolic because
they represent the person who does them. If the Colonel had ordered a

fruit salad with whipped cream, this too would have represented him in some way; given his other traits, it would have pointed to a complexity in his character that the hash did not suggest.

In the same way, the contrasting greens of my dress were a symbol of my taste in clothes and hence representative of me—all too representative, I suddenly saw, in the club car, when I got an "artistic" image of myself flashed back at me from the men's eyes. I had no wish to stylize myself as an artist, that is, to parade about as a symbol of flamboyant unconventionality, but apparently I had done so unwittingly when I picked those colors off a rack, under the impression that they suited me or "expressed my personality" as salesladies say.

My Clothes and the Two Nuns

My dress, then, was a symbol of the perplexity I found myself in with the Colonel; I did not want to be categorized as a member of a peculiar minority—an artist or a Jew; but brute fate and the Colonel kept resolutely cramming me into both those uncomfortable pigeonholes. I wished to be regarded as ordinary or rather as universal, to be anybody and therefore everybody (that is, in one sense, I wanted to be on the Colonel's side, majestically above minorities); but every time the Colonel looked at my dress and me in it with my pink earrings I shrank to minority status, and felt the dress in the heat shriveling me, like the shirt of Nessus, the centaur, that consumed Hercules.

But this is not what the students meant when they wanted the symbols "labeled." They were searching for a more recondite significance than that afforded by the trite symbolism of ordinary life, in which a dress is a social badge. They supposed that I was engaging in literary or artificial symbolism, which would lead the reader out of the confines of reality into the vast fairy tale of myth, in which the color green would have an emblematic meaning (or did the two greens signify for them what the teacher calls "shades" of prejudice), and the Colonel's hash, I imagine, would be some sort of Eucharistic mincemeat.

Apparently, the presence of the nuns assured them there were overtones of theology; it did not occur to them (a) that the nuns were there because pairs of nuns are a standardized feature of summer Pullman travel, like crying babies, and perspiring business men in the club car, and (b) that if I thought the nuns worth mentioning, it was also because of something very simple and directly relevant: the nuns and the Colonel and I all had something in common—we had all at one time been

Catholics—and I was seeking common ground with the Colonel, from which to turn and attack his position.

In any account of reality, even a televised one, which comes closest to being a literal transcript or replay, some details are left out as irrelevant (though nothing is really irrelevant). The details that are not eliminated have to stand as symbols of the whole, like stenogaphic signs, and of course there is an art of selection, even in a newspaper account: the writer, if he has any ability, is looking for the revealing detail that will sum up the picture for the reader in a flash of recognition.

But the art of abridgment and condensation, which is familiar to anybody who tries to relate an anecdote or give a direction—the art of natural symbolism, which is at the basis of speech and all representation —has at bottom a centripetal intention. It hovers over an object, an event, or series of events and tries to declare what it is. Analogy (that is, comparison to other objects) is inevitably one of its methods. "The weather was soupy," *i.e.*, like soup. "He wedged his way in," *i.e.*, he had to enter, thin edge first, as a wedge enters, and so on. All this is obvious. But these metaphorical aids to communication are a far cry from literary symbolism, as taught in the schools and practiced by certain fashionable writers. Literary symbolism is centrifugal and flees from the object, the event, into the incorporeal distance, where concepts are taken for substance and floating ideas and archetypes assume a hieratic authority.

In this dream-forest, symbols become arbitrary; all counters are interchangeable; anything can stand for anything else. The Colonel's hash can be a Eucharist or a cannibal feast or the banquet of Atreus, or all three, so long as the actual dish set before the actual man is disparaged. What is depressing about this insistent symbolization is the fact that while it claims to lead to the infinite, it quickly reaches very finite limits—there are only so many myths on record, and once you have got through Bulfinch, the Scandinavian, and the Indian, there is not much left. And if all stories reduce themselves to myth and symbol, qualitative differences vanish, and there is only a single, monotonous story.

American fiction of the symbolist school demonstrates this mournful truth, without precisely intending to. A few years ago, when the mode was at its height, chic novels and stories fell into three classes: those which had a Greek myth for their framework, which the reader was supposed to detect, like finding the faces in the clouds in old newspaper puzzle contests; those which had symbolic modern figures, dwarfs, hermaphrodites, and cripples, illustrating maiming and loneliness; and those which contained symbolic animals, cougars, wild cats, and monkeys. One young novelist, a product of the Princeton school of symbolism, had all three elements going at once, like the ringmaster of a three-ring circus, with the freaks, the animals, and the statues.

The Mystery of Mr. Bloom

The quest for symbolic referents had, as its object, of course the deepening of the writer's subject and the reader's awareness. But the result was paradoxical. At the very moment when American writing was penetrated by the symbolic urge, it ceased to be able to create symbols of its own. Babbitt, I suppose, was the last important symbol to be created by an American writer; he gave his name to a type that henceforth would be recognizable to everybody. He passed into the language. The same thing could be said, perhaps, though to a lesser degree, of Caldwell's Tobacco Road, Eliot's Prufrock, and possibly of Faulkner's Snopeses. The discovery of new symbols is not the only function of a writer, but the writer who cares about this must be fascinated by reality itself, as a butterfly collector is fascinated by the glimpse of a new specimen. Such a specimen was Mme. Bovary or M. Homais or M. de Charlus or Jupien: these specimens were precious to their discoverers, not because they repeated an age-old pattern but because their markings were new. Once the specimen has been described, the public instantly spots other examples of the kind, and the world seems suddenly full of Babbitts and Charlus, where none had been noted before,

A different matter was Joyce's Mr. Bloom. Mr. Bloom can be called a symbol of eternal recurrence—the wandering Jew, Ulysses the voyager— but he is a symbol thickly incarnate, fleshed out in a Dublin advertising canvasser. He is not *like* Ulysses or vaguely suggestive of Ulysses; he is Ulysses, circa 1905. Joyce evidently believed in a cyclical theory of history, in which everything repeated itself; he also subscribed in youth to the doctrine of the Incarnation, which declares that the Host, a piece of bread, is also God's body and blood. How it can be both things at the same time, consubstantially, is a mystery, and Mr. Bloom is just such a mystery: Ulysses in the visible appearance of a Dublin advertising-canvasser.

Mr. Bloom is not a symbol of Ulysses, but Ulysses-Bloom together, one and indivisible, symbolize or rather demonstrate eternal recurrence. I hope I make myself clear. The point is consubstantiation: Bloom and Ulysses are transfused into each other and neither reality is diminished. Both realities are locked together, like the protons and neutrons of an atom. *Finnegans Wake* is a still more ambitious attempt to create a fusion, this time a myriad fusion, and to exemplify the mystery of how a thing can be itself and at the same time be something else. The world is many and it is also one.

But the clarity and tension of Joyce's thought brought him closer in a way to the strictness of allegory than to the diffuse practices of latter-day symbolists. In Joyce, the equivalences and analogies are very sharp and distinct and the real world is almost querulously audible, like the voices of the washerwomen on the Liffey that come into Earwicker's dream. But this was not true of Joyce's imitators or of the imitators of his imitators, for whom reality is only a shadowy pretext for the introduction of a whole *corps de ballet* of dancing symbols in mythic draperies and animal skins.

Let me make a distinction. There are some great writers, like Joyce or Melville, who have consciously introduced symbolic elements into their work; and there are great writers who have written fables or allegories. In both cases, the writer makes it quite clear to the reader how he is to be read; only an idiot would take *Pilgrim's Progress* for a realistic story, and even a young boy, reading *Moby Dick,* realizes that there is something more than whale-fishing here, though he cannot be sure what it is. But the great body of fiction contains only what I have called natural symbolism, in which selected events represent or typify a problem, a kind of society or psychology, a philosophical theory, in the same way they do in real life. What happens to the hero becomes of the highest importance. This symbolism needs no abstruse interpretation and abstruse interpretation will only lead the reader away from the reality that the writer is trying to press on his attention.

I will give an example or two of what I mean by natural symbolism and I will begin with a rather florid one: Henry James's *The Golden Bowl.* This is the story of a rich American girl who collects European objects. One of these objects is a husband, a Prince Amerigo, who proves to be unfaithful. Early in the story, there is a visit to an antique shop in which the Prince picks out a gold bowl for his fiancée and finds, to his annoyance, that it is cracked. It is not hard to see that the cracked bowl is a symbol, both of the Prince himself, who is a valuable antique but a little flawed, morally, and also of the marriage, which represents an act of acquisition or purchase on the part of the heroine and her father. If the reader should fail to notice the analogy, James himself helps him out in the title.

I myself would not regard the introduction of this symbol as necessary to this particular history; it seems to me, rather, an ornament of the kind that was fashionable in the architecture and interior decoration of the period, like stylized sheaves of corn or wreaths on the façade of a house. Nevertheless, it is handsome and has an obvious appropriateness to the theme. It leads the reader into the gilded matter of the novel, rather than away from it. I think there is also a scriptural echo in the title that conveys the idea of punishment. But having seen and felt the weight of meaning that James put in this symbol, one must not be tempted to go further and look at the bowl as a female sex symbol, a chalice, the Holy Grail, and so on; a book is not a pious excuse for reciting a litany of associations.

My second example is from Tolstoy's *Anna Karenina*. At the beginning of the novel, Anna meets the man who will be her lover, Vronsky, on the Moscow-St. Petersburg express; as they meet, there has been an accident; a workman has been killed by the train coming into the station. This is the beginning of Anna's doom, which is completed when she throws herself under a train and is killed; and the last we see of Vronsky is in a train, with a toothache; he is being seen off by a friend to the wars. The train is necessary to the plot of the novel, and I believe it is also symbolic, both of the iron forces of material progress that Tolstoy hated so and that played a part in Anna's moral destruction, and also of those iron laws of necessity and consequence that govern human action when it remains on the sensual level.

One can read the whole novel, however, without being aware that the train is a symbol; we do not have to "interpret" to feel the import of doom and loneliness conveyed by the train's whistle—the same import we ourselves can feel when we hear a train go by in the country, even today. Tolstoy was a greater artist than James, and one cannot be certain that the train was a conscious device with him. The appropriateness to Anna's history may have been only a *felt* appropriateness; everything in Tolstoy has such a supreme naturalness that one shrinks from attributing contrivance to him, as if it were a sort of fraud. Yet he worked very hard on his novels—I forget how many times the Countess Tolstoy copied out *War and Peace* by hand.

The Right Tone

The impression one gets from his diaries is that he wrote by ear; he speaks repeatedly, even as an old man, of having to start a story over again because he has the wrong tone, and I suspect that he did not think of the train as a symbol but that it sounded "right" to him, because it was, in that day, an almost fearsome emblem of ruthless and impersonal force, not only to a writer of genius but to the poorest peasant who watched it pass through the fields. And in Tolstoy's case, I think it would be impossible, even for the most fanciful critic, to extricate the train from the novel and try to make it bear a meaning that the novel itself does not proclaim, explicitly and tacitly, on every page. Every detail in Tolstoy has an almost cruel and vise-like meaningfulness and truth to itself that makes it tautological to talk of symbolism; he was a moralist and to him the tiniest action, even the curiosities of physical appearance, Vronsky's bald spot, the small white hands of Prince Andrei, told a moral tale.

It is now considered very old-fashioned and tasteless to speak of an author's "philosophy of life" as something that can be harvested from his work. Actually, most of the great authors did have a "philosophy of life" which they were eager to communicate to the public: this was one of their motives for writing. And to disentangle a moral philosophy from a work that evidently contains one is far less damaging to the author's purpose and the integrity of his art than to violate his imagery by symbol-hunting, as though reading a novel were a sort of paper chase.

The images of a novel or a story belong, as it were, to a family, very closely knit and inseparable from each other; the parent "idea" of a story or a novel generates events and images all bearing a strong family resemblance. And to understand a story or a novel, you must look for the parent "idea," which is usually in plain view, if you read quite carefully and literally what the author says.

I will go back, for a moment, to my own story, to show how this can be done. Clearly, it is about the Jewish question, for that is what the people are talking about. It also seems to be about artists, since the title is "Artists in Uniform." Then there must be some relation between artists and Jews. What is it? They are both minorities that other people claim to be able to recognize by their appearance. But artists and Jews do not care for this categorization; they want to be universal, that is, like everybody else. But this aim is really hopeless, for life has formed them as Jews or artists, in a way that immediately betrays them to the majority they are trying to melt into. In my conversation with the Colonel, I was endeavoring to play a double game. I was trying to force him into a minority by treating anti-Semitism as an aberration, which, in fact, I believe it is. On his side, the Colonel resisted this attempt and tried to show that anti-Semitism was normal, and he was normal, while I was the queer one. He declined to be categorized as an anti-Semite; he regarded himself as an independent thinker, who by a happy chance thought the same as every-body else.

I imagined I had a card up my sleeve; I had guessed that the Colonel was Irish *(i.e.,* that he belonged to a minority) and presumed that he was a Catholic. I did not see how he could possibly guess that I, with my Irish name and Irish appearance, had a Jewish grandmother in the back-ground. Therefore when I found I had not convinced him by reasoning, I played my last card; I told him that the Church, his Church, forbade anti-Semitism. I went even further; I implied that God forbade it, though I had no right to do this, since I did not believe in God, but was only using Him as a whip to crack over the Colonel, to make him feel humble and inferior, a raw Irish Catholic lad under discipline. But the Colonel, it turned out, did not believe in God, either, and I lost. And since, in a sense, I had been cheating all along in this game we were playing, I had to concede the Colonel a sort of moral victory in the end; I let him think that my husband was Jewish and that that "explained" everything sat-isfactorily.

Better Than a Human Being

Now there are a number of morals or meanings in this little tale, starting with the simple one: don't talk to strangers on a train. The chief moral or meaning (what I learned, in other words, from this experience) was this: you cannot be a universal unless you accept the fact that you are a singular, that is, a Jew or an artist or what-have-you. What the Colonel and I were discussing, and at the same time illustrating and en-acting, was the definition of a human being. I was trying to be something better than a human being; I was trying to be the voice of pure reason; and pride went before a fall. The Colonel, without trying, was being something worse than a human being, and somehow we found ourselves on the same plane—facing each other, like mutually repellent twins. Or, put it another way: it is dangerous to be drawn into discussions of the Jews with anti-Semites: you delude yourself that you are spreading light, but you are really sinking into muck; if you endeavor to be dispassionate, you are really claiming for yourself a privileged position, a little moun-tain top, from which you look down, impartially, on both the Jews and the Colonel.

Anti-Semitism is a horrible disease from which nobody is immune, and it has a kind of evil fascination that makes an enlightened person draw near the source of infection, supposedly in a scientific spirit, but really to sniff the vapors and dally with the possibility. The enlightened person who lunches with the Colonel in order, as she tells herself, to improve him, is cheating herself, having her cake and eating it. This attempted cheat, on my part, was related to the question of the artist and the green dress; I wanted to be an artist but not to pay the price of looking like one, just as I was willing to have Jewish blood but not willing to show it, where it would cost me something—the loss of superiority in an argument.

These meanings are all there, quite patent, to anyone who consents to look *into* the story. They were *in* the experience itself, waiting to be found and considered. I did not perceive them all at the time the experience was happening; otherwise, it would not have taken place, in all probability—I should have given the Colonel a wide berth. But when I went back over the experience, in order to write it, I came upon these meanings, protruding at me, as it were, from the details of the occasion. I put in the green dress and my mortification over it because they were part of the truth, just as it had occurred, but I did not see how they were related to the general question of anti-Semitism and my grandmother until they *showed* me their relation in the course of writing.

Every short story, at least for me, is a little act of discovery. A cluster of details presents itself to my scrutiny, like a mystery that I will understand in the course of writing or sometimes not fully until afterward, when, if I have been honest and listened to these details carefully, I will find that they are connected and that there is a coherent pattern. This pattern is *in* experience itself; you do not impose it from the outside and if you try to, you will find that the story is taking the wrong tack, dribbling away from you into artificiality or inconsequence. A story that you do not learn something from while you are writing it, that does not illuminate something for you, is dead, finished before you started it. The "idea" of a story is implicit in it, on the one hand; on the other hand, it is always ahead of the writer, like a form dimly discerned in the distance; he is working *toward* the "idea."

It can sometimes happen that you begin a story thinking that you know the "idea" of it and find, when you are finished, that you have said something quite different and utterly unexpected to you. Most writers have been haunted all their lives by the "idea" of a story or a novel that they think they want to write and see very clearly: Tolstoy always wanted to write a novel about the Decembrists and instead, almost against his will, wrote *War and Peace*; Henry James thought he wanted to write a novel about Napoleon. Probably these ideas for novels were too set in their creators' minds to inspire creative discovery.

In any work that is truly creative, I believe, the writer cannot be omniscient in advance about the effects that he proposes to produce. The suspense in a novel is not only in the reader, but in the novelist himself, who is intensely curious too about what will happen to the hero. Jane Austen may know in a general way that Emma will marry Mr. Knightly in the end (the reader knows this too, as a matter of fact); the suspense for the author lies in the how, in the twists and turns of circumstance, waiting but as yet unknown, that will bring the consummation about. Hence, I would say to the student of writing that outlines, patterns, arrangements of symbols may have a certain usefulness at the outset for some kinds of minds, but in the end they will have to be scrapped. If the story does not contradict the outline, overrun the pattern, break the symbols, like an insurrection against authority, it is surely a still birth. The natural symbolism of reality has more messages to communicate than the dry Morse code of the disengaged mind.

The tree of life, said Hegel, is greener than the tree of thought; I have quoted this before but I cannot forbear from citing it again in this context. This is not an incitement to mindlessness or an endorsement of realism in the short story (there are several kinds of reality, including interior reality); it means only that the writer must be, first of all, a listener and observer, who can pay attention to reality, like an obedient pupil, and who is willing, always, to be surprised by the messages reality is sending through to him. And if he gets the messages correctly he will not have to go back and put in the symbols; he will find that the symbols are there, staring at him significantly from the commonplace.

Edward Sapir

LANGUAGE DEFINED

SPEECH is so familiar a feature of daily life that we rarely pause to define it. It seems as natural to man as walking, and only less so than breathing. Yet it needs but a moment's reflection to convince us that this naturalness of speech is but an illusory feeling. The process of acquiring speech is, in sober fact, an utterly different sort of thing from the process of learning to walk. In the case of the latter function, culture, in other words, the traditional body of social usage, is not seriously brought into play. The child is individually equipped, by the complex set of factors, that we term biological heredity, to make all the needed muscular and nervous adjustments that result in walking. Indeed, the very conformation of these muscles and of the appropriate parts of the nervous system may be said to be primarily adapted to the movements made in walking and in similar activities. In a very real sense the normal human being is predestined to walk, not because his elders will assist him to learn the art, but because his organism is prepared from birth, or even from the moment of conception, to take on all those expenditures of nervous energy and all those muscular adaptations that result in walking. To put it concisely, walking is an inherent, biological function of man.

Not so language. It is of course true that in a certain sense the individual is predestined to talk, but that is due entirely to the circumstance that he is born not merely in nature, but in the lap of a society that is certain, reasonably certain, to lead him to its traditions. Eliminate society and there is every reason to believe that he will learn to walk, if, indeed, he survives at all. But it is just as certain that he will never learn to talk, that is, to communicate ideas according to the traditional system

494

of a particular society. Or, again, remove the new-born individual from the social environment into which he has come and transplant him to an utterly alien one. He will develop the art of walking in his new environment very much as he would have developed it in the old. But his speech will be completely at variance with the speech of his native environment. Walking, then, is a general human activity that varies only within circumscribed limits as we pass from individual to individual. Its variability is involuntary and purposeless. Speech is a human activity that varies without assignable limit as we pass from social group to social group, because it is a purely historical heritage of the group, the product of long-continued social usage. It varies as all creative effort varies—not as consciously, perhaps, but none the less as truly as do the religions, the beliefs, the customs, and the arts of different peoples. Walking is an organic, an instinctive, function (not, of course, itself an instinct); speech is a non-instinctive, acquired, "cultural" function.

There is one fact that has frequently tended to prevent the recognition of language as a merely conventional system of sound symbols, that has seduced the popular mind into attributing to it an instinctive basis that it does not really possess. This is the well-known observation that under the stress of emotion, say of a sudden twinge of pain or of unbridled joy, we do involuntarily give utterance to sounds that the hearer interprets as indicative of the emotion itself. But there is all the difference in the world between such involuntary expression of feeling and the normal type of communication of ideas that is speech. The former kind of utterance is indeed instinctive, but it is non-symbolic; in other words, the sound of pain or the sound of joy does not, as such, indicate the emotion, it does not stand aloof, as it were, and announce that such and such an emotion is being felt. What it does is to serve as a more or less automatic overflow of the emotional energy; in a sense, it is part and parcel of the emotion itself. Moreover, such instinctive cries hardly constitute communication in any strict sense. They are not addressed to any one, they are merely overheard, if heard at all, as the bark of a dog, the sound of approaching footsteps, or the rustling of the wind is heard. If they convey certain ideas to the hearer, it is only in the very general sense in which any and every sound or even any phenomenon in our environment may be said to convey an idea to the perceiving mind. If the involuntary cry of pain which is conventionally represented by "Oh!" be looked upon as a true speech symbol equivalent to some such idea as "I am in great pain," it is just as allowable to interpret the appearance of clouds as an equivalent symbol that carries the definite message "It is likely to rain." A definition of language, however, that is so extended as to cover every type of inference becomes utterly meaningless.

The mistake must not be made of identifying our conventional interjections (our oh! and ah! and sh!) with the instinctive cries themselves. These interjections are merely conventional fixations of the natural sounds. They therefore differ widely in various languages in accordance with the specific phonetic genius of each of these. As such they may be considered an integral portion of speech, in the properly cultural sense of the term, being no more identical with the instinctive cries themselves than such words as "cuckoo" and "killdeer" are identical with the cries of the birds they denote or than Rossini's treatment of a storm in the overture to "William Tell" is in fact a storm. In other words, the interjections and sound-imitative words of normal speech are related to their natural prototypes as is art, a purely social or cultural thing, to nature. It may be objected that, though the interjections differ somewhat as we pass from language to language, they do nevertheless offer striking family resemblances and may therefore be looked upon as having grown up out of a common instinctive base. But their case is nowise different from that, say of the varying national modes of pictorial representation. A Japanese picture of a hill both differs from and resembles a typical modern European painting of the same kind of hill. Both are suggested by and both "imitate" the same natural feature. Neither the one nor the other is the same thing as, in any intelligible sense, a direct outgrowth of, this natural feature. The two modes of representation are not identical because they proceed from differing historical traditions, are executed with differing pictorial techniques. The interjections of Japanese and English are, just so, suggested by a common natural prototype, the instinctive cries, and are thus unavoidably suggestive of each other. They differ, now greatly, now but little, because they are builded out of historically diverse materials or techniques, the respective linguistic traditions, phonetic systems, speech habits of the two peoples. Yet the instinctive cries as such are practically identical for all humanity, just as the human skeleton or nervous system is to all intents and purposes a "fixed," that is, an only slightly and "accidentally" variable, feature of man's organism.

Interjections are among the least important of speech elements. Their discussion is valuable mainly because it can be shown that even they, avowedly the nearest of all language sounds to instinctive utterance, are only superficially of an instinctive nature. Were it therefore possible to demonstrate that the whole of language is traceable, in its ultimate historical and psychological foundations, to the interjections, it would still not follow that language is an instinctive activity. But, as a matter of fact, all attempts so to explain the origin of speech have been fruitless. There is no tangible evidence, historical or otherwise, tending to show that the mass of speech elements and speech processes has evolved out of the interjections. These are a very small and functionally insignificant proportion of the vocabulary of language; at no time and in no linguistic province that we have record of do we see a noticeable tendency towards their elaboration into the primary warp and woof of language. They are never more, at best, than a decorative edging to the ample, complex fabric.

What applies to the interjections applies with even greater force to the sound-imitative words. Such words as "whippoorwill," "to mew," "to caw" are in no sense natural sounds that man has instinctively or automatically reproduced. They are just as truly creations of the human mind, flights of the human fancy, as anything else in language. They do not directly grow out of nature, they are suggested by it and play with it. Hence the onomatopoetic theory of the origin of speech, the theory that would explain all speech as a gradual evolution from sounds of an imitative character, really brings us no nearer to the instinctive level than is language as we know it to-day. As to the theory itself, it is scarcely more credible than its interjectional counterpart. It is true that a number of words which we do not now feel to have a sound-imitative value can be shown to have once had a phonetic form that strongly suggests their origin as imitations of natural sounds. Such is the English word "to laugh." For all that, it is quite impossible to show, nor does it seem intrinsically reasonable to suppose, that more than a negligible proportion of the elements of speech or anything at all of its formal apparatus is derivable from an onomatopoetic source. However much we may be disposed on general principles to assign a fundamental importance in the languages of primitive peoples to the imitation of natural sounds, the actual fact of the matter is that these languages show no particular preference for imitative words. Among the most primitive peoples of aboriginal America, the Athabaskan tribes of the Mackenzie River speak languages in which such words seem to be nearly or entirely absent, while they are used freely enough in languages as sophisticated as English and

German. Such an instance shows how little the essential nature of speech is concerned with the mere imitation of things.

The way is now cleared for a serviceable definition of language. Language is a purely human and non-instinctive method of communicating ideas, emotions, and desires by means of a system of voluntarily produced symbols. These symbols are, in the first instance, auditory and they are produced by the so-called "organs of speech." There is no discernible instinctive basis in human speech as such, however much instinctive expressions and the natural environment may serve as a stimulus for the development of certain elements of speech, however much instinctive tendencies, motor and other, may give a predetermined range or mold to linguistic expression. Such human or animal communication, if "communication" it may be called, as is brought about by involuntary, instinctive cries is not, in our sense, language at all.

I have just referred to the "organs of speech," and it would seem at first blush that this is tantamount to an admission that speech itself is an instinctive, biologically predetermined activity. We must not be misled by the mere term. There are, properly speaking, no organs of speech; there are only organs that are incidentally useful in the production of speech sounds. The lungs, the larynx, the palate, the nose, the tongue, the teeth, and the lips, are all so utilized, but they are no more to be thought of as primary organs of speech than are the fingers to be considered as essentially organs of piano-playing or the knees as organs of prayer. Speech is not a simple activity that is carried on by one or more organs biologically adapted to the purpose. It is an extremely complex and ever-shifting network of adjustments—in the brain, in the nervous system, and in the articulating and auditory organs—tending towards the desired end of communication. The lungs developed, roughly speaking, in connection with the necessary biological function known as breathing; the nose, as an organ of smell; the teeth, as organs useful in breaking up food before it was ready for digestion. If, then, these and other organs are being constantly utilized in speech, it is only because any organ, once existent and in so far as it is subject to voluntary control, can be utilized by man for secondary purposes. Physiologically, speech is an overlaid function, or, to be more precise, a group of overlaid functions. It gets what service it can out of organs and functions, nervous and muscular, that have come into being and are maintained for very different ends than its own.

It is true that physiological psychologists speak of the localization of speech in the brain. This can only mean that the sounds of speech are localized in the auditory tract of the brain, or in some circumscribed portion of it, precisely as other classes of sounds are localized; and that the motor processes involved in speech (such as the movements of the glottal cords in the larynx, the movements of the tongue required to pronounce the vowels, lip movements required to articulate certain consonants, and numerous others) are localized in the motor tract precisely as are all other impulses to special motor activities. In the same way control is lodged in the visual tract of the brain over all those processes of visual recognition involved in reading. Naturally the particular points or clusters of points of localization in the several tracts that refer to any element of language are connected in the brain by paths of association, so that the outward, or psycho-physical, aspect of language is of a vast network of associated localizations in the brain and lower nervous tracts, the auditory localizations being without doubt the most fundamental of all for speech. However, a speech-sound localized in the brain, even when associated with the particular movements of the "speech organs" that are required to produce it, is very far from being an element of language. It must be further associated with some element or group of elements of experience, say a visual image or a class of visual images or a feeling of relation, before it has even rudimentary linguistic significance. This "element" of experience is the content or "meaning" of the linguistic unit; the associated auditory, motor, and other cerebral processes that lie immediately back of the act of speaking and the act of hearing speech are merely a complicated symbol of or signal for these "meanings," of which more anon. We see therefore at once that language as such is not and cannot be definitely localized, for it consists of a peculiar symbolic relation—physiologically an arbitrary one—between all possible elements of consciousness on the one hand and certain selected elements localized in the auditory, motor, and other cerebral and nervous tracts on the other. If language can be said to be definitely "localized" in the brain, it is only in that general and rather useless sense in which all aspects of consciousness, all human interest and activity, may be said to be "in the brain." Hence, we have no recourse but to accept language as a fully formed functional system within man's psychic or "spiritual" constitution. We cannot define it as an entity in psycho-physical terms alone, however much the psycho-physical basis is essential to its functioning in the individual.

From the physiologist's or psychologist's point of view we may seem to be making an unwarrantable abstraction in desiring to handle the subject of speech without constant and explicit reference to that basis.

However, such an abstraction is justifiable. We can profitably discuss the intention, the form, and the history of speech, precisely as we discuss the nature of any other phase of human culture—say art or religion—as an institutional or cultural entity, leaving the organic and psychological mechanisms back of it as something to be taken for granted. Accordingly, it must be clearly understood that this introduction to the study of speech is not concerned with those aspects of physiology and of physiological psychology that underlie speech. Our study of language is not to be one of the genesis and operation of a concrete mechanism; it is, rather, to be an inquiry into the function and form of the arbitrary systems of symbolism that we term languages.

I have already pointed out that the essence of language consists in the assigning of conventional, voluntarily articulated, sounds, or of their equivalents, to the diverse elements of experience. The word "house" is not a linguistic fact if by it is meant merely the acoustic effect produced on the ear by its constituent consonants and vowels, pronounced in a certain order; nor the motor processes and tactile feelings which make up the articulation of the word; nor the visual perception on the part of the hearer of this articulation; nor the visual perception of the word "house" on the written or printed page; nor the motor processes and tactile feelings which enter into the writing of the word; nor the memory of any or all of these experiences. It is only when these, and possibly still other, associated experiences are automatically associated with the image of a house that they begin to take on the nature of a symbol, a word, an element of language. But the mere fact of such an association is not enough. One might have heard a particular word spoken in an individual house under such impressive circumstances that neither the word nor the image of the house ever recur in consciousness without the other becoming present at the same time. This type of association does not constitute speech. The association must be a purely symbolic one; in other words, the word must denote, tag off, the image, must have no other significance than to serve as a counter to refer to it whenever it is necessary or convenient to do so. Such an association, voluntary and, in a sense, arbitrary as it is, demands a considerable exercise of self-conscious attention. At least to begin with, for habit soon makes the association nearly as automatic as any and more rapid than most.

But we have traveled a little too fast. Were the symbol "house"— whether an auditory, motor, or visual experience or image—attached but to the single image of a particular house once seen, it might perhaps, by an indulgent criticism, be termed an element of speech, yet it is obvious at the outset that speech so constituted would have little or no value for purposes of communication. The world of our experiences must be enormously simplified and generalized before it is possible to make a symbolic inventory of all our experiences of things and relations and this inventory is imperative before we can convey ideas. The elements of language, the symbols that ticket off experience, must therefore be associated with whole groups, delimited classes, of experience rather than with the single experiences themselves. Only so is communication possible, for the single experience lodges in an individual consciousness and is, strictly speaking, incommunicable. To be communicated it needs to be referred to a class which is tacitly accepted by the community as an identity. Thus, the single impression which I have had of a particular house must be identified with all my other impressions of it. Further, my generalized memory or my "notion" of this house must be merged with the notions that all other individuals who have seen the house have formed of it. The particular experience that we started with has now been widened so as to embrace all possible impressions or images that sentient beings have formed or may form of the house in question. This first simplification of experience is at the bottom of a large number of elements of speech, the so-called proper nouns or names of single individuals or objects. It is, essentially, the type of simplification which underlies, or forms the crude subject of, history and art. But we cannot be content with this measure of reduction of the infinity of experience. We must cut to the bone of things, we must more or less arbitrarily throw whole masses of experience together as similar enough to warrant their being looked upon—mistakenly, but conveniently—as identical. This house and that house and thousands of other phenomena of like character are thought of as having enough in common, in spite of great and obvious differences of detail, to be classed under the same heading. In other words, the speech element "house" is the symbol, first and foremost, not of a single perception, nor even of the notion of a particular object, but of a "concept," in other words, of a convenient capsule of thought that embraces thousands of distinct experiences and that is ready to take in thousands more. If the single significant elements of speech are the symbols of concepts, the actual flow of speech may be interpreted as a record of the setting of these concepts into mutual relations.

The question has often been raised whether thought is possible without speech; further, if speech and thought be not but two facets of the same psychic process. The question is all the more difficult because it has been hedged about by misunderstandings. In the first place, it is well to observe that whether or not thought necessitates symbolism, that is speech, the flow of language itself is not always indicative of thought. We have seen that the typical linguistic element labels a concept. It does not follow from this that the use to which language is put is always or even mainly conceptual. We are not in ordinary life so much concerned with concepts as such as with concrete particularities and specific relations. When I say, for instance, "I had a good breakfast this morning," it is clear that I am not in the throes of laborious thought, that what I have to transmit is hardly more than a pleasurable memory symbolically rendered in the grooves of habitual expression. Each element in the sentence defines a separate concept or conceptual relation or both combined, but the sentence as a whole has no conceptual significance whatever. It is somewhat as though a dynamo capable of generating enough power to run an elevator were operated almost exclusively to feed an electric doorbell. The parallel is more suggestive than at first sight appears. Language may be looked upon as an instrument capable of running a gamut of psychic uses. Its flow not only parallels that of the inner content of consciousness, but parallels it on different levels, ranging from the state of mind that is dominated by particular images to that in which abstract concepts and their relations are alone at the focus of attention and which is ordinarily termed reasoning. Thus the outward form only of language is constant; its inner meaning, its psychic value or intensity, varies freely with attention or the selective interest of the mind, also, needless to say, with the mind's general development. From the point of view of language, thought may be defined as the highest latent or potential content of speech, the content that is obtained by interpreting each of the elements in the flow of language as possessed of its very fullest conceptual value. From this it follows at once that language and thought are not strictly coterminous. At best language can but be the outward facet of thought on the highest, most generalized, level of symbolic expression. To put our viewpoint somewhat differently, language is primarily a pre-rational function. It humbly works up to the thought that is latent in, that may eventually be read into, its classifications and its forms; it is not, as is generally but naïvely assumed, the final label put upon the finished thought.

Most people, asked if they can think without speech, would probably answer, "Yes, but it is not easy for me to do so. Still I know it can be done." Language is but a garment! But what if language is not so much a garment as a prepared road or groove? It is, indeed, in the highest degree likely that language is an instrument originally put to uses lower than the conceptual plane and that thought arises as a refined interpretation of its content. The product grows, in other words, with the instrument, and thought may be no more conceivable, in its genesis and daily practice, without speech than is mathematical reasoning practicable without the lever of an appropriate mathematical symbolism. No one believes that even the most difficult mathematical proposition is inherently dependent on an arbitrary set of symbols, but it is impossible to suppose that the human mind is capable of arriving at or holding such a proposition without the symbolism. The writer, for one, is strongly of the opinion that the feeling entertained by so many that they can think, or even reason, without language is an illusion. The illusion seems to be due to a number of factors. The simplest of these is the failure to distinguish between imagery and thought. As a matter of fact, no sooner do we try to put an image into conscious relation with another than we find ourselves slipping into a silent flow of words. Thought may be a natural domain apart from the artificial one of speech, but speech would seem to be the only road we know of that leads to it. A still more fruitful source of the illusive feeling that language may be dispensed with in thought is the common failure to realize that language is not identical with its auditory symbolism. The auditory symbolism may be replaced, point for point, by a motor or by a visual symbolism (many people can read, for instance, in a purely visual sense, that is, without the intermediating link of an inner flow of the auditory images that correspond to the printed or written words) or by still other, more subtle and elusive, types of transfer that are not so easy to define. Hence the contention that one thinks without language merely because he is not aware of a coexisting auditory imagery is very far indeed from being a valid one. One may go so far as to suspect that the symbolic expression of thought may in some cases run along outside the fringe of the conscious mind, so that the feeling of a free, non-linguistic stream of thought is for minds of a certain type a relatively, but only a relatively, justified one. Psychophysically, this would mean that the auditory or equivalent visual or motor centers in the brain, together with the appropriate paths of association, that are the cerebral equivalent of speech, are touched off so lightly during the process of thought as not to rise into consciousness at all. This would be a limiting case—thought riding lightly on the submerged crests of speech, instead of jogging along with it, hand in hand.

The modern psychology has shown us how powerfully symbolism is at work in the unconscious mind. It is therefore easier to understand at the present time than it would have been twenty years ago that the most rarefied thought may be but the conscious counterpart of an unconscious linguistic symbolism.

One word more as to the relation between language and thought. The point of view that we have developed does not by any means preclude the possibility of the growth of speech being in a high degree dependent on the development of thought. We may assume that language arose pre-rationally—just how and on what precise level of mental activity we do not know—but we must not imagine that a highly developed system of speech symbols worked itself out before the genesis of distinct concepts and of thinking, the handling of concepts. We must rather imagine that thought processes set in, as a kind of psychic overflow, almost at the beginning of linguistic expression; further, that the concept, once defined, necessarily reacted on the life of its linguistic symbol, encouraging further linguistic growth. We see this complex process of the interaction of language and thought actually taking place under our eyes. The instrument makes possible the product, the product refines the instrument. The birth of a new concept is invariably foreshadowed by a more or less strained or extended use of old linguistic material; the concept does not attain to individual and independent life until it has found a distinctive linguistic embodiment. In most cases the new symbol is but a thing wrought from linguistic material already in existence in ways mapped out by crushingly despotic precedents. As soon as the word is at hand, we instinctively feel, with something of a sigh of relief, that the concept is ours for the handling. Not until we own the symbol do we feel that we hold a key to the immediate knowledge or understanding of the concept. Would we be so ready to die for "liberty," to struggle for "ideals," if the words themselves were not ringing within us? And the word, as we know, is not only a key; it may also be a fetter.

Language is primarily an auditory system of symbols. In so far as it is articulated it is also a motor system, but the motor aspect of speech is clearly secondary to the auditory. In normal individuals the impulse to speech first takes effect in the sphere of auditory imagery and is then transmitted to the motor nerves that control the organs of speech. The motor processes and the accompanying motor feelings are not, however, the end, the final resting point. They are merely a means and a control leading to auditory perception in both speaker and hearer. Communication, which is the very object of speech, is successfully effected only when the hearer's auditory perceptions are translated into the appropriate and intended flow of imagery or thought or both combined. Hence the cycle of speech, in so far as we may look upon it as a purely external instrument, begins and ends in the realm of sounds. The concordance between the initial auditory imagery and the final auditory perceptions is the social seal or warrant of the successful issue of the process. As we have already seen, the typical course of this process may undergo endless modifications or transfers into equivalent systems without thereby losing its essential formal characteristics.

The most important of these modifications is the abbreviation of the speech process involved in thinking. This has doubtless many forms, according to the structural or functional peculiarities of the individual mind. The least modified form is that known as "talking to one's self" or "thinking aloud." Here the speaker and the hearer are identified in a single person, who may be said to communicate with himself. More significant is the still further abbreviated form in which the sounds of speech are not articulated at all. To this belong all the varieties of silent speech and of normal thinking. The auditory centers alone may be excited; or the impulse to linguistic expression may be communicated as well to the motor nerves that communicate with the organs of speech but be inhibited either in the muscles of these organs or at some point in the motor nerves themselves; or, possibly, the auditory centers may be only slightly, if at all, affected, the speech process manifesting itself directly in the motor sphere. There must be still other types of abbreviation. How common is the excitation of the motor nerves in silent speech, in which no audible or visible articulations result, is shown by the frequent experience of fatigue in the speech organs, particularly in the larynx, after unusually stimulating reading or intensive thinking.

All the modifications so far considered are directly patterned on the typical process of normal speech. Of very great interest and importance is the possibility of transferring the whole system of speech symbolism into other terms than those that are involved in the typical process. This process, as we have seen, is a matter of sounds and of movements intended to produce these sounds. The sense of vision is not brought into play. But let us suppose that one not only hears the articulated sounds but sees the articulations themselves as they are being executed by the speaker. Clearly, if one can only gain a sufficiently high degree of adroitness in perceiving these movements of the speech organs, the way is opened for a new type of speech symbolism—that in which the sound is replaced by the visual image of the articulations that correspond to the sound. This sort of system has no great value for most of us because we are already possessed of the auditory-motor system of which it is at best but an imperfect translation, not all the articulations being visible to the eye. However, it is well known what excellent use deaf-mutes can make of "reading from the lips" as a subsidiary method of apprehending speech. The most important of all visual speech symbolisms is, of course, that of the written or printed word, to which, on the motor side, corresponds the system of delicately adjusted movements which result in the writing or typewriting or other graphic method of recording speech. The significant feature for our recognition in these new types of symbolism, apart from the fact that they are no longer a by-product of normal speech itself, is that each element (letter or written word) in the system corresponds to a specific element (sound or sound-group or spoken word) in the primary system. Written language is thus a point-to-point equivalence, to borrow a mathematical phrase, to its spoken counterpart. The written forms are secondary symbols of the spoken ones—symbols of symbols—yet so close is the correspondence that they may, not only in theory but in the actual practice of certain eye-readers and, possibly, in certain types of thinking, be entirely substituted for the spoken ones. Yet the auditory-motor associations are probably always latent at the least, that is, they are unconsciously brought into play. Even those who read and think without the slightest use of sound imagery are, at last analysis, dependent on it. They are merely handling the circulating medium, the money, of visual symbols as a convenient substitute for the economic goods and services of the fundamental auditory symbols.

The possibilities of linguistic transfer are practically unlimited. A familiar example is the Morse telegraph code, in which the letters of written speech are represented by a conventionally fixed sequence of longer or shorter ticks. Here the transfer takes place from the written word rather than directly from the sounds of spoken speech. The letter of the telegraph code is thus a symbol of a symbol of a symbol. It does not, of course, in the least follow that the skilled operator, in order to arrive at an understanding of a telegraphic message, needs to transpose the individual sequence of ticks into a visual image of the word before he experiences its normal auditory image. The precise method of reading off speech from the telegraphic communication undoubtedly varies widely with the individual. It is even conceivable, if not exactly likely, that certain operators may have learned to think directly, so far as the purely conscious part of the process of thought is concerned, in terms of the tick-auditory symbolism or, if they happen to have a strong natural bent toward motor symbolism, in terms of the correlated tactile-motor symbolism developed in the sending of telegraphic messages.

Still another interesting group of transfers are the different gesture languages, developed for the use of deaf-mutes, of Trappist monks vowed to perpetual silence, or of communicating parties that are within seeing distance of each other but are out of earshot. Some of these systems are one-to-one equivalences of the normal system of speech; others, like military gesture-symbolism or the gesture language of the Plains Indians of North America (understood by tribes of mutually unintelligible forms of speech) are imperfect transfers, limiting themselves to the rendering of such grosser speech elements as are an imperative minimum under difficult circumstances. In these latter systems, as in such still more imperfect symbolisms as those used at sea or in the woods, it may be contended that language no longer properly plays a part but that the ideas are directly conveyed by an utterly unrelated symbolic process or by a quasi-instinctive imitativeness. Such an interpretation would be erroneous. The intelligibility of these vaguer symbolisms can hardly be due to anything but their automatic and silent translation into the terms of a fuller flow of speech.

We shall no doubt conclude that all voluntary communication of ideas, aside from normal speech, is either a transfer, direct or indirect, from the typical symbolism of language as spoken and heard or, at the least, involves the intermediary of truly linguistic symbolism. This is a fact of the highest importance. Auditory imagery and the correlated motor imagery leading to articulation are, by whatever devious ways we follow the process, the historic fountain-head of all speech and of all thinking. One other point is of still greater importance. The ease with which speech symbolism can be transferred from one sense to another, from technique to technique, itself indicates that the mere sounds of speech are not the essential fact of language, which lies rather in the classification, in the formal patterning, and in the relating of concepts. Once more, language, as a structure, is on its inner face the mold of thought. It is this abstracted language, rather more than the physical facts of speech, that is to concern us in our inquiry.

There is no more striking general fact about language than its universality. One may argue as to whether a particular tribe engages in activities

that are worthy of the name of religion or of art, but we know of no
people that is not possessed of a fully developed language. The lowliest
South African Bushman speaks in the forms of a rich symbolic system
that is in essence perfectly comparable to the speech of the cultivated
Frenchman. It goes without saying that the more abstract concepts are
not nearly so plentifully represented in the language of the savage, nor is
there the rich terminology and the finer definition of nuances that reflect
the higher culture. Yet the sort of linguistic development that parallels
the historic growth of culture and which, in its later stages, we associate
with literature is, at best, but a superficial thing. The fundamental
groundwork of language—the development of a clear-cut phonetic system,
the specific association of speech elements with concepts, and the delicate
provision for the formal expression of all manner of relations—all this
meets us rigidly perfected and systematized in every language known to
us. Many primitive languages have a formal richness, a latent luxuriance
of expression, that eclipses anything known to the languages of modern
civilization. Even in the mere matter of the inventory of speech the layman must be prepared for strange surprises. Popular statements as to the
extreme poverty of expression to which primitive languages are doomed
are simply myths. Scarcely less impressive than the universality of speech
is its almost incredible diversity. Those of us that have studied French or
German, or, better yet, Latin or Greek, know in what varied forms a
thought may run. The formal divergences between the English plan and
the Latin plan, however, are comparatively slight in the perspective of
what we know of more exotic linguistic patterns. The universality and the
diversity of speech lead to a significant inference. We are forced to believe
that language is an immensely ancient heritage of the human race,
whether or not all forms of speech are the historical outgrowth of a single
pristine form. It is doubtful if any other cultural asset of man, be it the
art of drilling for fire or of chipping stone, may lay claim to a greater
age. I am inclined to believe that it antedated even the lowliest developments of material culture, that these developments, in fact, were not
strictly possible until language, the tool of significant expression, had
itself taken shape.

George Orwell

POLITICS AND THE
ENGLISH LANGUAGE

*M*ost people who bother with the matter at all would admit that
the English language is in a bad way, but it is generally assumed
that we cannot by conscious action do anything about it. Our civilization
is decadent and our language—so the argument runs—must inevitably
share in the general collapse. It follows that any struggle against the abuse
of language is a sentimental archaism, like preferring candles to electric
light or hansom cabs to aeroplanes. Underneath this lies the half-conscious
belief that language is a natural growth and not an instrument which
we shape for our own purposes.

Now, it is clear that the decline of a language must ultimately have
political and economic causes: it is not due simply to the bad influence
of this or that individual writer. But an effect can become a cause, re-
inforcing the original cause and producing the same effect in an intensified
form, and so on indefinitely. A man may take to drink because he feels
himself to be a failure, and then fail all the more completely because he
drinks. It is rather the same thing that is happening to the English language. It becomes ugly and inaccurate because our thoughts are foolish,
but the slovenliness of our language makes it easier for us to have foolish
thoughts. The point is that the process is reversible. Modern English,
especially written English, is full of bad habits which spread by imitation
and which can be avoided if one is willing to take the necessary trouble.
If one gets rid of these habits one can think more clearly, and to think
clearly is a necessary first step towards political regeneration: so that the
fight against bad English is not frivolous and is not the exclusive concern

of professional writers. I will come back to this presently, and I hope that by that time the meaning of what I have said here will have become clearer. Meanwhile, here are five specimens of the English language as it is now habitually written.

These five passages have not been picked out because they are especially bad—I could have quoted far worse if I had chosen—but because they illustrate various of the mental vices from which we now suffer. They are a little below the average, but are fairly representative samples. I number them so that I can refer back to them when necessary:

(1) I am not, indeed, sure whether it is not true to say that the Milton who once seemed not unlike a seventeenth-century Shelley had not become, out of an experience ever more bitter in each year, more alien [*sic*] to the founder of that Jesuit sect which nothing could induce him to tolerate.

> Professor Harold Laski (Essay in *Freedom of Expression*)

(2) Above all, we cannot play ducks and drakes with a native battery of idioms which prescribes such egregious collocations of vocables as the Basic *put up with* for *tolerate* or *put at a loss* for *bewilder*.

> Professor Lancelot Hogben (*Interglossa*)

(3) On the one side we have the free personality: by definition it is not neurotic, for it has neither conflict nor dream. Its desires, such as they are, are transparent, for they are just what institutional approval keeps in the forefront of consciousness; another institutional pattern would alter their number and intensity; there is little in them that is natural, irreducible, or culturally dangerous. But *on the other side,* the social bond itself is nothing but the mutual reflection of these self-secure integrities. Recall the definition of love. Is not this the very picture of a small academic? Where is there a place in this hall of mirrors for either personality or fraternity?

> Essay on psychology in *Politics* (New York)

(4) All the "best people" from the gentlemen's clubs, and all the frantic fascist captains, united in common hatred of Socialism and bestial horror of the rising tide of the mass revolutionary movement, have turned to acts of provocation, to foul incendiarism, to medieval legends of poisoned wells, to legalize their own destruction of proletarian organizations, and rouse the agitated petty-bourgeoisie to chauvinistic fervor on behalf of the fight against the revolutionary way out of the crisis.

> Communist pamphlet

(5) If a new spirit is to be infused into this old country, there is one thorny and contentious reform which must be tackled, and that is the humanization and galvanization of the B.B.C. Timidity here will bespeak canker and atrophy of the soul. The heart of Britain may be sound and of strong beat, for instance, but the British lion's roar at present is like that of Bottom in Shakespeare's *Midsummer Night's Dream*—as gentle as any sucking dove. A virile new Britain cannot continue indefinitely to be traduced in the eyes, or rather ears, of the world by the effete languors of Langham Place, brazenly masquerading as "standard English." When the Voice of Britain is heard at nine o'clock, better far and infinitely less ludicrous to hear aitches honestly dropped than the present priggish, inflated, inhibited, school-ma'amish arch braying of blameless bashful mewing maidens!

Letter in *Tribune*

Each of these passages has faults of its own, but, quite apart from avoidable ugliness, two qualities are common to all of them. The first is staleness of imagery; the other is lack of precision. The writer either has a meaning and cannot express it, or he inadvertently says something else, or he is almost indifferent as to whether his words mean anything or not. This mixture of vagueness and sheer incompetence is the most marked characteristic of modern English prose, and especially of any kind of political writing. As soon as certain topics are raised, the concrete melts into the abstract and no one seems able to think of turns of speech that are not hackneyed: prose consists less and less of *words* chosen for the sake of their meaning, and more and more of *phrases* tacked together like the sections of a prefabricated hen-house. I list below, with notes and examples, various of the tricks by means of which the work of prose-construction is habitually dodged:

Dying metaphors. A newly invented metaphor assists thought by evoking a visual image, while on the other hand a metaphor which is technically "dead" (e.g. *iron resolution*) has in effect reverted to being an ordinary word and can generally be used without loss of vividness. But in between these two classes there is a huge dump of worn-out metaphors which have lost all evocative power and are merely used because they save people the trouble of inventing phrases for themselves. Examples are: *Ring the changes on, take up the cudgels for, toe the line, ride roughshod over, stand shoulder to shoulder with, play into the hands of, no axe to grind, grist to the mill, fishing in troubled waters, on the order of the day, Achilles' heel, swan song, hotbed.* Many of these are used without knowledge of their meaning (what is a "rift," for instance?), and incompatible metaphors are frequently mixed, a sure sign that the writer is not interested in what he is saying. Some metaphors now current have been twisted out of their original meaning without those who use them even being aware of the fact. For example, *toe the line* is sometimes written *tow the line.* Another example is *the hammer and the anvil,* now always used with the implication that the anvil gets the worst of it. In real life it is always the anvil that breaks the hammer, never the other way about: a writer who stopped to think what he was saying would be aware of this, and would avoid perverting the original phrase.

Operators or *verbal false limbs.* These save the trouble of picking out appropriate verbs and nouns, and at the same time pad each sentence with extra syllables which give it an appearance of symmetry. Characteristic phrases are *render inoperative, militate against, make contact with, be subjected to, give rise to, give grounds for, have the effect of, play a leading part (role) in, make itself felt, take effect, exhibit a tendency to, serve the purpose of, etc., etc.* The keynote is the elimination of simple verbs. Instead of being a single word, such as *break, stop, spoil, mend, kill,* a verb becomes a *phrase,* made up of a noun or adjective tacked on to some general-purpose verb such as *prove, serve, form, play, render.* In addition, the passive voice is wherever possible used in preference to the active, and noun constructions are used instead of gerunds (*by examination of* instead of *by examining*). The range of verbs is further cut down by means of the *-ize* and *de-* formations, and the banal statements are given an appearance of profundity by means of the *not un-* formation. Simple conjunctions and prepositions are replaced by such phrases as *with respect to, having regard to, the fact that, by dint of, in view of, in the interests of, on the hypothesis that;* and the ends of sentences are saved by anticlimax by such resounding common-places as *greatly to be desired, cannot be left out of account, a development to be expected in the near future, deserving of serious consideration, brought to a satisfactory conclusion,* and so on and so forth.

Pretentious diction. Words like *phenomenon, element, individual* (as noun), *objective, categorical, effective, virtual, basic, primary, promote, constitute, exhibit, exploit, utilize, eliminate, liquidate,* are used to dress up simple statements and give an air of scientific impartiality to biased judgments. Adjectives like *epoch-making, epic, historic, unforgettable, triumphant, age-old, inevitable, inexorable, veritable,* are used to dignify the sordid processes of international politics, while writing that aims at glorifying war usually takes on an archaic color, its characteristic words being: *realm, throne, chariot, mailed fist, trident, sword, shield, buckler, banner, jackboot, clarion.* Foreign words and expressions such as *cul de sac, ancien régime, deus ex machina, mutatis mutandis, status quo, gleichschaltung, weltanschauung,* are used to give an air of culture and elegance. Except for the useful abbreviations *i.e., e.g.,* and *etc.,* there is no real need for any of the hundreds of foreign phrases now current in English. Bad writers, and especially scientific, political and sociological writers, are nearly always haunted by the notion that Latin or Greek words are grander than Saxon ones, and unnecessary words like *expedite, ameliorate, predict, extraneous, deracinated, clandestine, subaqueous* and hundreds of others constantly gain ground from their Anglo-Saxon opposite numbers.[1] The jargon peculiar to Marxist writing (*hyena, hangman, cannibal, petty bourgeois, these gentry, lacquey, flunkey, mad dog, White Guard,* etc.) consists largely of words and phrases translated from Russian, German or French; but the normal way of coining a new word is to use a Latin or Greek root with the appropriate affix and, where necessary, the size formation. It is often easier to make up words of this kind (*deregionalize, impermissible, extramarital, non-fragmentary* and so forth) than to think up the English words that will cover one's meaning. The result, in general, is an increase in slovenliness and vagueness.

Meaningless words. In certain kinds of writing, particularly in art criticism and literary criticism, it is normal to come across long passages which are almost completely lacking in meaning.[2] Words like *romantic, plastic, values, human, dead, sentimental, natural, vitality,* as used in art criticism, are strictly meaningless, in the sense that they not only do not

[1] An interesting illustration of this is the way in which the English flower names which were in use till very recently are being ousted by Greek ones, *snapdragon* becoming *antirrhinum, forget-me-not* becoming *myosotis,* etc. It is hard to see any practical reason for this change of fashion: it is probably due to an instinctive turning-away from the more homely word and a vague feeling that the Greek word is scientific.

[2] Example: "Comfort's catholicity of perception and image, strangely Whitmanesque in range, almost the exact opposite in aesthetic compulsion, continues to evoke that trembling atmospheric accumulative hinting at a cruel, an inexorably serene timelessness. . . . Wrey Gardiner scores by aiming at simple bull's-eyes with precision. Only they are not so simple, and through this contented sadness runs more than the surface bitter-sweet of resignation." (*Poetry Quarterly.*)

point to any discoverable object, but are hardly ever expected to do so by the reader. When one critic writes, "The outstanding feature of Mr. X's work is its living quality," while another writes, "The immediately striking thing about Mr. X's work is its peculiar deadness," the reader accepts this as a simple difference of opinion. If words like *black* and *white* were involved, instead of the jargon words *dead* and *living,* he would see at once that language was being used in an improper way. Many political words are similarly abused. The word *Fascism* has now no meaning except in so far as it signifies "something not desirable." The words *democracy, socialism, freedom, patriotic, realistic, justice,* have each of them several different meanings which cannot be reconciled with one another. In the case of a word like *democracy,* not only is there no agreed definition, but the attempt to make one is resisted from all sides. It is almost universally felt that when we call a country democratic we are praising it: consequently the defenders of every kind of régime claim that it is a democracy, and fear that they might have to stop using the word if it were tied down to any one meaning. Words of this kind are often used in a consciously dishonest way. That is, the person who uses them has his own private definition, but allows his hearer to think he means something quite different. Statements like *Marshal Pétain was a true patriot, The Soviet Press is the freest in the world, The Catholic Church is opposed to persecution,* are almost always made with intent to deceive. Other words used in variable meanings, in most cases more or less dishonestly, are: *class, totalitarian, science, progressive, reactionary, bourgeois, equality.*

Now that I have made this catalogue of swindles and perversions, let me give another example of the kind of writing that they lead to. This time it must of its nature be an imaginary one. I am going to translate a passage of good English into modern English of the worst sort. Here is a well-known verse from *Ecclesiastes:*

"I returned and saw under the sun, that the race is not to the swift, nor the battle to the strong, neither yet bread to the wise, nor yet riches to men of understanding, nor yet favour to men of skill; but time and chance happeneth to them all."

Here it is in modern English:

"Objective consideration of contemporary phenomena compels the conclusion that success or failure in competitive activities exhibits no tendency to be commensurate with innate capacity, but that a considerable element of the unpredictable must invariably be taken into account."

This is a parody, but not a very gross one. Exhibit (3), above, for instance, contains several patches of the same kind of English. It will be seen that I have not made a full translation. The beginning and ending of the sentence follow the original meaning fairly closely, but in the middle the concrete illustrations—race, battle, bread—dissolve into the vague phrase "success or failure in competitive activities." This had to be so, because no modern writer of the kind I am discussing—no one capable of using phrases like "objective consideration of contemporary phenomena"—would ever tabulate his thoughts in that precise and detailed way. The whole tendency of modern prose is away from concreteness. Now analyse these two sentences a little more closely. The first contains forty-nine words but only sixty syllables, and all its words are those of everyday life. The second contains thirty-eight words of ninety syllables: eighteen of its words are from Latin roots, and one from Greek. The first sentence contains six vivid images, and only one phrase ("time and chance") that could be called vague. The second contains not a single fresh, arresting phrase, and in spite of its ninety syllables it gives only a shortened version of the meaning contained in the first. Yet without a doubt it is the second kind of sentence that is gaining ground in modern English. I do not want to exaggerate. This kind of writing is not yet universal, and outcrops of simplicity will occur here and there in the worst-written page. Still, if you or I were told to write a few lines on the uncertainty of human fortunes, we should probably come much nearer to my imaginary sentence than to the one from *Ecclesiastes.*

As I have tried to show, modern writing at its worst does not consist in picking out words for the sake of their meaning and inventing images in order to make the meaning clearer. It consists in gumming together long strips of words which have already been set in order by someone else, and making the results presentable by sheer humbug. The attraction of this way of writing is that it is easy. It is easier—even quicker, once you have the habit—to say *In my opinion it is not an unjustifiable assumption that* than to say *I think.* If you use ready-made phrases, you not only don't have to hunt about for words; you also don't have to bother with the rhythms of your sentences, since these phrases are generally so arranged as to be more or less euphonious. When you are composing in a hurry—when you are dictating to a stenographer, for instance, or making a public speech—it is natural to fall into a pretentious, Latinized style. Tags like *a consideration which we should do well to bear in mind* or *a conclusion to which all of us would readily assent* will save many a sentence from coming down with a bump. By using stale metaphors,

similes and idioms, you save much mental effort, at the cost of leaving
your meaning vague, not only for your reader but for yourself. This is the
significance of mixed metaphors. The sole aim of a metaphor is to call up
a visual image. When these images clash—as in *The Fascist octopus has
sung its swan song, the jackboot is thrown into the melting pot*—it can
be taken as certain that the writer is not seeing a mental image of the
objects he is naming; in other words he is not really thinking. Look again
at the examples I gave at the beginning of this essay. Professor Laski (1)
uses five negatives in fifty-three words. One of these is superfluous, making
nonsense of the whole passage, and in addition there is the slip *alien* for
akin, making further nonsense, and several avoidable pieces of clumsiness
which increase the general vagueness. Professor Hogben (2) plays ducks
and drakes with a battery which is able to write prescriptions, and, while
disapproving of the everyday phrase *put up with,* is unwilling to look
egregious up in the dictionary and see what it means; (3), if one takes an
uncharitable attitude towards it, is simply meaningless: probably one
could work out its intended meaning by reading the whole of the article
in which it occurs. In (4), the writer knows more or less what he wants to
say, but an accumulation of stale phrases chokes him like tea leaves blocking a sink. In (5), words and meaning have almost parted company.
People who write in this manner usually have a general emotional meaning—they dislike one thing and want to express solidarity with another—
but they are not interested in the detail of what they are saying. A scrupulous writer, in every sentence that he writes, will ask himself at least four
questions, thus: What am I trying to say? What words will express it?
What image or idiom will make it clearer? Is this image fresh enough to
have an effect? And he will probably ask himself two more: Could I put
it more shortly? Have I said anything that is avoidably ugly? But you are
not obliged to go to all this trouble. You can shirk it by simply throwing
your mind open and letting the ready-made phrases come crowding in.
They will construct your sentences for you—even think your thoughts for
you, to a certain extent—and at need they will perform the important
service of partially concealing your meaning even from yourself. It is at
this point that the special connection between politics and the debasement
of language becomes clear.

In our time it is broadly true that political writing is bad writing.
Where it is not true, it will generally be found that the writer is some
kind of rebel, expressing his private opinions and not a "party line."
Orthodoxy, of whatever color, seems to demand a lifeless, imitative style.

The political dialects to be found in pamphlets, leading articles, manifestos, White Papers and the speeches of under-secretaries do, of course, vary from party to party, but they are all alike in that one almost never finds in them a fresh, vivid, home-made turn of speech. When one watches some tired hack on the platform mechanically repeating the familiar phrases—*bestial atrocities, iron heel, bloodstained tyranny, free peoples of the world, stand shoulder to shoulder*—one often has a curious feeling that one is not watching a live human being but some kind of dummy: a feeling which suddenly becomes stronger at moments when the light catches the speaker's spectacles and turns them into blank discs which seem to have no eyes behind them. And this is not altogether fanciful. A speaker who uses that kind of phraseology has gone some distance towards turning himself into a machine. The appropriate noises are coming out of his larynx, but his brain is not involved as it would be if he were choosing his words for himself. If the speech he is making is one that he is accustomed to make over and over again, he may be almost unconscious of what he is saying, as one is when one utters the responses in church. And this reduced state of consciousness, if not indispensable, is at any rate favorable to political conformity.

In our time, political speech and writing are largely the defence of the indefensible. Things like the continuance of British rule in India, the Russian purges and deportations, the dropping of the atom bombs on Japan, can indeed be defended, but only by arguments which are too brutal for most people to face, and which do not square with the professed aims of political parties. Thus political language has to consist largely of euphemism, question-begging and sheer cloudy vagueness. Defenceless villages are bombarded from the air, the inhabitants driven out into the countryside, the cattle machine-gunned, the huts set on fire with incendiary bullets: this is called *pacification*. Millions of peasants are robbed of their farms and sent trudging along the roads with no more than they can carry: this is called *transfer of population* or *rectification of frontiers*. People are imprisoned for years without trial, or shot in the back of the neck or sent to die of scurvy in Arctic lumber camps: this is called *elimination of unreliable elements*. Such phraseology is needed if one wants to name things without calling up mental pictures of them. Consider for instance some comfortable English professor defending Russian totalitarianism. He cannot say outright, "I believe in killing off your opponents when you get good results by doing so." Probably, therefore, he will say something like this:

"While freely conceding that the Soviet régime exhibits certain features which the humanitarian may be inclined to deplore, we must, I think, agree that a certain curtailment of the right to political opposition is an unavoidable concomitant of transitional periods, and that the rigors which the Russian people have been called upon to undergo have been amply justified in the sphere of concrete achievement."

The inflated style is itself a kind of euphemism. A mass of Latin words falls upon the facts like soft snow, blurring the outlines and covering up all the details. The great enemy of clear language is insincerity. When there is a gap between one's real and one's declared aims, one turns as it were instinctively to long words and exhausted idioms, like a cuttlefish squirting out ink. In our age there is no such thing as "keeping out of politics." All issues are political issues, and politics itself is a mass of lies, evasions, folly, hatred and schizophrenia. When the general atmosphere is bad, language must suffer. I should expect to find—this is a guess which I have not sufficient knowledge to verify—that the German, Russian, and Italian languages have all deteriorated in the last ten or fifteen years, as a result of dictatorship.

But if thought corrupts language, language can also corrupt thought. A bad usage can spread by tradition and imitation, even among people who should and do know better. The debased language that I have been discussing is in some ways very convenient. Phrases like *a not unjustifiable assumption, leaves much to be desired, would serve no good purpose, a consideration which we should do well to bear in mind,* are a continuous temptation, a packet of aspirins always at one's elbow. Look back through this essay, and for certain you will find that I have again and again committed the very faults I am protesting against. By this morning's post I have received a pamphlet dealing with conditions in Germany. The author tells me that he "felt impelled" to write it. I open it at random, and here is almost the first sentence that I see: "[The Allies] have an opportunity not only of achieving a radical transformation of Germany's social and political structure in such a way as to avoid a nationalistic reaction in Germany itself, but at the same time of laying the foundations of a co-operative and unified Europe." You see, he "feels impelled" to write—feels, presumably, that he has something new to say—and yet his words, like cavalry horses answering the bugle, group themselves automatically into the familiar dreary pattern. This invasion of one's mind by ready-made phrases (*lay the foundations, achieve a radical transformation*) can only be prevented if one is constantly on guard against them, and every such phrase anaesthetizes a portion of one's brain.

I said earlier that the decadence of our language is probably curable. Those who deny this would argue, if they produced an argument at all, that language merely reflects existing social conditions, and that we cannot influence its development by any direct tinkering with words and constructions. So far as the general tone or spirit of a language goes, this may be true, but it is not true in detail. Silly words and expressions have often disappeared, not through any evolutionary process but owing to the conscious action of a minority. Two recent examples were *explore every avenue* and *leave no stone unturned,* which were killed by the jeers of a few journalists. There is a long list of flyblown metaphors which could similarly be got rid of if enough people would interest themselves in the job; and it should also be possible to laugh the *not un-* formation out of existence,[3] to reduce the amount of Latin and Greek in the average sentence, to drive out foreign phrases and strayed scientific words, and, in general, to make pretentiousness unfashionable. But all these are minor points. The defence of the English language implies more than this, and perhaps it is best to start by saying what it does *not* imply.

To begin with it has nothing to do with archaism, with the salvaging of obsolete words and turns of speech, or with the setting up of a "standard English" which must never be departed from. On the contrary, it is especially concerned with the scrapping of every word or idiom which has outworn its usefulness. It has nothing to do with correct grammar and syntax, which are of no importance so long as one makes one's meaning clear, or with the avoidance of Americanisms, or with having what is called a "good prose style." On the other hand it is not concerned with fake simplicity and the attempt to make written English colloquial. Nor does it even imply in every case preferring the Saxon word to the Latin one, though it does imply using the fewest and shortest words that will cover one's meaning. What is above all needed is to let the meaning choose the word, and not the other way about. In prose, the worst thing one can do with words is to surrender to them. When you think of a concrete object, you think wordlessly, and then, if you want to describe the thing you have been visualizing you probably hunt about till you find the exact words that seem to fit it. When you think of something abstract

[3] One can cure oneself of the *not un-* formation by memorizing this sentence: *A not unblack dog was chasing a not unsmall rabbit across a not ungreen field.*

you are more inclined to use words from the start, and unless you make a conscious effort to prevent it, the existing dialect will come rushing in and do the job for you, at the expense of blurring or even changing your meaning. Probably it is better to put off using words as long as possible and get one's meaning as clear as one can through pictures or sensations. Afterwards one can choose—not simply *accept*—the phrases that will best cover the meaning, and then switch round and decide what impression one's words are likely to make on another person. This last effort of the mind cuts out all stale or mixed images, all prefabricated phrases, needless repetitions, and humbug and vagueness generally. But one can often be in doubt about the effect of a word or a phrase, and one needs rules that one can rely on when instinct fails. I think the following rules will cover most cases:

(i) Never use a metaphor, simile or other figure of speech which you are used to seeing in print.

(ii) Never use a long word where a short one will do.

(iii) If it is possible to cut a word out, always cut it out.

(iv) Never use the passive where you can use the active.

(v) Never use a foreign phrase, a scientific word or a jargon word if you can think of an everyday English equivalent.

(vi) Break any of these rules sooner than say anything outright barbarous.

These rules sound elementary, and so they are, but they demand a deep change of attitude in anyone who has grown used to writing in the style now fashionable. One could keep all of them and still write bad English, but one could not write the kind of stuff that I quoted in those five specimens at the beginning of this article.

I have not here been considering the literary use of language, but merely language as an instrument for expressing and not for concealing or preventing thought. Stuart Chase and others have come near to claiming that all abstract words are meaningless, and have used this as a pretext for advocating a kind of political quietism. Since you don't know what Fascism is, how can you struggle against Fascism? One need not swallow such absurdities as this, but one ought to recognize that the present political chaos is connected with the decay of language, and that one can probably bring about some improvement by starting at the verbal end. If you simplify your English, you are freed from the worst follies of orthodoxy.

You cannot speak any of the necessary dialects, and when you make a stupid remark its stupidity will be obvious, even to yourself. Political language—and with variations this is true of all political parties, from Conservatives to Anarchists—is designed to make lies sound truthful and murder respectable, and to give an appearance of solidity to pure wind. One cannot change this all in a moment, but one can at least change one's own habits, and from time to time one can even, if one jeers loudly enough, send some worn-out and useless phrase—some *jackboot, Achilles' heel, hotbed, melting pot, acid test, veritable inferno* or other lump of verbal refuse—into the dustbin where in belongs.

E. B. White

CALCULATING MACHINE

A PUBLISHER in Chicago has sent us a pocket calculating machine by which we may test our writing to see whether it is intelligible. The calculator was developed by General Motors, who, not satisfied with giving the world a Cadillac, now dream of bringing perfect understanding to men. The machine (it is simply a celluloid card with a dial) is called the Reading-Ease Calculator and shows four grades of "reading ease"— Very Easy, Easy, Hard, and Very Hard. You count your words and syllables, set the dial, and an indicator lets you know whether anybody is going to understand what you have written. An instruction book came with it, and after mastering the simple rules we lost no time in running a test on the instruction book itself, to see how *that* writer was doing. The poor fellow! His leading essay, the one on the front cover, tested Very Hard.

Our next step was to study the first phrase on the face of the calculator: "How to test Reading-Ease of written matter." There is, of course, no such thing as reading ease of written matter. There is the ease with which matter can be read, but that is a condition of the reader, not of the matter. Thus the inventors and distributors of this calculator get off to a poor start, with a Very Hard instruction book and a slovenly phrase. Already they have one foot caught in the brier patch of English usage.

Not only did the author of the instruction book score badly on the front cover, but inside the book he used the word "personalize" in an essay on how to improve one's writing. A man who likes the word "personalize" is entitled to his choice, but we wonder whether he should be in the business of giving advice to writers. "Whenever possible," he wrote, "personalize your writing by directing it to the reader." As for us, we would as lief Simonize our grandmother as personalize our writing.

In the same envelope with the calculator, we received another training aid for writers—a booklet called "How to Write Better," by Rudolf Flesch. This, too, we studied, and it quickly demonstrated the broncolike ability of the English language to throw whoever leaps cocksurely into the saddle. The language not only can toss a rider but knows a thousand tricks for tossing him, each more gay than the last. Dr. Flesch stayed in the saddle only a moment or two. Under the heading "Think Before You Write," he wrote, "The main thing to consider is your *purpose* in writing. Why are you sitting down to write?" And echo answered: Because, sir, it is more comfortable than standing up.

Communication by the written word is a subtler (and more beautiful) thing than Dr. Flesch and General Motors imagine. They contend that the "average reader" is capable of reading only what tests Easy, and that the writer should write at or below this level. This is a presumptuous and degrading idea. There is no average reader, and to reach down toward this mythical character is to deny that each of us is on the way up, is ascending. ("Ascending," by the way, is a word Dr. Flesch advises writers to stay away from. Too unusual.)

It is our belief that no writer can improve his work until he discards the dulcet notion that the reader is feeble-minded, for writing is an act of faith, not a trick of grammar. Ascent is at the heart of the matter. A country whose writers are following a calculating machine downstairs is not ascending—if you will pardon the expression—and a writer who questions the capacity of the person at the other end of the line is not a writer at all, merely a schemer. The movies long ago decided that a wider communication could be achieved by a deliberate descent to a lower level, and they walked proudly down until they reached the cellar. Now they are groping for the light switch, hoping to find the way out.

We have studied Dr. Flesch's instructions diligently, but we return for guidance in these matters to an earlier American, who wrote with more patience, more confidence. "I fear chiefly," he wrote, "lest my expression may not be *extra-vagant* enough, may not wander far enough beyond the narrow limits of my daily experience, so to be adequate to the truth of which I have been convinced. . . . Why level downward to our dullest perception always, and praise that as common sense? The commonest sense is the sense of men asleep, which they express by snoring."

Run that through your calculator! It may come out Hard, it may come out Easy. But it will come out whole, and it will last forever.

Dwight Macdonald

THE STRING UNTUNED

THE THIRD edition of Webster's New International Dictionary (Unabridged), which was published last fall by the G. & C. Merriam Co., of Springfield, Massachusetts, tells us a good deal about the changes in our cultural climate since the second edition appeared, in 1934. The most important difference between Webster's Second (hereafter called 2) and Webster's Third (or 3) is that 3 has accepted as standard English a great many words and expressions to which 2 attached warning labels: *slang, colloquial, erroneous, incorrect, illiterate.* My impression is that most of the words so labelled in the 1934 edition are accepted in the 1961 edition as perfectly normal, honest, respectable citizens. Between these dates in this country a revolution has taken place in the study of English grammar and usage, a revolution that probably represents an advance in scientific method but that certainly has had an unfortunate effect on such nonscientific activities as the teaching of English and the making of dictionaries—at least on the making of this particular dictionary. This scientific revolution has meshed gears with a trend toward permissiveness, in the name of democracy, that is debasing our language by rendering it less precise and thus less effective as literature and less efficient as communication. It is felt that it is snobbish to insist on making discriminations—the very word has acquired a Jim Crow flavor—about usage. And it is assumed that true democracy means that the majority is right. This feeling seems to me sentimental and this assumption unfounded.

There have been other recent dictionaries calling themselves "unabridged," but they are to Webster's 3 as a welterweight is to a heavy-

524

weight. 3 is a massive folio volume (thirteen inches by nine and a half by four) that weighs thirteen and a half pounds, contains four hundred and fifty thousand entries—an "entry" is a word plus its definition—in 2,662 pages, cast three and a half million dollars to produce, and sells for $47.50 up, according to binding. The least comparable dictionary now in print is the New Webster's Vest Pocket Dictionary, which bears on its title page the charmingly frank notation, "This dictionary is not published by the original publishers of Webster's Dictionary or by their successors." It measures five and a half inches by two and a half by a half, weighs two and a quarter ounces, has two hundred and thirty-nine pages, and costs thirty-nine cents. The only English dictionary now in print that *is* comparable to 3 is the great Oxford English Dictionary, a unique masterpiece of historical research that is as important in the study of the language as the King James Bible has been in the use of the language. The O.E.D. is much bigger than 3, containing sixteen thousand four hundred pages in thirteen folio volumes. It is bigger because its purpose is historical as well as definitive; it traces the evolution of each word through the centuries, illustrating the changes in meaning with dated quotations. The latest revision of the O.E.D. appeared in 1933, a year before Webster's 2 appeared. For the language as it has developed in the last quarter of a century, there is no dictionary comparable in scope to 3.

The editor of 2, Dr. William A. Neilson, president of Smith College, followed lexical practice that had obtained since Dr. Johnson's day and assumed there was such a thing as correct English and that it was his job to decide what it was. When he felt he had to include a sub-standard word because of its common use, he put it in, but with a warning label: *Slang, Dial.,* or even bluntly *Illit.* His approach was normative and his dictionary was an authority that pronounced on which words were standard English and which were not. Bets were decided by "looking it up in the dictionary." It would be hard to decide bets by appealing to 3, whose editor of fifteen years' standing, Dr. Philip Gove, while as dedicated a scholar as Dr. Neilson, has a quite different approach. A dictionary, he writes, "should have no traffic with . . . artificial notions of correctness or superiority. It must be descriptive and not prescriptive." Dr. Gove and the other makers of 3 are sympathetic to the school of language study that has become dominant since 1934. It is sometimes called Structural Linguistics and sometimes, rather magnificently, just Modern Linguistic Science. Dr. Gove gives its basic concepts as:

1. Language changes constantly.
2. Change is normal.
3. Spoken language is the language.
4. Correctness rests upon usage.
5. All usage is relative.

While one must sympathize with the counterattack the Structural Linguists have led against the tyranny of the schoolmarms and the purists, who have caused unnecessary suffering to generations of schoolchildren over such matters as *shall* v. *will* and the *who-whom* syndrome—someone has observed that the chief result of the long crusade against "It's me" is that most Americans now say "Between you and I"—it is remarkable what strange effects have been produced in 3 by following Dr. Gove's five little precepts, reasonable as each seems taken separately. Dr. Gove conceives of his dictionary as a recording instrument rather than as an authority; in fact, the whole idea of authority or correctness is repulsive to him as a lexical scientist. The question is, however, whether a purely scientific approach to dictionary-making may not result in greater evils than those it seeks to cure.

When one compares 2 and 3, the first difference that strikes one is that 2 is a work of traditional scholarship and hence oriented toward the past, while 3—though in many ways more scholarly, or at least more academic, than 2—exhales the breezy air of the present. This is hardly surprising, since the new school of linguistics is non-historical, if not anti-historical. Henry Luce's *Time* rather than Joseph Addison's *Spectator* was the hunting ground for 3's illustrative quotations. There is a four-and-a-half-page list of consultants. Its sheer bulk is impressive—until one begins to investigate. One can see why James W. Perry had to be consulted on Non-numerical Computer Applications and Margaret Fulford on Mosses and Liverworts, but it seems overdoing it to have *two* consultants on both Hardware and Salvation Army, and some people might even question the one apiece on Soft Drinks, Boy Scouts, Camp Fire Girls, and Girl Guiding, as well as the enrolling of Mr. Arthur B. LaFar, formerly president of the Angostura-Wuppermann bitters company, as consultant on Cocktails. Such padding is all the more odd, considering that the editors of 3 have forgotten to appoint anybody in Philosophy, Political Theory, or Theatre. The old-fashioned 2 had six consultants on Catholic Church and Protestant Churches. 3 has only one, on Catholic Church. But it also has one on Christian Science, a more up-to-date religion.

The G. & C. Merriam Co. has been publishing Webster's dictionaries since 1847, four years after Noah Webster died. Work on 3 began the day 2 went to press, but it gathered real momentum only fifteen years ago, when Dr. Gove began building up his staff of lexicographers. The first step was to sort out the words of 2 into a hundred and nine categories, so that specialized-definition writers could deal with them. It took five women two and a half years to do this. (" 'If seven maids with seven mops swept it for half a year, Do you suppose,' the Walrus said, 'That they could get it clear?' "—*Lewis Carroll.*) After that, all that had to be done was to write new definitions for most of the three hundred and fifty thousand entries that were taken over from 2, to select and write a hundred thousand new entries, to collect four and a half million quotations illustrating word usage, and to distribute them among the definition writers. The scope of the operation may be suggested by the fact that in chemistry alone the lexicographers gathered two hundred and fifty thousand quotations and took six and a half years to write the definitions. After that, it was up to the Lakeside Press, of Chicago, to set type from a manuscript that was as bristling with revisions and interlineations, mostly in longhand, as a Proust manuscript. At first they gave the printers clean, retyped copy, but they soon found that the extra step produced an extra crop of errors. The printing was done by the Riverside Press, of Cambridge, Massachusetts, a long-established firm, like Merriam, whose dictionaries it has been printing for almost a century. But antiquity is relative. There is no one at Riverside like the compositor at Oxford's Clarendon Press who began setting type for the O.E.D. in 1884 and was still at it when the last volume came off the presses in 1928.

In seeking out and including all the commonly used words, especially slang ones, the compilers of 3 have been admirably diligent. Their definitions, in the case of meanings that have arisen since 1900 or so, are usually superior (though, because of the tiny amount of a dictionary it is possible to read before vertigo sets in, all generalizations must be understood to be strictly impressionistic). They have also provided many more quotations (this is connected with the linguistic revolution), perhaps, indeed, too many more. It is quite true, as the promotional material for 3 claims, that this edition goes far beyond what is generally understood by the term "revision" and may honestly be termed a new dictionary. But I should advise the possessors of the 1934 edition to think carefully before they turn it in for the new model. Although the publishers have not yet destroyed the plates of 2, they do not plan to keep it in print, which is a pity. There are reasons, which will presently appear, that buyers should be given a choice between 2 and 3, and that, in the case of libraries and schools, 3 should be regarded as an up-to-date supplement to 2 rather than a replacement of it.

Quantitative comparison between 2 and 3 must be approached cautiously. On the surface, it is considerably in 2's favor: 3,194 pages v. 2,662. But although 2 has six hundred thousand entries to 3's four hundred and fifty thousand, its entries are shorter; and because 3's typography is more compact and its type page larger, it gets in almost as much text as 2. The actual number of entries dropped since 2 is not a hundred and fifty thousand but two hundred and fifty thousand, since a hundred thousand new ones have been added. This incredible massacre—almost half the words in the English language seem to have disappeared between 1934 and 1961—is in fact incredible. For the most part, the dropped entries fall into very special categories that have less to do with the language than with methods of lexicography. They are: variants; "nonce words," like *Shakespearolatry* ("excessive reverence or devotion to Shakespeare"), which seemed a good idea at the time, or for the nonce, but haven't caught on; a vast number of proper names, including nearly every one in both the King James and the Douay Bibles; foreign terms; and obsolete or archaic words. This last category is a large one, since 2 includes "all the literary and most of the technical and scientific words and meanings in the period of Modern English beginning with the year 1500," plus all the words in Chaucer, while 3, in line with its modernization program, has advanced the cut-off date to 1755. A great many, perhaps most, of the entries dropped from 2 were in a section of small type at the foot of each page, a sort of linguistic ghetto, in which the editors simply listed "fringe words"—the definitions being limited to a synonym or often merely a symbol—which they thought not important enough to put into the main text. 3 has either promoted them to the text or, more frequently, junked them.

Some examples of the kinds of words that are in 2 but not in 3 are: *arrousement, aswowe* (in a swoon), *dethronize, devoration* (act of devouring), *disagreeance, mummianize* (mummify), *noyous* (annoying), *punquetto* (strumpet), *ridiculize,* and *subsign* (subscribe). Two foreign words that one might expect to find in 3 were left out because of insufficient "backing"; i.e., the compilers didn't find enough usages to justify inclusion. They were *Achtung* and *niet;* the researchers must have skipped spy movies and Molotovian diplomacy. *Pot holder* was left out, after considerable tergiversating, because (a) for some reason the compilers found little backing for it, and (b) it was held to be self-explanatory (though considering some of the words they put in . . .). If it had been considered to be a single word, it would have been admitted, since one rule they followed was: No word written solid is self-explanatory.

The hundred thousand new entries in 3 are partly scientific or technical terms, partly words that have come into general use since 1934. The sheer quantity of the latter is impressive. English is clearly a living, growing language, and in this portion of their task the compilers of 3 have done an excellent job. Merriam-Webster has compiled some interesting lists of words in 3 that are not in 2.

Some of the political ones are:

character assassination	loyalty oath
desegregation	McCarthyism
freedom of speech	segregated
globalize	red-baiting
hatemonger	shoo-in
integrationist	sit-in
welfare capitalism	subsistence economy

Among the new entries in the cocktail-party area are:

club soda	name-dropping
elbow bending	pub crawler
gate-crasher	quick one
glad-hander	rumpot
good-time Charlie	silent treatment
Irish coffee	table-hop
jungle juice	yakety-yak

The most important new aspect of 3, the rock on which it has been erected, is the hundred thousand illustrative quotations—known professionally as "citations" or "cites"—drawn from fourteen thousand writers and publications. (Another hundred thousand "usage examples" were made up by the compilers.) Most of the cites are from living writers or speakers, ranging from Winston Churchill, Edith Sitwell, Jacques Maritain, J. Robert Oppenheimer, and Albert Schweitzer to Billy Rose, Ethel Merman, James Cagney, Burt Ives, and Ted Williams. Many are from publications, extending from the Dictionary of American Biography down to college catalogues, fashion magazines, and the annual report of the J. C. Penney Company. The hundred thousand cites were chosen from a collection of over six million, of which a million and a half were already in the Merriam-Webster files; four and a half million were garnered by Dr. Gove and his staff. (The O.E.D. had about the same number of cites in its files—drawn mostly from English literary classics—but used a much larger proportion of them, almost two million, which is why it is five or six times as long as 3.) For years everybody in the office did up to three hours of reading a day—the most, it was found, that was possible without attention lag. Dr. Gove presently discovered a curious defect in this method: the readers tended to overlook the main meanings of a word and concentrate on the peripheral ones; thus a hundred and fifty cite slips were turned in for *bump* as in burlesque stripping but not one for *bump* as in a road. To compensate for this, he created a humbler task force, whose job it was to go through the gutted carcasses of books and magazines after the first group had finished with them and arbitrarily enter on a slip one word—plus its context— in the first sentence in the fourth line from the top of each surviving page. The percentage of useful slips culled by this method approximated the percentage of useful slips made out by the readers who had used their brains. Unsettling.

The cites in 2 are almost all from standard authors. Its cite on *jocund* is from Shakespeare; 3's is from Elinor Wylie. Under *ghastly* 2 has cites from Gray (two), Milton (three), Poe, Wordsworth, Shakespeare, Shelley, Hawthorne, and—as a slight concession to modernity— Maurice Hewlett. 3 illustrates *ghastly* with cites from Louis Bromfield, Macaulay, Thackeray, Thomas Herbert, Aldous Huxley, H. J. Laski, D. B. Chidsey, and J. C. Powys. For *debonair,* 2 has Milton's "buxom, blithe and debonair," while 3 has H. M. Reynolds' "gay, brisk and debonair." One may think, as I do, that 3 has dropped far too many of the old writers, that it has overemphasized its duty of recording the current state of the language and skimped its duty of recording the past that is still alive (Mr. Reynolds would hardly have arrived at his threesome had not Mr. Milton been there before). A decent compromise would have been to include both, but the editors of 3 don't go in for compromises. They seem imperfectly aware of the fact that the past of a language is part of its present, that tradition is as much a fact as the violation of tradition.

The editors of 3 have labored heroically on pronunciation, since one of the basic principles of the new linguistic doctrine is that Language is Speech. Too heroically, indeed. For here, as in other aspects of their labors, the editors have displayed more valor than discretion. Sometimes they appear to be lacking in common sense. The editors of 2 found it necessary to give only two pronunciations for *berserk* and two for *lingerie*, but 3 seems to give twenty-five for the first and twenty-six for the second. (This is a rough estimate; the system of notation is very complex. Dr. Gove's pronunciation editor thinks there are approximately that number but says that he is unable to take the time to be entirely certain.) Granted that 2 may have shirked its duty, one may still find something compulsive in the amplitude with which 3 has fulfilled its obligations. Does anybody except a Structural Linguist need to know that much? And what use is such plethora to a reader who wants to know how to pronounce a word? The new list of pronunciation symbols in 3 is slightly shorter than the one in 2 but also—perhaps for that reason—harder to understand. 2 uses only those nice old familiar letters of the alphabet, with signs over them to indicate long and short and so on. (It also repeats its pronunciation guide at the foot of each page, which is handy; 3 does not, to save space and dollars, so one has to flop over as much as thirteen and a half pounds of printed matter to refer back to the one place the guide appears.) 3 also uses the alphabet, but there is one catastrophic exception. This is an upside-down "e," known in the trade as a "schwa," which stands for a faint, indistinct sound, like the "e" in *quiet,* that is unnervingly common and that can be either "a," "e," "i," "o," or "u," according to circumstance. Things get quite lively when you trip over a schwa. *Bird* is given straight as *bûrd* in 2, but in 3 it is *bərd, bəd,* and *bəid.* This last may be *boid,* but I'm not sure. Schwa trouble. ("Double, double schwa and trouble." —*Shakespeare.*)

Almost all 3's pictures are new or have been redrawn in a style that is superior to 2's—clearer and more diagrammatic. The new cut of "goose," with no less than twenty-four parts clearly marked, is a special triumph. The other animal illustrations, from *aardvark* to *zebu,* are less picturesque but more informative than those in 2. The illustrations are—rightly—chosen for utility rather than ornament. On facing pages we have pictures of *coracles, corbel,* and *corbiesteps,* all definitely needed, though, on another, *pail* might have been left to the imagination. One of the few illustrations repeated from 2 is *digestive organs,* and a fine bit of uncompromising realism it is, too.

I notice no important omissions in 3. *Namby-pamby* is in. However, it was coined—to describe the eighteenth-century Ambrose Philips' insipid verses—not "by some satirists of his time" but by just one of them, Henry Carey, whose celebrated parody of Philips is entitled "Namby-Pamby." *Bromide* is in ("a conventional and commonplace or tiresome person"), but not the fact that Gelett Burgess invented it. Still, he gets credit for *blurb* and *goop*. *Abstract expressionism* is in, but *Tachism* and *action painting* are not. The entries on Marxist and Freudian terms are skimpy. *Id* is in, but without citations and with too brief a definition. *Ego* is defined as Fichte, Kant, and Hume used it but not as Freud did. The distinction between *unconscious* and *subconscious* is muffed; the first is adequately defined and the reader is referred to the latter; looking that up, he finds "The mental activities just below the threshold of consciousness; *also:* the aspect of the mind concerned with such activities that is an entity or a part of the mental apparatus overlapping, equivalent to, or distinct from the unconscious." I can't grasp the nature of something that is overlapping, equivalent to, *or* distinct from something else. While *dialectical materialism* and *charisma* (which 2 treats only as a theological term, although Max Weber had made the word common sociological currency long before 1934) are in, there is no *mass culture,* and the full entry for the noun *masses* is "pl. of mass." There is no reference to Marx or even to Hegel under *reify,* and under *alienation* the closest 3 comes to this important concept of Marxist theory is "the state of being alienated or diverted from normal function," which is illustrated by "alienation of muscle." Marx is not mentioned in the very brief definition of *class struggle.*

The definitions seem admirably objective. I detected only one major lapse:

> McCarthyism—a political attitude of the mid-twentieth century closely allied to know-nothingism and characterized chiefly by opposition to elements held to be subversive and by the use of tactics involving personal attacks on individuals by means of widely publicized indiscriminate allegations esp. on the basis of unsubstantiated charges.

I fancy the formulator of this permitted himself a small, dry smile as he leaned back from his typewriter before trudging on to *McClellan saddle* and *McCoy* (the real). I'm not complaining, but I can't help remembering that the eponymous hero of *McCarthyism* wrote a little book with that title in which he gave a rather different definition. The tendentious treatment of *McCarthyism* contrasts with the objectivity of the definition of *Stalinism,* which some of us consider an even more reprehensible *ism:* "The political, economic and social principles and policies associated with Stalin; *esp*: the theory and practice of communism developed by Stalin from Marxism-Leninism." The first part seems to me inadequate and the second absurd, since Stalin never had a theory in his life. The definitions of *democratic* and *republican* seem fair: "policies of broad social reform and internationalism in foreign affairs" v. "usu. associated with business, financial, and some agricultural interests and with favoring a restricted governmental role in social and economic life." Though I wonder what the Republican National Committee thinks.

One of the most painful decisions unabridgers face is what to do about those obscene words that used to be wholly confined to informal discourse but that of late, after a series of favorable court decisions, have been cropping up in respectable print. The editors of 2, being gentlemen and scholars, simply omitted them. The editors of 3, being scientists, were more conscientious. All the chief four- and five-letter words are here, with the exception of perhaps the most important one. They defend this omission not on lexical grounds but on the practical and, I think, reasonable ground that its inclusion would have stimulated denunciations and boycotts. There are, after all, almost half a million other words in their dictionary—not to mention an investment of three and a half million dollars—and they reluctantly decided not to imperil the whole enterprise by insisting on that word.

Two useful features of 2 were omitted from 3: the gazetteer of place names and the biographical dictionary. They were left out partly to save money—they took up a hundred and seventy-six pages, and the biographical dictionary had to be brought up to date with each new printing—and partly because Dr. Gove and his colleagues, more severe than the easygoing editors of 2, considered such items "encyclopedic material" and so not pertinent to a dictionary. The force of this second excuse is weakened because although they did omit such encyclopedic features of 2 as the two pages on *grasses,* they put in a page-and-a-half table of currencies under *money* and three and a half pages of *dyes.* It is also worth noting that Merriam-Webster added a new item to its line in 1943—the Webster's Biographical Dictionary. While I quite understand the publishers' reluctance to give away what their customers would otherwise have to buy separately, I do think the biographical dictionary should have been included—from the consumer's point of view, at any rate.

However, the editors have sneaked in many proper names by the back door; that is, by entering their adjectival forms. *Walpolian* means

"1: of, relating to, or having the characteristics of Horace Walpole or his writings," and "2: of, relating to, or having the characteristics of Robert Walpole or his political policies," and we get the death dates of both men (but not the birth dates), plus the information that Horace was "Eng. man of letters" and Robert "Eng. statesman" (though it is not noted that Horace was Robert's son). This method of introducing proper names produces odd results. Raphael is in (*Raphaelesque, Raphaelism, Raphaelite*), as are Veronese (*Veronese green*) and Giotto and Giorgione and Michelangelo, but not Tintoretto and Piero della Francesca, because they had the wrong kind of names. Caravaggio had the right kind, but the editors missed him, though *Caravaggesque* is as frequently used in art criticism as *Giottesque*. All the great modern painters, from Cézanne on, are omitted, since none have appropriate adjectives. Yeats is in (*Yeatsian*) but not Eliot, Pound, or Frost (why not *Frosty?*). Sometimes one senses a certain desperation, as when *Smithian* is used to wedge in Adam Smith. *Menckenian* and *Menckenese* get an inch each, but there is no *Hawthornean*, no *Melvillesque*, no *Twainite*. All the twentieth-century presidents are in—Eisenhower by the skin of *Eisenhower jacket*—except Taft and Truman and Kennedy. Hoover has the most entries, all dispiriting: *Hoover apron* and *Hooverize,* because he was food administrator in the First World War; *Hooverville,* for the depression shanty towns; *Hoovercrat,* for a Southern Democrat who voted for him in 1928; and *Hooverism.*

This brings up the matter of capitalization. 2 capitalized proper names; 3 does not, with one exception. There may have been some esoteric reason of typographical consistency. Whatever their reasons, the result is that they must cumbersomely and forever add *usu. cap.* (Why *usu.* when it is *alw?*) The exception is *God,* which even these cautious linguisticians couldn't quite bring themselves to label *usu. cap. Jesus* is out because of adjectival deficiency, except for *Jesus bug,* a splendid slang term, new to me, for the waterbug ("fr. the allusion to his walking on water," the "his" being firmly lower case). He does get in via His second name, which, luckily, has given us a rather important adjective, *usu. cap.*

At first glance, 3's typography is cleaner and more harmonious. Dr. Gove estimates that the editors eliminated two million commas and periods (as after adj., n., and v.), or eighty pages' worth. A second glance shows a major and, from a utilitarian point of view, very nearly a fatal defect. Words that have more than one meaning—and many have dozens—are much easier to follow in 2, which gives a new paragraph to each meaning, than in 3, which runs the whole entry as one superparagraph. ("What! Will the line stretch out to the crack of doom?" —*Shakespeare.*) Thus 2 not only starts each new meaning of *cut* with a paragraph but also puts in an italicized heading: *Games & Sports, Bookbinding, Card Playing, Motion Pictures.* In 3 one has to look through a solid paragraph of nine inches, and there are no headings. The most extreme example I found was 3's entry on the transitive verb *take,* which runs on for a single paragraph two feet eight inches long, in which the twenty-one main meanings are divided only by boldfaced numerals; there follow, still in the same paragraph, four inches of the intransitive *take,* the only sign of this gear-shifting being a tiny printer's squiggle. *Take* is, admittedly, quite a verb. The Oxford English Dictionary gives sixty-three meanings in nine feet, but they are spaced out in separate paragraphs, as is the mere foot and a half that 2 devotes to *take.*

A second glance also suggests second thoughts about the richness of citations in 3. Often it seems *plethoric,* even *otiose* ("lacking use or effect"). The chief reason 3's entries on multiple-meaning words are so much longer than 2's is that it has so many more citations. Many are justified and do indeed enrich our sense of words, but a good thing can be overdone. The promotional material for 3 mentions the treatment of *freeze* as an improvement, but does anybody really need such illustrative richness as:

> 6a: to make (as the face) expressionless [with instructions to recognize no one; and in fact he did *freeze* his face up when an old acquaintance hailed him—Fletcher Pratt] [a look of incredulity *froze* his face . . . and his eyes went blank with surprise—Hamilton Basso] b. to preserve rigidly a particular expression on [he still sat, his face *frozen* in shame and misery—Agnes S. Turnbull]

The question is rhetorical.

One of the problems of an unabridger is where completeness ends and madness begins. The compilers of 2 had a weakness for such fabrications as *philomuse, philomythia* ("devotion to legends . . . sometimes, loquaciousness"), *philonoist* ("a seeker of knowledge"), *philophilosophos* ("partial to philosophers"), *philopolemic, philopornist* ("a lover of harlots"), and *philosopheress* (which means not only a woman philosopher, like Hannah Arendt, but a philosopher's wife, like Xantippe). These are omitted by the compilers of 3, though they could not resist *philoso-*

phastering ("philosophizing in a shallow or pretentious manner"). But why do we need *nooky* ("full of nooks") or *name-caller* ("one that habitually engages in name-calling") or all those "night" words, from *night clothes*—"garments worn in bed," with a citation from Jane Welsh Carlyle, of all people—through *nightdress, nightgear, nightgown, night-robe, nightshirt,* and *nightwear*? What need of *sea boat* ("a boat adapted to the open sea") or *sea captain* or *swimming pool* ("a pool suitable for swimming," lest we imagine it is a pool that swims) or *sunbath* ("exposure to sunlight,"—"or to a sun lamp," they add cautiously or *sunbather* ("one that takes sunbaths")? Why *kittenless* ("having no kitten")? Why need we be told that *white-faced* is "having the face white in whole or in part"? Or that *whitehanded* is "having white hands"? (They missed *whitelipped*.)

Then there are those terrible negative prefixes, which the unwary unabridger gets started on and slides down with sickening momentum. 3 has left out many of 2's absurdities: *nonborrower, nonnervous, non-Mohammedan, non-Welsh, non-walking.* But it adds some of its own: *nonscientist, nonphilatelic, non-inbred, nondrying* (why no *nonwetting?*), *nonbank* ("not being or done by a bank"), and many other nonuseful and nonsensical entries. It has thirty-four pages of words beginning with *un-*, and while it may seem carping to object to this abundance, since the O.E.D. has three hundred and eighty such pages, I think, given the difference in purpose, that many may be challenged. A reasonably bright child of ten will not have to run to Daddy's Unabridged to find the meaning of *unreelable* ("incapable of being wound on a reel"), *un-lustrous* ("lacking luster"), or *unpowdered* ("not powdered"). And if it's for unreasonably dumb children, why omit *unspinnable, unshining,* and *unsanded?*

For a minor example of Gnostomania, or scholar's knee, see the treatment of numbers. Every number from *one* to *ninety-nine* is entered and defined, also every numerical adjective. Thus when the reader hits *sixty* he goes into a skid fifteen inches long. *Sixty* ("being one more than 59 in number") is followed by the pronoun ("60 countable persons or things not specified but under consideration and being enumerated") and the noun ("six tens: twice 30: 12 fives," etc.). Then comes *sixty-eight* ("being one more than 67 in number") and *sixty-eighth* ("being number 68 in a countable series"), followed by *sixty-fifth, sixty-first,* and so on. The compilers of 2 dealt with the *sixty* problem in a mere two entries totalling an inch and a half. But the art of lexicography has mutated into a "science" since then. ("*Quotation mark* . . . sometimes used to enclose . . . words . . . in an . . . ironical . . . sense . . . or words for which a writer offers a slight apology.") In reading 3 one sometimes feels like a subscriber who gets two hundred and thirty-eight copies of the May issue because the addressing machine got stuck, and it doesn't make it any better to know that the operators jammed it on purpose.

My complaint is not that 3 is all-inclusive—that is, unabridged—but that *pedantry* is not a synonym of *scholarship*. I have no objection to the inclusion of such pomposities, mostly direct translations from the Latin, as *viridity* (greenness), *presbyopic* (farsighted because of old age), *vellication* (twitching), *pudency* (modesty), and *vulnerary* (wound-healing). These are necessary if only so that one can read James Gould Cozzens' "By Love Possessed," in which they all occur, along with many siblings. And in my rambles through these 2,662 pages I have come across many a splendid word that has not enjoyed the popularity it deserves. I think my favorites are *pilpul*, from the Hebrew *to search*, which means "critical analysis and hair-splitting; casuistic argumentation;" *dysphemism*, which is the antonym of *euphemism* (as, *axle grease* for *butter* or *old man* for *father*), *subfusc*, from the Latin *subfuscus*, meaning brownish, which is illustrated with a beautiful citation from Osbert Sitwell ("the moment when the word Austerity was to take to itself a new subfusc and squalid twist of meaning")—cf, the more familiar *subacid*, also well illustrated with "a little subacid kind of . . . impatience," from Laurence Sterne; *nanism*, which is the antonym of *gigantism; mesocracy*, which is the form of government we increasingly have in this country; and *lib-lab*, which means a Liberal who sympathizes with Labor—I wish the lexicographers had not restored the hyphen I deleted when I imported it from England twenty years ago. One might say, and in fact I will say, that H. L. Mencken, whose prose was dysphemistic but never subfusc, eschewed pilpul in expressing his nanitic esteem for lib-lab mesocracy. Unfortunately, 3 omits 2's *thob* ("to think according to one's wishes"), which someone made up from *think-opinion-believe*, or else I could also have noted Mencken's distaste for thobbery.

Dr. Gove met the problem of *ain't* head on in the best traditions of Structural Linguistics, labelling it—reluctantly, one imagines—*substandard* for *have not* and *has not*, but giving it, unlabelled, as a contraction of *am not, are not*, and *is not*, adding "though disapproved by many and more common in less educated speech, used orally in most parts of the U.S. by many cultivated speakers esp. in the phrase ain't I." This was courageous indeed; when Dr. C. C. Fries, the dean of Structural Linguists today, said, at a meeting of the Modern Language Association several years ago, that *ain't* was not wholly disreputable, a teapot tempest boiled up in the press. When Dr. Gove included a reference to the entry on *ain't* in the press announcement of 3, the newspapers seethed again, from the Houston *Press* ("It Ain't Uncouth To Say Ain't Now") to the San Francisco *Examiner* ("Ain't Bad at All—In Newest Revised Dictionary") and the *World-Telegram* ("It Just Ain't True That Ain't Ain't in the Dictionary"). But moral courage is not the only quality a good lexicographer needs. Once the matter of education and culture is raised, we are right back at the non-scientific business of deciding what is correct—*standard* is the modern euphemism—and this is more a matter of a feeling for language (what the trade calls *Sprachgefühl*) than of the statistics on which Dr. Gove and his colleagues seem to have chiefly relied. For what Geiger counter will decide who is in fact educated or cultivated? And what adding machine will discriminate between *ain't* used because the speaker thinks it is standard English and *ain't* used because he wants to get a special effect? "Survival must have quality, or it ain't worth a bean," Thornton Wilder recently observed. It doesn't take much *Sprachgefühl* to recognize that Mr. Wilder is here being a mite folksy and that his effect would be lost if *ain't* were indeed "used orally in most parts of the U.S. by many cultivated speakers." Though I regret that the nineteenth-century schoolteachers without justification deprived us of *ain't* for *am not,* the deed was done, and I think the *Dial.* or *Illit.* with which 2 labels all uses of the word comes closer to linguistic fact today.

The pejorative labels in 2 are forthright: *colloquial, erroneous, incorrect, illiterate.* 3 replaces these self-explanatory terms with two that are both fuzzier and more scientific-sounding: *substandard* and *nonstandard.* The first "indicates status conforming to a pattern of linguistic usage that exists throughout the American language community but differs in choice of word or form from that of the prestige group in that community," which is academese for "Not used by educated people." *Hisself* and *drownded* are labelled *substand.,* which sounds better than *erron.*—more democratic. *Nonstandard* "is used for a very small number of words that can hardly stand without some status label but are too widely current in reputable context to be labelled *substand.*" *Irregardless* is given as an example, which for me again raises doubts about the compilers' notion of a reputable context. I think 2's label for the word, *erron.* or *humorous,* more accurate.

The argument has now shifted from whether a dictionary should be an authority as against a reporter (in Dr. Gove's terms, prescriptive v. descriptive) to the validity of the prescriptive guidance that 3 does in fact give. For Dr. Gove and his colleagues have not ventured to omit all qualitative discriminations; they have cut them down drastically from 2, but they have felt obliged to include many. Perhaps by 1988, if the Structural Linguists remain dominant, there will be a fourth edition, which will simply record, without labels or warnings, all words and non-words that are used widely in "the American language community," including such favorites of a former President as *nucular* (warfare), *inviduous,* and *mischievious.* But it is still 1962, and 3 often does discriminate. The trouble is that its willingness to do so has been weakened by its scientific conscience, so that it palters and equivocates; this is often more misleading than would be the omission of all discriminations.

One drawback to the permissive approach of the Structural Linguists is that it impoverishes the language by not objecting to errors if they are common enough. ("And how should I presume?"—*T. S. Eliot.*) There is a natural tendency among human beings, who are *by def.* fallible, to confuse similar-sounding words. "One look at him would turn you nauseous," Phil Silvers said on television one night, as better stylists have written before. Up to now, dictionaries have distinguished *nauseous* (causing nausea) from *nauseated* (experiencing nausea); 2 labels *nauseous* in the sense of experiencing nausea *obs.,* but it is no longer *obs.* It is simply *erron.,* a fact you will not learn from 3, which gives as its first definition, without label, "affected with or inclining to nausea." So the language is *balled up* and *nauseous* is telescoped into *nauseated* and nobody knows who means which exactly. The magisterial Fowler—magisterial, that is, until the Structural Linguists got to work—has an entry on Pairs & Snares that makes sad reading now. He calls *deprecate* and *depreciate* "one of the altogether false pairs," but 3 gives the latter as a synonym of the first. It similarly blurs the distinction between Fowler's *forcible* ("effected by force") and *forceful* ("full of force"), *unexceptional* ("constituting no exception to the general rule") and *unexceptionable* ("not open or liable to objection," which is quite a different thing). A Pair & Snare Fowler doesn't give is *disinterested* (impartial) and *uninterested* (not interested); 2 lists the *uninterested* sense of *disinterested* but adds, *"now rare;"* even such permissive lexicographers as Bergen and Cornelia Evans, in their "Dictionary of Contemporary American Usage," state firmly, "Though *disinterested* was formerly a synonym for *uninter-*

ested, it is not now so used." But 3 gives *disinterested* as a synonym of
uninterested.

Each such confusion makes the language less efficient, and it is a
dictionary's job to *define words,* which means, literally, to set limits to
them. 3 still distinguishes *capital* from *capitol* and *principle* from *principal,* but how many more language-community members must join the
present sizable band that habitually confuses these words before they
go down the drain with the others? Perhaps nothing much is lost if
almost everybody calls Frankenstein the monster rather than the man
who made the monster, even though Mrs. Shelley wrote it the other way,
but how is one to deal with the *bimonthly* problem? 2 defines it as "once
in two months," which is correct. 3 gives this as the first meaning and
then adds, gritting its teeth, *"sometimes:* twice a month." (It defines
biweekly as "every two weeks" and adds "2: twice a week.") It does seem
a little awkward to have a word that can mean every two weeks *or* every
eight weeks, and it would have been convenient if 3 had compromised
with scientific integrity enough to replace its perfectly accurate *sometimes* with a firm *erroneous.* But this would have implied authority,
and authority is the last thing 3's modest recorders want. ("Let this cup
pass from me."—*New Testament.*)

The objection is not to recording the facts of actual usage. It is to
failing to give the information that would enable the reader to decide
which usage he wants to adopt. If he prefers to use *deprecate* and *depreciate* interchangeably, no dictionary can prevent him, but at least he
should be warned. Thus 3 has under *transpire*—"4: to come to pass; happen, occur." 2 has the same entry, but it is followed by a monitory
pointing hand: *"transpire* in this sense has been disapproved by most
authorities on usage, although the meaning occurs in the writings of
many authors of good standing." Fair enough. I also prefer 2's handling
of the common misuse of *infer* to mean *imply*—"5: loosely and erroneously, to imply." 3 sounds no warning, and twice under *infer* it advises
"compare imply." Similarly, 2 labels the conjunctive *like* "illiterate"
and "incorrect," which it is, adding that "in the works of careful writers
[it] is replaced by *as.*" 3 accepts it as a standard, giving such unprepossessing citations as "impromptu programs where they ask questions much
like I do on the air—*Art Linkletter"* and "wore his clothes like he was
. . . afraid of getting dirt on them—*St. Petersburg (Fla.) Independent."*
Enthuse is labelled *colloq.* in 2 but not in 3. It still sounds *colloq.* if not
godawf. to me, nor am I impressed by 3's citations, from writers named
L. G. Pine and Lawrence Constable and from a trade paper called

Fashion Accessories. Or consider the common misuse of *too* when *very* is meant, as "I was not too interested in the lecture." 2 gives this use but labels it *colloq.* 3 gives it straight and cites Irving Kolodin: "an episodic work without too consistent a texture;" Mr. Kolodin probably means "without a very consistent texture," but how does one know he doesn't mean "without an excessively consistent [or monotonous] texture"? In music criticism such ambiguities are not too helpful.

In dealing with words that might be considered slang, 2 uses the label wherever there is doubt, while 3 leans the other way. The first procedure seems to me more sensible, since no great harm is done if a word is labelled slang until its pretensions to being standard have been thoroughly tested (as long as it is admitted into the dictionary), while damage may be done if it is prematurely accepted as standard. Thus both 2 and 3 list such women's-magazine locutions as *galore, scads, scrumptious,* and *too-too,* but only 2 labels them slang. (Fowler's note on *galore* applies to them all: "Chiefly resorted to by those who are reduced to relieving the dullness of matter by oddity of expression.") Thus *rummy, spang* (in the middle of), and *nobby* are in both, but only 2 calls them slang.

Admittedly, the question is most difficult. Many words begin as slang and then rise in the world. Dean Swift, a great purist, objected to *mob* (from the Latin *mobile vulgus*), *banter, bully,* and *sham;* he also objected to *hyp,* which has disappeared as slang for *hypochondriac,* and *rep,* which persists for *reputation* but is still labelled slang even in 3. Some slang words have survived for centuries without bettering themselves, like the Jukes and the Kallikaks. *Dukes* (fists) and *duds* (clothes) are still slang, although they go back to the eighteenth and the sixteenth century, respectively.

The definition of *slang* in 3 is "characterized primarily by connotations of extreme informality . . . coinages or arbitrarily changed words, clipped or shortened forms, extravagant, forced, or facetious figures of speech or verbal novelties usu. experiencing quick popularity and relatively rapid decline into disuse." A good definition (Dr. Gove has added that slang is "linguistically self-conscious"), but it seems to have been forgotten in making up 3, most of whose discriminations about slang strike me as arbitrary. According to 3, *scram* is not slang, but *vamoose* is. "Goof 1" (to make a mistake or blunder") is not slang, but "goof 2" ("to spend time idly or foolishly") is, and the confusion is compounded when one finds that Ethel Merman is cited for the non-slang *goof* and James T. Farrell for the slang *goof.* "Floozy 1" ("an attractive young woman of loose morals") is standard, but "*floozy* 2" (a dissolute and sometimes slovenly woman") is slang. Can even a Structural Linguist make such fine distinctions about such a word? The many synonyms for *drunk* raise the same question. Why are *oiled, pickled,* and *boiled* labelled slang if *soused* and *spiflicated* are not? Perhaps cooking terms for *drunk* are automatically slang, but why?

I don't mean to *imply* (see *infer*) that the compilers of 3 didn't give much thought to the problem. When they came to a doubtful word, they took a staff poll, asking everybody to check it, after reviewing the accumulated cites, as either slang or standard. This resulted in *cornball's* being entered as slang and *corny's* being entered as standard. Such scientific, or quantitative, efforts to separate the goats from the sheep produced the absurdities noted above. Professor Austin C. Dobbins raised this point in *College English* for October, 1956:

> But what of such words as *boondoggle, corny, frisk, liquidate, pinched, bonehead, carpetbagger, pleb, slush fund,* and *snide?* Which of these words ordinarily would be considered appropriate in themes written by cultivated people? According to the editors of the ACD [the American College Dictionary, the 1953 edition, published by Random House] the first five of these words are slang; the second five are established usage. To the editors of WNCD [Webster's New Collegiate Dictionary, published by Merriam-Webster in the same year] the first five of these words represent established usage; the second five are slang. Which authority is the student to follow?

Mr. Dobbins is by no means hostile to Structural Linguistics, and his essay appears in a recent anthology edited by Dr. Harold B. Allen, of the University of Minnesota, an energetic proponent of the new school. "Perhaps the answer," Dr. Dobbins concludes, "is to advise students to study only one handbook, consult one dictionary, listen to one instructor. An alternate suggestion, of course, is for our textbooks more accurately to base their labels upon studies of usage." Assuming the first alternative is ironical, I would say the second is impractical unless the resources of a dozen Ford Foundations are devoted to trying to decide the matter scientifically—that is, statistically.

Short of this Land of Cockaigne, where partridge appear in the fields ready-roasted, I see only two logical alternatives: to label all doubtful words slang, as 2 does, or to drop the label entirely, as I suspect Dr. Gove would have liked to do. Using the label sparingly, if it is not to produce bizarre effects, takes a lot more *Sprachgefühl* than the editors of 3 seem to have possessed. Thus *horse* as a verb ("to engage in horseplay") they accept as standard. The citations are from Norman Mailer ("I never horse around much with the women") and J. D. Salinger ("I horse around quite a lot, just to keep from getting bored"). I doubt whether either Mr. Mailer or Mr. Salinger would use *horse* straight; in these cites, I venture, it is either put in the mouth of a first-person narrator or used deliberately to get a colloquial effect. Slang is concise and vivid—*jalopy* has advantages over *dilapidated automobile*—and a few slang terms salted in a formal paragraph bring out the flavor. But the user must know he *is* using slang, he must be aware of having introduced a slight discord into his harmonics, or else he coarsens and blurs his expression. This information he will not, for the most part, get from 3. I hate to think what monstrosities of prose foreigners and high-school students will produce if they take 3 seriously as a guide to what is and what is not standard English.

Whenever the compilers of 3 come up against a locution that some (me, or I) might consider simply wrong, they do their best, as Modern Linguists and democrats, to be good fellows. The softening-up process begins with substituting the euphemistic *substandard* for 2's blunt *erroneous* and *illiterate*. From there it expands into several forms. *Complected* (for *complexioned*) is *dialect* in 2, *not often in formal use* in 3. *Learn* (for *teach*) is *now a vulgarism* in 2, *now chiefly substand.* in 3. (*Chiefly* is the thin end of the wedge, implying that users of standard English on occasion exclaim, "I'll learn you to use bad English!") *Knowed* is listed as the past of *know,* though *broke* is labelled substandard for *broken*—another of those odd discriminations. While this picture is a bit idyllic—Clarence Barnhart's American College Dictionary, put out by Random House, is considered by many to be at least as good as the Webster Collegiate—it had some reality up to 1961. But as of today, courts that Look It Up In Webster will often find themselves little the wiser, since 3 claims no authority and merely records, mostly deadpan, what in fact every Tom, Dick, and Harry is now doing—in all innocence—to the language. That freedom or imprisonment should depend on 3 is an alarming idea. The secretary correcting her boss, if he is a magazine publisher, will collide with the unresolved *bimonthly* and *biweekly* problem, and the youngsters sprawled under the table will happily absorb from 3 the information that *jerk* is standard for "a stupid, foolish, naïve, or unconventional person." One imagines the themes: "Dr. Johnson admired Goldsmith's literary talent although he considered him a jerk." The editors of the New Webster's Vest Pocket Dictionary, thirty-nine cents at any cigar store, label *jerk* as *coll*. But then they aren't Structural Linguists.

The reviews of 3 in the lay press have not been enthusiastic. *Life* and the *Times* have both attacked it editorially as a "say-as-you-go" dictionary that reflects "the permissive school" in language study. The usually solemn editorialists of the *Times* were goaded to unprecedented wit:

> A passel of double-domes at the G. & C. Merriam Company joint in Springfield, Mass. [the editorial began], have been confabbing and yakking for twenty-seven years—which is not intended to infer that they have not been doing plenty work—and now they have finalized Webster's Third New International Dictionary, Unabridged, a new edition of that swell and esteemed word book.
>
> Those who regard the foregoing paragraph as acceptable English prose will find that the new Webster's is just the dictionary for them.

But the lay press doesn't always prevail. The irreverent may call 3 "Gove's Goof," but Dr. Gove and his editors are part of the dominant movement in the professional study of language—one that has in the last few years established strong beachheads in the National Council of Teachers of English and the College English Association. One may grant that for the scientific study of language the Structural Linguistic approach is superior to that of the old grammarians, who overestimated the importance of logic and Latin, but one may still object to its transfer directly to the teaching of English and the making of dictionaries. As a scientific discipline, Structural Linguistics can have no truck with values or standards. Its job is to deal only with The Facts. But in matters of usage, the evaluation of The Facts is important, too, and this requires a certain amount of general culture, not to mention common sense—commodities that many scientists have done brilliantly without but that teachers and lexicographers need in their work.

The kind of thinking responsible for 3 is illustrated by Dr. Gove's riposte, last week, to the many unfavorabler reviews of his dictionary: "The criticisms involve less than one per cent of the words in the dictionary." This quantitative approach might be useful to novelists who get bad reviews. It is foolproof here; a reviewer who tried to meet Dr. Gove's criterion and deal with a sizable proportion of 3's words—say, ten per cent—would need forty-five thousand words just to list them, and if his own comments averaged ten words apiece he would have to publish his five-hundred-thousand-word review in two large volumes. Some odd thinking gets done up at the old Merriam-Webster place in Springfield.

Dr. Gove's letter to the *Times* objecting to its editorial was also interesting. "The editors of *Webster's Third New International Dictionary* are not amused by the ingenuity of the first paragraph of your editorial," it began loftily, and continued, "Your paragraph obscures, or attempts to obscure, the fact that there are so many different degrees of standard usage that dictionary definitions cannot hope to distinguish one from another by status labelling." (But the *Times'* point was precisely that the editors did make such distinctions by status labelling, only they were the wrong distinctions; i.e., by omitting pejorative labels they accepted as standard words that, in the opinion of the *Times,* are not standard.) There followed several pages of citations in which Dr. Gove showed that the *Times* itself had often used the very words it objected to 3's including as standard language. "If we are ever inclined to the linguistic pedantry that easily fails to distinguish moribund traditions from genuine living usage [the adjectives here are perhaps more revealing than Dr. Gove intended] we have only to turn to the columns of the *Times,*" Dr. Gove concluded. The *Times* is the best newspaper in the world in the gathering and printing of news, but it has never been noted for stylistic distinction. And even if it were, the exigencies of printing a small book every day might be expected to drive the writers and editors of a newspaper into usages as convenient as they are sloppy—usages that people with more time on their hands, such as the editors of an unabridged dictionary, might distinguish from standard English.

There are several reasons that it is important to maintain standards in the use of a language. English, like other languages, is beautiful when properly used, and beauty can be achieved only by attention to form, which means setting limits, or de-fining, or dis-criminating. Language expresses the special, dis-tinctive quality of a people, and a people, like an individual, is to a large extent defined by its past—its traditions—whether it is conscious of this or not. If the language is allowed to shift too rapidly, without challenge from teachers and lexicographers, then the special character of the American people is blurred, since it tends to lose its past. In the same way a city loses its character if too much of it is torn down and rebuilt too quickly. "Languages are the pedigrees of nations," said Dr. Johnson.

The effect on the individual is also unfortunate. The kind of permissiveness that permeates 3 (the kind that a decade or two ago was more common in progressive schools than it is now) results, oddly, in less rather than more individuality, since the only way an individual can "express himself" is in relation to a social norm—in the case of language, to standard usage. James Joyce's creative distortions of words were possible only because he had a perfect ear for orthodox English. But if the very idea of form, or standards, is lacking, then how can one violate it? It's no fun to use *knowed* for *known* if everybody thinks you're just trying to be standard.

Counting cite slips is simply not the way to go about the delicate business of deciding these matters. If nine-tenths of the citizens of the United States, including a recent President, were to use *inviduous,* the one-tenth who clung to *invidious* would still be right, and they would be doing a favor to the majority if they continued to maintain the point. It is perhaps not democratic, according to some recent users, or abusers, of the word, to insist on this, and the question comes up of who is to decide at what point change—for language does indeed change, as the Structural Linguists insist—has evolved from *slang, dial., erron.,* or *substand.* to *standard.* The decision, I think, must be left to the teachers, the professional writers, and the lexicographers, and they might look up Ulysses' famous defense of conservatism in Shakespeare's "Troilus and Cressida":

> The heavens themselves, the planets and this centre
> Observe degree, priority and place,
> Insisture, course, proportion, season, form,
> Office and custom in all line of order. . . .
> Take but degree away, untune that string,
> And, hark, what discord follows! Each thing meets
> In mere oppugnancy. The bounded waters
> Should lift their bosoms higher than the shores
> And make a sop of all this solid globe.
> Strength should be lord of imbecility
> And the rude son should strike his father dead.
> Force should be right, or rather right and wrong
> (Between whose endless jar justice resides)
> Should lose their names, and so should justice too.
> Then every thing includes itself in power,
> Power into will, will into appetite
> And appetite, a universal wolf,
> So doubly seconded with will and power,
> Must make perforce a universal prey
> And, last, eat up himself. . . .

Dr. Johnson, a dictionary-maker of the old school, defined *lexicographer* as "a harmless drudge." Things have changed. Lexicographers may still be drudges, but they are certainly not harmless. They have untuned the string, made a sop of the solid structure of English, and encouraged the language to eat up himself.

The New Yorker, March 10, 1962

James Sledd

THE LEXICOGRAPHER'S UNEASY CHAIR

". . . this latest dictionary to bear the Merriam-Webster label is an intellectual achievement of the very highest order."

—Sumner Ives in *Word Study*

". . . the anxiously awaited work that was to have crowned cisatlantic linguistic scholarship with a particular glory turns out to be a scandal and a disaster."

—Wilson Follett in the *Atlantic*

"Somebody had goofed."

—Ethel Merman in *Webster's Third New International Dictionary*

*B*UT WHO? Is the goof trademarked, a Merriam-Webster, or is scholarship in Springfield trans-*Atlantic?* The experts will have to answer that question, and thoughtful laymen after using the new dictionary for a long time. This review has more modest aims. Mainly it examines a few issues which less inhibited critics have already raised, suggests some possible limitations of their criticisms, and urges that the serious work of serious scholars must be seriously judged.

Everyone knows that the *Third International* is an entirely new dictionary for use today. In this eighth member of a series which began in 1828, the Merriam Company has invested over $3,500,000, almost three times the cost of the 1934 *New International,* so that the statements in *Webster's Third* are backed by over a century of experience, by the evidence of more than 10,000,000 citations, and by the knowledge and skill of a large permanent staff and more than 200 special consultants. To a reviewer, those facts should be rather sobering.

Some editors, however, and some reviewers have not been restrained from prompt attacks. They have criticized the *Third International* for its failure to include expected encyclopedic matter, for its technique of definition, and especially for its treatment of what is called usage; and they have charged Dr. Gove and his associates with unwise innovations motivated by the desire to destroy all standards of better and worse in the use of English. While insisting upon the responsibility of lexicographers, some of the attackers have not been equally alert to the responsibility of critics.

The question of motives can be dismissed at once. The lexicographers at the Merriam Company, it may safely be assumed, have just one motive: to make the best possible dictionaries. They may have failed, in one respect or another; but such innovations as they actually have made have not been made without the most serious and responsible consideration.

The charge of unwise innovation has two parts: first, that an innovation has been made; and second, that it is unwise. Some of the critics have assumed that the editors of the *Third International* have departed from established lexicographical custom by assuming the role of historians, not lawgivers. One reviewer, indeed, to prove his accusation that the lexicographers had abandoned authority for permissiveness, quoted a part of their statement that "the standard of English pronunciation . . . is the usage that now prevails among the educated and cultured people to whom the language is vernacular." He had not bothered to read precisely the same statement in the 1934 *New International*.

More generally, too many of the unfavorable critics have ignored the whole history of English lexicography since Samuel Johnson: they have hurried to denounce an innovation as unwise before establishing the fact of innovation. Already in the eighteenth century, the ideal of the standard and standardizing dictionary had been sharply questioned. The encyclopedist Ephraim Chambers declared his view that "the Dictionary-Writer is not supposed to have any hand in the things he relates; he is no more concerned to make the improvements, or establish the significations, than the historian" to fight the battles he describes. Even Johnson said of himself that he did not "form, but register the language," that he did not "teach men how they should think, but relate how they have hitherto expressed their thoughts"; and when Englishmen a century later set out to make the great *Oxford Dictionary*, they assumed from the beginning that the lexicographer is "an historian" of the language, "not a critic." It may be that professional lexicographers have been on the wrong track for two centuries and that in two hours an amateur can set them straight; but in that event the amateur and not the lexicographer would be the innovator. He would do well, before attempting to put his lawgiving theory into practice, to face Johnson's doubts in that magnificent "Preface" and to ask himself the unanswerable question how rational choice among the resources of a language is possible for the man who does not know what those resources are.

The relation between a dictionary and an encyclopedia is another problem whose history should have been better known to some reviewers. Few lexicographers are likely to solve it either to their own full satisfaction or to the satisfaction of all their readers. From the *Third International,* the objectors miss the gazetteer and the biographical dictionary of the 1934 volume, and they dislike the new decision to restrict the word-list "to generic words . . . as distinguished from proper names that are not generic." Other readers might just as well make opposite complaints. The hairy-nosed wombat and the hickory shuck-worm do not greatly interest the average American, who has equally little need to know the incubation period of the ostrich or the gestation period of the elephant, to contemplate the drawing of a milestone marked "Boston 20 miles," or to examine a colorplate of fishes which is a slander to the catfish and the brook trout; and the occasional philologist might hope for a dictionary which explains words and leaves to the encyclopedia, as Murray said, the description of things. But who can say that he knows infallibly how such decisions should be made? Murray did not claim infallibility but admitted inconsistency in his omission of *African* and inclusion of *American.* Since man and the universe cannot be put between two covers, some things must be omitted; "selection is guided by usefulness"; and usefulness can be guessed at but not measured. Readers who can get the use of a Webster's unabridged will have access to an encyclopedia. They should consult it when they need to know about people and places. Meanwhile they may be grateful that the *Third International* has made space for as many quotations as it now includes. A dictionary without quotations is like a table of contents without a book.

There remain, of the critics' favorite subjects, the technique of definition and the matter of usage. The technique of definition is briefly explained in the editor's preface:

The primary objective of precise, sharp defining has been met through development of a new dictionary style based upon completely analytical one-phrase definitions throughout the book. Since the headword in the definition is intended to be modified only by structural elements restrictive in some degree and essential to each other, the use of commas either to separate or to group has been severely limited, chiefly to units in apposition or in series. The new defining pattern does not provide for a predication which conveys further expository comment. . . . Defining by synonym is carefully avoided by putting all unqualified or undifferentiated terms in small capital letters. Such a term in small capitals should not be considered a definition but a cross-reference to a definition of equivalent meaning that can be substituted for the small capitals.

A large number of verbal illustrations mostly from the mid-twentieth century has been woven into the defining pattern with a view to contributing considerably to the user's interest and understanding by showing a word used in context.

If it is not naively optimistic to expect most critics of a dictionary to agree on anything, general approval may be expected for careful synonymies and for the distinction between a synonym and a definition; and the value of illustrative quotations has been demonstrated by centuries of English lexicography. The objection that not many mid-century authors deserve quotation has already been answered, for it is only another form of the notion that the lexicographer should be a lawgiver and not a historian. It would, moreover, be rash to suggest either that many of the quotations are not particularly informative or that identification by the mere names of the authors makes it impossible to check the quotations or to examine them in their contexts: with 10,000,000 quotations to choose from, the editors must know the possibilities of choice more fully than any critic, and precise references would take up much valuable space.

The definitions themselves are another matter. Without advancing any claim to special competence, an ordinary reader may fairly report that he finds some of the definitions extraordinarily clumsy and hard to follow and that as an English teacher he would not encourage his students to follow the new Merriam-Webster model. The one-phrase definitions of nouns in particular may become confusing because in English it is hard to keep track of the relations among a long series of prepositional phrases, participial phrases, and relative clauses; the reader may simply forget what goes with what, if indeed he ever can find out. A less serious criticism is that the new typeface and the long entries unbroken by indentation are bad for middle-aged eyes. Real mistakes, of course, are extremely rare, but a fisherman may be pardoned an objection to the fourth numbered definition of the noun *keeper* as "a fish large enough to be legally caught." The crime is not catching but keeping an undersized or oversized fish.

Perhaps such a quibble is itself no keeper, and some criticism of the dictionary's treatment of usage has been equally frivolous. An excellent bad example appeared in *Life,* whose editors compressed a remarkable amount of confusion into a single sentence when they attacked "Editor Gove" for "saying that if a word is misused often enough, it becomes acceptable." Though one can argue how much use and by what speakers is enough, consistency would force *Life's* editors into silence. Their sacred kye are scrawnier than Pharaoh's seven kine, and it is shocking that the influence of such a magazine should force learning to debate with ignorance.

Yet so loud a stridulation of critics cannot simply be ignored. There is a real question whether the *Third International,* though justly called "the most comprehensive guide to usage currently available," has recorded usage as precisely as it might have done. Were the editors right to abandon "the status label *colloquial*"? Have they adequately reported not only what people say and write but also those opinions concerning speech and writing which properly enter into their own definitions of *standard* and of *Standard English?* Those are legitimate questions to ask of a dictionary "prepared with a constant regard for the needs of the high school and college student" and of the general reader. However diffidently and respectfully, a reviewer must give the best answers that he can.

Several reasons have been offered, by various authorities, for the abandonment of the label *colloquial.* Those reasons are not all alike. It is one thing to say that we cannot know "whether a word out of context is colloquial or not" (Gove), that lexicographers cannot distinguish the "many different degrees of standard usage" by status labels but can only suggest them by quotations (Gove), or that "the bases for discrimination are often too subtle for exact and understandable verbal statement" (Ives); it is quite another thing to argue against marking words *colloquial* because many readers have wrongly concluded that a word so marked is somehow bad (Ives). In a matter to which the editors must have given their best thought, the variety itself of these justifications and the failure to order them in any coherent and inclusive statement is somewhat puzzling; and the impertinent might be tempted to inquire how 200,000 quotations will enable the inexpert reader to do what

10,000,000 quotations did not make possible for the expert lexicographer or how a dictionary can be made at all if nothing can go into it which the ignorant might misinterpret. One reason for the widespread misinterpretation of the policy adopted is surely that the underlying theory has not been clearly explained.

And that is not all. The very defenses of the new policy appear sometimes to refute the contention that finer discriminations are not possible than those in *Webster's Third*. When the newspapers attack the dictionary for listing words like *double-dome* and *finalize* as standard, defenders reply by citing other slangy or colloquial or much reprobated terms from the columns of those same newspapers. What is the force of the attack or the defense unless the intelligent layman can draw precisely that distinction between "the formal and informal speech and writing of the educated" which the *Third International* refuses to draw for him? If he lacked that ability, both attackers and defenders would be wasting their citations.

Much can be said, of course, about the confusion of styles in modern writing. Perhaps distinctions among styles are now indeed less clear and stable than they were in a less troubled age; perhaps the clumsier writers do ignore the existing distinctions while the sophisticated use them to play sophisticated tunes; perhaps the scrupulously objective lexicographer cannot establish those distinctions from his quotation slips alone. For all that, distinctions do exist. They exist in good writing, and they exist in the linguistic consciousness of the educated. Dr. Gove's definers prove they exist when they give *egghead* as a synonym for *double-dome* but then define *egghead* in impeccably formal terms as "one with intellectual interests or pretensions" or as "a highly educated person." Such opposition between theory and practice strikes even a timid and generally admiring reviewer as rather odd, as though some notion of scientific objectivity should require the scientist to deny that he knows because he may not know how he knows it.

In the absence, then, of convincing argument to the contrary, a simple reader is left with the uneasy feeling that the abandonment of *"Colloq."* was a mistake which the introduction of more quotations does not quite rectify and that as a teacher he must now provide foreigners and inexperienced students both with some general principles of linguistic choice and with specific instruction in instances where the new dictionary does not discriminate finely enough among stylistic variants. The dictionary leaves unlabeled many expressions which this teacher would not allow a beginning writer to use in serious exposition or argument except for clearly intended and rather special effects: *(to be caught)* *with one's pants down, dollarwise, stylewise (s.v. -wise), (to give one) the bird, dog* "something inferior of its kind," *to enthuse, to level* "deal frankly," *schmaltz, chintzy, the catbird seat, to roll* "rob," *to send* "delight," *shindig, shook-up, square* "an unsophisticated person," *squirrelly, to goof,* and the like. Enforcing such modest niceties will now be more difficult; for classroom lawyers and irate parents will be able to cite the dictionary which the teacher has taught Johnny how to read but which has collapsed the distinction between formal and informal Standard English. Similar difficulties could occur with various mild obscenities, such as *pissed off* and *pisspoor,* which should be marked not only as slang but with some one of the warning labels that the dictionary attaches to the almost quite adequately recorded four-letter words; and the label *slang* itself might well be more freely used with the various synonyms for *drunk—stewed, stinko, stoned, tight, tanked, sozzled, potted, pie-eyed, feeling no pain, blind, looped, squiffed, boiled, fried, high,* etc. Odzooks!

The convenience of a classroom teacher, however, is a rather petty criterion by which to judge a great dictionary, and the tiny handful of evidence here alleged must not be taken as justifying the shrill lament that *Webster's Third* is "a scandal and a disaster." The wake has been distinctly premature. Both the dictionary and the language it records are likely to survive the keening critics, whose exaggerations are something of a stumbling block themselves. The mere extent of the information in a dictionary unabridged should fix in a reviewer's mind the salutary knowledge that as no one man can make such a book, so no one man can judge it; but the popular reviews of the *Third International* have merely skimmed its surface and have said little of its technical features or substantial accomplishments. The present discussion will conclude with a few slight remarks on some such matters and with the renewed insistence that longer use and more expert study will be necessary before the dictionary can be definitively judged.

Teachers of elementary composition may be especially interested in the dictionary's three well-filled pages on English punctuation. As several recent grammarians have done, the editors attempt to establish definite relations between pointing and intonation, and they pursue that end with some care and vigor: the theory that punctuation may in part be taught by relating it to pitch-contours and to pauses here receives a better-than-average statement.

Yet the composition teacher may still be sceptical. For one thing, no account of English intonation has deserved or won universal acceptance. The editors themselves thus seem to postulate more than the three "pauses" allowed in the Trager-Smith phonology, which their description directly or indirectly follows. What is worse is the failure of the proposed relationships between speech and pointing as one moves from dialect to dialect: rules that may hold in one region do not hold in another. For much Southern American speech and for much Southern British, it is simply not the case that "the rising pause . . . is usually indicated in writing by a comma"; for many speakers and writers in many areas, an exclamation point may correspond to a *low*-pitched "terminal stress" as well as to a high one; and a colon may be used in writing not just for "a fading or sustained pause in speech" but for a "rising pause" or for no pause at all. The editors have weakened their case by stating it too simply and too strongly.

For the linguistically inclined, Mr. Edwin Artin's extensive "Guide to Pronunciation" will have a particular attraction. The "Guide" is just that—a guide; "not a treatise on phonetics" or a structural dialectologist's systematic account of American pronunciation, but an explanation of the way the editors have used their new alphabet in their transcriptions. Though the forgetful will regret that the key is no longer before them at each opening, and though a stern phonemicist might call the whole system sloppy, the new alphabet is an arguable solution to an extremely complex theoretical and practical problem and a definite improvement over the more complicated yet less accurate and more misleading diacritical key in the *Webster's of* 1934. The objective in devising the alphabet "was a set of symbols which would represent each speech sound which distinguishes one word from another and each difference in sound which is associated with some large region of the country" (Ives), so that the editors might record both the formal and the informal pronunciations actually heard in cultivated conversation from speakers of the standard dialects in the various regions. The *Third International* can thus do fuller justice than its predecessor did to regional variation and to modes of speech less artificial than the "formal platform speech" of the earlier work.

Like every competent writer on American pronunciation, Mr. Artin will be criticized as well as praised. He writes, indeed, at a particularly difficult time, when phonological theory is so unsettled that rival groups among the linguists can scarcely communicate with one another. Since pleasing one group of theorists means displeasing its opponents, since it is easily possible to please neither or none, and since Mr. Artin does not include in his "Guide" the sort of general and historical information which could be found in the corresponding section of the 1934 dictionary, perhaps he will not have so large an audience as Kenyon reached. His readers will be the kind who will argue the results of equating the medial consonants of *tidal* and *title* because in some dialects they are phonetically identical or of distinguishing them because the preceding diphthongs may be of different lengths and because the consonants of *tide* and *titular* clearly differ. Other readers, if they find the "Guide" hard going, will not risk too much confusion by limiting their study to the table of symbols and to the short section on pronunciation in the "Explanatory Notes."

Within the dictionary proper, the word-list first invites examination. Like the addenda to the later editions of the *Second,* the vexing miscellaneous entries at the bottoms of the pages are now gone from *Webster's Third,* either dropped or worked into the main alphabet; numerous obsolete words have disappeared, since the cut-off date has been advanced from 1500 to 1755; and further space for additions has been found by rejecting many no longer useful terms from the rapidly changing and never generally current technical vocabulary with which both the *Second* and the *Third International* are stuffed. This plethora or scientific and technical terms, carefully gathered in an elaborate reading program, is of course no plethora at all but only a comfortable supply for the scientist and technologist, who seem pleased with the dictionary's coverage of their fields; and a general dictionary must make room as well for some regionalisms, for a certain amount of recent slang, and for the new words in general use which so eloquently damn our culture. When all this has been done, it would be unfair to complain that perhaps not enough attention has been paid to the distinctive vocabularies of English-speaking nations other than Britain and the United States.

Beyond the word-list, neither space nor the reviewer's competence will allow him to go. He has few complaints about spelling, the only loud one being against *alright;* as far as a layman's knowledge goes, the etymologies are accurate, and beyond that point they remain clear and comprehensible; the discrimination and the arrangement of senses impose silence on the reader who has not studied them with the same care that went into their making; and the synonymies have already proved their practical value. A sweeping conclusion will not be expected of a review whose thesis is that the prematurity of sweeping conclusions has already been sufficiently exemplified, but a moderately serious examination has made a few things perfectly plain about the *Third International.* As a completely new, independent, responsibly edited, unabridged dictionary, no other work can rival it on precisely its own ground. Its merits are infinitely greater than those of the reviews which have lightly questioned them. Time and the experts will ultimately decide its just rank in the world of English lexicography, whether above, below, or alongside its predecessor; but meanwhile it can usefully fill a place in the libraries of a generation.

College English, May, 1962

C. P. Snow

THE TWO CULTURES

JT IS about three years since I made a sketch in print of a problem which had been on my mind for some time. It was a problem I could not avoid just because of the circumstances of my life. The only credentials I had to ruminate on the subject at all came through those circumstances, through nothing more than a set of chances. Anyone with similar experience would have seen much the same things and I think made very much the same comments about them. It just happened to be an unusual experience. By training I was a scientist: by vocation I was a writer. That was all. It was a piece of luck, if you like, that arose through coming from a poor home.

But my personal history isn't the point now. All that I need say is that I came to Cambridge and did a bit of research here at a time of major scientific activity. I was privileged to have a ringside view of one of the most wonderful creative periods in all physics. And it happened through the flukes of war—including meeting W. L. Bragg in the buffet on Kettering station on a very cold morning in 1939, which had a determining influence on my practical life—that I was able, and indeed morally forced, to keep that ringside view ever since. So for thirty years I have had to be in touch with scientists not only out of curiosity, but as part of a working existence. During the same thirty years I was trying to shape the books I wanted to write, which in due course took me among writers.

There have been plenty of days when I have spent the working hours with scientists and then gone off at night with some literary colleagues. I mean that literally. I have had, of course, intimate friends among both scientists and writers. It was through living among these groups and much more, I think, through moving regularly from one to the other and back again that I got occupied with the problem of what, long before I put it on paper, I christened to myself as the "two cultures." For constantly I felt I was moving among two groups—comparable in intelligence, identical in race, not grossly different in social origin, earning about the same incomes, who had almost ceased to communicate at all, who in intellectual, moral and psychological climate had so little in common that instead of going from Burlington House or South Kensington to Chelsea, one might have crossed an ocean.

In fact, one had travelled much further than across an ocean—because after a few thousand Atlantic miles, one found Greenwich Village talking precisely the same language as Chelsea, and both having about as much communication with M.I.T. as though the scientists spoke nothing but Tibetan. For this is not just our problem; owing to some of our educational and social idiosyncrasies, it is slightly exaggerated here, owing to another English social peculiarity it is slightly minimised; by and large this is a problem of the entire West.

By this I intend something serious. I am not thinking of the pleasant story of how one of the more convivial Oxford greats dons—I have heard the story attributed to A. L. Smith—came over to Cambridge to dine. The date is perhaps the 1890's. I think it must have been at St. John's, or possibly Trinity. Anyway, Smith was sitting at the right hand of the President—or Vice-Master—and he was a man who liked to include all round him in the conversation, although he was not immediately encouraged by the expressions of his neighbours. He addressed some cheerful Oxonian chit-chat at the one opposite to him, and got a grunt. He then tried the man on his own right and got another grunt. Then, rather to his surprise, one looked at the other and said, "Do you know what he's talking about?" "I haven't the least idea." At this, even Smith was getting out of his depth. But the President, acting as a social emollient, put him at his ease, by saying, "Oh, those are mathematicians! We never talk to *them*."

No, I intend something serious. I believe the intellectual life of the whole of western society is increasingly being split into two polar groups. When I say the intellectual life, I mean to include also a large part of our practical life, because I should be the last person to suggest the two can at the deepest level be distinguished. I shall come back to the practical life a little later. Two polar groups: at one pole we have the literary intellectuals, who incidentally while no one was looking took to referring to themselves as "intellectuals" as though there were no others. I remember G. H. Hardy once remarking to me in mild puzzlement, some time in the 1930's: "Have you noticed how the word 'intellectual' is used nowadays? There seems to be a new definition which certainly doesn't include Rutherford or Eddington or Dirac or Adrian or me. It does seem rather odd, don't y' know."

Literary intellectuals at one pole—at the other scientists, and as the most representative, the physical scientists. Between the two a gulf of mutual incomprehension—sometimes (particularly among the young) hostility and dislike, but most of all lack of understanding. They have a curious distorted image of each other. Their attitudes are so different that, even on the level of emotion, they can't find much common ground. Non-scientists tend to think of scientists as brash and boastful. They hear Mr. T. S. Eliot, who just for these illustrations we can take as an archetypal figure, saying about his attempts to revive verse-drama, that we can hope for very little, but that he would feel content if he and his co-workers could prepare the ground for a new Kyd or a new Greene. That is the tone, restricted and constrained, with which literary intellectuals are at home: it is the subdued voice of their culture. Then they hear a much louder voice, that of another archetypal figure, Rutherford, trumpeting: "This is the heroic age of science! This is the Elizabethan age!" Many of us heard that, and a good many other statements beside which that was mild; and we weren't left in any doubt whom Rutherford was casting for the role of Shakespeare. What is hard for the literary intellectuals to understand, imaginatively or intellectually, is that he was absolutely right.

And compare "this is the way the world ends, not with a bang but a whimper"—incidentally, one of the least likely scientific prophecies ever made—compare that with Rutherford's famous repartee, "Lucky fellow, Rutherford, always on the crest of the wave." "Well, I made the wave, didn't I?"

The non-scientists have a rooted impression that the scientists are shallowly optimistic, unaware of man's condition. On the other hand, the scientists believe that the literary intellectuals are totally lacking in foresight, peculiarly unconcerned with their brother men, in a deep sense anti-intellectual, anxious to restrict both art and thought to the existential moment. And so on. Anyone with a mild talent for invective could produce plenty of this kind of subterranean back-chat. On each side there is some of it which is not entirely baseless. It is all destructive. Much of it rests on misinterpretations which are dangerous. I should like to deal with two of the most profound of these now, one on each side.

First, about the scientists' optimism. This is an accusation which has been made so often that it has become a platitude. It has been made by some of the acutest non-scientific minds of the day. But it depends upon a confusion between the individual experience and the social experience, between the individual condition of man and his social condition. Most of the scientists I have known well have felt—just as deeply as the non-scientists I have known well—that the individual condition of each of us is tragic. Each of us is alone: sometimes we escape from solitariness, through love or affection or perhaps creative moments, but those triumphs of life are pools of light we make for ourselves while the edge of the road is black: each of us dies alone. Some scientists I have known have had faith in revealed religion. Perhaps with them the sense of the tragic condition is not so strong. I don't know. With most people of deep feeling, however high-spirited and happy they are, sometimes most with those who are happiest and most high-spirited, it seems to be right in the fibres, part of the weight of life. That is as true of the scientists I have known best as of anyone at all.

But nearly all of them—and this is where the colour of hope genuinely comes in—would see no reason why, just because the individual condition is tragic, so must the social condition be. Each of us is solitary: each of us dies alone: all right, that's a fate against which we can't struggle—but there is plenty in our condition which is not fate, and against which we are less than human unless we do struggle.

Most of our fellow human beings, for instance, are underfed and die before their time. In the crudest terms, *that* is the social condition. There is a moral trap which comes through the insight into man's loneliness: it tempts one to sit back, complacent in one's unique tragedy, and let the others go without a meal.

As a group, the scientists fall into that trap less than others. They are inclined to be impatient to see if something can be done: and inclined to think that it can be done, until it's proved otherwise. That is their real optimism, and it's an optimism that the rest of us badly need.

In reverse, the same spirit, tough and good and determined to fight it out at the side of their brother men, has made scientists regard the other culture's social attitudes as contemptible. That is too facile: some of them are, but they are a temporary phase and not to be taken as representative.

I remember being cross-examined by a scientist of distinction. "Why do most writers take on social opinions which would have been thought distinctly uncivilised and démodé at the time of the Plantagenets? Wasn't that true of most of the famous twentieth-century writers? Yeats, Pound, Wyndham Lewis, nine out of ten of those who have dominated literary sensibility in our time—weren't they not only politically silly, but politically wicked? Didn't the influence of all they represent bring Auschwitz that much nearer?"

I thought at the time, and I still think, that the correct answer was not to defend the indefensible. It was no use saying that Yeats, according to friends whose judgment I trust, was a man of singular magnanimity of character, as well as a great poet. It was no use denying the facts, which are broadly true. The honest answer was that there is, in fact, a connection, which literary persons were culpably slow to see, between some kinds of early twentieth-century art and the most imbecile expressions of anti-social feeling. That was one reason, among many, why some of us turned our backs on the art and tried to hack out a new or different way for ourselves.

But though many of those writers dominated literary sensibility for a generation, that is no longer so, or at least to nothing like the same extent. Literature changes more slowly than science. It hasn't the same automatic corrective, and so its misguided periods are longer. But it is ill-considered of scientists to judge writers on the evidence of the period 1914–50.

Those are two of the misunderstandings between the two cultures. I should say, since I began to talk about them—the two cultures, that is —I have had some criticism. Most of my scientific acquaintances think that there is something in it, and so do most of the practising artists I know. But I have been argued with by non-scientists of strong down-to-earth interests. Their view is that it is an over-simplification, and that if one is going to talk in these terms there ought to be at least three cultures. They argue that, though they are not scientists themselves, they would share a good deal of the scientific feeling. They would have as little use —perhaps, since they knew more about it, even less use—for the recent literary culture as the scientists themselves. J. H. Plumb, Alan Bullock and some of my American sociological friends have said that they vigorously refuse to be corralled in a cultural box with people they wouldn't be seen dead with, or to be regarded as helping to produce a climate which would not permit of social hope.

I respect those arguments. The number 2 is a very dangerous number: that is why the dialectic is a dangerous process. Attempts to divide anything into two ought to be regarded with much suspicion. I have thought a long time about going in for further refinements: but in the end I have decided against. I was searching for something a little more than a dashing metaphor, a good deal less than a cultural map: and for those purposes the two cultures is about right, and subtilising any more would bring more disadvantages than it's worth.

At one pole, the scientific culture really is a culture, not only in an intellectual but also in an anthropological sense. That is, its members need not, and of course often do not, always completely understand each other; biologists more often than not will have a pretty hazy idea of contemporary physics; but there are common attitudes, common stand-ards and patterns of behaviour, common approaches and assumptions. This goes surprisingly wide and deep. It cuts across other mental patterns, such as those of religion or politics or class.

Statistically, I suppose slightly more scientists are in religious terms unbelievers, compared with the rest of the intellectual world—though there are plenty who are religious, and that seems to be increasingly so among the young. Statistically also, slightly more scientists are on the Left in open politics—though again, plenty always have called themselves conservatives, and that also seems to be more common among the young. Compared with the rest of the intellectual world, considerably more scien-tists in this country and probably in the U.S. come from poor families. Yet, over a whole range of thought and behaviour, none of that matters very much. In their working, and in much of their emotional life, their attitudes are closer to other scientists than to non-scientists who in religion or politics or class have the same labels as themselves. If I were to risk a piece of shorthand, I should say that naturally they had the future in their bones.

They may or may not like it, but they have it. That was as true of the conservatives J. J. Thomson and Lindemann as of the radicals Ein-stein or Blackett: as true of the Christian A. H. Compton as of the materialist Bernal: of the aristocrats Broglie or Russell as of the prole-tarian Faraday: of those born rich, like Thomas Merton or Victor Roths-child, as of Rutherford, who was the son of an odd-job handyman. With-out thinking about it, they respond alike. That is what a culture means.

At the other pole, the spread of attitudes is wider. It is obvious that between the two, as one moves through intellectual society from the physicists to the literary intellectuals, there are all kinds of tones of feeling on the way. But I believe the pole of total incomprehension of science radiates its influence on all the rest. That total incomprehension gives, much more pervasively than we realise, living in it, an unscientific flavour to the whole "traditional" culture, and that unscientific flavour is often, much more than we admit, on the point of turning anti-scientific. The feelings of one pole become the anti-feelings of the other. If the scientists have the future in their bones, then the traditional culture responds by wishing the future did not exist. It is the traditional culture, to an extent remarkably little diminished by the emergence of the scientific one, which manages the western world.

This polarisation is sheer loss to us all. To us as people, and to our society. It is at the same time practical and intellectual and creative loss, and I repeat that it is false to imagine that those three considerations are clearly separable. But for a moment I want to concentrate on the intellectual loss.

The degree of incomprehension on both sides is the kind of joke which has gone sour. There are about fifty thousand working scientists in the country and about eighty thousand professional engineers or applied scientists. During the war and in the years since, my colleagues and I have had to interview somewhere between thirty to forty thousand of these— that is, about 25 per cent. The number is large enough to give us a fair sample, though of the men we talked to most would still be under forty. We were able to find out a certain amount of what they read and thought about. I confess that even I, who am fond of them and respect them, was a bit shaken. We hadn't quite expected that the links with the traditional culture should be so tenuous, nothing more than a formal touch of the cap.

As one would expect, some of the very best scientists had and have plenty of energy and interest to spare, and we came across several who had read everything that literary people talk about. But that's very rare. Most of the rest, when one tried to probe for what books they had read, would modestly confess, "Well, I've *tried* a bit of Dickens," rather as though Dickens were an extraordinarily esoteric, tangled and dubiously rewarding writer, something like Rainer Maria Rilke. In fact that is exactly how they do regard him: we thought that discovery, that Dickens had been transformed into the type-specimen of literary incomprehensibility, was one of the oddest results of the whole exercise.

But of course, in reading him, in reading almost any writer whom we should value, they are just touching their caps to the traditional culture. They have their own culture, intensive, rigorous, and constantly in action. This culture contains a great deal of argument, usually much more rigorous, and almost always at a higher conceptual level, than literary persons' arguments—even though the scientists do cheerfully use words in senses which literary persons don't recognise, the senses are exact ones, and when they talk about "subjective," "objective," "philosophy" or "progressive," they know what they mean, even though it isn't what one is accustomed to expect.

Remember, these are very intelligent men. Their culture is in many ways an exacting and admirable one. It doesn't contain much art, with the exception, an important exception, of music. Verbal exchange, insistent argument. Long-playing records. Colour-photography. The ear, to some extent the eye. Books, very little, though perhaps not many would go so far as one hero, who perhaps I should admit was further down the scientific ladder than the people I've been talking about—who, when asked what books he read, replied firmly and confidently: "Books? I prefer to use my books as tools." It was very hard not to let the mind wander —what sort of tool would a book make? Perhaps a hammer? A primitive digging instrument?

Of books, though, very little. And of the books which to most literary persons are bread and butter, novels, history, poetry, plays, almost nothing at all. It isn't that they're not interested in the psychological or moral or social life. In the social life, they certainly are, more than most of us. In the moral, they are by and large the soundest group of intellectuals we have; there is a moral component right in the grain of science itself, and almost all scientists form their own judgments of the moral life. In the psychological they have as much interest as most of us, though occasionally I fancy they come to it rather late. It isn't that they lack the interests. It is much more that the whole literature of the traditional culture doesn't seem to them relevant to those interests. They are, of course, dead wrong. As a result, their imaginative understanding is less than it could be. They are self-impoverished.

But what about the other side? They are impoverished too—perhaps more seriously, because they are vainer about it. They still like to pretend that the traditional culture is the whole of "culture," as though the natural order didn't exist. As though the exploration of the natural order was of no interest either in its own value or its consequences. As though the scientific edifice of the physical world was not, in its intellectual depth, complexity and articulation, the most beautiful and wonderful collective work of the mind of man. Yet most non-scientists have no conception of that edifice at all. Even if they want to have it, they can't. It is rather as though, over an immense range of intellectual experience, a whole group was tone-deaf. Except that this tone-deafness doesn't come by nature, but by training, or rather the absence of training.

As with the tone-deaf, they don't know what they miss. They give a pitying chuckle at the news of scientists who have never read a major work of English literature. They dismiss them as ignorant specialists. Yet their own ignorance and their own specialisation is just as startling. A good many times I have been present at gatherings of people who, by the standards of the traditional culture, are thought highly educated and who have with considerable gusto been expressing their incredulity at the illiteracy of scientists. Once or twice I have been provoked and have asked the company how many of them could describe the Second Law of Thermodynamics. The response was cold: it was also negative. Yet I was asking something which is about the scientific equivalent of: *Have you read a work of Shakespeare's?*

I now believe that if I had asked an even simpler question—such as, What do you mean by mass, or acceleration, which is the scientific equivalent of saying, *Can you read?*—not more than one in ten of the highly educated would have felt that I was speaking the same language. So the great edifice of modern physics goes up, and the majority of the cleverest people in the western world have about as much insight into it as their neolithic ancestors would have had.

Just one more of those questions, that my nonscientific friends regard as being in the worst of taste. Cambridge is a university where scientists and non-scientists meet every night at dinner. About two years ago, one of the most astonishing experiments in the whole history of science was brought off. I don't mean the sputnik—that was admirable for quite different reasons, as a feat of organisation and a triumphant use of existing knowledge. No, I mean the experiment at Columbia by Yang and Lee. It is an experiment of the greatest beauty and originality, but the result is so startling that one forgets how beautiful the experiment is. It makes us think again about some of the fundamentals of the physical world. Intuition, common sense—they are neatly stood on their heads. The result is usually known as the contradiction of parity. If there were any serious communication between the two cultures, this experiment would have been talked about at every High Table in Cambridge. Was it? I wasn't here: but I should like to ask the question.

There seems then to be no place where the cultures meet. I am not going to waste time saying that this is a pity. It is much worse than that. Soon I shall come to some practical consequences. But at the heart of thought and creation we are letting some of our best chances go by default. The clashing point of two subjects, two disciplines, two cultures —of two galaxies, so far as that goes—ought to produce creative chances. In the history of mental activity that has been where some of the break-throughs came. The chances are there now. But they are there, as it were, in a vacuum, because those in the two cultures can't talk to each other. It is bizarre how very little of twentieth-century science has been assimi-lated into twentieth-century art. Now and then one used to find poets conscientiously using scientific expressions, and getting them wrong— there was a time when "refraction" kept cropping up in verse in a mysti-fying fashion, and when "polarised light" was used as though writers were under the illusion that it was a specially admirable kind of light.

Of course, that isn't the way that science could be any good to art. It has got to be assimilated along with, and as part and parcel of, the whole of our mental experience, and used as naturally as the rest.

I said earlier that this cultural divide is not just an English phenome-non: it exists all over the western world. But it probably seems at its sharpest in England, for two reasons. One is our fanatical belief in educa-tional specialisation, which is much more deeply ingrained in us than in any country in the world, west or east. The other is our tendency to let our social forms crystallise. This tendency appears to get stronger, not weaker, the more we iron out economic inequalities: and this is specially true in education. It means that once anything like a cultural divide gets established, all the social forces operate to make it not less rigid, but more so.

The two cultures were already dangerously separate sixty years ago; but a prime minister like Lord Salisbury could have his own laboratory at Hatfield, and Arthur Balfour had a somewhat more than amateur interest in natural science. John Anderson did some research in organic chemistry in Würzburg before passing first into the Civil Service, and incidentally took a spread of subjects which is now impossible. None of that degree of interchange at the top of the Establishment is likely, or indeed thinkable, now.

In fact, the separation between the scientists and non-scientists is much less bridgeable among the young than it was even thirty years ago. Thirty years ago the cultures had long ceased to speak to each other: but at least they managed a kind of frozen smile across the gulf. Now the politeness has gone, and they just make faces. It is not only that the young scientists now feel that they are part of a culture on the rise while the other is in retreat. It is also, to be brutal, that the young scientists know that with an indifferent degree they'll get a comfortable job, while their contemporaries and counterparts in English or History will be lucky to earn 60 per cent as much. No young scientist of any talent would feel that he isn't wanted or that his work is ridiculous, as did the hero of *Lucky Jim,* and in fact, some of the disgruntlement of Amis and his associates is the disgruntlement of the under-employed arts graduate.

There is only one way out of all this: it is, of course, by rethinking our education. In this country, for the two reasons I have given, that is more difficult than in any other. Nearly everyone will agree that our school education is too specialised. But nearly everyone feels that it is outside the will of man to alter it. Other countries are as dissatisfied with their education as we are, but are not so resigned.

The U.S. teach out of proportion more children up to eighteen than we do: they teach them far more widely, but nothing like so rigorously. They know that: they are hoping to take the problem in hand within ten years, though they may not have all that time to spare. The U.S.S.R. also teach out of proportion more children than we do: they also teach far more widely than we do (it is an absurd western myth that their school education is specialised) but much too rigorously. They know that —and they are beating about to get it right. The Scandinavians, in particular the Swedes, who would make a more sensible job of it than any of us, are handicapped by their practical need to devote an inordinate amount of time to foreign languages. But they too are seized of the problem.

Are we? Have we crystallised so far that we are no longer flexible at all?

Talk to schoolmasters, and they say that our intense specialisation, like nothing else on earth, is dictated by the Oxford and Cambridge scholarship examinations. If that is so, one would have thought it not utterly impracticable to change the Oxford and Cambridge scholarship examinations. Yet one would underestimate the national capacity for the intricate defensive to believe that that was easy. All the lessons of our educational history suggest we are only capable of increasing specialisation, not decreasing it.

Somehow we have set ourselves the task of producing a tiny *élite*— far smaller proportionately than in any comparable country—educated in one academic skill. For a hundred and fifty years in Cambridge it was mathematics: then it was mathematics or classics: then natural science was allowed in. But still the choice had to be a single one.

It may well be that this process has gone too far to be reversible. I have given reasons why I think it is a disastrous process, for the purpose of a living culture. I am going on to give reasons why I think it is fatal, if we're to perform our practical tasks in the world. But I can think of only one example, in the whole of English educational history, where our pursuit of specialised mental exercises was resisted with success.

It was done here in Cambridge, fifty years ago, when the old order-of-merit in the Mathematical Tripos was abolished. For over a hundred years, the nature of the Tripos had been crystallising. The competition for the top places had got fiercer, and careers hung on them. In most colleges, certainly in my own, if one managed to come out as Senior or Second Wrangler, one was elected a Fellow out of hand. A whole apparatus of coaching had grown up. Men of the quality of Hardy, Littlewood, Russell, Eddington, Jeans, Keynes, went in for two or three years' training for an examination which was intensely competitive and intensely difficult. Most people in Cambridge were very proud of it, with a similar pride to that which almost anyone in England always has for our existing educational institutions, whatever they happen to be. If you study the fly-sheets of the time, you will find the passionate arguments for keeping the examination precisely as it was to all eternity: it was the only way to keep up standards, it was the only fair test of merit, indeed, the only seriously objective test in the world. The arguments, in fact, were almost exactly those which are used today with precisely the same passionate sincerity if anyone suggests that the scholarship examinations might conceivably not be immune from change.

In every respect but one, in fact, the old Mathematical Tripos seemed perfect. The one exception, however, appeared to some to be rather important. It was simply—so the young creative mathematicians, such as Hardy and Littlewood, kept saying—that the training had no intellectual merit at all. They went a little further, and said that the Tripos had killed serious mathematics in England stone dead for a hundred years. Well, even in academic controversy, that took some skirting round, and they got their way. But I have an impression that Cambridge was a good deal more flexible between 1850 and 1914 than it has been in our time. If we had had the old Mathematical Tripos firmly planted among us, should we have ever managed to abolish it?

Douglas Bush

THE HUMANITIES

*N*o ONE would ever speak of "the plight of the natural sciences," or of "the plight of the social sciences," but it is always proper to speak of "the plight of the humanities," and in the hushed, melancholy tone of one present at a perpetual death bed. For something like twenty-five hundred years the humanities have been in more or less of a plight, not because they are themselves weak, but because their war is not merely with ignorance but with original sin; and as civilization has advanced, the means of stultifying the head and heart have multiplied in variety and power. As a sample of cultural leadership, or of a common attitude, I should like to read a declaration of faith delivered some years ago by the chairman of the department of humanities in a well-known technological institution. We will call him Professor X. This is most of the report, from the *New York Times,* of his speech to a convention of engineers:

> Professor X . . . asserted last night that it would be "morally wrong" for him to advise the reading of the literary classics in this fast-moving age of television, radio and movies. . . .
>
> One should read for the purpose of doing something with what one reads, he asserted: not of polishing one's mind like a jewel, but of improving the world around.
>
> Take up a book because it will tell you something of the world . . . ; read what you want to read, not what you think you should read. "This is the frame of mind that makes reading worthwhile and often deeply rewarding.
>
> "For example, it would be morally wrong of me to urge you to take up a classic like 'David Copperfield' and to settle yourselves in easy chairs for winter evenings' reading. If you tried 'David Copperfield' you

would grow restive; you would think of all the other things you might be doing more consistent with your daily environment—looking at television, listening to the radio, going to the movies.

"Moreover, you would wonder why you should spend so much time laboriously reading 'David Copperfield' when you could see the book as a film, should it return some time to the neighborhood movie." . . . .

"The single prescription for adult reading," he added, "should be to read something different, something that will change your mind. Herein lies compensation for the loss of the purely reflective life."

Engineers are not, to be sure, in common repute the most cultivated branch of mankind, but did even they deserve such counsel, and from such a source? The humanities, as I said, have always had to contend with the crude urges of the natural man, with his resistance to higher values than his own, but the speech I just quoted from reminds us of the many new ways there are of escaping from active thought and feeling into a state of lazy collapse, of passive surrender to unthinking action or external sensation. Many people would endorse our oracle's view that one should not read to polish one's mind like a jewel but for the sake of improving the world around. The humanistic tradition has always stood for improvement of the world, but it has always insisted that a man must make himself worthy of such an enterprise; one of our perennial troubles is that improvement of the world is undertaken by so many unpolished minds. Then our touching faith in machinery is illustrated by the quaint assumption that a movie is the same thing as a great book. And that *Ersatz* doctrine extends down through television to the comics, which have now joined the march of mind by reducing literary classics to capsule form. That sort of thing, by the way, was done, and done much better, a dozen centuries ago, and has been commonly labeled a symptom of the Dark Ages. But this is only a reminder; there is no need of enlarging upon such powerful elements in our popular civilization. The opposition to such elements comes from the humanities.

Negative terms, however, are not enough. The "humanities," in the original meaning of this and kindred words, embraced chiefly history, philosophy, and literature. These were the studies worthy of a free man, that ministered to *homo sapiens,* man the intellectual and moral being, and not *homo faber,* the professional and technical expert. And these, with divinity, completed the central circle of human knowledge and understanding. Divinity went overboard long ago; history, which once was literature, is now a social science; and philosophy, though still grouped with the humanities, has become a branch of mathematics.

Thus in common usage the humanities mean literature and the fine arts. That is an unfortunate narrowing but we may take things as we find them and concentrate on literature, which is central and representative.

One plain fact nowadays is that the study of literature, which in itself is comprehensive and complex, has had to take over the responsibilities that used to be discharged by philosophy and divinity. Most young people now get their only or their chief understanding of man's moral and religious quest through literature. Anyone who has been teaching literature for twenty-five or thirty years, as I have, can testify to the marked change there has been in the spiritual climate during that time. (A rigorously scientific colleague of mine, in psychology, will not permit the use of the word "spiritual," but I use it anyhow.) I am speaking mainly of the higher order of college students, but it would be hard to imagine even the better students of twenty-five or thirty years ago reading Dante and George Herbert and Milton and Hopkins and Eliot with the real sympathy that many now show. For the more intelligent and sensitive young people of today, and there are very many of that kind, are a serious and a conservative lot. They not only live in our unlovely world, they have no personal experience of any other. They are aware of hollowness and confusion all around them, and, what is still more real, of hollowness and confusion in themselves. They feel adrift in a cockboat on an uncharted sea, and they want a sense of direction, of order and integration. And in literature they find, as countless people have found before them, that their problems are not new, that earlier generations have been lost also. Most of the young people I see find in literature, literature of the remote past as well as of the present, what they cannot find in textbooks of psychology and sociology, the vision of human experience achieved by a great spirit and bodied forth by a great artist.

I apologize for elaborating what may be called clichés, but those familiar lists of courses in catalogues make one forget that the frigid label "English 10" or "French 20" may represent an illumination and a rebirth for John or Betty Doe. Not that courses are the only or even the main road to enriched experience and sensitivity, but they are one road; and a teacher can help as a guide or catalyst. Josiah Royce is said to have complained that a philosopher was expected to spiritualize the community. The modern philosopher is expected only to semanticize the community; the other function, as I said, falls upon the teacher of literature. I do not of course mean inspirational gush. I mean that teachers, conducting a critical discussion of a piece of great literature, necessarily deal not only with the artistic use of words and materials but with the moral and spiritual experience that are its subject matter. That is why, as President Pusey has said, the humanities must be the cornerstone of a liberal education. Naturally teachers will have their methods under constant scrutiny, but their material, the world's great literature, can hardly be improved; all it needs is a chance to work upon responsive minds and characters.

While I cannot guess the temper of this gathering, and while all the administrators present may, for all I know, regard the humanities as a pearl of great price, that is not their general reputation. Administrators are commonly said to prize the solid and tangible virtues of the natural and social sciences and to look upon the humanities as a nice luxury for the carriage trade. How far that general reputation is true or false I wouldn't know, but, just in case it has a modicum of truth, I have been insisting that the humanities are not a luxury; they are the most practical of necessities if men and women are to become fully human. The humanities commonly suffer in esteem because they do not lend themselves to statistical reports of achievement. You cannot demonstrate with graphs and charts that John or Betty Doe, through reacting to a piece of literature, became a person of richer moral and imaginative insight, of finer wisdom and discrimination and stability. For the experience of literature is an individual experience, and nothing that is really important can be measured.

When we look at the American educational scene, the diversity of standards is so great that generalizations about this or that part of it may be violently contradictory. At any rate educational history of the past fifty years seems to furnish a pretty good forecast of the bad effects of the deluge to be expected in the next fifteen. In school, college, and university, the results of the huge increase in the student body suggest that the principle of education for all, however fine in theory, in practice leads ultimately to education for none. An editorial in the *New York Times* of September 13, 1954, takes the usual line of defense. The principle of education for all, it says, forces us "to accept the principle, also, that the function of education is primarily social and political rather than purely intellectual." "It cannot be denied," the *Times* proceeds, "that this means a down-grading of the learning process. We are adjusting to an 'average' that must be spread so widely that it comes down automatically. Education is no longer the intellectual privilege of the gifted few. It is held to be the democratic right of all." The *Times* does go a little beyond this orthodox assent to express uneasiness over the sacrifice, in elementary and secondary schools, of quality to quantity.

To mention one of many results, there has been an appalling growth of illiteracy at all levels, even in the graduate school. (Somehow stenographers are still literate, even if their college-bred employers are not.) At every orgy of Commencements one wonders how many of the hordes of new bachelors of arts can speak and write their own language with elementary decency, or read it with understanding. After all, the polished mind is suspect, whether in a student, a professor, or a Presidential candidate. And illiteracy, and contentment with illiteracy, are only symptoms of general shoddiness.

Obviously one main cause of this state of things has been the sheer pressure of numbers, along with a deplorable shrinkage in the number of qualified teachers. But the situation would not be so bad as it has been if the downward pressure of numbers had not been powerfully strengthened by misguided doctrine and practice. The training of teachers and the control of school curricula have been in the hands of colleges of education and their products, and these have operated on principles extracted from John Dewey's philosophy of barbarism. (If that phrase seems unduly harsh, I may say that I have in mind Dewey's hostility to what he regarded as leisure-class studies; his anti-historical attitude, his desire—intensified in his followers—to immerse students in the contemporary and immediate; and his denial of a hierarchy of studies, his doctrine that all kinds of experience are equally or uniquely valuable; and it would not be irrelevant to add his notoriously inept writing.) The lowest common denominator has been, not an evil, but an ideal. The substantial disciplines have been so denuded of content that multitudes of students, often taught by uneducated teachers, have been illiterate, uninformed, and thoroughly immature. There is no use in priding ourselves on the operation of the democratic principle if education loses much of its meaning in the process. When we think, for instance, of education for citizenship, which has been the cry of modern pedagogy, we may think also of the volume and violence of popular support given to the anti-intellectual demagoguery of the last few years. Mass education tends to reflect mass civilization, instead of opposing it. Even if education were everywhere working on the highest level, it would still face tremendous odds.

The great problem has been, and will be, first, the preservation of minority culture against the many and insidious pressures of mass civilization, and, secondly, the extension of that minority culture through wider and wider areas. The rising flood of students is very much like the barbarian invasions of the early Middle Ages, and then the process of education took a thousand years. We hope for something less over-whelming, and for a less protracted cure, but the principle is the same; Graeco-Roman-Christian culture not only survived but triumphed, and with enrichment. If we think of our problem in the light of that one, we shall not be disheartened but recognize both as phases of man's perennial growing pains.

Throughout history it has been a more or less small minority that has created and preserved what culture and enlightenment we have, and, if adverse forces are always growing, that minority is always growing too. In spite of the low standards that have commonly prevailed in public education during the last fifty years, I think the top layer of college students now are proportionately more numerous than they were thirty years ago and are more generally serious and critical. There is a growing nucleus of fine minds, and teachers are concerned with the enlargement of that all-important group. At the same time, without retreating from that position, one wonders what it is in our educational process or in our culture at large that often causes a liberal education to end on Commencement Day.

I have no novel and dramatic remedy for the evils that have shown themselves so clearly already and will become more formidable still. But I might mention a few things of varying importance which do not seem utopian. Of course I represent no one but myself, and I cannot even say, like a member of the House of Lords, that I enjoy the full confidence of my constituents.

In the first place, I see no reason why the flood of students should be allowed to pour into college, why automatic graduation from school should qualify anyone for admission. We ought to recognize, and make people in general recognize, that a desire for economic or social advantage, or for merely four years of idle diversion, is not enough. Under such pressure as is coming, surely the state universities have the strength to set up bars and select their student body, instead of admitting all who choose to walk in the front door and then, with much trouble and expense, trying to get rid of some through the back door. Doubtless such procedure would require a campaign of enlightenment and persuasion, but legislators always have an alert ear for the cry of economy, and the public must be convinced that higher education, or what passes for that, is neither a birthright nor a badge of respectability, and that useful and happy lives can be led without a college degree. As things are, we have an army of misfits, who lower educational standards and increase expense, and no branch of a university staff has grown more rapidly of late years than the psychiatric squad.

Secondly, many people have grounds for the belief that the multiplying junior colleges can and will drain off a large number of the young who for various reasons are unfitted for a really strenuous four-year course. Junior colleges, however, should not be recreational centers for the subnormal.

Thirdly, I think the need for formal education beyond high school would be much lessened, and the quality of both secondary and higher education obviously improved, if the colleges and universities, getting the public behind them, made a concerted and effectual demand that the schools do their proper work and do it better than a great many schools have been doing it. Quite commonly, a distressing proportion of a college course now consists of high school work. We have grown so accustomed to a battalion of instructors teaching elementary composition to freshmen that we take it as a normal part of college education, whereas it is a monstrosity. Imagine a European university teaching the rudiments of expression! If high school graduates are illiterate, they have no business in college. For a long time, and for a variety of reasons, we have had slackness all along the line; somehow, some time, strictness and discipline have got to begin.

Increased enrollments have almost inevitably led to increased reliance upon large lecture courses. There are administrators who assume that here is no limit to the effectiveness of a lecture course except the size of the auditorium, and there are also teachers who see positive virtues in lectures and can themselves display them. Perhaps because I never remember anything I hear in a lecture, I do not share that faith. I favor classes small enough to allow discussion, and that is expensive. But there are possible economies that would be highly desirable in themselves. We do not need to maintain the naïve doctrine that there has to be a course in anything in which anyone ever has been or might be interested. Many catalogues list courses that can only be called fantastic, and I don't think I am guilty of partisan prejudice if I say that these are rarely found among the humanities. If we had fewer and less specialized courses, and if we did not have our armies of composition teachers, a considerable number of man-hours would be released for smaller classes.

One thing that has suffered grievously and conspicuously in this last generation has been the study of foreign languages. The usual reason given is again the pressure of numbers, the numbers who are not going beyond high school, but again a positive reason has been open or quiet hostility. Languages have been pretty well crowded out of the school curriculum, and of course there has been a corresponding decline in college study. Nothing has been commoner in recent decades than the applicant for admission to a graduate school who has had little or no acquaintance with any foreign language except possibly a year or two of Spanish. Serious study of a foreign language means work, and a first principle of modern pedagogy has been the elimination of work. Thus, during the years in which we have all become conscious of one small world, and in which this country has become the leader of that world, educational theory and practice have retreated into cultural parochialism. There is no need to argue how necessary for the ordinary citizen is some knowledge of a foreign language and a foreign people. In the last few years a good many parents have been aroused, and the Modern Language Association has been putting on a vigorous campaign, so that progress has been made; but there is a long way to go. It is encouraging that in some cities successful experiments have been made in the teaching of languages in elementary schools, where, for good psychological reasons, they ought to begin. I wish there were something encouraging to be said about the ancient languages, but we are concerned with actualities.

Finally, since I touched on the large number of young people who are in college and shouldn't be, I might mention those who are not and should be, and who may be lost in the oncoming flood. Educators and others are more conscious than they once were of our failure to recognize and foster promising students who cannot afford college, and increasing efforts are being made in that direction; but we are still very far behind England, where bright students are picked out at the age of ten or eleven and brought along on scholarships. If we spent on exceptional students a fraction of the time and money we have spent on nursing lame ducks, there would be a considerable change in the quality of education.

One last word on a different matter. Like everything else, the Ph.D. has been cheapened by quantitative pressure, and it might be earnestly wished that it were not a union card for the teaching profession. There are plenty of young men and women who would be good teachers without such a degree, and the degree itself ought to mean something more than it does. Along with that may go another earnest wish, that both administrators and members of departments would abandon the principle of "publish or perish." Socrates would never have had a chance at an assistant professorship.

R. S. Crane

THE IDEA OF THE HUMANITIES

*I*T HAS seemed to me that I could perhaps best inaugurate the Hill Foundation Visiting Professorship in this college by speaking to you briefly about a large question which is now being debated with great energy and much anxious concern by nearly everybody who is interested in the future of liberal education in America—the question of what, exactly, are the humanities. I shall take as my text those familiar words from Robert Louis Stevenson's *Child's Garden of Verses:* "The world is so full of a number of things, I am sure we should all be as happy as kings." And I shall argue that one of the reasons why so many of us are now unhappy about the state and prospects of the humanities is that we have not fully grasped, in a positive spirit, the wisdom of these simple lines.

There would seem at first sight to be an easy and wholly convincing answer to our question of what the humanities are. They are merely those subject matters or fields of study, in a college or university curriculum, which lie outside the generally recognized spheres of the natural and the social sciences. In the University of which I am a member, there have been for a good many years four administrative Divisions, each under a Dean: a Division of the Biological Sciences, a Division of the Physical Sciences, a Division of the Social Sciences, and a Division of the Humanities; and the humanities at the University of Chicago are simply those studies, comprising the languages and literatures, the fine arts, comparative linguistics, philosophy, and some parts of history, which fall under the jurisdiction of the Dean of the Humanities Division. This has come to be a rather common mode of classifica-

577

tion; I am told that it has great administrative and budgetary advantages in a large university; and it has the virtue, also, of letting everybody know, in an apparently clear way, who the humanists are. They are the people who teach in the Humanities Division and eat lunch at a certain table in the Faculty Club.

Unfortunately this kind of answer to our question, in terms merely of subject matters or departments, is much too easy, and it ceases to be convincing as soon as we begin to observe what actually goes on both in the so-called humanistic fields and in the admittedly non-humanistic fields of the natural and the social sciences. I suppose I must call myself a humanist, since I teach literature, and since I have no competence whatever in either of the two major fields of learning. But I have noticed two things in the course of my experience. On the one hand, some of my closest intellectual friends, now and in the past, have been biologists, physicists, psychologists, economists, and political scientists; and I have been impressed, in all of them, by a way of thinking about their non-humanistic subject matters that is indistinguishable from the way of thinking which I associate with the best practitioners I have known of the humanistic arts. I must admit that this is not true of all the natural and social scientists I know! And, on the other hand, I have met many humanists (in the sense of professors of the so-called humanistic subjects), or have read their works, who have seemed to me much less humanistic, in their essential ways of thinking, than the scientific friends I have alluded to. They are the students of language who refuse to entertain any questions of better or worse in speech; they are the philosophers who want to make philosophy a branch of mathematics; the historians who insist on explaining all human events in terms of impersonal social or natural forces; the professors of literature and the critics who would resolve the appreciation of literature into a play of the unconscious mind, and the literary arts themselves into vestiges of primitive ritual and myth. I don't mean to say that in doing any or all of these things the humanists I have in mind have not given us many valuable insights into the subjects they are professing to deal with. The point is not that. The point is merely that if we wish to be clear about what the humanities are, as distinguished from the sciences of nature and society, we won't get very far if we are content to identify the humanities merely with a certain list of subjects in the curriculum and let it go at that. You can study Greek or philosophy all your life and not be a humanist; and you can devote yourself to ophthalmology or political science with equal ardor and concentration and be recognized as a humanist by all discriminating men.

But if a simple consideration of subject matters—as humanistic and non-humanistic—will not give us an answer to our question, what about purposes or ends? Isn't it conceivable that there are certain general human values or utilities which are served more adequately by the so-called humanistic subjects than by either the natural or the social sciences, and in terms of which we can define the characteristics of these subjects that make them peculiarly humanistic? As a matter of fact, in the long history of discussions of the humanities from the Romans to our time, this has been the way in which the question has been most commonly approached. For Romans like Cicero and Quintilian, the humanities were those arts and subject matters which are best suited to the formation of the orator, who was, for them, the virtuous and wise man *par excellence:* they included, in the first place, grammar and rhetoric, and along with them subjects like music, geometry, astronomy, moral philosophy, civil law, history, and the customs of the state, but these last only to the extent that they were thought capable of giving to the orator the copious supply of words and matters which he needs. The ends which these Romans envisaged in their discussions of the humanities were thus intensely practical ends; and much the same thing is true of the various purposes that have been assigned to humanistic study since the Renaissance. The humanities have been looked upon, during most of the modern period, as means to the realization of some large ideal or use over and above the understanding and appreciation of whatever specific subject matters they have been thought to consist in. They have been recommended and defended on the ground that they restore man to humanity and raise him toward God (as in the Spanish humanist, Juan Luis Vives); or that they lead to the knowledge of man's self, with the end of well doing and not of well knowing only (as in Sir Philip Sidney); or that they induce a philosophic habit of mind (as in Cardinal Newman); or that they lead to a harmonious expansion and interrelation of all the powers which make the beauty and worth of human nature (as in Matthew Arnold). Or, again, in another line of writers, the peculiar values of the humanities have been stated in terms not so much of the intrinsic good of the soul as of some external utility: they are those pursuits and studies which, better than any others, prepare a man to be a prudent, just, and temperate magistrate (as in Sir Thomas Elyot); or which fit a man to perform justly, skillfully, and magnanimously all the offices both private and public of peace and war (as in John Milton); or which prepare and discipline men for active life by recognizing that they are men before they are lawyers or physicians or merchants (as in John

Stuart Mill and many others); or which preserve for us (in Walter Lippmann's phrase) "the ideas, the premises, the rationale, the logic, the method, the values" upon which our free civilization was founded—a society which will continue to be threatened by anarchy within and tyranny without until we have restored the ideals of reason and freedom which, because of the decline of the humanities, we have lost.

The great defect of all these attempts to define the humanities in terms of the useful or lofty ends they may be made to serve is their persistent vagueness about the means by which these ends are to be accomplished in the everyday affairs of education. We get from the writers who approach our question in this way a great deal of eloquent writing about *what* the humanities, or only the humanities, can do for us, but very little specific discussion of *how* they can be expected to do this that goes beyond the dogmatic statement that some subject matters are more humanistic than others and hence ought to be studied. Consider, for example, the great American apostle of humanism in the last generation, Professor Irving Babbitt of Harvard. The essential humanistic ideal, for Babbitt, was what he called the ideal of measure: the human power to harmonize in oneself opposite virtues and to occupy, as he liked to put it, all the space between them without falling into either of the extremes. He devoted many learned and eloquent volumes to stating and restating this ideal and especially to exhibiting, in rather unmeasured language, its absence from most of the great writers and men of action since the eighteenth century. But the educational program which he sets forth in his *Literature and the American College* as the proper discipline by which the aims of humanism may be achieved in American life turns out to be a rather simple one: we must preserve the traditional A. B. program with its emphasis on the classics, we must read widely in the great books of all ages before becoming specialists, we must avoid the excesses of scientific philology, and keep in mind that the end of all literary or humanistic study is the making of value judgments. I need hardly say that we can do all these things and yet do them in a spirit, and with results, which Professor Babbitt himself, or any one else, would never agree to call humanistic.

We have now tried out two common ways of answering our question of what exactly are the humanities—first, by pointing to certain subjects that are officially or conventionally designated as humanistic, and, second, by specifying the large and noble purposes which humanistic study may be supposed to serve; and we have found neither of them entirely satisfactory. There is, however, I think, a third, and more promising, way of approaching our question—a way which is suggested by one of the earliest documents in which the term "humanities" occurs (in its singular Latin form of *humanitas,* or humanity). The document is the work of a minor Latin grammarian (or professor of language and literature) of the second century A.D.; and in it "humanity" is defined simply as "education and training in the good arts" or disciplines; and the goodness of these arts is made to reside in the fact that those who earnestly desire and seek after them come to be most highly humanized, in the sense of being endowed with the virtues and knowledge that separate men most sharply from the lower animals. Let me try to say what I think this implies in modern terms.

It is a view, as you can easily see, that identifies the humanities, not with certain *subjects* of study merely, or with the pursuit of certain abstract *ends,* but with the proper cultivation of certain *arts* or *disciplines,* that is, of certain means; and it makes the humanistic character of such arts or methods to consist in their peculiar capacity to deal with those aspects of human experience that differentiate man most completely from the animals, to the end that individual men may actualize as fully as possible their potentialities as men.

But what are the aspects of human experience that distinguish men most completely, now and in the past, from the animals? I think the answer is not hard to give. They consist, generally, in all those things which, because not all men or all groups of men can, or do, do them, are therefore not amenable to adequate explanation in terms of general laws of natural processes, physical or biological, or in terms of collective social conditions or forces. They are the things which we cannot predict, in any scientific way, that men individually or in groups will do, but which, when they are done, we recognize as signs, not of any natural or social necessities, but of possibilities inherent in man's peculiar nature. They are, in short, what we commonly speak of as human achievements—whether in sciences, in institutions, or in the arts. And, more especially, they are those human achievements, like Newtonian or modern physics, the American constitution, or Shakespearean tragedy, to which we agree in attributing that kind of unprecedented excellence that calls forth wonder as well as admiration.

These, wherever we find them, are the distinctive objects of the humanities; and the aim of the humanities is precisely such an understanding, appreciation, and use of them as will most completely preserve their character as human achievements that cannot be completely resolved into either natural processes common to men and animals or into impersonal forces affecting all the members of a given society. In any field of study, however, whether in the natural sciences, the social sciences, or the humanities, everything depends on the kinds of questions we ask, and the habits of thinking about these which we bring to the study. We can read a tragedy of Shakespeare in such a way that it becomes hardly distinguishable from a Western melodrama or a high-school exercise in parsing; we can study the American constitution and miss everything that makes it unique in the world; we can, by our mode of examination, take away from Newton all that Newton peculiarly was. The mode of examination, therefore—the method of approach and discussion—is all-important; and that is why we cannot say what the humanities are, in general or at any time or in any college or university, without giving first place in our definition to the "good arts" or disciplines through which, and only through which, the humanistic aspects of human achievements are accessible to us or have power to nourish our minds, refine our sensibilities, or civilize our actions. For the humanities are, in a very real sense, identical with these arts or disciplines, and they prosper in any time or place in proportion as the disciplines prosper in which they have their tangible being.

The history of the humanities from the Greeks to the present is the story of how many philosophers, many rhetoricians, many logicians, many grammarians, philologists, critics, and historians have unconsciously co-operated in the discovery, formulation, and refinement of techniques of all sorts suited to the isolation and appreciation of the humanistic aspects of human achievements. These techniques are all available to us if we wish to use them; they may be classified very roughly into four principal groups of humanistic methods or arts. There are the arts, first of all, of language, comprising the many varied techniques we have for dealing with the symbolic media in which the achievements of men are embodied or through which they reach us, from grammar in the ordinary sense, through prosody, rhetoric, the simpler parts of logic, and textual criticism, to the refinements of modern general linguistics. There are the arts, in the second place, of which the special province is the analysis and appreciation of ideas—of the conceptions and reasons, of all kinds, which men have expressed either in the elaborate forms of philosophic, scientific, and religious systems or more informally in works of literature and fine art. In the third place, there are the arts of literary and artistic criticism—the numerous devices at our disposal for grasping and appreciating the aesthetic structures which men have made. And, finally, there are the arts that give us knowledge and understanding of the particular historical situations and causes in the midst of which the objects of humanistic study have emerged.

Linguistics, the analysis of ideas, literary and artistic criticism, and historiography—these are the four constituent elements of the humanities when the humanities are defined in terms of the "good arts" which their successful cultivation presupposes. I hope I shall not be misunderstood; I am not suggesting that humanistic study consists in learning techniques rather than in mastering concrete subjects. The techniques or arts are means; the ends are subjects. But it is never safe to dwell upon ends apart from means, for it is only through the use of adequate means that the ends can be attained, or even understood; and the relation between the arts of the humanities—the four groups of arts I have mentioned—and the various subject matters which have been conventionally set apart as humanistic is one in which, in a very important sense, the humanistic value of the subject matters depends upon the number and character of the humanistic arts that are brought to play upon them in our teaching and writing. The conception of the arts, in short, gives us a kind of measuring-rod by which we may judge how far, in any of the traditional fields of humanistic study, we are doing, humanistically speaking, an adequate rather than a merely partial job. We are doing a merely partial job in the teaching of literature, for example, when we are content to let our students see only those aspects of the great works we teach that can be brought out by asking questions concerning the language in which they are written or the historical circumstances that affected their writing, without also bringing to bear upon them, in a systematic way, the resources of the analysis of ideas and of the criticism of literary forms, or, conversely, when we approach literary works merely in terms of critical or philosophical analysis without adequate reference to problems of language and history. And it is the same in other fields. The best teachers of language are those, while being skilled in modern linguistic science, have also been trained to deal sensitively with the artistic and philosophical uses of language and are more than amateurs in historical method; and the best teachers of history are those who know not merely how historical facts are derived but also how to deal competently with problems of ideas, of literary and artistic techniques and structures, and of symbolic expression. The four arts are the arts of humanities, in short, because they are pertinent in varying degrees to all the subject matters with which humanists commonly deal; they thus cut across the boundaries dividing the subject matters from one another; and it is precisely the convergence of all of them upon any subject matter that makes it, in the completest degree, humanistic; just as in any scientific field we become scientific to the fullest extent in proportion as we have learned, not merely some, but all, of the various distinct skills that make up what we call, vaguely, scientific method.

We can define the humanities most exactly, then, by speaking in terms, not simply of subject matters or ends, but of the different but supplementary arts or disciplines the proper cultivation of which will enable us to discover the distinctively humanistic values that inhere in the subject matters to which we apply them. I must emphasize, however, the idea of proper cultivation. For there is nothing automatic about any art or method of inquiry or teaching, no matter what it may be; and the four humanistic arts I have mentioned cease to be humanistic just to the extent that their practitioners lose sight of what it is, after all, that justifies their development and use, namely, the ineradicable desire of men in all ages to understand and profit from what men have done when they have shown themselves to be most peculiarly human.

Now men have shown themselves to be most peculiarly human, as I have said, in those achievements, in arts, sciences, political and cultural institutions, and individual and collective actions, the causes of which are not completely reducible to the physical laws or the social necessities which are the principal objects of study in the natural and the social studies. I do not mean to imply by this any sharp separation between the world of the humanities and the worlds of natural law and social patterns. Everything that men do has a natural and social basis or context, which humanists can forget only at the peril of making their studies of human achievements unreal and abstract. Every writer, every artist, every scientist, every statesman, every moral agent knows well that there are limits to what he can do, fixed not by himself but by the natural conditions in which he lives, the state of his culture or language, the logic of inquiry or artistic creation, the uniformities of popular psychology. These causes operate, however, more or less regularly, upon everybody; and they are not sufficient to account for those attributes of human achievements with which the humanist is distinctively concerned—the uncommon and remarkable attributes that separate, for example, the Greek language, as written by Plato, from the languages of the American Indians, the science of Newton or Einstein from primitive magic, the tragedies of Shakespeare from the average of Hollywood melodramas, the American constitution from most earlier federations, the foreign statesmanship of Winston Churchill from that (say) of Stanley Baldwin. There is a very real sense, therefore, in which the direction of the humanistic arts, when they are properly cultivated, is the opposite of the direction properly taken by the sciences of nature and society. The sciences are most successful when they seek to move from the diversity and particularly of their observations toward as high a degree of unity, uniformity, simplicity, and necessity as their materials permit. The humanities, on the other hand, are most alive when they reverse this process, and look for devices of explanation and appreciation that will enable them to preserve as much as possible of the variety, the uniqueness, the unexpectedness, the complexity, the originality, that distinguish what men are capable of doing at their best from what they must do, or tend generally to do, as biological organisms or members of a community. The humanities therefore aim, characteristically, at that special kind of happiness suggested by my text from *The Child's Garden of Verses,* the happiness that goes with the habitual perception that the world of human experience can never be brought completely under the rule of uniform necessity or compulsion but will always remain—and, if we so will it, increasingly—"full of a number of things."

But only, let me say again, if we so will it. For although the diverse and uniquely valuable achievements of men will always, in a sense, be there, they will be there, for us as students, only if we are adequately equipped with the intellectual means of seeing, understanding, and appreciating them, discriminatingly, in all their richness and complexity of aspect. Hence the fate of the humanities in our education and culture is bound up with the fate of the "good arts" or disciplines of which I have spoken. And these, unfortunately, are always susceptible to decline and corruption.

It is natural enough for discouraged humanists—and there are a great many discouraged humanists nowadays—to put the chief blame for what they think is their sad lot either on the indifference of the outside world or on the undue prosperity and aggressiveness (as it seems to them) of the social and the natural sciences. I can't help believing that there is more emotion in this attitude than sound practical reason. After all, as the history of the humanities shows, the world in general has always been somewhat indifferent to what the best humanists were doing; and the humanities have always found themselves in more or less stiff competition with other subjects for the support of patrons and the younger generation. It was so in the Middle Ages, when the humanists and the dialecticians were constantly at odds; and it has been so in every generation since the rise of modern science in the seventeenth century. And the inevitable result of this attitude, now and in the past, is to cause us to shut our eyes to what is not as good as it should be, or could be, in the practice of humanists themselves, when this practice is judged by the great standard (given in the words of my text) of the extent to which it helps us to appreciate how "full of a number of things" the world really is.

For the most serious threats to the humanities, it seems to me, come from within rather than from without. The humanities are threatened, in the first place, whenever it is assumed that an adequate account of their objects can be obtained by methods of research and interpretation borrowed from the natural or social sciences; whenever it is thought, for example, that the emotional power of Shakespeare's tragedies can be satisfactorily explained by pointing to the similarities between them and primitive myths or fertility rituals, or that poetry is importantly illuminated by the devices of psychoanalysis, or that the philosophies of Plato, Aristotle, Descartes, or Marx can be significantly resolved into the pressure of the social forces at work in their times. The humanities are threatened, again, whenever any of the four humanistic arts are habitually neglected in the study of any subject matter, or whenever any of them, whether language, history, criticism, or philosophic analysis, is exalted over the others so that their independence, as distinct means for getting at different aspects of the same subject matter, is denied; as has happened, for example, in many courses in the humanities in which the organizing principles are taken exclusively from cultural history, or in which the concentration is exclusively on great issues or ideas. The various different arts of the humanities all have a distinctive work to do, which no one of them can do alone; the ideal is one of free co-operation among them upon the concrete objects of humanistic study; and this ideal is always in peril when philologists fight for supremacy with philosophers, historians with critics, or critics with historians. And the humanities are threatened, finally, whenever we fail to recognize that, although the four major humanistic arts have had a continuous history, many distinct versions of each of them, many different valid modes of criticism, many useful types of intellectual analysis, many sound varieties of approach in linguistics and in history, have emerged in the course of time, each of which has its peculiar virtues and is capable of revealing to us aspects of the truth about our objects which the other versions tend to conceal. There are no completely wrong or outdated ways of studying the achievements of men; the insights of the past are still insights today; and we unnecessarily impoverish ourselves when, by forgetting this, we neglect to employ as many as possible of the resources of analysis and appreciation which the long tradition of the humanities has made available to us.

I can sum this up by saying that the internal enemies of the humanities are mainly two in number. One of these is the spirit of dogmatism, or rather of sectarianism: the spirit that gives us so many rival schools of linguists, critics, historians, and philosophers, who frequently seem more intent on exposing each other's errors than on getting ahead with their own studies; the spirit, also, that inspires the many futile quarrels and jealousies, in departments and divisions of the humanities, among specialists in the various disciplines. These we shall doubtless always have with us in some degree, so long as human nature remains incompletely humanized through a proper study of the "good arts." The other enemy is perhaps more amenable, at least to a policy of containment. It is what I may call the spirit of reduction; the spirit that denies the essence of the humanities by seeking always to direct our attention away from the multiplicity and diversity of human achievements, in their rich concrete actuality, to some lower or lowest common denominator: the spirit that is ever intent on resolving the complex into the simple, the conscious into the unconscious, the human into the natural; the spirit for which great philosophic systems are nothing but the expression of personal opinions or class prejudices, the forms of art nothing but their materials or their sources in the unconscious mind, the acts of statesmen nothing but the reflections of economic forces, the moral virtues nothing but the *mores* or the functioning of the glands.

The idea of the humanities is incompatible with both of these subversive spirits, and it has its embodiment in the various arts and methods which, when properly cultivated, can at once liberate us from dogmatic sectarianism in education and culture and preserve for us, without simplifying reductions, the distinctive achievements of men. If the arts of the humanities are made to flourish, the ends of the humanities, upon which so many writers have exclusively concentrated, will take care of themselves; and we may even find that the very act of practicing the arts successfully will lead to the discovery, in the humanities, of values of a sort not prefigured in any of our statements of purpose. When the humanistic arts are given a central place in our definition, moreover, the question of what are the subject matters of the humanities is bound to receive a more comprehensive answer than is contained in any list of the subjects commonly called the "humanities" in the catalogues of colleges and universities. We are studying the humanities whenever we use methods of inquiry and interpretation that fix our attention upon those characteristics of any subject matter that reflect any of the possibilities of unusual excellence, beyond the necessities of nature and of the mass mind in which we all share, inherent in the varied activities of men. The subjects ordinarily called humanistic—the languages, the literatures, music, the graphic arts, philosophy, history—are doubtless those to which the humanistic arts are peculiarly appropriate, in the sense that they can account, among them, for the greater part of what these subjects contain. The subject matters of the sciences, both natural and social, make other primary demands, and require, if they are to be studied at all, quite different procedures. But it is hard to think of any good scientific teaching that does not employ at least some of the devices which humanists use as their principal means or which does not yield an essentially humanistic appreciation of what science or mathematics is and can be, considered as one of the distinctive achievements of men. And as for the social sciences, the best of them are at least partly humanistic already, and they are bound, I think, to become more so in the future.

In saying all this, I am aware that I am speaking in a place which is by its very nature, as a college devoted to the liberal arts, an illustration of the doctrine about the meaning of the humanities which I have been trying to set forth. The humanities, in the restricted sense of the word, are taught here, and so also are the various natural sciences and social studies; but the justifying faith of a college like this, the assumption upon which it is founded and continues to flourish, is that we can become educated men and women only by contemplating, in our youth, and learning the arts by which we may understand and emulate, the best achievements of all kinds of which men have been capable, in sciences, institutions, and arts. And that is the whole idea of the humanities, inasmuch as the world of the future would be much less "full of a number of things" did such colleges cease to exist.

Thomas Henry Huxley

SCIENCE AND CULTURE

Six years ago, as some of my present hearers may remember, I had the privilege of addressing a large assemblage of the inhabitants of this city, who had gathered together to do honour to the memory of their famous townsman, Joseph Priestley; and, if any satisfaction attaches to posthumous glory, we may hope that the names of the burnt-out philosopher were then finally appeased.

No man, however, who is endowed with a fair share of common sense, and not more than a fair share of vanity, will identify either contemporary or posthumous fame with the highest good; and Priestley's life leaves no doubt that he, at any rate, set a much higher value upon the advancement of knowledge, and the promotion of that freedom of thought which is at once the cause and the consequence of intellectual progress.

Hence I am disposed to think that, if Priestley could be amongst us to-day, the occasion of our meeting would afford him even greater pleasure than the proceedings which celebrated the centenary of his chief discovery. The kindly heart would be moved, the high sense of social duty would be satisfied, by the spectacle of well-earned wealth neither squandered in tawdry luxury and vainglorious show, nor scattered with the careless charity which blesses neither him that gives nor him that takes, but expended in the execution of a well-considered plan for the aid of present and future generations of those who are willing to help themselves.

We shall all be of one mind thus far. But it is needful to share Priestley's keen interest in physical science; and to have learned, as he had learned, the value of scientific training in fields of inquiry apparently far remote from physical science; in order to appreciate, as he would have appreciated, the value of the noble gift which Sir Josiah Mason has bestowed upon the inhabitants of the Midland district.

For us children of the nineteenth century, however, the establishment of a college under the conditions of Sir Josiah Mason's Trust, has a significance apart from any which it could have possessed a hundred years ago. It appears to be an indication that we are reaching the crisis of the battle, or rather of the long series of battles, which have been fought over education in a campaign which began long before Priestley's time, and will probably not be finished just yet.

In the last century, the combatants were the champions of ancient literature on the one side, and those of modern literature on the other; but, some thirty years[1] ago, the contest became complicated by the appearance of a third army, ranged round the banner of Physical Science.

I am not aware that any one has authority to speak in the name of this new host. For it must be admitted to be somewhat of a guerilla force, composed largely of irregulars, each of whom fights pretty much for his own hand. But the impressions of a full private, who has seen a good deal of service in the ranks, respecting the present position of affairs and the conditions of a permanent peace, may not be devoid of interest; and I do not know that I could make a better use of the present opportunity than by laying them before you.

From the time that the first suggestion to introduce physical science into ordinary education was timidly whispered, until now, the advocates of scientific education have met with opposition of two kinds. On the one hand, they have been pooh-poohed by the men of business who pride themselves on being the representatives of practicality; while, on the other hand, they have been excommunicated by the classical scholars, in their capacity of Levites in charge of the ark of culture and monopolists of liberal education.

The practical men believed that the idol whom they worship—rule of thumb—has been the source of the past prosperity, and will suffice for the future welfare of the arts and manufactures. They were of opinion that science is speculative rubbish; that theory and practice have nothing

[1] The advocacy of the introduction of physical science into general education by George Combe and others commenced a good deal earlier; but the movement had acquired hardly any practical force before the time to which I refer.

to do with one another; and that the scientific habit of mind is an impediment, rather than an aid, in the conduct of ordinary affairs.

I have used the past tense in speaking of the practical men—for although they were very formidable thirty years ago, I am not sure that the pure species has not been extirpated. In fact, so far as mere argument goes, they have been subjected to such a *feu d'enfer* that it is a miracle if any have escaped. But I have remarked that your typical practical man has an unexpected resemblance to one of Milton's angels. His spiritual wounds, such as are inflicted by logical weapons, may be as deep as a well and as wide as a church door, but beyond shedding a few drops of ichor, celestial or otherwise, he is no whit the worse. So, if any of these opponents be left, I will not waste time in vain repetition of the demonstrative evidence of the practical value of science; but knowing that a parable will sometimes penetrate where syllogisms fail to effect an entrance, I will offer a story for their consideration.

Once upon a time, a boy, with nothing to depend upon but his own vigorous nature, was thrown into the thick of the struggle for existence in the midst of a great manufacturing population. He seems to have had a hard fight, inasmuch as, by the time he was thirty years of age, his total disposable funds amounted to twenty pounds. Nevertheless, middle life found him giving proof of his comprehension of the practical problems he had been roughly called upon to solve, by a career of remarkable prosperity.

Finally, having reached old age with its well-earned surroundings of "honour, troops of friends," the hero of my story bethought himself of those who were making a like start in life, and how he could stretch out a helping hand to them.

After long and anxious reflection this successful practical man of business could devise nothing better than to provide them with the means of obtaining "sound, extensive, and practical scientific knowledge." And he devoted a large part of his wealth and five years of incessant work to this end.

I need not point the moral of a tale which, as the solid and spacious fabric of the Scientific College assures us, is no fable, nor can anything which I could say intensify the force of this practical answer to practical objections.

We may take it for granted then, that, in the opinion of those best qualified to judge, the diffusion of thorough scientific education is an absolutely essential condition of industrial progress; and that the College which has been opened to-day will confer an inestimable boon upon those whose livelihood is to be gained by the practise of the arts and manufactures of the district.

The only question worth discussion is, whether the conditions, under which the work of the College is to be carried out, are such as to give it the best possible chance of achieving permanent success.

Sir Josiah Mason, without doubt most wisely, has left very large freedom of action to the trustees, to whom he proposes ultimately to commit the administration of the College, so that they may be able to adjust its arrangements in accordance with the changing conditions of the future. But, with respect to three points, he has laid most explicit injunctions upon both administrators and teachers.

Party politics are forbidden to enter into the minds of either, so far as the work of the College is concerned; theology is as sternly banished from its precincts; and finally, it is especially declared that the College shall make no provision for "mere literary instruction and education."

It does not concern me at present to dwell upon the first two injunctions any longer than may be needful to express my full conviction of their wisdom. But the third prohibition brings us face to face with those other opponents of scientific education, who are by no means in the moribund condition of the practical man, but alive, alert, and formidable.

It is not impossible that we shall hear this express exclusion of "literary instruction and education" from a College which, nevertheless, professes to give a high and efficient education, sharply criticised. Certainly the time was that the Levites of culture would have sounded their trumpets against its walls as against an educational Jericho.

How often have we not been told that the study of physical science is incompetent to confer culture; that it touches none of the higher problems of life; and, what is worse, that the continual devotion to scientific studies tends to generate a narrow and bigoted belief in the applicability of scientific methods to the search after truth of all kinds? How frequently one has reason to observe that no reply to a troublesome argument tells so well as calling its author a "mere scientific specialist." And, as I am afraid it is not permissible to speak of this form of opposition to scientific education in the past tense; may we not expect to be told that this, not only omission, but prohibition, of "mere literary instruction and education" is a patent example of scientific narrow-mindedness?

I am not acquainted with Sir Josiah Mason's reasons for the action which he has taken; but if, as I apprehend is the case, he refers to the ordinary classical course of our schools and universities by the name of "mere literary instruction and education," I venture to offer sundry reasons of my own in support of that action.

For I hold very strongly by two convictions—The first is, that neither the discipline nor the subject-matter of classical education is of such direct value to the student of physical science as to justify the expenditure of valuable time upon either; and the second is, that for the purpose of attaining real culture, an exclusively scientific education is at least as effectual as an exclusively literary education.

I need hardly point out to you that these opinions, especially the latter, are diametrically opposed to those of the great majority of educated Englishmen, influenced as they are by school and university traditions. In their belief, culture is obtainable only by a liberal education; and a liberal education is synonymous, not merely with education and instruction in literature, but in one particular form of literature, namely, that of Greek and Roman antiquity. They hold that the man who has learned Latin and Greek, however little, is educated; while he who is versed in other branches of knowledge, however deeply, is a more or less respectable specialist, not admissible into the cultured caste. The stamp of the educated man, the University degree, is not for him.

I am too well acquainted with the generous catholicity of spirit, the true sympathy with scientific thought, which pervades the writings of our chief apostle of culture to identify him with these opinions; and yet one may cull from one and another of those epistles to the Philistines, which so much delight all who do not answer to that name, sentences which lend them some support.

Mr. Arnold tells us that the meaning of culture is "to know the best that has been thought and said in the world." It is the criticism of life contained in literature. That criticism regards "Europe as being, for intellectual and spiritual purposes, one great confederation, bound to a joint action and working to a common result; and whose members have, for their common outfit, a knowledge of Greek, Roman, and Eastern antiquity, and of one another. Special, local, and temporary advantages being put out of account, that modern nation will in the intellectual and spiritual sphere make most progress, which most thoroughly carries out this programme. And what is that but saying that we too, all of us, as individuals, the more thoroughly we carry it out, shall make the more progress?"[2]

We have here to deal with two distinct propositions. The first, that a criticism of life is the essence of culture; the second, that literature contains the materials which suffice for the construction of such criticism.

I think that we must all assent to the first proposition. For culture certainly means something quite different from learning or technical skill. It implies the possession of an ideal, and the habit of critically estimating the value of things by comparison with a theoretic standard. Perfect culture should supply a complete theory of life, based upon a clear knowledge alike of its possibilities and of its limitations.

But we may agree to all this, and yet strongly dissent from the assumption that literature alone is competent to supply this knowledge. After having learnt all that Greek, Roman, and Eastern antiquity have thought and said, and all that modern literature have to tell us, it is not self-evident that we have laid a sufficiently broad and deep foundation for that criticism of life, which constitutes culture.

Indeed, to any one acquainted with the scope of physical science, it is not at all evident. Considering progress only in the "intellectual and spiritual sphere," I find myself wholly unable to admit that either nations or individuals will really advance, if their common outfit draws nothing from the stores of physical science. I should say that an army, without weapons of precision and with no particular base of operations, might more hopefully enter upon a campaign on the Rhine, than a man, devoid of a knowledge of what physical science has done in the last century, upon a criticism of life.

When a biologist meets with an anomaly, he instinctively turns to the study of development to clear it up. The rationale of contradictory opinions may with equal confidence be sought in history.

It is, happily, no new thing that Englishmen should employ their wealth in building and endowing institutions for educational purposes. But, five or six hundred years ago, deeds of foundation expressed or implied conditions as nearly as possible contrary to those which have been thought expedient by Sir Josiah Mason. That is to say, physical science was practically ignored, while a certain literary training was enjoined as

[2] *Essays in Criticism.*

a means to the acquirement of knowledge which was essentially theological.

The reason of this singular contradiction between the actions of men alike animated by a strong and disinterested desire to promote the welfare of their fellows, is easily discovered.

At that time, in fact, if any one desired knowledge beyond such as could be obtained by his own observation, or by common conversation, his first necessity was to learn the Latin language, inasmuch as all the higher knowledge of the western world was contained in works written in that language. Hence, Latin grammar, with logic and rhetoric, studied through Latin, were the fundamentals of education. With respect to the substance of the knowledge imparted through this channel, the Jewish and Christian Scriptures, as interpreted and supplemented by the Romish Church, were held to contain a complete and infallibly true body of information.

Theological dicta were, to the thinkers of those days, that which the axioms and definitions of Euclid are to the geometers of these. The business of the philosophers of the middle ages was to deduce from the data furnished by the theologians, conclusions in accordance with ecclesiastical decrees. They were allowed the high privilege of showing, by logical process, how and why that which the Church said was true, must be true. And if their demonstrations fell short of or exceeded this limit, the Church was maternally ready to check their aberrations; if need were by the help of the secular arm.

Between the two, our ancestors were furnished with a compact and complete criticism of life. They were told how the world began and how it would end; they learned that all material existence was but a base and insignificant blot upon the fair face of the spiritual world, and that nature was, to all intents and purposes, the playground of the devil; they learned that the earth is the centre of the visible universe, and that man is the cynosure of things terrestrial, and more especially was it inculcated that the course of nature had no fixed order, but that it could be, and constantly was, altered by the agency of innumerable spiritual beings, good and bad, according as they were moved by the deeds and prayers of men. The sum and substance of the whole doctrine was to produce the conviction that the only thing really worth knowing in this world was how to secure that place in a better which, under certain conditions, the Church promised.

Our ancestors had a living belief in this theory of life, and acted upon it in their dealings with education, as in all other matters. Culture meant saintliness—after the fashion of the saints of those days; the education that led to it was, of necessity, theological; and the way to theology lay through Latin.

That the study of nature—further than was requisite for the satisfaction of everyday wants—should have any bearing on human life was far from the thoughts of men thus trained. Indeed, as nature had been cursed for man's sake, it was an obvious conclusion that those who meddled with nature were likely to come into pretty close contact with Satan. And, if any born scientific investigator followed his instincts, he might safely reckon upon earning the reputation, and probably upon suffering the fate, of a sorcerer.

Had the western world been left to itself in Chinese isolation, there is no saying how long this state of things might have endured. But, happily, it was not left to itself. Even earlier than the thirteenth century, the development of Moorish civilisation in Spain and the great movement of the Crusades had introduced the leaven which, from that day to this, has never ceased to work. At first, through the intermediation of Arabic translations, afterwards by the study of the originals, the western nations of Europe became acquainted with the writings of the ancient philosophers and poets, and, in time, with the whole of the vast literature of antiquity.

Whatever there was of high intellectual aspiration or dominant capacity in Italy, France, Germany, and England, spent itself for centuries in taking possession of the rich inheritance left by the dead civilisations of Greece and Rome. Marvellously aided by the invention of printing, classical learning spread and flourished. Those who possessed it prided themselves on having attained the highest culture then within the reach of mankind.

And justly. For, saving Dante on his solitary pinnacle, there was no figure in modern literature at the time of the Renascence to compare with the men of antiquity; there was no art to compete with their sculpture; there was no physical science but that which Greece had created. Above all, there was no other example of perfect intellectual freedom—of the unhesitating acceptance of reason as the sole guide to truth and the supreme arbiter of conduct.

The new learning necessarily soon exerted a profound influence upon education. The language of the monks and schoolmen seemed little better than gibberish to scholars fresh from Virgil and Cicero, and the study of Latin was placed upon a new foundation. Moreover, Latin itself ceased to afford the sole key to knowledge. The student who sought the highest thought of antiquity, found only a second-hand reflection of it in Roman literature, and turned his face to the full light of the Greeks. And after a battle, not altogether dissimilar to that which is at present being fought over the teaching of physical science, the study of Greek was recognised as an essential element of all higher education.

Then the Humanists, as they were called, won the day; and the great reform which they effected was of incalculable service to mankind. But the Nemesis of all reformers is finality; and the reformers of education, like those of religion, fell into the profound, however common, error of mistaking the beginning for the end of the work of reformation.

The representatives of the Humanists, in the nineteenth century, take their stand upon classical education as the sole avenue to culture, as firmly as if we were still in the age of Renascence. Yet, surely, the present intellectual relations of the modern and the ancient worlds are profoundly different from those which obtained three centuries ago. Leaving aside the existence of a great and characteristically modern literature, of modern painting, and, especially, of modern music, there is one feature of the present state of the civilised world which separates it more widely from the Renascence, than the Renascence was separated from the middle ages.

This distinctive character of our own times lies in the vast and constantly increasing part which is played by natural knowledge. Not only is our daily life shaped by it, not only does the prosperity of millions of men depend upon it, but our whole theory of life has long been influenced, consciously or unconsciously, by the general conceptions of the universe, which have been forced upon us by physical science.

In fact, the most elementary acquaintance with the results of scientific investigation shows us that they offer a broad and striking contradiction to the opinion so implicitly credited and taught in the middle ages.

The notions of the beginning and the end of the world entertained by our forefathers are no longer credible. It is very certain that the earth is not the chief body in the material universe, and that the world is not subordinated to man's use. It is even more certain that nature is the expression of a definite order with which nothing interferes, and that the chief business of mankind is to learn that order and govern themselves accordingly. Moreover this scientific "criticism of life" presents itself to us with different credentials from any other. It appeals not to authority, nor to what anybody may have thought or said, but to nature. It admits that all our interpretations of natural fact are more or less imperfect and symbolic, and bids the learner seek for truth not among words but among things. It warns us that the assertion which outstrips evidence is not only a blunder but a crime.

The purely classical education advocated by the representatives of the Humanists in our day, gives no inkling of all this. A man may be a better scholar than Erasmus, and know no more of the chief causes of the present intellectual fermentation than Erasmus did. Scholarly and pious persons, worthy of all respect, favour us with allocutions upon the sadness of the antagonism of science to their mediæval way of thinking, which betray an ignorance of the first principles of scientific investigation, an incapacity for understanding what a man of science means by veracity, and an unconsciousness of the weight of established scientific truths, which is almost comical.

There is no great force in the *tu quoque* argument, or else the advocates of scientific education might fairly enough retort upon the modern Humanists that they may be learned specialists, but that they possess no such sound foundation for a criticism of life as deserves the name of culture. And, indeed, if we were disposed to be cruel, we might urge that the Humanists have brought this reproach upon themselves, not because they are too full of the spirit of the ancient Greek, but because they lack it.

The period of the Renascence is commonly called that of the "Revival of Letters," as if the influences then brought to bear upon the mind of Western Europe had been wholly exhausted in the field of literature. I think it is very commonly forgotten that the revival of science, effected by the same agency, although less conspicuous, was not less momentous.

In fact, the few and scattered students of nature of that day picked up the clue to her secrets exactly as it fell from the hands of the Greeks a thousand years before. The foundations of mathematics were so well laid by them, that our children learn their geometry from a book written for the schools of Alexandria two thousand years ago. Modern astronomy is the natural continuation and development of the work of Hipparchus and of Ptolemy; modern physics of that of Democritus and of Archimedes; it was long before modern biological science outgrew the knowledge bequeathed to us by Aristotle, by Theophrastus, and by Galen.

We cannot know all the best thoughts and sayings of the Greeks unless we know what they thought about natural phænomena. We cannot fully apprehend their criticism of life unless we understand the extent to which that criticism was affected by scientific conceptions. We falsely pretend to be the inheritors of their culture, unless we are penetrated, as the best minds among them were, with an unhesitating faith that the free employment of reason, in accordance with scientific method, is the sole method of reaching truth.

Thus I venture to think that the pretensions of our modern Humanists to the possession of the monopoly of culture and to the exclusive inheritance of the spirit of antiquity must be abated, if not abandoned. But I should be very sorry that anything I have said should be taken to imply a desire on my part to depreciate the value of classical education, as it might be and as it sometimes is. The native capacities of mankind vary no less than their opportunities; and while culture is one, the road by which one man may best reach it is widely different from that which is most advantageous to another. Again, while scientific education is yet inchoate and tentative, classical education is thoroughly well organised upon the practical experience of generations of teachers. So that, given ample time for learning and estimation for ordinary life, or for a literary career, I do not think that a young Englishman in search of culture can do better than follow the course usually marked out for him, supplementing its deficiencies by his own efforts.

But for those who mean to make science their serious occupation; or who intend to follow the profession of medicine; or who have to enter early upon the business of life; for all these, in my opinion, classical education is a mistake; and it is for this reason that I am glad to see "mere literary education and instruction" shut out from the curriculum of Sir Josiah Mason's College, seeing that its inclusion would probably lead to the introduction of the ordinary smattering of Latin and Greek.

Nevertheless, I am the last person to question the importance of genuine literary education, or to suppose that intellectual culture can be complete without it. An exclusively scientific training will bring about a mental twist as surely as an exclusively literary training. The value of the cargo does not compensate for a ship's being out of trim; and I should be very sorry to think that the Scientific College would turn out none but lop-sided men.

There is no need, however, that such a catastrophe should happen. Instruction in English, French, and German is provided, and thus the three greatest literatures of the modern world are made accessible to the student.

French and German, and especially the latter language, are absolutely indispensable to those who desire full knowledge in any department of science. But even supposing that the knowledge of these languages acquired is not more than sufficient for purely scientific purposes, every Englishman has, in his native tongue, an almost perfect instrument of literary expression; and, in his own literature, models of every kind of literary excellence. If an Englishman cannot get literary culture out of his Bible, his Shakespeare, his Milton, neither, in my belief, will the profoundest study of Homer and Sophocles, Virgil and Horace, give it to him.

Thus, since the constitution of the College makes sufficient provision for literary as well as for scientific education, and since artistic instruction is also contemplated, it seems to me that a fairly complete culture is offered to all who are willing to take advantage of it.

But I am not sure that at this point the "practical" man, scotched but not slain, may ask what all this talk about culture has to do with an Institution, the object of which is defined to be "to promote the prosperity of the manufactures and the industry of the country." He may suggest that what is wanted for this end is not culture, nor even a purely scientific discipline, but simply a knowledge of applied science.

I often wish that this phrase, "applied science," had never been invented. For it suggests that there is a sort of scientific knowledge of direct practical use, which can be studied apart from another sort of scientific knowledge, which is of no practical utility, and which is termed "pure science." But there is no more complete fallacy than this. What people call applied science is nothing but the application of pure science to particular classes of problems. It consists of deductions from those general principles, established by reasoning and observation, which constitute pure science. No one can safely make these deductions until he has a firm grasp of the principles; and he can obtain that grasp only by personal experience of the operations of observation and of reasoning on which they are founded.

Almost all the processes employed in the arts and manufactures fall within the range either of physics or of chemistry. In order to improve them, one must thoroughly understand them; and no one has a chance of really understanding them, unless he has obtained that mastery of principles and that habit of dealing with facts, which is given by long-continued and well-directed purely scientific training in the physical and the chemical laboratory. So that there really is no question as to the necessity of purely scientific discipline, even if the work of the College were limited by the narrowest interpretation of its stated aims.

And, as to the desirableness of a wider culture than that yielded by science alone, it is to be recollected that the improvement of manufacturing processes is only one of the conditions which contribute to the prosperity of industry. Industry is a means and not an end; and mankind work only to get something which they want. What that something is depends partly on their innate, and partly on their acquired, desires.

If the wealth resulting from prosperous industry is to be sent upon the gratification of unworthy desires, if the increasing perfection of manufacturing processes is to be accompanied by an increasing debasement of those who carry them on, I do not see the good of industry and prosperity.

Now it is perfectly true that men's views of what is desirable depend upon their characters; and that the innate proclivities to which we give that name are not touched by any amount of instruction. But it does not follow that even mere intellectual education may not, to an indefinite extent, modify the practical manifestation of the characters of men in their actions, by supplying them with motives unknown to the ignorant. A pleasure-loving character will have pleasure of some sort; but, if you give him the choice, he may prefer pleasures which do not degrade him to those which do. And this choice is offered to every man, who possesses in literary or artistic culture a never-failing source of pleasures, which are neither withered by age, nor staled by custom, nor embittered in the recollection by the pangs of self-reproach.

If the Institution opened to-day fulfils the intention of its founder, the picked intelligences among all classes of the population of this district will pass through it. No child born in Birmingham, henceforward, if he have the capacity to profit by the opportunities offered to him, first in the primary and other schools, and afterwards in the Scientific College, need fail to obtain, not merely the instruction, but the culture most appropriate to the conditions of his life.

Within these walls, the future employer and the future artisan may sojourn together for a while, and carry, through all their lives, the stamp of the influences then brought to bear upon them. Hence, it is not beside the mark to remind you, that the prosperity of industry depends not merely upon the improvement of manufacturing processes, not merely upon the ennobling of the individual character, but upon a third condition, namely, a clear understanding of the conditions of social life, on the part of both the capitalist and the operative, and their agreement upon common principles of social action. They must learn that social phænomena are as much the expression of natural laws as any others; that no social arrangements can be permanent unless they harmonise with the requirements of social statics and dynamics; and that, in the nature of things, there is an arbiter whose decisions execute themselves.

But this knowledge is only to be obtained by the application of the methods of investigation adopted in physical researches to the investigation of the phænomena of society. Hence, I confess, I should like to see one addition made to the excellent scheme of education propounded for the College, in the shape of provision for the teaching of Sociology. For though we are all agreed that party politics are to have no place in the instruction of the College; yet in this country, practically governed as it is now by universal suffrage, every man who does his duty must exercise political functions. And, if the evils which are inseparable from the good of political liberty are to be checked, if the perpetual oscillation of nations between anarchy and despotism is to be replaced by the steady march of self-restraining freedom; it will be because men will gradually bring themselves to deal with political, as they now deal with scientific questions; to be as ashamed of undue haste and partisan prejudice in the one case as in the other; and to believe that the machinery of society is at least as delicate as that of a spinning-jenny, and as little likely to be improved by the meddling of those who have not taken the trouble to master the principles of its action.

In conclusion, I am sure that I make myself the mouthpiece of all present in offering to the venerable founder of the Institution, which now commences its beneficent career, our congratulations on the completion of his work; and in expressing the conviction, that the remotest posterity will point to it as a crucial instance of the wisdom which natural piety leads all men to ascribe to their ancestors.

Matthew Arnold

LITERATURE AND SCIENCE

*P*RACTICAL people talk with a smile of Plato and of his absolute ideas; and it is impossible to deny that Plato's ideas do often seem unpractical and unpracticable, and especially when one views them in connexion with the life of a great work-a-day world like the United States. The necessary staple of the life of such a world Plato regards with disdain; handicraft and trade and the working professions he regards with disdain; but what becomes of the life of an industrial modern community if you take handicraft and trade and the working professions out of it? The base mechanic arts and handicrafts, says Plato, bring about a natural weakness in the principle of excellence in a man, so that he cannot govern the ignoble growths in him, but nurses them, and cannot understand fostering any other. Those who exercise such arts and trades, as they have their bodies, he says, marred by their vulgar businesses, so they have their souls, too, bowed and broken by them. And if one of these uncomely people has a mind to seek self-culture and philosophy, Plato compares him to a bald little tinker, who has scraped together money, and has got his release from service, and has had a bath, and bought a new coat, and is rigged out like a bridegroom about to marry the daughter of his master who has fallen into poor and helpless estate.

Nor do the working professions fare any better than trade at the hands of Plato. He draws for us an inimitable picture of the working lawyer, and of his life of bondage; he shows how this bondage from his youth up has stunted and warped him, and made him small and crooked of soul, encompassing him with difficulties which he is not man enough to rely on justice and truth as means to encounter, but has recourse, for help out of them, to falsehood and wrong. And so, says Plato, this poor creature is bent and broken, and grows up from boy to man without a particle of soundness in him, although exceedingly smart and clever in his own esteem.

One cannot refuse to admire the artist who draws these pictures. But we say to ourselves that his ideas show the influence of a primitive and obsolete order of things, when the warrior caste and the priestly caste were alone in honour, and the humble work of the world was done by slaves. We have now changed all that; the modern majesty consists in work, as Emerson declares; and in work, we may add, principally of such plain and dusty kind as the work of cultivators of the ground, handicraftsmen, men of trade and business, men of the working professions. Above all is this true in a great industrious community such as that of the United States.

Now education, many people go on to say, is still mainly governed by the ideas of men like Plato, who lived when the warrior caste and the priestly or philosophical class were alone in honour, and the really useful part of the community were slaves. It is an education fitted for persons of leisure in such a community. This education passed from Greece and Rome to the feudal communities of Europe, where also the warrior caste and the priestly caste were alone held in honour, and where the really useful and working part of the community, though not nominally slaves as in the pagan world, were practically not much better off than slaves, and not more seriously regarded. And how absurd it is, people end by saying, to inflict this education upon an industrious modern community, where very few indeed are persons of leisure, and the mass to be considered has not leisure, but is bound, for its own great good, and for the great good of the world at large, to plain labour and to industrial pursuits, and the education in question tends necessarily to make men dissatisfied with these pursuits and unfitted for them!

That is what is said. So far I must defend Plato, as to plead that his view of education and studies is in the general, as it seems to me, sound enough, and fitted for all sorts and conditions of men, whatever their pursuits may be. "An intelligent man," says Plato, "will prize those studies which result in his soul getting soberness, righteousness, and wisdom, and will less value the others." I cannot consider *that* a bad description of the aim of education, and of the motives which should govern us in the choice of studies, whether we are preparing ourselves for a hereditary seat in the English House of Lords or for the pork trade in Chicago.

Still I admit that Plato's world was not ours, that his scorn of trade and handicraft is fantastic, that he had no conception of a great industrial community such as that of the United States, and that such a community must and will shape its education to suit its own needs. If the usual education handed down to it from the past does not suit it, it will certainly before long drop this and try another. The usual education in the past has been mainly literary. The question is whether the studies which were long supposed to be the best for all of us are practically the best now; whether others are not better. The tyranny of the past, many think, weighs on us injuriously in the predominance given to letters in education. The question is raised whether, to meet the needs of our modern life, the predominance ought not now to pass from letters to science; and naturally the question is nowhere raised with more energy than here in the United States. The design of abasing what is called "mere literary instruction and education," and of exalting what is called "sound, extensive, and practical scientific knowledge," is, in this intensely modern world of the United States, even more perhaps than in Europe, a very popular design, and makes great and rapid progress.

I am going to ask whether the present movement for ousting letters from their old predominance in education, and for transferring the predominance in education to the natural sciences, whether this brisk and flourishing movement ought to prevail, and whether it is likely that in the end it really will prevail. An objection may be raised which I will anticipate. My own studies have been almost wholly in letters, and my visits to the field of the natural sciences have been very slight and inadequate, although those sciences have always strongly moved my curiosity. A man of letters, it will perhaps be said, is not competent to discuss the comparative merits of letters and natural science as means of education. To this objection I reply, first of all, that his incompetence, if he attempts the discussion but is really incompetent for it, will be abundantly visible; nobody will be taken in; he will have plenty of sharp observers and critics to save mankind from that danger. But the line I am going to follow is, as you will soon discover, so extremely simple, that perhaps it may be followed without failure even by one who for a more ambitious line of discussion would be quite incompetent.

Some of you may possibly remember a phrase of mine which has been the object of a good deal of comment; an observation to the effect that in our culture, the aim being *to know ourselves and the world*, we have, as the means to this end, *to know the best which has been thought and said in the world*. A man of science, who is also an excellent writer and the very prince of debaters, Professor Huxley, in a discourse at the opening of Sir Josiah Mason's college at Birmingham, laying hold of this phrase, expanded it by quoting some more words of mine, which are these: "The civilised world is to be regarded as now being, for intellectual and spiritual purposes, one great confederation, bound to a joint action and working to a common result; and whose members have for their proper outfit a knowledge of Greek, Roman, and Eastern antiquity, and of one another. Special local and temporary advantages being put out of account, that modern nation will in the intellectual and spiritual sphere make most progress, which most thoroughly carries out this programme."

Now on my phrase, thus enlarged, Professor Huxley remarks that when I speak of the above-mentioned knowledge as enabling us to know ourselves and the world, I assert *literature* to contain the materials which suffice for thus making us know ourselves and the world. But it is not by any means clear, says he, that after having learnt all which ancient and modern literature have to tell us, we have laid a sufficiently broad and deep foundation for that criticism of life, that knowledge of ourselves and the world, which constitutes culture. On the contrary, Professor Huxley declares that he finds himself "wholly unable to admit that either nations or individuals will really advance, if their outfit draws nothing from the stores of physical science. An army without weapons of precision, and with no particular base of operations, might more hopefully enter upon a campaign on the Rhine, than a man, devoid of a knowledge of what physical science has done in the last century, upon a criticism of life."

This shows how needful it is for those who are to discuss any matter together, to have a common understanding as to the sense of the terms they employ,—how needful, and how difficult. What Professor Huxley says, implies just the reproach which is so often brought against the study of *belles lettres,* as they are called: that the study is an elegant one, but slight and ineffectual; a smattering of Greek and Latin and other ornamental things, of little use for any one whose object is to get at truth, and to be a practical man. So, too, M. Renan talks of the "superficial humanism" of a school-course which treats us as if we were all going to be poets, writers, preachers, orators, and he opposes this humanism to positive science, or the critical search after truth. And there is always a tendency in those who are remonstrating against the predominance of letters in education, to understand by letters *belles lettres,* and by *belles lettres* a superficial humanism, the opposite of science or true knowledge.

But when we talk of knowing Greek and Roman antiquity, for instance, which is the knowledge people have called the humanities, I for my part mean a knowledge which is something more than a superficial humanism, mainly decorative. "I call all teaching *scientific*," says Wolf, the critic of Homer, "which is systematically laid out and followed up to its original sources. For example: a knowledge of classical antiquity is scientific when the remains of classical antiquity are correctly studied in the original languages." There can be no doubt that Wolf is perfectly right; that all learning is scientific which is systematically laid out and followed up to its original sources, and that a genuine humanism is scientific.

When I speak of knowing Greek and Roman antiquity, therefore, as a help to knowing ourselves and the world, I mean more than a knowledge of so much vocabulary, so much grammar, so many portions of authors in the Greek and Latin languages, I mean knowing the Greeks and Romans, and their life and genius, and what they were and did in the world; what we get from them, and what is its value. That, at least, is the ideal; and when we talk of endeavouring to know Greek and Roman antiquity, as a help to knowing ourselves and the world, we mean endeavouring so to know them as to satisfy this ideal, however much we may still fall short of it.

The same also as to knowing our own and other modern nations, with the like aim of getting to understand ourselves and the world. To know the best that has been thought and said by the modern nations, is to know, says Professor Huxley, "only what modern *literatures* have to tell us; it is the criticism of life contained in modern literature." And yet "the distinctive character of our times," he urges, "lies in the vast and constantly increasing part which is played by natural knowledge." And how, therefore, can a man, devoid of knowledge of what physical science has done in the last century, enter hopefully upon a criticism of modern life?

Let us, I say, be agreed about the meaning of the terms we are using. I talk of knowing the best which has been thought and uttered in the world; Professor Huxley says this means knowing *literature*. Literature is a large word; it may mean everything written with letters or printed in a book. Euclid's *Elements* and Newton's *Principia* are thus literature. All knowledge that reaches us through books is literature. But by literature Professor Huxley means *belles lettres*. He means to make me say, that knowing the best which has been thought and said by the modern nations is knowing their *belles lettres* and no more. And this is no sufficient equipment, he argues, for a criticism of modern life. But as I do not mean, by knowing ancient Rome, knowing merely more or less of Latin *belles lettres,* and taking no account of Rome's military, and political, and legal, and administrative work in the world; and as, by knowing ancient Greece, I understand knowing her as the giver of Greek art, and the guide to a free and right use of reason and to scientific method, and the founder of our mathematics and physics and astronomy and biology,—I understand knowing her as all this, and not merely knowing certain Greek poems, and histories, and treatises, and speeches,—so as to the knowledge of modern nations also. By knowing modern nations, I mean not merely knowing their *belles lettres,* but knowing also what has been done by such men as Copernicus, Galileo, Newton, Darwin. "Our ancestors learned," says Professor Huxley, "that the earth is the centre of the visible universe, and that man is the cynosure of things terrestrial; and more especially was it inculcated that the course of nature had no fixed order, but that it could be, and constantly was, altered." "But for us now," continues Professor Huxley, "the notions of the beginning and the end of the world entertained by our forefathers are no longer credible. It is very certain that the earth is not the chief body in the material universe, and that the world is not subordinated to man's use. It is even more certain that nature is the expression of a definite order, with which nothing interferes." "And yet," he cries, "the purely classical education advocated by the representatives of the humanists in our day gives no inkling of all this."

In due place and time I will just touch upon that vexed question of classical education; but at present the question is as to what is meant by knowing the best which modern nations have thought and said. It is not knowing their *belles lettres* merely which is meant. To know Italian *belles lettres* is not to know Italy, and to know English *belles lettres* is not to know England. Into knowing Italy and England there comes a great deal more, Galileo and Newton amongst it. The reproach of being a superficial humanism, a tincture of *belles lettres,* may attach rightly enough to some other disciplines; but to the particular discipline recommended when I proposed knowing the best that has been thought and said in the world, it does not apply. In that best I certainly include what in modern times has been thought and said by the great observers and knowers of nature.

There is, therefore, really no question between Professor Huxley and me as to whether knowing the great results of the modern scientific study of nature is not required as a part of our culture, as well as knowing the products of literature and art. But to follow the processes by which those results are reached, ought, say the friends of physical science, to be made the staple of education for the bulk of mankind. And here there does arise a question between those whom Professor Huxley calls with playful sarcasm "the Levites of culture," and those whom the poor humanist is sometimes apt to regard as its Nebuchadnezzars.

The great results of the scientific investigation of nature we are agreed upon knowing, but how much of our study are we bound to give to the processes by which those results are reached? The results have their visible bearing on human life. But all the processes, too, all the items of fact, by which those results are reached and established, are interesting. All knowledge is interesting to a wise man, and the knowledge of nature is interesting to all men. It is very interesting to know, that, from the albuminous white of the egg, the chick in the egg gets the materials for its flesh, bones, blood, and feathers; while, from the fatty yolk of the egg, it gets the heat and energy which enable it at length to break its shell and begin the world. It is less interesting, perhaps, but still it is interesting, to know that when a taper burns, the wax is converted into carbonic acid and water. Moreover, it is quite true that the habit of dealing with facts, which is given by the study of nature, is, as the friends of physical science praise it for being, an excellent discipline. The appeal, in the study of nature, is constantly to observation and experiment; not only is it said that the thing is so, but we can be made to see that it is so. Not only does a man tell us that when a taper burns the wax is converted into carbonic acid and water, as a man may tell us, if he likes, that Charon is punting his ferry-boat on the river Styx, or that Victor Hugo is a sublime poet, or Mr. Gladstone the most admirable of statesmen; but we are made to see that the conversion into carbonic acid and water does actually happen. This reality of natural knowledge it is, which makes the friends of physical science contrast it, as a knowledge of things, with the humanist's knowledge, which is, say they, a knowledge of words. And hence Professor Huxley is moved to lay it down that, "for the purpose of attaining real culture, an exclusively scientific education is at least as effectual as an exclusively literary education." And a certain President of the Section for Mechanical Science in the British Association is, in Scripture phrase, "very bold," and declares that if a man, in his mental training, "has substituted literature and history for natural science, he has chosen the less useful alternative." But whether we go these lengths or not, we must all admit that in natural science the habit gained of dealing with facts is a most valuable discipline, and that every one should have some experience of it.

More than this, however, is demanded by the reformers. It is proposed to make the training in natural science the main part of education, for the great majority of mankind at any rate. And here, I confess, I part company with the friends of physical science, with whom up to this point I have been agreeing. In differing from them, however, I wish to proceed with the utmost caution and diffidence. The smallness of my own acquaintance with the disciplines of natural science is ever before my mind, and I am fearful of doing these disciplines an injustice. The ability and pugnacity of the partisans of natural science make them formidable persons to contradict. The tone of tentative inquiry, which befits a being of dim faculties and bounded knowledge, is the tone I would wish to take and not to depart from. At present it seems to me, that those who are giving to natural knowledge, as they call it, the chief place in the education of the majority of mankind, leave one important thing out of their account: the constitution of human nature. But I put this forward on the strength of some facts not at all recondite, very far from it; facts capable of being stated in the simplest possible fashion, and to which, if I so state them, the man of science will, I am sure, be willing to allow their due weight.

Deny the facts altogether, I think, he hardly can. He can hardly deny, that when we set ourselves to enumerate the powers which go to the building up of human life, and say that they are the power of conduct, the power of intellect and knowledge, the power of beauty, and the power of social life and manners,—he can hardly deny that this scheme, though drawn in rough and plain lines enough, and not pretending to scientific exactness, does yet give a fairly true representation of the matter. Human nature is built up by these powers; we have the need for them all. When we have rightly met and adjusted the claims of them all, we shall then be in a fair way for getting soberness and righteousness, with wisdom. This is evident enough and the friends of physical science would admit it.

But perhaps they may not have sufficiently observed another thing: namely, that the several powers just mentioned are not isolated, but there is, in the generality of mankind, a perpetual tendency to relate them one to another in divers ways. With one such way of relating them I am particularly concerned now. Following our instinct for intellect and knowledge, we acquire pieces of knowledge; and presently, in the generality of men, there arises the desire to relate these pieces of knowledge to our sense for conduct, to our sense for beauty,—and there is weariness and dissatisfaction if the desire is baulked. Now in this desire lies, I think, the strength of that hold which letters have upon us.

All knowledge is, as I said just now, interesting; and even items of knowledge which from the nature of the case cannot well be related, but must stand isolated in our thoughts, have their interest. Even lists of exceptions have their interest. If we are studying Greek accents, it is interesting to know that *pais* and *pas,* and some other monosyllables of the same form of declension, do not take the circumflex upon the last syllable of the genitive plural, but vary, in this respect, from the common rule. If we are studying physiology, it is interesting to know that the pulmonary artery carries dark blood and the pulmonary vein carries bright blood, departing in this respect from the common rule for the division of labour between the veins and the arteries. But every one knows how we seek naturally to combine the pieces of our knowledge together, to bring them under general rules, to relate them to principles; and how unsatisfactory and tiresome it would be to go on for ever learning lists of exceptions, or accumulating items of fact which must stand isolated.

Well, that same need of relating our knowledge, which operates here within the sphere of our knowledge itself, we shall find operating, also, outside that sphere. We experience, as we go on learning and knowing,— the vast majority of us experience,—the need of relating what we have learnt and known to the sense which we have in us for conduct, to the sense which we have in us for beauty.

A certain Greek prophetess of Mantineia in Arcadia, Diotima by name, once explained to the philosopher Socrates that love, and impulse, and bent of all kinds, is, in fact, nothing else but the desire in men that good should for ever be present to them. This desire for good, Diotima assured Socrates, is our fundamental desire, of which fundamental desire every impulse in us is only some one particular form. And therefore this fundamental desire it is, I suppose,—this desire in men that good should be for ever present to them,—which acts in us when we feel the impulse for relating our knowledge to our sense for conduct and to our sense for beauty. At any rate, with men in general the instinct exists. Such is human nature. And the instinct, it will be admitted, is innocent, and human nature is preserved by our following the lead of its innocent instincts. Therefore, in seeking to gratify this instinct in question, we are following the instinct of self-preservation in humanity.

But, no doubt, some kinds of knowledge cannot be made to directly serve the instinct in question, cannot be directly related to the sense for beauty, to the sense for conduct. These are instrument-knowledges; they lead on to other knowledge, which can. A man who passes his life in instrument knowledges is a specialist. They may be invaluable as instruments to something beyond, for those who have the gift thus to employ them; and they may be disciplines in themselves wherein it is useful for every one to have some schooling. But it is inconceivable that the generality of men should pass all their mental life with Greek accents or with formal logic. My friend Professor Sylvester, who is one of the first mathematicians in the world, holds transcendental doctrines as to the virtue of mathematics, but those doctrines are not for common men. In the very Senate House and heart of our English Cambridge I once ventured, though not without an apology for my profaneness, to hazard the opinion that for the majority of mankind a little of mathematics, even, goes a long way. Of course this is quite consistent with their being of immense importance as an instrument to something else; but it is the few who have the aptitude for thus using them, not the bulk of mankind.

The natural sciences do not, however, stand on the same footing with these instrument-knowledges. Experience shows us that the generality of men will find more interest in learning that, when a taper burns, the wax is converted into carbonic acid and water, or in learning the explanation of the phenomenon of dew, or in learning how the circulation of the blood is carried on, than they find in learning that the genitive plural of *pias* and *pas* does not take the circumflex on the termination. And one piece of natural knowledge is added to another, and others are added to that, and at last we come to propositions so interesting as Mr. Darwin's famous proposition that "our ancestor was a hairy quadruped furnished with a tail and pointed ears, probably arboreal in his habits." Or we come to propositions of such reach and magnitude as those which Professor Huxley delivers, when he says that the notions of our forefathers about the beginning and the end of the world were all wrong and that nature is the expression of a definite order with which nothing interferes.

Interesting, indeed, these results of science are, important they are, and we should all of us be acquainted with them. But what I now wish you to mark is, that we are still, when they are propounded to us and we receive them, we are still in the sphere of intellect and knowledge. And for the generality of men there will be found, I say, to arise, when they have duly taken in the proposition that their ancestor was "a hairy quadruped furnished with a tail and pointed ears, probably arboreal in his habits," there will be found to arise an invincible desire to relate this proposition to the sense in us for conduct, and to the sense in us for beauty. But this the men of science will not do for us, and will hardly even profess to do. They will give us other pieces of knowledge, other facts, about other animals and their ancestors, or about plants, or about stones, or about stars; and they may finally bring us to those great "general conceptions of the universe, which are forced upon us all," says Professor Huxley, "by the progress of physical science." But still it will be *knowledge* only which they give us; knowledge not put for us into relation with our sense for conduct, our sense for beauty, and touched with emotion by being so put; not thus put for us, and therefore, to the majority of mankind, after a certain while, unsatisfying, wearying.

Not to the born naturalist, I admit. But what do we mean by a born naturalist? We mean a man in whom the zeal for observing nature is so uncommonly strong and eminent, that it marks him off from the bulk of mankind. Such a man will pass his life happily in collecting natural knowledge and reasoning upon it, and will ask for nothing, or hardly anything, more. I have heard it said that the sagacious and admirable naturalist whom we lost not very long ago, Mr. Darwin, once owned to a friend that for his part he did not experience the necessity for two things which most men find so necessary to them,—religion and poetry; science and the domestic affections, he thought, were enough. To a born naturalist, I can well understand that this should seem so. So absorbing is his occupation with nature, so strong his love for his occupation, that he goes on acquiring natural knowledge and reasoning upon it, and has little time or inclination for thinking about getting it related to the desire in man for conduct, the desire in man for beauty. He relates it to them for himself as he goes along, so far as he feels the need; and he draws from the domestic affections all the additional solace necessary. But then Darwins are extremely rare. Another great and admirable master of natural knowledge, Faraday, was a Sandemanian. That is to say, he related his knowledge to his instinct for conduct and to his instinct for beauty, by the aid of that respectable Scottish sectary, Robert Sandeman. And so strong, in general, is the demand of religion and poetry to have their share in a man, to associate themselves with his knowing, and to relieve and rejoice it, that, probably, for one man amongst us with the disposition to do as Darwin did in this respect, there are at least fifty with the disposition to do as Faraday.

Education lays hold upon us, in fact, by satisfying this demand. Professor Huxley holds up to scorn mediæval education, with its neglect of the knowledge of nature, its poverty even of literary studies, its formal logic devoted to "showing how and why that which the Church said was true and must be true." But the great mediæval Universities were not brought into being, we may be sure, by the zeal for giving a jejune and contemptible education. Kings have been their nursing fathers, and queens have been their nursing mothers, but not for this. The mediæval Universities came into being, because the supposed knowledge, delivered by Scripture and the Church, so deeply engaged men's hearts, by so simply, easily, and powerfully relating itself to their desire for conduct, their desire for beauty. All other knowledge was dominated by this supposed knowledge and was subordinated to it, because of the surpassing strength of the hold which it gained upon the affections of men, by allying itself profoundly with their sense for conduct, their sense for beauty.

But now, says Professor Huxley, conceptions of the universe fatal to the notions held by our forefathers have been forced upon us by physical science. Grant to him that they are thus fatal, that the new conceptions must and will soon become current everywhere, and that every one will finally perceive them to be fatal to the beliefs of our forefathers. The need of humane letters, as they are truly called, because they serve the paramount desire in men that good should be for ever present to them,—the need of humane letters, to establish a relation between the new conceptions, and our instinct for beauty, our instinct for conduct, is only the more visible. The Middle Age could do without humane letters, as it could do without the study of nature, because its supposed knowledge was made to engage its emotions so powerfully. Grant that the supposed knowledge disappears, its power of being made to engage the emotions will of course disappear along with it,—but the emotions themselves, and their claim to be engaged and satisfied, will remain. Now if we find by experience that humane letters have an undeniable power of engaging the emotions, the importance of humane letters in a man's training becomes not less, but greater, in proportion to the success of modern science in extirpating what it calls "mediæval thinking."

Have humane letters, then, have poetry and eloquence, the power here attributed to them of engaging the emotions, and do they exercise it? And if they have it and exercise it, *how* do they exercise it, so as to exert an influence upon man's sense for conduct, his sense for beauty? Finally, even if they both can and do exert an influence upon the senses in question, how are they to relate to them the results,—the modern results,—of natural science? All these questions may be asked. First, have poetry and eloquence the power of calling out the emotions? The appeal is to experience. Experience shows that for the vast majority of men, for mankind in general, they have the power. Next, do they exercise it? They do. But then, *how* do they exercise it so as to affect man's sense for conduct, his sense for beauty? And this is perhaps a case for applying the Preacher's words: "Though a man labour to seek it out, yet he shall not find it; yea, farther, though a wise man think to know it, yet shall he not be able to find it."[1] Why should it be one thing, in its effect upon the emotions, to say, "Patience is a virtue," and quite another thing, in its effect upon the emotions, to say with Homer,

$$\tau\lambda\eta\tau o\nu \ \gamma\alpha\rho \ \mathrm{M}o\iota\rho\alpha\iota \ \theta\upsilon\mu o\nu \ \theta\epsilon\sigma\alpha\nu \ \alpha\nu\theta\rho\omega\pi o\iota\sigma\iota\nu—[2]$$

"for an enduring heart have the destinies appointed to the children of men"? Why should it be one thing, in its effect upon the emotions, to say with the philosopher Spinoza, *Felicitas in eo consistit quod homo suum esse conservare potest*—"Man's happiness consists in his being able to preserve his own essence," and quite another thing, in its effect upon the emotions, to say with the Gospel, "What is a man advantaged, if he gain the whole world, and lose himself, forfeit himself?" How does this difference of effect arise? I cannot tell, and I am not much concerned to know; the important thing is that it does arise, and that we can profit by it. But how, finally, are poetry and eloquence to exercise the power of relating the modern results of natural science to man's instinct for conduct, his instinct for beauty? And here again I answer that I do not know *how* they will exercise it, but that they can and will exercise it I am sure. I do not mean that modern philosophical poets and modern philosophical moralists are to come and relate for us, in express terms, the results of modern scientific research to our instinct for conduct, our instinct for beauty. But I mean that we shall find, as a matter of experience, if we know the best that has been thought and uttered in the world, we shall find that the art and poetry and eloquence of men who

[1] *Ecclesiastes*, viii. 17.
[2] *Iliad*, xxiv, 49.

lived, perhaps, long ago, who had the most limited natural knowledge, who had the most erroneous conceptions about many important matters, we shall find that this art, and poetry, and eloquence, have in fact not only the power of refreshing and delighting us, they have also the power, —such is the strength and worth, in essentials, of their authors' criticism of life,—they have a fortifying, and elevating, and quickening, and suggestive power, capable of wonderfully helping us to relate the results of modern science to our need for conduct, our need for beauty. Homer's conceptions of the physical universe were, I imagine, grotesque; but really, under the shock of hearing from modern science that "the world is not subordinated to man's use, and that man is not the cynosure of things terrestrial," I could, for my own part, desire no better comfort than Homer's line which I quoted just now,

τλητον γαρ Μοιραι θυμον θεσαν ανθρωποισιν—

"for an enduring heart have the destinies appointed to the children of men"!

And the more that men's minds are cleared, the more that the results of science are frankly accepted, the more that poetry and eloquence come to be received and studied as what in truth they really are,— the criticism of life by gifted men, alive and active with extraordinary power at an unusual number of points;—so much the more will the value of humane letters, and of art also, which is an utterance having a like kind of power with theirs, be felt and acknowledged, and their place in education be secured.

Let us therefore, all of us, avoid indeed as much as possible any invidious comparison between the merits of humane letters, as means of education, and the merits of the natural sciences. But when some President of a Section for Mechanical Science insists on making the comparison, and tells us that "he who in his training has substituted literature and history for natural science has chosen the less useful alternative," let us make answer to him that the student of humane letters only, will, at least, know also the great general conceptions brought in by modern physical science; for science, as Professor Huxley says, forces them upon us all. But the student of the natural sciences only, will, by our very hypothesis, know nothing of humane letters; not to mention that in setting himself to be perpetually accumulating natural knowledge, he sets himself to do what only specialists have in general the gift for doing genially. And so he will probably be unsatisfied, or at any rate incomplete, and even more incomplete than the student of humane letters only.

I once mentioned in a school-report, how a young man in one of our English training colleges having to paraphrase the passage in *Macbeth* beginning,

"Can'st thou not minister to a mind diseased?"
turned this line into, "Can you not wait upon the lunatic?" And I remarked what a curious state of things it would be, if every pupil of our national schools knew, let us say, that the moon is two thousand one hundred and sixty miles in diameter, and thought at the same time that a good paraphrase for

"Can'st thou not minister to a mind diseased?"
was, "Can you not wait upon the lunatic?" If one is driven to choose, I think I would rather have a young person ignorant about the moon's diameter, but aware that "Can you not wait upon the lunatic?" is bad, than a young person whose education had been such as to manage things the other way.

Or to go higher than the pupils of our national schools. I have in my mind's eye a member of our British Parliament who comes to travel here in America, who afterwards relates his travels, and who shows a really masterly knowledge of the geology of this great country and of its mining capabilities, but who ends by gravely suggesting that the United States should borrow a prince from our Royal Family, and should make him their king, and should create a House of Lords of great landed proprietors after the pattern of ours; and then America, he thinks, would have her future happily and perfectly secured. Surely, in this case, the President of the Section for Mechanical Science would himself hardly say that our member of Parliament, by concentrating himself upon geology and mineralogy, and so on, and not attending to literature and history, had "chosen the more useful alternative."

If then there is to be separation and option between humane letters on the one hand, and the natural sciences on the other, the great majority of mankind, all who have not exceptional and overpowering aptitudes for the study of nature, would do well, I cannot but think, to choose to be educated in humane letters rather than in the natural sciences. Letters will call out their being at more points, will make them live more.

I said that before I ended I would just touch on the question of classical education, and I will keep my word. Even if literature is to retain a large place in our education, yet Latin and Greek, say the friends of progress, will certainly have to go. Greek is the grand offender in the eyes of these gentlemen. The attackers of the established course of study think that against Greek, at any rate, they have irresistible arguments. Literature may perhaps be needed in education, they say; but why on earth should it be Greek literature? Why not French or German? Nay, "has not an Englishman models in his own literature of every kind of excellence?" As before, it is not on any weak pleadings of my own that I rely for convincing the gainsayers; it is on the constitution of human nature itself, and on the instinct of self-preservation in humanity. The instinct for beauty is set in human nature, as surely as the instinct for knowledge is set there, or the instinct for conduct. If the instinct for beauty is served by Greek literature and art as it is served by no other literature and art, we may trust to the instinct of self-preservation in humanity for keeping Greek as part of our culture. We may trust to it for even making the study of Greek more prevalent than it is now. Greek will come, I hope, some day to be studied more rationally than at present; but it will be increasingly studied as men increasingly feel the need in them for beauty, and how powerfully Greek art and Greek literature can serve this need. Women will again study Greek, as Lady Jane Grey did; I believe that in that chain of forts, with which the fair host of the Amazons are now engirdling our English universities, I find that here in America, in colleges like Smith College in Massachusetts, and Vassar College in the State of New York, and in the happy families of the mixed universities out West, they are studying it already.

Defuit una mihi symmetria prisca,—"The antique symmetry was the one thing wanting to me," said Leonardo da Vinci; and he was an Italian. I will not presume to speak for the Americans, but I am sure that, in the Englishman, the want of this admirable symmetry of the Greeks is a thousand times more great and crying than in any Italian. The results of the want show themselves most glaringly, perhaps, in our architecture, but they show themselves, also, in all our art. *Fit details strictly combined, in view of a large general result nobly conceived;* that is just the beautiful *symmetria prisca* of the Greeks, and it is just where we English fail, where all our art fails. Striking ideas we have, and well-executed details we have; but that high symmetry which, with satisfying and delightful effect, combines them, we seldom or never have. The glorious beauty of the Acropolis at Athens did not come from single fine things stuck about on that hill, a statue here, a gateway there;—no, it arose from all things being perfectly combined for a supreme total effect. What must not an Englishman feel about our deficiencies in this respect, as the sense for beauty, whereof this symmetry is an essential element, awakens and strengthens within him! what will not one day be his respect and desire for Greece and its *symmetria prisca,* when the scales drop from his eyes as he walks the London streets, and he sees such a lesson in meanness as the Strand, for instance, in its true deformity! But here we are coming to our friend Mr. Ruskin's province, and I will not intrude upon it, for he is its very sufficient guardian.

And so we at last find, it seems, we find flowing in favour of the humanities the natural and necessary stream of things, which seemed against them when we started. The "hairy quadruped furnished with a tail and pointed ears, probably arboreal in his habits," this good fellow carried hidden in his nature, apparently, something destined to develop into a necessity for humane letters. Nay, more; we seem finally to be even led to the further conclusion that our hairy ancestor carried in his nature, also, a necessity for Greek.

And therefore, to say the truth, I cannot really think that humane letters are in much actual danger of being thrust out from their leading place in education, in spite of the array of authorities against them at this moment. So long as human nature is what it is, their attractions will remain irresistible. As with Greek, so with letters generally: they will some day come, we may hope, to be studied more rationally, but they will not lose their place. What will happen will rather be that there will be crowded into education other matters besides, far too many; there will be, perhaps, a period of unsettlement and confusion and false tendency; but letters will not in the end lose their leading place. If they lose it for a time, they will get it back again. We shall be brought back to them by our wants and aspirations. And a poor humanist may possess his soul in patience, neither strive nor cry, admit the energy and brilliancy of the partisans of physical science, and their present favour with the public, to be far greater than his own, and still have a happy faith that the nature of things works silently on behalf of the studies which he loves, and that, while we shall all have to acquaint ourselves with the great results reached by modern science, and to give ourselves as much training in its disciplines as we can conveniently carry, yet the majority of men will always require humane letters; and so much the more, as they have the more and the greater results of science to relate to the need in man for conduct, and to the need in him for beauty.

Carl Becker

PROGRESS

𝒯HOUGHT, says Pascal, "makes the greatness of man." The universe can destroy an individual by a mere breath; but even if the entire force of the universe were employed to destroy a single man, the man "would still be more noble than that which destroys him, since he is aware of his own death and of the advantage which the universe has over him: of all this the universe knows nothing." This awareness of himself and of the universe is no doubt what chiefly distinguishes man from all other forms of life. Man alone is conscious in the sense that he alone can stand outside of himself, as it were, and watch himself functioning for a brief span in the universe of which he is part. Man alone can coördinate memory of things past, perception of things present, anticipation of things to come, sufficiently so at least to know that he, like generations before him and after him, will live his brief span and will die. It is in virtue of this awareness, and somewhat in proportion to its intensity, that man alone asks the fundamental questions. Why and for what purpose this brief and precarious existence in a universe that endures? What is man's relation to the universe that is sometimes friendly, sometimes hostile, but in the end always fatal to him? How may he elude its hostility, win its favor, find compensations for the intolerable certainty of the death which it will inflict upon him? The answers which men have given to these questions are to be found in the various myths, religious doctrines, philosophical and ethical interpretations which they have accepted, and in those unconsciously held preconceptions which in every age so largely shape their thought and conduct. The modern idea of progress belongs in this category of answers to necessary but insoluble questions. Like the myths of primitive peoples and the religious and philosophical beliefs of more advanced societies, it springs from the nature of man as a conscious creature, who finds existence intolerable unless he can enlarge and enrich his otherwise futile activities by relating them to something more enduring and significant than himself.

Although grounded in the nature of man as a conscious creature, the idea of progress belongs historically to the European tradition, and its origin may be derived from two sources. One of these is the classical conception of history as an endless series of cycles; the other is the Hebraic-Christian doctrine of messianic intervention and salvation.

In Greek mythology the reign of Cronus was regarded as a golden age when men lived like gods free from toil and grief. The present appeared to be a period of degeneration, and improvement or progress could be conceived only in terms of regeneration—a return to the lost golden age. After the myth ceased to be believed, the Greeks continued to look back to the time of great lawgivers, such as Lycurgus and Solon, whose work they idealized, and forward to the time when other great lawgivers would appear and give them better laws again. "Until philosophers become kings . . . ," said Plato, "cities will not cease from ill." Yet however often restoration was accomplished by inspired lawgivers or philosopher-kings, fate and human frailty would again bring degeneration; so that, since "time is the enemy of man," most classical writers regarded human history as an endless series of cycles, a continual repetition of the familiar phenomena of recovery and degeneration. The rational mind, according to Marcus Aurelius, "stretches forth into the infinitude of Time, and comprehends the cyclical Regeneration of all things, and . . . discerns that our children will see nothing fresh, just as our fathers too never saw anything more than we" (*The Communings with Himself of Marcus Aurelius Antonius,* tr. by C. R. Haines, Loeb Classical Library, London 1916, bk. XI, sect. I). To regenerate the Roman Empire was obviously less easy than to construct a constitution for a small city-state; and Marcus Aurelius, philosopher-king though he was, instead of giving new laws to society recommended that the individual cultivate resignation. The later centuries of the Roman Empire, when resignation became at once more necessary and more difficult, were therefore a suitable time for the hopeless classical doctrine of endless cycles to be replaced by the Hebraic-Christian doctrine of messianic intervention and salvation.

The Jews like the Greeks looked back to a golden age, but it was identified with the creation of the world and with the Garden of Eden, in which the first men lived in innocence. Like the Greeks the Jews regarded the present as a period of degeneration, but they attributed the "fall" to Adam's disobedience to God's commands. God was at once the omniscient creator of the world and the supreme lawgiver, so that regeneration was identified with the coming of a God-inspired king of the house of David. Multiplied reverses and the destruction of the Hebraic state gave to this doctrine a less political, a more mystical and transcendent character. The once actual but now vanished kingdom was replaced by an ideal Israel, symbolized as the "son of man"; and the idea of a God-inspired king was replaced by the idea of a messiah who would effect a catastrophic intervention in the affairs of men and pronounce a doomlike judgment on the world. The Christian myth was but an elaboration of these ideas. Jesus, son of man, son of God, was the Messiah. But the end was not yet. The death of Jesus was expiation for the sins of men, faith in Him the means of salvation. Jesus the man was dead, but Christ the Lord still lived and would come again; then the earthly city would be destroyed and all the faithful be gathered with God in the heavenly city, there to dwell in perfection forever.

The weakness of the classical version of degeneration and recovery was that it offered no ultimate hope; of the Jewish, that its promise was for the chosen people only. The strength of the Christian version was that, conceiving human history as a cosmic drama in which all men played their predestined part, it offered to all the hope of eternal life as a compensation for the frustrations of temporal existence: by transferring the golden age from the past to the future it substituted an optimistic for a disillusioned view of human destiny. It is easily to be understood that such a view won wide assent in the Roman Empire during the centuries (300–500) of declining prosperity and increasing oppression or that it served so well to make existence tolerable in the relatively anarchic, isolated and static society of western Europe from the dissolution of the Roman Empire to the Renaissance of classical learning. But it lost its hold on the imaginations of men as a result of profound changes in the outward conditions of life which occurred in western Europe from the fourteenth to the nineteenth century. Among these changes were the rise of ordered secular governments, the growth of towns and industry, the geographical discoveries and the extension of commerce which brought western Europe into direct contact with alien customs and ideas, and above all the rise of an educated middle class whose interests were hampered by a form of society in which both the power and the doctrines of the Christian church supported the autocracy of kings and the privileges of a landed aristocracy. It was in this time of revolt against ecclesiastical and secular authority that the Christian doctrine of salvation was gradually transformed into the modern idea of progress.

So long as Christian philosophy was little questioned, men could afford to ignore the factual experience of mankind since they were so well assured of its ultimate significance. But the declining influence of the church was accompanied by an increasing interest in the worldly activities of men in the past. Italian humanists turned to the study of classical writers; Protestant reformers appealed from current theologians to the beliefs and practises of the primitive church. Thus was born the modern historical approach to problems, and human life came increasingly to be regarded rather as a historical process than as a finished drama to be played out according to a divine plan. Seen in historical perspective, classical civilization emerged for the humanists as a resplendent epoch from which the middle period of ecclesiastical ascendancy was manifestly a degeneration. Until the seventeenth century secular thought and learning turned for inspiration to the past—to the golden ages of Pericles and Augustus; and classical writers were idealized as models to be imitated, to be equaled if possible but hardly to be surpassed. In all this there was nothing that could not be found in the Greek notion of history with its cycles of recovery and degeneration, and but for two general influences modern thought might have been no more than a return to the classical view of human destiny.

One of these influences was Christian philosophy itself. Although it was gradually discredited as an account of events historically verifiable, Christian philosophy had so thoroughly habituated men to the thought of an ultimate happy destiny that they could never be content with a pale imitation of Greek pessimism. The other influence was experimental science which, in proportion as it displaced the Christian notion of a utopian existence after death to be brought about by the miraculous intervention of God, opened up the engaging prospect of indefinite improvement in this life to be effected by the application of human reason to the mastery of the physical and social environment which determines men's lives for good or ill.

In the seventeenth century Galileo and Newton made possible a new attitude toward nature. Nature was now seen to be friendly to man since the universe behaved in a uniform way according to universal natural laws—a behavior capable of being observed and measured and subjected to the uses of men. God was still the supreme lawgiver, the author of the universe; but His will was revealed in the great book of nature which men were to study in order to interpret, and to interpret in order that their ideas and customs might attain an increasing perfection by being brought into greater harmony with the laws of nature and of nature's God. God's revelation to men was thus made not through an inspired book or a divinely established church but through His works, and man had been endowed with reason precisely that he might learn through the course of the centuries what that revelation was. It was therefore no longer so necessary to think of the golden age of Greece and Rome as unsurpassable. "Those whom we call the ancients were really those who lived in the youth of the world," said Pascal, and "as we have added the experience of the ages between us and them to what they knew, it is in ourselves that is to be found that antiquity which we venerate in others." In the ascription of antiquity to the race there is still the implication of degeneration; but if a continuously richer experience made the moderns wiser than the ancients, it was not difficult to hit upon the idea that future generations would, in virtue of the same advantages, surpass the moderns. "We have admired our ancestors less," said Chastellux, "but we have loved our contemporaries better, and have expected more of our descendants" (*De la félicité publique*, 2 vols., new ed. Paris 1822, vol. ii, p. 71). Thus in the eighteenth century the modern idea of progress was born. Under the pressure of social discontents the dream of perfection, that necessary compensation for the limitations of the present state, having long been identified with the golden age of the Garden of Eden or life eternal in the heavenly city of God, was at last projected into the temporal life of man on earth and identified with the desired and hoped for regeneration of society.

As formulated by the *philosophes* the doctrine of progress was but a modification, however important, of the Christian doctrine of redemption; what was new in it was faith in the goodness of man and the efficacy of conscious reason to create an earthly utopia. The French Revolution was the outward expression of this faith. In the nineteenth century the doctrine of progress still reigned and won even a wider popular support, but it was somewhat differently conceived. After the disillusionment occasioned by the revolution and the Napoleonic conquests the prevailing desire was for social stability and national independence. The rationalization of this desire was provided by the historians and jurists who formulated the notion of historical continuity and deprecated the attempt to transform institutions according to a rational plan. Change was considered necessary but was thought to be beneficial only when it issued spontaneously from national tradition; the concept of natural law was not abandoned, but it was regarded as implicit in historical evolution rather than as a conclusion from abstract reason. Law is not made by the legislator, said Savigny, any more than language is made by the grammarian. Ranke, who influenced three generations of historians, viewed progress as something to be discovered by tracing the history of each nation just as it had occurred and by noting the peculiar contribution which each nation at the appropriate moment had made to European civilization. Hegel formulated the point of view of early nineteenth century jurists and historians in his *Philosophie der Geschichte*. A reason of nature working over the heads of men, a transcendent *Vernunft* reconciling within its cloudy recesses innumerable and conflicting *Verstände*, progressively realized itself in the actual events of history.

After the middle of the century natural science invested the doctrine of progress with a more materialistic implication. Progress was still regarded as the result of a force external to man; but the force was to be found not above but inherent in the phenomenal world. This view found support in the Darwinian theory of struggle for existence and survival of the fittest and in Schopenhauer's doctrine of the will as an aspect of a universal blind force. Guided by these preconceptions thinkers abandoned the effort to hasten progress by describing utopias and turned to the search for the inevitable law by which progress had been and would be achieved. Of the many efforts of this sort the most important were those of Auguste Comte and Karl Marx. Comte looked upon history as the result of the instinctive effort of men to ameliorate their condition —an effort which could be observed to fall into three stages of culture, the theological, the metaphysical and the positive, or scientific. Marx, interpreting the historic process in terms of Hegel's famous dialectic, found the determining force in the economic class conflict which, having substituted the nineteenth century capitalist competitive society for the aristocratic landed society of the Middle Ages and early modern times, would in turn replace the capitalist competitive society of the nineteenth century by the proletarian communist society of the future.

Of the many theories of progress formulated in the nineteenth century the only one that had much influence on the thought of common men was that of Marx. Yet the idea of progress, vaguely conceived as a rapid improvement in general prosperity and happiness, became a living force.

The chief reason for this was no doubt the rapid changes in the outward conditions of life consequent upon the technological revolution. The common man, before whose eyes the marvels of science and invention were constantly displayed, noted the unprecedented increase in wealth, the growth of cities, the new and improved methods of transportation and communication, the greater security from disease and death and all the conveniences of domestic life unknown to previous generations, and accepted the doctrine of progress without question: the world was obviously better than it had been, obviously would be better than it was. The precise objective toward which the world was progressing remained, however, for the common man and for the intellectual, somewhat vague.

Thus the nineteenth century doctrine of progress differed somewhat from that of the eighteenth. The difference may be expressed, with some exaggeration in the contrast, by saying that whereas the eighteenth century held that man can by taking thought add a cubit to his stature, the nineteenth century held that a cubit would be added to his stature whether he took thought or not. This latter faith that the stars were carrying men on to better things received a rude shock during the World War and subsequently; and there may be noted two significant changes in the present attitude toward the doctrine of progress. Certain thinkers, notably Spengler, are returning to the Greek notion of cycles, now formulated in terms of the rise, flourishing and decline of "cultures." Others are reverting to the eighteenth century idea that by deliberate purpose and the rational use of knowledge man can reconstruct society according to a more just and intelligible design. To this class belong those who have faith in communism, fascism and the planned capitalist society.

The doctrine of progress is peculiarly suited to western society in modern times; that is, a highly dynamic society capable of seeing its achievements against a long historical background. From the practical and from the rational point of view there is no reason to suppose that it will have a more enduring virtue than other doctrines which it has supplanted. If, as may well happen, the possibilities of scientific discovery and of technological invention should sometime be exhausted, the outward conditions of life might become sufficiently stabilized so that the idea of progress would cease to be relevant. Rationally considered, the idea of progress is always at war with its premises. It rests upon the notion of a universe in perpetual flux; yet the idea of progress has always carried the implication of finality, for it seems to be meaningless unless there is movement toward some ultimate objective. The formal theories of progress are all vitiated by this radical inconsistency. In Hegel's scheme the objective was freedom, already realized in the Prussian state. In Comte's theory the objective was the final positive stage into which Europe had already entered. Marx criticized Hegel for explaining history by a process which would not explain the future, but he is himself open to the criticism of having explained history in terms of a class conflict which would end with the establishment of a classless society. It is easy to picture history as a process working toward an ultimate good if the world is to come to an end when that good is attained; but if the universe as presented by modern science is to be accepted—a universe in perpetual flux—then a law of history which at some determinate time ceases to apply leaves much to be desired.

Thus the final good, absolute standards of value, are sought in vain; there is merely a universe in which the ideas of things as well as the things themselves arise out of temporary conditions and are transformed with the modification of the conditions out of which they arose. On this assumption we must dispense with the notion of finality, must suppose that the idea of progress and all of its special formulations are but temporary insights useful for the brief moment in which they flourish. "In escaping from the illusion of finality, is it legitimate to exempt that dogma itself? Must not it, too, submit to its own negation of finality? Will not that process of change, for which Progress is the optimistic name, compel 'Progress' too to fall from the commanding position in which it is now, with apparent security, enthroned?" (Bury, J. B., *The Idea of Progress*, p. 352). The price we pay for escaping from the illusion of finality is the recognition that nothing, not even the belief that we have escaped that illusion, is likely to endure. All philosophies based upon the absolute and the unconditioned have their defects; but all philosophies based upon the universal relativity of things have their defects also, a minor one being that they must be prepared, at the appropriate moment, to commit hara-kiri in deference to the ceaseless change which they postulate.

Belief in progress as a fact depends upon the standard of value chosen for measuring it and upon the time perspective in which it is measured. If we look back a hundred years, it is obvious that there has been progress in the mastery of physical forces. If we look back two thousand years, it is uncertain whether there has been much if any progress in intelligence and the art of living. If we look back two hundred and fifty thousand years, it is apparent that there has been progress in all those aspects of life which civilized men regard as valuable. All these judgments are based on standards of value appreciable by the mind of civilized man. But if we take a still longer perspective and estimate the universe as a whole, as an omniscient intelligence indifferent to human values might estimate it, in terms of cosmic energy, then progress and the very existence of man himself become negligible and meaningless. In such a perspective we should see the whole life of man on the earth as a mere momentary ripple on the surface of one of the minor planets in one of the minor stellar systems.

Edward Gibbon

GENERAL OBSERVATIONS ON THE FALL
OF THE ROMAN EMPIRE IN THE WEST
From *The Decline and Fall of the Roman Empire*

*T*HE GREEKS, after their country had been reduced into a province, imputed the triumphs of Rome not to the merit but to the *Fortune* of the republic. The inconstant goddess, who so blindly distributes and resumes her favours, had *now* consented (such was the language of envious flattery) to resign her wings, to descend from her globe, and to fix her firm and immutable throne on the banks of the Tiber. A wiser Greek [Polybius], who has composed with a philosophic spirit the memorable history of his own times, deprived his countrymen of this vain and delusive comfort by opening to their view the deep foundations of the greatness of Rome. The fidelity of the citizens to each other and to the state was confirmed by the habits of education and the prejudices of religion. Honour, as well as virtue, was the principle of the republic; the ambitious citizens laboured to deserve the solemn glories of a triumph; and the ardour of the Roman youth was kindled into active emulation as often as they beheld the domestic images of their ancestors. The temperate struggles of the patricians and plebeians had finally established the firm and equal balance of the constitution, which united the freedom of popular assemblies with the authority and wisdom of a senate and the executive powers of a regal magistrate. When the consul displayed the standard of the republic, each citizen bound himself, by the obligation of an oath, to draw his sword in the cause of his country till he had discharged the sacred duty by a military service of ten years. This wise institution continually poured into the field the rising generations of freemen and

629

soldiers; and their numbers were reinforced by the warlike and populous states of Italy, who after a brave resistance had yielded to the valour and embraced the alliance of the Romans.

The sage historian, who excited the virtue of the younger Scipio and beheld the ruin of Carthage, has accurately described their military system, their levies, arms, exercises, subordination, marches, encampments, and the invincible legion, superior in active strength to the Macedonian phalanx of Philip and Alexander. From these institutions of peace and war Polybius has deduced the spirit and success of a people incapable of fear and impatient of repose. The ambitious design of conquest, which might have been defeated by the seasonable conspiracy of mankind, was attempted and achieved; and the perpetual violation of justice was maintained by the political virtues of prudence and courage. The arms of the republic, sometimes vanquished in battle, always victorious in war, advanced with rapid steps to the Euphrates, the Danube, the Rhine, and the ocean; and the images of gold, or silver, or brass that might serve to represent the nations and their kings were successively broken by the *iron* monarchy of Rome.

The rise of a city which swelled into an empire may deserve, as a singular prodigy, the reflection of a philosophic mind. But the decline of Rome was the natural and inevitable effect of immoderate greatness. Prosperity ripened the principle of decay; the causes of destruction multiplied with the extent of conquest; and as soon as time or accident had removed the artificial supports, the stupendous fabric yielded to the pressure of its own weight. The story of its ruin is simple and obvious; and instead of inquiring *why* the Roman empire was destroyed, we should rather be surprised that it had subsisted so long. The victorious legions, who in distant wars acquired the vices of strangers and mercenaries, first oppressed the freedom of the republic and afterwards violated the majesty of the purple. The emperors, anxious for their personal safety and the public peace, were reduced to the base expedient of corrupting the discipline which rendered them alike formidable to their sovereign and to the enemy; the vigour of the military government was relaxed and finally dissolved by the partial institutions of Constantine; and the Roman world was overwhelmed by a deluge of barbarians.

The decay of Rome has been frequently ascribed to the translation of the seat of empire; but this history has already shown that the powers of government were *divided* rather than *removed*. The throne of Constantinople was erected in the East; while the West was still possessed by a series of emperors who held their residence in Italy and claimed their equal inheritance of the legions and provinces. This dangerous novelty impaired the strength and fomented the vices of a double reign; the instruments of an oppressive and arbitrary system were multiplied; and a vain emulation of luxury, not of merit, was introduced and supported between the degenerate successors of Theodosius. Extreme distress, which unites the virtue of a free people, embitters the factions of a declining monarchy. The hostile favourites of Arcadius and Honorius betrayed the republic to its common enemies; and the Byzantine court beheld with indifference, perhaps with pleasure, the disgrace of Rome, the misfortunes of Italy, and the loss of the West. Under the succeeding reigns the alliance of the two empires was restored; but the aid of the Oriental Romans was tardy, doubtful, and ineffectual; and the national schism of the Greeks and Latins was enlarged by the perpetual difference of language and manners, of interests, and even of religion. Yet the salutary even approved in some measure the judgment of Constantine. During a long period of decay his impregnable city repelled the victorious armies of barbarians, protected the wealth of Asia, and commanded, both in peace and war, the important straits which connect the Euxine and Mediterranean Seas. The foundation of Constantinople more essentially contributed to the preservation of the East than to the ruin of the West.

As the happiness of a *future* life is the great object of religion, we may hear without surprise or scandal that the introduction, or at least the abuse, of Christianity had some influence on the decline and fall of the Roman empire. The clergy successfully preached the doctrines of patience and pusillanimity; the active virtues of society were discouraged; and the last remains of military spirit were buried in the cloister. A large portion of public and private wealth was consecrated to the specious demands of charity and devotion, and the soldiers' pay was lavished on the useless multitudes of both sexes who could plead the merits of abstinence and chastity. Faith, zeal, curiosity, and more earthly passions of malice and ambition kindled the flame of theological discord; the church and even the state were distracted by religious factions, whose conflicts were sometimes bloody and always implacable; the attention of the emperors was diverted from camps to synods; the Roman world was oppressed by a new species of tyranny, and the persecuted sects became the secret enemies of their country.

Yet party spirit, however pernicious or absurd, is a principle of union as well as of dissension. The bishops, from eighteen hundred pulpits, inculcated the duty of passive obedience to a lawful and orthodox sovereign; their frequent assemblies and perpetual correspondence maintained the communion of distant churches; and the benevolent temper of the Gospel was strengthened, though confined, by the spiritual alliance of the catholics. The sacred indolence of the monks was devoutly embraced by a servile and effeminate age; but if superstition had not afforded a decent retreat, the same vices would have tempted the unworthy Romans to desert, from baser motives, the standard of the republic. Religious precepts are easily obeyed which indulge and sanctify the natural inclinations of their votaries; but the pure and genuine influence of Christianity may be traced in its beneficial though imperfect effects on the barbarian proselytes of the North. If the decline of the Roman empire was hastened by the conversion of Constantine, his victorious religion broke the violence of the fall and mollified the ferocious temper of the conquerors.

This awful revolution may be usefully applied to the instruction of the present age. It is the duty of a patriot to prefer and promote the exclusive interest and glory of his native country; but a philosopher may be permitted to enlarge his views and to consider Europe as one great republic whose various inhabitants have attained almost the same level of politeness and cultivation. The balance of power will continue to fluctuate, and the prosperity of our own or the neighbouring kingdoms may be alternately exalted or depressed; but these partial events cannot essentially injure our general state of happiness, the system of arts and laws and manners which so advantageously distinguish, above the rest of mankind, the Europeans and their colonies. The savage nations of the globe are the common enemies of civilized society; and we may inquire, with anxious curiosity, whether Europe is still threatened with a repetition of those calamities which formerly oppressed the arms and institutions of Rome. Perhaps the same reflections will illustrate the fall of that mighty empire, and explain the probable causes of our actual security.

The Romans were ignorant of the extent of their dangers and the number of their enemies. Beyond the Rhine and Danube the northern countries of Europe and Asia were filled with innumerable tribes of hunters and shepherds, poor, voracious, and turbulent, bold in arms and impatient to ravish the fruits of industry. The barbarian world was agitated by the rapid impulse of war, and the peace of Gaul or Italy was shaken by the distant revolutions of China. The Huns, who fled before a victorious enemy, directed their march towards the West; and the torrent was swelled by the gradual accession of captives and allies. The flying tribes who yielded to the Huns assumed in *their* turn the spirit of conquest; the endless column of barbarians pressed on the Roman empire with accumulated weight; and if the foremost were destroyed the vacant space was instantly replenished by new assailants. Such formidable emigrations no longer issue from the North; and the long repose, which has been imputed to the decrease of population, is the happy consequence of the progress of arts and agriculture. Instead of some rude villages thinly scattered among its woods and morasses, Germany now produces a list of two thousand three hundred walled towns; the Christian kingdoms of Denmark, Sweden, and Poland have been successively established; and the Hanse merchants, with the Teutonic knights, have extended their colonies along the coast of the Baltic as far as the Gulf of Finland. From the Gulf of Finland to the Eastern Ocean, Russia now assumes the form of a powerful and civilized empire. The plough, the loom, and the forge are introduced on the banks of the Volga, the Oby, and the Lena; and the fiercest of the Tartar hordes have been taught to tremble and obey. The reign of independent barbarism is now contracted to a narrow span; and the remnant of Calmucks or Uzbecks, whose forces may be almost numbered, cannot seriously excite the apprehensions of the great republic of Europe. Yet this apparent security should not tempt us to forget that new enemies and unknown dangers may *possibly* arise from some obscure people, scarcely visible in the map of the world. The Arabs or Saracens, who spread their conquests from India to Spain, had languished in poverty and contempt till Mahomet breathed into those same bodies the soul of enthusiasm.

The empire of Rome was firmly established by the singular and perfect coalition of its members. The subject nations, resigning the hope and even the wish of independence, embraced the character of Roman citizens; and the provinces of the West were reluctantly torn by the barbarians from the bosom of their mother country. But this union was purchased by the loss of national freedom and military spirit; and the servile provinces, destitute of life and motion, expected their safety from the mercenary troops and governors who were directed by the orders of a distant court. The happiness of an hundred millions depended on the personal merit of one or two men, perhaps children, whose minds were corrupted by education, luxury, and despotic power. The deepest wounds were inflicted on the empire during the minorities of the sons and grandsons of Theodosius; and after those incapable princes seemed to attain the age of manhood they abandoned the church to the bishops, the state to the eunuchs, and the provinces to the barbarians. Europe is now divided into twelve powerful though unequal kingdoms, three respectable commonwealths, and a variety of smaller though independent states; the chances of royal and ministerial talent are multiplied, at least, with the number of its rulers; and a Julian or Semiramis may reign in the North, while Arcadius and Honorius again slumber on the thrones of the South. The abuses of tyranny are restrained by the mutual influence of fear and shame; republics have acquired order and stability; monarchies have imbibed the principles of freedom, or at least of moderation; and some sense of honour and justice is introduced into the most defective constitutions by the general manners of the times. In peace, the progress of knowledge and industry is accelerated by the emulation of so many active rivals; in war, the European forces are exercised by temperate and undecisive contests. If a savage conqueror should issue from the deserts of Tartary, he must repeatedly vanquish the robust peasants of Russia, the numerous armies of Germany, the gallant nobles of France, and the intrepid freemen of Britain, who, perhaps, might confederate for their common defence. Should the victorious barbarians carry slavery and desolation as far as the Atlantic Ocean, ten thousand vessels would transport beyond their pursuit the remains of civilized society; and Europe would revive and flourish in the American world, which is already filled with her colonies and institutions.

Cold, poverty, and a life of danger and fatigue fortify the strength and courage of barbarians. In every age they have oppressed the polite and peaceful nations of China, India, and Persia, who neglected, and still neglect, to counterbalance these natural powers by the resources of military art. The warlike states of antiquity, Greece, Macedonia, and Rome, educated a race of soldiers: exercised their bodies, disciplined their courage, multiplied their forces by regular evolutions, and converted the iron which they possessed into strong and serviceable weapons. But this superiority insensibly declined with their laws and manners; and the feeble policy of Constantine and his successors armed and instructed, for the ruin of the empire, the rude valour of the barbarian mercenaries. The military art has been changed by the invention of gunpowder, which enables man to command the two most powerful agents of nature, air and fire. Mathematics, chemistry, mechanics, architecture, have been applied to the service of war, and the adverse parties oppose to each other the most elaborate modes of attack and of defence. Historians may indignantly observe that the preparations of a siege would found and maintain a flourishing colony; yet we cannot be displeased that the subversion of a city should be a work of cost and difficulty, or that an industrious people should be protected by those arts which survive and supply the decay of military virtue. Cannon and fortifications now form an impregnable barrier against the Tartar horse; and Europe is secure from any future irruption of barbarians, since, before they can conquer, they must cease to be barbarous. Their gradual advances in the science of war would always be accompanied, as we may learn from the example of Russia, with a proportionable improvement in the arts of peace and civil policy; and they themselves must deserve a place among the polished nations whom they subdue.

Should these speculations be found doubtful or fallacious, there still remains a more humble source of comfort and hope. The discoveries of ancient and modern navigators, and the domestic history or tradition of the most enlightened nations, represent the *human savage* naked both in mind and body, and destitute of laws, of arts, of ideas, and almost of language. From this abject condition, perhaps the primitive and universal state of man, he has gradually arisen to command the animals, to fertilize the earth, to traverse the ocean, and to measure the heavens. His progress in the improvement and exercise of his mental and corporeal faculties has been irregular and various, infinitely slow in the beginning and increasing by degrees with redoubled velocity; ages of laborious ascent have been followed by a moment of rapid downfall; and the several climates of the globe have felt the vicissitudes of light and darkness. Yet the experience of four thousand years should enlarge our hopes and diminish our apprehensions. We cannot determine to what height the human species may aspire in their advance towards perfection; but it may safely be presumed that no people, unless the face of nature is changed, will relapse into their original barbarism.

The improvements of society may be viewed under a threefold aspect: 1. The poet or philosopher illustrates his age and country by the efforts of a *single* mind; but these superior powers of reason or fancy are rare and spontaneous productions, and the genius of Homer or Cicero or Newton would excite less admiration if they could be created by the will of a prince or the lessons of a preceptor. 2. The benefits of law and policy, of trade and manufactures, of arts and sciences, are more solid and permanent; and *many* individuals may be qualified, by education and discipline, to promote in their respective stations the interest of the community. But this general order is the effect of skill and labour; and the complex machinery may be decayed by time or injured by violence. 3. Fortunately for mankind, the more useful or at least more necessary arts can be performed without superior talents or national subordination, without powers of *one* or the union of *many*. Each village, each family, each individual, must always possess both ability and inclination to perpetuate the use of fire and of metals; the propagation and service of domestic animals; the methods of hunting and fishing; the rudiments of navigation; the imperfect cultivation of corn or other nutritive grain; and the simple practice of the mechanic trades. Private genius and public industry may be extirpated, but these hardy plants survive the tempest and strike an everlasting root into the most unfavourable soil. The splendid days of Augustus and Trajan were eclipsed by a cloud of ignorance, and the barbarians subverted the laws and palaces of Rome. But the scythe, the invention or emblem of Saturn, still continued annually to mow the harvests of Italy; and the human feasts of the Læstrigons have never been renewed on the coast of Campania.

Since the first discovery of the arts, war, commerce, and religious zeal have diffused among the savages of the Old and New World these inestimable gifts. They have been successively propagated; they can never be lost. We may therefore acquiesce in the pleasing conclusion that every age of the world has increased and still increases the real wealth, the happiness, the knowledge, and perhaps the virtue of the human race.

E. M. Forster

CAPTAIN EDWARD GIBBON

*T*HE GARDEN where I am writing slopes down to a field, the field to a
road, and along that road exactly a hundred and seventy years ago
passed a young officer with a rather large head. If he had turned the
head to the right, he would have seen not me, not the garden, but he
would have seen the elms that still border the garden—they were already
recognizable trees. And on his left, outrunning him as it has outlived
him, ran a little stream called the Tillingbourne. The gorse and the
may were just over when he passed, the dog roses coming out, the
bracken rising, but although he was unusually observant he has left no
record of these events. "June was absolutely lost" is his only comment;
June, which he might have spent reading Strabo, he was condemned to
spend marching across Kent, Surrey and Hants.

He does, however, mention that the previous night he slept at
Dorking, and visited there "a whimsical pretty place in the style of
Vauxhall." I am glad he should have had that relaxation. The pretty
place was Denbighs, on the slope of the downs. It was not merely in the
style of the Vauxhall gardens. It actually belonged to the proprietor, an
ingenious gentleman who contrived at every turn some "singularity,"
something that amused and amazed, and the last turn was the most
marvellous of all, for it was none other than the Valley of the Shadow
of Death itself. A guide book of the period thus describes the scene:

> "The view on a descent into this gloomy vale was awful. There
> was a large alcove, divided into two compartments, in one of which
> the Unbeliever was represented dying in great agony. Near him were
> his books which encouraged him in his libertine course, such as

Hobbes, Tindal, etc. In the other was the good Christian, calm and
serene, taking a solemn leave of the World, and anticipating the joys
of immortality."

The young officer must have regarded the alcove with an easy and
equal smile. He was rather conceited and he may have foreseen that
before long, in the Libertine's library, a work of his own would be lying,
a work more suggestive than even Tindal and Hobbes, and entitled *The
Decline and Fall of the Roman Empire*.

Yes; it is Edward Gibbon who passes at the bottom of this garden
on June 8, 1761. He strikes me as a little dissatisfied. He is fresh from a
wretched love affair; he wanted to marry a Swiss girl, and his father
objected. "I sighed as a lover, I obeyed as a son," he will write in after
years, but the episode is not yet an epigram. He is vaguely unhappy, and
his father has married again—depressing. Then there is money—he needs
it for books and dissipation, and has consented to cutting off an entail in
return for £300 a year—a bad bargain. Then there is religion—it is all
very well to smile at the alcove, but one must belong somewhere, and
he has already changed from Protestantism to Catholicism and back
again; the Swiss girl was a Protestant. And then—overshadowing everything—is a vexatious war. England is at war with France. Our ally,
Prussia, is beating France, yet we are afraid of a French invasion, and a
militia Bill has been passed authorizing the raising of troops for home
defence. It seemed an excellent measure, and he and his father were both
enthusiastic. Alas! Their services have been accepted, and here they are, a
captain and a major in the South Hampshire Militia, and they are
making constant route marches, drilling, recruiting, guarding dirty prisoners, entertaining people whom they do not want to meet, quarrelling
with people whom they have never seen, and engaged in a war otherwise
unknown to history—the war between the South Hampshire Militia and
the North. The major is bored—still, he wastes his life wherever he is,
and we need not pity him. The captain wants to read, study, think, but
this aggravating little trap has caught him. Nor is he feeling physically
well—the grotesque disease which will finally carry him off has already
declared itself. However, this he mentions to no one, any more than he
mentions the love affair, and his outward deportment is frigid and bland.
Westward he goes, and, looked at through all those years and those
myriads of fallen leaves, he seems romantic to me—the greatest historian
England has ever produced, trying his paces on the English roads. But
he found no romance in them himself, nor anywhere until he heard

vespers in the church of Ara Coeli. His head—moving away from mine by now—is not yet concentrated on the decline and fall. Other schemes contend inside it, such as the life of Sir Walter Raleigh, or a history of that noble people, the Swiss, or a monograph of the talented Medici at Florence. And his little book about literature has just come out written in French, and he will present a copy to the Duke of York if opportunity offers. Nursing his secrets, he disappears in the direction of Guildford and I lose him as a neighbour. It is surprising he ever came so near.

Now, when Gibbon wrote his famous Autobiography (or—to be more accurate—when he wrote the various memoirs which were afterwards combined into an autobiography by his executor), he had become a great man with a fixed attitude towards life and an assured style, and such a man can never interpret his own youth. He has ripened but he has hardened. Gibbon did not harden into a prig, he never concealed immaturities through hypocrisy. But he often omitted them because they no longer interested him, and were unlikely to interest his public, and if he did refer to them it was jestingly and in general terms, as befitted an eminent and sarcastic historian. "By degrees a mimic Bellona unveiled her naked deformity, and before our final dissolution I had longed, sighed for my release." That was how the South Hampshire Militia appeared in retrospect but how did it appear to the militiaman? Did he "sigh" for release, any more than he "sighed" as a lover? We can answer these questions, thanks to the militiaman's journal, which was published not long ago. It is like anyone else's journal, the author never intended us to see it and that is its value, because if Gibbon has a literary fault it is the fault of presenting himself to us too commandingly. His mastery of style entails a mastery of his audience which becomes monotonous. Even when he is personally appealing—as in the passage that describes the inception of the *Decline and Fall* at Rome or in the still more touching passage that describes its conclusion in the summer-house at Lausanne—we are conscious of reacting precisely as he intended, we have no chance of bringing a free-will offering to that august shrine, all has been prearranged. He insists on our hearing what he says to us until we long for a chance of hearing what he says to himself, and thanks to the Journal that chance is now ours. We find not a new Gibbon but a more vulnerable one, and the mere fact that he does not finish all his sentences endears him to me. When he was worried and when he was young, he did not always know what he wanted to say. Nor did he always know where things lead to. For instance, on Sunday, December 22, 1762, we get the entry: "Captain Perkins dined with us today, and led us into an intemperance we have not known for some time past," followed on Monday by: "I could do nothing this morning but spew. I scarce wonder at the Confessor who enjoined getting drunk as a pennance."

But I must keep to more serious matters. I have already mentioned a war between England and France. It occasioned little inconvenience, but the war between Sir Thomas and the Duke was a very different affair, and some account of it is necessary if we are to understand Gibbon's military career.

Charles Paulet, fifth Duke of Bolton, and Lord Lieutenant of the County of Hampshire, was admittedly Colonel of the North Hampshire Militia. But he wanted to be Colonel of the South Hampshires as well, to which Sir Thomas Worsley objected. Sir Thomas had already been instituted as colonel by another authority, and nothing would induce him to resign. In vain did the Duke argue that the two battalions really constituted a single regiment, so that he commanded both. Sir Thomas retorted from his cups that, by Act of Parliament, no regiment could exceed a certain size, and that if the two battalions were added together that size would be exceeded; consequently the South Hampshires were an individual unit, which he commanded. The Duke was a Whig, Sir Thomas a Tory. Both of them had influential friends in London, to whom they wrote, and since Sir Thomas was not good at letters, his were drafted for him by Captain Gibbon. Both colonels complained to their general, who affected not to understand them, and finally Pitt was asked to lay the dispute before the King. Pitt declined to do this—perhaps the rival contest between England and France distracted him—and the struggle had to go on as best it might. We can read the details in Gibbon's journal. The Duke had begun the campaign with a notable success; he split the enemy ranks by imposing on the South Hampshires as adjutant an officer of his own, McCombe by name, and instructing him to make all the official returns to himself, and not to Sir Thomas. But he had reckoned without honest Sergeant Firth. Firth, on hearing that McCombe was coming, "said publicly he had been a prizefighter and an alehouse keeper, and that when they had been together in another regiment McCombe was broke for having cheated as Paymaster." This came to McCombe's ears. He demanded a court-martial on Firth. Sir Thomas countered by demanding a court-martial on McCombe because he insisted on sending his official returns to the Duke; all Hampshire society was rent in twain, and before the court-martial could be held King George II died and a truce had to be called while the belligerents went into mourning. Gibbon was actually coming back from the King's funeral at the moment I visualize him—the funniest funeral that Westminster Abbey has ever seen, if Horace Walpole is correct, the funeral where the Duke of Newcastle stood on the Duke of Cumberland's train for fear of catching a chill from the marble. The courts-martial were finally held at Southampton; both Firth and McCombe were reprimanded and Gibbon was made a burgess of the city, and entertained the Corporation to dinner in the Old Assembly room: "six dishes of turtle, eight of Game with jellies, Syllabubs, tarts, puddings, pineapples, in all three and twenty things besides a large piece of roast of beef on the side table. The whole made a pretty appearance and (reckoning port, white wine and punch) cost me only thirteen pounds odd." McCombe was invited, the Duke began to weary and the war died out by common consent.

While the gentlemen of England thus rallied in her hour of need, the common people showed no enthusiasm. Recent events were fresh in their mind, and they knew that though they had been called up for home service they might be drafted overseas. Recruits were difficult to get. Each parish had to provide its quota, they were chosen by lot, and each man chosen had either to serve or to provide a substitute or pay £10. Men with three children born in wedlock were exempt, and it was extraordinary how prolific and how moral the population proved; nearly all the weavers of Alton got off. Finally a reluctant crowd of three hundred yokels were collected, in place of the scheduled five hundred, and were marched about their native soil, and sometimes given uniforms. "I am afraid," writes an anonymous satirist of the period, "if you should take your firearms with you, that John in the Rear will be firing his Piece into the Back-side of his friend Tom in the Front; or which would be still worse, blow out the brains of his noble Captain." No such disaster occurred to Captain Gibbon. He did no good, but came to no harm, and when, after three wasted years, the militia was disbanded, he could return with a good conscience to his studies, and to his beloved Europe.

He had studied, as best he could, in the midst of his duties, and the list of the books he read and the extracts he compiled are formidable. As yet, he scarcely knew what he was reading for, but he had grasped his vocation, and, if historians did nothing but read, he might well have complained that the militia nearly stultified him with its pettiness, its scrappiness, and "more than all, the disagreeable society I was obliged to live in. No manners, no conversation, they were only a set of fellows all whose behaviour was low, and most of whose characters were despicable. Luckily I was their superior in every sense, and through Sir Thomas (whose prime minister I was) in fact I commanded the Battalion."

A severe, unattractive young man! But a just one. He goes on to summarize the advantages. His health seems better, he has had amusement and change of scene, he has become conscious of "a new field, that of military affairs which, both in my studies and travels, will give me eyes for a new world of things. . . . But what I value most, is the knowledge it has given me of mankind in general, and of my own country in particular. So that the sum of all is, that I am glad the militia has been, and glad it is no more."

This is the summary not so much of a philosopher as of a historian who realizes that it is impossible, through reading alone, to interpret the past. Nor is emotion enough. The historian must have a third quality as well: some conception of how men who are not historians behave. Otherwise he will move in a world of the dead. He can only gain that conception through personal experience, and he can only use his personal experiences when he is a genius. In Gibbon, as in no other English historian, this tenuous circle was complete. He was a genius who read, dreamed, and also knew—knew by direct contact, a fragment of the rough stuff of society, and extended his knowledge through the ages. Thus the lane that passes under this garden reminds me at moments of the enormous stretches of road he was later to traverse—the roads that led all over Europe and back through the centuries into Rome, then all over Europe again until they frayed out in the forests of Germany and the sands of Syria. As he jogged away through Surrey and Hampshire, he had already in his mind premonitions of a larger route, though its direction remained obscure, and when Sergeant Firth accused McCombe or Sir Thomas dictated another letter about the Duke, his mind was preparing for brawls where the disputants were Caesars and the prize the civilized world.

Herbert J. Muller

THE FALL OF ROME:
ITS IMPLICATIONS FOR US

*F*ROM THE melancholy spectacle of the decline and fall of Rome, the skeptical Gibbon was able to derive comfort by reflecting on the manifest superiority of his own enlightened age, and by drawing "the pleasing conclusion that every age of the world has increased and still increases the real wealth, the happiness, the knowledge, and perhaps the virtue, of the human race." Today we are no longer so complacent, at least about the increase in happiness and virtue. The fashion now is to dwell on the deadly analogies between the Roman world and our own, in the suspicion that history may repeat itself after all. We have reason to feel that we too may have lost control of our destiny. We know the "schism in the soul" that Toynbee analyzes in disintegrating societies— the common symptoms of abandon and truancy, drift and promiscuity, vulgarity and barbarism. ("Bongo, bongo," ran the popular song; then "Enjoy yourself, it's later than you think.") We are now prone, indeed, to overlook the essential differences between our civilization and the Roman, which have become much more conspicuous since Gibbon wrote. Yet we might well begin with the analogies. We always have to deal with the invariable basic problems of rulers and ruled, haves and have-nots, and to struggle with the invariable enemies, selfishness and greed. More specifically, we have retraced the Roman adventure of brutal conquest and exploitation, followed by ideal aspirations to a universal commonwealth. If the barbarian hordes that finally overran Rome have dwindled to a negligible power, the West has been breeding its own barbarians, of a type still more dangerous. I assume that no thoughtful person believes we

643

shall escape the fate of Rome because the Huns have technically disappeared from history.

Gibbon wrote that the fall of Rome was "the natural and inevitable effect of immoderate greatness." Spengler and Toynbee specifically regard empire itself as a historic sign of decadence, instead of the vigorous growth it appears to be. It breeds the disease of gigantism as well as militarism— a swaggering in size and quantity and material power, which corrupts artistic, intellectual, political, and moral standards alike. It gives rise to the great world-city and the city masses. "There is a new sort of nomad," wrote Spengler, "cohering unstably in fluid masses: the parasitical city-dweller, traditionless, utterly matter-of-fact, without religion, clever, unfruitful. . ." The man on the street is in fact likely to be a shallower and shoddier type than the simple peasant, lacking piety, lacking a genuine folk culture. In ancient Rome he demanded only bread and circuses; he hardly noticed the fall of Rome because the games went on. In America today he glances at the headlines and then turns to the sports page and the comics.

Another consequence of Roman imperialism was the rise of the businessman and the rule of money. Although the growing materialism was cloaked by the traditional contempt of trade, as today it is cloaked by the conventions of Christian service, it corroded the old traditions and cheapened the tone of the national life. The rising bourgeoisie had the limitations typical of their class. At worst, their notion of grandeur was the vulgar ostentation satirized by Juvenal and Petronius; at best, their civic ideals were exemplified by the beloved Antoninus Pius, who was a kind of benign Coolidge. To the administration of the empire they contributed some practical ability but little vision or statesmanship. The plainest analogy is the complacency of the bourgeoisie, rooted in their material well-being, their civic pride, their superficial culture, and their economic ignorance. The voice of Rome under the Antonines, just before the deluge, sounds much like the voice of Victorian England.

It is America, however, that offers the happy hunting ground for the analogist. America too has risen, without conscious plan, to a position of world leadership; and while some of its senators want to pull back and escape the responsibilities of this role, others call for an aggressive leadership that to Europeans looks like Roman imperialism. As the inheritor of a great culture, it stands to Europe much as Rome did to Greece. The Americans too are a practical people who have distinguished themselves by their material contributions, notably their engineering feats; they glory in their roads, bridges, and dams, and in their plumbing. They have the same ambivalent attitude toward Europeans as the Romans had toward the Greeks, now humbly admiring their superior culture, now scorning them as corrupt and effete. They are prone to the same narrow, short view of the useful, the same distrust of theory and "brain trusts." Their common sense is as cloudy a sense of the theories they live by.

Hence Americans were as unprepared for the economic and political problems that resulted from their rapid expansion. Both nations entered a feverish get-rich-quick era, marked by prodigies of exploitation and orgies of speculation. On the morning after, both woke up to chronic unemployment, inflation, the cycle of boom and crash, and bitter class war. Rome tried to solve its problems by *ad hoc* "new deal" measures, which outraged wealthy conservatives but brought only temporary or superficial relief to the poor. (Among the experiments outlined in Haskell's *The New Deal in Ancient Rome* were debt moratoriums, farm-labor acts, resettlement administrations, the ever-normal granary, work relief, and public subsidies or doles.) The outcome was the dictatorship of Augustus, which some Americans saw coming under Franklin D. Roosevelt. Now America faces the further problem that beset the Roman Republic, the necessity of adapting its democratic institutions to its new responsibilities as a world power. Its problem is complicated by reverence for a Constitution designed for a much simpler society, and specifically by the elaborate system of checks and balances that it inherited from Rome. It has a deep-rooted fear of strong government. But the chief bogey of its conservatives remains the kind of prophecy that Macaulay made a century ago. Once there was no longer a frontier to absorb the discontented and unemployed, he wrote, America would be rent by class war and its prosperity destroyed by demagogues bent on despoiling the rich; whereupon either some Caesar or Napoleon would seize the reins of government or the republic would be laid waste by its own barbarians.

So it might be. But now we need to pause in this popular hunt of analogies, and return to the obvious. There is literally a world of difference between America and ancient Rome—politically, economically, socially, culturally. Western civilization as a whole is still more different, sprawling over whole continents, impinging on all other societies, involving the entire world in its destiny; by comparison the mighty Roman Empire was a piddling local affair. Never before has there been a civilization so vast and dynamic, with such immense powers and incalculable possibilities. Never again will there be such a civilization, one might add, given an atomic war; but this possibility only emphasizes the profound differences in our situation. Such differences are not necessarily in our favor and by no means guarantee our success. The point is merely that they must be taken into account before we draw any final lessons from the failure of Rome. They make nonsense of all neat patterns got by analogy, and more especially of the efforts of Spengler and Toynbee to locate the exact position of our civilization on the downcurve of their historic cycles. We cannot even count on the time that Toynbee gives us when he calculates that Western Christendom has experienced only one-and-a-half of the standard three-and-a-half beats he makes out in the rhythm of disintegrating societies.

Briefly, the major differences may be traced to the growth of democracy, science, and technology. These achievements Toynbee dismisses as "an almost meaningless repetition of something that the Greeks and Romans did before us and did supremely well." In fact, they are strictly, profoundly unique. Rome experienced nothing like the political, scientific, and industrial revolutions that have created the modern world, and that are still revolutionizing it. Even in its periods of anarchy the Roman world was not a revolutionary world. Even in times of peace the modern world is.

The Industrial Revolution alone has brought the most radical changes in human life since the Urban Revolution with which civilization began. Like all other great societies, Rome ultimately rested on the manual labor of slaves or serfs. However immoderate its greatness, it was spared the problem of managing an immense machine civilization. Likewise its subject peoples were spared the profound disruption that the impact of Western civilization has caused in other societies today; Roman rule brought a change in masters but relatively little economic, cultural, or social change in the Eastern provinces. By the same token, however, the Roman Empire had nothing like our material resources. Its famed wealth and power were negligible in comparison—the imperial revenues were a mere fraction of the annual income of United States Steel, or the annual budget of the city of New York. Lacking the basic idea of systematically applied knowledge, the Romans had no real command of their physical environment; and as their material resources were depleted by extravagance, plague, war, and exhaustion of mine and soil, they were helpless. They could only turn to magic and prayer. (Thus the medical science developed so brilliantly by the Greeks was swamped by superstition as the empire was devastated by plagues; it was lost to Europe for a thousand years.) A major symptom of their impotence was a sharp decline in population, which further weakened the empire; whereas another unparalleled consequence of the Industrial Revolution has been an enormous increase in population, which has continued even through the unparalleled slaughter of the world wars.

This immense population is utterly dependent upon science and industry. Its masses, however, are by no means so slavish or inert as the masses of the Roman Empire. Spengler's 'megalopolis' is now productive, not parasitic, and there is no longer a great gulf between it and the country. If the city masses are rootless and formless, they are nevertheless energetic and busy; they earn their bread and enjoy their circuses in their leisure. When they go on relief or demand social security, conservatives are like to fear for their character, pointing out how the Roman masses were demoralized by hereditary doles and free grain; yet what the modern worker is demanding first of all is the opportunity to work.[1] Hence there is some reason for optimism even in the "spiritual barrenness" that Toynbee notes in the proletariat today. Since spirituality in his analysis is a portent of worldly doom, our perverse failure to exhibit some of the appropriate symptoms of distintegration (such as a resurgence of asceticism and the sense of sin) leads him to venture the "cynical conclusion" that our case has not yet reached the advanced stage; but at least he grants that the schism in the soul of the workers seems to have been repaired. Unlike the Roman masses who took to Oriental gods, they have not lost faith in their society.

One reason for this obstinate faith is that common men now enjoy political rights, or at least the illusion of political power. Nietzsche and Spengler pictured the rise of democracy and socialism as a typical mark of a society in decay, signifying the dominance of the herd-values of the mass-man; but on the face of it this is an astonishing misreading of history. Until recent centuries the masses have had no real political power in any civilization except the Greco-Roman, and there democracy was steadily on the decline after the fall of Athens. The Roman Republic was essentially a timocracy, which in diplomacy and in conquest supported local oligarchies everywhere. The Roman Empire granted a kind of equality before the law, but it granted the masses no rights whatever

[1] It is worth recalling that the millions of WPA workers who were pictured leaning on their shovels, reveling in the taxpayers' money, flocked back to the factories as soon as war production offered jobs again. Their character proved to be as sturdy as that of the businessmen who had rushed to Washington for help early in the depression, when relief to workers was still stigmatized as a "dole"; and businessmen are notable for a peculiarly stalwart character, which enables them to enjoy without loss of self-reliance the benefits of tariffs, franchises, and even outright government subsidies.

in the making of the law. As for the socialism of its last phase, with the regimentation that now serves as a horrid example for Chambers of Commerce, this was a far cry from an experiment in the "welfare state." It was neither demanded by the common man nor designed for his benefit; it was designed to aid the imperial government, and merely sealed his slavery to the State. In short, never before our own time has virtually the entire population of large nations been a genuine citizenry, with a voice in selecting its rulers and deciding its destiny.

With the rise of democracy has come an unprecedented humanitarianism, in the name of the dignity and worth of the individual. It is often sentimental and unenlightened, seldom a match for prejudice or the profit motive. It makes more hideous such contradictions as the unprecedented horrors of modern war—the barbarism that we cannot afford to regard as a mere "reversion," or incidental relic of our primitive ancestry. Still the humanitarianism is a real force, which has brought real changes. The Roman ideal of *humanitas* was an intellectual concept that involved little concern for the individual; under the formal ideals of classicism, the individual was merely an example of some formal 'type.' Good Romans were seldom disturbed by the wretchedness of the masses and saw no particular evil in gladiatorial games, judicial torture, slavery, or war. In the democracies today there are still plenty of social evils, but they are commonly regarded as evils that should be remedied. The barbarism of our times is at least called by that name.

Most important, however, is the active faith on which democracy is based—the faith in reason, freedom, individualism, with its stress on "opportunity" and the active effort to improve life. The Romans clung to an essentially passive ideal, relying on discipline rather than initiative, encouraging patient endurance rather than wilful endeavor. Their characteristic wisdom was the wisdom of Epictetus: "Seek not that the things which happen to you should happen as you wish, but wish the things that happen to be as they are, and you will find tranquillity." This is always a genuine kind of wisdom, and may be the best kind of life in the atomic age; it is no longer necessary to emphasize the dangers of Western wishfulness and wilfulness. Here, at any rate, is the basic difference between the Roman world and ours, the ultimate source of all the specific economic, political, and cultural differences. Rome had no faith in progress, expecting the future to be merely a recurrence; it sought to keep things as they were, and when things went wrong it looked backward, to a Utopian past. We keep looking forward, much less hopefully than we used to, but still with a vivid sense of possibilities, of things that could or should be done. Rome suffered from a lack of energy and enterprise, a stagnation; its decline was a creeping paralysis. We suffer from an excess of energy, or misguided enterprise; and we are likely to end with a bang.

In this perspective, the apparent analogies between the Roman world and our own may take on a quite different aspect. Thus the skepticism and irreligion of the educated class, which Spengler and many others view as a symptom of disease, is not the same old story. In Rome such skepticism was apt to be unhealthy because it was primarily negative, reflecting only a loss of faith. Today it is often as unhealthy or even more so, springing from a deeper confusion or a stronger aversion; it is more apt to produce a cynical indifference than a stoical resignation. Yet it commonly springs from a positive faith in reason and science. Many men are critical of the traditional absolutes because of this faith; they insist on the principle of uncertainty implied in the method of science, and in the ideals of freedom and the open society. Modern skepticism has therefore produced much creative criticism, as in Rome it did not. Modern irreligion has generally been an optimistic religion of humanity. Both have been a positive moral force.

For such reasons the ancient faiths may also have a vitality that traditionalism obscures. The genius of Christianity has been more enterprising, resourceful, and versatile than the orthodox make it out to be. It has known a Protestant Reformation—something of which Roman piety was wholly incapable. Today millions of churchgoers recall this piety as they go through their routine rituals, recite ancient Creeds that they do not really believe or even understand; yet many leaders of Christianity are striving to readapt it to the needs of a revolutionary world. Similarly with the arts. Whereas Roman art suffered from a sterile classicism, modern art suffers from a feverish confusion, intensified by the romantic tradition of individualism, self-expression, and free imagination; the obvious trouble with it is not lifeless formality but strain and excess. I should not predict what will come out of all this experimentation. The point is simply that something rich may come out of it—it is a live growth, however deformed.

Again, the social enterprise of modern democracy has always been more extensive and energetic than champions of private enterprise seem to realize. In pointing to the obvious evils of Roman bureaucracy, and the failure of the final experiment in state socialism, they forget that until this experiment the imperial policy was more consistently laissez faire than that of capitalistic America in its nineteenth-century heydey.

The Roman government did not restrict free enterprise by patent laws, hamper free trade by tariffs, or interfere in business by giving franchises or subsidies to a favored few. Neither did it enter the postal business or provide socialized education through public schools. Certainly its mismanagement of its economic resources were not due to rage for "planning"—it was due rather to a lack of any plan. The Romans were more consistent than conservatives today in their obedience to Nature or Necessity, even though they had not consciously formulated the Laws of Competition and of Supply and Demand. For modern capitalism has never really respected these sacrosanct laws that it has written into its bill of rights. It has always tended to evade them by seeking monopoly; it has always got more or less government protection against them. And if conservatives have stubbornly resisted every measure to extend similar protection to workers and consumers, they have steadily lost ground, and by now take for granted a great deal of social legislation that horrified their fathers. When the national economy is threatened by a rugged individualist like John L. Lewis, who still believes in free private enterprise, they are the first to demand that the government should do something about it. In spite of themselves, they are committed to the Western faith in active intelligence—the faith that man can make his own laws, control his society, and determine his future.

Hence the experience of the Roman Empire is hardly a guide in our experiment of a democratically planned society. It does suggest, however, that the experiment is worth trying. It supports John Stuart Mill's argument that a benevolent autocracy is inferior to self-government, and in the long run even more harmful than a vicious autocracy, because more enervating. Self-government makes for a vigorous, self-reliant people; whereas a people deprived of political life loses energy, becomes mentally passive, at length becomes helpless—as helpless as the Romans proved to be after the reign of Marcus Aurelius.

But Mill also raised the final issue, of the objects of democratic energy and enterprise, the goods sought by free men; and here the testimony of Rome is less clear. In one sense the Roman masses had the last word: their mentality, based on religion, in time dominated their masters. To Toynbee this was a triumph of transcendence, the victory of Christ over Caesar. Worldlier historians have dwelt rather on its immediate meaning, which was the death of a civilization. Rostovtzeff summarizes the whole story of the decline of the Roman Empire as "the gradual absorption of the educated classes by the masses and the consequent simplification of all the functions of political, social, economic, and intellectual life, which we call the barbarization of the ancient world." The lesson of Rome, he believes, is that a civilization cannot endure if it rests on a small class, not on the masses; but then he points out that the masses debase a civilization. He concludes with a question: "Is not every civilization bound to decay as soon as it begins to penetrate the masses?"

It is an open question. The creative achievements of civilization to date have been primarily the work of an elite, and the greatest achievements will always be due immediately to the gifted few. Ideally, democracy would mean not merely a general rise in the culture of the masses but an elite that is freely recruited, that may be enlarged and constantly invigorated by special talents from the ranks. Actually, democracy has indeed enlisted vast reserves of energy and talent, but it has also meant a lowering of standards of excellence, a blurring of the all-important distinction between common and uncommon men. It has produced the half-educated man—a type relatively rare in other societies—who is apt to have less respect for learning and culture than the uneducated man. And with industrialism has come a universal vulgarization. An immense machinery is now geared to the tastes and desires of common men, which are an offense by the standards of all civilizations before ours. It produces the appalling confusion of values reflected in radio programs, on which a breathless announcement of impending world catastrophe is preceded by a jingle in praise of some eyewash and followed by a popular comic.

Let us spell out the worst about this notorious mass-man and his mass-culture. He has a meager idea of the abundant life, confusing quantity with quality, size with greatness, comfort with culture, gadgetry with genius. He has as little appreciation of pure science as of the fine arts, and as little capacity for the discipline that both require; although he may stand in awe of them his real veneration goes to the engineers and inventors, the manufacturers of True Romances and Tin Pan Alley airs. He is frequently illiberal, suspicious of "radical" ideas, scornful of "visionary" ideals, hostile to "aliens"; in America he has developed a remarkable vocabulary of contempt that manages to embrace most of mankind—the nigger, the mick, the chink, the wop, the kike, et cetera. He is the chief foe of the individualism he boasts of, a patron of standard brands in tastes and opinions as in material possessions, with a morbid fear of being thought queer or different from the Joneses; individuality to him is "personality," which may be acquired in six easy lessons or his money back, is then turned on to win friends and influence people, and is confirmed by the possession of "personalized" objects, which are distinguished only by having his initials on them. In short, he appears to be a spoiled child, fundamentally ungrateful to the scientists, political philosophers, social reformers, and religious idealists who have given him his unprecedented opportunities. He is therefore the natural prey of advertisers, politicians, millionaire publishers, and would-be dictators.

Yet he is much more than this, else he would never have got where he has. The "mass-man" is also a bogey—a monstrous abstraction that conceals the infinite varieties of common men, in interest, ability, character, and aspiration. It conceals all the degrees in culture, the frequent lustiness of the low-brow, the earnestness of the middle-brow. In particular it conceals the idealism that underlies the obvious materialism. This expresses itself in such commonplace sentiments as that every man ought to have a fair chance—a very novel commonplace, in the light of history. In times of crisis it has enabled such loyalty, fortitude, and unpretentious heroism as won the Battle for Britain. At all times it inspires an enthusiasm for vast co-operative enterprises, kindles the energy and imagination that have made the kingdom of common men the most adventurous in history. "An idealist working on matter" Santayana has called the American; and his fine enthusiasm might be touched to finer issues. Meanwhile it is again an inhuman spirituality that cannot see idealism in the effort to eliminate the poverty and wretchedness once accepted as the will of God, and to enable all men to enjoy the material well-being once enjoyed only by a privileged few—by aristocrats who could afford to exalt non-economic interests and values because they took for granted their wealth and luxury, and seldom had to earn it.

Rostovtzeff's question remains open for the simple reason that common men are having their first real chance in history, and have not had it long. It is hardly surprising if they still fall short of their opportunities and their responsibilities—as throughout history their masters consistently did. In judging this new adventure, accordingly, we must at least face squarely the historic alternatives. Many critics of democratic culture are not candid. They yearn for all the advantages of an aristocratic society without being willing to commit themselves to the moral and intellectual responsibilities of arguing for an aristocratic government, shouldering the human cost. Even T. S. Eliot, who frankly condemns the ideal of equality of opportunity and maintains that a hereditary privileged class is essential to culture, is vague or irresponsible at the critical points of his argument. He arbitrarily dismisses the "myth" of the mute, inglorious Milton, ignoring the plain reasons for believing that a great deal of potential talent or even genius went to waste among the illiterate masses of the past. He merely asserts that his privileged elite will have special responsibilities, ignoring the historic fact that they usually evaded these responsibilities, and suggesting no safeguards against the historic abuses of privilege. He declares very simply that "no sane person can be consumed with bitterness at not having had more exalted ancestors," ignoring the very good reasons for bitterness that millions of poor devils have had. Possibly Eliot's kind of culture does require a hereditary aristocracy; but given the historic record, I should say that a more reasonable ideal is culture and education for all, within their capacities, even if democracy is not the best soil for the very choicest flowers of the human spirit.

As for Rome, at any rate, the masses cannot be held responsible for its fall. If they "absorbed" the educated classes, the fault lay with these privileged classes, who had failed to educate or uplift them, failed to maintain either the material prosperity or the spiritual health of the nation. Rome illustrates the maxim that societies die at the top. As it rose to greatness it rehearsed the old story of the selfishness and shortsightedness of the elite. The aristocratic families who ran the senatorial machine proved utterly incapable of the statesmanship that the rising empire called for. They turned on their liberal members, such as the Gracchi, with the kind of fury that was inspired by "that man" Roosevelt; they rejected the compromises that might have preserved the privileges they jealously clung to; and so they perversely brought on the military dictatorship that destroyed their power. The bourgeois class that replaced them was less suicidal, if only because it had less political power, but ulimately it proved as incapable of enlightened leadership. Nor was it enlightened by Roman intellectuals. If the cultivated class was well-intentioned, it proved wanting in creative intelligence and imagination.

For the Romans, we may then speak the last word in charity, and even in awe. They had nothing like our material and intellectual resources; the wonder is not that their empire fell but that it endured so long and so grandly. For us, the last word is a challenge to the educated, privileged classes. The problem today is not merely a matter of improving the minds and tastes of common men. It is also a question of whether the elite can provide better political, intellectual, and spiritual leadership than it has in all previous societies. For if the creative achievements of civilization have been due primarily to the elite, so too have the failures of civilization. "No civilized minority," observed Leonard Woolf, "has yet been found willing to make the necessary sacrifices."

INDEX

Afterthoughts on the Rosenbergs, 255
Allen, Frederick Lewis, 193
The Army Ant, 130
Arnold, Matthew, 603
The Art of Political Lying, 334
The Arts of Selling, 338

Baldwin, Hanson, 181
Baldwin, James, 431
Becker, Carl, 620
Beerbohm, Max, 236
Benjamin Franklin, 451
Boswell, James, 224
The Boys' Ambition, 241
Burke, Edmund, 306
Bush, Douglas, 569

Calculating Machine, 522
Captain Edward Gibbon, 637
Carson, Rachel, 169
The Case for the Daydreamer, 369
Christmas Trees, 421
Churchill, Winston, 71
Clemens, Samuel, 241
A Cloud of Smoke, 346
Collingwood, R. G., 110
*Constitutional Rights of Racial
    Minorities in the United States,*
    402
Cooke, Alistair, 245, 374

Crane, R. S., 577
Crash!, 193
The Crisis, No. 1, 298

De Quincey, Thomas, 442
*The Discovery of What it Means
    to be an American,* 431
Dunkirk, 71

Edmund G. Ross, 281
Einstein, Albert, 106, 395
*An Enquiry into the Origins of
    Moral Virtue,* 325

*The Fall of Rome: Its Implications
    for Us,* 643
The Federalist, No. 10, 27
Fiedler, Leslie, 255
The First "Fireside Chat," 84
Forster, E. M., 637
Franklin, Benjamin, 65
Freedom and the Colleges, 48

*General Observations on the Fall of
    the Roman Empire in the West,*
    629
Gibbon, Edward, 629
Gibel, Inge Lederer, 410
The Gray Beginnings, 169

A Hanging, 209
History's Nature, Object, Method, and Value, 110
How Not to Integrate the Schools, 410
The Humanities, 569
Hume, David, 123
Huxley, Aldous, 338
Huxley, Thomas Henry, 589

The Idea of the Humanities, 577
The Idler, No. 103, 36
Individualism in America, 19
The Invention of the Steamboat, 115

Joe Louis, 245
Johnson, Samuel, 36

Kennedy, John F., 89, 281
The Kinsey Report, 379
Kroeber, A. L., 115
Kronenberger, Louis, 19
Krutch, Joseph Wood, 439

Language Defined, 494
Lawrence, D. H., 451
The Laws of Science and the Laws of Ethics, 106
The Lexicographer's Uneasy Chair, 547
Literature and Science, 603

McCarthy, Mary, 481
Macaulay, Thomas Babington, 159
Macdonald, Dwight, 524
McGinley, Phyllis, 40
Madison, James, 27
Malinowski, Bronislaw, 140
The Man Who Knew Everybody, 216
Mandeville, Bernard, 325
Mathematical Creation, 146
The Meaning of Treason, 273
Mill, John Stuart, 13
The Monster, 447

Motherhood and the Temptations of Incest, 140
Muller, Herbert J., 643

Nicolson, Harold, 216, 421

Of Tragedy, 123
On the Knocking at the Gate in Macbeth, 442
Orwell, George, 209, 509

Paine, Thomas, 298
Palos Verdes, 3, 4, 7
Piel, Gerard, 130
Poincaré, Henri, 146
Politics and the English Language, 509
Progress, 620

From *Reflections on the Revolution in France*, 306
Roosevelt, Franklin D., 84
Roughing It, 374
R.M.S. Titanic, 181
Russell, Bertrand, 48

Sapir, Edward, 494
Schneirla, T. C., 130
Schorer, Mark, 461
Science and Culture, 589
The Scottish Highlands in the Seventeenth Century, 159
Settling the Colonel's Hash, 481
Slavery in Ohio and Kentucky, 60
Sledd, James, 547
Snow, C. P., 557
Something Defeasible, 236
The Soviet Threat to the Americas, 89
Speech in the Convention on the Subject of Salaries, 65
The String Untuned, 524
Suburbia, of Thee I Sing, 40
Sutherland, Arthur E., 402
Swift, Jonathan, 334

Taylor, Deems, 447
Thoreau, Henry David, 57
*Three Examples of Persecution for
    Belief,* 13
Thurber, James, 369
de Tocqueville, Alexis, 60, 97
Trilling, Lionel, 379
The Two Cultures, 557
*Two Houses, Two Ways: The
    Florentine Villas of Lewis and
    Lawrence, Respectively,* 461
Two Women, 425

The War of the Ants, 57
West, Rebecca, 273
What Is a Good Review?, 439
White, E. B., 522
Whiteside, Thomas, 346
*Why Democratic Nations Naturally
    Desire Peace, and Democratic
    Armies, War,* 97
Why Do They Hate the Jews?, 395
The Wilkes Episode, 224
Woolf, Virginia, 425